Introduction to the Fundamental Liberal Arts

Introduction to the Fundamental Liberal Arts:

Grammar, Logic, and Rhetoric

Jonathan Sammartino
and
Gideon Rappaport

2015
Whole Mind Press

Introduction to the
Fundamental Liberal Arts:
Grammar, Logic and Rhetoric

This volume has been compiled and edited by Jonathan Sammartino and Gideon Rappaport.

Whole Mind Press is an imprint of Adventures in Tranquility, LLC. Any inquiries about the text should be mailed to: Whole Mind Press, PO Box 955, Littleton, New Hampshire, 03561.

ISBN: 978-0-9966307-1-9

To Angelo Joseph Sammartino

Born in Philadelphia, Pennsylvania, in 1920, Jonathan Sammartino's grandfather (Pa), after graduating high school from Girard College, a boarding school for orphaned boys, began college at Drexel University. Following the German invasion of Poland in late 1939, he enlisted as a private in the United States Marine Corps on April 2, 1940. Assigned to the 1st Marine Division, the oldest and largest division of the Corps, he landed on Guadalcanal on August 7, 1942, in the first major American Pacific campaign in World War II. In 1943 he was commissioned as a 2nd Lieutenant. At the end of the war, he was deployed to Nagasaki, Japan, just five weeks after the atomic bomb was dropped there. He fought in the Korean War serving as a battalion commander and helping to train Korean soldiers. He retired from the Marine Corps in 1965, having attained the rank of major and having served for 25 years.

After graduating from San Diego State University, he taught history and geography at Oceanside High School for 13 years. History and education were always important to him. For 16 years, he served as the editor of over 400 "School Days" articles, a weekly column on education that his wife, Marion, wrote for the *Blade Tribune* (later the *Blade Citizen*). He was always learning and was never without the latest books on history or current events.

When his elder grandson, Joseph, entered middle school, he gave him an old fluorescent desk lamp from his office, inscribed (by means of his manual typewriter and double-stick tape) with one of his favorite quotations, by George Santayana, "Those who cannot remember the past are condemned to repeat it." When his younger grandson, Jonathan, entered middle school, he received from his grandfather a nearly identical desk lamp, this one inscribed with another favorite quotation, by Thucydides, "We must remember that one man is much the same as another, and that he is best who is trained at the severest school."

Because he thought that Winston Churchill had given so many good speeches, he recommended that we include at least two in this volume. Looking over the table of contents of a nearly complete draft of the book, he remarked that he thought the class based on it was "shaping up to be a very interesting class, one that I'd like to take." Less than a month later, surrounded by his family, he died peacefully at the age of 93.

Major Angelo J. Sammartino
November 4, 1920–April 14, 2014

Table of Contents

Nineteenth Century

Twentieth Century

Contents

Acknowledgements

We would like to thank the following individuals for their many
and various contributions to this work.

Dr. Bruce Mangan, for numerous suggested sources to include in the
Rhetoric portion (specifically, Ecclesiastes, Thucydides, Montaigne, Simone
Weil, JFK, Malcolm X), and for myriad other comments that helped to
shape this volume, including an echo of Angelo Sammartino's suggestion for
multiple speeches by Churchill.

Dr. Wayne A. Davis, for education in the study of logic, for
encouraging us to bring logic to high school students, and for providing
invaluable comments and suggestions.

Joseph Sammartino, for comments on copyright and legal information,
and for assistance with some details of the dedication.

Dr. Jessica Thierman, for support and encouragement, for comments
on layout, and for the early suggestion to include more variety—especially
women authors—in the Rhetoric portion.

John McClure, for conversation and comments on teaching Logic to
high school students, and for the specific suggestion that broad
presuppositions be addressed in "Basic Concepts of Logic."

Tim Monaco, for general comments and suggestions about content,
and for furnishing a list of "Speeches that Changed the World," on which
the Pankhurst and Curie speeches were found.

Victor Boft, for comments, encouragement, and conversation on many
different aspects of the book.

Christopher Maron, for intellectual and moral support and suggestions
about content and contribution of "On Reading Historically."

Rev. Andy Shamel, for comments, suggestions, and technical advice on
layout and typesetting.

Seunghee Erin Kim, for comments on layout and design from a
student's perspective.

The students in the first offering of our course, Trivium, at La Jolla
Country Day School, who caught many errors and whose questions
prompted us to rewrite and expand several of the introductions in the
Rhetoric portion.

Special thanks to Dr. Greg Martin at La Jolla Country Day School for
the opportunity to offer and teach the course for which this is the textbook,
and for financial support for the publication of this book.

Introduction

What are the Liberal Arts?

"Liberal Arts" is a classical term applied during the Middle Ages to the the seven branches of knowledge that "initiate the young into a life of learning." These arts are called "liberal" (from the Latin *liber*, meaning free) because their goal is to liberate human beings from intellectual bondage, to allow them to be able to think for themselves instead of, like slaves, depending on others for their knowledge and opinions.

The seven liberal arts are made up of the Trivium (from the Latin *tri* and *via*, "three ways"), which are the arts of language pertaining to the mind, and the Quadrivium (Latin "four ways"), the arts of quantity pertaining to matter.

The trivium consists of the three arts grammar, logic, and rhetoric. Grammar is the art of combining the symbols that we call words into sentences; it is concerned with the thing as it is symbolized, and its norm is correctness. Logic is the art of reasoning to achieve knowledge of reality as it is; it is concerned with the thing as it is known, and its norm is truth. Rhetoric is the art of sharing ideas and of persuasion; it is concerned with the thing as it is communicated, and its norm is effectiveness.

The four arts of the Quadrivium are two of discrete quantity or number—arithmetic, the theory of number; and music, the application of the theory of number—and two of continuous quantity—geometry, the theory of space; and astronomy, the application of the theory of space. These four arts made up what today we would call mathematics and all the sciences of the physical world.

"The function of the trivium is the training of the mind for the study of matter and spirit, which together constitute the sum of reality."[1]

---

[1] Sister Miriam Joseph, *The Trivium*, ed. Marguerite McGlinn (Philadelphia: Paul Dry Books, 2002), p. 8.

About Our Text

An introduction to the fundamental liberal arts ought to be spread across years, not just a single volume. In the educational tradition as practiced from the Middle Ages, grammar—in Latin —was taught to young children (who love to show off what they have memorized), logic to somewhat older children (who love to argue and to prove adults wrong), and rhetoric to young teens (who are filled with desire and are capable of poetry and idealism and therefore of rhetoric).[2] These three arts were followed by the Quadrivium, then by philosophy, and finally by theology, called the queen of the arts. The entire course of study was pursued only by the most intelligent and intellectually gifted of children, but all children who had any pretense to education completed at least the Trivium.

Because we are not the masters of these arts that we should be, and because this is only a single volume, it is not possible to train our readers thoroughly in the three arts of the Trivium. However, we hope to introduce them to you enough to help you, if you are so inclined, to pursue them as intellectual support for a "lifetime of learning." At least you will know well that there are such things as correct grammar, sound logic, and effective rhetoric, and perhaps be the better able to detect their opposites and so to live as freer and more intellectually responsible adults, friends, spouses, parents, and citizens.

Finally, it becomes apparent when reviewing the table of contents that there are comparatively few women authors included in this text. Indeed, the documentary history of civilization has privileged men over women: in many different cultures at many different times, women were not granted the same education as men and so did not produce as many works. Thus, our selection necessarily reflects that history.

---

[2] See Dorothy Sayers, "The Lost Tools of Learning," presented at Oxford, 1947, first published by E.T. Heron, 1948, available at www.accsedu.org/files/Documents/ TheLostToolsofLearning.pdf.

Important Texts and Further Reading

In addition to the selections reproduced here, the following books proved invaluable in crafting portions of the course and this book, and are recommended reading for anyone who wants to plumb these topics in greater depth:

Sister Miriam Joseph, *The Trivium: The Liberal Arts of Grammar, Logic, and Rhetoric*, ed. Marguerite McGlinn (Philadelphia: Paul Dry Books, 2002).

Part I: Grammar

Jane E. Aaron, H. Ramsey Fowler. *The Little Brown Handbook.* 12th ed. (London: Longman, 2011).

Part II: Logic

Wayne A. Davis with the Georgetown Logic Group, *An Introduction to Logic*, 2nd ed., (Kunos Press, 2007).

Part III: Rhetoric

Ward Farnsworth, *Farnsworth's Classical English Rhetoric,* (Boston: David R. Godine, 2010).

Part I: Grammar

Grammatica, Cornelis Cort, 1565, engraving.

Introduction: Grammar

Grammar is the art of inventing and combining the symbols we call words, and its norm is correctness. Thus grammar prescribes how to combine words so as to form sentences correctly.

Why is it so valuable to understand grammar?

Grammar is the foundation of logic (the art of thinking, whose norm is truth) and rhetoric (the art of communication, whose norm is effectiveness). These three arts form the trivium, the foundation of the liberal arts by which human beings become free, able to reason for themselves instead of depending on others for truth. Without grammar, both logic and rhetoric dissolve into nonsense.

Grammar is essential for the understanding of meaning in the sentences of others (reading) and for the expression of meaning in one's own sentences (writing).

Grammar is a reflection of the structure of the mind and its processes of thought and communication. Hence, not to know grammar is to be ignorant of how one's own and others' minds work when it comes to symbol-making with words. The ability to speak and write grammatically is the ability to convey ideas, feelings, and experience rationally.

Grammar is a body of knowledge basic to human culture and as such is as valuable an inheritance as arithmetic, the periodic table, musical notation, and cooking.

Basic Concepts of English Grammar

I

Parts of Speech

Every English word falls into one of eight categories called the **parts of speech:**

1. Noun: person, place, thing, concept:

> **Common noun:** not capitalized
> > *horse, banana, element, consciousness, growth, elation*

> **Proper noun:** capitalized names
> > *Idaho, St. Thomas Aquinas, Molly, Maxwell House Coffee*

2. Pronoun: stands in place of a noun in various ways:

Note: The Personal, Reflexive, and Demonstrative Prounoun must agree with its antecedent in number.

> **Personal pronoun:** referring to a specified person or thing

> > **Subjective case** (Latin: nominative):
> > singular: *I, you, he, she, it* (also called "impersonal")
> > plural: *we, you, they*

> > **Objective case** (Latin: accusative):
> > singular: *me, you, him, her, it*
> > plural: *us, you, them*

> > **Possessive case** (Latin: genitive):
> > singular: *my, mine, your, yours, his, her, hers, its*
> > plural: *our, ours, your, yours, their, theirs*

> **Reflexive pronoun:** reflecting back on someone or something previously mentioned:
> > singular: *myself, yourself, himself, herself, itself, oneself*
> > plural: *ourselves, yourselves, themselves*
> > > Please help *yourself*.
> > > He thought *himself* impaired. — C.S. Lewis, *A Preface to* Paradise Lost
> > > Once powered on, the machines run *themselves*.

> **Demonstrative pronoun:** pointing to or indicating someone or something
> > singular: *this, that*
> > plural: *these, those*

singular or plural: *the former, the latter, the first, the second, same, so, such*

> *This* is a novel.
> *That* is an epic poem.
> Of the two, *the former* is longer, but *the latter* is more
> challenging.
> *Those* belong to George.

Note: *former* and *latter* together may be treated as correlative demonstratives (cf., correlative conjunctions, p. 11).

Indefinite pronoun: referring to a non-specified person or thing:
all, another, any, anybody, anyone, anything, both, each, each one, either, everybody, everyone, everything, few, many, more, most, much, neither, nobody, none, no one, nothing, one, other, several, some, somebody, someone, something, such

Intensive pronoun: emphasizing the substantive to which it refers and functioning as an appositive
> singular: *myself, yourself, himself, herself, itself, oneself*
> plural: *ourselves, yourselves, themselves*
> I can do it *myself*.
> He *himself* does not speak French, but his wife does.

Relative pronoun: modifying by relating a subordinate clause to a substantive

> Person:
> > Subjective case (Latin: nominative): *who, whoever, whichever*
> > > The doctor *who* cured me is a genius.
> > Objective case (Latin: accusative): *whom, whomever, whichever*
> > > The king *whom* he served was a good king.
> > Possessive case (Latin: genitive): *whose*
> > > Whose woods these are I think I know.
> > > > -Robert Frost, "Stopping by Woods on a Snowy Evening"

> Thing or concept:
> > Subjective and objective cases: *that* (restrictive),
> > *which* (non-restrictive)
> > Possessive case: *whose, of that, of which*
> > > The question *that* I am often asked has no answer.

> The familiar question of free will, *which* you have
> now posed in a new way, requires some study.

(See also "The Four *That*'s," p. 46)

Note: The **case** of a relative pronoun is determined by its use in its own subordinate clause (cf., Adjective Clause, p. 26).

Interrogative pronoun: asking a question
who? whom? whose? what? which? whoever? whomever? whatever?

> *Who* is at the door?
> *What* are you eating?
> *Which* is the car you bought?

Reciprocal pronoun: indicating interrelation (used as objects only)
each other, one another

> They wrote to *one another* for years.
> They like *each other*.

3. Adjective: modifies noun, pronoun, or other substantive
The *blue* notebook is filled with *cursive* writing.
The *green* one has only *uneven* printing.
The *drama* critic found the *new* play a *total* bore.

A phrase can become an adjectival modifier by the use of hyphens: a *turn-of-the-century* house, a *devil-may-care* attitude.

Article: The three words that introduce nouns to limit, individualize, or give definiteness or indefiniteness to their application:

> Definite article: *the*, referring to a particular item
> Indefinite articles: referring to a general item or one not already mentioned:
>> *a* (before a noun beginning with a consonant sound)
>> *an* (before a noun beginning with a vowel sound)

4. Adverb: modifies
a verb or verbal:

> *Weekly* he would do a budget.
> The snow fell *softly* upon the *slowly* whitening field.

an adjective:

> I have not seen you in a *very* long time.

9

The opera was *relatively* short.

It is *entirely* possible that I was *completely* wrong.

or another adverb:

He *quite* quickly realized his mistake.

Conjunctive adverb: implies a relation but acts as an adverb rather than as a conjunction:

accordingly, also, anyhow, anyway, besides, consequently, further, furthermore, hence, however, indeed, likewise, moreover, namely, nevertheless, so, still, then, thence, thus, therefore

When it introduces a new independent clause, a conjunctive adverb is preceded by a semicolon and followed by a comma:

I found the new phone extremely versatile; *however,* I had no idea how to work it.

The rains washed out the bridge; *consequently,* we were stranded at the cabin for nearly a week.

It is true that students are extremely busy these days; *nonetheless,* they must strive to turn their work in on time.

5. Preposition: relates its object (a substantive—noun, pronoun, gerund, noun clause) to another element of the sentence (usually a verb, noun, or adjective):

one-word prepositions:

about, across, after, against, along, amid, amidst, among, apropos, around, at, before, behind, below, beneath, beside, between, beyond, by, concerning, despite, down, during, except, for, from, in, inside, into, like, near, of, off, on, onto, over, past, per, since, through, throughout, till, to, toward, under, until, up, upon, via, with, within

multiple-word prepositions:

according to, ahead of, apart from, as far as, as to, because of, by means of, by reason of, contrary to, due to, for the sake of, in place of, in regard to, in spite of, instead of, on account of, out of, owing to, up to

The squirrel *in* the tree was rolling a nut *with* its paw.

Over the river and *through* the woods *to* Grandmother's house we go.

My eyes are tired *from* reading the small print *under* a weak lamp.

6. Conjunction: joins words, phrases, and clauses in three ways (see "Adverb" on the previous page for conjunctive adverbs):

Coordinating conjunction: joins two parallel grammatical elements (noun to noun, verb to verb, adjective to adjective, clause to clause, etc.) or precedes the last element in a parallel series: *and, but, yet, or, for, nor,* and *so* (remembered as a rhyme in that order or as the acronym FANBOYS)

The boys *and* the girls are in school today.

I want vanilla *or* chocolate, not strawberry.

It is a stirring *yet* sentimental story.

Note: Use a comma before a coordinating conjunction only when it joins two independent clauses or introduces the last item in a series.

The painter set up the ladder, *and* then he began to paint.

I cannot see the logic of your convoluted argument, *but* I believe there is a point in it somewhere.

They conversed through the night, *yet* the topic was not exhausted even at the break of day.

Correlative conjunction: a subset of coordinating conjunction involving two words or phrases that join parallel elements:

although/still, both/and, either/or, if/then, just as/so, neither/nor, not/but, no sooner/than, not only/but also, whether/or

I love *not only* Bach *but also* Beethoven.

I *neither* know whether you have plagiarized in the past *nor* care to find out, so long as from now on you *both* use quotations judiciously *and* give proper credit where it is due.

Note: What follows the first part of the correlative must grammatically parallel what follows the second: *both* [noun] *and* [noun]; *neither* [clause] *nor* [clause]; *not only* [verb] *but* [verb] (cf., "Parallel Structure," pp. 43–45).

Subordinating: joins a subordinate adverbial or noun clause to an independent (main) clause:

Adverbial clause conjunctions:

after, although, as, as if, as long as, as soon as, as though, because, before, even though, if, in order that, since, so, so

11

that, that, though, unless, until, when, whenever, where,
whereby, wherefore, wherein, wherever, wherewith, whether
> *Because* it was raining, I opened my umbrella.
> I will fold it up *when* the rain stops.
> *Unless* you open yours too, you will get wet.
> I suggest you do it now *so that* you don't forget.

Noun clause conjunctions:
that, how, if, when, where, whether, why
> I believe *that* the sun rises in the east.
> You may ask *why* it does so.
> *Whether* that question should be answered by a
> philosopher, a psychologist, or a kindergarten
> teacher I don't know, and *when, where,* or *how*
> he might answer it is not my concern.

Note: These conjunctions and certain pronouns are
sometimes called **Noun clause identifiers** (cf., "Noun
clause," pp. 26–27).

7. Interjection: exclamatory word or phrase with no grammatical
connection to the sentence; it may be punctuated with a
following exclamation point or comma:
yes, no, ouch, wow, drat, pooh, hot diggety, no way, and various
curse words and obscenities
> *Ouch!*
> *Yes,* we have no bananas.
> *Jumping Jehoshaphat,* it's hot out there!
> *Tsk, tsk,* you know better than to do that.

8. Verb: indicates action or state of being, the basis of the
predicate of a sentence:

Transitive verb is an action verb that takes a direct object.

Intransitive verb may be any of the following kinds of verb
taking no direct object:

Verbs may be understood in four categories:

Action verb: indicating a physical or mental movement
with or without an object as complement

transitive: swings (the bat)
> Joey *hit* the ball out of the park.

I *passed* my test.

The Americans *landed* a space ship on Mars.

intransitive: swings (on a swing)

Jamie *is swinging* on the tether ball rope!

Helicopters *fly* without wings.

The Americans *landed* on the moon.

Helping (or **Auxiliary**) **verb**: indicates tense or mode of a main verb:

is, be, am, are, was, were, been, being, will, would, can, could, shall, should, may, might, must, have, has, had, do, does, did

Have you traveled to Texas?

She *might* meet us at the theater.

They *could* not join us tonight.

I *am* arriving by plane

Could you pick me up?

Modal Auxiliaries are helping verbs that indicate the mode of a verb, such as necessity (*must*), obligation (*should*), permission (*may*), probability (*might*), possibility (*could*), ability (*can*), or tentativeness (*would*).

Linking verb: indicates identity (like an equal sign), linking or equating the subject to something in the predicate and taking a predicate nominative or predicate adjective as complement:

is, be, am, are, was, were, been, being, appear, become, feel, grow, look, remain, seem, smell, sound, stay, taste, etc.

Joey *is* a baseball player.

Sally *grew* rather tall last year.

I *am feeling* rather weak today.

Roses *smell* sweet.

She *became* a news reporter.

Verbs of being: usually forms of *to be* indicating a state of being with no complement, often with a deferred subject:

She *is* in the garden.

There *were* flowers in the pot.

Verbs convey several qualities:

Tense: time of the verb
> Present: Joey *hits* the ball.
> Past: Joey *hit* the ball.
> Future: Joey *will hit* the ball.
> Present perfect: Joey *has hit* the ball.
> Past perfect: Joey *had hit* the ball.
> Future perfect: Joey *will have hit* the ball.
> Present progressive: Joey *is hitting* the ball.
> Past progressive: Joey *was hitting* the ball.
> Future progressive: Joey *will be hitting* the ball.

Voice: active or passive attribute of the verb:
> Active: Joey *hit* the ball.
> Passive: The ball *was hit* by Joey.

Mood: manner in which the action or state of being is conceived:
> Indicative: Joey *hit* the ball.
> Imperative: Joey, please *hit* the ball!
> Subjunctive: If Joey *were* a good hitter . . .

Verbal: Made from the verb, and therefore capable of taking its own complements (see "Complement," p. 18, and "Verbal phrase," p. 22) and modifiers, it comes in three forms and functions as a noun, adverb, or adjective:

Infinitive: non-finite form of the verb in its most abstract form indicating no specific tense; except with certain verbs, always accompanied by the particle *to* (the "sign of the infinitive"), and used as

noun:
> *To tame* a horse requires skill.
> He tried *to tame* a horse.

adverb:
> She took a course *to learn* French.
> They stayed *to hear* the speech.
> A good book is fun *to read*.

adjective:
> There were sights *to see*.
> We had popcorn *to eat*.
> He had a strong desire *to win*.

Participle: verbal adjective, modifying a noun, pronoun, or other substantive:

>The *babbling* brook seems to sing.
>
>*Running,* she caught the bus.
>
>*Hitting* a homerun, he won the game.

>Participles may be active or passive:

>>Active:
>>>*sailing* ship (*sailing* modifies *ship*)
>>>
>>>*Skating* to the music, she lost her sense of time. (*Skating* modifies *she*)

>>Passive:
>>>*reserved* seat (*reserved* modifies *seat*)
>>>
>>>*Invited* to the party, he dressed in a tuxedo. (*Invited* modifies *he*)

>Participles may be of various tenses, most commonly

>>**Present active participle:**
>>>*Hitting* the ball, the runner runs. (*Hitting* modifies *runner*)

>>**Present passive participle:**
>>>*Being hit* by the batter, the ball flies into left field. (*Being hit* modifies *ball*)

>>**Perfect active participle:**
>>>*Having jumped* the fence, the horse ran away. (*Having jumped* modifies *horse*)
>>>
>>>*Having hit* the ball, the runner ran. (*Having hit* modifies *runner*)

>>**Perfect passive participle:**
>>>*Having been elected,* the club president thanked the members. (*Having been elected* modifies *president*)
>>>
>>>*Having been hit* by the batter, the ball flew into left field. (*Having been hit* modifies *ball*)

Gerund: verbal noun that can perform any function a noun can perform: subject, direct object, object of a preposition, predicate nominative, appositive, etc.

>subject:
>>*Flying* makes me nervous.
>>
>>*Taking* French is both useful and enjoyable.

direct object:
>I enjoy *hiking.*
>She had never much liked *fishing.*

object of a preposition:
>Many people get pleasure from *reading.*
>He had learned about *buying* and *selling* cars.

predicate nominative:
>The most challenging activity on the ranch is *riding.*

appositive:
>He hoped to get on the varsity team in his favorite sport, swimming.

Gerunds may be of various tenses, most commonly

Present active gerund:
>*Hitting* a baseball requires skill.

Present passive gerund:
>*Being hit* by a baseball is painful.

Perfect active gerund:
>I enjoyed *having eaten* that dessert.

Perfect passive gerund:
>I have to believe that the dessert enjoyed *having been eaten.*

II

Sentence Structure

The basic structure of the English sentence is

subject	predicate
Julia	runs

A **substantive** is a word or group of words that performs the function of a noun: noun, pronoun, gerund, gerund phrase, noun clause.

Subject: the substantive about which a sentence predicates something—the subject does the action of, or is in the condition indicated by, the verb. **Complete subject**: the subject with all of its modifiers. **Compound subject**: two or more subjects joined by coordinate or correlative conjunctions.

Predicate: the verb that predicates something about the subject.

	subject	predicate (verb)
Noun:	Julia	runs
Compound subject:	Julia and Alex	run
Pronoun:	They	play
Pronoun & modifier:	Those who are young	discover
Gerund:	Swimming	pleases
Gerund phrase:	Swimming in a lake	pleases
Noun clause:	That it is hot out	surprises

Complete predicate: the verb with all its modifiers and complements (see next page).

subject	predicate	
	verb	complement
Alex	quickly swings	the bat (direct object)
Those who are young	become	adults (predicate nominative)
Almost all children	grow	big (predicate adjective)
Sally	sent	me a letter (indirect and direct object)

Complement (from L. *complere*, to fill up, complete) fills out the predicate by completing the sense of the verb. It may be any of six types:

After an action verb—the object of an action verb, receiving the action, is in the objective (Latin: accusative) case:

Direct object: receives the action of an action verb:

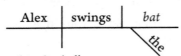

George hit the *ball.*
Stephanie telephoned her *cousin.*
Do you expect *anyone* to believe that?
Americans love *ice cream.*
When will Grandpa sell that old *jalopy* he drives?
I do not know *why yet I live to say "this thing's to do."*
    (noun clause as direct object) — Shakespeare, Hamlet
It is not possible that I could count *the ways* I love
    you. (*the ways [that] I love you* is the complete
    direct object)

Indirect object: the person or thing to or for whom an action is done. In order for there to be an indirect object, there must be an actual or implied direct object:

Sally	sent	a letter
	me	

George hit *me* the ball.
Stephanie asked *her cousin* an important question.
I do not know why I ever tell *you* my secrets.
I do not owe *her* an apology; she owes *me* one.
Tell *me* the time.
Tell *us* [something implied].

Note: When the person or thing to or for whom the action is done follows a preposition, it is not an indirect object but the object of a preposition (see "Preposition," p. 10–11):

George hit the ball *to me.*
Stephanie asked an important question *of her cousin.*
I do not know why I ever tell my secrets *to you.*
Do a favor *for me.*

Objects of Verbals: Objects of verbals (participles, gerunds, infinitives—see "Verbal," pp. 14–16) are not called "direct" objects. In the sentence *Do you expect anyone to believe that,* the word *that* is the object of the infinitive "to believe." A verbal can have both an object and an indirect object:

Infinitive complements:

> **Object of the infinitive:**
> I have decided to buy a *car.* (*car* is the object of the infinitive)

> **Indirect object of the infinitive:**
> I have decided to buy *myself* a car. (*myself* is the indirect object of the infinitive)

Participle complements:

> **Object of the participle** is the noun that *receives* the action of the participle, not the noun that the participle modifies:
> Having jumped the *fence,* the horse ran away.
> > (*Having jumped* modifies *horse;* the object of the participle is *fence.*)

> **Indirect object of the participle** is the noun to or for whom the action of the participle is done:
> Giving *myself* a pep talk, I signed the check.
> > (*Giving* modifies *I; myself* is the indirect object of the participle; *talk* is the object of the participle)

Gerund complements:

> **Object of the gerund:**
> Flying a *plane* makes me nervous. (*plane* is the object of the gerund *flying*)
> I enjoy flying *kites.* (*kites* is the object of the gerund *flying*)
> Many people get pleasure from reading *books.*
> > (*books* is the object of the gerund *reading*)
> The most challenging activity is riding *horses.*
> > (*horses* is the object of the gerund *riding*)

Indirect object of the gerund:

Giving *myself* a car was an expensive proposition.
(*myself* is the indirect object of the gerund
Giving; *car* is the object of the gerund)

After a linking verb: **Subjective complement.** (Because the linking verb makes the complement equal to the subject, the complement of a linking verb will be in the subjective—Latin: nominative—case.):

Predicate nominative: a substantive (noun, pronoun, noun clause):

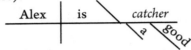

(Note: *good* modifies the predicate nominative; it is not a predicate adjective)

Joey is a baseball *player*. (*player* is the predicate
nominative after the linking verb *is*)
Marcie became a theatrical *director*. (*director* is the
predicate nominative after the linking verb *became*)
The seven deadly sins are a serious *threat* to us all.
(*threat* is the predicate nominative after the
linking verb *are*; see note, below)
A serious threat to us all is the seven deadly *sins*. (*sins*
is the predicate nominative after the linking verb *is*)

Note: A verb must always agree with the subject, not the predicate nominative. Hence the verb in the third sentence above is plural (seven deadly sins *are*) and the verb in the fourth is singular (threat *is*).

Predicate adjective: an adjective or participle

Sally | feels \confident

Joey is extremely *bright*. (*bright* is the predicate
adjective modifying the subject *Joey* after the
linking verb *is*)
Marcie became *irate* when the actors canceled. (*irate*
is the predicate adjective modifying the subject
Marcie after the linking verb *became*)

The seven deadly sins are *serious* and *important*. (*serious* and *important* are predicate adjectives modifying the subject *sins* after the linking verb *are*)
Sally grew rather *tall* last year.
I am feeling *weak* today.
Roses smell *sweet*.

After certain verbs (like *make, name, call, choose, elect,* etc.):

Objective complement: a noun or adjective complementing (referring to and completing) the direct object:
We elected Lincoln *president*.
They called her *a winner*.
I made the ornament *shiny*.

After a passive verb:

Retained object: The direct object in an active sentence that is retained when the verb is made passive:
He was given *a dangerous mission*. [from "They gave him a dangerous mission."]
They were told *the truth*. [from "Someone told them the truth."]

Appositive: a noun or pronoun that renames a noun or pronoun:
My cousin *Sally* came to visit.
Charles Dickens, *the author*, is well known.

III
Phrases

A **phrase** is a group of words forming a modifying or substantive unit but not containing a subject and a finite verb (cf., "Clauses," p. 25).

Prepositional phrase: a preposition with its object and any modifiers;
> *to the tree; from the hot oven; over the rainbow; above the clouds*

Prepositional phrases may be either adverbial or adjectival:
> Adverbial: Forward the email *to your friends*. (modifies the verb *Forward*)
> Adjectival: The letter *from my friend* was postmarked yesterday (modifies the noun *letter*)

Verbal phrase: a verbal with any complements and modifiers (see "Verbal," pp. 14–16, and "Complement," pp. 18–21)
> **Infinitive phrase**: an infinitive with its object (if any) and any modifiers, as *to buy a new car* or *to paddle quickly*
>> as a noun:
>>> *To tame a horse* requires skill.
>>> He tried *to tame a horse*.
>> as an adverb:
>>> She took a course *to learn French*.
>>> They stayed *to hear the speech*.
>>> A good book is fun *to read when alone*.
>> as an adjective:
>>> There were sights *to see first*.
>>> We had enough popcorn *to eat to our hearts' content*.
>>> He had a strong desire *to win the race for his team*.

Note: In formal writing it is preferable to avoid splitting an infinitive (i.e., avoid inserting an adverb or phrase between the *to* and the infinitive form) as "*to* boldly *go*," "*to* completely *forget*," "*to* quickly and easily *learn*"
> Informal: *To really know* what it was like you had *to actually be* there.
> Formal: *Really to know* what it was like, you *actually* had *to be* there.

Participial phrase: a participle with its complements (if any) and any modifiers:

> With adverbial modifier: The *quickly running* brook was cold.
> With adverbial prepositional phrase: The brook *running through the woods* was cold.
> With object of the participle: *Buying a new car,* George felt successful.
> Participle with objective complement: *Voting him president,* the club completes its agenda.
> Participle with retained object: *Being given a birthday present,* she blushes.

Gerund phrase: a gerund with its complements (if any) and any modifiers:

> With adverbial modifier: *Swimming upstream* was difficult.
> With adverbial prepositional phrase: *His arriving from the beach* meant the importation of a lot of sand.
> With object of the gerund: *Failing the test* was not an option.
> With object and indirect object of the gerund: I disapprove of your sending *them* my email *address.* (*them* is the indirect object of the gerund *sending*; *address* is the object of the gerund; the gerund phrase *your sending them my email address* is the object of the preposition *of*)
> Gerund with objective complement: *Electing him president* was relatively painless.
> Gerund with retained object: She does not enjoy *being given birthday presents.*

Note: The implied subject of a verbal needs to be the same as the subject of the sentence. If the subjects are different, the result is a **dangling modifier.**

Dangling infinitive phrase:

> Faulty: To play tennis well, the racquet must be tightly strung.
> Correct: *If one wants to play tennis well, one's racquet must be tightly strung.* (infinitive phrase changed to a clause with its own subject)
> Correct: *To play tennis well, one must use a tightly strung racquet.* (subject of the sentence changed to be the same as the implied subject of the infinitive.)

Dangling participial phrase:

Faulty: *Walking down the street,* the house came into view.

Correct: *As I walked down the street,* the house came into view. (participial phrase changed to a clause with its own subject)

Correct: *Walking down the street,* I saw the house come into view. (subject of the sentence changed to be the same as the implied subject of the participle)

Dangling gerund phrase:

Faulty: *By blinding the Cyclops,* Odysseus' escape remained possible.

Correct: *Because Odysseus blinded the Cyclops,* his escape remained possible. (gerund phrase changed to a clause with its own subject)

Correct: *By blinding the Cyclops,* Odysseus preserved the possibility of escape. (subject of the sentence changed to be the same as the implied subject of the gerund)

Appositive phrase: an appositive with any modifiers:

My only cousin, *Sally of the blue eyes,* came for a visit.

Charles Dickens, *the author of <u>Great Expectations</u>,* is well known.

IV

Clauses

A **clause** is a group of words containing a subject and a predicate with a finite verb (not just a verbal).

Independent or **Main clause:** a clause that can stand by itself without being a fragment—the foundation that makes a sentence.

> *We journeyed to the frozen wastes of Antarctica.*
> *I once saw a hawk.*
> When we looked out the window, *we saw a hawk.*
> *The hawk* that was above our heads *swooped down into the field* as if he were about to catch a mouse in his talons.

Dependent or **Subordinate clause:** a clause that *cannot* stand by itself without being a fragment. It performs one of three functions within an independent (main) clause: adverb, adjective, or noun. It is introduced by a subordinate conjunction (usually adverbial), a relative pronoun (usually adjectival), or a noun clause identifier (subordinate conjunction or pronoun):

> **Adverbial clause:** functions as an adverb modifier of the independent (main) clause. It is introduced by a subordinate conjunction and usually modifies the verb (or sometimes an adjective or an adverb) of the independent clause:
>
> > *When we journeyed to the frozen wastes of Antarctica,* we wondered at its beauty. (The *when* clause modifies the verb *wondered*.)
> > *Because we journeyed to the frozen wastes of Antarctica,* we discovered great beauty. (The *because* clause modifies the verb *discovered*.)
> > *If you ever journey to the frozen wastes of Antarctica,* you too will experience wonders. (The *if* clause modifies the verb *will experience*.)
> > *If we arrive on time,* we will be admitted.
> > We will go hungry *because we caught no fish.*
> > *When we looked out the window,* we saw a hawk.
> > The hawk that was above our heads swooped down into the field *as if he were about to catch a mouse in his talons.*

Adjective clause: functions as an adjective modifier of the independent (main) clause, modifying a noun or pronoun in the independent clause. It is most often a **relative clause** introduced by a relative pronoun (*who, whom, whose, that, which,* see "Parts of Speech," pp. 8–9) or a subordinate conjunction:

> The adventurer *who journeyed to Antarctica* returned without harm. (The relative *who* clause modifies the noun *adventurer.*)
>
> The adventurer *whom we followed to Antarctica* led us home. (The relative *whom* clause modifies the noun *adventurer.*)
>
> The journey *that we took to Antarctica* was thrilling. (The relative *that* clause modifies the noun *journey.*)
>
> The club *whose members traveled* honors its charter. (The relative *whose* clause modifies the noun *club.*)
>
> The journey to Antarctica, *which we took last spring,* rewarded us greatly. (The relative *which* clause modifies the noun *journey.*)
>
> That is the place *where he was last seen.* (The subordinate conjunction *where* introduces an adjective clause modifying the noun *place*)
>
> The doctor *who diagnosed the disease* found its cure.
>
> I could not remember the name of the doctor *whom you recommended last week.*
>
> What are the ingredients of the dish *that you served us*?
>
> The hawk *that was above our heads* swooped into the field as if he were about to catch a mouse in his talons.

Note: The case of the relative pronoun (who/whom, whoever/whomever) is determined by its function in its own subordinate clause:

> Subjective case: Give the book to *whoever wants it.*
>
> Objective case: Give the book to *whomever you choose.*

Noun clause: performs within the independent (main) clause any function that a noun may perform (i.e., subject, direct object, indirect object, object of preposition, predicate nominative, objective complement, retained object, or appositive). It is introduced by a **noun clause identifier,** which may be either a subordinate conjunction (*that, how, when, where, whether, why*) or a pronoun (*what, whatever, who, whoever, which, whose, whom, whomever*):

Subject:

> *That we journeyed to Antarctica* was remarkable. (Noun
> clause subject of the verb *was*)
> *That the orchestra is ready* must be obvious.

Direct object:

> I will tell you *how we journeyed to Antarctica.* (Noun
> clause direct object of the verb *will tell*)
> I request *that you be seated.*
> The professor recommended *that we read his short story,*
> but he would not tell us *why we ought to do so.*
> Will he ever know *whether we have read it?*

Indirect object:

> They sent *whoever wanted one* a copy of the book.

Object of preposition:

> I am happy to tell you about *what we saw there.* (Noun
> clause object of the preposition *about*)
> You may relay the message to *whoever will benefit from it*
> (*whoever* is in the subjective case because it is the
> subject of the noun clause; the object of the
> preposition *to* is the whole noun clause)

Predicate nominative:

> The inventor of the device was *whom we needed.*

Objective complement:

> She called the experiment *exactly what was required.*

Retained object:

> The children were given *what they wanted*—a pony.

Appositive phrase:

> His plan, *that we should all play hooky,* got us into trouble.

V

Sentence Types

Structural

Simple sentence: one independent clause:

> *I saw a hawk yesterday.*
> *"Never give a sucker an even break."*

with compound verb:

> *He may be captured but will never talk.*
> *Never give a sucker an even break or smarten up a chump.*
> — W.C. Fields, *You Can't Cheat an Honest Man*

with compound subject:

> *The Capulets and the Montagues agreed to have a battle.*

Compound sentence: two or more independent clauses

> *He may be captured, but he will never talk.*
> *I never see a hawk without thinking about the Rocky Mountains; I*
> *grew up in the Rockies, and they were my home for twenty years.*

Complex sentence: one independent clause with one or more dependent (subordinate) clauses:

> *Though Capulets hated Montagues, Juliet fell in love with Romeo.*
> *Yesterday, before the sun began to set, I saw a hawk that also saw me.*

Compound-Complex sentence: two or more independent clauses with one or more dependent clauses:

> *Although Capulets hated Montagues, Juliet fell in love with Romeo,*
> *and he, in spite of the fact that Montagues hated Capulets, fell*
> *equally in love with Juliet.*
> *Yesterday, before the sun began to set, I saw a hawk that also no doubt*
> *saw me, and I watched it swoop down as if to catch a mouse.*

Rhetorical

Declarative: makes a statement

> *The sky is blue.*
> *You cannot make omelets without breaking eggs.*

Interrogative: asks a question

> *Where are you going?*
> *"When shall we three meet again?"* — Shakespeare, *Macbeth*

Imperative: makes a command

Go to the window.

"Never give a sucker an even break or smarten up a chump."

Exclamatory: expresses an intense emotion or attitude

How beautiful the sunset is tonight!

Over my dead body!

Stylistic

Loose sentence: A sentence that begins with the main clause and attaches modifiers, qualifiers, and details following it:

The ballgame ended in the cheers of the home team, the dejection of the visitors, and a rash of honking in the parking lot that signified the joy of an unexpected victory.

Periodic sentence: A sentence that expresses the main clause at the end after introductory subordinate ideas:

When the couple had departed and all the visitors had left the banquet hall, and as the staff was cleaning up, among the drooping flowers and the empty bottles, sitting dejected in a corner and wondering how he was going to pay for it all, sat the father of the bride.

Suspended sentence: A sentence that interrupts the main clause with intervening subordinate ideas:

The completion of the transcontinental railroad, long in coming and fraught with labor and danger, succeeded in uniting the nation.

Sentence fragment: any group of words not grammatically a complete sentence but punctuated as if it were one:

So unlike the concerns of most of us, the investors' moods rising and falling, depending on whether the stock market went up or down.

VI

Punctuation

Essential rules about punctuation include the following:

Comma (,):
General rule: The comma, being a precise instrument, should not be used unless there is a specific rule that calls for it.

Specific rules:

1. No comma between subject and verb.
> Faulty: *The woodman I saw yesterday marking a tree,*
> *chopped it down today.*
> Correct: *The woodman I saw yesterday marking a tree*
> *chopped it down today.*

2. Always place a comma or a period inside the closing quotation mark. (Question mark and exclamation point may go inside or outside the quotation mark depending on the sense intended.)
> Faulty: *"To be or not to be. That is the question", says Hamlet.*
> Correct: *"To be or not to be. That is the question," says Hamlet.*
> Faulty: *Hamlet says, "The readiness is all".*
> Correct: *Hamlet says, "The readiness is all."*
> Correct: *"What do you want me to do?" asked Joey.*
> Correct: *Did Jane say "I love you"?*
> Correct: *Jane actually said "I love you" to me!*
> Correct: *My response to Jane was an eloquent "Gosh!"*

3. Place a comma before a coordinating conjunction joining two independent clauses. (No comma before a coordinate conjunction joining anything less than two independent clauses.)
> Correct: *He may be captured, but he will never talk.*
> Faulty: *He may be captured but he will never talk.*
> Faulty: *I saw a hawk, and a blue heron yesterday.*
> Faulty: *I saw a hawk yesterday, and shouted at it.*

4. Place commas before and after **non-restrictive** (non-essential) appositives and relative clauses. No commas before or after **restrictive** (essential) appositives and relative clauses:

Non-restrictive appositive:
> My horse, *Flicka*, is a beauty. (I own only one horse)
> My only dog, *Spot*, is extremely loyal to me.
> <u>A Tale of Two Cities</u>, *a novel by Dickens*, is worth
> reading a second time.

Restrictive appositive:
> My horse *Flicka* is a beauty. (I own several horses)
> Of the three canines in my house, my dog *Spot* is the
> most loyal to me.
> Shakespeare's play <u>*Othello*</u> is a great tragedy.

Non-restrictive relative clause (uses *which*):
> The ending of <u>A Tale of Two Cities</u>, *which I was
> reading last night*, is very exciting.
> Mr. Sapsucker, *whom I saw marking a tree yesterday,*
> felled that tree today.

Restrictive relative clause (uses *that*):
> The book *that I read last night* was <u>A Tale of Two
> Cities</u>.
> The woodman *whom I saw marking a tree yesterday*
> felled that tree today.

5. The serial (Oxford) comma—i.e., before a coordinate conjunction introducing the last item in a series—is recommended.
> *We bought lettuce, tomatoes, carrots, cucumbers, and celery for
> the salad.*

6. Place a comma after an *introductory* adverbial dependent (subordinate) clause and after an introductory participial phrase. (No comma before an adverbial dependent clause that *follows* the main clause.)
> Correct: *If we arrive on time,* we will be admitted.
> Correct: We will go hungry *because we caught no fish.*
> Correct: *Looking out the window,* we saw a hawk.

7. Place a comma before and after a noun of direct address.
> Correct: *George,* can you help me for a minute?
> Correct: I must tell you, *Ladies and Gentlemen of the jury,*
> that the defendant cannot possibly be guilty.

8. Place parenthetical phrases between commas, never omitting the second comma:

> *When you go hiking, whether in the woods or in the desert, take water with you.*

For brief, easily integrated phrases, omit the commas:

> *Take water if you can whenever you go hiking.*

Use parentheses instead if the parenthetical phrase is a significant interruption of the sentence:

> *Whenever you go hiking (a form of recreation very popular in summer in almost any climate) take water with you.*

9. Use commas before *and* after the year in a date:

> *The Declaration was dated July 4, 1776, at Philadelphia.*

No comma is necessary when the month and date are reversed:

> *4 July 1776*

10. Use commas after scholarly abbreviations (*etc., i.e., e.g.*):

> *Have notebooks, pens, paper, etc., always at hand.*

Use commas before academic degrees and titles that follow names (B.A., M.A., Ph.D., S.J., OBE, etc.):

> *Jason Briggs, M.A., will lecture tonight.*
> *George Franco, Vice-Chair of Development, will also be speaking.*

The term *Junior* and its abbreviation *Jr.* used to be set off by commas as a parenthetical, but since it is essentially a restrictive appositive, publishing style now eliminates it.

> *Martin Luther King Jr.*

11. Do not use a comma after a coordinate conjunction:

> *The situation is comical, yet there is a moral to be learned from it.*

There should be no comma after the coordinate conjunction even if it is followed by an introductory dependent clause introducing an independent clause:

> *There are several alternatives we may choose, but if we do not act quickly, it will be too late to make any choice at all.*

12. Do not use a comma to join independent clauses where there is no coordinate conjunction; this error is called a comma splice:

> Faulty: *We put on our ice skates and tied them, then we carefully hobbled to the rink.*

Use a semicolon instead (see Semicolon, below). If the two independent clauses are very short and closely related, a comma is permitted:

Correct: *Fly now, pay later.*

13. Do not use periods for commas, turning sentences into fragments:

Faulty: *They were typical travelers. Teenagers away from home for the first time.*

Correct: *They were typical travelers, teenagers away from home for the first time.*

A word or brief phrase may be punctuated as a sentence for emphasis, but this device should be used sparingly and only where informal style is appropriate (as in dialogue):

I haled one taxi after another. None stopped. I waved, whistled, and jumped. No luck.

Semicolon (;): a heavier point than the comma and having only two uses:

1. The semicolon joins two independent clauses where there is no coordinating conjunction. (Note: Use of a comma in place of a semicolon here constitutes the error called the comma splice)

Faulty: *I never see a hawk without thinking about the Rocky Mountains, I grew up in the Rockies.*

Correct: *I never see a hawk without thinking about the Rocky Mountains; I grew up in the Rockies.*

2. The semicolon is used for clarity in place of commas that would normally separate elements that have their own internal comma punctuation.

Correct: *For the salad we bought lettuce, the red leaf kind that Josie likes; tomatoes, of which the label said they were organic; carrots; those crispy Persian cucumbers, which you can't get in most stores; and celery.*

Colon (:): a final punctuation mark to be used at the end of a complete sentence to introduce another way of saying the same thing or a list. What follows the colon may, but need not, be a complete sentence.

Faulty: *I can tell you the one thing you need to know for the exam;*
    Shakespeare did not write novels.

Correct: *I can tell you the one thing you need to know for the exam:*
    Shakespeare did not write novels.

Faulty: *The five ingredients we bought for the salad were: lettuce,*
    tomatoes, carrots, cucumbers, and celery.

Correct: *We bought five ingredients for the salad: lettuce, tomatoes,*
    carrots, cucumbers, and celery.

Exclamation Point (!): used to indicate exclamations, commands, or very strong emotion.

What a magnificent sunset!
Ouch!
Get out of my house!

Avoid exclamation points for mere emphasis. It is better to let the words do their work:

Faulty: *I loved that art exhibition!*
Correct: *I loved that art exhibition.*

Parentheses (( )): used to set off words, phrases, or sentences more heavily parenthetical than commas would indicate. Punctuate a sentence containing parentheses outside the final parenthesis mark as if the parenthetical phrase were not there:

Correct: *We have found a fossil (having looked everywhere else) in*
    the least likely spot.

Correct: *We have found a fossil in an unlikely spot (having looked*
    everywhere else with no luck), and the team has decided to donate
    it to the Museum of Archaeology.

Punctuate the parenthetical phrase or sentence as if it were its own sentence, omitting the final comma or period but including any question mark or exclamation point:

Correct: *We have found a fossil (you will never believe where!)*
    under a parking lot.

Correct: *We have found a fossil (will you believe me?) under a*
    parking lot.

When a parenthetical sentence in a paragraph stands by itself, its final punctuation comes inside the closing parenthesis:

Correct: *After seeking for three years we discovered evidence for our*
    theory. (We found the fossil under a parking lot.) The Museum of
    Archaeology will be pleased.

Use parentheses for scholarly references within your text. (See under "Scholarly References," p. 48)

Quotation Marks (" "): used to indicate an exact quotation of someone else's written or spoken words. Quotations may be formally introduced with a colon:

> *The Declaration of Independence lists three unalienable rights: "Life, Liberty and the Pursuit of Happiness."*

Most often a quotation is the direct object of a verb of writing (*he reiterated*) or speaking (*she said*) or in apposition. In these cases, the quotation is introduced by a comma:

> *The author of the Declaration wrote, "We hold these truths to be self-evident . . . ."*
>
> *George said, "There is no way I will jump into that pond."*
>
> *Sally replied, "You will if you know what is good for you," staring at him fiercely.*
>
> *"You will if you know what is good for you," Sally said, staring at him fiercely.*

Publishers' style is now to place ending commas and periods *before* the closing quotation mark, as above. Exclamation points and question marks that are part of the quotation itself go before the closing quotation mark:

> *"Save my puppy!" Sally shouted.*

If the quotation is part of a larger question or exclamantion, then the punctuation comes after the quotation mark:

> *As long as you live here, you will never again say to me "No, I won't"!*
>
> *How can you tell me "I do not and cannot love you"?*

Quotations of three lines or fewer (prose or verse) are placed in quotation marks. Quotations of more than three lines are indented within the paragraph and have no quotation marks except those indicating dialogue within the quotation. (See "Slash" below.)

Indirect quotations, usually introduced by *that,* have no quotation marks:

> *I said that I will never speak to you again if you do not save my puppy.*

Quotations within quotations are indicated by single quotation marks (' '). Quotations within them are indicated by double quotation marks, and so on. (" ' " ' . . . ' " ' ").

Expressions in common use are not usually placed within quotation marks:

She advised me to look before you leap.

Avoid using quotation marks for slang expressions or to apologize for a usage. Have the courage of your diction.

Faulty: *Students who "kiss up" to teachers at that school are wasting their energy.*

Brave: *Students who kiss up to teachers at that school are wasting their energy.*

Similarly, avoid treating the reader with the nod and wink with what are called "scare quotes," quotation marks indicating an ironic intention in the writer:

Avoid: *He told her father that they were "friends."*

It is better to use words to indicate irony:

Better: *He told her father with a straight face that they were friends.*

Use quotation marks for titles of poems, short stories, or any short work published as part of a larger work. (See also "Italics," p. 48)

Ellipsis (. . .): indicates some specific word or passage left out of a quotation. The series of periods is formed with spaces between them (. . . not ...). When the ellipsis includes the end of a sentence, a fourth period is added:

"We hold these truths to be self-evident, that all men . . . are endowed by their Creator . . . ."

Slash (/): used to indicate a line break when more than one line of verse is quoted within a paragraph. Place a space before the slash and one after it:

As Ogden Nash writes, "The cow is of the bovine ilk; / One end is moo, the other, milk."

A quotation of more than three lines from a poem should be indented and printed line for line as in the original with no slash marks:

Coleridge begins his Kubla Khan

In Xanadu did Kubla Khan
A stately pleasure dome decree:
Where Alph, the sacred river, ran
Through caverns measureless to man
Down to a sunless sea.

Hyphen (-): the shortest horizontal line, used

1. to indicate compound words:
   self-reliance
   cul-de-sac

2. to join multiple words forming an adjective preceding a noun:
   a well-documented observation
   an out-of-the-box thinker

3. In determining whether a two-word phrase should be treated as two words (*jump rope*), one word (*jumpsuit*), or a hyphenated phrase (*jump-start*) the best guide is a good dictionary. We recommend the latest edition of *Merriam Webster's Collegiate Dictionary*.

N-dash (–): the middle-sized horizontal line (named so because in the old typesetting it was the width of the letter *N*), used to indicate continuous numbers:
   38–42; 3,675–76; etc.

M-dash (—): the longest horizontal line (named so because in the old typesetting it was the width of the letter *M*), used to indicate a break in the grammar of a sentence and, if necessary, the resumption of the original grammar:
   Students of Shakespeare—at least those who wish to understand his plays as he meant them to be understood—must know something about Ptolemaic astronomy.
   As the train pulled in to the station and the crowd—are you listening to this?—leaned forward for a look, guess who was the first to shout "hurrah!"
   I'm not sure when we can expect Joey to—oh, there he is now!

VII
Additional Points of Grammar and Form

Subject-Verb Agreement

Relevant Rules:

1. A verb must always agree in **number** with its subject.

2. Even where there is a linking verb followed by a predicate nominative, Rule 1 still applies.
> My worry *is* the flies. (not *are*)
> The flies *are* my worry. (not *is*)

3. Even where there is an object of a preposition of a different number from the subject, Rule 1 still applies.
> Each of the girls *has* a locker. (not *have*)
> The location of the safes full of rich jewels *is* not known. (not *are*)

4. Where there is a compound subject, Rule 1 still applies; the verb must be plural.
> The classroom on the second floor and the library *were* empty. (not *was*)

5. A prepositional phrase does not make a single subject compound.
> The classroom in addition to the library *was* empty. (not *were*)

Pronoun-Antecedent Agreement

Relevant Rules:

1. A pronoun must agree with its antecedent (the word to which it refers) in number.

2. *Their* is plural, not singular. (*Theirself* and *theirselves* are not valid English words.)

3. Each of the following words is singular: *every, each, everybody, everyone, anyone, no one, none.*

Faulty: Everybody who ate of it lost their will to do
anything else. (*their* should be *his* or *his or her*)

Faulty: Every human will make mistakes, whether or
not they are a hero. (*he is* or *he or she is*)

Faulty: All of these concepts working together is
how the poet got their point across. (*are* how the
poet got *his* or *are* how the poet got *her*)

Faulty: Someone came snooping around the house
last night and left their footprints in the sand.
(*his* or *her* or *his or her*)

Faulty: The crowd rose to its feet and shouted their
approval of the catch. (either *its* feet ... *its*
approval or *their* feet ... *their* approval)

Faulty: A group of famous musicians want to express
its appreciation. (*want ... their* or *wants ... its*)

Faulty: One need not clarify every detail of his/her speech.
(*one's*; *his/her* is not acceptable in formal writing)

Faulty: The chairman asked everyone who had
recently delivered a speech to make a note of
their contribution. (*his or her*)

Faulty: The proprietors of the smorgasbord
restaurant urged everybody to return to the
revolving table as often as they liked. (*he or she*)

Faulty: One who lacks a sense of direction will usually lose
your way on this campus. (*one's* or *his* or *her* or *his or her*)

Faulty: I know that no one will believe me if I tell
them that the exam was easy. (*him or her*)

Faulty: Each of the states that had suffered heavy
losses during the hurricane received federal aid for
their restoration programs. (*its*)

Faulty: The reporters were interested in anyone who
would give their opinions of the city's baseball team.
(*his opinion* or *her opinion* or *his or her opinion*)

Faulty: Those kind of women can easily adjust
theirselves to changes in fashion. (*Those kinds of
women ... themselves* or *That kind of woman ... herself*)

Case of Pronouns
(see Personal and Relative pronouns under "Parts of Speech," pp. 7–9)

Use the correct case of pronouns: subjective case for subjects, objective case for objects, and possessive case for possession and subjects of gerunds:

Correct: *Did you or she call me?*
Correct: *Did anyone call you or her?*
Correct: *We students of grammar care about case.*
Correct: *Case is crucial to us students of grammar.*
Correct: *Someone stole my bicycle.*
Correct: *Someone watched my awkward swimming.*

In the comparison of the subjects of implied verbs, the proper case is the subjective:

George swims better than I. [implied verb *swim*]
Sally is taller than he. [implied verb *is tall*]

Avoid reflexive pronouns to hide ignorance of the proper case:

Faulty: *Sally and myself arrived at the meeting early.* [*Sally and I*]
Faulty: *They failed to call on either Sally or myself.* [*Sally or me*]
Faulty: *Sally and yourself were expected to vote no.* [*Sally and you*]

The case of the relative pronouns *who, whom, whoever, whomever* is determined by the pronoun's function in its own clause, no matter what function the clause itself performs in the sentence:

Faulty: *Give the gavel to whomever wants to run the meeting.*
Correct: *Give the gavel to whoever wants to run the meeting.*
    [*whoever* the subject of *wants*]
Correct: *Give the book to him who is eager to read it.* [*who* the subject of *is*]
Correct: *Give the book to him whom you choose.* [*whom* the object of *choose*]

Intervening phrases like *you think* or *I believe* or *we know* or *they said* are treated as parenthetical and do not affect the case of the pronoun:

Faulty: *Vote for the candidate whom you think can win.*
Correct: *Vote for the candidate who you think can win.* [*who* the subject of *can win*]
Faulty: *Whom did she say proposed the amendment?*
Correct: *Who did she say proposed the amendment?* [*who* the subject of *proposed*]

The subject of a gerund (the person doing the action of the gerund) is in the possessive case:

Faulty: *I appreciate you coming on time.*

Correct: *I appreciate your coming on time.*

Faulty: *Was their objection to him being a fencing instructor unfounded?*

Correct: *Was their objection to his being a fencing instructor unfounded?*

Faulty: *Do you think that we not being there was noticed?*

Faulty: *Do you think that us not being there was noticed?*

Correct: *Do you think that our not being there was noticed?*

Subordinating Conjunctions vs. Relative Pronouns— What's the Difference?

Dependent (subordinate) clauses usually begin with either a subordinating conjunction or a pronoun. A subordinating conjunction is a logical connector joining the dependent clause to the independent (main) clause (cf., "Conjunction," pp. 11–12); a pronoun is a substantive standing in for a noun and usually referring to some noun previously mentioned in the sentence (cf., "Pronoun," pp. 7–9).

Subordinating Conjunctions:

A subordinating conjunction is always followed by a dependent clause. The most common subordinating conjunctions are:

after	*because*	*provided (that)*	*when*
although	*before*	*since*	*whenever*
as	*even if*	*so that*	*where*
as if	*even though*	*than*	*wherever*
as long as	*how*	*that*	*while*
as much as	*if*	*though*	
as soon as	*in order that*	*unless*	
as though	*lest*	*until* (or *till*)	

A subordinating conjunction will most often introduce an **adverb clause:**

> *When* you enter, please give your ticket to the usher. (the *When* clause modifies the verb *give*)

A subordinating conjunction can introduce a **noun clause,** in which case it is sometimes called a **noun clause identifier:**

> He inquired *whether* he needed a ticket to enter. (the *whether* clause is the direct object of the verb *inquired*)

A subordinating conjunction can introduce an **adjective clause**:

> She remembered the time *when* she first put on roller skates. (the *when* clause modifies the noun *time*)

Note: depending on their use, some words that serve as subordinating conjunctions may also serve as other parts of speech, specifically prepositions and adverbs:

> Adelaide raised her hand *before* Sam did. (*before* is a subordinating conjunction introducing an adverb clause)
>
> Adelaide stood *before* the class. (*before* is a preposition whose object is *class*)
>
> Adelaide ran before. (*before* is an adverb modifying the verb *ran*)

Relative Pronouns:

Relative pronouns are called "relative" because they relate a dependent (subordinate) clause to a noun or pronoun elsewhere in the sentence. The relative pronouns are:

> *who, whom, whose, that, which, whoever, whomever, whichever*

Relative pronouns most often introduce adjective clauses:

> The adventurer *who journeyed to Antarctica* returned without harm. (the *who* clause modifies the noun *adventurer*)
>
> The adventurer *whom we followed to Antarctica* led us home again. (the *whom* clause modifies the noun *adventurer*)
>
> The journey *that we took to Antarctica* was thrilling. (the *that* clause modifies the noun *journey*)
>
> The club *whose members journeyed to Antarctica* honors its charter. (the *whose* clause modifies the noun *club*)
>
> The journey to Antarctica, *which we took last spring,* rewarded us greatly. (the *which* clause modifies the noun *journey*)

In deciding between *that* and *which*, treat *that* as restrictive and *which* as non-restrictive.

> The book that I have just read is *A Tale of Two Cities* by Charles Dickens.
>
> *A Tale of Two Cities*, which I have just read, is by Charles Dickens.

(see also "Relative Pronoun," pp. 8–9, and "Comma Rule #4," pp. 30-31, and "The Four *That*'s," p. 46)

Ambiguous and Vague Pronoun Reference

Ambiguous: Where a pronoun could refer to more than one person or thing previously mentioned, the reader cannot tell which of them is intended.

> Faulty: Argos, Odysseus' dog, was lying on a dung heap when he recognized his old master, although *he* looked old and decrepit. (Who looked old and decrepit?)

> To fix ambiguous pronoun references, use nouns:

> Correct: . . . although *Argos* looked old and decrepit.

> Correct: . . . although *Odysseus* looked old and decrepit

Vague: A pronoun must refer to some specific previous noun; it cannot refer to an unnamed abstract idea implied in a previous clause or sentence without causing confusion and obscurity.

> Faulty: Odysseus pretended not to know Argos in order to avoid being recognized by the suitors. *This* was hard for the returning hero. (What was hard for the returning hero? There is no noun to which the word *this* refers.)

> Faulty: When Odysseus proclaims who he is to Polyphemus, *it* gets him into trouble. (What gets him into trouble? There is no noun to which the word *it* refers.)

> To fix vague pronoun references, use nouns:

> Correct: Odysseus pretended not to know Argos in order to avoid being recognized by the suitors. *This suppression of feeling* was hard for the returning hero.

> Correct: When Odysseus proclaims who he is to Polyphemus, *his bragging* gets him into trouble.

Parallel Structure

Grammatical (as opposed to stylistic) parallel structure refers to the use of parallel elements:

> a. with coordinating conjunctions,
> b. with correlative conjunctions, and
> c. in a series.

1. Any two grammatical elements joined by a coordinating conjunction (*and, but, yet, or, for, nor,* and sometimes *so*—see "Coordinating Conjunctions" under "Parts of Speech," p. 11) must be parallel: nouns parallel to nouns, adjectives to adjectives, clauses to clauses, verbs to verbs, prepositional phrases to prepositional phrases, etc.

Faulty: We practiced *pitching tents* and *how to build a fire.*
Correct: We practiced *pitching tents* and *building fires.*
Correct: We practiced *how to pitch a tent* and *how to build a fire.*
Correct (informal): We practiced *how to pitch a tent* and *build a fire.*
Faulty: The teacher was *amused* but *skeptical about* the student's excuse.
Correct: The teacher was *amused by* but *skeptical about* the student's excuse.

2. Any two elements joined by a correlative conjunction—*not only/but (also), both/and, either/or, neither/nor, whether/or, if/then*—must be grammatically parallel; what follows the first part of the conjunction must be the same grammatical element as what follows the second part.

Not only [noun] but also [noun]
    not only *dogs* but also *cats.*
both [adverbial clause] and [adverbial clause]
    not only *when they arrive* but *after they settle in*
neither [infinitive phrase] nor [infinitive phrase]
    neither *to brush his teeth* nor *to wash his face*
either [object of preposition] or [object of preposition]
    either *under the bed* or *behind the dresser*
Faulty: In therapy, I think both *talking* and *to listen* are important.
Correct: In therapy, I think both *talking* and *listening* are important.
Faulty: We are not *for war* but *peace*
Correct: We are not *for war* but *for peace*
Faulty: This car is not only *fast* but also *it is safe to drive.*
Correct: This car is not only *fast* but also *safe.*
Faulty: The trip to the city is neither *a long one* nor *expensive.*
Correct: The trip to the city is neither *long* nor *expensive.*
Faulty: Either *you must stay home* or *go with us.*
Correct: You must either *stay home* or *go with us.*

3. All elements in a series must be parallel. For example,
[noun], [noun], and [noun]
    dogs, cats, and *ponies*
[gerund phrase], [gerund phrase], or [gerund phrase]
    fishing for trout, hiking on trails, or *climbing mountains*
[adjective], [adjective], [adjective], and [adjective]
    solitary, poor, nasty, brutish, and *short* — Hobbes, *Leviathan*

Faulty: In his first week at camp George most loved pitching tents, building fires, and to ride the zip line. (gerund, gerund, infinitive)

Correct: In his first week at camp George most loved pitching tents, building fires, and riding the zip line. (all gerunds)

Correct: In his first week at camp George most loved to pitch tents, to build fires, and to ride the zip line. (all infinitives)

Faulty: The restaurant owner greeted and seated us politely, efficiently, and in less than a minute. (adverb, adverb, and prepositional phrase)

Correct: The restaurant owner greeted and seated us politely, efficiently, and quickly. (all adverbs)

Faulty: The reporter stated that the politician resisted answering questions, responded impolitely, and his staff was surly. (verb, verb, and independent clause)

Correct: The reporter stated that the politician resisted answering questions, responded impolitely, and commanded a surly staff. (all verbs).

Faulty: The instruction booklet for my new TV tells me that I should first check all its connections, that I should then plug it in, and to register it online. (noun clause, noun clause, and infinitive)

Correct: The instruction booklet for my new TV tells me that I should first check all its connections, that only then should I plug it in, and that lastly I should register it online. (all noun clauses)

Correct: The instruction booklet for my new TV tells me that I should first check all its connections, then plug it in, and lastly register it online. (all verbs)

Faulty: The Periodic Table of the Elements can be used to learn various facts about the chemical elements: to learn the atomic number of an element, its atomic weight, seeing the position in relation to an inert gas, heavy metals, etc. (infinitive, noun, gerund phrase, noun)

Correct: The Periodic Table of the Elements can be used to learn various facts about the chemical elements: their atomic numbers, atomic weights, and positions in relation to inert gasses, heavy metals, and other categories. (all nouns)

The Four *That*'s

The word *that* can be:

A demonstrative pronoun:
> *That* is my car.

A demonstrative adjective:
> *That* car is mine.

A relative pronoun:
> The car *that* I bought last week is a beauty. (*that* introduces the relative clause *that I bought last week*)
> The book [ ] I read last night was exciting. (understood *that* is the direct object of the relative clause *[that] I read last night*)

A subordinate conjunction (also called a noun clause identifier):
> I believe *that* we have met. (noun clause *that we have met* is the direct object of the verb *believe*)
> *That* the movie was entertaining goes without saying. (noun clause *That the movie was entertaining* is the subject of the verb *goes*)

The Four *As*'s (based on *Merriam-Webster's Collegiate Dictionary*)

The word *as* can be:

As—Adverb (modifying an adjective):
> "To the same extent," "in equal degree" (the first *as* in comparisons):
>> *as* high as a mountain
>> *as* thick as thieves
>> *as* honest as he could be

As—Conjunction:
> "To which extent," "in which degree" (the second *as* in comparisons, introducing a clause or the noun or pronoun of an elliptical clause):
>> as honest *as* he could be
>> as high *as* a mountain [is high]
>> as thick *as* thieves [are thick]
> "In the way or manner":
>> Do *as* I do.
>> *as* the crow flies
> "While" or "when":
>> She spilled the milk *as* she got up.

As—Pronoun:

"That," "who," or "which," following *same* or *such*:

the same building *as* my brother

tears such *as* angels weep

As—Preposition:

"Like":

All rose *as* one man.

His face was *as* a mask.

"In the capacity of," "in the role of":

He works *as* an editor.

Possessives

Add apostrophe and the letter *s* to form the possessive of most nouns:

the boy's bike

the girl's kite

If the word already ends in *s* and would sound awkward if another *s* were added, add the apostrophe only:

Achilles' heel

Gyges' ring

Jesus' parables

for roundness' sake

The possessive pronouns (*his, hers, its, ours, yours, theirs*) have no apostrophe.

Note: *it's* is a contraction of "it is"; *its* is the possessive pronoun—they are not to be confused.

The indefinite pronouns do form the possessive with apostrophe *s*

one's house

another's yard

somebody's phone

Numbers

Spell out the first number of a sentence. In ordinary text, spell out numbers from one to ninety-nine and whole numbers followed by *hundred, thousand, million,* etc. Use numerals instead of words in most other cases:

*Sixty-five members showed up at the meeting out of the total
membership of 148.*

Sixty-five members out of seventy-three were present.
We counted eight thousand ballots today, of which 7,642 were valid ones.
Our second edition will be about eight hundred pages, with thirty
*   illustrations.*
Of those eight hundred pages 770 will not have illustrations.

Use figures for dates except when they appear in quotations:
The Declaration of Independence is traditionally dated July 4, 1776.
"Were you watching TV on September eleventh?"

For detailed instructions on proper publishing form for numbers and all other matters, consult the latest edition of the *Chicago Manual of Style* (University of Chicago Press).

Italics

Use italic font for titles of works published under their own names (novels, epic poems, plays, collections, non-fiction works, etc.). In writing or typing on a machine without an italic font, substitute underlining for italics. (see also "Quotation Marks," pp. 35–36)
>   Correct: In the third act of *Hamlet*, Hamlet finds the king
>   apparently praying.

Use italics to refer to a word as a word (rather than to its meaning).
>   Correct: You use *liberty* in an odd sense of that word.

Use italics (sparingly) to stress a word or phrase.
>   Correct: Joey, I want you in the house this minute, and I
>   mean *now*.

Scholarly References

Use abbreviated titles and line references in parentheses within your text and punctuate as follows. Give full citations in footnotes or endnotes.
>   *When Hamlet says "the readiness is all" (V.ii.222), he is talking to*
>   *Horatio.*

Spell out *act* and *scene* and *line(s)* only when introducing a discussion of one particular passage:
>   *In Act III, Scene iii, of* Hamlet, *we find Hamlet contemplating the*
>   *apparently praying king.*
>   *In* Hamlet *III.iii, we find Hamlet contemplating the apparently*
>   *praying king.*

In long poems (the *Iliad, Paradise Lost,* etc.), give the book and line number(s) in parentheses:

Milton's Satan says "Evil be thou my good" (IV.110).

Capitalization

Capitalize the first letter of any sentence. Capitalize all proper nouns.

For titles of people, capitalize both title and name:
General Eisenhower
President Charles De Gaulle

Do not capitalize the title of a person when it is used in apposition:
the emperor Constantine
French president Charles De Gaulle.

In titles of works, capitalize the first word, the last word, and all nouns, pronouns, adjectives, verbs, adverbs, and subordinate conjunctions. Do not capitalize articles (*a, an, the*), coordinating conjunctions (*and, but, yet, or, for, nor*), or prepositions (of any length) unless they are the first or last words of the title.

When referring to a title whose first word is *A* or *The*, omit that word when the title follows a possessive:
A Tale of Two Cities, the novel by Charles Dickens, is read
during sophomore year.
Charles Dickens' *Tale of Two Cities* is read during sophomore year.

Syllabication

There are correct and incorrect places in which to divide words when, for reasons of space, the whole word will not fit on a line. Consult a dictionary to find where to divide a word. (Note: there is a letter in Russian whose sound is *shch.* The correct division of the name Krushchev would be *Kru-shchev.*)

VIII
Usage

In this section we will address words and phrases often misused. See the section, "Style: Twenty-Five Guidelines for Good Rhetoric (Plus Six on Oral Presentation)" for additional suggestions about usage in relation to style. Interested readers are advised to consult the following works for further clarification:

Merriam Webster's Collegiate Dictionary (latest edition)
Webster's Second (or Third) New International Dictionary (unabridged)
Fowler's Modern English Usage, edited by R.W. Burchfield
Modern American Usage by Wilson Follett and Erik Wensberg

Affect and Effect
Verbs:

To affect—transitive verb meaning to have an influence upon something or someone.

The legislature's decision affected my life greatly: I went out of business.

To effect—transitive verb meaning to cause something to happen, to accomplish something

My adoption of new rules effected a big change in my classroom: the students stopped chewing gum.

Nouns:

affect—a term in psychology for human emotion or feeling

The patient, on several different drugs, ceased to demonstrate any affect.

effect—the result of an influence on the thing affected

The effect of the legislation on my life was great: I went out of business.

The secondary effect was that I went into a different field.

Adjectives:

affective—Psych.: having to do with human emotion or feeling

The patient's affective behavior was perplexing.

effective—successful in accomplishing its intended use, of utility

The taser was highly effective in getting the Martian to stop making bad puns in English.

Note the spelling of the two most common uses:

The cut in pay affected me; it had a big effect on me.

Aggravate: from the Latin *ad* (to, toward) + *gravare* (to burden), from *gravis* (heavy)—to make a condition or situation worse. It does not mean to irritate or to annoy.

All right: Two words, never *alright*.

Allude/Allusion, Elude, Illusion: *Allude* is from the Latin *ad* (to, toward) + *ludere* (to play, mock at)—to make an indirect reference, as to some biblical or classical myth or idea familiar to the reader. *To refer* is to make a direct reference with a citation. *Elude* is from the Latin *ex* (from, out from) + *ludere* (to play, mock at)—to avoid, escape from. *Illusion* is from the Latin *in* (into) + *ludere* (to play, mock at)—deceptive or misleading image.

Alternate, Alternative—nouns and adjectives: *Alternate* refers to succession by turns, every other, every second.
> *She drives the carpool on alternate days.*

Alternative refers to one of two (or sometimes more) possible choices of things, courses, or propositions or to the situation offering a choice where only one of two (or more) possibilities may be chosen.
> *He had no alternative but to risk his life or turn back.*

Among, between—*Among* implies more than two in a group, *between* only two.
> *She walked among the trees. He sat between the pine and the poplar.*

And/or—Avoid this formula. It forces the reader to guess at your meaning. Choose one or the other word.

Anybody, somebody, nobody, everybody—as one word: any (some, no, every) person; as two words, any (some, no, every) physical body or group. Similarly, *anyone, someone, everyone* as one word refer to any (some, every) person; as two words, any particular single thing or person. Note, *no one* is always two words.
> *Anybody can do it.*
> *Any body will feel pain when stuck with a pin.*
> *Everyone is welcome.*
> *Every one shoe has another as its mate.*

Based on: Not *based off* or *based off of*.

Can/may: *Can* means "is able"; *may* means "is permitted" or "is possible."
> *You can fall asleep during class, but you may not.*

Could care less: Always an error that contradicts the actual intention. That one could not care less asserts how little one cares. That one could care less implies that one does care.

Compare to, compare with: *Compare to* implies pointing out a similarity or difference between two things expected to be essentially different:

> *Fresh tomatoes cannot compare to canned tomatoes* [implying the former are much better].
>
> *Going on a first date may be compared to leaping from a high diving board* [though essentially different, the experiences are similar in feeling risky].

Compare with implies the enumeration of similarities and differences:

> *The sonnets of Shakespeare may be compared with those of Donne* [implying that both similarities and differences are to be observed in them].

Composed of, comprised of, divided into: *Compose*, from the Latin *com* (with) + *ponere* (to put, place), means to form by putting together; *comprise*, from the Latin *com* + *prehendere* (to grasp), means to include within a particular scope, to be made up of; *divide*, from the Latin *dis* + *videre* (to separate), means to split or separate apart. A water molecule is composed of (not divided into) two hydrogen atoms and an oxygen atom; an apartment complex comprises many apartments (the apartments do not comprise the complex); a pie is composed of crust and filling, is divided into slices.

Cope: In standard English prose, *cope* must be accompanied with the preposition *with* (since the verb is intransitive). One does not cope, nor does one cope difficulties; one copes with difficulties.

Data: Originally the plural of *datum*, from the Latin for "given." The word is now treated as either a plural noun (*these data, many data*) or a singular abstract mass noun like *information* (*there is data to show, that data is valid*), though the plural form is more common in formal writing.

Different from: Never *different than* (except in comparisons of degrees of difference):

> Faulty: *Your experience of surfing is very different than mine.*
> Correct: *Your experience of surfing is very different from mine.*
> Correct: *Our two experiences are more different than they are similar.*

Disinterested: impartial, having no investment in or likelihood of gaining from. Not to be confused with *uninterested*, which means lacking interest in, bored by.

Due to: as an adjective *due* means "owed" or "owing," used with *to* it means "ascribable to"; it is preferable not to use *due to* as a prepositional phrase to mean "because of."
> Correct: *The floods were due to the heavy rains.*
> Faulty: *I was late due to the traffic.*
> Correct: *I was late because of the traffic.*

Elude: see *Allude*

Enormity, enormousness: *Enormity* means a monstrous, outrageously immoral or vicious act or the quality of such an act. It is imprecise to use it to mean large size. When describing the characteristic of large size, *enormousness* should be used instead.

Etc., et al.: *Etc.* is an abbreviation of the Latin *et cetera* (no *x* in it), meaning "and the rest." *Et al.* is an abbreviation of the Latin *et alia*, meaning "and the others" (i.e., other people). They should be used at the ends of lists only when sufficient particulars have been given to make the idea clear, and, being vague, never after *for example*.

Fact: Use the word only for verifiable realities, not to stress one's belief in the truth of an opinion or judgment.

Farther, further: Use *farther* for physical distance, *further* for abstract comparisons:
> Correct: *I could walk no farther.*
> Correct: *That day we read no further.*

Flammable, inflammable: Both mean combustible, able to burn. *Inflammable*, from the Latin *in* (in, into) + *flamma* (flame), is the more precise term; *flammable* is often used on signs to avoid misunderstanding, since the Latin *in-* can also mean non-, though not in this case. For the opposite meaning use *nonflammable*.

Fortuitous, fortunate: *Fortuitous* means happening by chance; *fortunate* means lucky, characterized by good luck.

Gratuitous: meaning undeserved, unmerited, uncalled for (as a *gratuity* is a tip given above and beyond the charges on a bill, or as gratuitous violence is violence not evoked by any particular cause). Not to be confused with *grateful*, meaning thankful.

Hopefully: This word means "in a hopeful manner" or "in a hopeful state of mind." It does not mean "I hope" or "we hope" or "it is to be hoped" or "one hopes" etc.

Faulty: *Hopefully she will arrive on time.*

Correct: *I hope she will arrive on time. We may hope that she will arrive on time.*

Faulty: *I'll get the paper in by Tuesday hopefully.*

Correct: *I hope to get the paper in by Tuesday. You may hope that I will get the paper in by Tuesday.*

Faulty: *Hopefully there will not be a war.*

Correct: *Let us hope there will not be a war. One would hope there will not be a war. It is to be hoped that there will not be a war.*

Illusion: see *Allude*

Imply, infer: To *imply* is intentionally to suggest or point to a meaning not explicitly stated; to *infer* is to take or understand a meaning suggested or to deduce it from the givens. Generally, the speaker or writer implies, the listener or reader infers.

In regard to, as regards, regarding: All correct. Notice, no *s* in the first phrase.

Inside, inside of: Avoid the *of* except to mean "in less than a certain amount of time."

Correct: *Inside the house, the air was warm.*

Correct: *Inside of an hour it rained twelve inches.*

Irregardless: Not a word. The correct word is *regardless*. (*-less* is already a negation, wrongly duplicated by the addition of *ir-*).

Is When: Used as a tool for defining something, *is when* is a grammatically impossible construction because *is* is a linking verb that takes a predicate nominative and *when* is a subordinate conjunction that introduces an adverbial clause. So the construction becomes

noun   linking verb (=)   adverbial clause

Such a construction is impossible. Replace the *when* clause with some form of substantive.

Faulty: *Chemical bonding is when two molecules are joined together.*

Correct: *Chemical bonding is the joining of two molecules.*

Faulty: *An example is when Odysseus tells Polyphemus his name.*

Correct: *An example is Odysseus' revelation of his name to Polyphemus.*

Faulty: *The end of the game is when the king is in checkmate.*
Correct: *The end of the game comes when the king is in checkmate.*
Correct: *The end of the game is the checkmate of the king.*

Lie, Lay: The verb *to lie* is intransitive. The verb *to lay* is transitive. *Lie, lay, lain*—intransitive verb: what you are doing when prone or supine on a surface.

I *lie* down.
I *lay* in bed all day yesterday.
I have *lain* in bed all week.
I will be *lying* in the hospital after my operation.
I will have *lain* in bed for days once it's all over.
You look as if you have been *lying* on a bed of nails.
Lie down! (to the dog).

Lay, laid, laid—transitive verb: what you do to something else that you place on a surface.

I *lay* the book on the table.
I have *laid* that subject to rest.
The chicken *lays* an egg.
Are you *laying* a trap for me?
They have *laid* us in chains.
Now I *lay* me down to rest.

Note: If you tell a dog "Lay down!" don't be surprised if a dog who knows grammar better than you do asks, "Lay *what* down?"

Note: Neither of the above verbs is to be confused with the verb *lie, lied, lied,* meaning to tell lies:

Because I *lie* to her, she *lies* to me.
Because she *lied* to me, I *lied* to her.
Though we have *lied* to one another about many things, we
    have never been caught *lying* about the dog.
(Knowing the above enhances one's appreciation of the triple puns in the couplet of Shakespeare's Sonnet 138.)

Less, fewer: *Less* refers to quantity of a single substance or a quality; *fewer* refers to number of discrete items.
Less peanut butter. Fewer peanuts. Less satisfaction.

Like, as: Do not use the preposition *like* in place of the conjunction *as*. *Like* introduces nouns and pronouns; *as* introduces clauses and phrases:

Faulty: *"Winston tastes good like a cigarette should."*
Correct: *These cherries taste good, as fresh fruit should.*
Faulty: *Like I always say, one should never start smoking.*
Correct: *As I always say, one should never start smoking.*
Faulty: *I was able to water ski like in my youth.*
Correct: *I was able to water ski as [I did understood] in my youth.*

Literal, literally: Use to indicate that something is actual or factual rather than metaphorical. Avoid using as hyperbole for mere emphasis. The metaphor itself often does the work without the need for misuse of the adverb:

Faulty: *I literally flew out of the office to get home in time for dinner.*
Correct: *I flew out of the office to get home in time for dinner.*
Correct: *I literally hugged the mast for an hour before I was rescued.*
(I actually held the mast to my chest with my arms.)

Memento: not "momento," (from the imperative of the Latin verb *meminisse*, remember)

Nauseous, nauseated: *Nauseous* means causing nausea. *Nauseated* means feeling nausea. "I am nauseous" means I am making you sick.

Nor: After a negative, use *or* instead of *nor*:

Faulty: *She cannot fix her own bicycle nor buy a new one.*
Correct: *She cannot fix her own bicycle or buy a new one.*
Correct: *She can neither fix her own bicycle nor buy a new one.*
Correct: *She cannot fix her own bicycle, nor can she buy a new one.*

One: Refer back to *one* with *one's* rather than with *his* or *her* or *his or her*.

Correct: *One cannot always fix one's own bicycle.*

Partially, Partly: Though often interchangeable in common speech, *partially* tends to imply "not completely," "to some extent," "in some degree," in relation to abstractions; *partly* tends to imply a particular part of a usually material or physical whole:

Faulty: *I partly agree with your position on the issue.*
Correct: *I partially agree with your position on the issue.*
Faulty: *The Great Dane only partially fits under the table.*
Correct: *The Great Dane only partly fits under the table.*

Presently: can mean both "soon" and "now, currently"; sticklers prefer that formal writers use it only in the first sense.

Refer: see *Allude*

Regretful, regrettable: *Regretful* means full of regret; *regrettable* means to be regretted, meriting regret.

> *George was regretful when he discovered that, regrettably, he had forgotten to mute the phone before uttering his curses.*

Relatable to: *Relatable* cannot be substituted for *relatable to*. *Relatable* as an adjective does not describe something to which one can relate; rather, it means that one can relate it to something else. "The story is relatable" means "the story can be told, related" *not* "you will find you can relate to the story." The latter idea requires adding the word *to*: e.g., "The book is very relatable to." However, it will almost always be better to use the verb phrase *relate to* than the adjective phrase *relatable to*.

Secondly: When numbering examples at the beginnings of paragraphs, use *First, Second, Third* for transition words, rather than *Firstly, Secondly, Thirdly*, etc.

That, which: *That* is used in restrictive relative clauses; *which* is used in non-restrictive relative clauses.

> Faulty: *The car which I bought yesterday is a convertible.*
> Correct: *The car that I bought yesterday is a convertible.*
> Faulty: *The Fourth of July, that celebrates the signing of the Declaration of Independence, is my favorite holiday.*
> Correct: *The fourth of July, which celebrates the signing of the Declaration of Independence, is my favorite holiday.*

Tortuous, torturous: Both words come from the Latin *torquere* (to twist), but *tortuous* means twisting, winding, crooked, tricky, convoluted, devious, circuitous; *torturous* means relating to torture, agonizing, unbearably painful.

Try to: not *try and*.

Unique: means one of a kind, nonpareil, nothing like it. Therefore it is erroneous to imply degrees of uniqueness: one cannot be more or less unique. Also, avoid *unique* as a complimentary adjective: since every human being, and every work of art by a human being, is unique, to assert that a person or work of art is unique does not distinguish it from any other person or work of art in the world or in history. Strive to describe or define in what way or by what qualities a particular subject is distinguished from all others.

Verbal, Oral: *Verbal* refers to words; *oral* refers to words spoken (from the Latin *os,* mouth). A *verbal* agreement is an agreement in words, whether written, spoken, or otherwise; an *oral* agreement is one made by speaking it aloud.

While: Avoid using *while* to mean "and" or "but." It should be reserved for the meaning "at the time that" or, in certain cases, "although" (if the context makes the contrast clear):

Faulty: *Writing in English, which reads from left to right, left-handed people tend to smudge the ink, while writing in Hebrew, which reads from right to left, they have an advantage.*

Correct: *Writing in English, which reads from left to right, left-handed people tend to smudge the ink; writing in Hebrew, which reads from right to left, they have an advantage.*

Faulty: *Both chemistry and history involve numbers, but while numbers in chemistry appear in calculations, in history they appear more significantly as dates.*

Correct: *Both chemistry and history involve numbers: in chemistry they appear in calculations, in history as dates.*

Faulty: *While the summers there are warm and balmy, the winters are notoriously cold.*

Correct: *While the city's air quality has indeed improved, the number of its drivers has increased.*

Part II: Logic

Dialectica, Cornelis Cort, 1565, engraving.

Introduction: Logic

Having mastered grammar, the art of inventing and combining symbols, we must next learn how to arrange these symbols to make true statements about the world. We must learn how to reason.

Reasoning is essential to our lives as human beings. As Aristotle observes, the specific function of a human being is not merely to eat, grow, and survive, for we share these functions with plants. Neither is the specific function of a human being to have sensations and awareness, for we share these functions with animals. The particular function proper to a human being, he says, "is an activity of the soul in accordance with, or implying, a rational principle."[1]

In other words, reasoning is the essence of what it means to be human.

Certainly our ability to gain knowledge about the world around us contributes to our survival. Unlike the instincts of animals, our instincts are not sufficient to do that job alone. With reason we can anticipate consequences based on past experience and arrive at new knowledge based on prior knowledge. For example, we can directly apprehend whether an apple we are looking at is red or green. To determine how nutritious the apple is, however, we need to use reasoning.

But human reason extends beyond the realm of survival to the realm of knowledge about the meaning and value of all things, including of our own lives. The majority of our knowledge is based upon reasoning.

In order to lead to knowledge, whether practical or theoretical, reasoning must be correct, for if our reasoning is faulty, we will be unable to differentiate between unfounded opinions and truth.

The art of correct reasoning is called Logic. It is the art of being able to move reliably from certain sets of symbols that illuminate a truth to others. If this is true, is that true? In the

---

[1] J.A.K. Thomson, tr., *The Ethics of Aristotle: The Nicomachean Ethics* (London: Penguin Classics, 1955, Rev. Hugh Tredennick, 1976), pp.75–76.

most famous example of a logical argument, if I know that "Socrates is a human being" is a true statement, and I know that "human beings are mortal" is also a true statement, then I can reason correctly—logically—that "Socrates is mortal" is also a true statement.

The norm of logic is truth; the medium of logic is arguments; the judgments of logic are validity and soundness. The goal is to prove true one or more conclusions based on evidence.

As we grow up, we learn to reason correctly to a certain extent, just as we learn language, in the context of training by parents and others and by observation and experience. But our ability to reason correctly can be improved with study and reflection. As with any trait, the ability to reason logically varies from individual to individual. The goal of studying logic is to attain mastery of reasoning, regardless of one's starting point.

Basic Concepts of Logic

Adapted in large part from *An Introduction to Logic* by Wayne A. Davis with the Georgetown Logic Group, Georgetown University. 2nd ed. Kunos Press, 2007.

I
Building Blocks of Logic:
Propositions and Arguments

Propositions

As stated in the introduction to this portion of the text, the medium of logic is arguments. Generally, an argument attempts to prove the truth of something on the basis of something else. But what is meant by "something"? We will call this "something" a *proposition* (in some logic textbooks the word "statement" is used, but "statement" is often used colloquially, so we will not use it here). It might seem at first that a "proposition" could be any sentence about the world. However, a proposition is not just any grammatical sentence; it has a specific structure and characteristics.

There are four rhetorical kinds of sentences:

Declarative: Plants need water to live.

Interrogative: How are you today?

Imperative: Sit on that chair.

Exclamatory: What a beautiful day!

If the goal of an argument is to prove the truth of one proposition on the basis of other propositions, then immediately, we can eliminate three of these kinds of sentences. It would be impossible to prove the truth of any question, because the question itself does not contain any *truth-value* (truth, falsity, or uncertainty) about the world. Neither do imperatives; determining whether "Sit down" is a true statement is nonsensical. Finally, exclamations will be excluded. Cases where an exclamation point is used at the end of a declarative sentence will not necessarily be excluded.

The table is made of wood.

People do not always make rational decisions.

This sentence is a proposition.

It might seem that we are left only with declarative sentences, then, to serve as propositions. But propositions do not have to be entire sentences; in fact, any independent clause could serve just as well. With a few examples, it will become clear that even a single sentence could contain multiple truth-values.

> The sun is now behind the hills, so it will be time to go home soon.
>
> This self-referential sentence contains a comma and a coordinating conjunction, and so it likely contains two independent clauses.
>
> The car could get from San Diego to San Francisco, but it needs a new engine.

Each of these sentences is saying two things, one before the comma, and one after. Leaving aside the coordinating conjunction, each clause within each sentence could stand on its own as an assertion about some aspect of the world. Each assertion could be true or false. Thus, each of these sentences contains two propositions.

Arguments

Now that we have the proper terminology, we can define an *argument*: An argument is an attempt to demonstrate the truth of a proposition based on evidence found in at least one other proposition. The propositions that provide evidence are called *premises*, and the proposition that is being supported is called the *conclusion*. This is a technical definition different from the colloquial meaning of argument as a verbal altercation. Let's look at how we could craft an argument from multiple propositions.

> Milton has a fever, so he is sick.

"Milton has a fever" is the premise. From the truth of this premise, we conclude that "he is sick." Note that identical propositions could be expressed in other grammatically-correct ways:

> Milton has a fever. Therefore, he is sick.
>
> Because Milton has a fever, he is sick.

The grammatical differences make no difference to the logic of the argument.

A proposition could be stated in a way that is unrelated to any argument:

> Milton lives down the street. He has a fever. He has never set foot in the zoo.

These three sentences, though all propositions, do not form an argument. None of the propositions is providing evidence for any of the others.

A proposition may be a conclusion in one argument and at the same time a premise in another:

> Milton has a fever. Therefore he is sick, and so he should go to bed early.

"He is sick" is the conclusion of the argument formed by the first and second propositions, and the premise of the argument formed by the second and third propositions. We will call such a proposition an *intermediate conclusion,* and we will learn about it later on. Thus, we will say that "premise" and "conclusion" are relative terms. They can be described in relation to each other only in a particular context.

All arguments *must* contain at least one premise. They *may* contain many premises.

> This dog has floppy ears. This dog has brown and white spots. This dog weighs 60 pounds. This dog has a curved sabre tail. This dog is quite short of stature given its weight. This dog has droopy eyes. Therefore, this dog is a bassett hound.

There is no limit to the number of premises that a single argument can have, but all simple arguments contain only one conclusion.

Recognizing Arguments

Arguments are the fundamental building blocks of logic. Thus, it is critical to be able to recognize the presence of arguments in written and spoken language.

Recognizing the conclusion is often an easy place to start because there is only one conclusion in each argument. What is being claimed? What is the author or speaker attempting to prove? Often the conclusion takes the first or last position in a paragraph (a matter of style and rhetoric, which we will observe in Part III).

Premises can often be recognized by their scope. They will provide specific evidence for the conclusion. They will tend not to be general statements but instead will have a clear relation to the conclusion. We will learn more about general and specific statements when we cover induction and deduction in Section 5.

Note that premises and conclusions will not necessarily be in separate sentences. Our knowledge of grammar and syntax will guide us as we *parse* passages; that is, as we break them down into their component parts and determine the parts of speech of each word and the function of each word or phrase, demarcate each proposition, and examine the logic at work. Punctuation marks like colons, semicolons, and commas help us to distinguish different propositions and to assess the identity of each as a premise, a conclusion, or a statement that is irrelevant to a given argument.

Often certain words are used to signify that a proposition is being offered as evidence or that a proposition forms a conclusion. These signifiers, called *argument indicators*, are of two types: words that signify the premise are called *premise leaders*, and words that signify the conclusion are called *conclusion leaders*.

If we look back at some of the earlier arguments, we notice some of these words:

Milton has a fever. Therefore, he is sick.

Milton has a fever, so he is sick.

Because Milton has a fever, he is sick.

"Therefore" and "so" are conclusion leaders, and "because" is a premise leader. Note that these words are not part of the propositions; they simply change the relation between propositions.

Conclusion leaders can occur anywhere at the beginning, middle, or end of the conclusion:

Milton has a fever. Therefore, he is sick.

Milton has a fever; he is therefore sick.

Milton has a fever; he is sick therefore.

Premise leaders always occur at the beginning of the premise:

Because Milton has a fever, he is sick.

Since Milton has a fever, he is sick.

Milton is sick, for he has a fever.

Keep in mind that arguments will sometimes have no indicators at all:

> Mickey is on the fencing team. He will probably be at the tournament this weekend.

Arguments without indicators will be inherently more difficult to recognize. In the next section, we will discuss some principles for interpreting such arguments.

Premise Leaders	Conclusion Leaders
for	therefore
because	thus
since	then
as	consequently
inasmuch as	hence
as indicated by the fact that	as a result
which follows from the fact that	it follows that
which is proven by the fact that	which shows that

A table of common argument indicators. It is not exhaustive.

Interpreting Arguments

Brevity, novelty, and other concerns of style can all lead to an argument's being presented without argument indicators. Nonetheless, the same argument structure of premise-and-conclusion will apply. Consider the following passage from one of John F. Kennedy's messages to Congress (as cited and analyzed in Davis' *Introduction to Logic*, p. 4):

> A strong and sound Federal tax system is essential to America's future. Without such a system, we cannot maintain our defenses and give leadership to the free world. Without such a system, we cannot render the public services necessary for enriching the lives of our people and furthering the growth of our economy. (From Kennedy, *To Turn the Tide*, 1962, p. 108)

The conclusion of this argument is "A strong and sound Federal tax system is essential to America's future." After the conclusion are two propositions that are premises. But if there are no premise leaders, how can we be sure that this is the case? There is no way to be positive. However, we know that the claim that a strong Federal tax system is essential is not self-evident. Indeed, it has been actively debated throughout American history. Rationality therefore demands that Kennedy defend his position, and we would expect that he would provide premises supporting his claim. The propositions that assert that such a tax system is required for the maintenance of defense, the giving of leadership, and rendering public services are potentially relevant. Furthermore, they support the conclusion. Thus, it makes sense to interpret these propositions as premises. This interpretation is further bolstered by the fact that if a premise indicator like "because" or "since" is inserted before "Without such a system…" the sense of the passage does not change. However, the insertion of a conclusion indicator like "therefore" in the same place would make the passage seem obviously fallacious.

Two principles should guide our interpretation of arguments: *fidelity* and *charity*. Fidelity requires that an interpretation be as faithful as possible to the author's express intention. Charity demands that if two interpretations of the author's intentions are compatible with the evidence, but one interpretation makes the author's argument more reasonable than the other, then we should assume that the more reasonable interpretation is the intended one. Charity guided our interpretation of the above passage from Kennedy on taxes.

These principles are only rough guidelines. Even when they are used, there will be many cases in which it is simply not clear whether an interpretation of a passage is correct, especially when that passage is quoted out of context.

Even when argument indicators are present, the identification of premises and conclusions is not an automatic process. Consider the following passage from Robert J. Ringer's *Restoring the American Dream* (as cited and analyzed in Davis, *Introduction to Logic*, p.5):

> I also feel duty bound, at the outset, to remind the reader that no system of philosophy is perfect, because man himself is imperfect.

Ringer is making an argument, and it is fairly easy to see that the premise is "man himself is imperfect." The conclusion, however, is not so straightforward. Parsing the propositions in the simplest way, the conclusion seems to be "I (Ringer) also feel duty bound, at the outset, to remind the reader that no system of philosophy is perfect." But this is not quite correct. The actual conclusion is "No system of philosophy is perfect." By omitting the reference to personal characteristics, we take into account that Ringer's book is not about himself but about political philosophy. He has no reason to offer a proof for his feelings. Claiming that no system of philosophy is perfect, on the other hand, certainly requires evidence. *Personal intrusions,* such as "I believe," or "I think," ought to be omitted when arguments are parsed.

Non-Arguments

A passage of writing may contain several propositions that are not linked to one another or propositions that do not provide support for any other proposition. If that is the case, then such a passage does not contain an argument. However, such passages are often difficult to distinguish from other passages that do in fact contain arguments but lack argument indicators. To add to this difficulty, many words that often serve as argument indicators have secondary senses. Here, we will review alternative functions of several indicators: conditionals; temporal sequences, examples, and comparisons; and explanations.

Conditionals

"Then" is a adverb with several different functions. Let us revisit an earlier example:

Milton has a fever. Then he is sick.

There is an argument here, and "then" is a conclusion leader. "Therefore," "thus," or several other conclusion leaders could be substituted without changing the meaning of the sentence. But "then" also serves as an adverb in conditional statements (see the next page for "then" as a temporal indicator):

If Milton has a fever, then he is sick.

This is nearly identical to the earlier version; formally, all that has been added is an "if" in the beginning, and the period has been changed to a comma. However, there is now but a single proposition: *if* Milton has a fever, he is sick. We are not asserting that Milton *is* sick, nor are we stating that he *has* a fever; we are simply describing that if a certain condition is met (having a fever), we would be able to assume a consequence (his being sick). The condition in question is called the *antecedent* of the conditional. The antecedent is almost always immediately preceded by the "if." The consequence in question is called the *consequent* of the conditional. It is almost always immediately preceded by "then."

Conditionals are never arguments in and of themselves, though we will see examples of arguments that use conditionals as premises:

> If Milton has a fever, then he is sick. Milton does in fact have a fever. Therefore, Milton is sick.

Now there is a complete argument. The first premise is a single conditional statement: If Milton has a fever, then he is sick. The second premise asserts the satisfaction of the antecedent of the conditional: Milton has a fever. The conclusion asserts the truth of the consequent: Milton is sick. This is a perfectly good argument, called *modus ponens* ("the method of affirming" in Latin).

There is another way in which a conditional could be used in an argument:

> If you read the instructions, you will succeed in assembling the computer. You failed to assemble the computer. Therefore, you didn't read the instructions.

Here the second premise asserts the negation of the consequent of the conditional: You failed to assemble the computer. The conclusion asserts the falsity of the antecedent: You didn't read the instructions. This also is a perfectly good argument, called *modus tollens* ("the method of denying" in Latin).

Conditionals may be chained together in greater lengths, as well; so long as the structure of assertions is maintained, the argument is still a fine argument:

> If Morton goes to the store, he will buy a bag of peanuts. If Morton buys a bag of peanuts, he will eat all of them. If he eats an entire bag of peanuts, he will get sick. Therefore, if Morton goes to the store, he will get sick.

"If… then…" is the most common formulation for a conditional statement, but it is not the only one. "If" could be replaced with "suppose":

> Suppose Milton has a fever. Then he is sick.

We cannot reasonably replace "then" with "therefore" in this case; doing so would assume that a hypothetical state implied an actual one. Hence the example is a conditional, not an argument. This substitution of "therefore" for "then" is one way to disambiguate conditionals from arguments.

Sometimes other variations on the conditional structure are used for the sake of brevity: the "then" can be implied but unstated, as in "If you have a ticket on your record, your insurance premiums will be higher." Other times, the "then" is replaced by a future-pointing phrase such as "will happen," as in "If you do that, something will happen."

Finally, arguments will often omit the repetition of if-clauses for purposes of style and clarity:

> Suppose Milton has a fever. Then he is sick, and therefore he should take it easy.

This is an argument, clearly marked by "therefore." The premise is a conditional: If Milton has a fever, then he is sick. The conclusion is also a conditional: Milton should rest if he has a fever. Joining the two, we have a complete argument. To restate this argument making all the propositions explicit: If Milton has a fever, then he is sick. If Milton is sick, then he should rest. Therefore, if Milton has a fever, then he should rest.

Temporal Sequences, Examples, and Comparisons

In addition to its role as a premise leader, "since" has a temporal meaning:

> Since *The Jazz Singer* was released into theaters in 1927, synchronized dialogue tracks have become commonplace in films.

This sounds like an argument, but if it is, it's a very weak one. Our maxim of charity dictates that we not interpret this sentence as claiming that the release date of *The Jazz Singer* being 1927, and not 1926 or 1928 or any other year, somehow caused the trend of recorded audio to catch on. Nor was it the commercial release of *The Jazz Singer*, as opposed to another movie from 1927—for example, *Metropolis* or *The Unknown*—or some other hypothetical movie with a synchronized dialogue track that caused this change. Instead, we should interpret "since" as marking an event that came before another event.

Similarly, "then" also has a temporal meaning. If I say, "First, I will go to the store; then I will go home," I am not arguing for or against any proposition; rather, I am saying what will happen and in what order.

"Thus," despite its common usage as a conclusion leader, also can serve to introduce an example:

> Many filmmakers draw inspiration from situations and circumstances they are familiar with. Thus, Fellini's 8½, one of his most revered films, is about a filmmaker.

"Thus" cannot reasonably be interpreted as a conclusion leader in this example: that many filmmakers draw inspiration from real life does not provide much support for the fact that Fellini did, and it provides no support at all for the content of 8½. Here, "thus" simply marks an example, and could have been replaced with "in this way," or "in this manner."

Explanations

"Because," "as a result of," and several other premise leaders are commonly used in explanations. Compare the following sentences:

> The missing person died, because the body was found.

> The missing person died because he ran out of food.

The first sentence is certainly an argument; the assertion that the person died is supported by the evidence that his body was found. We could restate the assertion more clearly as "We know the missing person died because the body was found." The second sentence is an explanation. Its assertion is the cause of the person's death itself. In order to turn that explanation into an argument, we would have to add evidence to support the assertion about the cause of death.

Explanations are often the trickiest non-arguments to recognize. However, keeping in mind a fundamental concept about the nature of premises and conclusions will help in this endeavor. In arguments, conclusions tend to be propositions that require some support, and premises are already well established (or in good arguments ought to be). In explanations, by contrast, the explanatory factors tend to be uncertain and the fact being explained is already well established. An additional technique for distinguishing arguments from explanations is to try substituting "as a result of" for "because." In an explanation, doing so will not change the meaning at all. In our example, saying "the person died as a result of running out of food" does not change the meaning of "the person died because he ran out of food." In an argument, however, saying "the missing person died as a result of the body's being found" makes an unreasonable change of meaning from "the person died, because the body was found."

> The people of Northern Ireland are fed up with the violence that has wrecked their country. Support for the IRA and for militant Protestant groups is the lowest it has ever been.

Here, we return to the maxim of charity to aid in our interpretation. Which construction is the better argument? Is it better to claim that low support has caused the people to be fed up, or that the people being fed up has caused low support? If it is not yet clear, think about another way to view the information: would it make more sense to say that I dislike violence as a result of not supporting certain violent groups, or that I do not support certain violent groups as a result of disliking violence? Clearly, the latter is the better argument, and thus it is the interpretation we will use.

II

More About Arguments

Simple versus Complex Arguments

Thus far, we have focused on cases where a single conclusion is drawn from some number of premises. This is called a *simple argument*. Here are two simple arguments:

Morton is shivering, so he is too cold.

Morton is too cold, so he should put on a jacket.

The conclusion of the first argument is identical to the premise of the second argument, so these two simple arguments could well be combined into a single *complex argument*:

Morton is shivering, so he is too cold, and thus he should put on a jacket.

Any number of simple arguments can be combined into a complex argument. When that happens, some propositions become *intermediate conclusions*: conclusions other than the *main conclusion* of the argument (almost always the final conclusion). In the example above, "he is too cold" is an intermediate conclusion, and "he should put on a jacket" is the main conclusion. Note that an intermediate conclusion, in addition to serving the function of a conclusion in one simple argument, will also serve as a premise in a different simple argument.

Summarizing Arguments

It is often useful, in interpreting an argument, to restate the premises and conclusions without any other unnecessary pieces. Thus, the sentence

Morton is shivering, so he is too cold, and thus, he should put on a jacket.

could be broken down in the following way:

Premise: Morton is shivering.
Intermediate Conclusion: Morton is too cold.
Main Conclusion: Morton should put on a jacket.

By removing the conclusion and premise leaders and labeling the propositions for purposes of analysis, we have made it easier to see exactly what is being claimed. As we will soon see, this technique will be invaluable for determining what is going on in more complex arguments. It is important to remember when summarizing that certain words, which may be omitted from the original text of the argument for purposes of brevity, should be included when expanding and separating each proposition. In the previous example, the full and proper intermediate and main conclusions about Morton, even though the original text uses "he." This is a point we will return to when we discuss the analysis and diagramming of arguments.

Suppressed Premises, Suppressed Conclusions, and Broad Presuppositions

When summarizing arguments, fidelity and charity will occasionally lead to seeming violations of the rules about propositions we discussed earlier. Examine the following argument from Herbert L. Petri's *Motivation: Theory, Research, and Applications* (Stamford: Wadsworth Publishing Company, 1991), p. 76:

> Though it is possible that REM sleep and dreaming are not necessary in the adult, REM deprivation studies seem to suggest otherwise. Why would REM pressure increase with deprivation if the system is unimportant in the adult?

If we were not reading closely or carefully, we might think that this passage did not contain an argument. After all, there is not much of an argument in the first sentence—a vague statement about studies that "seem to suggest otherwise" does not reach the level of support that is necessary for premises—and the second sentence is a question. However, the second sentence, though phrased as a question, has content that, *if interpreted charitably*, does lend credibility to the truth of the first sentence. It is not the case that the author is genuinely wondering why REM pressure would increase with deprivation if the system were unimportant in adults; rather, the author is implying that because REM pressure *does* increase with deprivation, the system *likely is* of importance to adults. If we were to summarize the argument and remove the rhetorical device of the question, we would say:

> Premise: REM deprivation studies show that REM pressure increases with deprivation in adults. Conclusion: REM sleep and dreaming are important in adults.

In this way, the conclusion in our summary above is a *suppressed conclusion* in the initial rendering of the argument; it functions as a conclusion but is not stated explicitly.

It is also possible—and more common—to have a *suppressed premise*:

> If people acted rationally, marketing would be much less effective. Thus, advertising has a large impact on people's decisions.

Here the conclusion only follows from the premise if a second (suppressed) premise is assumed to be true as well: People do not act rationally.

There are two reasons that a premise or conclusion may be suppressed in an argument: the author may believe that the premise or conclusion is made obvious by the rest of the argument and may be trying to spare the audience redundant language, or the author may be trying to hide the premise or conclusion because stating it outright would open the author up to criticism.

Recognizing suppressed premises and conclusions can be difficult. Doing so is the more difficult because there are also always unstated assumptions on which an argument is based. We call these *broad presuppositions*. In addition to "People do not act rationally," we could say that "marketing and advertising are pretty much the same thing" is another suppressed premise in the argument above, as is "Something that has a large impact must be effective." The identification of such broad presuppositions could go on ad nauseam if we were picky enough. However, for our purposes, premises and conclusions will be described as suppressed only if they are directly related to the stated argument and are not simply a matter of associating terms (e.g., "marketing" is the same as "advertising," or "less effective" is the opposite of "large impact").

Often the presented conclusion of an argument follows if the premises are taken to be true, and the true source of the dispute is about the truth of a particular suppressed premise (for example, that the legality of abortion is a concern of personal liberty and not of morality) or a broad presupposition (for example, that life is a basic good that ought to be valued over all else). One of the skills of a good student of logic, then, is to be able to uncover that particular suppressed premise or presupposition which ought not be taken for granted as true.

Analyzing and Diagramming Arguments

Arguments require analysis, and the nature of language is such that analysis can become unnecessarily complex if the argument is especially verbose. Thus, it is common practice to number each proposition in an argument and then to use arrows and brackets to describe the relationships between them. Here's a simple example:

Milton has a fever, so he is sick and therefore should take it easy.

We start by numbering each proposition, keeping in mind that premise and conclusion leaders are not included. Here, we have also underlined them:

1 Milton has a fever, so 2 he is sick, and therefore 3 [he] should take it easy.

Note that these numbered propositions stand for complete propositions. That is, 3 stands for "Milton should take it easy," and not just "should take it easy," which in itself would not be a complete proposition.

Next, if there are any premise or conclusion leaders, we can use them to determine which propositions are premises and which are conclusions. 2 is preceded by "so," and 3 is preceded by "therefore," so both are conclusions. 2 is the intermediate conclusion. We can visualize this argument in this way:

$$1 \rightarrow 2 \rightarrow 3$$

The arrows designate the line of reasoning. Based on 1, the author concludes 2. Based on 2, the author concludes 3.

Here is another example:

1 Morton failed his final exam. As a result, 2 he will not pass the course this semester. 3 He will be placed on academic probation.

Here a single premise leads to two separate conclusions. This argument would be diagrammed with separate arrows for each conclusion.

$$\begin{array}{c} 1 \\ \swarrow \searrow \\ 2 \quad 3 \end{array}$$

In other cases, two premises lead to a single conclusion. The two premises may be independent or conjoint. *Independent premises* lead to the conclusion each on its own:

1 This tree is an apple tree. 2 It is bearing apples as fruit, and 3 it grew from the seed of an apple.

Each independent premise is sufficient, but not necessary, in making a complete argument.

Each of the two *conjoint premises* is necessary, but not sufficient on its own:

1 <u>Socrates is a man.</u> 2 <u>All men are mortal.</u> 3 Therefore, <u>Socrates is mortal.</u>

$$\overset{\textstyle 1 \quad 2}{\underbrace{\qquad}}$$
$$3$$

If we removed either **1** or **2**, we would no longer have a coherent argument. For such an argument, we use a bracket when diagramming to show that the premises are conjoint, that is, they require each other in order to form a complete argument.

Natural language can often make arguments seem more complicated than they really are. For example:

1 Human beings who do right because it pleases them are not yet intrinsically moral. For 2 had it pleased them they would have done wrong.[1]

These two sentences are fairly dense. There is a conditional involving how people behave based on pleasure, and information about people being moral in and of themselves. The "yet" implies that people who are not moral beings of this sort have the potential to become that way in the future. In short, there is a lot to discuss and unpack in this argument. But the structure of the argument is nevertheless fairly straightforward: the second proposition is given as evidence for the first. Our diagram of this complex language would be quite simple: **2 → 1**.

This demonstrates one great benefit of diagramming: it very quickly illustrates the structure of the argument without any ambiguities or complexities brought about by the language of the argument. It is much easier to write **2 → 1** and then to write about "proposition 2" or even "2" than to have to recopy or even restate the proposition itself.

Especially as arguments get longer, analysis and diagramming become even more important as aids to understanding:

History has shown repeatedly that you cannot legislate morality, nor does anyone have a right to. The real problem is the people

---

[1] Christina Sommers and Fred Sommers, "Good Will, Duty, and the Categorical Imperative." In *Vice and Virtue in Everyday Life: Introductory Readings in Ethics*, 2nd ed., Robert J. Fogelin, ed. (San Diego: Harcourt Brace Jovanovich, 1989), p. 122.

who have a vested interest in sustaining the multibillion-dollar drug industry created by the laws against drugs. The legalization of drugs would remove the thrill of breaking the law; it would end the suffering caused by unmetered doses, impurities, and substandard paraphernalia. A huge segment of the underground and extralegal economy would move into a legitimate economy, taking money away from criminals, eliminating crime and violence, and restoring many talented people to useful endeavor.
— Thomas L. Wayburn, "Letter to the Editor: Crackdown on Drugs," 1986, *TIME*, 128(10), p. 9.

The conclusion in this argument is buried in the language and is not stated explicitly. In cases like this, it can be helpful to extract and number each proposition.

1: History demonstrates that morality cannot be legislated, nor does anyone have a right to legislate it.

2: The laws against drugs were created by people who have a vested interest in sustaining the drug industry.

3: Legalizing drugs would remove the thrill of breaking the law.

4: Legalizing drugs would end the suffering caused by unmetered doses, impurities, and substandard paraphernalia.

5: If drugs were legalized, much of the underground and extralegal economy would move into a legitimate economy.

6: This in turn would take money away from criminals, would eliminate crime and violence, and would restore many talented people to useful endeavor.

So, with this breakdown in mind, what is the conclusion of the argument? It is implied, but not stated. Nonetheless, it should be included in any summary or analysis of the argument. It is simply this: drugs ought to be legalized. (Note also that statement 1 could be viewed as having a suppressed premise, which is that drug legality is a moral matter rather than one of, say, public health.)

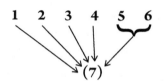

Proposition 7 is placed in parentheses because it is suppressed. Propositions 1 through 4 are each drawn with an arrow to 7 because each provides separate evidence for concluding 7. Propositions 5 and 6, however, are drawn with a bracket because they conjointly provide evidence for 7.

III
Soundness and Validity

If the person making an argument reasons well and properly, his or her argument will be sound. A *sound argument* is an argument in which the premises provide sufficient reason to believe the conclusion. Any argument that is not sound is *fallacious.*

A sound argument meets three criteria, each with an associated fallacy, committed when a criterion is not met:

1. The first criterion is that all of its premises are justified and true. If this is not the case, the argument is a *nonstarter.* Here is the premise of an argument:

All human beings are invertebrates.

Without even seeing the rest of the argument, we know that the argument lacks proper reasoning because the premise is false.

Here are two premises from a different argument:

All human beings are mammals. All mammals are warm-blooded.

Do we know from these two premises whether the argument is sound? Of course not; it depends on what conclusion is drawn from these premises. Perhaps the conclusion of the argument is:

Therefore, jellyfish are invertebrates.

In that case, this argument would not be sound; the premises would provide no reason to believe the conclusion. Only if the conclusion were something related to the premises would the argument be sound:

All human beings are mammals. All mammals are warm-blooded. Therefore, all human beings are warm-blooded.

2. This brings us to the second criterion: the conclusion of an argument should logically follow from its premises with probability. What do we mean by probability? We will address argument strength and modality in section 5, but for now, it means that there must be a greater than 50% likelihood that the conclusion follows from the premises. There is a special term, *validity,* that refers to this particular criterion. We will explore validity further in Section 5. An argument that violates this criterion is a *non sequitur* (literally, "does not follow" in Latin).

3. To illustrate the need for one final criterion for soundness, consider the following argument:

Because human beings are mammals, human beings are mammals.

This certainly doesn't look like a good argument. But why? The premise is "human beings are mammals," which we know to be true. And it stands to reason that if "human beings are mammals" (the first instance) is true, then, by the same law of identity we learn about in mathematics, "human beings are mammals" (the second instance) must also be true. But even though it is true, it is not sound because it is an identity. So we say that the conclusion of a sound argument cannot be the same as any of the premises. An argument that violates this criterion *begs the question*.

Furthermore, to be sound, the conclusion may not even be assumed by any of the premises. This guards against simple reformulations:

Elves do not exist because there is no such thing as an elf.

And against premises that assume the truth of the conclusion:

God created the universe in six days. So, God created the universe.

Attending to these three criteria—the truth of the premises, the probability of the conclusion following from the premises, and the lack of identity or reformulation between the premises and conclusion—will allow us to evaluate the reasoning behind an argument and thus to fulfill one of the main purposes of logic. The three failures to meet these criteria—nonstarter, non sequitur, and begging the question—are called *fallacies*.

Note: That an argument is fallacious does not necessarily mean that its premises are false or that its conclusion is false. To make such a claim is to commit a fallacy called **argumentum ad logicam** (argument to logic; see Section 8).

Inductive and Deductive Soundness

A sound argument requires that the conclusion follow from the premises at least with probability. As we will see in the next section under "Modality," probability is one of several degrees of strength of an argument. A conclusion may follow with necessity, a conclusion may follow with certainty, or a conclusion may follow with probability. Consider the following three arguments:

A ball drawn from the pit will be blue because:

Premise version 1: all of the balls in the pit are blue.
Premise version 2: eighty percent of the balls in the pit are blue.
Premise version 3: ten percent of the balls in the pit are blue.

Assuming the truth of the first premise, it is impossible that the conclusion is false. Thus, we could say that the conclusion "necessarily follows" or "logically follows" from the premise. Such an argument is *deductively sound*. Assuming the truth of the second premise, the conclusion follows with probability but not with necessity. Such an argument is *inductively sound*. Assuming the truth of the third premise makes the argument neither deductively nor inductively sound; it is fallacious because it is a non sequitur.

Deductive reasoning uses general statements as evidence for a necessary conclusion. Inductive reasoning uses specific examples as evidence for a probable conclusion. We will explore induction in much more detail in later sections.

Validity

Earlier, we discussed soundness and its three criteria. Now, we will expand the second of those criteria: a conclusion must follow from premises at least with probability. An argument that meets this requirement has *validity*.

Colloquially, "validity" and "soundness" are often used interchangeably. However, in logic, validity has the narrower definition given above. Given this definition, validity is necessary but not sufficient for soundness. Arguments may be valid without being sound, but no argument can be sound without also being valid.

Here is an argument that is valid but not sound:

All animals are walruses. All walruses have tusks. Therefore, all animals have tusks.

The judgment of validity is concerned only with whether the conclusion follows from the premises and not whether the premises are true. Put another way, when judging validity, we assume premises to be true. The argument above would be considered valid even though its false premise makes it unsound and therefore a fallacy.

IV
Argument Strength and Modality

Argument Strength

Evaluating the soundness of an argument is not the only judgment we can make in logic. Within the realm of sound arguments, we can distinguish between arguments that are stronger and arguments that are weaker. That is, some sound arguments provide more reason to believe the conclusion than others. Though all sound arguments provide sufficient reason to believe their conclusions, not all sound arguments are equal.

For example, imagine a theme park with a large ball pit filled with colored plastic balls. In addition to having fun playing in such a place, we could make arguments about its contents and about what color ball we might have if we drew a ball at random from the pit. Here are two arguments that should sound familiar:

A ball drawn from the pit will be blue, because all of the balls in the pit are blue.

A ball drawn from the pit will be blue, because eighty percent of the balls in the pit are blue.

If we assume that the premises are true in both cases, then both arguments meet the three criteria for soundness. However, the first argument provides complete certainty about the conclusion that a ball drawn from the pit will be blue; if all the balls are blue, then it is impossible for any ball taken out of the pit to be any other color. The fact that eighty percent of the balls are blue, however, does not provide the same level of certainty. While the conclusion of the second argument follows from the premise with probability, the ball could be another color. If the percentage given in the premise is reduced enough, the argument will cease to be sound:

The ball drawn from the pit will be blue, because ten percent of the balls in the pit are blue.

The premise no longer provides sufficient reason to believe the conclusion. As we learned in the last section, this is a non sequitur.

When we talk of the *strength* of a particular ***proposition***, we are not talking about whether it is supported or justified, but instead about how much that proposition asserts or implies. This will often be a measure of comparison. One proposition is stronger than another if the former entails or implies the latter, but not vice versa. For example, the proposition that all balls in the pit are blue is stronger than the proposition that at least eighty percent of them are blue, which in turn is stronger than the proposition that ten percent of them are blue.

While proposition strength (how much is implied or necessitated by a given proposition) and argument strength (how well the premises support the conclusion) refer to different quantities, they are related: the strength of the propositions that comprise an argument (premises and conclusion) determines the strength of the argument as a whole. Argument strength is directly related to the strength of its premises. *Ceteris paribus* (literally, "other things being equal," in Latin), as the strength of premises increases, the argument strength increases.

Consider the following arguments, all sound, which increase in strength from first to last:

> A ball drawn from the pit will be blue, because at least sixty percent of the balls in the pit are blue.

> A ball drawn from the pit will be blue, because at least eighty percent of the balls in the pit are blue.

> A ball drawn from the pit will be blue, because all of the balls in the pit are blue.

Argument strength is also related to the strength of the conclusion. Let us see what happens if we hold all else constant and vary the strength of the conclusion:

> The first ball drawn from the pit will be blue, because at least eighty percent of the balls in the pit are blue.

> The first four balls drawn from the pit will be blue, because at least eighty percent of the balls in the pit are blue.

> The first eight balls drawn from the pit will be blue, because at least eighty percent of the balls in the pit are blue.

These conclusions increase in strength from first to last (the claim is greater). Consequently, the arguments decrease in strength from first to last. The premise that eighty percent of the balls are blue does not support the conclusion that the first eight balls will be blue as well as it supports the conclusion that the first ball will be blue. Thus, we can say that argument strength is inversely related to the strength of its conclusion.

It is worth noting that these judgments of argument strength and premise strength are purely comparative. We cannot make such judgments in isolation. We also cannot make such comparative judgments in cases that do not meet *ceteris paribus* rules. Here are two arguments:

> The first ball drawn from the pit will be blue, because at least eighty percent of the balls in the pit are blue.

> The first four balls drawn from the pit will be blue, because at least ninety percent of the balls in the pit are blue.

Because the strength of the premise and the strength of the conclusion are both different, we cannot compare the strength of each complete argument.

Finally, the strength of an argument depends not just on the strength of its premises and conclusion, but also on how much evidence there is for its premises. Consider the following argument:

> Milton broke a mirror today. He will have bad luck for the next seven years, because whenever anyone breaks a mirror, he has bad luck for seven years.

There is no evidence provided for the premise that breaking a mirror causes bad luck. If it *were* true, then this argument would be a strong one, but it is (likely) not. As such, this is a fairly weak argument. To be fair, evidence could be presented to support this premise, but it would be difficult to test such a claim properly (see Section 7). We could also strengthen the argument by weakening the claim of the premise, perhaps substituting "because whenever anyone breaks a mirror," with "because sometimes when a person breaks a mirror." This difference leads us to our next topic, modality.

Modality

As we learned in Section 1, all propositions assert something about the world. The *modality* of a proposition refers to whether its assertion is that something in the world must be the case, will definitely be the case, will probably be the case, will possibly be the case, or is the case. In order, these assertions are referred to as modalities of necessity, certainty, probability, possibility, or actuality.

Treating these assertions as propositions, we can rank them based on their strength. The strongest is necessity, then certainty, then probability, then possibility. The strongest assertion we can make is necessity, for it entails the truth of all other modalities: if something is necessary, then it is also certainly the case, probably the case, and possibly the case. Certainty is weaker than necessity: It is certain that Washington, DC, is the capital of the United States, but it is not necessary. It is certain that the magnolia tree in my backyard has a trunk that is four feet in diameter, but it is not necessary. Probability is weaker than certainty. To illustrate, we can rely on percentages. If something is certainly the case, then it is as likely to occur as it can be, 100%. In order for something to be probable, its likelihood must be greater than 50%. Possibility is the weakest modality. In order for something to be possible, its likelihood must only be greater than 0%.

The modality of actuality is a special case. Actuality is weaker than necessity. That Washington, DC, is actually the capital of the United States does not mean that it is necessarily the capital. San Francisco could be the capital city; it just isn't. And actuality is stronger than possibility, for anything that is actually the case must be possible, even if it is unlikely. If two lines intersect, then it must be possible for the two lines to intersect (and thus, necessary that the two lines are not parallel). However, despite how it may appear, actuality does not entail certainty or probability. The fact that the tree was actually struck by lightning does not mean that it was probable or improbable (perhaps the size and location of the tree makes it a freak occurrence; perhaps they made it certain to happen). Alternatively, the fact that something is probable does not necessitate it actually being the case. Consider the following pairs of arguments.

The first two arguments use probability as the modality in the premises and actuality as the modality in the conclusions:

The weather reports stated that it would probably rain today. Therefore, it is raining.

The weather reports stated that it would probably not rain today. Therefore, it is not raining.

In the next two arguments the modality is actuality in the premises and probability in the conclusions:

It is raining today. Therefore, it was probable that it would rain today.

It is not raining today. Therefore, it was probable that it would not rain today.

None of these four arguments is sound.

The most troubling characteristic of modality for students of logic seems to be that certainty does not entail actuality and thus cannot be compared to actuality in terms of strength. Unlike other orderings of strength, we cannot make judgments of these two modalities in either direction (from actuality to certainty or from certainty or probability to actuality). It is possible to be certain of something that is not actually the case: that is, perhaps all the evidence points to the fact that something would be the case, but in the end it turns out not to be the case.

The thermometer reads 101° and I feel hot. Therefore, it is certain that I have a fever.

That I have a fever is both certain and likely. However, if the thermometer is broken and the A/C is broken, then in actuality I have no fever. So certainty and probability do not imply actuality. Conversely what actually occurs may or may not be certain or even likely:

It is neither certain nor likely that I do not have a fever, given the evidence of my thermometer.

In fact, because the thermometer and A/C are broken, I have no fever. Thus, actuality must be separated from certainty and probability.

Sometimes in arguments, for the sake of variety, other terms will be substituted for the formal terms of modality ("necessary," "certain," "probable," "possible," and "actual"). For example, "must" may indicate necessity or "could" may indicate possibility. The best way to assess modality in such sentences is to substitute the modality term for the alternative term used. For "What goes up must come down" substitute "It is necessary that something thrown into the air fall down again." For "If the clouds continue to darken, it could rain before dark" substitute "If the clouds continue to darken, it is possible that it will rain before dark." At the same time, some terms that seem to be alternative modality terms are actually being used in senses having nothing to do with modality. For example, in the sentence "Because it was drafted under false pretenses, the man may break his contract" the word "may" does not indicate what the man might possibly do but rather what it is legally or morally permissible for him to do.

Term or Phrase	Modality Expressed
must	Necessity
have to	Necessity
definitely	Certainty
bound to	Certainty
should	Probability
likely to	Probability
may	Possibility
might	Possibility
could	Possibility

Hierarchy of Modalities

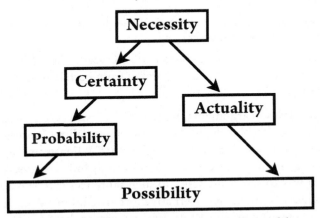

A representation of the relationship between the five modalities. Within each side, the height of each modality represents its strength. Arrows represent implication.

–Adapted from Davis, *Introduction to Logic*, p. 37.

V

Deductive Logic: Categorical Propositions and Syllogisms

In earlier sections of the book, we learned about propositions. Many of them dealt with the identity of a particular object. Here is one example from before, along with two new examples:

All mammals are warm-blooded.

Some tree is an apple tree.

No people are plants.

Each of these propositions contains two logical terms, a subject and a predicate. Note that while we have seen the terms "subject" and "predicate" in the grammar section, they have a slightly different application in logic. In grammar, the subject of the second proposition given above is "some tree," and the predicate is "is an apple tree." In logic, the *subject* (S) and *predicate* (P) would be a bit more restricted: "tree" and "apple tree," respectively. Unsurprisingly, these propositions are sometimes called subject-predicate propositions. We will refer to these propositions by their more common logical name, *categorical propositions,*[1] so named because each is an assertion that some or all members of one category do or do not belong to another category. In the propositions, for example, some members of the category "tree" are asserted to belong to the category "apple tree," all members of the category "mammal" are asserted to belong to the category "warm-blooded [thing]," and all members of the "people" category are asserted not to belong to the category "plants."

The portions of the proposition we removed when defining the logical subject and predicate would have different names. The "some" is called a *quantifier,* since it refers to the quantity of objects in question, and the "is" is called a *copula,* which is Latin for a link or tie between two things.

---

[1] Subject-predicate propositions can be simple, as in the above examples, or compound, as in these examples: "If these trees over here are apple trees, then those trees over there must not be apple trees," or "All mammals are warm blooded and all reptiles are cold-blooded." We will limit our discussion here to simple subject-predicate propositions.

Only three quantifiers will be of concern to us: every, no, and some. The quantifier will determine what is called the **quantity** of the categorical proposition (answering the question: "How many things are we talking about?"). As far as copulas go, we will discuss only two: is, and is not. The copulas will determine the **quality** of the categorical proposition, which will either be **affirmative** (meaning the predicate is affirmed of the subject) or **negative** (meaning the predicate is denied of the subject). Thus, there will be four categorical propositions that we will discuss. The structure of these four categorical propositions could be used to create an infinite number of actual propositions for argumentation. The letters S and P below could stand for any subject or any predicate, respectively. Labeled with their traditional names, which are letters, here are the four forms of categorical propositions:

A: Every S is a P.

E: No S is a P.

I: Some S is a P.

O: Some S is not a P.

In terms of quality, the A and I propositions are affirmative, while the E and O propositions are negative. In all likelihood, the letter names for the propositions come from Latin words: "**AffIrmo**," which means "I affirm," and "**nEgO**," which means "I deny." In terms of quantity, the A and E propositions are universal, since they affirm or deny the predicate of the entire category of thing that the subject is. The I and O propositions are particular, since they affirm or deny the predicate only from part of the category of thing that the subject is. If the quality and quantity are known, the categorical proposition is precisely determined.

A: universal and affirmative

E: universal and negative

I: particular and affirmative

O: particular and negative

Forms of Opposition

When working with categorical propositions, it can be useful to determine how different categorical propositions logically relate to each other. One broad limit is necessary to start: for one categorical proposition to logically relate to another, the two propositions must have the same subject and predicate. In his *On Interpretation*, Aristotle detailed the logical relationships between these four propositions.

For example, "all mammals are vertebrates" is a fine categorical proposition (an A proposition, in fact). Other categorical propositions that logically relate to this one must have mammals and vertebrates as their subjects and predicates, respectively. Thus, "some mammal is a vertebrate" relates logically to this first proposition because the truth of the first proposition affects and is affected by the truth of the second proposition. On the other hand, a proposition that does not use mammals and vertebrates as subjects and predicates, like "this dog has black fur," or one that perhaps shares only the subject or only the predicate but not both, such as "those frogs are vertebrates" cannot logically relate to the first proposition. The truth of the first proposition does not affect and is not affected by a proposition that does not share both the subject and the predicate.

The general rule is that categorical propositions logically relate to each other if they share both subject and predicate but differ in some other way. Given the composition of categorical propositions, there are only two other ways in which they could differ: quality and quantity. The logical relation between categorical propositions that share subject and predicate but differ in quality or quantity is called *opposition*. Now we will detail the different oppositions that can occur, and point out the truth values that are associated with these relations.

Contradiction is the form of opposition that occurs between two propositions that have *different qualities* and *different quantities*. Because of the nature of their quantity and quality, opposing A and O propositions are *incompatible*, that is, they cannot both be true:

> All mammals are vertebrates.
> Some mammals are vertebrates.

Similarly, opposing E and I propositions cannot both be true:

> No fish is a mammal.
> Some fish is a mammal.

It is also impossible for contradictory propositions both to be false. They would be said to be *complementary* because each must have a different state in the world: if one is true, the other must be false:

> Every reptile is a turtle.
> Some reptile is not a turtle.

Categorical propositions can also differ from each other in quantity only or quality only.

If two propositions differ in *quantity only*, each is an **altern** of the other. Alterns cannot be incompatible, nor can they be complementary. The altern of "All mammals are vertebrates" (A, called **superaltern** because it is universal) is "some mammals are vertebrates." (I, called **subaltern** because it is particular). It is possible for both of these propositions to be true:

> Every turtle is a reptile.
> Some turtles are reptiles.

It is possible for both of them to be false:

> Every turtle is a mammal.
> Some turtles are mammals.

It is possible for the particular proposition (I) to be true while the universal proposition (A) is false:

> Some reptiles are turtles.
> Every reptile is a turtle.

If the universal proposition (A) is true, the particular proposition (I) is implied to be true:

> Every turtle is a reptile.
> Some turtles are reptiles.

The same pattern holds for propositions with negative quality:

> No turtle is a mammal.
> Some turtles are not mammals.

If two propositions differ in *quality only*, then the propositions are **contrary** if their quantity is universal, and **subcontrary** if their quantity is particular. Contrary propositions cannot both be true:

> All flowers are plants.
> No flowers are plants.

but both can be false:

> All music teachers are pianists.
> No music teachers are pianists.

Subcontraries cannot both be false:

> Some turtles are reptiles.
> Some turtles are not reptiles.

but both can be true:

> Some music teachers are pianists
> Some music teachers are not pianists.

Square of Opposition

The traditional visualization of the relationships between categorical propositions is called the Square of Opposition.

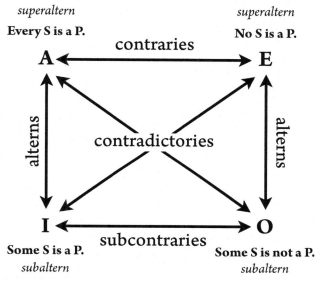

Three Transformations: Conversion, Contraposition, and Obversion

Categorical propositions that are not opposed—that is, propositions with different subjects or predicates from each other —can still have important logical relationships. We will discuss three important transformations that can be done to propositions: conversion, contraposition, and obversion.

Two propositions are said to be the *converse* of each other if the subject and predicate of one proposition are the predicate and the subject of the other, while the quantity and quality are identical in each. Sometimes, the truth of a proposition implies the truth of its converse: "No mammal is a reptile" is *equivalent* to its converse, which would be "No reptile is a mammal." But this equivalence is not true for just any proposition, which is easy to see if we change the quality: "Every turtle is a reptile" is not equivalent to "Every reptile is a turtle." With analysis, it becomes clear that E and I propositions are equivalent, while A and O propositions are not.

Conversion

Converse A's (non-equivalent):
Every turtle is a reptile.   Every reptile is a turtle.

Converse E's (equivalent):
No mammal is a reptile.   No reptile is a mammal.

Converse I's (equivalent):
Some turtles are reptiles.   Some reptiles are turtles.

Converse O's (non-equivalent):
Some reptiles are not turtles.   Some turtles are not reptiles.

(A) Every S is a P. ⟷ ≢ ⟷ (A) Every P is a S.
(E) No S is a P. ⟷ ≡ ⟷ (E) No P is a S.
(I) Some S is a P. ⟷ ≡ ⟷ (I) Some P is a S.
(O) Some S is not a P. ⟷ ≢ ⟷ (O) Some P is a S.

Sometimes when examining propositions and their components, it becomes useful to reverse a subject or predicate category. That is, if something is known about reptiles, it is possible for something else to be implied about all things that are not reptiles, or non-reptiles. This reversal is called the *complement*. Just as the complement of "reptiles" is "non-reptiles," the complement of any category S is "non-S."

Complements can sometimes run counter to the way we would typically speak: the complement of "men" is not "women" but is, logically, "non-men," since it includes all things that are not men, not just women. Additionally, turning a subject or predicate into its complement is unaffected by the quality of the proposition.

There are two more relations we will mention: contrapositive and obverse. The *contrapositive* of a proposition is created by replacing the subject with the complement of the predicate and the predicate with the complement of the subject. The contrapositive of "Every turtle is a reptile" would be "Every non-reptile is a non-turtle." For contrapositives, A and O propositions are equivalent, while I and E propositions are not (note that this is the opposite of the equivalence for converses).

The *obverse* of a proposition is created by changing the quality and replacing its predicate with the complement of the predicate. The obverse of "Every turtle is a reptile" would be "No turtles are non-reptiles." Obversion is a special logical property because it is the only transformation that will produce an equivalent proposition regardless of the quality and quantity of the starting proposition.

Contraposition

Contrapositive A's (equivalent):
Every turtle is a reptile.   Every non-reptile is a non-turtle.

Contrapositive E's (non-equivalent):
No mammal is a reptile.   No non-reptile is a non-mammal.

Contrapositive I's (non-equivalent):
Some turtles are reptiles.   Some non-reptiles are non-turtles.

Contrapositive O's (equivalent):
Some reptiles are not turtles. Some non-turtles are not non-reptiles.

(A) Every S is a P. ⟷ ≡ ⟷ (A) Every non-P is a non-S.

(E) No S is a P. ⟷ ≢ ⟷ (E) No non-P is a non-S.

(I) Some S is a P. ⟷ ≢ ⟷ (I) Some non-P is a non-S.

(O) Some S is not a P. ⟷ ≡ ⟷ (O) Some non-P is not a non- S.

Obversion

Obverse A's (equivalent):
Every turtle is a reptile.   No turtles are non-reptiles.

Obverse E's (equivalent):
No mammal is a reptile.   Every mammal is a non-reptile.

Obverse I's (equivalent):
Some turtles are reptiles.   Some turtles are not non-reptiles.

Obverse O's (equivalent):
Some reptiles are not turtles. Some reptiles are non-turtles.

(A) Every S is a P. ⟷ ≡ ⟷ (E) No S is a non-P.

(E) No S is a P. ⟷ ≡ ⟷ (A) Every S is a non-P.

(I) Some S is a P. ⟷ ≡ ⟷ (O) Some S is not a non-P.

(O) Some S is not a P. ⟷ ≡ ⟷ (I) Some S is a non-P.

Two propositions that are non-equivalent can still be true if their subjects and predicates are both at the same level of generality/specificity—both genus or both species. For example, "reptiles" and "turtles" are genus and species, so the converse A propositions above would be inequivalent and could not both be true. However, "authors" and "Americans" are both species-level characteristics, and so the converse O propositions that are non-equivalent ("Some authors are not Americans" and "Some Americans are not authors") are in this case both true. See pp. 95–96, above.

Syllogisms

A *syllogism* is a specific kind of argument that uses deductive reasoning to prove a conclusion based on two or more premises. The most common form of syllogism has three propositions: two premises and one conclusion:

First premise: All mammals are warm-blooded.
Second premise: All monkeys are mammals.
Conclusion: Therefore, all monkeys are warm-blooded.

A *categorical syllogism* is a syllogistic argument that consists of three categorical propositions that contain a total of three terms, each of which is used twice. The *minor term* will be the subject of the conclusion; the *major term* will be the predicate of the conclusion; and the *middle term* (M) does not appear in the conclusion but must appear somewhere in each of the two premises. One premise of the syllogism must link the major and middle terms and the other must link the minor and middle terms. The premise that contains the major term is called the *major premise,* and the premise that contains the minor term is called the *minor premise.*

Major premise:
  All mammals (middle term) are warm-blooded (major term).
Minor premise:
  All monkeys (minor term) are mammals (middle term).
Conclusion:
  Therefore, all monkeys (minor term) are warm-blooded (major term).

Major premise:
  All amphibians (middle term) are animals (major term).
Minor premise:
  All frogs (minor term) are amphibians (middle term).
Conclusion:
  Therefore, all frogs (minor term) are animals (major term).

The particular makeup of a syllogism—that is, the kind of proposition it has in each of its three positions—is called the *mood* of the syllogism. The mood is written as a combination of three of the four letters that refer to the four forms of categorical proposition (A, E, I, and O, see p. 92). The first of the three letters describes the major premise, the second describes the minor premise, and the third describes the conclusion. The monkey syllogism would be described as AAA, as would the frog syllogism. Here is a syllogism that would be described as AII:

Major premise:
All dogs (middle term) have fur (major term).
Minor premise:
Some dogs (middle term) are cuddly (minor term).
Conclusion:
Therefore, some cuddly things (minor term) have fur (major term).

The middle term of a syllogism can have four possible positions in the premises. That position of the middle term determines the *figure* of the syllogism. In the *first figure* the middle term is the subject of the major premise and the predicate of the minor premise (like "mammals" and "amphibians"). In the *second figure* the middle term is the predicate of both premises. In the *third figure* the middle term is the subject of both premises (like "dogs"). In the *fourth figure* the middle term is the predicate of the major premise and the subject of the minor premise.

The figure of a syllogism is typically given as a number (1 through 4) after the mood. Hence, the first two syllogisms above (middle terms: mammals, amphibians) would be described as AAA1, the third syllogism (middle term: dogs) as AII3.

1st Figure:
Major premise:
S (middle) P (Major)
Minor premise:
S (Minor) P (middle)
Conclusion:
S(Minor) P(Major)

2nd Figure:
Major premise:
S (Major) P (middle)
Minor premise:
S (Minor) P (middle)
Conclusion:
S(Minor) P(Major)

3rd Figure:
Major premise:
S (middle) P (Major)
Minor premise:
S (middle) P (Minor)
Conclusion:
S(Minor) P(Major)

4th Figure:
Major premise:
S (Major) P (middle)
Minor premise:
S (middle) P (Minor)
Conclusion:
S(Minor) P(Major)

Figure	Middle Term
1	$S\ p$
2	$P\ p$
3	$S\ s$
4	$P\ s$

MAJOR premise
minor premise

Given the varieties of form, mood, and figure, there are many possible permutations of the categorical syllogism. There are four forms of proposition (A, E, I, or O), any of which could be in any of three positions (major premise, minor premise, conclusion). Multiplying the possibilities (4 x 4 x 4) leads to 64 different possible moods. Multiplying the possible moods by the four figures (positions of the middle term) yields 256 possible types of categorical syllogism! However, logicians have shown that only 24 of them can form valid arguments.

There are six valid forms for each figure:

1st fig.	2nd fig.	3rd fig.	4th fig.	
AAA	AEE	*AAI*	**AAI***	Note: The 15 forms in regular type are
AAI	AOO	OAO	AEE	unconditionally valid. The nine others are
AII	**AEO**	AII	**AEO**	<valid only if the following conditions are
EAO	**EAO**	*EAO*	*EAO*	met:
EIO	EIO	EIO	EIO	**Bold**: valid so long as S actually exists.
EAE	EAE	IAI	IAI	*Italic*: valid so long as M actually exists.
				AAI* is valid so long as P actually exists.

Rules of Inference

A *rule of inference* is a rule by which a valid deduction can be made about an argument using the forms of opposition and the transformations that we have discussed.

Most of the transformations and other relationships mentioned in this chapter lead to a rule of inference.

Subalternation: from an A or E proposition, we can infer its subaltern:

> Every turtle is a reptile.
> Therefore, some turtle is a reptile.

Conversion: from an E or I proposition, we can infer its converse:

> Some turtle is a reptile.
> Therefore, some reptile is a turtle.

Contraposition: from an A or O proposition, we can infer its contrapositive:

> All turtles are reptiles.
> Therefore, all non-reptiles are non-turtles.

Obversion: from any categorical proposition, we can infer its obverse:

> All turtles are reptiles.
> Therefore, no turtles are non-reptiles.

Finally, there are two syllogisms that can be shown to be deductively valid directly from their structure and from their assertions about category membership: AAA1 and AII1.

AAA1:

All mammals are warm-blooded.
All monkeys are mammals.
Therefore, all monkeys are warm-blooded.

AII1:

All dogs have fur.
Some dogs are cuddly.
Therefore, some cuddly things have fur.

The rule asserting the validity of these syllogisms is called *transitivity of implication*. It can also be referred to as the *chain rule*, or *general categorical syllogism*.

How might we use these rules to prove the validity of an argument? Imagine the following argument:

Every turtle is a reptile.
Therefore some reptile is a turtle.

From the starting premise "Every turtle is a reptile," we can infer by *subalternation* that "Some turtle is a reptile." From there, we could infer by *conversion* that "Some reptile is a turtle." This would constitute a deductive proof of the validity of that argument.

Refutation by Counterexample

If the form of a syllogism is invalid, then any syllogism with that form will be invalid no matter what the content of its propositions. Thus, it is possible to refute an invalid syllogism by the use of a counterexample, that is, by substituting for its propositions more self-evidently illogical ones. This technique makes it unnecessary to memorize the table of valid syllogism forms in order to refute a syllogism. Indeed, in common usage, telling someone that his or her particular argument is an invalid form of categorical syllogism would likely not lead to a meaningful response (unless the person were well-versed in logic).

The power of refutation by counterexample is that it does not require any knowledge or background in the original content of the argument. Take the following argument:

Some films are directed by Alejandro Jodorowsky.
Some films have a score that consists only of diegetic music.
Therefore, some movies by Alejandro Jodorowsky have a score that consists only of diegetic music.

Perhaps you have no idea who Alejandro Jodorowsky is, or what "diegetic music" is, either. But you hear the argument being made, and because of its form, it strikes you as a bad argument. You do not want to enter into a discussion of syllogistic structure and logic, nor to ask what diagetic music is, but you still want to prove that the argument is wrong. You can formulate another argument of the same form with true premises and a false conclusion:

> Some animals are dogs.
> Some animals are cats.
> Therefore, some dogs are cats.

The above conclusion about dogs and cats could be recognized as false by just about anyone. The counterexample argument demonstrates that in that form of argument (in this case, III3), the premises can be true (which, in the counterexample, they certainly are) and the conclusion can be false (which, in the counterexample, it certainly is). Therefore, it is a good example of why the statements intended as evidence in the film example cannot prove the truth (or falsity) of the conclusion, and why the argument can be dismissed.

Categorical Propositions: Singular vs. General

So far, we have examined categorical propositions whose subjects and predicates are *general terms*, such as "tree," "pets," "dogs," and "turtles." But some terms that could appear in arguments would not qualify as general terms, because they are too specific, such as "the tree in my front yard," "California," "Luna, the dog," or "Socrates." These are called *singular terms*, because they refer to individual, concrete things. A *singular categorical proposition* has a subject that is a singular term and a predicate that is a general term.

Because singular categorical propositions refer only to a single object, they only have one quantity. Their quality can be affirmative or negative in the same way that general categorical propositions can. A *quasi-syllogism* is a syllogism where one of the terms is singular.

In the same way that we determined AAA1 and AII1 syllogisms to be valid, there are two forms of quasi syllogism that are valid simply by their structure. For both forms of quasi-syllogism, the validity only holds if there are only three terms, as in a standard syllogism. In one instance the major premise is an A proposition, the minor premise is an affirmative singular proposition, and the conclusion is an affirmative singular proposition. Here's an example:

All men are mortal.
Socrates is a man.
Therefore, Socrates is mortal.

In the other instance the major and minor premises are affirmative singular propositions, and the conclusion is an I proposition. Here's an example:

My friend is a man.
My friend has a beard.
Therefore, some men have a beard.

Some Thoughts on Common Usage

As was stated early on, every argument is made up of propositions. As we learned in this section, every proposition is made up of a subject, a copula, and a predicate. However, the propositions we saw in this section of the text are a bit easier to break down into subject, copula, and predicate than others that we might come across. For example "All dogs are mammals" is easy to parse into the subject (dogs), the copula (are), and the predicate (mammals). But what if we go back to one of the very first sentences we discussed in terms of propositions? "The car could get from San Diego to San Francisco, but it needs a new engine." This sentence contains two propositions, but how could we break each proposition down into its components? The car is clearly the subject of both, but what about the copulae and the predicates? In cases such as these, each proposition ought to be reworded in order to illustrate its predicate and copula. An equivalent proposition to the first one given is "The car is a thing that could get from San Diego to San Francisco." An equivalent proposition to the second one given is "The car is a thing that needs a new engine." Now it is clear that the copula is "is" in both cases, even though the "is" was unstated in the original wording. The predicates are "thing that could get from San Diego to San Francisco" and "thing that needs a new engine." It is rarely necessary to reword propositions in this way, but the purpose here is to show that the subject, copula, predicate structure is always present even if hidden by the structure or style of the proposition.

VI
Inductive Logic I:
Argument From Analogy, Enumerative Induction, and Statistical Syllogism

The Argument from Analogy

Arguments from analogy entail highlighting similarities between two things—making an analogy—and drawing a conclusion from one to the other. There are several different forms that such an argument can take.

Basic Argument from Analogy

It's a summer day and you're thirsty. You buy a bottle of *Quench* and are delighted at how cool and refreshing it tastes. Unfortunately, it's a relatively small bottle and it's a very hot day, and you find yourself wanting more refreshment. You buy a second bottle with the reasonable expectation that it will be as good as the first. In this case, your reasonable conclusion is supported by an *argument from analogy*, a form of inductive reasoning. Your argument goes something like this:

> The first bottle of *Quench* is similar to the second bottle of *Quench*. The first bottle was very refreshing. Therefore, the second bottle will be very refreshing too.

Analogical arguments all have similar components: a *data object*, an *inference object*, and an *attribute* that the former is *known* to possess and the latter is *concluded* to possess. Their structure includes a *similarity premise*, which asserts that the data object is similar to the inference object, and an *attribute premise*, which asserts that the data object has a certain attribute (the *given attribute*). The conclusion is then made that the inference object has the attribute that the data object has (the *projected attribute*). In order to be a valid argument, the data object and inference object must be similar to each other in relevant respects.

Note that both the similarity and the relevance of the similarity are necessary to crafting a valid argument from analogy. In the *Quench* example, the first bottle and the second bottle are identical in every relevant regard: the same product, packaged the same way, bought relatively close in time to each other. If the two bottles were bought several months apart, the conclusion would be less certain; similarly, if one were bottled and the other were canned, there might be more room for the conclusion to be false. Clearly, if the two bottled drinks were not the same drink—one was *Quench* and the other was tomato juice—the similarities of packaging and time of purchase would not be relevant enough to the claim for the argument to retain its validity.

Varieties of Analogical Arguments

Though all analogical arguments share the same components and general structure, there are different ways in which to make an argument from analogy. Most relevant to our purposes is the nature of the projected attribute. Typically, in what is called the **straight** form of analogical argument, the projected attribute is identical to the given attribute. This is the form used in our initial example. The projected and given attributes are both "very refreshing."

However, we could be more careful about our assertions, accounting for unknown differences between any two objects, and end up either with a projected attribute that is less specific than the given attribute, or with a weaker modality in the conclusion. Such an argument would read as follows:

> The first bottle of *Quench* is similar to the second bottle of *Quench*. The first bottle was very refreshing. Therefore, the second bottle will be at least somewhat refreshing. (modality variations: "might be," "likely to be." See "Modality," pp. 87–90)

This form of argument from analogy is called the **cautious** form.

A final form goes in the other direction, in which the projected attribute is more specific than the given attribute. This form of argument, the so-called **rash** form of analogical argument, is fallacious because it is a non sequitur:

> The first bottle of *Quench* is similar to the second bottle of *Quench*. The first bottle was slightly refreshing. Therefore, the second bottle will be very refreshing.

Analogical Arguments Involving Groups of Objects

It is possible—and quite common, in fact—to make an argument from analogy that involves many objects. In these cases, what we referred to previously as the data object and inference object will become the **data group** and **inference group**. Additionally, our criteria for validity will grow: in addition to having sufficient and relevant similarity, certain characteristics of the objects within each group will be important. We will refer to the entire set of objects in the data and inference groups combined as the **population,** whether they are people or bottles, movies, umbrellas, etc. The objects in the data group, by definition a subset of the population, are referred to as the **sample.** In arguments from analogy we look at some properties of the sample and infer that the rest of the population has the same properties. These terms—sample and population—are commonly used in scientific research, which we will discuss in the next section.

Say we want to make an argument about a group of students:

> Students in Dr. R's English class are similar to students in Dr. S's English class. Students in Dr. R's class enjoy reading *Hamlet.* Therefore, students in Dr. S's class enjoy reading *Hamlet.*

This may be a valid argument, but in addition to the similarity and the relevance of the similarity between the data and inference groups, there are two additional criteria for validity. The first additional criterion for validity is the number of objects in each group. If Dr. R's English class has five students in it, and Dr. S's class has fifty, then there is likely insufficient evidence for the conclusion. There is a direct relation between the size of the data group and the strength of an argument from analogy involving groups; as the data group gets larger, the argument gets stronger because we are increasing the amount of evidence we have. On the other hand, there is an inverse relation between the size of the inference group and the strength of the argument. In general then, the larger the data group and the smaller the inference group, the stronger the argument.

Consider the following variations. The first three arguments have data groups that increase in size and thus the arguments get stronger from the first to the third:

> All the students in Dr. R's English class enjoy reading *Hamlet* because ten similar students enjoy reading *Hamlet.*

> All the students in Dr. R's English class enjoy reading *Hamlet* because fifty similar students enjoy reading *Hamlet.*

> All the students in Dr. R's English class enjoy reading *Hamlet* because thousands of similar students enjoy reading *Hamlet.*

The second set of three arguments have inference groups that increase in size and thus the arguments get weaker from the first to the third:

> One student in Dr. R's English class enjoys reading *Hamlet* because fifty similar students enjoy reading *Hamlet*.

> Ten students in Dr. R's English class enjoy reading *Hamlet* because fifty similar students enjoy reading *Hamlet*.

> Fifty students in Dr. R's English class enjoy reading *Hamlet* because fifty similar students enjoy reading *Hamlet*.

The second additional criterion for validity is the amount of variation in the data group. If the population itself is very homogeneous, then the argument will be stronger because there is less variability that might interfere with our inference. However, if there is variation in the population, we want the data group to share that variation. If I wish to conclude that my ten-person cooking class will enjoy eating chocolate, it will be stronger if my evidence is that everyone in the world enjoys eating chocolate than if I draw evidence only from last year's ten-person cooking class.

In analogical arguments involving groups of objects, proportions and statistics become relevant. In *pure* arguments from analogy, every member of the data group is claimed to exhibit the given attribute. As the proportion of the data group that exhibits the given attribute decreases, the argument becomes weaker, and when the proportion dips below 50%, the argument from analogy becomes fallacious. If an argument from analogy is not pure, it is *statistical*, and the strength of the argument is directly related to the proportion of the data group that exhibits the given attribute, and inversely related to the proportion of the inference group that is claimed to exhibit the projected attribute.

> Last year, 80% of the students in my Logic class enjoyed this example. Last year's Logic class is very similar to this year's Logic class. Therefore, X% of students this year will enjoy this example.

It would be fallacious to substitute any number higher than 80 for X. The lower that X is, the stronger the argument becomes.

Enumerative Induction

Enumerative induction is a form of inductive logic in which evidence is gathered from some specified number of instances and a conclusion is drawn about a larger group of instances. As before, the group that provides the evidence is called the data group or the sample, and the larger group, which contains the data group but also contains other instances (an important difference between argument from analogy and enumerative induction), is called the inference group or the population.

The *pure* form of enumerative induction involves a conclusion that generalizes to all other cases. For example:

> Over the course of many years, I have seen 1000 dogs. All of the dogs I have seen have four legs. Therefore, all dogs have four legs.

The other form is *statistical enumerative induction*; in place of a generalization to all members—observed and unobserved—of a particular set of cases, a conclusion is given with a *probability* of some unobserved cases. For example:

> In a sample of 400 students, 80% enjoyed taking a course on logic. Therefore, 80% of the students in this class will enjoy this course on logic.

This example highlights two important criteria for a valid enumerative induction. The first criterion is that the sample group be similar to the population in relevant characteristics. The second criterion is that the sample be large and varied.

Similarity between the Sample and the Population

How can we determine whether the sample and population are similar enough? Were the students in the sample college students? If so, then the conclusion should be describing college students as well and not, for example, high school students. More generally, if there are variations in the population, the sample should be large enough to include similar proportions of these variations. Put another way, the variation present in the sample should be representative of the variation present in the population. Samples that meet this criterion are called *representative samples*. Samples that do not, either by chance or by design, are called *biased samples*. Note that what constitutes a representative sample is based on what the population is, which in turn affects the scope of a valid conclusion. If I wish to conclude something about men, a sample that consists of all men and no women is perfectly fine; if I wish to conclude something about people, a sample that consists of all men and no women is a biased sample that will not provide sufficient support to my conclusion.

The similarity between the sample and the population has been the subject of much discussion in the sciences. We will not delve into all of the different theories of proper sampling here. However, across disciplines, the value of two specific methods of sampling is widely accepted: random and stratified.

In *random sampling* every individual (or object) within a population has an equal chance of being selected in the sample. While this equal chance does not in itself guarantee a representative sample, it certainly increases the chances of obtaining one if the sample is large enough. Opinion polls are often randomized across the relevant area. For example, the media in the city of Polis are interested in gauging the public support of two mayoral candidates. They use a computer to dial phone numbers randomly within the relevant area codes, and after polling 300 people in this way, they generalize to the population and say that Candidate A is favored by 35% of the population, while Candidate B is favored by 50%, with 15% undecided. This would be a random sample. It would be much more reliable than having two pollsters go door-to-door in a single neighborhood of the city. Even if more people were polled that way, the sample would not be representative of the entire city, and variation in the rest of the city's population would not be present in the poll.

Let's take an even more extreme example: Candidate A wants to know what her chances of election are, so she hires someone to make a poll. The pollster tells her that she is winning 72% of the vote. Understandably, Candidate A is elated. However, after she loses the election by 20% and looks into the methods used by the pollster, she finds that the poll was conducted at one of Candidate A's own fundraisers. A random sample was not used, and thus the conclusion that she would be elected would not be well-founded (in fact, 72% from a fundraiser sample would be embarrassingly low!).

Random sampling is especially useful when little is known about variation (relevant and irrelevant) in a population. When specific relevant variations are known in advance, *stratified sampling* can be better. In this method, the population is divided up into different *strata* (plural of stratum, literally, "a layer of rock or soil" in Latin), and samples are taken randomly within each of those strata. Let's say we want to gather data on student behavior in high school, and we have enough time and money to poll 16 people. If we take a random sample, our sample is small enough that there is a good probability that we would end up with only one or two students from a given grade level. However, we know in advance that the high school is equally divided between 9th, 10th, 11th, and 12th graders. Thus, we could stratify the population by grade, and randomly select 4 people from each grade. This would be a better sample.

Large and Varied Sample

The second criterion for a valid enumerative induction is that the sample be large and varied. The variation is necessary for purposes of satisfying the first criterion; the size is necessary for purposes of providing sufficient strength to the conclusion. Suppose I want to conclude something about people's enjoyment of watching *Citizen Kane*. I talk to eight of my friends, all of whom say they like the movie, and I conclude that everyone likes *Citizen Kane*. Even if my sample is somewhat representative in terms of potentially relevant characteristics (age, gender, etc.), it cannot be large enough, simply by virtue of its size, to make a conclusion about all people. In this case, I have committed a fallacy known as *hasty generalization*. I have generalized from my small sample to a large population too quickly; I needed to collect more data. Much work in statistics has been spent determining exactly how large a sample ought to be to provide a defensible conclusion about a population of a certain size, but that question is beyond the scope of our interests here.

Statistical Syllogism

We can invert the relationship between the data group and the inference group and end up with a *statistical syllogism*. This is a form of induction in which evidence is provided in the form of a generalization about some large proportion of instances and a conclusion is drawn about a specific instance. Thus, the data group is the same as the population, and the inference group is contained within that data group. In order to be valid, the percentage of the data group with the given attribute should be more than 50%, and the inference group should not be too large. For example,

> Ninety percent of the trees in Fantastica have purple leaves. This tree is in Fantastica. Therefore, it probably has purple leaves.

Note that both enumerative induction and statistical syllogism are inductive arguments; as such, their conclusions follow with probability, but not certainty. In the earlier example of enumerative induction, it is possible to produce a dog with three legs (either by genetic defect or unfortunate accident); such an event does not invalidate the argument. Similarly, the conclusion of a statistical syllogism will never be introduced with the modalities of necessity or certainty.

Fallacy of Exclusion

There is another major fallacy that must be avoided when one makes any sort of inductive argument. Remember that the purpose of an argument is to provide evidence to support a conclusion. If the argument is inductive, that is, if the conclusion does not follow with necessity from the premises, then there will always be some uncertainty involved in the conclusion.

An argument will often provide evidence only in support of its conclusion. Evidence that goes against the conclusion is called *counterevidence*. In debates, for example, one goal of each side is to provide counterevidence to the other side's conclusions. In a sound argument, the counterevidence does not outweigh the positive evidence for the conclusion. Consider the following argument:

> Martin lives on the coast in California. Most people who live on the coast in California vote Democratic, so Martin probably votes Democratic.

This could be a reasonable argument, especially if we assume that the premises are true.

However, suppose we find some fairly strong counterevidence:

> Martin lives on the coast in California, in Orange County. Most people who live in Orange County vote Republican.

The counterevidence is strong enough that even if the premises are true, the conclusion would still be false. Then, we could describe this as *undermining counterevidence,* and the initial argument, which omitted it, would have committed the *fallacy of exclusion.*

Returning to a term from our discussion of samples and populations, the premises in arguments that commit this fallacy are biased in the information that they present. Presenting only evidence that supports the conclusion and omitting counterevidence makes the argument appear to be stronger than it really is. This fallacy is very common. Undermining evidence can be left out for many different reasons: conscious deception (think of advertisements or political speeches), unconscious bias (in psychology, the phrase "confirmation bias" refers to people's tendency to favor information that confirms what they already believe), a lack of rigorous background research, etc.

Visualizing the Varieties of Inductive Argument

In this section, we've seen several varieties of logical comparison between individual objects and groups of objects. Below are illustrations of the relationships between data and inference groups in these forms of argumentation (from Davis' *Introduction to Logic*, p. 81, 95, 99):

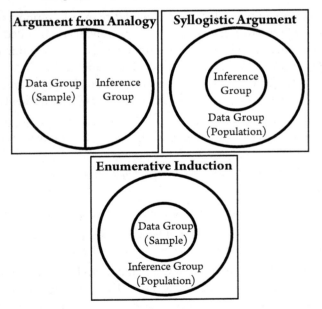

VII
Inductive Logic II:
Causes and Hypotheses

Causal Induction

If the previous section's discussion of populations and samples reminded you of things you may have heard in a science class, it is because inductive logic is the cornerstone of much scientific reasoning and experimentation. Because of the nature of human beings and most of the natural world, we cannot observe every single instance of any given thing. Yet with sound logic and good scientific practices, we can make very well-reasoned conclusions about things in the world.

There are a few characteristics of causes and effects that are part of their definitions. First, because we assume (and rightly so, according to most physicists) that time is linear, a cause must always either precede or accompany an effect. An effect cannot precede its cause. Second, the effect cannot be present without its cause; that is, Effect B cannot be present without Cause A. Finally, for A to be the cause of B, the presence of A must reliably lead to B. If A leads to B only some of the time, it cannot be the cause of B.

With these definitions in mind, Here is a sound argument ascribing causality between two events or actions, A and B:

> B occurred when and only when A occurred (in context C). Therefore, A caused B.

This sort of argument requires three criteria to be met. First, event A must be a possible cause of event B. Second, event B cannot be a possible cause of event A. Third, there cannot be any confounding factors. None of these criteria is easy to prove definitively; if they were, we could talk about causal deduction, but as it stands, we must always leave room for alternatives. Thus, we will call this sort of argument *causal induction*.

The first two criteria may sound somewhat broad; however, the concept of correlation can help limit what possible causes may be. For the sake of illustration, let us return to Milton, who is sick.

Perhaps Milton wants to figure out what caused his sickness, so he starts keeping a daily log of his activities, his diet, and his sleep schedule. He is looking for a relationship between any of these factors and his health. He finds that on days when he reports eating meals that contain dairy (A), he also reports poor health (B). This is the first step in determining the cause, but this is not yet proof of causation. At this stage, Milton has found a *correlation* between two events. As the one event occurs more frequently, there is either an increase or decrease in the occurrence of another event.

Next, Milton must be sure that he does not report poor health on days that he does not eat meals that contain dairy, for the correlation he has found could be due to coincidence. Put more generally, the cause cannot appear without the effect. If it turns out to be the case that eating dairy occurs on days that he feels sick and that it does not occur on days that he does not feel sick, Milton is that much closer to determining cause. But we do not yet know that A causes B. Perhaps it is the case that whenever he feels sick, Milton eats ice cream as a means of comforting himself. Then there would be the same correlation between A and B, but B would be the cause of A. Thus, it is important to remember that *correlation is not the same as causation*.[1] As his logs become more detailed, Milton discovers that B (feeling sick) is not a possible cause of A (eating dairy) because A always occurs before B, sometimes by a few hours.

To continue his exploration—and to satisfy the third criterion—Milton decides to rule out other potential causes. Milton believes that in order to be possible causes, they must still occur when (or before) and only when (or before) the effect occurs. He finds no such factors, and he brings his argument to the conclusion that eating dairy causes him to feel sick. But perhaps there is a *confounding factor* (or simply a *confound*), which is a possible cause of B that meets the first two criteria and was not previously accounted for. In this case, if Milton concludes that eating dairy causes him to feel sick, he may be ignoring the confounding factor that whenever he eats dairy, be it drinking a

---

[1] As human beings, we are predisposed to look for causation even when none is explicitly stated. If we are presented with the sentence, "First A happened, then B happened," it is in our nature to assume that A caused B. Even a more general phrasing that leaves out the temporal relationship—"When A happens, B happens"—tends to lead to the same conclusion. But if we want to reason logically, we must divorce ourselves from this habit.

glass of milk or eating a bowl of ice cream, he does so very quickly because he likes it so much, and he never eats anything else that quickly. Then we could imagine a version of this story in which it is the speed with which he eats, and not what he eats, that is making him sick. It just happened that speed of consumption was confounded with what was being consumed.

For a final illustration, let's ignore the speed-of-eating factor and use a different version of this scenario: Imagine that Milton drinks a liter of orange juice at the start of every day. Since this event occurs on days on which he does feel sick and on days on which he doesn't, he ruled it out. But since it occurred every day that he logged, Milton does not know whether there might be an interaction between the orange juice and eating dairy. It could be the case that eating dairy only makes him feel sick because it is mixing with the acidic orange juice in his stomach. In order to rule out this sort of joint cause, Milton would have to experiment with the temporary removal of any potentially relevant component of his daily routine. Then he would find that he can eat dairy just fine on days when he does not start his day with a liter of orange juice. Thus, the dairy and orange juice would each be *necessary*, but not separately *sufficient* to cause his sickness. We would call them *jointly sufficient causes* of his sickness.

It is difficult to overstate both the importance of ruling out confounds and the difficulty of doing so. What constitutes a satisfactory methodology will vary widely based on the relevant domain of knowledge: psychology, sociology, anthropology, physics, chemistry, meteorology, etc. Often the strength of an argument will hinge much more on its satisfaction of the third criterion and the rigor with which various confounds have been eliminated than on any other characteristic. In some cases, it might be more useful to determine what is *not* the cause rather than what is the cause. Then, our initial argument would be altered to take the following form, called *causal elimination*:

A occurred without B. B occurred without A (in context C). Therefore, A is not a cause of B.

Another aspect of our example argument is what we termed "context C." This leaves room for the fact that a certain cause might lead to an effect in one set of circumstances but not in another. For example, drinking water might meet all the criteria for being a cause of satisfaction when one is thirsty, but not when one isn't thirsty. Lying down and closing your eyes could cause you to go to sleep if you are tired, but not if you have just woken up from a good night's sleep. Note that a different role of an event in a different context does not necessarily imply joint causes; in the example of drinking water, it would be quite odd to conclude that the thirst jointly caused its own satisfaction. At the same time, thirst is a necessary condition for the satisfaction of thirst; if you were not thirsty to begin with, you could not satisfy your thirst.

Finally, it is worth highlighting a very common fallacy associated with the ascription of causality. In the *post hoc fallacy* (literally, "after this" in Latin), causality is ascribed to an event or action merely because it preceded or accompanied an effect. This is fallacious because a nearly infinite number of events precede any given effect; to pick A and highlight a characteristic (preceding or accompanying the effect) that A shares with so many others does not provide sufficient reason to believe the conclusion that A is the cause. It is indeed true that causes always precede or accompany their effects, but while precedence or accompaniment is necessary for something to be a cause, it is not sufficient. Sir James George Frazier, an early social anthropologist who studied mythologies and religions, pointed out the role of post-hoc reasoning as applied to belief in magic and various religious practices:

> The reader may well be tempted to ask, How was it that intelligent men did not sooner detect the fallacy of magic? ... Why cling to beliefs which were so flatly contradicted by experience? How dare to repeat experiments that had failed so often? The answer seems to be that the fallacy was far from easy to detect, the failure by no means obvious, since in many, perhaps in most cases, the desired event did actually follow, at a longer or shorter interval, the performance of the rite which was designed to bring it about; and a mind of more than common acuteness was needed to perceive that, even in these cases, the rite was not necessarily the cause of the event. A ceremony intended to make the wind blow or the rain fall, or to work the death of an enemy, will always be followed, sooner or later, by the occurrence it is meant to bring to pass; and primitive man may be excused for regarding the occurrence as a direct result of the ceremony, and the best possible proof of its efficacy.[2]

---

[2] Sir James George Frazier, *The Golden Bough: A Study in Magic and Religion*, abridged ed. (New York: The Macmillan Co., 1922), p. 59.

Hypothetical Induction

Depending on the particular thing we wish to make inferences about, it might be most useful to come up with a possible hypothesis or theory and then test it. When we test a hypothesis by seeing what would follow if we assume it to be the case, we are using *hypothetical induction*. Imagine a large set of facts about the physical world. We could test a theory of physics by seeing whether each of the facts we know to be true can be accounted for by the theory. If it fails to account for some of the data, then it cannot be a complete theory. Hypothetical induction is a form of *indirect reasoning* because it is focused on the consequences of assuming the truth or falsity of a conclusion. The other forms of inductive and deductive logic that we have discussed so far comprise *direct reasoning*. In its most basic form, hypothetical induction is the following kind of argument:

X is true. T would explain X. Therefore, T is true.

T represents the theory or hypothesis in question. But we know that a theory being possibly true is not a sufficient reason to claim that it is true. If, however, T can explain X better than any other explanation can, then the threshold has been crossed and the argument is valid. How, then, are we to define "better"? Here, as with eliminating confounds, specific measures might vary with different examples, but in general, the better explanation is the one that demonstrates five characteristics (from Davis, *Introduction to Logic*, pp. 157–167): consistency, completeness, simplicity, direct support, and confirmability.

Consistency

A good explanation must be internally consistent; that is, it must not contradict itself. Put another way, it must not predict two mutually exclusive occurrences. Additionally, a good explanation should be consistent with other facts that are already known (or assumed) to be true.

Completeness

Better explanations are those that account for more of the relevant data. The best explanations account for all relevant data. Of course, there can be competing explanations each of which can account for all the data in a given case.

Simplicity

Ceteris paribus, simpler explanations are better than more complicated explanations. The classic statement of this characteristic is named after William of Occam, a friar and logician in the 14th Century. There are many formulations of "Occam's Razor": "One formulation… says 'Entities are not to be multiplied beyond necessity.' Another says 'Plurality is not to be assumed without necessity.'"[3] Explanations that are unnecessarily complex or that require postulating multiple things are less simple, and thus often "worse" or less likely to be true,[4] than explanations that are simpler or that postulate only a single thing.

Direct Support

Any good candidate for an explanation will draw upon some amount of evidence that supports the truth of the explanation via direct reasoning. The more direct support an explanation has, the better an explanation it is.

Confirmability

A good explanation will allow for predictions to be made about future occurrences. If the prediction turns out to be true, it strengthens the explanation; if it turns out to be false, it weakens —or eliminates—the explanation.

It is very difficult to assess the worth of explanations that are not confirmable. The philosopher Karl Popper famously took falsifiability (the ability to be falsified, a sort of inverted definition of confirmability) as the criterion that separated scientific theories from non-scientific theories.

A Note About Evaluative Characteristics

Many explanations do not have every single one of these five characteristics. Consistency is the only characteristic that is necessary for an explanation. The absence of completeness, simplicity, direct support, or confirmability is not sufficient to eliminate an explanation. When judging which explanation is

---

[3] From Davis, *Introduction to Logic*, p. 160.

[4] There are, of course, exceptions to this rule, especially in the scientific literature, in which a more complicated explanation is proven to be true.

better than another, the demonstration of each of these characteristics should be taken into account. There is no easy formula that can be used to evaluate explanations.

Scientific Experimentation

In hypothetical induction, we assume a hypothesis to be true and then evaluate it based on what might follow if it were true. In the scientific method, we craft hypotheses and then test them in actuality—in a laboratory setting or elsewhere—to determine whether they are true or false. Scientific experimentation brings together components of enumerative induction and elements of causal and hypothetical induction. Broadly speaking, a good experiment typically uses random or stratified sampling and controls for confounding variables by holding as much constant as possible while varying a single factor at a time. The specific design of a scientific experiment varies widely with the scope and nature of the hypothesis being tested. In many ways, scientific experimentation is the culmination of inductive logic.

VIII
Fallacies and Biasing Influences

What follows is a list of common logical fallacies and biasing influences. All are common, all are often well-disguised, and all are to be avoided. When available and commonly used, the original Latin phrase for the fallacy is given. Other common names of the fallacy are given in parentheses.

Affirming the Consequent: This fallacy occurs when an argument is based on a conditional along with the truth of the consequent. The general form is, "If A, then B. B. Therefore, A." "If the mailman is approaching, my dog barks. My dog is barking. So the mailman is approaching." Note that a conditional can form the basis of a valid argument if a premise asserts the truth of the antecedent ("If the mailman is approaching, my dog barks. The mailman is approaching. So my dog barks.").

Argumentum ad Auctoritate **(argument from authority):** This fallacious argument takes the following structure: Person A says X about topic Y. Person A should be trusted about topic Y. Therefore X is true. This is a fallacy only when the statement about trusting the person is unsupported; indeed the statement of trust in the person is often a suppressed premise: "Dr. Honeydew is a dentist. He says that brushing teeth with baking soda is best. Therefore, it is best to use baking soda when brushing one's teeth." That someone has an occupation related to a claim does not in itself support that claim. However, if the statement about trusting the person is well-supported, this argument, still based on authority, is no longer fallacious: "Dr. Honeydew is a dentist who has published many peer-reviewed articles about the pros and cons of brushing teeth with different substances. Based on these studies, he says that baking soda is best. Therefore, it is best to use baking soda when brushing teeth." Now the credibility of the authority has been demonstrated and the argument is sound.

Argumentum ad Consequentiam **(appeal to consequences):** This fallacy occurs when an argument is formed in which the consequences of a proposition are used as evidence for or against the truth of the proposition. With positive consequences: "If it rained more frequently, then a higher water level would be a result. A higher water level would be a great thing for many people. So it will rain more frequently." With negative consequences: "If God did not exist, my life would be less meaningful. A less meaningful life is undesirable. Therefore, God exists." A variation on this argument follows:

Argumentum ad Baculum (**appeal to force**): Literally "argument to the cudgel." "If you say that Proposition X should be passed, then you will be fired. Being fired would lead to lots of problems in your life. So Proposition X should not be passed."

Note that consequences can be part of a logical argument if one is careful about the relation of the evidence to the conclusions. For example, with one adjustment, the example given for an argumentum ad baculum can be made valid: "If you say that Proposition X should be passed, then you will be fired. Being fired would lead to lots of problems in your life. Therefore, *you should not say that* Proposition X should be passed." Similar adjustments can salvage any fallacious appeal to the consequences.

Argumentum ad Hominem (**argument to the person**): The soundness of arguments does not depend on the particular people who make them. When someone claims that an argument is not sound because of the person arguing, this fallacy is committed. It is an attack on the character of the arguer rather than the content of the argument. There are four main varieties of ad hominem argument:

Abusive: attacking the personality traits or character of an opponent: "She's been convicted of theft, so her argument about how to treat the budget must be wrong." A person's character, moral standards, political viewpoint, or past or current transgressions may be relevant to all manner of assessments, but such assessments do not affect the logic of the person's argument. In this way, this particular version of the fallacy includes poisoning the well, which is covered below.

Circumstantial: asserting that the position a person takes in an argument is one that the person is disposed to take: "He's a Republican; of course he would say that. So what he is saying is false." The truth of such statements about an arguer does not affect the logic of the statements made by that arguer. Note that if the second sentence were eliminated, and we crafted an argument saying "He's a Republican, thus, he would be likely to say that," it could be a valid argument rather than an ad hominem attack, albeit with a suppressed premise that "Republicans tend to say that."

Tu Quoque: Literally, "you also." This variety claims that because the speaker has acted in a way inconsistent with an argument, he cannot make that argument. Basically, it is an argument of hypocrisy: "Your argument against smoking is clearly incorrect; you used to be a smoker." Clearly, this is a fallacious argument; people are permitted—encouraged, in fact—to learn from their mistakes, and this form of argument contradicts that principle. More to the point, whether or not the arguer smokes or has smoked is irrelevant to the question whether smoking is to be avoided. In fact, in this case the arguer's experience may add authority to his argument.

Guilt by association: This variety of *ad hominem* argument works to discredit an argument because the arguer's views are shared by some disliked other entity: "She argues that the death penalty is wrong, a view that is shared by murderers and other criminals." Sometimes, the arguer is associated directly with a disliked entity: "Sure, he gives some reasons that this law would be beneficial, but he is a member of the Evil Deeds Corporation. Thus, his argument is wrong."

Note that many cases of *ad hominem* argument might fall into more than one variety of it. The example given for "guilt by association" could be broadened to include both association and personal character: "He gives some reasons that this law would be beneficial, but he is a member of the Evil Deeds Company and clearly must be dishonest. Thus, his argument is wrong." This argument would demonstrate both the "guilt by association" and "abusive" varieties.

Argumentum ad Ignorantiam **(argument from ignorance)**: Lack of proof is not proof. This fallacy is committed whenever the conclusion that something is false is drawn from the premise that its truth has not been demonstrated. These arguments are often offered by hunters of witches, communists, terrorists, and other groups. The same mistake is made when someone claims a new or unfamiliar product to be unsafe, dangerous, or ineffective simply because it has not been adequately tested.

If the argument from ignorance were not considered fallacious *eo ipso* (in itself), then simultaneously contradictory conclusions could result from a given argument. For example, scientists do not currently have enough evidence to establish whether there is extra-terrestrial life in the universe. The argument from ignorance would then lead to both the conclusion that there is extra-terrestrial life (because the contrary has not been proven) and the conclusion that there is no such thing (for the same reason).

In the American legal system, the argument from ignorance is avoided by presuming innocence. While it is possible to prove guilt in various ways, it is much more difficult to prove that one did *not* commit a particular crime (especially depending on the nature and timing of said crime). This shifts the burden of proof to the prosecution, which must provide positive evidence that the crime was committed by the defendant.

But beware: it can be tempting to over-assign the label of "argument from ignorance." We all believe that leprechauns are fictitious creatures. If asked why, it might be reasonable to say simply that no one has ever seen or found evidence of a leprechaun. This sounds like the argument from ignorance, but it is not. There is a crucial suppressed premise: namely, that people have looked in all of the places that leprechauns are likely to live. Failure to find something *after a thorough search for it* indeed constitutes proof that it is not there. Note, however, that this argument does presuppose that the thing in question is something that can be sought after and found.

Two fallacies related to the argument from ignorance are the **argument from incredulity** and the **argument from self-knowledge**. The argument from incredulity occurs when a person concludes that because it is difficult to imagine the truth of a proposition, the proposition must be false. "I can't fathom that there is extra-terrestrial life. Therefore, there probably isn't extra-terrestrial life." This fallacy is sometimes inadvertent; there may be suppressed premises that would render the argument valid. For example, if I believe in the laws of physics, then if something would violate the laws of physics, it is reasonable to say that it is unlikely to occur for that reason. However, if the argument is structured such that the evidence given for the conclusion is that I cannot believe in something rather than that it would violate the laws of physics, then the argument is badly structured. The argument from self-knowledge occurs when people claim that if something were true, they would know it and that because they don't know it, it must be false. As with the argument from authority, if sufficient evidence is provided that the arguer has a large body of relevant knowledge and it is in fact reasonable to believe that the claim at hand would be present in that body of knowledge, then there is not necessarily a fallacy at work.

Argumentum ad Logicam (**argument to logic; argument from fallacy; the "fallacy fallacy"**): This fallacy occurs when the claim is made that because an argument is fallacious, its conclusion must be false. It is a tempting but false assumption that one cannot reach a correct conclusion for an incorrect reason.

Argumentum ad Naturam (**appeal to nature**): This fallacy occurs when a person argues that simply because something occurs in nature it is justified or good. If the assumption is addressed in the argument—for example, one describes exactly why something that occurs in nature is a good—then it is no longer a fallacy. However, in most uses of this argument, that if it occurs in nature it must be good, there is a suppressed premise.

Argumentum ad Passiones (**appeal to emotion**): This fallacy occurs when people seek to elicit a strong emotional response in listeners and have that emotional response stand in place of a logical argument. People who commit this fallacy are relying on listeners' inherent enjoyment of positive emotions and inherent dislike of negative emotions, and then are attempting to link the feelings to the truth or falsity of some conclusion.

Argumentum ad Populum (**appeal to the people, appeal to popularity, the bandwagon fallacy**): This argument assumes that if a belief is popular or widely-held, it must be true: "Fifty million people believe that this policy will not solve our problems; therefore, it will not solve our problems." If the argument has to do with the popularity of a given statement, saying something about how many people agree or disagree with the statement may be useful; in other cases, it is fallacious.

An *argumentum ad populum* can also be used as a biasing influence, to the extent that some people might alter their opinions and thoughts to be in accord with popular opinion. Two forms of social influence can be at work when this occurs.

Normative social influence occurs when a person says that he agrees with a given argument when he in fact does not. He is accepting the conclusion of the argument not because he genuinely believes it, but because he does not wish to go against the popular opinion openly. **Informational social influence** occurs when a person's opinion has changed as the result of the argument. He is accepting the conclusion of the argument because he genuinely believes it to be true.

Begging the Question: This is a fallacy that occurs when the truth of the conclusion of an argument is presupposed by one or more premises in the argument (see p. 83). Certainly, making the same statement twice would never pass as a sound argument: "Spending state money on this program would not solve the problem because spending state money on this program will not solve the problem." However, question begging often uses a different phrasing in the conclusion from that used in the premise: "Spending state money on this program will not solve the problem because this problem will persist even if money is spent on it." Deceitful arguers will often hide question begging in a much longer chain of premises, or will use vague or unfamiliar terminology to obfuscate their logical shortcomings.

Note that colloquially "begs the question" will often be used to mean "raises the question" or "calls for the question to be asked." This is an incorrect usage.

Either-Or Fallacy (black-or-white thinking, false choice, false dilemma): This is the fallacy of the false dilemma. Note that despite its name, the fallacy is not limited to oversimplification to only two options. A reduction to three options (trilemma) or to four options (tetralemma) would still be an example of this fallacy, so long as those three or four options are not the only options.

Either we pass this law, or the economy will collapse.

You are either against capital punishment or you are ignorant.

Equivocation (fallacy of four terms): This fallacy is committed when the premises of an argument assume a misleading transitivity between terms. *Term* is the word we use to refer to the elements of a syllogism. This fallacy occurs when there are multiple interpretations of terms in the premises and conclusion, and the truth of the premise assumes an interpretation that is different from the interpretation assumed by the conclusion. Consider the following argument:

> A cookie is better than nothing. Nothing is better than eternal happiness. Therefore, a cookie is better than eternal happiness.

It seems like there are only three terms in this argument: cookie, nothing, and eternal happiness. In this argument, the transitivity causes the argument to seem valid. If we reduce the argument to a basic sequence, we are left with: A is better than B. B is better than C. Therefore A is better than C. This structure is valid. However, the sense of B in the first premise is not the same as the sense of B in the second premise; in the first, the proposition says that it is better to have a cookie than to have nothing at all to eat, while in the second, the proposition says that there is literally no thing that can be experienced by a human being that is better than eternal happiness. It is only because the term "nothing" can be used in both senses that such a fallacious argument can be made. Hence the "four terms" name for the fallacy: the argument would be valid with only three terms, but in reality, it has four.

Exclusion (fallacy of suppressed evidence): A fallacy that results when evidence that would undermine the conclusion of an argument is omitted from the argument. Note that this is only relevant for inductive arguments (see pp.111–112).

Hasty Generalization (hasty induction, fallacy of insufficient sample): a fallacy that results when the observation group in an enumerative induction is not large enough sufficiently to support the conclusion about the inference group or population (see p. 110).

Loaded Question Fallacy (complex question fallacy, fallacy of presupposition): Despite its name, this in many ways is more of a biasing influence than a fallacious argument. It occurs when a question presupposes information that is unjustified. Because it is a question, there is usually not an argument that follows directly from it. Most commonly, any sort of answer to the question legitimizes the unjustified information. For example, "Have you stopped embezzling money from your work?" If you say "yes," then you are acknowledging that in the past you embezzled money from your work; if you say "no," then you are acknowledging that you still embezzle. If you say "I never embezzled money," and go on to argue your innocence, you are not answering the question in the way it was posed (though that might be a perfectly reasonable way to respond).

Non Sequitur: Literally, "it does not follow." This fallacy occurs when the conclusion of an argument does not follow with probability from its premises. Sometimes it results from a simple modality mismatch: "5% of the balls in the pit are blue; therefore, a ball taken from the pit will be blue." At other times it results from premises that do not relate to the conclusion: "The humidity today is 85%. Therefore, dogs are mammals."

Nonstarter: This fallacy occurs when the premises of an argument are false. If that is the case, then—from the start—the argument cannot be sound.

Poisoning the Well: This is a biasing influence (technically, a rhetorical device) that offers negative information about a position or person—often before that position is advanced or that person speaks—in order to bias the audience against believing what is said or against being included in the group that holds that position. The full metaphor is that if you add poison to a well, no one will drink any of its water; thus, if you have poisoned the source of all possible arguments, people will not be receptive to a person's speech or a particular point of view. It can be combined with other rhetorical devices, such as a rhetorical question: "What reasonable person could think that this action should be taken?"

Note that poisoning the well against a person becomes a special case of *argumentum ad hominem*. "Postlethwaite is a communist and a psychopath; don't believe what he says about fossil fuel emissions."

Post Hoc **Fallacy (post hoc reasoning, post hoc ergo propter hoc)**: Literally, "after this," or in the longer form, "after this, therefore because of this." This fallacy occurs when causality is ascribed to an event or action merely because it preceded or accompanied an effect (see p.115).

Red Herring: This is a kind of biasing influence that attempts to distract the listener with irrelevant but gripping content. The fallacy is named for the distractingly strong smell of certain varieties of smoked fish. Note that the two appeals described earlier (appeal to nature and appeal to emotion) could be classified as types of red herring. The phrase is most commonly used for misleading clues in mystery novels or films.

Slippery Slope Fallacy: This fallacy occurs when an event is said to follow from another event with some likelihood (often inevitability) without any actual evidence provided to link the two events, aside from the similarity in the kind of event. For example: "If we permit this increase of tuition, before you know it we'll be paying $80,000 a year. It would be awful to have to pay $80,000 a year. So we can't allow this tuition increase." Note that if there is evidence supporting a link (even several events long) between the first event and the final event, this would no longer be a fallacy: "If A happens, B will happen. If B happens, C will happen. If C happens, D will happen. We don't want D to happen. So, we should not allow A to happen."

Straw Man: A man of straw is easier to knock down than a real man. The straw man argument accuses the opposition of having a position that is easily refuted and then refutes it to imply that thereby the opposition's entire argument is similarly demolished. "People who think abortion should be made illegal have no respect for women's rights. Clearly, women's rights must be upheld, and so abortion must remain legal." This argument assumes that the opponents, rather than simply being against abortion, are not supportive of women's rights. While the two are related, abortion is one potential right that a woman has, while "women's rights" encompasses much more than just abortion. This fallacy can be woven into a rhetorical question: "Why is it that these lawmakers don't value freedom?"

Subjectivist Fallacy: This fallacy occurs when something is claimed to be true for one person or group and false for another person or group when, in actuality, it has been demonstrated by empirical evidence to be true for everyone. For example, "I know studies show that talking on your phone or texting while driving leads to accidents, but I'm very careful when I do it, so I will be fine." Note that if the claim in question actually is subjective (e.g., discussion of the taste of food, or enjoyment of a certain book or movie), it would not be a fallacious argument: "I know lots of people liked that book, but I really didn't like it, so I shouldn't read the sequel."

Ten Fallacious Arguments or Invalid Topics
(Based on Aristotle)

1. Concluding an argument as if having proved it without actually having gone through the process of arguing it

2. Playing on using a word in a different (illogical, fortuitous) sense—e.g., "A saucepan must be noble for so was the great god Pan."[a]

3. Making a statement of a whole that is true only of parts, or of parts true only of the whole—e.g., Anyone who knows all the letters of a word knows the word since the letters make up the word.[b]

4. Using indignant language: exclaiming that something is insulting, outrageous, or unfair is not an argument

5. Using a single unrepresentative example—e.g., "Dionysius is a thief since he is a vicious man."[b]

6. Treating an accidental as an essential—e.g., text messages are upsetting to me because I was upset when I got the text message that you were breaking up with me.

7. Arguing from consequences—e.g., Beggars must be happy because not having to pay taxes makes us happy and beggars don't pay taxes on the money they get.

8. Arguing *post hoc ergo propter hoc* (after it, therefore because of it) —that one event follows another in time does not prove the earlier caused the later.

9. Ignoring crucial circumstances—e.g., Autolycus must not be a thief because he will not accept the gift of any money from the shepherd (Autolycus had already picked the shepherd's pocket).

10. Arguing based on confusion of general and particular—e.g., it is probable that things improbable will happen, therefore improbable things are probable (fallacious because the sense of probable in the conclusion is not specified)

This list has been adapted from Richard A. Lanham, *A Handlist of Rhetorical Terms* (Berkeley: University of California Press, 1969), pp. 109–110, and from Aristotle's *Rhetoric*, Book II, Ch. 23, ed. Lee Honeycutt, tr. W. Rhys Roberts. Quotations marked a are from Lanham. Quotations marked b are from Honeycutt.

On Talmudic Logic

The tradition of logical discourse in Judaism is both ancient and unbroken through more than two millennia. It begins with God's teaching as written in the Five Books of Moses and the teachings in the accompanying oral tradition, believed to be equally authoritative and eventually written during successive ages into the other books of the Bible, the Mishnah, the Talmud, and countless works that have commented and built upon them down to the present day. It is impossible here to give more than the merest hint about the hermeneutics of Talmudic reasoning. First we provide a short list of the basic foundational categories of works to introduce the relevant terminology. Next we give one of several ancient lists of principles intended to guide the logical interpretation of the Torah and the derivation of laws from scripture.

The specific rules given here are meant to serve as rules of inference for proper interpretation of scripture. They will not be found in any traditional logic book; however, their style and intended use would fit right in with other traditional techniques in inferential logic, which may themselves have been influenced by Talmudic reasoning. The Thirteen Principles given below serve a similar role to the rules of inference discussed in "Basic Concepts of Logic" (pp. 100-101) in the sense that if they are adhered to, the resulting conclusions will be trustworthy.

Our hope is that this list illustrates some of the subtle logic of the rabbinic tradition, which combines the authority of scripture, the responsibility—and the freedom—to apply that authority to the ever-changing realities of human life in time, and the proper use of human reason as a guide in determining the right thought and right action in response to those realities.

Above: *At the Rabbi's*, Carl Schleicher, ca. 1860, oil on panel.

Adapted from Rabbi Nosson Scherman and Rabbi Meir Zlotowitz, eds. *The Complete ArtScroll Siddur* (Brooklyn, NY: Mesorah Publications, 2000), pp. 48–53; Philip Birnbaum, *Daily Prayer Book* (New York: Hebrew Publishing Co., 1949), pp. 41–46; Rabbi Nissen Mangel, ed., *Siddur Tehillat Hashem* (Brooklyn, NY: Merkos L'Inyonei Chinuch, 2013), p. 25; and Adin Steinsaltz, *The Talmud: The Steinsaltz Edition: A Reference Guide*, ed. and tr. Israel V. Berman (New York: Random House, 1989), passim.

Basic Terminology

Written *Torah*: Believed to have been given by God to Moses and recorded in five books. The Hebrew name of each book is the first key word of its first sentence:

B'reishit ("in the beginning")—Genesis

Shemot ("names")—Exodus

Vayikra ("He called")—Leviticus

Bamidbar ("in the desert")—Numbers

Devarim ("words")—Deuteronomy

Oral *Torah*: Believed to have been given by God to Moses and passed down from teacher to student through the ages until finally recorded in written form.

Talmud: the multi-volume compendium of interpretation (*Midrash*) of the Torah and the application of its laws. Talmud is comprised of

> *Mishnah*: a compendium of the laws of behavior and ritual, derived from the Torah and established by the *Tanaim* (early sages, 20–200 C.E.), collected by Rabbi Judah the Prince (170–200 C.E.); and

> *Gemara*: commentaries on the *Mishnah*, established by the *Amoraim* (later sages, 220–500 C.E.) and collected in the shorter and earlier Jerusalem Talmud compiled in the Land of Israel and in the longer and later Babylonian Talmud compiled in the exile in Babylonia. Gemara is comprised of

>> *Halachah* ("the way to go" = normative laws)— discussions of the logic behind the laws of the *Mishnah* and of their application, intertwined with

>> *Aggadah* ("tellings" = homiletics, legends, speculations) — discussions of theology, philosophy, and ethics and stories about individual people

The Thirteen Principles of Rabbi Ishmael

Rabbi Ishmael's principles focus not on the statement of laws themselves but on the logic behind their derivation from the Torah.

Rabbi Ishmael says: By means of thirteen rules is the Torah interpreted:

1. Conclusion from *Kal va'chomer*—"light and heavy" (lenient and strict): A strictness or leniency that applies in a less obvious situation will apply all the more in a more obvious situation.

> An example: If an act is forbidden on regular festival days, one may conclude that it is all the more forbidden on Yom Kippur, the Day of Atonement (the holiest day of the Jewish year). Conversely, if an act is permitted on Yom Kippur, one may conclude that it is permitted on the lesser festival days.

> Another example: Moses says to God, "Behold, the Children of Israel have not listened to me; how then will Pharaoh listen to me?" (Exodus 6:12).

2. Conclusion from *G'zeirah shavah*—"similar root" (similarity of words or phrases in two different contexts): In certain cases, it may be concluded that two different laws are meant to shed light on one another if a) they appear in two different places but use similar terms, or b) are on different subjects but appear near one another.

> An example of a): The phrase "Hebrew bondsman" at Exodus 21:2 is taken to mean not a non-Hebrew bondsman owned by a Hebrew but a bondsman who is a Hebrew. This is because the law limiting the bondage to six years that appears there reappears at Deuteronomy 15:12, where it applies to "your brother, a Hebrew man or a Hebrew woman."

> An example of b): Many laws pertaining to betrothal and divorce are derived from one another because at Deuteronomy 24:2 a single phrase ("she shall go out [by divorce] and go and become betrothed to another man") juxtaposes the two actions, betrothal and divorce.

3. Conclusion from *Binyan av*—"parent building" (general principle—the full rule is "from a general principle from a single writing and from a general principle from two writings"): A

general principle derived from either a) a law written in one place, or b) a law written in two places, applies to all cases that appear logically similar.

> An example of a): Deuteronomy 24:6 has the law "One shall not take a lower or upper millstone as a pledge, for he would be taking a life as a pledge." From this it is concluded that anything used for preparing food is forbidden to be taken as a pledge.

> An example of b): Exodus 21:26–27 has the law "If a man shall strike the eye of his indentured servant or the eye of his maidservant and destroy it, he shall set him free in compensation for his eye. And if he knocks out the tooth of his indentured servant or the tooth of his maidservant, he shall set him free in compensation for his tooth." From this it is concluded that an indentured servant or maidservant must be set free in compensation for the master's mutilation of any part of the servant's body.

4. Conclusion from *Klal u'phrat*—"general and particular" (a general law followed in scripture by a particular case): When a general rule is followed by a specific case, the law applies only in that specific case.

> An example: The Torah says that sacrificial offerings may be brought "from the animals, from the cattle and the flock [i.e., sheep and goats]" (Leviticus 1:2). By this rule no animals but cattle, sheep, and goats may be used. The general term (animals) is given only to indicate that no animals from the general category may be used but those specified. Similarly, Leviticus 18:6 says, "no one shall marry a close relative." This general rule is followed by a long list of specific relatives forbidden as marriage partners. By this rule the prohibition applies only to those relatives mentioned.

5. Conclusion from *Prat u'chlal*—"particular and general" (a particular case or cases followed by a general law): When particulars are followed by a general law, the law applies to all instances of the general law (the reverse of the previous rule).

> An example: The Torah says about returning another man's lost objects that one should return "his donkey . . . his garment . . . any lost object" that belongs to him

(Deuteronomy 22:3). By this rule, the law applies to any lost item without exception that belongs to another person.

Another example: Exodus 22:9 says "if a man give to his neighbor an ass, or an ox, or a sheep, or any animal to safeguard . . . ," and so the general rule that follows applies not only to the animals specified but to all kinds of animal.

6. Conclusion from *Klal u'phrat u'chlal*—"general and particular and general" (general law followed by a particular case followed by a general law): Where two general laws sandwich a particular case or cases, judgment must be governed by the implication of the particulars. While the two general laws would imply that everything is included and the particular between them that only it is included, the contradiction is resolved thus: everything is included provided it is essentially similar to the particular item specified.

An example: In the question of imposing a fine on a thief, where Exodus 22:8 says "For any thing stolen [general]— whether an ox, an ass, a sheep, a garment [particulars]—for any lost thing [general] . . ." it is concluded based on the particulars listed that the following law applies to any movable object that has intrinsic value but not to real estate, which is not movable, or to contracts, which have no intrinsic value.

7. Conclusion from *Klal she'hu tzarich li'phrat* and *prat she'hu tzarich li'chlal*—"general that requires a particular and particular that requires a general" (a general rule that requires a particular to make its meaning clear and a particular that requires a general rule to make its meaning clear): Where a general law requires a particular, or a particular requires a general law, to make its meaning clear, Rules 4 and 5 above do not apply.

An example: Leviticus 17:13 says that after slaughtering a fowl that may be eaten, one must "pour out its blood and cover it with earth." Cover is a general term that can mean both to cover and to conceal. The particular "with earth" indicates that it is not enough to hide the blood in a vessel and cover it with wood or another solid; "with earth" indicates that the covering must be a soft substance that can mix with the blood. Hence Rule 4 (by which we might have concluded that the blood must be covered by nothing but earth) does not apply since "with earth" is needed to define "cover" clearly.

8. Conclusion from *Kol davar sh'hayah bi'chlal v'yatzah ... l'lameid*—"everything that is included in a general rule and singled out ... to teach" (When any particular case included in a general rule is singled out to teach us something new, what it teaches applies not only to itself but to all cases implied in the general rule):

> An example: Deuteronomy 22:1–2 gives the general rule that one must return any item of lost property to its owner, to do which one must announce the finding of the item. In verse 3, the Torah adds, "so shall you do for his garment." Though a garment is included in the rule that applies to any item of lost property, the specific mention of it implies that the duty to announce its finding applies only to items that, like a garment, are likely to have an owner and marks by which it could be identified.

9. Conclusion from *V'yatzah l't'on ... ch'inyano*—"and singled out to require [something] like the principle" (When a particular case of a general rule is singled out to add a provision similar to the general rule, it is being specified to lessen, not increase, the severity of that provision):

> An example: Exodus 35:2–3 says, "Whoever does work on [the Sabbath day] shall be put to death. You shall not kindle fire in any of your dwellings on the Sabbath day." The provision about not kindling fire, though already implied by "work," is added to indicate that the penalty for kindling fire is less severe than for other kinds of work.

> Another example: Though Leviticus 24:21 imposes the death penalty on one who kills a person, Deuteronomy 19:5 makes exile the punishment for one man's killing another through carelessness. Though the second case is a particular instance of the first, this rule indicates that the accidental killer has been singled out for more lenient punishment (exile instead of death).

10. Conclusion from *V'yatzah l't'on ... she'lo ch'inyano*—"and singled out to require [something] unlike the principle" (When a particular case of a general rule is singled out to add a provision

that is not similar to the general rule, it is being specified in some respects to lessen and in some respects to increase the severity of that provision):

> An example: In Exodus 21:1–6, the Torah says that an indentured servant shall go free after six years of service. In verses 7–11 the Torah adds different provisions for a maidservant, to whom the previous rules for any servant might have been assumed to apply. The added rules for the maidservant are in one respect more lenient—under certain circumstances she may go free even before six years of service —and in another respect more severe—she may be betrothed against her will to her master or his son.

> Another example: In Exodus 21:29–30, the owner of a vicious animal that kills a man or woman must pay a compensation imposed by the court. In verse 32, the Torah adds that if the animal kills an indentured servant or maidservant, the penalty shall be thirty silver shekels. This fixed penalty would be a more lenient provision if the servant's worth were more than thirty shekels and more stringent if the servant's worth were less.

11. Conclusion from *V'yatzah li'don ba'davar he'chadash*—"and singled out in a new thing" (When a particular case of a general rule is singled out with a new matter, the general rule no longer applies to it unless Torah expressly stipulates that it does)

> An example: The entire family of a priest (*kohen*) is permitted to eat of the priestly tithe, but if the priest's daughter marries a non-priest, she is no longer permitted to eat of that tithe (Leviticus 22:11–12). If she were widowed or divorced and returned to her father's house, her status would prevent her from eating of the tithe again unless the Torah had specifically returned her to the status of a member of her father's family (which it does at 22:13).

12. Conclusion from *Davar ha'lameid mei'inyano, v'davar ha'lameid mi'sopho*—"a thing learned from its context and a thing learned from the following passage" (A dubious implication is elucidated from a) its context and b) a subsequent passage):

> An example of a): The same noun, *tinshemet*, occurs both in the context of a list of ritually forbidden birds (Leviticus

11:18) and in the context of a list of ritually forbidden reptiles (Leviticus 11:30), from which it is concluded that the name *tinshemet* was that of both a particular kind of bird and a particular kind of reptile.

An example of b): Leviticus 14:33ff. describes the process for determining whether a house afflicted with the spiritual punishment of a leprosy-like condition must be demolished. From verse 45, "He shall demolish the house—its stones, its timber, and all the mortar of the house," we conclude that the law applies only to houses made of stone, wood, and mortar.

13. Conclusion from *Shnei ch'tuvim ha'mach'chishim zeh et zeh* — "two passages that contradict one another" (Two passages that seem to contradict one another remain contradictory until a third passage comes to reconcile them):

An example: God tells Abraham that his descendants would come through his son Isaac (Genesis 21:12) and then commands Abraham to offer up Isaac as a sacrificial offering (Genesis 22:2). The *Midrash* to Genesis 22:12 reconciles them by showing that the wording of the command to offer Isaac as a sacrifice was literally to "raise him up as an offering" rather than "slay him," so that both the passages remain true without contradiction.

Another example: Exodus 13:6 says, "Matzah you shall eat for seven days"; Deuteronomy 16:8 says "For six days you shall eat matzah." The contradiction is resolved by a third passage (Leviticus 23:14), which forbids the use of new produce until the second day of Passover, after the Omer offering. If the matzah was prepared from new grain, it could be eaten for only six days of Passover, so the Exodus passage must be referring to matzah prepared from the produce of a previous year; hence both passages remain valid without contradiction.

Part III: Rhetoric

Rhetorica, Cornelis Cort, 1565, engraving.

Introduction: Rhetoric

Built upon grammatical correctness and logical truth, the art of rhetoric seeks to communicate to an audience or reader the knowledge, opinion, or idea of the speaker or writer in a way that persuades of its validity.

Rhetoric was originally the study of the principles of oratory, including composition and delivery. It came to be thought of in the ancient world as the art of persuasion and in the medieval period as the art and principles of all discourse and literary composition, including, for orators, principles of delivery, posture, and even gesture, which also affect the impact of a speech. At its best, the art of rhetoric seeks to persuade us of truth. Familiarity with its principles helps us both to communicate truth persuasively to others and to resist being persuaded of falsehood ourselves.

If an argument lacks good rhetoric, it will not be as successful as it could be. However, the use of effective rhetoric does not necessarily imply that a work is logical or its message true. Because the art of persuasion can be used for both good and bad purposes, some societies, ancient and modern, have sought to discredit rhetoric as an art of deception. Indeed, in common usage "rhetoric" is often used as a derisive term to suggest that what is being said or written sounds good but that there is no logic in the content itself—or that perhaps there is a deliberately misleading attempt to make faulty logic appear sound. Logic and rhetoric are separable disciplines, and it is possible to have either one without the other.

As you read the following selections, remember the importance of the starting assumptions of arguments. From three different starting assumptions, "Personal liberty is the highest good," "Equality is the highest good," and "Happiness is the highest good," three different arguments that are grammatically correct, logically sound, and rhetorically effective could be made, each of which could have its conclusion be diametrically opposed to the others. It would be impossible to choose one over another as more sensible simply by looking at the grammar, logic, and rhetoric of the arguments themselves given their respective underlying assumptions.

The examples we have chosen here include works meant to be heard and works meant to be read, works ancient and modern, works nonfictional and fictional, works philosophical, ethical, and political. We urge you to take these works seriously not only as examples of the art of rhetoric but as challenges to achieve correctness in your own thinking, which means "conformity of thought with things as they are—with reality."[1]

Starting with the selections from Hebrew Scriptures, the order of the selections within Part III is chronological rather than thematic.

Note: Because of similar content and related themes, in your reading you may wish to juxtapose

Allegory of the Charioteer excerpt from Plato's *Phaedrus* and the Allegory of the Charioteer in the Katha Upanishad.

Excerpts from Homer's *Iliad* and Weil's essay "The *Iliad*, or Poem of Force."

Excerpts from Kant, Benedict's essay, and Pojman's essay.

Declaration of Independence, Bill of Rights, Declaration of the Rights of Man and of the Citizen, Roosevelt's Second Bill of Rights, and UN's Declaration of Human Rights.

Stanton's speeches and Pankhurst's speech.

---

[1] Sister Miriam Joseph, *The Trivium*, ed. Marguerite McGlinn (Philadelphia: Paul Dry Books, 2002), p. 10.

Style:
Twenty-five Guidelines for Good Rhetoric (Plus Six on Oral Presentation)

Introduction to Style

Style is a matter of judgment and taste, so guidelines for good style are more fluid than the firmer rules of correct grammar. Nonetheless, the underlying principles of rhetorical effectiveness hold true, and the following guidelines will be found to help a writer adhere to them. Note: Except in Part IV, where oral presentation is specifically discussed, all the guidelines apply to speaker and audience as well as to writer and reader; we use the latter terms for convenience.

There are ways of making one's message more persuasive to an audience that go beyond any of the techniques mentioned here. Gesture of the hands can be used to add to the persuasiveness of a message. Called *chironomia* in Greek, it was studied and detailed by the Greeks and Romans. Body posture as well is important for conveying a proper mood and setting the stage for one's message to be well received. Imagine the same well-reasoned argument put forth to you by a person who is standing excitedly at a podium, leaning toward you, gesturing, and speaking more loudly as the speech reaches its climax, and alternatively by a person who is speaking in a soft monotone and looking away from you with his or her arms hanging limp the entire time.

As you practice communicating messages, both orally and in writing, you will craft your own style. You will find some techniques mentioned here that you are able to employ more easily than others, that feel more natural to you to use than others, and that are more effective given your particular context. Over time, you will develop a rhetorical style that is most effective for you. Some aspects of your style may permeate all of your communications; other aspects may change in different environments or for different messages.

I

The Whole Work

1. Unity

Know the ultimate purpose of your essay or speech or argument. Every work of art, whether fictional or not, whether spoken or written, whether in verse or in prose, no matter how much variety it contains, must convey to its audience some unity of purpose. The writer's confusion about what that unity is will cause confusion in the reader. Only once you know what you are really trying to say will all the parts come together in an effective whole.

For whom are you writing? What is the central point? Are you engaging in description, narration, argumentation, self-examination, accusation, defense? Even if there are elements of all of these in a single piece of writing, they must all be tending to a single purpose. Why are you writing this piece? Whom are you trying to persuade and of exactly what? The answer to these essential questions will form the substance of your thesis. And the thesis will usually come at the end of your first paragraph, setting the terms and limits of the discourse and pointing its direction.

If you find you are trying to do several things at once, either look for what the goals have in common and make that the central idea, or eliminate the ancillary or irrelevant elements. There may certainly be digressions within the piece, but every digression or side note must be related to the central thrust of your argument and be seen to be so eventually even if not at first.

Unity must also be present in each paragraph, of which the central idea should be expressed in the thesis sentence of the paragraph, wherever it comes, and everything in the paragraph must be in some way—and clearly—related to that unifying idea. No paragraph should have anything so beside the point that the reader will lose the thread of the argument or question the relevance of the sentences.

Without unity, all the specific support and development in the world will evoke from a reader the question "But what is your point?"

2. Development

Any point, if it is going to stick, must be supported. This means that your reader must not merely understand your idea in the abstract but must experience it as real and present, visible to the mind's eye or audible to the mind's ear. The reason is that for human beings, incarnate spirits in physical bodies, only seeing is believing. We can conceive of an abstract idea, but we cannot truly grasp it, believe it, know its substance, if we cannot see or feel or hear it, as we say, in the flesh.

But the writer, like any other artist, can cause us to experience his idea in the flesh and so to believe it if he or she appeals to what is called our empathy (from the Greek "to feel into"). Empathy is our capacity to feel the present reality of something through our mind's version of our senses almost as vividly as if we were experiencing it with our physical senses in fact. It is this capacity that makes any work of art—writing, picture, sculpture, building, film, music, dance, etc.—come alive for us.

If I say "I had a near-miss on the road today," you perfectly understand the idea, but you are not experiencing it except as an abstraction. Your heart does not speed up. But if I say "I was driving at about seventy-five miles per hour in the left lane on the northbound side of the interstate when a red Porsche convertible, driven by a man in sunglasses with a long-haired blonde in the passenger seat, zoomed past me on the left shoulder at ninety-five and then cut in front of me and straight across the other lanes of traffic to exit at the racetrack"—now you can actually feel what I meant by "near-miss on the road." The first quoted sentence was my thesis; the second was its development.

What are called the body paragraphs of your essay or speech or argument are its development, the particular supporting evidence or descriptions or examples or illustrations that allow us to experience empathically the reality of the abstract idea of the thesis and thereby to make it stick. Every paragraph must have sufficient detail and specifics to convince the reader of the reality of its claims.

Without thorough development, the reader will say about the thesis, "show me. I don't get it. What do you mean?"

3. Structure

The overall structure of any written work will depend on the intellectual content, the purpose, the audience, the form of delivery, and the tone. But whatever these may be, once the writer is aware of them, planning the overall structure is essential. Some people plan with outlines, others with mind mapping (connected balloons of ideas), others with physical shapes like the column (capital as thesis, column as body, base as conclusion) or the hamburger (burger body paragraphs between the two buns of thesis and conclusion). One well-known journalistic simplification of structure is "Tell them what you're going to tell them, tell them, then tell them what you've told them." Whatever the kind of writing, you must have a clear knowledge of its structure (even if you only find that out in the process of writing), so that every part fits harmoniously and effectively into the whole.

The basic unit of the structure of any written work is the paragraph. Paragraphs are not made by writing a whole and then adding random indentations. A paragraph too is a unit, beginning with a transitional sentence or phrase tying it to the previous paragraphs and leading in to this paragraph's idea. The thesis idea of the paragraph will usually come in its first sentence, though if it is more effective to lead to the thesis by steps, the thesis may come later and may even come at the end of the paragraph as the point to which the paragraph has been moving. The length of a paragraph should depend not on quantitative calculations but on the unity of thought within the paragraph. However, avoid single-sentence paragraphs except in dialogue, where each change in speaker begins a new paragraph.

Arrange paragraphs in the most appropriate way to develop and support your thesis idea. How can the supporting paragraphs be best arranged to lead the reader to accept the conclusion and believe the thesis? Put yourself in the reader's place and ask what it would take to convince you.

If it is a description of an event, chronological order may be best. If it is a logical argument, paragraphs may be arranged from weakest to strongest point, or from strongest to weakest, or from most to least familiar, or vice versa, or from most narrowly applicable to most broadly applicable, or from easiest to hardest or hardest to easiest. If the essay is a comparison, support may be arranged item by item (everything to be said about Dickens first, then everything to be said about Thackeray) or point by point (Dickens and Thackeray in relation to satire, Dickens and Thackeray in relation to social conscience, Dickens and Thackeray in relation to sentence structure, etc.). Whatever arrangement is chosen, it must have a logic to it that fits the purpose of the piece and that will be visible to the reader.

4. Coherence

The word *cohere*, from the Latin *co* (together) + *haerere* (to stick), means to stick together. Readers do not like to be confused or bewildered in the middle of their reading. They want to know where they are. The writer must make sure the order of paragraphs, and of sentences within paragraphs, not only makes sense but is visible to the reader. Paragraphs or sentences that seem unrelated to one another interrupt the flow of thought and experience that the writer is striving to make happen in the reader's mind. Some methods of achieving coherence include

Enumeration:

> *First ... Second ... Third ...*
> *In width ... In height ... In depth ...*
> *Before the show ... During the show ... Immediately after the show ... The next day ...*

Pronoun Reference:

> *There are some people who ... They ... But whether they ... or they ... they nonetheless ...*
> *In a good marriage ... When he comes home and she is asleep ... When she comes home and he is asleep ... When she comes home and he is frantically cooking ... When he comes home and she is in the office ...*

Sentence Modifiers:

> *Of course, As a result, However, Nevertheless, Now, In other words, So, After all, etc.*

Initial Coordinating Conjunctions:

> *And, But, Yet, Or, For, Nor*

Correlative Conjunctions:

> *Not only ... but (also); Both ... and; If ... then; Neither ... nor; Either ... or*

Repetition of Words, Phrases, Ideas:

The big difference is between insiders and outsiders . . . Insiders will . . . Outsiders will . . . Though insiders . . . yet they . . . Outsiders, however, . . .

Parallel Structure:

If they were rich . . . If they were getting along . . . If they were poor . . .

An example of Paragraph Coherence: Here is a paragraph without coherence, and with minimal development, abstracted from a passage in Virginia Woolf:

We are also aware of the person he is writing to, though we don't hear him speak. This makes the letters more interesting. He has been getting letters since he was seven. By now he is older and more serious. He is interested in politics and in reading. He tries to live up to his father's expectations and follow his advice but fails. He died young and his wife had to tell his father who she was and that she had children. Then we have the Earl's letters to her and her sons.

Now here is the original passage, coherent and developed:

But while we amuse ourselves with this brilliant nobleman and his views on life we are aware, and the letters owe much of their fascination to this consciousness, of a dumb yet substantial figure on the farther side of the page. Philip Stanhope is always there. It is true that he says nothing, but we feel his presence in Dresden, in Berlin, in Paris, opening the letters and poring over them and looking dolefully at the thick packets which have been accumulating year after year since he was a child of seven. He had grown into a rather serious, rather stout, rather short young man. He had a taste for foreign politics. A little serious reading was rather to his liking. And by every post the letters came — urbane, polished, brilliant, imploring and commanding him to learn to dance, to learn to carve, to consider the management of his legs, and to seduce a lady of fashion. He did his best. He worked very hard in the school of the Graces, but their service was too exacting. He sat down half-way up the steep stairs which lead to the glittering hall with all the mirrors. He could not do it. He failed in the House of Commons; he subsided into some small post in Ratisbon; he died untimely. He left it to his widow to break the news which he had lacked the heart or the courage to tell his father — that he had been married all these years to a lady of low birth, who had borne him children.

The Earl took the blow like a gentleman. His letter to his daughter-in-law is a model of urbanity. He began the education of his grandsons.

—from Virginia Woolf, "Lord Chesterfield's Letters to His Son"[1]

---

[1] from *The Common Reader*, Second Series, accessed 7/23/15 at https://ebooks.adelaide.edu.au/w/woolf/virginia/w91c2/chapter8.html

5. Transitions

While the structure and coherence of an essay form its map, the reader, like a driver, also needs road signs. It does no good to see on the map that you must turn left from Central Parkway onto Roberts Road if there are no road signs along Central Parkway to tell you which intersection is Roberts Road. Similarly, after making clear how the order of your paragraphs will go and seeing that the paragraphs and sentences cohere, you must alert the reader to where he or she is now.

Transitions may be obvious and explicit:

First . . . Second . . . Third . . . Last

The most obvious reason . . . Another reason . . . A surprising reason . . . Finally, the most dramatic reason . . .

Or they may be subtle:

The common attitude was . . . The attitude of the inner circle differed in being . . . When we come to my own attitude at the time . . .

Whatever the method, transitions keep the reader aware of where he or she is in relation to the whole.

6. Hook the Reader

Any written work, just as any speech, needs to grab the attention of its audience from the beginning. If the audience is known to be interested in the subject (for example, a speech on bioengineering to a convention of bioengineers), the hook need not be dramatic. Almost any introduction to the topic will serve. But it is not wise to depend upon a reader's pre-existing interest. Therefore, the first sentence of the work ought to hook or grab the attention and cause any reader to want to keep reading to satisfy the interest that the hook evokes. Unless you are famous and much in demand, it is probably not wise to begin

Well, I guess I should say something about Shakespeare's last play.

Much better to begin

At the peak of his phenomenal career of imaginative inventions, Shakespeare, in his last play, with no loss of dramatic and poetic power, looks back at the world of man with an angel's perspective and the serenity of a child at home in its mother's lap.

7. Conclusion Is the Fruit

The answer to most difficulties about conclusions lies in Guideline #1 above. If unity is lacking, any conclusion will seem either forced or irrelevant, and certainly disappointing. When inexperienced writers have trouble with conclusions, it is usually for one of a very few reasons. If the essay is forced or canned, the conclusion will be little but a boring repetition of the thesis paragraph. If the thesis of the essay is not an arguable claim that needs proving, the conclusion will be obvious from the start. If the essay had no central thesis or unity at all, the conclusion will feel random or abrupt.

Think of a conclusion as the fruit of the tree that is the essay. The roots are the introductory foundations of the argument and its underlying assumptions; the trunk is the structure of that argument; the branches and leaves and flowers are the development and support and ramifications of the argument's claims. The conclusion then will be the ultimate and satisfying purpose for which the reader has moved through the argument. It will seem sweet in its completion of the process of reading, as the apple is the sweet fruit of the process of growth in the apple tree. And it will have the freshness of surprise in its fulfillment of the expectations that the introduction and body of the piece have promised, as it is surprising, when we think about it, that invisible roots, hard wood, inedible branches, and tasteless leaves should produce something so crisp and delicious as an apple.

An artificial conclusion arising from a work with no unity or coherence assures disappointment in the reader. It makes us feel as we would approaching an apple tree and finding that the apple we looked forward to tasting is in fact a cardboard cutout, colored red with crayon, Scotch-taped to a twig.

There can be no formula for a good conclusion, for its quality depends on the kind of tree on which it grows. Difficulties with conclusions almost always arise from the writer's confusion about audience, purpose, and structure, and no conclusion, however eloquent, can be effective if it is trying to make up for such structural flaws.

8. Revision

It has been said that all good writing is rewriting. The assertion is true for almost everyone. There are a few natural geniuses who work at their best under extreme inspiration and pressure and for whom revision can be counterproductive. Chances are this is not you or anyone you know. So to produce your best work, reread and revise your writing. And reread aloud, if possible, because often the ear will hear what the eye may skip.

Writing, the ancients pointed out, begins with invention. When the mind is in invention mode, its critical mode should be silenced. The process of invention needs freedom for the imagination to work, and a critical eye looking over its shoulder is hampering. However, once invention is complete, before the work is finished, it must be read with fiercely strict standards by a nitpicking critical intellect. Now the voice of pride ("I wrote this! It's now done! I'm so pleased with myself") must be silenced, and the voice of perfectionism must be invited to check every comma, every word, sentence, and paragraph for error, weakness, and self-indulgence. Only when writers have thoroughly revised in this spirit are they likely to present their best possible work to their audiences.

9. Avoid Avoidance

One of the greatest enemies of good writing is diffidence in the writer, the fear of being caught saying something wrong, something that will be disagreed with or refuted, or of being thought ignorant or, worse, stupid. Bringing such fear into the writing process is guaranteed to produce writing that is ineffective because it is vague and therefore dull, if not also obscure. It leads to excessive use of the passive voice:

> *It is believed by some that a measure of responsibility was to be placed upon the inhabitants for their role in the city's becoming polluted, due to certain chemicals being used without safeguards having been put in place.*

Such sentences kill the energy of the argument and feel like droning. Use the active voice, therefore, wherever possible; use vivid and specific diction; and have the courage of your argument:

> *I conclude that the inhabitants of the city contributed to its pollution by using benzene and fluorine without proper safeguards.*

10. Be a Medium

Students often ask whether it is appropriate to use the first person. When they were children, they were told to avoid it. That was the grammar school teacher's technique for forcing children to write about facts instead of only about personal feelings or impressions. Older students and adults can decide for themselves when and how the first person is appropriate.

In general, unless the writer's own life and experience are specifically relevant to the discussion, the "I" is best kept out of the picture. However, this does not mean the writing should be impersonal, vague, or passionless. The more specifically and precisely the writer addresses the ideas to be communicated, the more personal and compelling will be the writing.

One does not disappear from one's writing just because the first person is avoided. Every work of art reveals the character and mind of its maker to some extent, all the more effectively when the artist is conveying his or her thought honestly. This is because anything we make is as much stamped with our unique self as is our signature. The writer cannot *not* be expressing himself or herself in anything he or she writes. Hence, as art historian Mary Holmes taught, self-expression is a false goal of all art no matter the medium. It is superfluous because we express ourselves in everything we do anyway, and it is distracting because it turns the reader's attention from what matters more.

Instead, the writer's goal should be to become a vehicle through which the ideas demanding to be conveyed may reach the intended audience. As in public speaking or any other performing art, in writing one must in a sense disappear, surrendering the aims of the self-regarding ego to the higher purpose of becoming a transparent medium for the truth as the writer sees it. Just as actors can become so preoccupied with what the audience thinks of them that they forget their lines and flub their parts, so writers concerned with impressing readers with their own brilliance or wit will end by calling attention away from their ideas toward their own need for approval. While we all want approval, we hardly ever approve of approval-seeking in others. What we do approve of is being moved by truth and meaning, and we give our most sincere approval to those who provide us with experiences of them.

11. Generosity and Politeness

There is a middle path here: good writers will give readers all they need but not more than they need. If you do not assume that your readers already know what you have not said, you will avoid making them feel ignorant. At the same time, you want to avoid overfeeding them, making the same point too many times or too imperatively. Once again this is a matter of judgment and taste. Put yourself into the reader's shoes to see whether you have said not enough or too much.

It is a cop-out to think "I know what I mean; let the reader figure it out." It is the writer's job to make things so clear that the reader cannot possibly misunderstand. Yet the reader needs to be treated with respect and not with condescension. While refusing to explain is a cop-out, treating the reader as childish or ignorant and oneself as superior will become offensive to a reader and put an end to the reader's charity toward the writer. Instead, think of the reader as a partner in a conversation, one who is interested in knowing exactly what you mean but who has a respectable mind of his or her own.

Avoid forcing the reader to agree by overstatement. In rational readers a writer's unreasonable stress or hyperbole tends to evoke resistance instead of trust.

Overstatement: *Yesterday I saw the greatest, most beautiful sunset that anyone has ever seen; not to have been there to see it is to have missed a peak experience of life.*

Reasonable: *Yesterday I saw a sunset that moved me with its beauty more any I have seen.*

Overstatement: *This president is a complete moron about international affairs, the most thoroughly incompetent leader the nation could possibly have elected.*

Reasonable: *According to at least three recent polls, a majority of voters find this president to be incompetent in leading the nation in relation to international affairs.*

Another form of politeness is to avoid quirkiness in one's writing. Unless one is fairly certain of being an imaginative genius whom the world will eventually recognize as such, it is best not to think "Well, that's just me; get used to it."

12. Natural vs. Artificial

Every work of art is in a sense artificial, coming into being as a made thing, not an outgrowth of nature. But to be effective a work of art must feel natural, must not be artificial in the sense that it seems forced or contrived or deceptive. Readers appreciate a natural voice, one that expresses what the writer actually is and that fits the subject. A voice might strike a reader as artificial if the writer is being pretentious, pompous, and condescending, or self-conscious and over-apologetic, or disingenuously politically or socially correct, or pseudo-pious, or any other form of speaking indirectly and dishonestly. As Jacques Barzun recommends, be "simple and direct."

Another word for what is wanted here is integrity. The essay or speech should be at one with its author, its true intentions, and its audience. A third word for the same quality is decorum, an old rhetorical term signifying that the form of a work and its level and style of discourse were appropriate to its topic, time, place, and audience. A letter to the editor in the form of an epic poem in rhymed heroic couplets would show a lack of decorum, as would a funeral oration in the form of a limerick.

In general, write as simply and directly as you can about what you have to say, and write in your own natural voice. But direct that voice as if to a wide audience rather than to an intimate friend, recognizing that most readers and listeners are people not so very unlike you.

13. Be Serious or Funny, not Folksy

One form of lack of integrity is folksiness, the pretense that one is speaking to one's cronies at home, in undress, as it were. Beginning a speech or essay with "Hey, guys, guess what? I'm about to give a speech!" may entertain one's close friends, but it will alienate anyone else.

14. Avoid Mechanical Habits and Shortcuts

Some phrases can get into the mind of the writer and not want to leave it without appearing on every page: *of course, indeed, that is to say, it may be the case that,* etc. Sometimes a writer may latch on to a particular figure of speech, which may then appear sentence after sentence, page after page, to annoy and finally exasperate the reader: *not only . . . but also; both . . . and; however . . . however . . . however; having said as much . . . this being said . . . having said so;* etc. Here the ear is as important as the eye, and the good stylist will detect habitual repetitions and eliminate them where possible.

Shortcuts are best avoided. Examples are

acronyms: These may be familiar to some readers and unfamiliar to others. They may be used if the writer gives the full phrase at the first use: National Association for Stock Car Auto Racing (NASCAR), United Arab Emirates (UAE), Best Friend Forever (BFF), etc.

abbreviations: Similarly some may recognize an abbreviation, others may not. Use only those that significantly reduce length where there are space considerations and that are unlikely to cause perplexity, always spelling them out at first use unless they are likely to be universally recognized. *Etc.* and *e.g.* are well enough known to all readers. But *Rep.* might mean Representative or Republican, *B.C.* might mean Before Christ or British Columbia, *trans.* might mean translation or transition or transit or transportation.

one-word modifiers: Often inexperienced writers will assume that a one-word modifier carries the full significance of a phrase in which it often appears. For example, a *nuclear agreement*, except in a context in which it has already been thoroughly explained, does not mean "an agreement to limit nuclear arms." In a different context, it could as easily mean "an agreement made by members of a nuclear family" or "an agreement by physicists on facts about the nucleus of the atom." None of these ideas is well expressed by the phrase *nuclear agreement,* and so the shortcut is counterproductive.

II
Paragraphs and Sentences

15. Sentence Variety

When all the sentences of a paragraph have the same length, shape, or style, the reader loses focus, then patience, then consciousness in sleep. Repetition of short subject-verb sentences leads to the washboard effect, as if one were driving over a transversely rutted dirt road (ridged like an old-fashioned washboard).

> *Odysseus came ashore in the land of the Cyclops. Odysseus and his men found shelter in a cave. Then the Cyclops returned. He treated Odysseus' men badly. He ate them. They were horrified. Odysseus figures out a means of escape.*

Too much repetition of loose or suspended sentences, or of long convoluted sentences, can be similarly soporific. In fact any kind of sentence that is too often repeated without variation has a dulling effect. Thus good rhetorical style requires an ear for variation in kinds of sentence and the willingness to use variation to produce a complex and fluid succession of sentences that keep the reader engaged and interested.

Forms of sentence to choose from include the following:
Simple, compound, complex and compound-complex (see p. 28)
Subject-verb sentence: *The cock crew at dawn.*
Loose, Periodic, Suspended, Fragment (see p. 29)
Declarative, Interrogative, Imperative, Exclamatory (see pp. 28–29)

Except for the fragmentary sentence, which should be avoided under most circumstances, all of these kinds of sentence are available to help the writer achieve sentence variety.

16. Sentence Emphasis

The first rule about emphasis within a sentence is that all emphasis is no emphasis: to emphasize everything is to emphasize nothing:

> *And there it was! Right in the very densest part of that absolutely impenetrable spruce swamp I had practically stumbled on a really*

more than perfect specimen of the extremely rare Orchis
rotundifolia, *incredibly unusual so early in the summer.*

The writer has a variety of ways of emphasizing the most important idea or ideas in a sentence. Since the first and the last word in any sentence will carry particular emphasis in comparison with words in the middle of the sentence, altering the position of a phrase within the sentence alters the emphasis:

> *The state office demanded the release of the fliers after a week's delay.*
> *After a week's delay, the state office demanded the release of the fliers.*
> *The state office, after a week's delay, demanded the release of the fliers.*
>
> *The hawk's small and weak talons confine its attention to little animals.*
> *The hawk's talons, small and weak, confine its attention to little animals.*
> *Small and weak, the hawk's talons confine its attention to little animals.*

Other options for emphasis include the following:

Periodic sentence: The first and third sentences of Lincoln's Second Inaugural Address (see p. 492) are periodic, beginning with phrases that defer the main clause until the end of the sentence:

> *At this second appearing to take the oath of the Presidential office, there is less occasion for an extended address than there was at the first. Then a statement somewhat in detail of a course to be pursued seemed fitting and proper. Now, at the expiration of four years, during which public declarations have been constantly called forth on every point and phase of the great contest which still absorbs the attention and engrosses the energies of the nation, little that is new could be presented.*

Suspended sentence: In the second sentence of the previous example, Lincoln uses a suspended sentence, in which phrases intervene between the subject and the verb.

Deferred subject: Compare the effects of deferring the subject in each of the following pairs of sentences:

> *There are many people who read history to raise their self-esteem.*
> *Many people read history to raise their self-esteem.*
>
> *There is some evidence pointing to the gradual disappearance of hazing.*
> *Some evidence points to the gradual disappearance of hazing.*
>
> *To quarrel about words is silly.*
> *It is silly to quarrel about words.*

Notice how in the next example deferring the subject is essential to the emphasis:

A number of interfering, fanatical, greedy, reckless, brutal people, who, given the chance, will behave in such a way as to make life intolerable and civilization impossible, are in the world.

There are in the world a number of interfering, fanatical, greedy, reckless people, who, given the chance, will behave in such a way as to make life intolerable and civilization impossible.

Inversion: Inverting the normal word order can result in the emphasis wanted:

Charles he had beaten twice, but never Charles' brother.
Last of all came the man they had expected would be first.
Cut is the branch that might have grown full straight.
 —Chistopher Marlow, *Doctor Faustus*, V.Chorus.1
So blazes out a man's life and becomes ashes.
 —from Thomas Carlisle, *The French Revolution*, 2.III

Voice: Most often the active voice is more emphatic than the passive voice:

A good bit of autobiographical information is contained in his latest novel, which appeared yesterday.

His latest novel, which appeared yesterday, contains a good bit of autobiographical information.

In the basement of the library a leak in the new boiler is indicated by a small puddle of water on the floor.

A small puddle of water on the floor in the basement of the library indicates a leak in the new boiler.

The legislators complained and procrastinated but finally a large amount was appropriated by them.

The legislators complained and procrastinated but finally appropriated a large amount.

Sometimes, however, the passive voice is essential to the point:

The band stopped playing, the lights grew dim, and the queen of the ball was seen stepping out of a gigantic paper heart.

Few men are given the chance to become heroes.

Repetition: Well managed, repetition can be useful, but often emphasis is achieved by removing it:

This dam was definitely going to be the largest dam in the world.
This dam was definitely going to be the largest in the world.

The problem of feeding her ever increasing population is one of Japan's most acute problems.
One of Japan's most acute problems is feeding her ever increasing population.

Separation: Sometimes the breaking of a related idea into two sentences can provide dramatic emphasis:

You do not revise dogmas. You smash them.

Parallel structure can be used for clarifying emphasis (and see Guideline 18, "Clarify Coordination," pp. 165–166). In the first example here, the emphasis is on the three nations visited, in the second it is on each of the nations individually:

I traveled last year to China, India, and Japan.
I traveled last year to China, to India, and to Japan.

Climax: Arranging the parts of a sentence to build to a climax is an essential method of assuring proper emphasis:

The young twins set the kitchen on fire, spilled the soup, and left the refrigerator door open.
The young twins left the refrigerator door open, spilled the soup, and set the kitchen on fire.

Mechanical devices: When overused, mechanical devices— exclamation points, dashes, capital letters, italics—break the first rule: All emphasis is no emphasis:

"I go on through!" he repeated earnestly. I have suffered—but I know that I am Destiny's darling! . . . You have suffered but you, too, can carry on through! . . . Take it from me! I know! In spite of all the little detainments, disappointments, disillusionments—I get the lucky breaks! I get the signal to go forward! I have been delayed—long —long—long—but—at length—I get the GREEN LIGHT!!!"

However, a well placed mechanical device—in this case one exclamation point—makes a great difference:

I know not what course others may take, but as for me, give me liberty or give me death.
I know not what course others may take, but as for me, give me liberty or give me death!
—Patrick Henry, speech to the Virginia Convention, 1775, at St. John's Church, Richmond Virginia

Intensives (*so* and *such*): Paradoxically, most commonly used intensives reduce rather than increase emphasis. Though the writer uses them to convince the reader, the reader is likelier to doubt the validity or force of the statement because of them. Consider the following pairs of examples :

> *We had such a lovely time at your party.*
> *We had a lovely time at your party.*
>
> *She had the nicest manners.*
> *She had refined manners.*
>
> *All of us were so happy to hear your news.*
> *All of us were happy to hear your news.*

Automatic qualifiers (*somewhat, very, a little, pretty, rather*): Mechanically adding imprecise qualifiers mechanically leads to dull and unpersuasive prose:

> *Feeling somewhat better today, I was very intent on getting out of bed, which was pretty hard to do, but I succeeded rather well at it, and after I was up for a while, I felt a little proud of myself.*

Avoid *a most* by substituting *the* for *a* or by removing *most:*

> *He is a most important figure in the book.*
> *He is the most important figure in the book.*
> *He is an important figure in the book.*

Finally, emphasis is usually not achieved by overstatement. Exaggeration leads not to persuasion but to mistrust. The truth always moves more powerfully than inauthentic hyperbole.

17. Sentence Economy

No guideline for writing and public speaking is more important than this one: Cut deadwood. Or omit needless words. Or reduce unnecessary diction. Or be concise. However you put it, do not say in more words what you can say in fewer. Examples are plentiful:

Throughout means "all the way through," so "throughout the entire book" is redundant.

Eliminate the *but* in phrases with *cannot help:*

> Faulty: *I could not help but find the situation funny.*
> Correct (formal): *I could not but find the situation funny.*
> Correct (informal): *I could not help finding the situation funny.*

Character and *nature* in phrases like "of a useful character" and "of a stubborn nature" should be cut in favor of "useful" and "stubborn."

Avoid *as* following *consider* or *regard*:
> *I considered my third cousin as part of our nuclear family.*
> *I considered my third cousin part of our nuclear family.*

Each and every can be safely limited to *each* or *every*.
> *After today's game I am happy to say that I am proud of each and every one of you.*
> *After today's game I am happy to say that I am proud of every one of you.*

Factor is often an unnecessary filler word:
> *We had prepared both sides of the question, and that was a major factor in our winning the debate.*
> *Our preparation of both sides of the question helped us win the debate.*

Avoid *–oriented* and *–wise* as add-ons:
> *It was a tourist-oriented city.*
> *The city catered to tourists.*

> *Identity-wise, Plato's Euthyphro was somewhat lacking.*
> *Plato's Euthyphro was somewhat lacking in self-knowledge.*

Apart from using it in its specific sense in logic (see "Syllogism," pp. 98–99), avoid the word *terms* in the phrase *in terms of*:
> *In terms of friendships, I did much better at my new school than at my old.*
> *I made more friends at my new school than at my old.*

> *The latest space probe was highly successful in terms of the amount of data that was gathered.*
> *The latest space probe was highly successful in gathering data.*

As yet should be *Yet* except when it means "until now" (in time) at the beginning of a clause. *As of yet* should always be cut:
> *They have not seen the fireworks as yet (or as of yet).*
> *They have not yet seen the fireworks.*
> *As yet (meaning "up until now") we have not seen the fireworks.*
> *Yet (meaning "however") we have not seen the fireworks.*

Eliminate *so* and *such* as mere intensifiers (see "Intensives" above under "Sentence Emphasis," p. 162).

Eliminate circumlocution, talking around the point instead of just saying it:

Every thinking person these days seems inclined to agree with the conception that the world has gone mad.

Every thinking person agrees that the world has gone mad.

Anyone acquainted with violin construction knows that the better the wood is seasoned, the better the result will be as far as the tone of the instrument is concerned.

In violin making, the better the seasoning of the wood, the better the tone of the instrument.

At the end of an hour we arrived at the spot where the red flag was situated.

After an hour we reached the red flag.

The way in which psychologists measure ability is by tests.

Psychologists use tests to measure ability.

It has some of the best ski trails in the country, and as far as the other cold weather sports are concerned, it has them too, along with one of the most fashionable hotels in the country.

In addition to other cold weather sports, it has some of the best ski trails and one of the most fashionable hotels in the country.

In addition to other cold weather sports, it has excellent ski trails and a fashionable hotel.

Reduce predication (the number of clauses), especially with unnecessarily deferred subjects: *There are those who . . .; There are some cases in which . . .* (but see "Deferred Subject" under Guideline 16, "Sentence Emphasis," pp. 159–160):

There is one fraternity president who works with mentally impaired children; he teaches them songs and games.

One fraternity president teaches songs and games to mentally impaired children.

There was snow, which lay like a blanket. It covered the countryside.

The snow, which lay like a blanket, covered the countryside.

The snow covered the countryside like a blanket.

The snow blanketed the countryside.

Except for specific rhetorical purposes, as when contrasting with a falsehood or illusion in the previous sentence, avoid *The truth is* and *The fact is*:

The truth is that I had worked a twelve-hour shift the night before and was tired.

I had worked a twelve-hour shift the night before and was tired.

Avoid unnecessary repetition:

The modern college student of today

The resultant effect

I know officers who try to give you any possible assistance that they can.

18. Clarify Coordination

As in Grammar (see pp. 43–45) so in style parallel ideas should be expressed in parallel structural elements, so that the reader finds in the sentence a harmony between form and content, and hence integrity.

In Europe the students are assigned to schools by the system of tracking them from a young age, whereas in America the system of free choice among kinds of school is used.

Europe uses a tracking system to place students in schools whereas America uses a free choice system.

Idiom requires the use of particular prepositions with certain words:

different from	*confidence in*	*nervous about*
agree with	*conform to*	*interested in*
prepare for	*belief in*	*conscious of*
excited about	*content with*	*disgusted at*

Therefore do not omit the relevant prepositions in compounds unless they take the same preposition:

Faulty: *All the children in that school agree and conform to its principles.*

Correct: *All the children in that school agree with and conform to its principles.*

Faulty: *The trustees expressed confidence and approval of the headmaster.*

Correct: *The trustees expressed confidence in and approval of the headmaster.*

Correct: *Membership in that sect requires belief and interest in its tenets.*

As ... than: The second *as* is required for parallel structure:

Faulty: *He was as fast or faster than his twin brother.*

Correct: *He was as fast as, or faster than, his twin brother.*

Than: When a comparison is made, avoid ambiguity by completing clauses:

Faulty: *George loves his dog more than his cat.*

Correct: *George loves his dog more than he loves his cat.*

Correct: *George loves his dog more than his cat does.*

Likewise, when using different tenses of the same verb in coordinate sentences, be sure to include both necessary forms of the verb:

> Faulty: *I always have and always will remember my trip to London.*
> Correct: *I always have remembered and always will remember my trip to London.*

When using comparative adjectives like *more* and *better*, do not omit the second term.

> *In this novel by Dickens there is much more description.*
>> [than *what*? more description than narration? more description than in another Dickens novel? more description than in a novel by another author?]

19. Placement Matters

For the effect of placement on emphasis see Guideline 16, "Sentence Emphasis," pp. 158–162.

Unlike in Latin, the meaning of whose sentences depends on the inflection of individual words (declension of nouns and adjectives, conjugation of verbs), in English the sense of a sentence depends on word order. Hence the placement of modifying words and phrases is significant to the meaning of the sentence. In general, a modifier should be placed as close as possible to the word it modifies. Misplaced modifiers and squinting modifiers (which can modify either forward or backward) are common and often comical errors.

Misplaced modifiers:

> Faulty: *He knocked a hole in the fence that was two feet wide.*
> Correct: *He knocked a two-foot-wide hole in the fence.*
> Faulty: *Because he was quick and clever, the goose was outwitted by the fox.*
> Correct: *Because he was quick and clever, the fox outwitted the goose.*

> *The teacher erased all the compromising documents she had saved with the aid of the technology assistant.* (Did the technology assistant aid her in saving or in erasing?)
> *The teacher, with the aid of the technology assistant, erased all the compromising documents she had saved.*

> *The Ethics Council found that the student had in fact cheated on a test after deliberating for half an hour.* (Did the Council deliberate for half an hour or did the cheater? See "Dangling Gerunds" in Grammar, p. 24)

After deliberating for half an hour, the Ethics Council found that the student had in fact cheated on a test.

It has been reported to police that the interstate has been blocked by a truck driver. (Did the truck driver report the blockage or cause it?)

It has been reported to police by a truck driver that the interstate has been blocked.

It has been reported to police that a truck driver has blocked the interstate.

He stood in the deep snow, looking up at the new building, which had fallen the night before. (Had the snow fallen, or the building?)

He stood in the deep snow, which had fallen the night before, looking up at the new building.

A book has been written on the misuse of the vice-presidency by the former vice-president. (Did the former VP write the book or misuse the vice-presidency?)

The former vice-president has written a book on the misuse of the vice-presidency.

Be particularly careful with words like *just, only, hardly, barely, nearly,* and *scarcely*.

I only saw one of the children of the family. (only saw but did not speak to)

I saw only one of the children of the family. (only one and not the others)

We had barely been at school for ten minutes when the fire bell rang.
We had been at school for barely ten minutes when the fire bell rang.

They just came here a week ago.
They came here just a week ago.

He nearly ate all of the ice cream.
He ate nearly all of the ice cream.

I only want to see you win once.
I want only to see you win once.
I want to see only you win once.
I want to see you only win once
I want to see you win only once.

Ambiguous modifiers (often found in news headlines):

> *Hospital staff repair man injured by reckless driver.* (Did the hospital staff repair the man, or was the injured person a hospital staff repair man?)
>
> *Dog bites nose of owner; man says he will keep biting dog.* (Will the man keep the dog that is a biter, or will he keep on biting his dog?)

Squinting modifiers are ambiguous because they may modify either of two words or phrases, the one the comes before the modifier and the one that comes after it. Even if the writer intends the modifier to modify both, the sentence should be revised to avoid confusion and uncertainty in the reader:

> Faulty: *They agreed on the following day to go to the beach.* (They agreed on the following day, or they would go to the beach on the following day?)
>
> Correct: *On the following day, they agreed to go to the beach.*
>
> Correct: *They agreed to go to the beach on the following day.*
>
> Faulty: *I asked my sister on Sunday to help me with my homework.* (asked on Sunday, or to help on Sunday?)
>
> Correct: *On Sunday I asked my sister to help me with my homework.*
>
> Correct: *I asked my sister to help me with my homework on Sunday.*

20. Avoid Tense Shifts

Keep to the same tense in narrating a succession of events in the same ongoing time sequence. The shifting of tenses is confusing to the reader.

> Faulty: *We arrived at the foot of the mountain at about 6:00 a.m. By about 7:30 we climbed to 2000 feet. We look down and see that someone breaks in to our car. We are furious, but we knew we can't descend the mountain fast enough to have caught the thief.*
>
> Correct: *We arrived at the foot of the mountain at about 6:00 a.m. By about 7:30 we had climbed to 2000 feet. We looked down and saw that someone was breaking in to our car. We were furious, but we knew we could not descend the mountain fast enough to catch the thief.*

In writing essays that include discussion of the plot of a novel or a short story, use the historical present tense rather than the past:

> *Toward the end of* A Tale of Two Cities *Sidney Carton develops (not developed) a plan to save Charles Darnay, but Carton does not share the details with anyone.*

III
Words

21. Diction

In choosing your words be aware of your purpose and your audience so that your diction strikes the right level of discourse and tone: formal or informal; public or private; serious or light; passionate, ironical, inquisitive, bemused, irate, detached, etc. Above all, use the most precise word you can find for what you wish to say.

Where there is any doubt about a word, double-check in a good dictionary. We recommend the latest edition of *Merriam-Webster's Collegiate Dictionary*. In it you will find not only the meanings of a word in its various senses but its division into syllables, pronunciation, part of speech, and derivation, all of which may prove useful. Historical dictionaries like the *Collegiate* will give the senses of the word in the approximate order of development so that you can see how relatively old or recent the word in that sense is. For some words the dictionary will add a section on usage, including synonyms and subtle distinctions of sense.

The thesaurus too is a valuable tool, but also a dangerous one. It is good for finding a word that you want but cannot call to mind. If you can think of a synonym, you will find near it in the thesaurus the exact word you were looking for, or perhaps another word that will fit even better. The thesaurus is also useful for learning in how many ways and at what different levels of discourse a similar idea may be expressed.

However, there are two pitfalls into which the thesaurus may invite one to fall: pretense and elegant variation. If you look up synonyms for the purpose of using words to sound more erudite than you think you are, the effect on the reader will be the thought "This writer is trying to show off," and the reader will cease to trust you. The writer cannot hide from the reader. What you write reveals your thought, even if your thought is to fool the reader. Readers cannot be trusted to be fooled. Good ones will always catch on. So it is important never to try to show off unless you want your reader to know you are doing so.

The second temptation for inexperienced writers, called elegant variation, is the effort to use synonyms out of a fear of excessively repeating the accurate word. The effect of this use of the thesaurus will be confusion for the reader. For example, there are differences in the senses of the words *worried* and *anxious*. If you begin with one word and shift to another merely for variation's sake, the reader will think you intend a distinction that you do not intend:

> I was worried that we would be late, and my anxiety kept me from concentrating on the map.

It would be better to use the word *worry* here instead of *anxiety* lest we think that in addition to worrying about being late, you tend to suffer from an pre-existing psychological problem. If you find that the same word is reappearing over and over in a passage of your writing, the thesaurus will not help. What is called for instead is a recasting of sentences or a restructuring of the argument of the paragraph, or both.

22. Be Specific and Concrete, Avoiding Vagueness and Unintentional Ambiguity

Because it is essential to appeal with vivid images to the reader's senses through the imagination, it is to the writer's advantage to be as specific in word choices as possible and to avoid all forms of vagueness.

First of all, write with nouns and verbs more than with adjectives, adverbs, and pronouns. All words are rooted in the metaphorical nature of the human mind: *Revolution* derives from the word meaning "to roll or spin." Nonetheless, a noun naming a concrete thing (*wagon wheel*) causes us to imagine touching, seeing, smelling, tasting, and hearing what it names more vividly than an abstraction (*revolution*). The more concrete the noun, the likelier it is to reach us through empathy (*salmon tail*); the more abstract the noun, the more it gets stuck in our intellect without ever reaching our senses (*bargain*). Similarly, verbs naming actions potentially visible or audible (*dive*) are likelier to stimulate our empathy than more abstract verbs (*descend*). Nouns and verbs are also more vivid than adjectives (*lesser, faulty*), adverbs (*sensibly, well*), and much more vivid than mere function words (*but, because, whenever*). All these words are useful in their places, of course, but without vivid and specific nouns and verbs, a paragraph will sink into blandness and the reader into sleep. In particular, avoid dependence on adjectives. As Mark Twain wrote,

> When you catch an adjective, kill it. No, I don't mean utterly, but kill most of them—then the rest will be valuable. They weaken when they are close together. They give strength when they are wide apart. An adjective habit, or a wordy, diffuse, flowery habit, once fastened upon a person, is as hard to get rid of as any other vice.
>
> —Mark Twain, Letter to D. W. Bowser, March 20, 1880

Second, avoid vagueness. The more possible meanings a word can have in a particular context, the weaker and less vivid it will be. The word *nice* is a good example. How much do we learn about a friend's new acquaintance if the friend says "She is nice" or "He's a nice person." Compare to "She cares for her aged mother and her orphaned niece" or "She is an accomplished chef" or "He donates not only money but time to the Rotary Club's fund raisers" or "He wears a handlebar moustache." (See Jane Austen's *Northanger Abbey* for a disquisition on the decline of the word *nice* from its original meaning of precise, delicate, refined, subtle, exacting, etc. to a catch-all word for vaguely positive feelings.) Avoid the word in its debased sense.

The most common form of habitual vagueness is using pronouns like *it, this, which,* and *that* in place of concrete nouns in referring to an idea in a previous clause or sentence. Pronouns stand in for nouns. They cannot be expected to stand in for a noun that has not been written. So it is impolite to expect a reader to guess to what particular idea or thing the pronoun refers or to supply the imaginary antecedent that might name the idea being referred to. This imposition on the reader interrupts the flow of the reader's understanding of the content and forces him or her to guess at what the writer meant. Turn the pronouns into pronominal adjectives and supply the missing noun: e.g., "This imposition on the reader" rather than merely "This" in the previous sentence.

Faulty: *Odysseus pretended not to know Argos in order to avoid being recognized by the suitors. This was hard for the returning hero.* [What was hard for the returning hero? There is no noun to which the word *this* refers.]

Correct: *Odysseus pretended not to know Argos in order to avoid being recognized by the suitors. This suppression of feeling was hard for the returning hero.*

Faulty: *When Odysseus proclaims who he is to Polyphemus, it gets him into trouble.* [What gets him into trouble? There is no noun to which the word *it* refers.]

Correct: *When Odysseus proclaims who he is to Polyphemus, his bragging gets him into trouble.*

Finally avoid unintentional ambiguity, particularly with pronouns. Where a pronoun could refer to more than one person or thing previously mentioned, the reader cannot tell which of them is intended. It is the writer's job to prevent that confusion.

Faulty: *Argos, Odysseus' dog, was lying on a dung heap when he recognized his old master, although he looked old and decrepit.* [Who looked old and decrepit?]

Correct: *Argos, Odysseus' dog, was lying on a dung heap when he recognized his old master, although Argos looked old and decrepit.*

Correct: *Argos, Odysseus' dog, was lying on a dung heap when he recognized his old master, although Odysseus looked old and decrepit.*

Here is a sentnce from George Orwell's essay "Politics and the English Language" in which he translates a passage from Ecclesiastes into what he calls "modern English of the worst sort" because of the use of vague abstract terms in favor of concrete, specific language:

> *Objective considerations of contemporary phenomena compel the conclusion that success or failure in competitive activities exhibits no tendency to be commensurate with innate capacity, but that a considerable element of the unpredictable must invariably be taken into account.*

The original reads thus:

> *I returned and saw under the sun, that the race is not to the swift, nor the battle to the strong, neither yet bread to the wise, nor yet riches to men of understanding, nor yet favor to men of skill; but time and chance happeneth to them all.* —Ecclesiastes 9:11 (KJV)

23. Avoid Pretentious, Colloquial, and Cliché Diction

The writer cannot hide from the reader. What is in the writer's mind will be experienced by the reader. That includes any temptation to impress through big or fancy words, to ingratiate through the pseudo-familiarity of colloquialism, and to treat with carelessness or disrespect through the lazy use of clichés.

Where the natural, normal, common, and precise word will serve, use it (rather than *utilizing* it). For example, use *beautiful* instead of *beauteous*, *huge* instead of *humongous*:

> Pretentious: *The commentator gifted us with his presence on our program.*
>
> Appropriate: *The commentator agreed to be interviewed on our program.*
>
> Pretentious: *Her boyfriend would not state why he wanted to live in Alaska.*
>
> Appropriate: *Her boyfriend would not say why he wanted to live in Alaska.*
>
> Appropriate: *Under oath, the senator stated his objections to being cross-examined, without counsel, by the opposition party.*

Colloquialisms should be reserved for realistic dialogue. Avoid *kind of* and *sort of* to mean "rather," "somewhat," or "moderately." More generally, avoid using colloquialisms that are appropriate to a particular in-group but not to your actual audience:

> *In Shakespeare's last four plays, which, though technically comedies, are sometimes also called romances, the author's tone makes him seem more chill.*

Avoid clichés except in the dialogue of a character who uses them. Examples include:

> *last but not least*
> *one and only*
> *pardon my French*
> *it is what it is*
> *now or never*
> *not product but process*
> *cutting edge*

24. Spell Correctly

Once again, the dictionary is your best friend here. When in doubt, use it. Misspelling causes loss of respect in the reader.

25. Above All—Be Clear

Following the guidelines offered here will help you to achieve ever increasing clarity in your writing. Clarity depends upon correct grammar, spelling, and punctuation. It depends upon unity, sufficient but not excessive development, visible coherence, and accurate transitions. It depends upon proper sentence structure, emphasis, diction, and tone. But any of the above guidelines must yield to clarity as the ultimate value in writing. Only you know what you intend to say, even if you are discovering what that is in the course of attempting to put it into words. But the words you put it into must be wrought into precision, effectiveness, and clarity. The by-products of the harmony of all these will be truth and, if you are also talented and fortunate, beauty.

IV

Six Additional Guidelines for Speakers

Here are six additional guidelines for speeches intended to be delivered orally:

26. Pace Yourself

The ear and brain of English-speaking people will follow a well-written speech at approximately 2.5 minutes per double-spaced page in 12-point type. Read slower and they will lose concentration. Read faster and they will lose the thread of the argument. This rate will seem excessively slow to inexperienced speakers, whose nervous energy will tempt them to speed up. Resist the temptation. The best method to avoid rushing is to time oneself in reading the speech aloud beforehand.

27. Articulate

Audiences, without the benefit of seeing a text to reinforce their hearing of it, depend upon precisely articulated consonants to understand words. The fuzzier the pronunciation, the likelier the audience is to mishear what is said.

28. Don't Bury Emphasis

As mentioned in Guideline 16, the beginnings and ends of sentences are the positions of greatest potential emphasis. Avoid letting your voice die away at the ends of sentences and paragraphs, including the last.

29. Reveal the Structure

Making explicit the structure of a speech at its beginning and recapitulating its main points at the end can contribute to the audience's appreciation, so long as they do not perceive your doing so as excessively repetitive.

30. Eye Contact

Because eye contact with the audience enhances the hearer's experience, a well-memorized speech is more effective than one merely read. Even if a speech is read, however, the speaker should take time to look up and connect with the audience. If one knows one's topic especially well and speaks well extemporaneously, it can be effective to have only brief notes in front of one during the speech to be sure all main points are covered. More diffident speakers should write out their speeches beforehand and practice delivering them.

31. Stage Fright

The most common cause of nervousness in public speaking is the conscious or unconscious fear of being judged by the audience. It is the same for actors, musicians, and any other public performers. The only sure cure for this nervousness, which can range from mere jitters to paralyzing panic, is to conceive of oneself as the medium not the focus of the speech.

We all want to be loved and win approval. But an audience that perceives a speaker to be speaking to them only out of ego will remain unmoved by the content of the speech, and a speaker whose main motive is to win approval can become distracted by the fear of failing to win that approval; that distraction will then lead to errors and confusion, and so to loss of approval. But winning approval is a false goal, and audiences know it. Applause sought for its own sake will be weak and grudging, and such an audience response will lead to yet more fear in the speaker in a vicious circle of inauthenticity.

The cure is for the speaker to get ego out of the way. Just as the true goal of an actor is to cause the audience to experience the character, not to win applause, so the speaker's true goal is the audience's experience and absorption of the content of the speech. When the speaker has that as a goal, fear will fall away, concentration will be rewarded, and applause will come as a byproduct of an authentic performance and will mean something when it does. (See also Guideline 10, "Be a Medium" p. 154.)

Divisions and Devices of Rhetoric

Adapted from Richard A. Lanham, *A Handlist of Rhetorical Terms* (Berkeley: University of California Press, 1969), pp. 107–109; from Aristotle's *Rhetoric*, Book II, Ch. 23, ed. Lee Honeycutt, tr. W. Rhys Roberts; and from Ward Farnsworth, *Farnsworth's Classical English Rhetoric* (Boston: David R. Godine, 2011). Quotations marked a are from Lanham. Quotations marked b are from Honeycutt. Quotations marked c are from Farnsworth.

Divisions of Rhetoric

Here are some of the divisions in rhetoric which ancient, medieval, and modern authors have discerned and discussed.

Five Parts of Rhetoric (based on Cicero)[a]

English	Latin	Greek
Invention	*inventio*	*heuresis*
Arrangement	*dispositio*	*taxis*
Style	*elocutio*	*lexis*
Memory	*memoria*	*mneme*
Delivery	*actio*	*hypocrisis*

Three Modes of Persuasion (from Aristotle's *On Rhetoric*)

Ethos—persuading that the speaker has proper authority or good character and is therefore credible

Logos—persuading by the rational logic of the argument

Pathos—persuading by rousing and appealing to the feelings of the audience

Twenty-eight Useful Rhetorical Techniques (based on Aristotle)[b]

1. Restating proposition in an opposite way—e.g., "Temperance is beneficial; for licentiousness is hurtful."

2. Redefining a term or providing a synonym—e.g., "Just does not always mean beneficial or justly would always mean beneficially, whereas it is not beneficial to be justly put to death."

3. Using a correlative argument—e.g., "Where it is right to command obedience, it [is] right to obey the command," or A deserves no credit for winning a battle, for B has all the credit for losing it.

4. Using an argument *a fortiori*—"If a quality does not in fact exist where is it more likely to exist, it clearly does not exist where it is less likely" or if it does exist where it is less likely, it probably exists where it is more likely—e.g., if the man often strikes his own father in anger, he is likely to strike his neighbors when angry. (cf., Rabbi Ishmael Rule 1, p. 132)

5. Using circumstance of past time—The promise to do some behavior, made or implied under past circumstances if some event should occur, ought to be kept if that event does occur even though circumstances have changed—e.g., Since before the battle you would have promised to pay me if I should win it, you should pay me now that I have won it.

6. Turning the accusation back upon the accuser to undermine his supposed moral superiority—e.g., If you, who are known to have taken bribes for advancing relatives, would never take a bribe to betray your country, would I, who am known never to have taken a bribe to advance anyone, take a bribe to betray my country? (This only works if the speaker is known to be superior to his opponent.)

7. Defining terms—e.g., Socrates: "What is the supernatural? Surely it is either a god or the work of a god. Well, anyone who believes that the work of a god exists cannot help also believing that gods exist."

8. Playing upon the senses of a word.

9. Dividing the argument into logical parts—"All men do wrong from one of three motives, A, B, or C: in my case A and B are out of the question, and even the accusers do not allege C."[b]

10. Arguing from induction—using one or more cases to conclude about all similar cases including the present one.

11. Arguing from the authority of previous decisions on similar cases, particularly decisions by all or most or wise authorities.

12. Arguing by parts—e.g., You accuse Socrates of profanation, but "What temple has he profaned? What gods recognized by the state has he not honored?"

13. Arguing from good or bad consequences

14. Arguing the opposite of good or bad consequences (divarication) —e.g., "the priestess enjoined upon her son not to take to public speaking: 'For,' she said, 'if you say what is right, men will hate you; if you say what is wrong, the gods will hate you." The reply might be 'you ought to take to public speaking: for if you say what is right the gods will love you; if you say what is wrong, men will love you.'"

15. Arguing from the difference between the outward show and the inward reality, between common public opinion and personal secret opinion. Depending on the position of the opponent, argue that things either are or are not what they seem.

16. Arguing from logical correspondence—e.g., If you treat tall boys as men, you will next be treating short men as boys.

17. Arguing that similarity of results implies similarity of causes

18. Using the opponent's earlier position in a different case to his disadvantage in this case—e.g., "When we were exiles, we fought in order to return; now [that] we have returned, it would be strange to choose exile in order not to have to fight."[b]

19. Taking a possible motive for the actual motive—e.g., the "gift was given [not out of kindness but] in order to cause pain by its withdrawal."[b]

20. Arguing motives from inducements and deterrents—men act in ways that are "possible, easy, and useful" to themselves or harmful to their enemies so long as the benefits outweigh the losses. A speaker can stress the benefits to support an action and the losses to oppose it, and likewise stress either to argue the likelihood of a person's motives.

21. Arguing truth from incredibility—"If . . . a thing that is believed is improbable and even incredible, it must be true, since it is certainly not believed because it is at all probable or credible."[b] "Make people believe an improbability by pointing to an even greater one that is yet true."[a]

22. Arguing from an opponent's contradictions or inaccuracies.

23. Refuting slander by showing that the actual facts are different from the supposed facts, which would, if true, admittedly support the slander.

24. Arguing "that if the cause is present, the effect [must be] present, and if absent, absent."[b]

25. Arguing that a defendant's having a better argument than he has used and failing to use it is evidence of his innocence. (The argument is fallacious if the unused better argument is discovered only after the outcome.)

26. Arguing from inconsistency of past actions—e.g., "When the people of Elea asked Xenophanes if they should or should not sacrifice to Leucothea and mourn for her, he advised them not to mourn for her if they thought her a goddess, and not to sacrifice to her if they thought her a mortal woman."[b]

27. Making previous mistakes grounds for accusation or defense.

28. Playing on the meaning of names—e.g., "Herodicus said of . . . the legislator Draco that his laws were those not of a human being but of a dragon [L. draco], so savage were they . . . and Chaeremon writes 'Pentheus—a name foreshadowing grief (G. penthos) to come.'"[a]

Sixteen Basic Topics (based on Cicero's *Topica*)

Cicero gives the following sixteen bases of argumentation:

Argument from

1. definition—delimiting the kind of thing something is by specifying both the genus of which it is a species and the distinguishing property of the species. E.g., Freedom of religion is a subset of the human rights claimed for all men by the Declaration of Independence and can be distinguished from other freedoms (of speech, press, assembly, etc.) in being focused on the right to worship as one sees fit without government interference.

2. partition—analysis of a class into subclasses. E.g., Human rights may be seen as consisting of the specific rights to freedom of religion, freedom of speech, freedom of the press, etc.

3. etymology—the root meaning of a word and the history of its usage. E.g., The word right is derived from the Anglo-Saxon *riht*, and is akin to Latin *rectus* (straight, right), Greek *orektos* (stretched out, upright), Old Irish *recht* (law), Sanskrit *rju* (straight, right), Latin *regere* (to guide or rule), Greek *oregein* (to stretch out), Latin *rogare* (to stretch after, ask, beg).

4. conjugates—words similar in derivation and therefore in meaning. E.g., We cannot enjoy our rights if the abuse of them is not rectified, for rectification, in its root meaning, intends the restoration of right.

5. genus—the more general category of which something is a species. E.g., The right to live unhindered by government is ours because it is one of the human rights implied by the Declaration of Independence under "unalienable rights."

6. species—the specific qualities that distinguish something from other members of its class. E.g., Freedom of religion is a particularly precious right because, unlike speech, assembly, and press, worship is one of the most private and intimate human activities.

7. similarity—Something is the case because something like it is the case. E.g., Just as a tree must have water to grow strong, so must human rights, whose roots are deeply imbedded in the nature of things, be watered regularly with our attention.

8. difference—The particular qualities or characteristics that distinguish one member of a species from another. E.g., There is no need to name freedom of thought as a fundamental human right because, unlike other human activities protected by the Bill of Rights (like worship, assembly, speech, etc.), thought by its nature is invisible to government.

9. contraries—A proposition related to another such that both cannot be true can be used to argue for the truth or falsehood of a proposition. E.g., The fundamental source of human rights is nature and nature's God; the fundamental source of human rights is government: the first statement being true, the second is shown to be false.

10. adjuncts—Qualities that are accidental or non-essential to something can be used to defend a proposition about that thing. E.g., It is not necessary for government to specify that a citizen may wear clothing of any color; the color of one's clothes is not relevant to arguments for the freedoms secured by the Bill of Rights.

11. antecedents—A precondition for the truth of a proposition can be shown to exist as proof that the consequent may be true. More generally, support from a foregoing fact known to be true. "Four score and seven years ago our fathers brought forth on this continent, a new nation, conceived in liberty, and dedicated to the proposition that all men are created equal. Now we are engaged in a great civil war, testing whether that nation, or any nation so conceived and so dedicated, can long endure."—Abraham Lincoln

12. consequents—The hypothetical conclusion of a conditional proposition; a conclusion or inference arrived at by logical deduction. E.g., If we are to preserve the union dedicated to the proposition that all men are created equal, the North must win the Civil War.

13. contradictions—Self-contradictory propositions can be shown to be false.

14. efficient cause—Of Aristotle's four causes (formal—the plan of a house in the mind of the builder; material—the wood,

beams, nails; efficient—the hammering of the carpenter; and final—to live in the house), the third may be used to argue for something. E.g., The founders proclaimed that our rights come from nature and God; that we are aware of this truth is a function of their writing and signing and risking everything to produce the Declaration of Independence.

15. effects—The reality of effects that can spring only from a particular cause serve as evidence for the reality or presence of that cause. E.g., The fact that there are shards of glass on the floor and no vase on the table proves that someone or something must have knocked the vase off the table.

16. comparison—Something may be demonstrated by pointing to one or many similarities to something else already known. E.g., The republican form of government, unlike that of a monarchy, is constrained in many ways: a monarchy may tax without representation, a republic may not; a monarchy may confiscate property arbitrarily, a republic may not; etc.

Seven Elements or Circumstances (based on Hermagoras of Temnos, 1st century BCE) from which modern journalism derives its six questions: who, what, when, where, why, and how:

Actor (who, L. *quis*)
Action (what, L. *quid*)
Time (when, L. *quando*)
Place (where, L. *ubi*)
Cause (why, L. *cur*)
Manner (how, in what way, L. *quem ad modum*)
Means (by what means, L. *quibus adminiculis*)

Arrangement: Seven Parts of an Oration[a]

1. Entrance or Proœmium (L. *exordium*)—grabbing the audience's attention, sometimes called the hook

2. Narration (L. *praecognitio* or *narratio*)—setting out the facts

3. Exposition or Definition (L. *explicatio* or *definitio*)—opening the issues and defining the terms

4. Proposition (L. *partitio*)—clarifying the issue and stating what is to be proved, sometimes subdivided into primary (about things) and secondary (about other propositions)

5. Confirmation (L. *amplificatio*)—setting out the arguments for and against

6. Confutation or Refutation (L. *refutatio* or *reprehensio*)—disarming the opposition, refuting the opponent's arguments

7. Conclusion or Epilogue (L. *peroratio* or *epilogus*)—summing up the arguments and stirring the audience to agreement

Style[a]

The Three Types—based on subject, diction, effect on audience, syntax, composition,

> Low or Plain (*genus humile* or *extenuatum*), also called Attic (unornamented, brief)—negative counterpart: Meager
>
> Middle (*genus medium* or *modicum* or *mediocre* or *temperatum*), also called Rhodian—negative counterpart: Loose (*dissolutum*)
>
> Grand (*genus grande* or *grave*), also called Asiatic (ornamented, full)—negative counterpart: Swollen

or Four Types (according to Demetrius):

> Plain
> Grand
> Elegant
> Forceful

Rhetorical Virtues

The Four Virtues of Rhetorical Style based on Theophrastus, *On Style* (lost), via Cicero, *De Oratore*, each of which has a corresponding opposite vice. As Lanham argues, though many other writers have labored to list particular virtues of oratorical style, "they all seem reducible to the four of Theophrastus."[a]

> Purity (correctness)—Correctness of grammar, as opposed to grammatical error and solecism
>
> Clarity—as opposed to obscurity, confusion, obfuscation
>
> Decorum—appropriateness to the time, the place, the audience, the situation, the intention, etc., as opposed to that which is inappropriate or not fitting (like telling a joke at a funeral or discussing death and decay at a wedding)

Ornament—the appropriate use of rhetorical devices (figures of speech), opposite to excessive and overindulgent elaboration with figurative language and also to the dull and dry lack of any rhetorical elegance

Figures [a]

of Words

Trope—use of word meaning something other than its ordinary meaning—e.g., metaphor

Scheme—use of words in ordinary meanings but specially arranged

of Thought

large-scale trope or scheme—e.g., allegory

E.g., *Richard II* is structured as a chiasmus of thought (AB,BA structure, see p. 190) formed by the fall of Richard and the rise of Henry. The point of crossing, when Richard surrenders the crown to Henry, is a chiasmus of words ("Ay, no, no, ay; for I must nothing be," IV.i.201).

Rhetorical Devices

The art of Rhetoric as effective and persuasive communication has been studied for thousands of years. One element in the long tradition of the study of this art has been the observation, articulation, and collection of specific techniques for achieving rhetorical effects. These techniques, called rhetorical devices or figures of speech, can be seen in two ways: On the one had, figures of speech are often the natural forms of human speech when speech is used to describe, persuade, or dramatize. We all use the forms of our speaking to help get across our meanings. In this sense, every effective speaker is a rhetorician, whether or not he or she has studied the art and is aware of rhetorical devices as devices. On the other hand, rhetoricians have elaborated definitions, illustrations, and instructions for their students in order to help them enhance, with given techniques, their competence and effectiveness in the various forms of speech. From such compilations we have chosen the following list of rhetorical devices that you are most likely to read about, to see used, and to use yourselves in speaking or writing effectively. The list is intended to be not exhaustive or prescriptive but rather informative and useful. These devices, however thoroughly mastered, cannot in themselves guarantee effective rhetorical speech or writing. The speaker's or writer's art calls for judgment, taste, sensitivity, imagination, and so on. This list is offered to serve the purposes of observation, analysis, and experimentation. To hope that any device or system of devices can substitute mechanical technique for a living art is to see a great fountain as mere plumbing or the Parthenon as nothing but marble. And yet the fountain does use plumbing and the Parthenon marble. How they do so is worth studying.

Acyrologia: use of incorrect word; malapropism (*deep-seeded* for *deep-seated, doggy dog world* for *dog-eat-dog world*)

Adage: see Proverb

Allegory: extending a metaphor throughout a passage; a story told in symbols; one of three senses or levels of interpretation beyond the literal: Allegorical, Moral (homiletic, tropological), and Anagogical (spiritual, mystical)

Alliteration: repetition of initial sounds of words (*"When I do count the clock that tells the time"* —Shakespeare, Sonnet 12, l. 1)

Allusion: hint or reference to a classical, biblical, or other work likely to be familiar to the audience

Ambiguity: suggesting more than one meaning with a word or phrase (*I cannot say enough about this student.*)

Amphibologia: ambiguity of grammatical structure, often by mispunctuation (*Hubert fed his dog Max.*)

Anacoluthon: shifting the structure of a sentence in the middle (*If you do not come on time—but why should I expect today to be different?*)

Anadiplosis: repeating the last word of one line as the first word of the next (*"Foul words is but foul wind, and foul wind is but foul breath, and foul breath is noisome; therefore I will depart unkissed"* — Shakespeare, *Much Ado about Nothing* V.ii.52–54)

Analogy: bringing together two cases, even from different disciplines, that exhibit some similar structure, concept, or characteristic

Anaphora: repetition of the same word at the beginning of each of two or more lines

> Queen Margaret: ...
> > *I had an Edward, till a Richard killed him;*
> > *I had a Harry, till a Richard killed him.*
> > *Thou hadst an Edward, till a Richard killed him.*
> > *Thou hadst a Richard, till a Richard killed him.*
>
> Dutchess: *I had a Richard too, and thou didst kill him;*
> > *I had a Rutland too, thou holp'st to kill him.*
>
> Queen Margaret: *Thou hadst a Clarence too, and Richard killed him.*
> > —Shakespeare, *Richard III* IV.iii.40–46

Anastrophe: inversion or unusual arrangement of word order in a sentence (*"Cut is the branch that might have grown full straight"* — Marlowe, *Doctor Faustus* V.Chorus.1)

Antanaclasis: repetition of a word in a different sense (*"You have dancing shoes / With nimble soles; I have a soul of lead . . . I am too sore enpierced with his shaft / To soar with his light feathers"* —Shakespeare *Romeo and Juliet* I.iii.14–15, 19–20) cf., Paronomasia

Antimetabole: inverting word order to make a contrasting point (*"Ask not what your country can do for you; ask what you can do for your country"* —J.F. Kennedy Inaugural Address, see p. 693), cf., Chiasmus

Antinomy: setting one law, or part of a law, against another

Antiphrasis: one-word irony (*"some mollification for your giant"* about the diminutive Maria, in Shakespeare's *Twelfth Night* I.v.204)

Antistasis: repetition of a word in an opposite sense (*"A kleptomaniac is a person who helps himself because he can't help himself."* —Henry Morgan)

Antistrophe: repetition of word or phrase at the ends of several lines, clauses, or sentences (not to be confused with its use in Greek tragedy to mean a choral dance or chant answering a strophe) (*"in spite of all she could say to me, [I] went to bed despairing. I got up despairing, and went out despairing."*—Dickens, *David Copperfield*; *"government of the people, by the people, for the people"*— Lincoln, Gettysburg Address), often a synonym for Epistrophe

Antithesis: contrasting ideas juxtaposed within one or several lines

Antonomasia: using a proper name for a quality or a quality for a proper name (*"That technician is a regular Einstein"*; *"Well, Mr. Smarty-pants, solve this!"*; *"Your Majesty"*)

Aphaeresis: omitting a syllable from the beginning of a word (*mid* for *amid*; *twas* for *it was*; *round* for *around*; *lone* for *alone*; *I couldn't 'scribe it to you 'f I tried.*)

Aphorismus: see Proverb

Apocope: omitting the last syllable or letter from a word (*street cred* for *credit*; *chile* for *child*; *barbie* for *barbecue*; *photo* for *photograph*)

Apoplanesis: evading the issue by digressing

Aposiopesis: stopping the the middle of a line or thought, leaving the rest unfinished

Apostrophe: breaking off to address directly someone or something present or absent

Assonance: repetition of vowel sounds in the middles of words (*"And see the brave day sunk in hideous night"*—Shakespeare, Sonnet 12, l. 2)

Asyndeton: omitting conjunctions between words, phrases, clauses (*"And that must sleep, shriek, struggle to escape"*—Yeats, "Among School Children," l. 35)

Brachylogia: abbreviated construction or brevity of diction (*morning* for *good morning*; *s'up?* for *what's up?*; *"Grates me, the sum"* —Shakespeare, *Antony and Cleopatra* I.i.18, for *"Your slowness grates on me, get to the point"*), sometimes used for Asyndeton

Brevitas: concision of phrasing

Cacophony: sounds unpleasing to the ear (opposite of euphony)

Cacozelia: affectation of style with inflated diction (see *Hamlet* V.ii.112–20)

Caesura: pause, usually punctuated, in the middle of a verse line (*"Admit impediments; love is not love"*—Shakespeare, Sonnet 116, l. 2)

Catachresis: metaphor using words "wrenched from common usage, as when Hamlet says, 'I will speak daggers to her'"—III.ii. 396; farfetched metaphor[a]

Chiasmus: mirror-image structure (AB-BA) of words or phrases, from the Latin letter *X* (*chi*) (*"Ay, no, no, ay"* *Richard II* IV.i.201)

Circumlocution: talking around a subject rather than getting to the point (see *Hamlet* II.ii.86ff.), Periphrasis

Climax: by degrees increasing tension, significance, or weight

Comprobatio: complimenting the audience to win trust

Conceit: farfetched or ingenious comparison of dissimilar things

Concessio: conceding a point to strengthen a following point

Conduplicatio: repeating words or phrases for emphasis or amplification

Connotation: a non-literal, implied sense of a word

Consonance: repetition of consonant sounds within words (*"This thou perceiv'st which makes thy love more strong"*—Shakespeare, Sonnet 73, l. 13)

Consonantal rhyme: repetition of consonant groups where the vowels differ (*simple/supple*)

Contrarium: using a statement to prove its opposite (*"Now how should you expect one who has ever been hostile to his own interests to be friendly to another's?"* [*Rhetorica ad Herennium*, IV.xviii, 25])[a]

Declamatio: elaborate, ornamented, rehearsed speech

Decorum: making style of language, tone, diction, and gesture fit with one another and with the time, place, speaker, subject, and audience.

Denotation: literal sense of a word

Diacope: repetition of a word or phrase on both sides of another word or phrase (*Patience, my friend, patience*), cf., Tmesis

Diaeresis: dividing genus into species; dividing adjacent vowels from one syllable into two; the two-dot mark indicating this division (as in *preëminent*); in prosody, a verse line where "the end of a foot corresponds with the end of a word"[a]

Dialogismus: speaking as if in the person of someone else

Dialysis: "A figure in which one argues from a series of disjunctive (compound hypothetical) propositions (e.g.: Either Bill ran out of gas or he ran out of money) directly to a conclusion. Henry V says before Agincourt:
> *If we are mark'd to die, we are enow*
> *To do our country loss; and if to live,*
> *The fewer men, the greater share of honour.*
> *God's will, I pray thee wish not one man more.*
> [—Shakespeare, *Henry V* IV.iii.20–23]
see also Dilemma [next entry]"[a]

Dilemma: "Any technique of argument which offers an opponent a choice, or a series of them, all of which are unacceptable. The counterargument ('taking the dilemma by the horns') is to deny the premise by which choice is restricted to unacceptable alternatives. For example, the boss argues: I will not give you a raise; either it will make you lazy and less efficient, or [it will make you] avaricious and less content. The employee replies: No, it will make me more energetic, because less discontent. . . . [In logic:] A syllogism in which the major premise is a compound hypothetical proposition and the minor a disjunctive proposition. If the conclusion is a disjunctive proposition, the syllogism is called *complex*; if the conclusion is a categorical proposition, *simple*. For example, if the welfare legislation feeds the people, they will grow lazy; if it does not feed the people, it will be a failure. It either will or will not feed the people. Therefore, the legislation will either make people lazy or it will be a failure. A dilemma with the minor premise left out makes the figure Dialysis [see previous entry]."[a]

Divisio: division into kinds or classes

Ellipsis: omitting a word that is understood though not said (*"Can thy dam?—may't be?—"*; *"Inch-thick, knee-deep, o'er head and ears a forked one"* for *"I am a forked one"*—Shakespeare, *The Winter's Tale* I.ii.137, 186)

Emphasis: "Stress of language in such a way as to imply more than is actually stated"[a] (*"Send us your prisoners, or you will hear of it."*—Shakespeare *I Henry IV* I.iii.124)

End rhyme: rhyming words ending two or more lines of verse

End-stopped line: verse line ending with the end of a grammatical unit or with a pause, usually punctuated (opposite of enjambment)

Enigma: riddle

Enjambment: where the sense or grammar of a verse line runs onto the next line with no pause or punctuation (opposite of end-stopped line), synonym: Run-on line.

Enumeratio: "dividing subjects into adjuncts, causes into effects, antecedents into consequents"[a]

Epanalepsis: repeating at the end of a line the word that began it
> . . . hear *me for my*
> cause, and be silent, that you may hear. Believe *me*
> *for mine honour, and have respect to mine honour, that*
> *you may* believe . . . .
> —Shakespeare *Julius Caesar* III.ii.13–16

Epigram: short, pithy poem, often humorous or satirical, capturing a thought with witty brevity:

> *The humanist whom no belief constrained*
> *Grew so broad-minded, he was scatterbrained.*
>   —J.V. Cunningham

Epimone: frequent repetition of a word, phrase, or question to emphasize an idea or point

> *How now, wife? . . .*
> *Soft, take me with you, take me with you, wife.*
> *How, will she none? Doth she not give us thanks?*
> *Is she not proud? Doth she not count her blest . . . ?*
> *How how, how how, chopped logic! What is this?*
> *"Proud," and "I thank you" and "I thank you not."*
> *And yet "not proud," mistress minion you?*
>   —Shakespeare *Romeo and Juliet* III.v.137–51

Epitheton: epithet, "qualifying the subject with an appropriate adjective; an adjective that frequently or habitually accompanies a certain noun"[a] (*Olympian Jove, Alexander the Great, green-eyed jealousy* [from Shakespeare, *Othello* III.iii.165–66])

Epistrophe: repetition of word or phrase at ends of several lines, often a synonym for Antistrophe

Epiphora: repetition of the same word or phrase at the ends of successive clauses, sentences, or lines of verse, as in I Corinthians 13:11 (see p. 353), opposite of Anaphora[a]

Epizeuxis: repetition for emphasis of a word with no other words between (*"Never, never, never, never, never"*—Shakespeare, *King Lear* V.iii.309)

Erotema / Erotesis: "rhetorical question implying strong affirmation or denial, as when Laertes laments Ophelia's madness: 'O heavens, is't possible a young maid's wits / Should be as mortal as an old man's life?' (*Hamlet*, IV.v.[160–61])[a]

Eulogia: commending someone or something

Euphemismus: predicting something good; using a pleasant word to name something unpleasant (*rest room; visually challenged; sleep together; undertaker*)

Euphony: sounds pleasing to the ear (opposite of cacophony)

Euphuism: "The elaborately patterned prose style of John Lyly's prose romance *Euphues* (1579). It emphasizes the figures of words that create balance, and makes frequent use of antithesis, paradox, repetitive patterns with single words, sound-plays of various sorts, amplification of all sorts, unremitting use of the sententia and . . . simile[s] from traditional natural history. Euphuism has now come to mean any highly figured, Asiatic style."[a] Adjective: Euphuistic

Exemplum: example (true or made up), illustrative story

Expeditio: rejecting all but one of various alternatives to bring an argument to a speedy close

Eye rhyme: a rhyme based on similar spelling despite difference in sound (*prove/love; on the sly/certainly*)

Fable: short tale, usually involving animals, to illustrate a moral lesson

Feminine rhyme: two-syllable rhyme with a stressed syllable followed by an unstressed syllable (*utter/shutter, despising/arising*)

Gnome: see Proverb

Hendyadis: Using two nouns or two adjectives connected by *and* instead of a noun and modifier (nouns: *"youth and observation"* [*Hamlet* I.v.101] for "youthful observation," *"book and volume of my brain"* [I.v.103]; adjectives: *"ponderous and marble jaws"* [I.iv.50] for "ponderous marble jaws")

Hyperbole: exaggeration for emphasis or irony (not meant to be taken literally)

Hypophora: raising and answering arguments or questions against another's contention (see *I Henry IV* V.i.130ff) cf., Ratiocinatio

Hypozeugma: using one verb in a final clause to govern previous elliptical clauses (*"Hours, days, weeks, months, and years do pass away"* [Sherry's *Treatise of the Figures of Grammar and Rhetorike* (1555)])[a]

Hypozeuxis: "every clause in a sentence has its own subject and verb"

> Madam, the guests are come, supper serv'd up, you call'd,
> my young lady ask'd for, the nurse curs'd in
> the pantry, and everything in extremity.
> [—Shakespeare, *Romeo and Juliet* I.iii.100–102].[a]

Hysteron proteron: phrases out of normal logical or temporal word order, the later coming earlier, the earlier later (*"Moriamur, et in media arma ruamus"* [*Let us die, and rush into the midst of the weapons*]—Virgil, *Aeneid* II. 353; *put on your shoes and socks*)

Indignatio: indignant (loud, angry, impassioned) speech

Irony: using words or phrases that say the opposite of what is intended to be understood

Isocolon: using two or more parallel phrases of the same length and usually the same structure ("pleasant without scurrility, witty without affection, audacious without impudency, learned without opinion, and strange without heresy"—Shakespeare, *Love's Labour's Lost* V. i.3–6)[a]

Litotes: denying the contrary ("you can't be serious," "not to mention Mr. Jack Guilford") or understatement that intensifies ("he likes his wife not a little")

Malapropism: "vulgar error through an attempt to seem learned; not, properly speaking, a rhetorical term. The word comes from Mrs. Malaprop, a character in Sheridan's *The Rivals* (1775)"[a]; see Acyrologia.

Masculine rhyme: rhyming on the final stressed syllable (*grant/scant, remove/disprove, oxidate/agitate*)

Maxim: see Proverb

Meiosis: belittling with a demeaning word or phrase, using an "intentionally and aggressively plain" word or phrase[a]

Metanoia: qualifying a statement by revising it (*"But two months dead, nay, not so much, not two"* —Shakespeare, *Hamlet* I.ii.138)

Metaphor: applying a word in a non-literal connotation to something different from it, implying an identity with something it is normally thought of as unlike; Aristotle: "Midway between the unintelligible and the commonplace, it is a metaphor which most produces knowledge" (*Rhetoric*, III.1410b)[a], cf., Simile

Metaphysical conceit: using commonplace physical objects to carry extremely abstract spiritual or metaphysical ideas; conceit (see above) as used by the Metaphysical poets in England in the 17th century (Donne, Herbert, Marvel)

Metastasis: "passing over an issue quickly" or "turning back an insult or objection against the person who made it, as when Adam answers Oliver's 'Get you with him, you old dog!' with 'Is "old dog" my reward? Most true, I have lost my teeth in your service'[—Shakespeare] *As You Like It* I.i.[81–83]"[a]

Metonymy: (lit. change of name) using a cause to indicate an effect or vice versa, using a proper name to indicate a quality or vice versa; in practice, substituting an attribute or associated quality for the thing itself (*crown* for the king or the royal government; *The White House* for the president and administration); cf., Synecdoche

Mimesis: imitation of word, gesture, pronunciation, speech

Occupatio: emphasizing something by seeming to pass over it (*"In introducing our next speaker, I need not mention that he has taught for forty years, written six books, and won a Pulitzer Prize . . .*), cf., Praeteritio

Off rhyme: rhyme words in which the final consonant sounds are the same but the vowels different (*bard/heard*)

Onomatopoeia: using words whose sound imitates or recreates the sound of their meaning (*busy buzzing bees*)

Oxymoron: a self-contradictory phrase often made of two words of contradictory meaning (*"O brawling love! O loveing hate! . . . O heavy lightness, serious vanity . . . bright smoke, cold fire, sick health"*— Shakespeare, *Romeo and Juliet* I.i.175–80)

Parable: "teaching a moral lesson by means of an extended metaphor"[a]

Paradox: self-contradictory statement that in some sense is true nonetheless

Parechesis: "'the repetition of the same sound in words in close or immediate succession'" ([H.W.] Smythe, *Greek Grammar*, [Cambridge, MA, 1956], p. 680). E.g., 'Gaunt as the ghastliest of glimpses that gleam through the gloom of the gloaming when ghosts go aghast' (Swinburne, *Nephelidia*)"[a]

Parenthesis: "word, phrase, or sentence inserted as an aside in a sentence complete in itself"[a]

Paronomasia: punning, play on words based on their similar sound (*"Now is the winter of our discontent / Made glorious summer by this sun* [son] *of York"*—Shakespeare *Richard III* I.i.1) cf., Antanaclasis

Periphrasis: talking around a subject rather than getting to the point (see *Hamlet* II.ii.86ff.), Circumlocution

Peristrophe: "Converting an opponent's argument to one's own use. So a peculating tax-collector might say: 'Yes, I took bribes; on my salary I had to.'"[a]

Peroration: last of the seven parts of a formal oration, conclusion, usually with impassioned speech, see "Arrangement" in "Divisions of Rhetoric," p. 184–85.

Personification: treating an animal or object as if it had human characteristics, or addressing it as if it were human

Philophronesis: "attempt to mitigate anger by gentle speech and humble submission"[a]

Pleonasmus: unnecessary repetition ("I spoke the words with my own mouth"[a])

Ploce: emphatic repetition of a word, sometimes in a different sense, to imply its special significance (*Now this cigar is really a cigar; When I say jump, I mean jump.*)

Polyptoton: repeating a word with different case endings or in varied forms (*sweetly she sweetened the coffee with sweetener*)

Polysyndeton: connecting a series of words, phrases, or clauses with conjunctions ("And swims, or sinks, or wades, or creeps, or flies"—Milton, *Paradise Lost*, II.950)[a], opposite of Asyndeton

Praeteritio: Pretending to pass over a point in order to make it, describing something by describing what one will not be saying (*"Of course I'm not going to threaten you, but if this Budget passes the rents will go up."*—in G. K. Chesterton, *A Miscellany of Men* [1912])[c] cf., Occupatio

Pragmatographia: "vivid description of an action or event"[a]

Progressio: "advancing by steps of comparison to the most important point of a series."[a] (*She rides bareback, you ride side-saddle; she takes risks, you take none; she flies to the aid of wounded soldiers, you wait to be invited; of course I will marry her and not you.*)

Prolepsis: "applying now an attribute or epithet that will have relevancy later"[a]

> *Benedick: They swore that you were almost sick for me.*
> *Beatrice: They swore that you were well-nigh dead for me.*
> —Shakespeare, *Much Ado about Nothing* V.iv.81–82

also anticipation of another's objection in order to reduce its force (*You will accuse me of oversensitivity, but I remind you that . . .*; "*I do not like the fashion of your garments. You will say they are Persian, but let them be changed.*"—Shakespeare, *King Lear* III.vi.79–81)

Proverb: "A short, pithy statement of a general truth . . . that condenses into memorable form common experience"[a]; synonyms of varying degress of congruence include Gnome, Maxim, Sententia, Aphorismus, Adage, all of which (as Lanham points out) were used not merely as ornament but as means of *proof*, though in later literature they may be used ironically.

Pun: see Antanaclasis and Paronomasia

Pysma: "asking many questions that require diverse answers. Imogen to Pisanio, in *Cymbeline*: '. . . What shall I do the while? Where bide? how live? / Or in my life what comfort . . .?' (III.iv. 128–29)"[a]

Ratiocinatio: discursive reasoning with oneself

> *To be or not to be, that is the question:*
> —Shakespeare, *Hamlet* III.i.55ff.
> *This entertainment*
> *May a free face put on, derive a liberty*
> *From heartiness, from bounty, fertile bosom,*
> *And well become the agent; 't may, I grant.*
> *But to be paddling palms and pinching fingers,*
> *As now they are . . .*
> —Shakespeare, *The Winter's Tale* I.ii.111–116

cf., Hypophora

Run-on line: see Enjambment

Sarcasmus: "bitter gibe or taunt"[a], sarcasm

Sententia: see Proverb

Simile: a comparison of something to a dissimilar thing, often in a non-literal connotation, expressed by use of *like* or *as*, used (as is Metaphor) to show a similarity between two things normally thought of as unlike

Slant rhyme: see Off rhyme

Solecismus: incorrect use of case, gender, tense, etc., grammatical error, cf., Malapropism

Symbol: using one thing to suggest another: a symbol remains what it is but carries with it another level of significance or sense.

Symploce: "Repetition of one word or phrase at the beginning, and of another at the end, of successive clauses, sentences, or passages; a combination of Anaphora and Epistrophe"[a] (*"We do not need a censorship of the press. We have a censorship by the press."* —G.K. Chesterton, *Orthodoxy* (1908); *"I am not afraid of you; but I am afraid for you."*—Anthony Trollope, *The Prime Minister* (1876); *"We are fighting by ourselves alone; but we are not fighting for ourselves alone."*—Winston Churchill, London radio broadcast (1940); *"In that room he found three gentlemen; number one doing nothing particular, number two doing nothing particular, number three doing nothing particular."*—Charles Dickens, *Little Dorrit* (1857); *"I am a donkey, that's what I am. I am as obstinate as one, I am more stupid than one, I get as much pleasure as one, and I should like to kick like one."*—Charles Dickens, *Hard Times* (1854)

Syncope: removing letters or syllables from the middle of a word: *inomy* for *ignomy*; *heartly* for *heartily*[a]

Synecdoche: using a part to indicate the whole (*sail* for ship, *hands* for sailors, *wheels* for automobile) or vice versa, a species to indicate the genus or the genus to indicate a species (*cutthroat* for assassin, *creature* for a human being or a particular person), or the container for the contained or material for the thing made of it (*classroom* for its pupils, *boards* for stage); cf., Metonymy

Tautology: repetition of the same idea in different or even in the same words, an identity (*Whatever will be will be*; *"There's nothing you can do that can't be done. There's nothing you can sing that can't be sung."*—The Beatles; *"Rose is a rose is a rose"*—Gertrude Stein; *" 'A tautology is a tautology' is a tautology"*—Gideon Rappaport)

Threnos: a lamentation, often lyrical

Tmesis: insertion of one or more words between the components of a compound word (*what case soever*), cf., Diacope

Triple rhyme: a three-syllable rhyme (*Petronius/Euphonious, unfortunate/importunate, tonsilectomy/come direct to me/send a check to me*—from a Groucho Marx song in *A Day at the Races*)

Understatement: a form of verbal irony in which one represents something as less important than it really is in order to emphasize it

Zeugma: using one word, usually a verb, in different senses to govern several different words or clauses (*"Here thou, great Anna! whom three realms obey, / Dost sometimes counsel take—and sometimes Tea."*—Alexander Pope, *The Rape of the Lock* III.7–8)

Elements of Debate

with Todd Ballaban

Debate is a form of structured argument. It is one of the oldest forms of rhetoric, growing out of the tradition of political speeches in ancient Greece. To be successful, a debater needs to demonstrate mastery of the complete trivium: mastery of grammar, so that arguments are expressed clearly; mastery of logic, so that arguments are sound and reasoning is correct; mastery of rhetoric, so that the audience is convinced of what is said.

There are many different forms of debate, which derive from the different purposes of debate over the course of history. The Lincoln-Douglas format is based on the 1858 debate between Abraham Lincoln and Stephen Douglas. Because that debate focused heavily on the morality and ethics of slavery, this format is sometimes called Values Debate. The Parliamentary format is modeled on British parliamentary procedure. The Policy format is so named because its resolution often calls for a change in federal government policy; since there is time set aside for questioning of each side by the other, it is sometimes called Cross Examination Debate.

The format that we will describe here, adapted from the High School Public Debate Program that originated at Claremont McKenna College, contains elements from several different formats.

Format and Rules

Two teams debate a motion given in advance. One team, the Proposition, argues in favor of the motion. The other team, the Opposition, argues against. Though the motion is known in advance, teams will not know their side until the day of the debate.

The debate consists of six speeches, three from each side. The first speech is given by the Proposition. Its goal is to make a case for the motion. Next, the Opposition attempts to refute the arguments of the Proposition while presenting new arguments for the Opposition's case. The third speech is given by the Proposition, supporting and supplementing the case presented by the first Proposition speaker and refuting the arguments presented by the Opposition. The fourth speech is given by the Opposition, refuting again the arguments presented by the Proposition and bringing in new information to support the Opposition's case. The fifth and sixth speeches are Rebuttals, first by the Opposition, then by the Proposition. In the rebuttals, the speaker refutes the other side's arguments and attempts to convince the judges and the audience that his or her side has won the debate.

1) 1st Proposition Speaker
Makes a case for the motion. Provides assertions, reasoning, and evidence (ARE) in support of the motion. May offer a specific interpretation of the motion.

2) 1st Opposition Speaker
Presents arguments against the case presented by the other team. Uses direct and indirect refutation to undermine the case and show why the proposition is wrong.

3) 2nd Proposition Speaker
Supports the case presented by the first proposition speaker. Should answer all arguments made by the previous speaker. Should bring in new ideas to bolster the proposition's side.

4) 2nd Opposition Speaker
Extends partner's arguments against the case. Continues to refute proposition's arguments. Should bring in new ideas to bolster the opposition's side.

5) Opposition Rebuttal
Continues to refute proposition's major points. Should explain how, given the arguments advanced in the debate, the opposition wins the debate.

6) Proposition Rebuttal
Refutes the arguments advanced and extended by the opposition. Extends partners' arguments. Shows how, given the arguments advanced in debate, the proposition wins the debate.

The standard format is that each of the first four speeches is five minutes long; the rebuttals are each four minutes long. As for the teams, the standard format is to have teams of three. In that case, each speech is given by a different member of each team. If teams of two are used, the same person may deliver two speeches, or the three-minute rebuttals may be split into two two-minute speeches, each given by one member of the team. If teams of four are used, the first speech for each side is lengthened to six minutes and two people speak for three minutes each.

Rebuttal speakers must summarize and clearly state to the judge why the team has won. No new arguments may be made in the rebuttal speech; still, the speaker must help with his or her team's research and know the main points of his or her side.

In this format of debate, people have the opportunity to interrupt. These interruptions are called Points of Information (POI). Any member of the opposing team may ask for permission to speak by standing up. If the speaker takes a point by acknowledging the person standing for the POI, 15 seconds are allowed for that person to deliver a thoughtful challenge. POIs can be delivered only during the middle three minutes of the first four speeches. No POIs are allowed in the rebuttal speeches.

The winner of the debate is not the team with the most arguments. Rather, it is the team that successfully defended its claims with sound reasoning and evidence and refuted the other team's points. Absence of any refutation results in an automatic loss. The burden of proof rests with the proposition: no proof, no win.

ARE Method: Assertion, Reasoning, Evidence

The ARE method provides the backbone of a debate. An Assertion is the debate-related term for a conclusion. That is, what are you trying to prove? Reasoning and Evidence together form the premises. Reasoning consists of the steps that lead toward proof of the assertion. Evidence supports the reasoning every step of the way.

Using this ARE structure as you speak will ensure that your research is effectively and thoroughly presented. Using this ARE structure as you craft your presentation will ensure that you employ good logic and make strong points.

On Reading Historically

Christopher Maron

History inquires into the writings of the past. Some of the writings of the past are actual histories—works that order the events of a discrete past into a narrative using names, dates, origins, causes, and effects. Most of the writings of the past are not histories, but, whether they are essays, transcripts of speeches, law codes, letters, or even recipes, they can be read historically.

How does one read historically? Historians examine change over time. What happened? What happened before? What happened after? What changed? What remained constant? The answers to these questions give context to what we read. Literally, the text is the written word; the context is that which precedes and follows the text. The text is the thread; the context is the fabric. Historically, context is everything that we can know about the times of which the text is a product.

Why is context important? We use words to order and to communicate our thoughts and our perception of the world. To explain what a particular word means, we use other words: "This is not that." The words that we use depend upon each other for meaning. That interdependence is context. For example, we use contrast to describe what we experience through our senses: bright versus dark, rough versus smooth, loud versus quiet, fragrant versus pungent, savory versus sweet. These characteristics

Above: *Portrait of a Scholar*, Domenico Fetti, first half of 17th Century, oil on canvas.

are relational and fluid. We describe them, rather than define them, and convey their meanings to one another on the basis of shared experience. "Today is warmer than yesterday, but not as warm as the day before." I understand the meaning of the sentence without quantifying the temperature in degrees or defining *absolute* warmness, but it makes a difference whether the sentence is said at Mammoth Mountain in January or in Death Valley in August. The more I know about the context, the greater my understanding.

In the act of reading historically we take for granted that we share enough in common with the people of the past that we can understand what they wrote. We also accept historical change as axiomatic. Ideas, attitudes, cultures, and institutions as well as the words used to describe them may change over time. We look for similarities, aware of differences. Hence reading historically requires that one be an honest and careful reader. And that honesty begins with awareness of one's own presuppositions and those of one's own time and place.

What agenda do I bring with me to the reading? What assumptions do I start with? Do I believe in historical progress— that human beings and human society are ever advancing and improving? If so, do I believe that human beings of my time know more than those of the past? Do I know more than Aristotle did? Or do I believe that the world in which I live is decadent and corrupt? If so, do I look to the past in the hope of finding a golden age when people knew and revered the good, the beautiful, and the true? Or do I bring a mixture of these two assumptions, or one set to one historical period and another to a different period?

Do I consider myself an objective collector of historical facts? Or do I doubt that historical texts can teach me anything other than the opinion of the author? Then do I assume that every author is telling truth as best he or she can, or do I assume that every author is hiding some unsavory ulterior motive? Whatever my assumptions, they can color and distort historical reading.

Once one is aware of one's own assumptions, historical reading requires awareness of historical context. Abraham Lincoln justified civil war for the preservation of freedom, liberty, and democratic government. So did Jefferson Davis. What criteria do we use to understand what they meant? What do we mean by these terms? If we use the standards of our own time, we can argue that neither the Union nor the Confederacy was a democracy, since Davis fought to preserve slavery and even Lincoln's "government of the people, by the people, for the people" excluded women and blacks. But "the standards of our own time" are in part a product of the outcome of the argument between the Lincoln and the Davis positions. We make the arguments we make partly as a result of their having made the arguments they made. So instead of judging the past as if the present were its only measure, is it not more useful to compare the Union with the Confederacy to determine what the words that both used actually meant then and would mean now if we consider their context?

If we do not take Jefferson Davis and Abraham Lincoln (and every other historical figure) at their word and in the context of their own time, then either we reduce history to a fable, in which the outcome is predetermined and the story exists only for the sake of a moral that reinforces our own bias, or we abandon history as irrelevant entirely.

It may or may not be true that, in the words of George Santayana, "those who cannot remember the past are condemned to repeat it." We may be condemned to repeat the past, or to repeat it with variations, in any case. But to see the past only as an opaque mirror of ourselves is to condemn ourselves to unnecessary and potentially fatal ignorance. To see it through the window of historical reading is to be led out of ourselves toward richer, more comprehensive, and we may hope truer knowledge—in short, to be educated.

from the
Hebrew Scriptures

Genesis 1–4
Job 1–14, 29–42
Psalms 23, 90, 148
Ecclesiastes 1–3, 12

King James Version

The King James translation of the Bible was commissioned by James I of England and produced by an illustrious committee of scholars in 1611. A masterpiece of Renaissance poetry, the "KJV" became for English-speaking Christians the authoritative version of the Bible for four centuries, its phrases the ones most often quoted and alluded to by writers and speakers of English, including many in this volume.

In Genesis the creation of the world is figured as a wondrous preparation and context for the life of man on earth, which is meant to be lived in worship of the Creator rather than in human self-worship. Man's failure is then recorded as a moral disaster from which redemption comes through repentance and penance.

The Psalms, traditionally ascribed to King David, are poetic songs in praise of God. Psalm 23 celebrates God as man's protector, as a shepherd protects his sheep; Psalm 90 declares man's insignificance by comparison with the eternal divine reality; Psalm 148 figures the whole of creation as a great chorus of praise of God, ending in a reiteration of the mission of the people of Israel to lead and exemplify that chorus.

Ecclesiastes, traditionally ascribed to King Solomon, is a litany of the vanity of all worldly things, including man and all his works as experienced in time, in which all things pass away and all pretensions end in dust. The recognition of the vanity of things is not meant to evoke despair but rather a renewed commitment to the simple virtues of faith and obedience to the laws of God.

Job, sometimes called a tragedy, is partly an allegory of and partly a dialogue on the justice of God. Why is a good man afflicted with sufferings if God is just? After defending himself from the unjust accusations of his "comforters," who wish to justify God by maligning the innocent Job, the book ends with a powerful and humbling proclamation that God, the source of man and man's ideas of justice, is beyond the judgments of men—ineffable and absolute, not to be measured in human terms.

Above: *Holkham Hebrew Bible* Genesis title page, Joshua Solomon Soncino, 1491–1492.

Genesis

Chapter 1

¹ In the beginning God created the heaven and the earth. ² And the earth was without form, and void; and darkness was upon the face of the deep. And the Spirit of God moved upon the face of the waters. ³ And God said, Let there be light: and there was light. ⁴ And God saw the light, that it was good: and God divided the light from the darkness. ⁵ And God called the light Day, and the darkness he called Night. And the evening and the morning were the first day.

⁶ And God said, Let there be a firmament in the midst of the waters, and let it divide the waters from the waters. ⁷ And God made the firmament, and divided the waters which were under the firmament from the waters which were above the firmament: and it was so. ⁸ And God called the firmament Heaven. And the evening and the morning were the second day.

⁹ And God said, Let the waters under the heaven be gathered together unto one place, and let the dry land appear: and it was so. ¹⁰ And God called the dry land Earth; and the gathering together of the waters called he Seas: and God saw that it was good. ¹¹ And God said, Let the earth bring forth grass, the herb yielding seed, and the fruit tree yielding fruit after his kind, whose seed is in itself, upon the earth: and it was so. ¹² And the earth brought forth grass, and herb yielding seed after his kind, and the tree yielding fruit, whose seed was in itself, after his kind: and God saw that it was good. ¹³ And the evening and the morning were the third day.

¹⁴ And God said, Let there be lights in the firmament of the heaven to divide the day from the night; and let them be for signs, and for seasons, and for days, and years: ¹⁵ And let them be for lights in the firmament of the heaven to give light upon the earth: and it was so. ¹⁶ And God made two great lights; the greater light to rule the day, and the lesser light to rule the night: he made the stars also. ¹⁷ And God set them in the firmament of the heaven to give light upon the earth, ¹⁸ And to rule over the day and over the night, and to divide the light from the darkness: and God saw that it was good. ¹⁹ And the evening and the morning were the fourth day.

[20] And God said, Let the waters bring forth abundantly the moving creature that hath life, and fowl that may fly above the earth in the open firmament of heaven. [21] And God created great whales, and every living creature that moveth, which the waters brought forth abundantly, after their kind, and every winged fowl after his kind: and God saw that it was good. [22] And God blessed them, saying, Be fruitful, and multiply, and fill the waters in the seas, and let fowl multiply in the earth. [23] And the evening and the morning were the fifth day.

[24] And God said, Let the earth bring forth the living creature after his kind, cattle, and creeping thing, and beast of the earth after his kind: and it was so. [25] And God made the beast of the earth after his kind, and cattle after their kind, and every thing that creepeth upon the earth after his kind: and God saw that it was good.

[26] And God said, Let us make man in our image, after our likeness: and let them have dominion over the fish of the sea, and over the fowl of the air, and over the cattle, and over all the earth, and over every creeping thing that creepeth upon the earth.

[27] So God created man in his own image, in the image of God created he him; male and female created he them.

[28] And God blessed them, and God said unto them, Be fruitful, and multiply, and replenish the earth, and subdue it: and have dominion over the fish of the sea, and over the fowl of the air, and over every living thing that moveth upon the earth. [29] And God said, Behold, I have given you every herb bearing seed, which is upon the face of all the earth, and every tree, in the which is the fruit of a tree yielding seed; to you it shall be for meat. [30] And to every beast of the earth, and to every fowl of the air, and to every thing that creepeth upon the earth, wherein there is life, I have given every green herb for meat: and it was so. [31] And God saw every thing that he had made, and, behold, it was very good. And the evening and the morning were the sixth day.

Chapter 2

[1] Thus the heavens and the earth were finished, and all the host of them. [2] And on the seventh day God ended his work which he had made; and he rested on the seventh day from all his

work which he had made. 3 And God blessed the seventh day, and sanctified it: because that in it he had rested from all his work which God created and made.

4 These are the generations of the heavens and of the earth when they were created, in the day that the Lord God made the earth and the heavens,

5 And every plant of the field before it was in the earth, and every herb of the field before it grew: for the Lord God had not caused it to rain upon the earth, and there was not a man to till the ground. 6 But there went up a mist from the earth, and watered the whole face of the ground. 7 And the Lord God formed man of the dust of the ground, and breathed into his nostrils the breath of life; and man became a living soul. 8 And the Lord God planted a garden eastward in Eden; and there he put the man whom he had formed.

9 And out of the ground made the Lord God to grow every tree that is pleasant to the sight, and good for food; the tree of life also in the midst of the garden, and the tree of knowledge of good and evil.

10 And a river went out of Eden to water the garden; and from thence it was parted, and became into four heads. 11 The name of the first is Pison: that is it which compasseth the whole land of Havilah, where there is gold; 12 And the gold of that land is good: there is bdellium and the onyx stone. 13 And the name of the second river is Gihon: the same is it that compasseth the whole land of Ethiopia. 14 And the name of the third river is Hiddekel: that is it which goeth toward the east of Assyria. And the fourth river is Euphrates.

15 And the Lord God took the man, and put him into the garden of Eden to dress it and to keep it.

16 And the Lord God commanded the man, saying, Of every tree of the garden thou mayest freely eat: 17 But of the tree of the knowledge of good and evil, thou shalt not eat of it: for in the day that thou eatest thereof thou shalt surely die.

18 And the Lord God said, It is not good that the man should be alone; I will make him an help meet for him. 19 And out of the ground the Lord God formed every beast of the field, and every

fowl of the air; and brought them unto Adam to see what he would call them: and whatsoever Adam called every living creature, that was the name thereof. 20 And Adam gave names to all cattle, and to the fowl of the air, and to every beast of the field; but for Adam there was not found an help meet for him. 21 And the Lord God caused a deep sleep to fall upon Adam, and he slept: and he took one of his ribs, and closed up the flesh instead thereof; 22 And the rib, which the Lord God had taken from man, made he a woman, and brought her unto the man.

23 And Adam said, This is now bone of my bones, and flesh of my flesh: she shall be called Woman, because she was taken out of Man.

24 Therefore shall a man leave his father and his mother, and shall cleave unto his wife: and they shall be one flesh. 25 And they were both naked, the man and his wife, and were not ashamed.

Chapter 3

1 Now the serpent was more subtil than any beast of the field which the Lord God had made. And he said unto the woman, Yea, hath God said, Ye shall not eat of every tree of the garden? 2 And the woman said unto the serpent, We may eat of the fruit of the trees of the garden: 3 But of the fruit of the tree which is in the midst of the garden, God hath said, Ye shall not eat of it, neither shall ye touch it, lest ye die. 4 And the serpent said unto the woman, Ye shall not surely die: 5 For God doth know that in the day ye eat thereof, then your eyes shall be opened, and ye shall be as gods, knowing good and evil. 6 And when the woman saw that the tree was good for food, and that it was pleasant to the eyes, and a tree to be desired to make one wise, she took of the fruit thereof, and did eat, and gave also unto her husband with her; and he did eat. 7 And the eyes of them both were opened, and they knew that they were naked; and they sewed fig leaves together, and made themselves aprons.

8 And they heard the voice of the Lord God walking in the garden in the cool of the day: and Adam and his wife hid themselves from the presence of the Lord God amongst the trees of the garden. 9 And the Lord God called unto Adam, and said unto

him, Where art thou? 10 And he said, I heard thy voice in the garden, and I was afraid, because I was naked; and I hid myself.

11 And he said, Who told thee that thou wast naked? Hast thou eaten of the tree, whereof I commanded thee that thou shouldest not eat?

12 And the man said, The woman whom thou gavest to be with me, she gave me of the tree, and I did eat. 13 And the Lord God said unto the woman, What is this that thou hast done? And the woman said, The serpent beguiled me, and I did eat.

14 And the Lord God said unto the serpent, Because thou hast done this, thou art cursed above all cattle, and above every beast of the field; upon thy belly shalt thou go, and dust shalt thou eat all the days of thy life: 15 And I will put enmity between thee and the woman, and between thy seed and her seed; it shall bruise thy head, and thou shalt bruise his heel.

16 Unto the woman he said, I will greatly multiply thy sorrow and thy conception; in sorrow thou shalt bring forth children; and thy desire shall be to thy husband, and he shall rule over thee.

17 And unto Adam he said, Because thou hast hearkened unto the voice of thy wife, and hast eaten of the tree, of which I commanded thee, saying, Thou shalt not eat of it: cursed is the ground for thy sake; in sorrow shalt thou eat of it all the days of thy life; 18 Thorns also and thistles shall it bring forth to thee; and thou shalt eat the herb of the field; 19 In the sweat of thy face shalt thou eat bread, till thou return unto the ground; for out of it wast thou taken: for dust thou art, and unto dust shalt thou return.

20 And Adam called his wife's name Eve; because she was the mother of all living. 21 Unto Adam also and to his wife did the Lord God make coats of skins, and clothed them. 22 And the Lord God said, Behold, the man is become as one of us, to know good and evil: and now, lest he put forth his hand, and take also of the tree of life, and eat, and live for ever: 23 Therefore the Lord God sent him forth from the garden of Eden, to till the ground from whence he was taken. 24 So he drove out the man; and he placed at the east of the garden of Eden Cherubims, and a flaming sword which turned every way, to keep the way of the tree of life.

Chapter 4

¹ And Adam knew Eve his wife; and she conceived, and bare Cain, and said, I have gotten a man from the Lord. ² And she again bare his brother Abel. And Abel was a keeper of sheep, but Cain was a tiller of the ground. ³ And in process of time it came to pass, that Cain brought of the fruit of the ground an offering unto the Lord. ⁴ And Abel, he also brought of the firstlings of his flock and of the fat thereof. And the Lord had respect unto Abel and to his offering: ⁵ But unto Cain and to his offering he had not respect. And Cain was very wroth, and his countenance fell. ⁶ And the Lord said unto Cain, Why art thou wroth? and why is thy countenance fallen? ⁷ If thou doest well, shalt thou not be accepted? and if thou doest not well, sin lieth at the door. And unto thee shall be his desire, and thou shalt rule over him.

⁸ And Cain talked with Abel his brother: and it came to pass, when they were in the field, that Cain rose up against Abel his brother, and slew him. ⁹ And the Lord said unto Cain, Where is Abel thy brother? And he said, I know not: Am I my brother's keeper? ¹⁰ And he said, What hast thou done? the voice of thy brother's blood crieth unto me from the ground. ¹¹ And now art thou cursed from the earth, which hath opened her mouth to receive thy brother's blood from thy hand; ¹² When thou tillest the ground, it shall not henceforth yield unto thee her strength; a fugitive and a vagabond shalt thou be in the earth. ¹³ And Cain said unto the Lord, My punishment is greater than I can bear. ¹⁴ Behold, thou hast driven me out this day from the face of the earth; and from thy face shall I be hid; and I shall be a fugitive and a vagabond in the earth; and it shall come to pass, that every one that findeth me shall slay me. ¹⁵ And the Lord said unto him, Therefore whosoever slayeth Cain, vengeance shall be taken on him sevenfold. And the Lord set a mark upon Cain, lest any finding him should kill him. ¹⁶ And Cain went out from the presence of the Lord, and dwelt in the land of Nod, on the east of Eden.

¹⁷ And Cain knew his wife; and she conceived, and bare Enoch: and he builded a city, and called the name of the city, after the name of his son, Enoch. ¹⁸ And unto Enoch was born Irad: and Irad begat Mehujael: and Mehujael begat Methusael: and Methusael begat Lamech. ¹⁹ And Lamech took unto him two wives: the name of the one was Adah, and the name of the other

Zillah. 20 And Adah bare Jabal: he was the father of such as dwell in tents, and of such as have cattle. 21 And his brother's name was Jubal: he was the father of all such as handle the harp and organ. 22 And Zillah, she also bare Tubal-cain, an instructer of every artificer in brass and iron: and the sister of Tubal-cain was Naamah.

23 And Lamech said unto his wives, Adah and Zillah, Hear my voice; ye wives of Lamech, hearken unto my speech: for I have slain a man to my wounding, and a young man to my hurt. 24 If Cain shall be avenged sevenfold, truly Lamech seventy and sevenfold.

25 And Adam knew his wife again; and she bare a son, and called his name Seth: For God, said she, hath appointed me another seed instead of Abel, whom Cain slew. 26 And to Seth, to him also there was born a son; and he called his name Enos: then began men to call upon the name of the Lord.

Job

Chapter 1

¹ There was a man in the land of Uz, whose name was Job; and that man was perfect and upright, and one that feared God, and eschewed evil. ² And there were born unto him seven sons and three daughters. ³ His substance also was seven thousand sheep, and three thousand camels, and five hundred yoke of oxen, and five hundred she asses, and a very great household; so that this man was the greatest of all the men of the east.

⁴ And his sons went and feasted in their houses, every one his day; and sent and called for their three sisters to eat and to drink with them. ⁵ And it was so, when the days of their feasting were gone about, that Job sent and sanctified them, and rose up early in the morning, and offered burnt offerings according to the number of them all: for Job said, It may be that my sons have sinned, and cursed God in their hearts. Thus did Job continually.

⁶ Now there was a day when the sons of God came to present themselves before the Lord, and Satan came also among them. ⁷ And the Lord said unto Satan, Whence comest thou? Then Satan answered the Lord, and said, From going to and fro in the earth, and from walking up and down in it. ⁸ And the Lord said unto Satan, Hast thou considered my servant Job, that there is none like him in the earth, a perfect and an upright man, one that feareth God, and escheweth evil? ⁹ Then Satan answered the Lord, and said, Doth Job fear God for nought? ¹⁰ Hast not thou made an hedge about him, and about his house, and about all that he hath on every side? thou hast blessed the work of his hands, and his substance is increased in the land. ¹¹ But put forth thine hand now, and touch all that he hath, and he will curse thee to thy face. ¹² And the Lord said unto Satan, Behold, all that he hath is in thy power; only upon himself put not forth thine hand. So Satan went forth from the presence of the Lord.

¹³ And there was a day when his sons and his daughters were eating and drinking wine in their eldest brother's house: ¹⁴ And there came a messenger unto Job, and said, The oxen were plowing, and the asses feeding beside them: ¹⁵ And the Sabeans fell upon them, and took them away; yea, they have slain the servants with the edge of the sword; and I only am escaped alone

to tell thee. 16 While he was yet speaking, there came also another, and said, The fire of God is fallen from heaven, and hath burned up the sheep, and the servants, and consumed them; and I only am escaped alone to tell thee. 17 While he was yet speaking, there came also another, and said, The Chaldeans made out three bands, and fell upon the camels, and have carried them away, yea, and slain the servants with the edge of the sword; and I only am escaped alone to tell thee. 18 While he was yet speaking, there came also another, and said, Thy sons and thy daughters were eating and drinking wine in their eldest brother's house: 19 And, behold, there came a great wind from the wilderness, and smote the four corners of the house, and it fell upon the young men, and they are dead; and I only am escaped alone to tell thee.

20 Then Job arose, and rent his mantle, and shaved his head, and fell down upon the ground, and worshipped, 21 And said, Naked came I out of my mother's womb, and naked shall I return thither: the Lord gave, and the Lord hath taken away; blessed be the name of the Lord. 22 In all this Job sinned not, nor charged God foolishly.

Chapter 2

1 Again there was a day when the sons of God came to present themselves before the Lord, and Satan came also among them to present himself before the Lord. 2 And the Lord said unto Satan, From whence comest thou? And Satan answered the Lord, and said, From going to and fro in the earth, and from walking up and down in it. 3 And the Lord said unto Satan, Hast thou considered my servant Job, that there is none like him in the earth, a perfect and an upright man, one that feareth God, and escheweth evil? and still he holdeth fast his integrity, although thou movedst me against him, to destroy him without cause. 4 And Satan answered the Lord, and said, Skin for skin, yea, all that a man hath will he give for his life. 5 But put forth thine hand now, and touch his bone and his flesh, and he will curse thee to thy face. 6 And the Lord said unto Satan, Behold, he is in thine hand; but save his life.

7 So went Satan forth from the presence of the Lord, and smote Job with sore boils from the sole of his foot unto his crown. 8 And he took him a potsherd to scrape himself withal; and he sat down among the ashes.

⁹ Then said his wife unto him, Dost thou still retain thine integrity? curse God, and die. ¹⁰ But he said unto her, Thou speakest as one of the foolish women speaketh. What? shall we receive good at the hand of God, and shall we not receive evil? In all this did not Job sin with his lips.

¹¹ Now when Job's three friends heard of all this evil that was come upon him, they came every one from his own place; Eliphaz the Temanite, and Bildad the Shuhite, and Zophar the Naamathite: for they had made an appointment together to come to mourn with him and to comfort him. ¹² And when they lifted up their eyes afar off, and knew him not, they lifted up their voice, and wept; and they rent every one his mantle, and sprinkled dust upon their heads toward heaven. ¹³ So they sat down with him upon the ground seven days and seven nights, and none spake a word unto him: for they saw that his grief was very great.

Chapter 3

¹ After this opened Job his mouth, and cursed his day. ² And Job spake, and said, ³ Let the day perish wherein I was born, and the night in which it was said, There is a man child conceived. ⁴ Let that day be darkness; let not God regard it from above, neither let the light shine upon it. ⁵ Let darkness and the shadow of death stain it; let a cloud dwell upon it; let the blackness of the day terrify it. ⁶ As for that night, let darkness seize upon it; let it not be joined unto the days of the year, let it not come into the number of the months. ⁷ Lo, let that night be solitary, let no joyful voice come therein. ⁸ Let them curse it that curse the day, who are ready to raise up their mourning. ⁹ Let the stars of the twilight thereof be dark; let it look for light, but have none; neither let it see the dawning of the day: ¹⁰ Because it shut not up the doors of my mother's womb, nor hid sorrow from mine eyes.

¹¹ Why died I not from the womb? why did I not give up the ghost when I came out of the belly? ¹² Why did the knees prevent me? or why the breasts that I should suck? ¹³ For now should I have lain still and been quiet, I should have slept: then had I been at rest, ¹⁴ With kings and counsellors of the earth, which build desolate places for themselves; ¹⁵ Or with princes that had gold, who filled their houses with silver: ¹⁶ Or as an hidden untimely birth I had not been; as infants which never saw light. ¹⁷ There the wicked cease

from troubling; and there the weary be at rest. 18 There the prisoners rest together; they hear not the voice of the oppressor. 19 The small and great are there; and the servant is free from his master.

20 Wherefore is light given to him that is in misery, and life unto the bitter in soul; 21 Which long for death, but it cometh not; and dig for it more than for hid treasures; 22 Which rejoice exceedingly, and are glad, when they can find the grave? 23 Why is light given to a man whose way is hid, and whom God hath hedged in? 24 For my sighing cometh before I eat, and my roarings are poured out like the waters. 25 For the thing which I greatly feared is come upon me, and that which I was afraid of is come unto me. 26 I was not in safety, neither had I rest, neither was I quiet; yet trouble came.

Chapter 4

1 Then Eliphaz the Temanite answered and said, 2 If we assay to commune with thee, wilt thou be grieved? but who can withhold himself from speaking? 3 Behold, thou hast instructed many, and thou hast strengthened the weak hands. 4 Thy words have upholden him that was falling, and thou hast strengthened the feeble knees. 5 But now it is come upon thee, and thou faintest; it toucheth thee, and thou art troubled. 6 Is not this thy fear, thy confidence, thy hope, and the uprightness of thy ways?

7 Remember, I pray thee, who ever perished, being innocent? or where were the righteous cut off? 8 Even as I have seen, they that plow iniquity, and sow wickedness, reap the same. 9 By the blast of God they perish, and by the breath of his nostrils are they consumed. 10 The roaring of the lion, and the voice of the fierce lion, and the teeth of the young lions, are broken. 11 The old lion perisheth for lack of prey, and the stout lion's whelps are scattered abroad.

12 Now a thing was secretly brought to me, and mine ear received a little thereof. 13 In thoughts from the visions of the night, when deep sleep falleth on men, 14 Fear came upon me, and trembling, which made all my bones to shake.15 Then a spirit passed before my face; the hair of my flesh stood up: 16 It stood still, but I could not discern the form thereof: an image was before mine eyes, there was silence, and I heard a voice, saying, 17 Shall mortal man be more just than God? shall a man be more

pure than his maker? 18 Behold, he put no trust in his servants; and his angels he charged with folly: 19 How much less in them that dwell in houses of clay, whose foundation is in the dust, which are crushed before the moth? 20 They are destroyed from morning to evening: they perish for ever without any regarding it. 21 Doth not their excellency which is in them go away? they die, even without wisdom.

Chapter 5

1 Call now, if there be any that will answer thee; and to which of the saints wilt thou turn? 2 For wrath killeth the foolish man, and envy slayeth the silly one. 3 I have seen the foolish taking root: but suddenly I cursed his habitation. 4 His children are far from safety, and they are crushed in the gate, neither is there any to deliver them. 5 Whose harvest the hungry eateth up, and taketh it even out of the thorns, and the robber swalloweth up their substance.

6 Although affliction cometh not forth of the dust, neither doth trouble spring out of the ground; 7 Yet man is born unto trouble, as the sparks fly upward. 8 I would seek unto God, and unto God would I commit my cause: 9 Which doeth great things and unsearchable; marvellous things without number: 10 Who giveth rain upon the earth, and sendeth waters upon the fields: 11 To set up on high those that be low; that those which mourn may be exalted to safety. 12 He disappointeth the devices of the crafty, so that their hands cannot perform their enterprise. 13 He taketh the wise in their own craftiness: and the counsel of the froward is carried headlong. 14 They meet with darkness in the day time, and grope in the noonday as in the night. 15 But he saveth the poor from the sword, from their mouth, and from the hand of the mighty. 16 So the poor hath hope, and iniquity stoppeth her mouth.

17 Behold, happy is the man whom God correcteth: therefore despise not thou the chastening of the Almighty: 18 For he maketh sore, and bindeth up: he woundeth, and his hands make whole. 19 He shall deliver thee in six troubles: yea, in seven there shall no evil touch thee. 20 In famine he shall redeem thee from death: and in war from the power of the sword. 21 Thou shalt be hid from the scourge of the tongue: neither shalt thou be afraid of destruction when it cometh. 22 At destruction and famine thou shalt laugh: neither shalt thou be afraid of the beasts of the earth.

23 For thou shalt be in league with the stones of the field: and the beasts of the field shall be at peace with thee. 24 And thou shalt know that thy tabernacle shall be in peace; and thou shalt visit thy habitation, and shalt not sin. 25 Thou shalt know also that thy seed shall be great, and thine offspring as the grass of the earth. 26 Thou shalt come to thy grave in a full age, like as a shock of corn cometh in in his season. 27 Lo this, we have searched it, so it is; hear it, and know thou it for thy good.

Chapter 6

1 But Job answered and said, 2 Oh that my grief were throughly weighed, and my calamity laid in the balances together! 3 For now it would be heavier than the sand of the sea: therefore my words are swallowed up. 4 For the arrows of the Almighty are within me, the poison whereof drinketh up my spirit: the terrors of God do set themselves in array against me. 5 Doth the wild ass bray when he hath grass? or loweth the ox over his fodder? 6 Can that which is unsavoury be eaten without salt? or is there any taste in the white of an egg? 7 The things that my soul refused to touch are as my sorrowful meat.

8 Oh that I might have my request; and that God would grant me the thing that I long for! 9 Even that it would please God to destroy me; that he would let loose his hand, and cut me off! 10 Then should I yet have comfort; yea, I would harden myself in sorrow: let him not spare; for I have not concealed the words of the Holy One. 11 What is my strength, that I should hope? and what is mine end, that I should prolong my life? 12 Is my strength the strength of stones? or is my flesh of brass? 13 Is not my help in me? and is wisdom driven quite from me?

14 To him that is afflicted pity should be shewed from his friend; but he forsaketh the fear of the Almighty. 15 My brethren have dealt deceitfully as a brook, and as the stream of brooks they pass away; 16 Which are blackish by reason of the ice, and wherein the snow is hid: 17 What time they wax warm, they vanish: when it is hot, they are consumed out of their place. 18 The paths of their way are turned aside; they go to nothing, and perish. 19 The troops of Tema looked, the companies of Sheba waited for them. 20 They were confounded because they had hoped; they came

thither, and were ashamed. 21 For now ye are nothing; ye see my casting down, and are afraid.

22 Did I say, Bring unto me? or, Give a reward for me of your substance? 23 Or, Deliver me from the enemy's hand? or, Redeem me from the hand of the mighty? 24 Teach me, and I will hold my tongue: and cause me to understand wherein I have erred. 25 How forcible are right words! but what doth your arguing reprove? 26 Do ye imagine to reprove words, and the speeches of one that is desperate, which are as wind? 27 Yea, ye overwhelm the fatherless, and ye dig a pit for your friend. 28 Now therefore be content, look upon me; for it is evident unto you if I lie. 29 Return, I pray you, let it not be iniquity; yea, return again, my righteousness is in it. 30 Is there iniquity in my tongue? cannot my taste discern perverse things?

Chapter 7

1 Is there not an appointed time to man upon earth? are not his days also like the days of an hireling? 2 As a servant earnestly desireth the shadow, and as an hireling looketh for the reward of his work: 3 So am I made to possess months of vanity, and wearisome nights are appointed to me. 4 When I lie down, I say, When shall I arise, and the night be gone? and I am full of tossings to and fro unto the dawning of the day. 5 My flesh is clothed with worms and clods of dust; my skin is broken, and become loathsome. 6 My days are swifter than a weaver's shuttle, and are spent without hope.

7 O remember that my life is wind: mine eye shall no more see good. 8 The eye of him that hath seen me shall see me no more: thine eyes are upon me, and I am not. 9 As the cloud is consumed and vanisheth away: so he that goeth down to the grave shall come up no more. 10 He shall return no more to his house, neither shall his place know him any more. 11 Therefore I will not refrain my mouth; I will speak in the anguish of my spirit; I will complain in the bitterness of my soul. 12 Am I a sea, or a whale, that thou settest a watch over me? 13 When I say, My bed shall comfort me, my couch shall ease my complaints; 14 Then thou scarest me with dreams, and terrifiest me through visions: 15 So that my soul chooseth strangling, and death rather than my life. 16 I loathe it; I would not live alway: let me alone; for my days are vanity.

17 What is man, that thou shouldest magnify him? and that thou shouldest set thine heart upon him? 18 And that thou shouldest visit him every morning, and try him every moment? 19 How long wilt thou not depart from me, nor let me alone till I swallow down my spittle? 20 I have sinned; what shall I do unto thee, O thou preserver of men? why hast thou set me as a mark against thee, so that I am a burden to myself? 21 And why dost thou not pardon my transgression, and take away my iniquity? for now shall I sleep in the dust; and thou shalt seek me in the morning, but I shall not be.

Chapter 8

1 Then answered Bildad the Shuhite, and said, 2 How long wilt thou speak these things? and how long shall the words of thy mouth be like a strong wind? 3 Doth God pervert judgment? or doth the Almighty pervert justice? 4 If thy children have sinned against him, and he have cast them away for their transgression; 5 If thou wouldest seek unto God betimes, and make thy supplication to the Almighty; 6 If thou wert pure and upright; surely now he would awake for thee, and make the habitation of thy righteousness prosperous. 7 Though thy beginning was small, yet thy latter end should greatly increase.

8 For enquire, I pray thee, of the former age, and prepare thyself to the search of their fathers: 9 (For we are but of yesterday, and know nothing, because our days upon earth are a shadow:) 10 Shall not they teach thee, and tell thee, and utter words out of their heart? 11 Can the rush grow up without mire? can the flag grow without water? 12 Whilst it is yet in his greenness, and not cut down, it withereth before any other herb. 13 So are the paths of all that forget God; and the hypocrite's hope shall perish: 14 Whose hope shall be cut off, and whose trust shall be a spider's web. 15 He shall lean upon his house, but it shall not stand: he shall hold it fast, but it shall not endure. 16 He is green before the sun, and his branch shooteth forth in his garden. 17 His roots are wrapped about the heap, and seeth the place of stones. 18 If he destroy him from his place, then it shall deny him, saying, I have not seen thee. 19 Behold, this is the joy of his way, and out of the earth shall others grow.

20 Behold, God will not cast away a perfect man, neither will he help the evil doers: 21 Till he fill thy mouth with laughing, and

thy lips with rejoicing. 22 They that hate thee shall be clothed with shame; and the dwelling place of the wicked shall come to nought.

Chapter 9

1 Then Job answered and said, 2 I know it is so of a truth: but how should man be just with God? 3 If he will contend with him, he cannot answer him one of a thousand. 4 He is wise in heart, and mighty in strength: who hath hardened himself against him, and hath prospered? 5 Which removeth the mountains, and they know not: which overturneth them in his anger. 6 Which shaketh the earth out of her place, and the pillars thereof tremble. 7 Which commandeth the sun, and it riseth not; and sealeth up the stars. 8 Which alone spreadeth out the heavens, and treadeth upon the waves of the sea. 9 Which maketh Arcturus, Orion, and Pleiades, and the chambers of the south. 10 Which doeth great things past finding out; yea, and wonders without number. 11 Lo, he goeth by me, and I see him not: he passeth on also, but I perceive him not. 12 Behold, he taketh away, who can hinder him? who will say unto him, What doest thou? 13 If God will not withdraw his anger, the proud helpers do stoop under him.

14 How much less shall I answer him, and choose out my words to reason with him? 15 Whom, though I were righteous, yet would I not answer, but I would make supplication to my judge. 16 If I had called, and he had answered me; yet would I not believe that he had hearkened unto my voice. 17 For he breaketh me with a tempest, and multiplieth my wounds without cause. 18 He will not suffer me to take my breath, but filleth me with bitterness. 19 If I speak of strength, lo, he is strong: and if of judgment, who shall set me a time to plead? 20 If I justify myself, mine own mouth shall condemn me: if I say, I am perfect, it shall also prove me perverse. 21 Though I were perfect, yet would I not know my soul: I would despise my life.

22 This is one thing, therefore I said it, He destroyeth the perfect and the wicked. 23 If the scourge slay suddenly, he will laugh at the trial of the innocent. 24 The earth is given into the hand of the wicked: he covereth the faces of the judges thereof; if not, where, and who is he?

25 Now my days are swifter than a post: they flee away, they see no good. 26 They are passed away as the swift ships: as the eagle that hasteth to the prey. 27 If I say, I will forget my complaint, I will leave off my heaviness, and comfort myself: 28 I am afraid of all my sorrows, I know that thou wilt not hold me innocent. 29 If I be wicked, why then labour I in vain? 30 If I wash myself with snow water, and make my hands never so clean; 31 Yet shalt thou plunge me in the ditch, and mine own clothes shall abhor me. 32 For he is not a man, as I am, that I should answer him, and we should come together in judgment. 33 Neither is there any daysman betwixt us, that might lay his hand upon us both. 34 Let him take his rod away from me, and let not his fear terrify me: 35 Then would I speak, and not fear him; but it is not so with me.

Chapter 10

1 My soul is weary of my life; I will leave my complaint upon myself; I will speak in the bitterness of my soul. 2 I will say unto God, Do not condemn me; shew me wherefore thou contendest with me. 3 Is it good unto thee that thou shouldest oppress, that thou shouldest despise the work of thine hands, and shine upon the counsel of the wicked? 4 Hast thou eyes of flesh? or seest thou as man seeth? 5 Are thy days as the days of man? are thy years as man's days, 6 That thou enquirest after mine iniquity, and searchest after my sin? 7 Thou knowest that I am not wicked; and there is none that can deliver out of thine hand.

8 Thine hands have made me and fashioned me together round about; yet thou dost destroy me. 9 Remember, I beseech thee, that thou hast made me as the clay; and wilt thou bring me into dust again? 10 Hast thou not poured me out as milk, and curdled me like cheese? 11 Thou hast clothed me with skin and flesh, and hast fenced me with bones and sinews. 12 Thou hast granted me life and favour, and thy visitation hath preserved my spirit. 13 And these things hast thou hid in thine heart: I know that this is with thee.

14 If I sin, then thou markest me, and thou wilt not acquit me from mine iniquity. 15 If I be wicked, woe unto me; and if I be righteous, yet will I not lift up my head. I am full of confusion; therefore see thou mine affliction; 16 For it increaseth. Thou huntest me as a fierce lion: and again thou shewest thyself marvellous upon me. 17 Thou renewest thy witnesses against me,

and increasest thine indignation upon me; changes and war are against me. 18 Wherefore then hast thou brought me forth out of the womb? Oh that I had given up the ghost, and no eye had seen me! 19 I should have been as though I had not been; I should have been carried from the womb to the grave. 20 Are not my days few? cease then, and let me alone, that I may take comfort a little, 21 Before I go whence I shall not return, even to the land of darkness and the shadow of death; 22 A land of darkness, as darkness itself; and of the shadow of death, without any order, and where the light is as darkness.

Chapter 11

1 Then answered Zophar the Naamathite, and said, 2 Should not the multitude of words be answered? and should a man full of talk be justified? 3 Should thy lies make men hold their peace? and when thou mockest, shall no man make thee ashamed? 4 For thou hast said, My doctrine is pure, and I am clean in thine eyes. 5 But oh that God would speak, and open his lips against thee; 6 And that he would shew thee the secrets of wisdom, that they are double to that which is! Know therefore that God exacteth of thee less than thine iniquity deserveth.

7 Canst thou by searching find out God? canst thou find out the Almighty unto perfection? 8 It is as high as heaven; what canst thou do? deeper than hell; what canst thou know? 9 The measure thereof is longer than the earth, and broader than the sea. 10 If he cut off, and shut up, or gather together, then who can hinder him? 11 For he knoweth vain men: he seeth wickedness also; will he not then consider it? 12 For vain men would be wise, though man be born like a wild ass's colt.

13 If thou prepare thine heart, and stretch out thine hands toward him; 14 If iniquity be in thine hand, put it far away, and let not wickedness dwell in thy tabernacles. 15 For then shalt thou lift up thy face without spot; yea, thou shalt be stedfast, and shalt not fear: 16 Because thou shalt forget thy misery, and remember it as waters that pass away: 17 And thine age shall be clearer than the noonday: thou shalt shine forth, thou shalt be as the morning. 18 And thou shalt be secure, because there is hope; yea, thou shalt dig about thee, and thou shalt take thy rest in safety. 19 Also thou shalt lie down, and none shall make thee afraid; yea, many shall make suit unto thee.

20 But the eyes of the wicked shall fail, and they shall not escape, and their hope shall be as the giving up of the ghost.

Chapter 12

1 And Job answered and said, 2 No doubt but ye are the people, and wisdom shall die with you. 3 But I have understanding as well as you; I am not inferior to you: yea, who knoweth not such things as these? 4 I am as one mocked of his neighbour, who calleth upon God, and he answereth him: the just upright man is laughed to scorn. 5 He that is ready to slip with his feet is as a lamp despised in the thought of him that is at ease.

6 The tabernacles of robbers prosper, and they that provoke God are secure; into whose hand God bringeth abundantly. 7 But ask now the beasts, and they shall teach thee; and the fowls of the air, and they shall tell thee: 8 Or speak to the earth, and it shall teach thee: and the fishes of the sea shall declare unto thee. 9 Who knoweth not in all these that the hand of the Lord hath wrought this? 10 In whose hand is the soul of every living thing, and the breath of all mankind. 11 Doth not the ear try words? and the mouth taste his meat?

12 With the ancient is wisdom; and in length of days understanding. 13 With him is wisdom and strength, he hath counsel and understanding. 14 Behold, he breaketh down, and it cannot be built again: he shutteth up a man, and there can be no opening. 15 Behold, he withholdeth the waters, and they dry up: also he sendeth them out, and they overturn the earth. 16 With him is strength and wisdom: the deceived and the deceiver are his. 17 He leadeth counsellors away spoiled, and maketh the judges fools. 18 He looseth the bond of kings, and girdeth their loins with a girdle. 19 He leadeth princes away spoiled, and overthroweth the mighty. 20 He removeth away the speech of the trusty, and taketh away the understanding of the aged. 21 He poureth contempt upon princes, and weakeneth the strength of the mighty. 22 He discovereth deep things out of darkness, and bringeth out to light the shadow of death. 23 He increaseth the nations, and destroyeth them: he enlargeth the nations, and straiteneth them again. 24 He taketh away the heart of the chief of the people of the earth, and causeth them to wander in a wilderness where there is no way. 25 They grope in the dark without light, and he maketh them to stagger like a drunken man.

Chapter 13

¹ Lo, mine eye hath seen all this, mine ear hath heard and understood it. ² What ye know, the same do I know also: I am not inferior unto you. ³ Surely I would speak to the Almighty, and I desire to reason with God. ⁴ But ye are forgers of lies, ye are all physicians of no value. ⁵ O that ye would altogether hold your peace! and it should be your wisdom. ⁶ Hear now my reasoning, and hearken to the pleadings of my lips. ⁷ Will ye speak wickedly for God? and talk deceitfully for him? ⁸ Will ye accept his person? will ye contend for God? ⁹ Is it good that he should search you out? or as one man mocketh another, do ye so mock him? ¹⁰ He will surely reprove you, if ye do secretly accept persons. ¹¹ Shall not his excellency make you afraid? and his dread fall upon you? ¹² Your remembrances are like unto ashes, your bodies to bodies of clay.

¹³ Hold your peace, let me alone, that I may speak, and let come on me what will. ¹⁴ Wherefore do I take my flesh in my teeth, and put my life in mine hand? ¹⁵ Though he slay me, yet will I trust in him: but I will maintain mine own ways before him.¹⁶ He also shall be my salvation: for an hypocrite shall not come before him. ¹⁷ Hear diligently my speech, and my declaration with your ears. ¹⁸ Behold now, I have ordered my cause; I know that I shall be justified. ¹⁹ Who is he that will plead with me? for now, if I hold my tongue, I shall give up the ghost. ²⁰ Only do not two things unto me: then will I not hide myself from thee. ²¹ Withdraw thine hand far from me: and let not thy dread make me afraid. ²² Then call thou, and I will answer: or let me speak, and answer thou me.

²³ How many are mine iniquities and sins? make me to know my transgression and my sin. ²⁴ Wherefore hidest thou thy face, and holdest me for thine enemy? ²⁵ Wilt thou break a leaf driven to and fro? and wilt thou pursue the dry stubble? ²⁶ For thou writest bitter things against me, and makest me to possess the iniquities of my youth. ²⁷ Thou puttest my feet also in the stocks, and lookest narrowly unto all my paths; thou settest a print upon the heels of my feet. ²⁸ And he, as a rotten thing, consumeth, as a garment that is moth eaten.

Chapter 14

1 Man that is born of a woman is of few days and full of trouble.
2 He cometh forth like a flower, and is cut down: he fleeth also as a
shadow, and continueth not. 3 And doth thou open thine eyes upon
such an one, and bringest me into judgment with thee? 4 Who can
bring a clean thing out of an unclean? not one. 5 Seeing his days are
determined, the number of his months are with thee, thou hast
appointed his bounds that he cannot pass; 6 Turn from him, that he
may rest, till he shall accomplish, as an hireling, his day.

7 For there is hope of a tree, if it be cut down, that it will
sprout again, and that the tender branch thereof will not cease.
8 Though the root thereof wax old in the earth, and the stock
thereof die in the ground; 9 Yet through the scent of water it will
bud, and bring forth boughs like a plant. 10 But man dieth, and
wasteth away: yea, man giveth up the ghost, and where is he? 11 As
the waters fail from the sea, and the flood decayeth and drieth up:
12 So man lieth down, and riseth not: till the heavens be no more,
they shall not awake, nor be raised out of their sleep. 13 O that
thou wouldest hide me in the grave, that thou wouldest keep me
secret, until thy wrath be past, that thou wouldest appoint me a
set time, and remember me! 14 If a man die, shall he live again? all
the days of my appointed time will I wait, till my change come.
15 Thou shalt call, and I will answer thee: thou wilt have a desire
to the work of thine hands.

16 For now thou numberest my steps: dost thou not watch
over my sin? 17 My transgression is sealed up in a bag, and thou
sewest up mine iniquity. 18 And surely the mountains falling
cometh to nought, and the rock is removed out of his place.
19 The waters wear the stones: thou washest away the things
which grow out of the dust of the earth; and thou destroyest the
hope of man. 20 Thou prevailest for ever against him, and he
passeth: thou changest his countenance, and sendest him away.
21 His sons come to honour, and he knoweth it not; and they are
brought low, but he perceiveth it not of them. 22 But his flesh
upon him shall have pain, and his soul within him shall mourn.

Chapter 29

¹ Moreover Job continued his parable, and said, ² Oh that I were as in months past, as in the days when God preserved me; ³ When his candle shined upon my head, and when by his light I walked through darkness; ⁴ As I was in the days of my youth, when the secret of God was upon my tabernacle; ⁵ When the Almighty was yet with me, when my children were about me; ⁶ When I washed my steps with butter, and the rock poured me out rivers of oil;

⁷ When I went out to the gate through the city, when I prepared my seat in the street! ⁸ The young men saw me, and hid themselves: and the aged arose, and stood up. ⁹ The princes refrained talking, and laid their hand on their mouth. ¹⁰ The nobles held their peace, and their tongue cleaved to the roof of their mouth. ¹¹ When the ear heard me, then it blessed me; and when the eye saw me, it gave witness to me: ¹² Because I delivered the poor that cried, and the fatherless, and him that had none to help him. ¹³ The blessing of him that was ready to perish came upon me: and I caused the widow's heart to sing for joy. ¹⁴ I put on righteousness, and it clothed me: my judgment was as a robe and a diadem. ¹⁵ I was eyes to the blind, and feet was I to the lame. ¹⁶ I was a father to the poor: and the cause which I knew not I searched out. ¹⁷ And I brake the jaws of the wicked, and plucked the spoil out of his teeth.

¹⁸ Then I said, I shall die in my nest, and I shall multiply my days as the sand. ¹⁹ My root was spread out by the waters, and the dew lay all night upon my branch. ²⁰ My glory was fresh in me, and my bow was renewed in my hand. ²¹ Unto me men gave ear, and waited, and kept silence at my counsel. ²² After my words they spake not again; and my speech dropped upon them. ²³ And they waited for me as for the rain; and they opened their mouth wide as for the latter rain. ²⁴ If I laughed on them, they believed it not; and the light of my countenance they cast not down. ²⁵ I chose out their way, and sat chief, and dwelt as a king in the army, as one that comforteth the mourners.

Chapter 30

¹ But now they that are younger than I have me in derision, whose fathers I would have disdained to have set with the dogs of

my flock. 2 Yea, whereto might the strength of their hands profit me, in whom old age was perished? 3 For want and famine they were solitary; fleeing into the wilderness in former time desolate and waste. 4 Who cut up mallows by the bushes, and juniper roots for their meat. 5 They were driven forth from among men, (they cried after them as after a thief;) 6 To dwell in the cliffs of the valleys, in caves of the earth, and in the rocks. 7 Among the bushes they brayed; under the nettles they were gathered together. 8 They were children of fools, yea, children of base men: they were viler than the earth. 9 And now am I their song, yea, I am their byword. 10 They abhor me, they flee far from me, and spare not to spit in my face. 11 Because he hath loosed my cord, and afflicted me, they have also let loose the bridle before me. 12 Upon my right hand rise the youth; they push away my feet, and they raise up against me the ways of their destruction. 13 They mar my path, they set forward my calamity, they have no helper. 14 They came upon me as a wide breaking in of waters: in the desolation they rolled themselves upon me.

15 Terrors are turned upon me: they pursue my soul as the wind: and my welfare passeth away as a cloud. 16 And now my soul is poured out upon me; the days of affliction have taken hold upon me. 17 My bones are pierced in me in the night season: and my sinews take no rest. 18 By the great force of my disease is my garment changed: it bindeth me about as the collar of my coat. 19 He hath cast me into the mire, and I am become like dust and ashes. 20 I cry unto thee, and thou dost not hear me: I stand up, and thou regardest me not. 21 Thou art become cruel to me: with thy strong hand thou opposest thyself against me. 22 Thou liftest me up to the wind; thou causest me to ride upon it, and dissolvest my substance. 23 For I know that thou wilt bring me to death, and to the house appointed for all living. 24 Howbeit he will not stretch out his hand to the grave, though they cry in his destruction. 25 Did not I weep for him that was in trouble? was not my soul grieved for the poor? 26 When I looked for good, then evil came unto me: and when I waited for light, there came darkness. 27 My bowels boiled, and rested not: the days of affliction prevented me. 28 I went mourning without the sun: I stood up, and I cried in the congregation. 29 I am a brother to dragons, and a companion to owls. 30 My skin is black upon me,

and my bones are burned with heat. 31 My harp also is turned to mourning, and my organ into the voice of them that weep.

Chapter 31

1 I made a covenant with mine eyes; why then should I think upon a maid? 2 For what portion of God is there from above? and what inheritance of the Almighty from on high? 3 Is not destruction to the wicked? and a strange punishment to the workers of iniquity? 4 Doth not he see my ways, and count all my steps? 5 If I have walked with vanity, or if my foot hath hasted to deceit; 6 Let me be weighed in an even balance that God may know mine integrity. 7 If my step hath turned out of the way, and mine heart walked after mine eyes, and if any blot hath cleaved to mine hands; 8 Then let me sow, and let another eat; yea, let my offspring be rooted out.

9 If mine heart have been deceived by a woman, or if I have laid wait at my neighbour's door; 10 Then let my wife grind unto another, and let others bow down upon her. 11 For this is an heinous crime; yea, it is an iniquity to be punished by the judges. 12 For it is a fire that consumeth to destruction, and would root out all mine increase. 13 If I did despise the cause of my manservant or of my maidservant, when they contended with me; 14 What then shall I do when God riseth up? and when he visiteth, what shall I answer him? 15 Did not he that made me in the womb make him? and did not one fashion us in the womb?

16 If I have withheld the poor from their desire, or have caused the eyes of the widow to fail; 17 Or have eaten my morsel myself alone, and the fatherless hath not eaten thereof; 18 (For from my youth he was brought up with me, as with a father, and I have guided her from my mother's womb;) 19 If I have seen any perish for want of clothing, or any poor without covering; 20 If his loins have not blessed me, and if he were not warmed with the fleece of my sheep; 21 If I have lifted up my hand against the fatherless, when I saw my help in the gate: 22 Then let mine arm fall from my shoulder blade, and mine arm be broken from the bone. 23 For destruction from God was a terror to me, and by reason of his highness I could not endure.

24 If I have made gold my hope, or have said to the fine gold, Thou art my confidence; 25 If I rejoice because my wealth was great, and because mine hand had gotten much; 26 If I beheld the sun when it shined, or the moon walking in brightness; 27 And my heart hath been secretly enticed, or my mouth hath kissed my hand: 28 This also were an iniquity to be punished by the judge: for I should have denied the God that is above. 29 If I rejoice at the destruction of him that hated me, or lifted up myself when evil found him: 30 Neither have I suffered my mouth to sin by wishing a curse to his soul. 31 If the men of my tabernacle said not, Oh that we had of his flesh! we cannot be satisfied. 32 The stranger did not lodge in the street: but I opened my doors to the traveller.

33 If I covered my transgressions as Adam, by hiding mine iniquity in my bosom: 34 Did I fear a great multitude, or did the contempt of families terrify me, that I kept silence, and went not out of the door? 35 Oh that one would hear me! behold, my desire is, that the Almighty would answer me, and that mine adversary had written a book. 36 Surely I would take it upon my shoulder, and bind it as a crown to me. 37 I would declare unto him the number of my steps; as a prince would I go near unto him. 38 If my land cry against me, or that the furrows likewise thereof complain; 39 If I have eaten the fruits thereof without money, or have caused the owners thereof to lose their life: 40 Let thistles grow instead of wheat, and cockle instead of barley. The words of Job are ended.

Chapter 32

1 So these three men ceased to answer Job, because he was righteous in his own eyes. 2 Then was kindled the wrath of Elihu the son of Barachel the Buzite, of the kindred of Ram: against Job was his wrath kindled, because he justified himself rather than God. 3 Also against his three friends was his wrath kindled, because they had found no answer, and yet had condemned Job. 4 Now Elihu had waited till Job had spoken, because they were elder than he. 5 When Elihu saw that there was no answer in the mouth of these three men, then his wrath was kindled.

6 And Elihu the son of Barachel the Buzite answered and said, I am young, and ye are very old; wherefore I was afraid, and durst not shew you mine opinion. 7 I said, Days should speak, and multitude of years should teach wisdom. 8 But there is a spirit in

man: and the inspiration of the Almighty giveth them understanding. ⁹ Great men are not always wise: neither do the aged understand judgment. ¹⁰ Therefore I said, Hearken to me; I also will shew mine opinion. ¹¹ Behold, I waited for your words; I gave ear to your reasons, whilst ye searched out what to say. ¹² Yea, I attended unto you, and, behold, there was none of you that convinced Job, or that answered his words: ¹³ Lest ye should say, We have found out wisdom: God thrusteth him down, not man. ¹⁴ Now he hath not directed his words against me: neither will I answer him with your speeches.

¹⁵ They were amazed, they answered no more: they left off speaking. ¹⁶ When I had waited, (for they spake not, but stood still, and answered no more;) ¹⁷ I said, I will answer also my part, I also will shew mine opinion. ¹⁸ For I am full of matter, the spirit within me constraineth me. ¹⁹ Behold, my belly is as wine which hath no vent; it is ready to burst like new bottles. ²⁰ I will speak, that I may be refreshed: I will open my lips and answer. ²¹ Let me not, I pray you, accept any man's person, neither let me give flattering titles unto man. ²² For I know not to give flattering titles; in so doing my maker would soon take me away.

Chapter 33

¹ Wherefore, Job, I pray thee, hear my speeches, and hearken to all my words. ² Behold, now I have opened my mouth, my tongue hath spoken in my mouth. ³ My words shall be of the uprightness of my heart: and my lips shall utter knowledge clearly. ⁴ The spirit of God hath made me, and the breath of the Almighty hath given me life. ⁵ If thou canst answer me, set thy words in order before me, stand up. ⁶ Behold, I am according to thy wish in God's stead: I also am formed out of the clay. ⁷ Behold, my terror shall not make thee afraid, neither shall my hand be heavy upon thee.

⁸ Surely thou hast spoken in mine hearing, and I have heard the voice of thy words, saying, ⁹ I am clean without transgression, I am innocent; neither is there iniquity in me. ¹⁰ Behold, he findeth occasions against me, he counteth me for his enemy, ¹¹ He putteth my feet in the stocks, he marketh all my paths. ¹² Behold, in this thou art not just: I will answer thee, that God is greater

than man. 13 Why dost thou strive against him? for he giveth not account of any of his matters.

14 For God speaketh once, yea twice, yet man perceiveth it not. 15 In a dream, in a vision of the night, when deep sleep falleth upon men, in slumberings upon the bed; 16 Then he openeth the ears of men, and sealeth their instruction, 17 That he may withdraw man from his purpose, and hide pride from man. 18 He keepeth back his soul from the pit, and his life from perishing by the sword.

19 He is chastened also with pain upon his bed, and the multitude of his bones with strong pain: 20 So that his life abhorreth bread, and his soul dainty meat. 21 His flesh is consumed away, that it cannot be seen; and his bones that were not seen stick out. 22 Yea, his soul draweth near unto the grave, and his life to the destroyers. 23 If there be a messenger with him, an interpreter, one among a thousand, to shew unto man his uprightness: 24 Then he is gracious unto him, and saith, Deliver him from going down to the pit: I have found a ransom. 25 His flesh shall be fresher than a child's: he shall return to the days of his youth: 26 He shall pray unto God, and he will be favourable unto him: and he shall see his face with joy: for he will render unto man his righteousness. 27 He looketh upon men, and if any say, I have sinned, and perverted that which was right, and it profited me not; 28 He will deliver his soul from going into the pit, and his life shall see the light.

29 Lo, all these things worketh God oftentimes with man, 30 To bring back his soul from the pit, to be enlightened with the light of the living. 31 Mark well, O Job, hearken unto me: hold thy peace, and I will speak. 32 If thou hast anything to say, answer me: speak, for I desire to justify thee. 33 If not, hearken unto me: hold thy peace, and I shall teach thee wisdom.

Chapter 34

1 Furthermore Elihu answered and said, 2 Hear my words, O ye wise men; and give ear unto me, ye that have knowledge. 3 For the ear trieth words, as the mouth tasteth meat. 4 Let us choose to us judgment: let us know among ourselves what is good. 5 For Job hath said, I am righteous: and God hath taken away my judgment. 6 Should I lie against my right? my wound is incurable without

transgression. 7 What man is like Job, who drinketh up scorning like water? 8 Which goeth in company with the workers of iniquity, and walketh with wicked men. 9 For he hath said, It profiteth a man nothing that he should delight himself with God.

10 Therefore hearken unto me ye men of understanding: far be it from God, that he should do wickedness; and from the Almighty, that he should commit iniquity. 11 For the work of a man shall he render unto him, and cause every man to find according to his ways. 12 Yea, surely God will not do wickedly, neither will the Almighty pervert judgment. 13 Who hath given him a charge over the earth? or who hath disposed the whole world? 14 If he set his heart upon man, if he gather unto himself his spirit and his breath; 15 All flesh shall perish together, and man shall turn again unto dust.

16 If now thou hast understanding, hear this: hearken to the voice of my words. 17 Shall even he that hateth right govern? and wilt thou condemn him that is most just? 18 Is it fit to say to a king, Thou art wicked? and to princes, Ye are ungodly? 19 How much less to him that accepteth not the persons of princes, nor regardeth the rich more than the poor? for they all are the work of his hands. 20 In a moment shall they die, and the people shall be troubled at midnight, and pass away: and the mighty shall be taken away without hand. 21 For his eyes are upon the ways of man, and he seeth all his goings. 22 There is no darkness, nor shadow of death, where the workers of iniquity may hide themselves. 23 For he will not lay upon man more than right; that he should enter into judgment with God. 24 He shall break in pieces mighty men without number, and set others in their stead. 25 Therefore he knoweth their works, and he overturneth them in the night, so that they are destroyed. 26 He striketh them as wicked men in the open sight of others; 27 Because they turned back from him, and would not consider any of his ways: 28 So that they cause the cry of the poor to come unto him, and he heareth the cry of the afflicted. 29 When he giveth quietness, who then can make trouble? and when he hideth his face, who then can behold him? whether it be done against a nation, or against a man only: 30 That the hypocrite reign not, lest the people be ensnared.

31 Surely it is meet to be said unto God, I have borne chastisement, I will not offend any more: 32 That which I see not

teach thou me: if I have done iniquity, I will do no more.
33 Should it be according to thy mind? he will recompense it,
whether thou refuse, or whether thou choose; and not I: therefore
speak what thou knowest. 34 Let men of understanding tell me,
and let a wise man hearken unto me. 35 Job hath spoken without
knowledge, and his words were without wisdom. 36 My desire is
that Job may be tried unto the end because of his answers for
wicked men. 37 For he addeth rebellion unto his sin, he clappeth
his hands among us, and multiplieth his words against God.

Chapter 35

1 Elihu spake moreover, and said, 2 Thinkest thou this to be
right, that thou saidst, My righteousness is more than God's?
3 For thou saidst, What advantage will it be unto thee? and, What
profit shall I have, if I be cleansed from my sin? 4 I will answer
thee, and thy companions with thee. 5 Look unto the heavens,
and see; and behold the clouds which are higher than thou.
6 If thou sinnest, what doest thou against him? or if thy
transgressions be multiplied, what doest thou unto him? 7 If thou
be righteous, what givest thou him? or what receiveth he of thine
hand? 8 Thy wickedness may hurt a man as thou art; and thy
righteousness may profit the son of man.

9 By reason of the multitude of oppressions they make the
oppressed to cry: they cry out by reason of the arm of the mighty.
10 But none saith, Where is God my maker, who giveth songs in
the night; 11 Who teacheth us more than the beasts of the earth,
and maketh us wiser than the fowls of heaven? 12 There they cry,
but none giveth answer, because of the pride of evil men. 13 Surely
God will not hear vanity, neither will the Almighty regard it.

14 Although thou sayest thou shalt not see him, yet judgment
is before him; therefore trust thou in him. 15 But now, because it
is not so, he hath visited in his anger; yet he knoweth it not in
great extremity: 16 Therefore doth Job open his mouth in vain; he
multiplieth words without knowledge.

Chapter 36

1 Elihu also proceeded, and said, 2 Suffer me a little, and I will
shew thee that I have yet to speak on God's behalf. 3 I will fetch
my knowledge from afar, and will ascribe righteousness to my

Maker. 4 For truly my words shall not be false: he that is perfect in knowledge is with thee.

5 Behold, God is mighty, and despiseth not any: he is mighty in strength and wisdom. 6 He preserveth not the life of the wicked: but giveth right to the poor. 7 He withdraweth not his eyes from the righteous: but with kings are they on the throne; yea, he doth establish them for ever, and they are exalted. 8 And if they be bound in fetters, and be holden in cords of affliction; 9 Then he sheweth them their work, and their transgressions that they have exceeded. 10 He openeth also their ear to discipline, and commandeth that they return from iniquity. 11 If they obey and serve him, they shall spend their days in prosperity, and their years in pleasures. 12 But if they obey not, they shall perish by the sword, and they shall die without knowledge. 13 But the hypocrites in heart heap up wrath: they cry not when he bindeth them. 14 They die in youth, and their life is among the unclean.

15 He delivereth the poor in his affliction, and openeth their ears in oppression. 16 Even so would he have removed thee out of the strait into a broad place, where there is no straitness; and that which should be set on thy table should be full of fatness. 17 But thou hast fulfilled the judgment of the wicked: judgment and justice take hold on thee. 18 Because there is wrath, beware lest he take thee away with his stroke: then a great ransom cannot deliver thee. 19 Will he esteem thy riches? no, not gold, nor all the forces of strength. 20 Desire not the night, when people are cut off in their place. 21 Take heed, regard not iniquity: for this hast thou chosen rather than affliction. 22 Behold, God exalteth by his power: who teacheth like him? 23 Who hath enjoined him his way? or who can say, Thou hast wrought iniquity?

24 Remember that thou magnify his work, which men behold. 25 Every man may see it; man may behold it afar off. 26 Behold, God is great, and we know him not, neither can the number of his years be searched out. 27 For he maketh small the drops of water: they pour down rain according to the vapour thereof: 28 Which the clouds do drop and distil upon man abundantly. 29 Also can any understand the spreadings of the clouds, or the noise of his tabernacle? 30 Behold, he spreadeth his light upon it, and covereth the bottom of the sea. 31 For by them judgeth he the people; he giveth meat in abundance. 32 With clouds he covereth the light;

and commandeth it not to shine by the cloud that cometh betwixt. 33 The noise thereof sheweth concerning it, the cattle also concerning the vapour.

Chapter 37

1 At this also my heart trembleth, and is moved out of his place. 2 Hear attentively the noise of his voice, and the sound that goeth out of his mouth. 3 He directeth it under the whole heaven, and his lightning unto the ends of the earth. 4 After it a voice roareth: he thundereth with the voice of his excellency; and he will not stay them when his voice is heard. 5 God thundereth marvellously with his voice; great things doeth he, which we cannot comprehend.

6 For he saith to the snow, Be thou on the earth; likewise to the small rain, and to the great rain of his strength. 7 He sealeth up the hand of every man; that all men may know his work. 8 Then the beasts go into dens, and remain in their places. 9 Out of the south cometh the whirlwind: and cold out of the north.

10 By the breath of God frost is given: and the breadth of the waters is straitened. 11 Also by watering he wearieth the thick cloud: he scattereth his bright cloud: 12 And it is turned round about by his counsels: that they may do whatsoever he commandeth them upon the face of the world in the earth. 13 He causeth it to come, whether for correction, or for his land, or for mercy.

14 Hearken unto this, O Job: stand still, and consider the wondrous works of God. 15 Dost thou know when God disposed them, and caused the light of his cloud to shine? 16 Dost thou know the balancings of the clouds, the wondrous works of him which is perfect in knowledge? 17 How thy garments are warm, when he quieteth the earth by the south wind? 18 Hast thou with him spread out the sky, which is strong, and as a molten looking glass? 19 Teach us what we shall say unto him; for we cannot order our speech by reason of darkness. 20 Shall it be told him that I speak? if a man speak, surely he shall be swallowed up.

21 And now men see not the bright light which is in the clouds: but the wind passeth, and cleanseth them. 22 Fair weather cometh out of the north: with God is terrible majesty. 23 Touching the Almighty, we cannot find him out: he is excellent

in power, and in judgment, and in plenty of justice: he will not afflict. ²⁴ Men do therefore fear him: he respecteth not any that are wise of heart.

Chapter 38

¹ Then the Lord answered Job out of the whirlwind, and said, ² Who is this that darkeneth counsel by words without knowledge? ³ Gird up now thy loins like a man; for I will demand of thee, and answer thou me.

⁴ Where wast thou when I laid the foundations of the earth? declare, if thou hast understanding. ⁵ Who hath laid the measures thereof, if thou knowest? or who hath stretched the line upon it? ⁶ Whereupon are the foundations thereof fastened? or who laid the corner stone thereof; ⁷ When the morning stars sang together, and all the sons of God shouted for joy? ⁸ Or who shut up the sea with doors, when it brake forth, as if it had issued out of the womb? ⁹ When I made the cloud the garment thereof, and thick darkness a swaddlingband for it, ¹⁰ And brake up for it my decreed place, and set bars and doors, ¹¹ And said, Hitherto shalt thou come, but no further: and here shall thy proud waves be stayed?

¹² Hast thou commanded the morning since thy days; and caused the dayspring to know his place; ¹³ That it might take hold of the ends of the earth, that the wicked might be shaken out of it? ¹⁴ It is turned as clay to the seal; and they stand as a garment. ¹⁵ And from the wicked their light is withholden, and the high arm shall be broken. ¹⁶ Hast thou entered into the springs of the sea? or hast thou walked in the search of the depth? ¹⁷ Have the gates of death been opened unto thee? or hast thou seen the doors of the shadow of death? ¹⁸ Hast thou perceived the breadth of the earth? declare if thou knowest it all. ¹⁹ Where is the way where light dwelleth? and as for darkness, where is the place thereof, ²⁰ That thou shouldest take it to the bound thereof, and that thou shouldest know the paths to the house thereof? ²¹ Knowest thou it, because thou wast then born? or because the number of thy days is great? ²² Hast thou entered into the treasures of the snow? or hast thou seen the treasures of the hail, ²³ Which I have reserved against the time of trouble, against the day of battle and war? ²⁴ By what way is the light parted, which scattereth the east wind upon the earth?

25 Who hath divided a watercourse for the overflowing of waters, or a way for the lightning of thunder; 26 To cause it to rain on the earth, where no man is; on the wilderness, wherein there is no man; 27 To satisfy the desolate and waste ground; and to cause the bud of the tender herb to spring forth? 28 Hath the rain a father? or who hath begotten the drops of dew? 29 Out of whose womb came the ice? and the hoary frost of heaven, who hath gendered it? 30 The waters are hid as with a stone, and the face of the deep is frozen. 31 Canst thou bind the sweet influences of Pleiades, or loose the bands of Orion? 32 Canst thou bring forth Mazzaroth in his season? or canst thou guide Arcturus with his sons? 33 Knowest thou the ordinances of heaven? canst thou set the dominion thereof in the earth? 34 Canst thou lift up thy voice to the clouds, that abundance of waters may cover thee? 35 Canst thou send lightnings, that they may go and say unto thee, Here we are? 36 Who hath put wisdom in the inward parts? or who hath given understanding to the heart? 37 Who can number the clouds in wisdom? or who can stay the bottles of heaven, 38 When the dust groweth into hardness, and the clods cleave fast together? 39 Wilt thou hunt the prey for the lion? or fill the appetite of the young lions, 40 When they couch in their dens, and abide in the covert to lie in wait? 41 Who provideth for the raven his food? when his young ones cry unto God, they wander for lack of meat.

Chapter 39

1 Knowest thou the time when the wild goats of the rock bring forth? or canst thou mark when the hinds do calve? 2 Canst thou number the months that they fulfil? or knowest thou the time when they bring forth? 3 They bow themselves, they bring forth their young ones, they cast out their sorrows. 4 Their young ones are in good liking, they grow up with corn; they go forth, and return not unto them. 5 Who hath sent out the wild ass free? or who hath loosed the bands of the wild ass? 6 Whose house I have made the wilderness, and the barren land his dwellings. 7 He scorneth the multitude of the city, neither regardeth he the crying of the driver. 8 The range of the mountains is his pasture, and he searcheth after every green thing. 9 Will the unicorn be willing to serve thee, or abide by thy crib? 10 Canst thou bind the unicorn with his band in the furrow? or will he harrow the valleys after thee? 11 Wilt thou trust him, because his strength is great? or wilt

thou leave thy labour to him? 12 Wilt thou believe him, that he will bring home thy seed, and gather it into thy barn?

13 Gavest thou the goodly wings unto the peacocks? or wings and feathers unto the ostrich? 14 Which leaveth her eggs in the earth, and warmeth them in dust, 15 And forgetteth that the foot may crush them, or that the wild beast may break them. 16 She is hardened against her young ones, as though they were not her's: her labour is in vain without fear; 17 Because God hath deprived her of wisdom, neither hath he imparted to her understanding. 18 What time she lifteth up herself on high, she scorneth the horse and his rider.

19 Hast thou given the horse strength? hast thou clothed his neck with thunder? 20 Canst thou make him afraid as a grasshopper? the glory of his nostrils is terrible. 21 He paweth in the valley, and rejoiceth in his strength: he goeth on to meet the armed men. 22 He mocketh at fear, and is not affrighted; neither turneth he back from the sword. 23 The quiver rattleth against him, the glittering spear and the shield. 24 He swalloweth the ground with fierceness and rage: neither believeth he that it is the sound of the trumpet. 25 He saith among the trumpets, Ha, ha; and he smelleth the battle afar off, the thunder of the captains, and the shouting.

26 Doth the hawk fly by thy wisdom, and stretch her wings toward the south? 27 Doth the eagle mount up at thy command, and make her nest on high? 28 She dwelleth and abideth on the rock, upon the crag of the rock, and the strong place. 29 From thence she seeketh the prey, and her eyes behold afar off. 30 Her young ones also suck up blood: and where the slain are, there is she.

Chapter 40

1 Moreover the Lord answered Job, and said, 2 Shall he that contendeth with the Almighty instruct him? he that reproveth God, let him answer it.

3 Then Job answered the Lord, and said, 4 Behold, I am vile; what shall I answer thee? I will lay mine hand upon my mouth. 5 Once have I spoken; but I will not answer: yea, twice; but I will proceed no further.

6 Then answered the Lord unto Job out of the whirlwind, and said, 7 Gird up thy loins now like a man: I will demand of thee, and declare thou unto me. 8 Wilt thou also disannul my judgment? wilt thou condemn me, that thou mayest be righteous? 9 Hast thou an arm like God? or canst thou thunder with a voice like him? 10 Deck thyself now with majesty and excellency; and array thyself with glory and beauty. 11 Cast abroad the rage of thy wrath: and behold every one that is proud, and abase him. 12 Look on every one that is proud, and bring him low; and tread down the wicked in their place. 13 Hide them in the dust together; and bind their faces in secret. 14 Then will I also confess unto thee that thine own right hand can save thee. 15 Behold now behemoth, which I made with thee; he eateth grass as an ox.

16 Lo now, his strength is in his loins, and his force is in the navel of his belly. 17 He moveth his tail like a cedar: the sinews of his stones are wrapped together. 18 His bones are as strong pieces of brass; his bones are like bars of iron. 19 He is the chief of the ways of God: he that made him can make his sword to approach unto him. 20 Surely the mountains bring him forth food, where all the beasts of the field play. 21 He lieth under the shady trees, in the covert of the reed, and fens. 22 The shady trees cover him with their shadow; the willows of the brook compass him about. 23 Behold, he drinketh up a river, and hasteth not: he trusteth that he can draw up Jordan into his mouth. 24 He taketh it with his eyes: his nose pierceth through snares.

Chapter 41

1 Canst thou draw out leviathan with an hook? or his tongue with a cord which thou lettest down? 2 Canst thou put an hook into his nose? or bore his jaw through with a thorn? 3 Will he make many supplications unto thee? will he speak soft words unto thee? 4 Will he make a covenant with thee? wilt thou take him for a servant for ever? 5 Wilt thou play with him as with a bird? or wilt thou bind him for thy maidens? 6 Shall the companions make a banquet of him? shall they part him among the merchants? 7 Canst thou fill his skin with barbed irons? or his head with fish spears? 8 Lay thine hand upon him, remember the battle, do no more. 9 Behold, the hope of him is in vain: shall not

one be cast down even at the sight of him? ¹⁰ None is so fierce that dare stir him up: who then is able to stand before me?

¹¹ Who hath prevented me, that I should repay him? whatsoever is under the whole heaven is mine. ¹² I will not conceal his parts, nor his power, nor his comely proportion. ¹³ Who can discover the face of his garment? or who can come to him with his double bridle? ¹⁴ Who can open the doors of his face? his teeth are terrible round about. ¹⁵ His scales are his pride, shut up together as with a close seal. ¹⁶ One is so near to another, that no air can come between them. ¹⁷ They are joined one to another, they stick together, that they cannot be sundered. ¹⁸ By his neesings a light doth shine, and his eyes are like the eyelids of the morning. ¹⁹ Out of his mouth go burning lamps, and sparks of fire leap out. ²⁰ Out of his nostrils goeth smoke, as out of a seething pot or caldron. ²¹ His breath kindleth coals, and a flame goeth out of his mouth. ²² In his neck remaineth strength, and sorrow is turned into joy before him. ²³ The flakes of his flesh are joined together: they are firm in themselves; they cannot be moved. ²⁴ His heart is as firm as a stone; yea, as hard as a piece of the nether millstone. ²⁵ When he raiseth up himself, the mighty are afraid: by reason of breakings they purify themselves. ²⁶ The sword of him that layeth at him cannot hold: the spear, the dart, nor the habergeon. ²⁷ He esteemeth iron as straw, and brass as rotten wood. ²⁸ The arrow cannot make him flee: slingstones are turned with him into stubble. ²⁹ Darts are counted as stubble: he laugheth at the shaking of a spear. ³⁰ Sharp stones are under him: he spreadeth sharp pointed things upon the mire. ³¹ He maketh the deep to boil like a pot: he maketh the sea like a pot of ointment. ³² He maketh a path to shine after him; one would think the deep to be hoary. ³³ Upon earth there is not his like, who is made without fear. ³⁴ He beholdeth all high things: he is a king over all the children of pride.

Chapter 42

¹ Then Job answered the Lord, and said, ² I know that thou canst do every thing, and that no thought can be withholden from thee. ³ Who is he that hideth counsel without knowledge? therefore have I uttered that I understood not; things too wonderful for me, which I knew not. ⁴ Hear, I beseech thee, and I will speak:

I will demand of thee, and declare thou unto me. ⁵ I have heard of thee by the hearing of the ear: but now mine eye seeth thee. ⁶ Wherefore I abhor myself, and repent in dust and ashes.

⁷ And it was so, that after the Lord had spoken these words unto Job, the Lord said to Eliphaz the Temanite, My wrath is kindled against thee, and against thy two friends: for ye have not spoken of me the thing that is right, as my servant Job hath. ⁸ Therefore take unto you now seven bullocks and seven rams, and go to my servant Job, and offer up for yourselves a burnt offering; and my servant Job shall pray for you: for him will I accept: lest I deal with you after your folly, in that ye have not spoken of me the thing which is right, like my servant Job. ⁹ So Eliphaz the Temanite and Bildad the Shuhite and Zophar the Naamathite went, and did according as the Lord commanded them: the Lord also accepted Job.

¹⁰ And the Lord turned the captivity of Job, when he prayed for his friends: also the Lord gave Job twice as much as he had before. ¹¹ Then came there unto him all his brethren, and all his sisters, and all they that had been of his acquaintance before, and did eat bread with him in his house: and they bemoaned him, and comforted him over all the evil that the Lord had brought upon him: every man also gave him a piece of money, and every one an earring of gold. ¹² So the Lord blessed the latter end of Job more than his beginning: for he had fourteen thousand sheep, and six thousand camels, and a thousand yoke of oxen, and a thousand she asses. ¹³ He had also seven sons and three daughters. ¹⁴ And he called the name of the first, Jemima; and the name of the second, Kezia; and the name of the third, Kerenhappuch. ¹⁵ And in all the land were no women found so fair as the daughters of Job: and their father gave them inheritance among their brethren. ¹⁶ After this lived Job an hundred and forty years, and saw his sons, and his sons' sons, even four generations. ¹⁷ So Job died, being old and full of days.

Psalms

Psalm 23

A Psalm of David

¹ The Lord is my shepherd; I shall not want.

² He maketh me to lie down in green pastures: he leadeth me beside the still waters.

³ He restoreth my soul: he leadeth me in the paths of righteousness for his name's sake.

⁴ Yea, though I walk through the valley of the shadow of death, I will fear no evil: for thou art with me; thy rod and thy staff they comfort me.

⁵ Thou preparest a table before me in the presence of mine enemies: thou anointest my head with oil; my cup runneth over.

⁶ Surely goodness and mercy shall follow me all the days of my life: and I will dwell in the house of the Lord for ever.

Psalm 90

A Psalm of Moses the man of God

¹ Lord, thou hast been our dwelling place in all generations.

² Before the mountains were brought forth, or ever thou hadst formed the earth and the world, even from everlasting to everlasting, thou art God.

³ Thou turnest man to destruction; and sayest, Return, ye children of men.

⁴ For a thousand years in thy sight are but as yesterday when it is past, and as a watch in the night.

⁵ Thou carriest them away as with a flood; they are as a sleep: in the morning they are like grass which groweth up.

⁶ In the morning it flourisheth, and groweth up; in the evening it is cut down, and withereth.

⁷ For we are consumed by thine anger, and by thy wrath are we troubled.

⁸ Thou hast set our iniquities before thee, our secret sins in the light of thy countenance.

⁹ For all our days are passed away in thy wrath: we spend our years as a tale that is told.

¹⁰ The days of our years are threescore years and ten; and if by reason of strength they be fourscore years, yet is their strength labour and sorrow; for it is soon cut off, and we fly away.

11 Who knoweth the power of thine anger? even according to thy fear, so is thy wrath.

12 So teach us to number our days, that we may apply our hearts unto wisdom.

13 Return, O Lord, how long? and let it repent thee concerning thy servants.

14 O satisfy us early with thy mercy; that we may rejoice and be glad all our days.

15 Make us glad according to the days wherein thou hast afflicted us, and the years wherein we have seen evil.

16 Let thy work appear unto thy servants, and thy glory unto their children.

17 And let the beauty of the Lord our God be upon us: and establish thou the work of our hands upon us; yea, the work of our hands establish thou it.

Psalm 148

1 Praise ye the Lord. Praise ye the Lord from the heavens: praise him in the heights.

2 Praise ye him, all his angels: praise ye him, all his hosts.

3 Praise ye him, sun and moon: praise him, all ye stars of light.

4 Praise him, ye heavens of heavens, and ye waters that be above the heavens.

5 Let them praise the name of the Lord: for he commanded, and they were created.

6 He hath also stablished them for ever and ever: he hath made a decree which shall not pass.

7 Praise the Lord from the earth, ye dragons, and all deeps:

8 Fire, and hail; snow, and vapour; stormy wind fulfilling his word:

9 Mountains, and all hills; fruitful trees, and all cedars:

10 Beasts, and all cattle; creeping things, and flying fowl:

11 Kings of the earth, and all people; princes, and all judges of the earth:

12 Both young men, and maidens; old men, and children:

13 Let them praise the name of the Lord: for his name alone is excellent; his glory is above the earth and heaven.

14 He also exalteth the horn of his people, the praise of all his saints; even of the children of Israel, a people near unto him. Praise ye the Lord.

Ecclesiastes

Chapter 1

¹ The words of the Preacher, the son of David, king in Jerusalem. ² Vanity of vanities, saith the Preacher, vanity of vanities; all is vanity. ³ What profit hath a man of all his labour which he taketh under the sun?

⁴ One generation passeth away, and another generation cometh: but the earth abideth for ever. ⁵ The sun also ariseth, and the sun goeth down, and hasteth to his place where he arose. ⁶ The wind goeth toward the south, and turneth about unto the north; it whirleth about continually, and the wind returneth again according to his circuits. ⁷ All the rivers run into the sea; yet the sea is not full; unto the place from whence the rivers come, thither they return again. ⁸ All things are full of labour; man cannot utter it: the eye is not satisfied with seeing, nor the ear filled with hearing.

⁹ The thing that hath been, it is that which shall be; and that which is done is that which shall be done: and there is no new thing under the sun. ¹⁰ Is there any thing whereof it may be said, See, this is new? it hath been already of old time, which was before us. ¹¹ There is no remembrance of former things; neither shall there be any remembrance of things that are to come with those that shall come after.

¹² I the Preacher was king over Israel in Jerusalem. ¹³ And I gave my heart to seek and search out by wisdom concerning all things that are done under heaven: this sore travail hath God given to the sons of man to be exercised therewith. ¹⁴ I have seen all the works that are done under the sun; and, behold, all is vanity and vexation of spirit. ¹⁵ That which is crooked cannot be made straight: and that which is wanting cannot be numbered. ¹⁶ I communed with mine own hearth, saying, Lo, I am come to great estate, and have gotten more wisdom than all they that have been before me in Jerusalem: yea, my heart had great experience of wisdom and knowledge. ¹⁷ And I gave my heart to know wisdom, and to know madness and folly: I perceived that this also is vexation of spirit. ¹⁸ For in much wisdom is much grief: and he that increaseth knowledge increaseth sorrow.

Chapter 2

¹ I said in mine heart, Go to now, I will prove thee with mirth, therefore enjoy pleasure: and, behold, this also is vanity. ² I said of laughter, It is mad: and of mirth, What doeth it? ³ I sought in mine heart to give myself unto wine, yet acquainting mine heart with wisdom; and to lay hold on folly, till I might see what was that good for the sons of men, which they should do under the heaven all the days of their life. ⁴ I made me great works; I builded me houses; I planted me vineyards: ⁵ I made me gardens and orchards, and I planted trees in them of all kind of fruits: ⁶ I made me pools of water, to water therewith the wood that bringeth forth trees: ⁷ I got me servants and maidens, and had servants born in my house; also I had great possessions of great and small cattle above all that were in Jerusalem before me: ⁸ I gathered me also silver and gold, and the peculiar treasure of kings and of the provinces: I gat me men singers and women singers, and the delights of the sons of men, as musical instruments, and that of all sorts. ⁹ So I was great, and increased more that all that were before me in Jerusalem: also my wisdom remained with me. ¹⁰ And whatsoever mine eyes desired I kept not from them, I withheld not my heart from any joy; for my heart rejoiced in all my labour: and this was my portion of all my labour. ¹¹ Then I looked on all the works that my hands had wrought, and on the labour that I had laboured to do: and, behold, all was vanity and vexation of spirit, and there was no profit under the sun.

¹² And I turned myself to behold wisdom, and madness, and folly: for what can the man do that cometh after the king? even that which hath already been done. ¹³ Then I saw that wisdom excelleth folly, as far as light excelleth darkness. ¹⁴ The wise man's eyes are in his head; but the fool walketh in darkness: and I perceived also that one event happeneth to them all. ¹⁵ Then I said in my heart, As it happeneth to the fool, so it happeneth even to me; and why was I then more wise? Then I said in my heart, that this also is vanity. ¹⁶ For there is no remembrance of the wise more than of the fool for ever; seeing that which now is in the days to come shall all be forgotten. And how dieth the wise man? as the fool.

[17] Therefore I hated life; because the work that is wrought under the sun is grievous unto me: for all is vanity and vexation of spirit.

[18] Yea, I hated all my labour which I had taken under the sun: because I should leave it unto the man that shall be after me. [19] And who knoweth whether he shall be a wise man or a fool? yet shall he have rule over all my labour wherein I have laboured, and wherein I have shewed myself wise under the sun. This is also vanity. [20] Therefore I went about to cause my heart to despair of all the labour which I took under the sun. [21] For there is a man whose labour is in wisdom, and in knowledge, and in equity; yet to a man that hath not laboured therein shall he leave it for his portion. This also is vanity and a great evil. [22] For what hath man of all his labour, and of the vexation of his heart, wherein he hath laboured under the sun? [23] For all his days are sorrows, and his travail grief; yea, his heart taketh not rest in the night. This is also vanity.

[24] There is nothing better for a man, than that he should eat and drink, and that he should make his soul enjoy good in his labour. This also I saw, that it was from the hand of God. [25] For who can eat, or who else can hasten hereunto, more than I? [26] For God giveth to a man that is good in his sight wisdom, and knowledge, and joy: but to the sinner he giveth travail, to gather and to heap up, that he may give to him that is good before God. This also is vanity and vexation of spirit.

Chapter 3

[1] To every thing there is a season, and a time to every purpose under the heaven: [2] A time to be born, and a time to die; a time to plant, and a time to pluck up that which is planted; [3] A time to kill, and a time to heal; a time to break down, and a time to build up; [4] A time to weep, and a time to laugh; a time to mourn, and a time to dance; [5] A time to cast away stones, and a time to gather stones together; a time to embrace, and a time to refrain from embracing; [6] A time to get, and a time to lose; a time to keep, and a time to cast away; [7] A time to rend, and a time to sew; a time to keep silence, and a time to speak; [8] A time to love, and a time to hate; a time of war, and a time of peace. [9] What profit hath he that

worketh in that wherein he laboureth? 10 I have seen the travail, which God hath given to the sons of men to be exercised in it.

11 He hath made every thing beautiful in his time: also he hath set the world in their heart, so that no man can find out the work that God maketh from the beginning to the end. 12 I know that there is no good in them, but for a man to rejoice, and to do good in his life. 13 And also that every man should eat and drink, and enjoy the good of all his labour, it is the gift of God. 14 I know that, whatsoever God doeth, it shall be for ever: nothing can be put to it, nor any thing taken from it: and God doeth it, that men should fear before him. 15 That which hath been is now; and that which is to be hath already been; and God requireth that which is past.

16 And moreover I saw under the sun the place of judgment, that wickedness was there; and the place of righteousness, that iniquity was there. 17 I said in mine heart, God shall judge the righteous and the wicked: for there is a time there for every purpose and for every work. 18 I said in mine heart concerning the estate of the sons of men, that God might manifest them, and that they might see that they themselves are beasts. 19 For that which befalleth the sons of men befalleth beasts; even one thing befalleth them: as the one dieth, so dieth the other; yea, they have all one breath; so that a man hath no preeminence above a beast: for all is vanity. 20 All go unto one place; all are of the dust, and all turn to dust again. 21 Who knoweth the spirit of man that goeth upward, and the spirit of the beast that goeth downward to the earth? 22 Wherefore I perceive that there is nothing better, than that a man should rejoice in his own works; for that is his portion: for who shall bring him to see what shall be after him?

• • •

Chapter 12

1 Remember now thy Creator in the days of thy youth, while the evil days come not, nor the years draw nigh, when thou shalt say, I have no pleasure in them; 2 While the sun, or the light, or the moon, or the stars, be not darkened, nor the clouds return after the rain: 3 In the day when the keepers of the house shall tremble, and the strong men shall bow themselves, and the grinders cease because they are few, and those that look out of the

windows be darkened, 4 And the doors shall be shut in the streets, when the sound of the grinding is low, and he shall rise up at the voice of the bird, and all the daughters of musick shall be brought low; 5 Also when they shall be afraid of that which is high, and fears shall be in the way, and the almond tree shall flourish, and the grasshopper shall be a burden, and desire shall fail: because man goeth to his long home, and the mourners go about the streets: 6 Or ever the silver cord be loosed, or the golden bowl be broken, or the pitcher be broken at the fountain, or the wheel broken at the cistern. 7 Then shall the dust return to the earth as it was: and the spirit shall return unto God who gave it.

8 Vanity of vanities, saith the preacher; all is vanity. 9 And moreover, because the preacher was wise, he still taught the people knowledge; yea, he gave good heed, and sought out, and set in order many proverbs. 10 The preacher sought to find out acceptable words: and that which was written was upright, even words of truth. 11 The words of the wise are as goads, and as nails fastened by the masters of assemblies, which are given from one shepherd. 12 And further, by these, my son, be admonished: of making many books there is no end; and much study is a weariness of the flesh.

13 Let us hear the conclusion of the whole matter: Fear God, and keep his commandments: for this is the whole duty of man. 14 For God shall bring every work into judgment, with every secret thing, whether it be good, or whether it be evil.

The *Iliad*

Excerpts from:
Book I
Book XVI
Book XXII
Book XXIV

Homer

Dating to approximately the 8th Century BCE, the Iliad is the oldest work of Western literature and is considered by many the greatest. A long epic poem, depicting the men of a heroic age in conflict with one another, loved and protected or hated and betrayed by the gods, it tells of a particular period in the ten-year war between the Achaeans and the Trojans over the possession of the most beautiful woman in the world. The narration begins with the anger of the greatest of the Greek heroes, Achilles, and ends with the death and funeral of the greatest of the Trojan heroes, Hector. In between, in perhaps the most effective combination of vivid dramatic intensity and cool detachment, immediacy and perspective, subtlety and power in all Western literature, it provides an image of man in his condition as subject to the immortal gods and to the myriad forces of his own thoughts, emotions, and actions under the perennial threat of death and meaninglessness. For the Greek imagination, informed by Homer for a thousand years from the archaic through the Hellenistic period, human life in the world is an agon, *a contest, ending inevitably in death. The only lasting meaning lies in the heroism of winning that contest, which can be accomplished only by those who possess the quality of* arete *or excellence, comprising the virtues of strength, courage, self-control, reverence of the gods, artfulness, and self-confidence. The reward is to earn the only immortality available to man—a place in the story.*

Above: Achilles tending Patroclus wounded by an arrow, attributed to Sosias, 500BCE, Tondo of an Attic red-figure kylix.

Composed ca. 8th century, BCE; translated by Samuel Butler, 1898

Book I (Greek lines 1–222)

Sing, O goddess, the anger of Achilles son of Peleus, that brought countless ills upon the Achaeans. Many a brave soul did it send hurrying down to Hades, and many a hero did it yield a prey to dogs and vultures, for so were the counsels of Zeus fulfilled from the day on which the son of Atreus, king of men, and great Achilles, first fell out with one another.

And which of the gods was it that set them on to quarrel? It was the son of Zeus and Leto; for he was angry with the king and sent a pestilence upon the host to plague the people, because the son of Atreus had dishonored Chryses his priest. Now Chryses had come to the ships of the Achaeans to free his daughter, and had brought with him a great ransom: moreover he bore in his hand the scepter of Apollo wreathed with a suppliant's wreath, and he besought the Achaeans, but most of all the two sons of Atreus, who were their chiefs.

"Sons of Atreus," he cried, "and all other Achaeans, may the gods who dwell in Olympus grant you to sack the city of Priam, and to reach your homes in safety; but free my daughter, and accept a ransom for her, in reverence to Apollo, son of Zeus."

On this the rest of the Achaeans with one voice were for respecting the priest and taking the ransom that he offered; but not so Agamemnon, who spoke fiercely to him and sent him roughly away. "Old man," said he, "let me not find you tarrying about our ships, nor yet coming hereafter. Your scepter of the god and your wreath shall profit you nothing. I will not free her. She shall grow old in my house at Argos far from her own home, busying herself with her loom and visiting my couch; so go, and do not provoke me or it shall be the worse for you."

The old man feared him and obeyed. Not a word he spoke, but went by the shore of the sounding sea and prayed apart to King Apollo whom lovely Leto had borne. "Hear me," he cried, "O god of the silver bow, that protects Chryse and holy Cilla and rules Tenedos with thy might, hear me oh thou of Sminthe. If I have ever decked your temple with garlands, or burned your thigh-bones in fat of bulls or goats, grant my prayer, and let your arrows avenge these my tears upon the Danaans."

Thus did he pray, and Apollo heard his prayer. He came down furious from the summits of Olympus, with his bow and his quiver upon his shoulder, and the arrows rattled on his back with the rage that trembled within him. He sat himself down away from the ships with a face as dark as night, and his silver bow rang death as he shot his arrow in the midst of them. First he smote their mules and their hounds, but presently he aimed his shafts at the people themselves, and all day long the pyres of the dead were burning.

For nine whole days he shot his arrows among the people, but upon the tenth day Achilles called them in assembly—moved thereto by Hera, who saw the Achaeans in their death-throes and had compassion upon them. Then, when they were got together, he rose and spoke among them.

"Son of Atreus," said he, "I deem that we should now turn roving home if we would escape destruction, for we are being cut down by war and pestilence at once. Let us ask some priest or prophet, or some reader of dreams (for dreams, too, are of Zeus) who can tell us why Phoebus Apollo is so angry, and say whether it is for some vow that we have broken, or hecatomb that we have not offered, and whether he will accept the savor of lambs and goats without blemish, so as to take away the plague from us."

With these words he sat down, and Calchas son of Thestor, wisest of augurs, who knew things past present and to come, rose to speak. He it was who had guided the Achaeans with their fleet to Ilius, through the prophesyings with which Phoebus Apollo had inspired him. With all sincerity and goodwill he addressed them thus:—

"Achilles, loved of heaven, you bid me tell you about the anger of King Apollo, I will therefore do so; but consider first and swear that you will stand by me heartily in word and deed, for I know that I shall offend one who rules the Argives with might, to whom all the Achaeans are in subjection. A plain man cannot stand against the anger of a king, who if he swallow his displeasure now, will yet nurse revenge till he has wreaked it. Consider, therefore, whether or no you will protect me."

And Achilles answered, "Fear not, but speak as it is borne in upon you from heaven, for by Apollo, Calchas, to whom you pray, and whose oracles you reveal to us, not a Danaan at our ships shall lay his hand upon you, while I yet live to look upon the face of the earth—no, not though you name Agamemnon himself, who is by far the foremost of the Achaeans."

Thereon the seer spoke boldly. "The god," he said, "is angry neither about vow nor hecatomb, but for his priest's sake, whom Agamemnon has dishonored, in that he would not free his daughter nor take a ransom for her; therefore has he sent these evils upon us, and will yet send others. He will not deliver the Danaans from this pestilence till Agamemnon has restored the girl without fee or ransom to her father, and has sent a holy hecatomb to Chryse. Thus we may perhaps appease him."

With these words he sat down, and Agamemnon rose in anger. His heart was black with rage, and his eyes flashed fire as he scowled on Calchas and said, "Seer of evil, you never yet prophesied smooth things concerning me, but have ever loved to foretell that which was evil. You have brought me neither comfort nor performance; and now you come seeing among Danaans, and saying that Apollo has plagued us because I would not take a ransom for this girl, the daughter of Chryses. I have set my heart on keeping her in my own house, for I love her better even than my own wife Clytemnestra, whose peer she is alike in form and feature, in understanding and accomplishments. Still I will give her up if I must, for I would have the people live, not die; but you must find me a prize instead, or I alone among the Argives shall be without one. This is not well; for you behold, all of you, that my prize goes elsewhere."

And Achilles answered, "Most noble son of Atreus, covetous beyond all mankind, how shall the Achaeans find you another prize? We have no common store from which to take one. Those we took from the cities have been awarded; we cannot disallow the awards that have been made already. Give this girl, therefore, to the god, and if ever Zeus grants us to sack the city of Troy we will requite you three and fourfold."

Then Agamemnon said, "Achilles, valiant though you be, you shall not thus outwit me. You shall not overreach and you shall not persuade me. Are you to keep your own prize, while I sit tamely under my loss and give up the girl at your bidding? Let the Achaeans find me a prize in fair exchange to my liking, or I will come and take your own, or that of Ajax or of Ulysses; and he to whomsoever I may come shall rue my coming. But of this we will take thought hereafter; for the present, let us draw a ship into the sea, and find a crew for her expressly; let us put a hecatomb on board, and let us send Chryseis also; further, let some chief man among us be in command, either Ajax, or Idomeneus, or yourself, son of Peleus, mighty warrior that you are, that we may offer sacrifice and appease the anger of the god."

Achilles scowled at him and answered, "You are steeped in insolence and lust of gain. With what heart can any of the Achaeans do your bidding, either on foray or in open fighting? I came not warring here for any ill the Trojans had done me. I have no quarrel with them. They have not raided my cattle nor my horses, nor cut down my harvests on the rich plains of Phthia; for between me and them there is a great space, both mountain and sounding sea. We have followed you, Sir Insolence! for your pleasure, not ours—to gain satisfaction from the Trojans for your shameless self and for Menelaus. You forget this, and threaten to rob me of the prize for which I have toiled, and which the sons of the Achaeans have given me. Never when the Achaeans sack any rich city of the Trojans do I receive so good a prize as you do, though it is my hands that do the better part of the fighting. When the sharing comes, your share is far the largest, and I, forsooth, must go back to my ships, take what I can get and be thankful, when my labour of fighting is done. Now, therefore, I shall go back to Phthia; it will be much better for me to return home with my ships, for I will not stay here dishonored to gather gold and substance for you."

And Agamemnon answered, "Fly if you will, I shall make you no prayers to stay you. I have others here who will do me honor, and above all Zeus, the lord of counsel. There is no king here so hateful to me as you are, for you are ever quarrelsome and ill-affected. What though you be brave? Was it not heaven that made you so? Go home, then, with your ships and comrades to lord it over the Myrmidons. I care neither for you nor for your anger; and thus will I do: since Phoebus Apollo is taking Chryseis from me, I shall send her with my ship and my followers, but I shall come to your tent and take your own prize Briseis, that you may learn how much stronger I am than you are, and that another may fear to set himself up as equal or comparable with me."

The son of Peleus was furious, and his heart within his shaggy breast was divided whether to draw his sword, push the others aside, and kill the son of Atreus, or to restrain himself and check his anger. While he was thus in two minds, and was drawing his mighty sword from its scabbard, Athena came down from heaven (for Hera had sent her in the love she bore to them both), and seized the son of Peleus by his yellow hair, visible to him alone, for of the others no man could see her. Achilles turned in amaze, and by the fire that flashed from her eyes at once knew that she was Athena. "Why are you here," said he, "daughter of aegis-bearing Zeus? To see the pride of Agamemnon, son of Atreus? Let me tell you—and it shall surely be—he shall pay for this insolence with his life."

And Athena said, "I come from heaven, if you will hear me, to bid you stay your anger. Hera has sent me, who cares for both of you alike. Cease, then, this brawling, and do not draw your sword; rail at him if you will, and your railing will not be vain, for I tell you—and it shall surely be—that you shall hereafter receive gifts three times as splendid by reason of this present insult. Hold, therefore, and obey."

"Goddess," answered Achilles, "however angry a man may be, he must do as you two command him. This will be best, for the gods ever hear the prayers of him who has obeyed them."

He stayed his hand on the silver hilt of his sword, and thrust it back into the scabbard as Athena bade him. Then she went back to Olympus among the other gods, and to the house of aegis-bearing Zeus.

Book XVI (Greek Lines 780–867)

So long as the sun was still high in mid-heaven the weapons of either side were alike deadly, and the people fell; but when he went down towards the time when men loose their oxen, the Achaeans proved to be beyond all forecast stronger, so that they drew Cebriones out of range of the darts and tumult of the Trojans, and stripped the armor from his shoulders. Then Patroclus sprang like Ares with fierce intent and a terrific shout upon the Trojans, and thrice did he kill nine men; but as he was coming on like a god for a time, then, O Patroclus, was the hour of your end approaching, for Phoebus fought you in fell earnest. Patroclus did not see him as he moved about in the crush, for he was enshrouded in thick darkness, and the god struck him from behind on his back and his broad shoulders with the flat of his hand, so that his eyes turned dizzy. Phoebus Apollo beat the helmet from off his head, and it rolled rattling off under the horses' feet, where its horse-hair plumes were all begrimed with dust and blood. Never indeed had that helmet fared so before, for it had served to protect the head and comely forehead of the godlike hero Achilles. Now, however, Zeus delivered it over to be worn by Hector. Nevertheless the end of Hector also was near. The bronze-shod spear, so great and so strong, was broken in the hand of Patroclus, while his shield that covered him from head to foot fell to the ground as did also the band that held it, and Apollo undid the fastenings of his breastplate.

On this his mind became clouded; his limbs failed him, and he stood as one dazed; whereon Euphorbus son of Panthous a Dardanian, the best spearman of his time, as also the finest horseman and fleetest runner, came behind him and struck him in the back with a spear, midway between the shoulders. This man as soon as ever he had come up with his chariot had dismounted twenty men, so proficient was he in all the arts of war—he it was, O knight Patroclus, that first drove a weapon into you, but he did not quite overpower you. Euphorbus then ran back into the crowd, after drawing his ashen spear out of the wound; he would not stand firm and wait for Patroclus, unarmed though he now was, to attack him; but Patroclus unnerved, alike by the blow the god had given him and by the spear-wound, drew back under cover of his men in fear for his life. Hector on this, seeing him to be wounded and giving ground, forced his way through the ranks, and when close up with him struck him in the lower part of the belly with a spear, driving the bronze point right through it, so that he fell heavily to the ground to the great grief of the Achaeans. As when a lion has fought some fierce wild-boar and worsted him—the two fight furiously upon the mountains over some little fountain at which they would both drink, and the lion has beaten the boar till he can hardly breathe—even so did Hector son of Priam take the life of the brave son of Menoetius who had killed so many, striking him from close at hand, and vaunting over him the while. "Patroclus," said he, "you deemed that you should sack our city, rob our Trojan women of their freedom, and carry them off in your ships to your own country. Fool; Hector and his fleet horses were ever straining their utmost to defend them. I am foremost of all the Trojan warriors to stave the day of bondage from off them; as for you, vultures shall devour you here. Poor wretch, Achilles with all his bravery availed you nothing; and yet I ween when you left him he charged you straitly saying, 'Come not back to the ships, knight Patroclus, till you have rent the bloodstained shirt of murderous Hector about his body.' Thus I ween did he charge you, and your fool's heart answered him 'yea' within you."

Then, as the life ebbed out of you, you answered, O knight Patroclus: "Hector, vaunt as you will, for Zeus the son of Cronus and Apollo have vouchsafed you victory; it is they who have vanquished me so easily, and they who have stripped the armor from my shoulders; had twenty such men as you attacked me, all of them would have fallen before my spear. Fate and the son of Leto have overpowered me, and among mortal men Euphorbus; you are yourself third only in the killing of me. I say further, and lay my saying to your heart, you too shall live but for a little season; death and the day of your doom are close upon you, and they will lay you low by the hand of Achilles son of Aeacus."

When he had thus spoken his eyes were closed in death, his soul left his body and flitted down to the house of Hades, mourning its sad fate and bidding farewell to the youth and vigor of its manhood. Dead though he was, Hector still spoke to him saying, "Patroclus, why should you thus foretell my doom? Who knows but Achilles, son of lovely Thetis, may be smitten by my spear and die before me?"

As he spoke he drew the bronze spear from the wound, planting his foot upon the body, which he thrust off and let lie on its back. He then went spear in hand after Automedon, squire of the fleet descendant of Aeacus, for he longed to lay him low, but the immortal steeds which the gods had given as a rich gift to Peleus bore him swiftly from the field.

Book XXII (Greek Lines 1–375)

Thus the Trojans in the city, scared like fawns, wiped the sweat from off them and drank to quench their thirst, leaning against the goodly battlements, while the Achaeans with their shields laid upon their shoulders drew close up to the walls. But stern fate bade Hector stay where he was before Ilius and the Scaean gates. Then Phoebus Apollo spoke to the son of Peleus saying, "Why, son of Peleus, do you, who are but man, give chase to me who am immortal? Have you not yet found out that it is a god whom you pursue so furiously? You did not harass the Trojans whom you had routed, and now they are within their walls, while you have been decoyed hither away from them. Me you cannot kill, for death can take no hold upon me."

Achilles was greatly angered and said, "You have baulked me, Far-Darter, most malicious of all gods, and have drawn me away from the wall, where many another man would have bitten the dust ere he got within Ilius; you have robbed me of great glory and have saved the Trojans at no risk to yourself, for you have nothing to fear, but I would indeed have my revenge if it were in my power to do so."

On this, with fell intent he made towards the city, and as the winning horse in a chariot race strains every nerve when he is flying over the plain, even so fast and furiously did the limbs of Achilles bear him onwards. King Priam was first to note him as he scoured the plain, all radiant as the star which men call Orion's Hound, and whose beams blaze forth in time of harvest more brilliantly than those of any other that shines by night; brightest of them all though he be, he yet bodes ill for mortals, for he brings fire and fever in his train—even so did Achilles' armor gleam on his breast as he sped onwards. Priam raised a cry and beat his head with his hands as he lifted them up and shouted out to his dear son, imploring him to return; but Hector still stayed before the gates, for his heart was set upon doing battle with Achilles. The old man reached out his arms towards him and bade him for pity's sake come within the walls. "Hector," he cried, "my son, stay not to face this man alone and unsupported, or you will meet death at the hands of the son of Peleus, for he is mightier than you. Monster that he is; would indeed that the gods loved him no better than I do, for so, dogs and vultures would soon

devour him as he lay stretched on earth, and a load of grief would
be lifted from my heart, for many a brave son has he reft from me,
either by killing them or selling them away in the islands that are
beyond the sea: even now I miss two sons from among the
Trojans who have thronged within the city, Lycaon and
Polydorus, whom Laothoe peeress among women bore me.
Should they be still alive and in the hands of the Achaeans, we
will ransom them with gold and bronze, of which we have store,
for the old man Altes endowed his daughter richly; but if they are
already dead and in the house of Hades, sorrow will it be to us
two who were their parents; albeit the grief of others will be more
short-lived unless you too perish at the hands of Achilles. Come,
then, my son, within the city, to be the guardian of Trojan men
and Trojan women, or you will both lose your own life and afford
a mighty triumph to the son of Peleus. Have pity also on your
unhappy father while life yet remains to him—on me, whom the
son of Cronus will destroy by a terrible doom on the threshold of
old age, after I have seen my sons slain and my daughters haled
away as captives, my bridal chambers pillaged, little children
dashed to earth amid the rage of battle, and my sons' wives
dragged away by the cruel hands of the Achaeans; in the end
fierce hounds will tear me in pieces at my own gates after some
one has beaten the life out of my body with sword or spear-
hounds that I myself reared and fed at my own table to guard my
gates, but who will yet lap my blood and then lie all distraught at
my doors. When a young man falls by the sword in battle, he may
lie where he is and there is nothing unseemly; let what will be
seen, all is honorable in death, but when an old man is slain there
is nothing in this world more pitiable than that dogs should defile
his grey hair and beard and all that men hide for shame."

The old man tore his grey hair as he spoke, but he moved not
the heart of Hector. His mother hard by wept and moaned aloud
as she bared her bosom and pointed to the breast which had
suckled him. "Hector," she cried, weeping bitterly the while,
"Hector, my son, spurn not this breast, but have pity upon me
too: if I have ever given you comfort from my own bosom, think
on it now, dear son, and come within the wall to protect us from
this man; stand not without to meet him. Should the wretch kill
you, neither I nor your richly dowered wife shall ever weep, dear

offshoot of myself, over the bed on which you lie, for dogs will devour you at the ships of the Achaeans."

Thus did the two with many tears implore their son, but they moved not the heart of Hector, and he stood his ground awaiting huge Achilles as he drew nearer towards him. As a serpent in its den upon the mountains, full fed with deadly poisons, waits for the approach of man—he is filled with fury and his eyes glare terribly as he goes writhing round his den—even so Hector leaned his shield against a tower that jutted out from the wall and stood where he was, undaunted.

"Alas," said he to himself in the heaviness of his heart, "if I go within the gates, Polydamas will be the first to heap reproach upon me, for it was he that urged me to lead the Trojans back to the city on that awful night when Achilles again came forth against us. I would not listen, but it would have been indeed better if I had done so. Now that my folly has destroyed the host, I dare not look Trojan men and Trojan women in the face, lest a worse man should say, 'Hector has ruined us by his self-confidence.' Surely it would be better for me to return after having fought Achilles and slain him, or to die gloriously here before the city. What, again, if I were to lay down my shield and helmet, lean my spear against the wall and go straight up to noble Achilles? What if I were to promise to give up Helen, who was the fountainhead of all this war, and all the treasure that Alexandrus brought with him in his ships to Troy, aye, and to let the Achaeans divide the half of everything that the city contains among themselves? I might make the Trojans, by the mouths of their princes, take a solemn oath that they would hide nothing, but would divide into two shares all that is within the city—but why argue with myself in this way? Were I to go up to him he would show me no kind of mercy; he would kill me then and there as easily as though I were a woman, when I had off my armor. There is no parleying with him from some rock or oak tree as young men and maidens prattle with one another. Better fight him at once, and learn to which of us Zeus will vouchsafe victory."

Thus did he stand and ponder, but Achilles came up to him as it were Mars himself, plumed lord of battle. From his right shoulder he brandished his terrible spear of Pelian ash, and the bronze gleamed around him like flashing fire or the rays of the rising sun. Fear fell upon Hector as he beheld him, and he dared not stay longer where he was but fled in dismay from before the gates, while Achilles darted after him at his utmost speed. As a mountain falcon, swiftest of all birds, swoops down upon some cowering dove—the dove flies before him but the falcon with a shrill scream follows close after, resolved to have her—even so did Achilles make straight for Hector with all his might, while Hector fled under the Trojan wall as fast as his limbs could take him.

On they flew along the wagon-road that ran hard by under the wall, past the lookout station, and past the weather-beaten wild fig-tree, till they came to two fair springs which feed the river Scamander. One of these two springs is warm, and steam rises from it as smoke from a burning fire, but the other even in summer is as cold as hail or snow, or the ice that forms on water. Here, hard by the springs, are the goodly washing-troughs of stone, where in the time of peace before the coming of the Achaeans the wives and fair daughters of the Trojans used to wash their clothes. Past these did they fly, the one in front and the other giving chase behind him: good was the man that fled, but better far was he that followed after, and swiftly indeed did they run, for the prize was no mere beast for sacrifice or bullock's hide, as it might be for a common foot-race, but they ran for the life of Hector. As horses in a chariot race speed round the turning-posts when they are running for some great prize—a tripod or woman —at the games in honor of some dead hero, so did these two run full speed three times round the city of Priam. All the gods watched them, and the sire of gods and men was the first to speak.

"Alas," said he, "my eyes behold a man who is dear to me being pursued round the walls of Troy; my heart is full of pity for Hector, who has burned the thigh-bones of many a heifer in my honor, one while on the crests of many-valleyed Ida, and again on the citadel of Troy; and now I see noble Achilles in full pursuit of him round the city of Priam. What say you? Consider among yourselves and decide whether we shall now save him or let him fall, valiant though he be, before Achilles, son of Peleus."

Then Athena said, "Father, wielder of the lightning, lord of cloud and storm, what mean you? Would you pluck this mortal whose doom has long been decreed out of the jaws of death? Do as you will, but we others shall not be of a mind with you."

And Zeus answered, "My child, Trito-born, take heart. I did not speak in full earnest, and I will let you have your way. Do without let or hindrance as you are minded."

Thus did he urge Athena who was already eager, and down she darted from the topmost summits of Olympus.

Achilles was still in full pursuit of Hector, as a hound chasing a fawn which he has started from its covert on the mountains, and hunts through glade and thicket. The fawn may try to elude him by crouching under cover of a bush, but he will scent her out and follow her up until he gets her—even so there was no escape for Hector from the fleet son of Peleus. Whenever he made a set to get near the Dardanian gates and under the walls, that his people might help him by showering down weapons from above, Achilles would gain on him and head him back towards the plain, keeping himself always on the city side. As a man in a dream who fails to lay hands upon another whom he is pursuing—the one cannot escape nor the other overtake—even so neither could Achilles come up with Hector, nor Hector break away from Achilles; nevertheless he might even yet have escaped death had not the time come when Apollo, who thus far had sustained his strength and nerved his running, was now no longer to stay by him. Achilles made signs to the Achaean host, and shook his head to show that no man was to aim a dart at Hector, lest another might win the glory of having hit him and he might himself come in second. Then, at last, as they were nearing the fountains for the fourth time, the father of all balanced his golden scales and placed a doom in each of them, one for Achilles and the other for Hector. As he held the scales by the middle, the doom of Hector fell down deep into the house of Hades—and then Phoebus Apollo left him. Thereon Athena went close up to the son of Peleus and said, "Noble Achilles, favored of heaven, we two shall surely take back to the ships a triumph for the Achaeans by slaying Hector, for all his lust of battle. Do what Apollo may as he lies groveling before his father, aegis-bearing Zeus, Hector cannot escape us longer. Stay here and take breath, while I go up to him and persuade him to make a stand and fight you."

Thus spoke Athena. Achilles obeyed her gladly, and stood still, leaning on his bronze-pointed ashen spear, while Athena left him and went after Hector in the form and with the voice of Deiphobus. She came close up to him and said, "Dear brother, I see you are hard pressed by Achilles who is chasing you at full speed round the city of Priam, let us await his onset and stand on our defense."

And Hector answered, "Deiphobus, you have always been dearest to me of all my brothers, children of Hecuba and Priam, but henceforth I shall rate you yet more highly, inasmuch as you have ventured outside the wall for my sake when all the others remain inside."

Then Athena said, "Dear brother, my father and mother went down on their knees and implored me, as did all my comrades, to remain inside, so great a fear has fallen upon them all; but I was in an agony of grief when I beheld you; now, therefore, let us two make a stand and fight, and let there be no keeping our spears in reserve, that we may learn whether Achilles shall kill us and bear off our spoils to the ships, or whether he shall fall before you."

Thus did Athena inveigle him by her cunning, and when the two were now close to one another great Hector was first to speak. "I will no longer fly you, son of Peleus," said he, "as I have been doing hitherto. Three times have I fled round the mighty city of Priam, without daring to withstand you, but now, let me either slay or be slain, for I am in the mind to face you. Let us, then, give pledges to one another by our gods, who are the fittest witnesses and guardians of all covenants; let it be agreed between us that if Zeus vouchsafes me the longer stay and I take your life, I am not to treat your dead body in any unseemly fashion, but when I have stripped you of your armor, I am to give up your body to the Achaeans. And do you likewise."

Achilles glared at him and answered, "Fool, prate not to me about covenants. There can be no covenants between men and lions, wolves and lambs can never be of one mind, but hate each other out and out all through. Therefore there can be no understanding between you and me, nor may there be any covenants between us, till one or other shall fall and glut grim Mars with his life's blood. Put forth all your strength; you have need now to prove yourself indeed a bold soldier and man of war.

You have no more chance, and Pallas Athena will forthwith vanquish you by my spear: you shall now pay me in full for the grief you have caused me on account of my comrades whom you have killed in battle."

He poised his spear as he spoke and hurled it. Hector saw it coming and avoided it; he watched it and crouched down so that it flew over his head and stuck in the ground beyond; Athena then snatched it up and gave it back to Achilles without Hector's seeing her; Hector thereon said to the son of Peleus, "You have missed your aim, Achilles, peer of the gods, and Zeus has not yet revealed to you the hour of my doom, though you made sure that he had done so. You were a false-tongued liar when you deemed that I should forget my valor and quail before you. You shall not drive your spear into the back of a runaway—drive it, should heaven so grant you power, drive it into me as I make straight towards you; and now for your own part avoid my spear if you can—would that you might receive the whole of it into your body; if you were once dead the Trojans would find the war an easier matter, for it is you who have harmed them most."

He poised his spear as he spoke and hurled it. His aim was true for he hit the middle of Achilles' shield, but the spear rebounded from it, and did not pierce it. Hector was angry when he saw that the weapon had sped from his hand in vain, and stood there in dismay for he had no second spear. With a loud cry he called Deiphobus and asked him for one, but there was no man; then he saw the truth and said to himself, "Alas! the gods have lured me on to my destruction. I deemed that the hero Deiphobus was by my side, but he is within the wall, and Athena has inveigled me; death is now indeed exceedingly near at hand and there is no way out of it—for so Zeus and his son Apollo the far-darter have willed it, though heretofore they have been ever ready to protect me. My doom has come upon me; let me not then die ingloriously and without a struggle, but let me first do some great thing that shall be told among men hereafter."

As he spoke he drew the keen blade that hung so great and strong by his side, and gathering himself together be sprang on Achilles like a soaring eagle which swoops down from the clouds on to some lamb or timid hare—even so did Hector brandish his sword and spring upon Achilles. Achilles mad with rage darted towards him, with his wondrous shield before his breast, and his gleaming helmet, made with four layers of metal, nodding fiercely forward. The thick tresses of gold with which Vulcan had crested the helmet floated round it, and as the evening star that shines brighter than all others through the stillness of night, even such was the gleam of the spear which Achilles poised in his right hand, fraught with the death of noble Hector. He eyed his fair flesh over and over to see where he could best wound it, but all was protected by the goodly armor of which Hector had spoiled Patroclus after he had slain him, save only the throat where the collar-bones divide the neck from the shoulders, and this is a most deadly place: here then did Achilles strike him as he was coming on towards him, and the point of his spear went right through the fleshy part of the neck, but it did not sever his windpipe so that he could still speak. Hector fell headlong, and Achilles vaunted over him saying, "Hector, you deemed that you should come off scatheless when you were spoiling Patroclus, and recked not of myself who was not with him. Fool that you were: for I, his comrade, mightier far than he, was still left behind him at the ships, and now I have laid you low. The Achaeans shall give him all due funeral rites, while dogs and vultures shall work their will upon yourself."

Then Hector said, as the life ebbed out of him, "I pray you by your life and knees, and by your parents, let not dogs devour me at the ships of the Achaeans, but accept the rich treasure of gold and bronze which my father and mother will offer you, and send my body home, that the Trojans and their wives may give me my dues of fire when I am dead."

Achilles glared at him and answered, "Dog, talk not to me neither of knees nor parents; would that I could be as sure of being able to cut your flesh into pieces and eat it raw, for the ill you have done me, as I am that nothing shall save you from the dogs—it shall not be, though they bring ten or twenty-fold ransom and weigh it out for me on the spot, with promise of yet more hereafter. Though Priam son of Dardanus should bid them offer me your weight in gold, even so your mother shall never lay you out and make lament over the son she bore, but dogs and vultures shall eat you utterly up."

Hector with his dying breath then said, "I know you what you are, and was sure that I should not move you, for your heart is hard as iron; look to it that I bring not heaven's anger upon you on the day when Paris and Phoebus Apollo, valiant though you be, shall slay you at the Scaean gates."

When he had thus said the shrouds of death enfolded him, whereon his soul went out of him and flew down to the house of Hades, lamenting its sad fate that it should enjoy youth and strength no longer. But Achilles said, speaking to the dead body, "Die; for my part I will accept my fate whensoever Zeus and the other gods see fit to send it."

As he spoke he drew his spear from the body and set it on one side; then he stripped the blood-stained armor from Hector's shoulders while the other Achaeans came running up to view his wondrous strength and beauty; and no one came near him without giving him a fresh wound. Then would one turn to his neighbor and say, "It is easier to handle Hector now than when he was flinging fire on to our ships"—and as he spoke he would thrust his spear into him anew.

Book XXIV (Greek Lines 1–187, 386–804)

The assembly now broke up and the people went their ways each to his own ship. There they made ready their supper, and then bethought them of the blessed boon of sleep; but Achilles still wept for thinking of his dear comrade, and sleep, before whom all things bow, could take no hold upon him. This way and that did he turn as he yearned after the might and manfulness of Patroclus; he thought of all they had done together, and all they had gone through both on the field of battle and on the waves of the weary sea. As he dwelt on these things he wept bitterly and lay now on his side, now on his back, and now face downwards, till at last he rose and went out as one distraught to wander upon the seashore. Then, when he saw dawn breaking over beach and sea, he yoked his horses to his chariot, and bound the body of Hector behind it that he might drag it about. Thrice did he drag it round the tomb of the son of Menoetius, and then went back into his tent, leaving the body on the ground full length and with its face downwards. But Apollo would not suffer it to be disfigured, for he pitied the man, dead though he now was; therefore he shielded him with his golden aegis continually, that he might take no hurt while Achilles was dragging him.

Thus shamefully did Achilles in his fury dishonor Hector; but the blessed gods looked down in pity from heaven, and urged Mercury, slayer of Argus, to steal the body. All were of this mind save only Hera, Neptune, and Zeus's grey-eyed daughter, who persisted in the hate which they had ever borne towards Ilius with Priam and his people; for they forgave not the wrong done them by Alexandrus in disdaining the goddesses who came to him when he was in his sheepyards, and preferring her who had offered him a wanton to his ruin.

When, therefore, the morning of the twelfth day had now come, Phoebus Apollo spoke among the immortals saying, "You gods ought to be ashamed of yourselves; you are cruel and hard-hearted. Did not Hector burn you thigh-bones of heifers and of unblemished goats? And now dare you not rescue even his dead body, for his wife to look upon, with his mother and child, his father Priam, and his people, who would forthwith commit him to the flames, and give him his due funeral rites? So, then, you would all be on the side of mad Achilles, who knows neither right nor ruth? He is like some savage lion that in the pride of his great strength and daring springs upon men's flocks and gorges on them. Even so has Achilles flung aside all pity, and all that conscience which at once so greatly banes yet greatly boons him that will heed it. A man may lose one far dearer than Achilles has lost—a son, it may be, or a brother born from his own mother's womb; yet when he has mourned him and wept over him he will let him bide, for it takes much sorrow to kill a man; whereas Achilles, now that he has slain noble Hector, drags him behind his chariot round the tomb of his comrade. It were better of him, and for him, that he should not do so, for brave though he be we gods may take it ill that he should vent his fury upon dead clay."

Hera spoke up in a rage. "This were well," she cried, "O lord of the silver bow, if you would give like honor to Hector and to Achilles; but Hector was mortal and suckled at a woman's breast, whereas Achilles is the offspring of a goddess whom I myself reared and brought up. I married her to Peleus, who is above measure dear to the immortals; you gods came all of you to her wedding; you feasted along with them yourself and brought your lyre—false, and fond of low company, that you have ever been."

Then said Zeus, "Hera, be not so bitter. Their honor shall not be equal, but of all that dwell in Ilius, Hector was dearest to the gods, as also to myself, for his offerings never failed me. Never was my altar stinted of its dues, nor of the drink-offerings and savor of sacrifice which we claim of right. I shall therefore permit the body of mighty Hector to be stolen; and yet this may hardly be without Achilles coming to know it, for his mother keeps night and day beside him. Let some one of you, therefore, send Thetis to me, and I will impart my counsel to her, namely that Achilles is to accept a ransom from Priam, and give up the body."

On this Iris fleet as the wind went forth to carry his message. Down she plunged into the dark sea midway between Samos and rocky Imbrus; the waters hissed as they closed over her, and she sank into the bottom as the lead at the end of an ox-horn, that is sped to carry death to fishes. She found Thetis sitting in a great cave with the other sea-goddesses gathered round her; there she sat in the midst of them weeping for her noble son who was to fall far from his own land, on the rich plains of Troy. Iris went up to her and said, "Rise Thetis; Zeus, whose counsels fail not, bids you come to him." And Thetis answered, "Why does the mighty god so bid me? I am in great grief, and shrink from going in and out among the immortals. Still, I will go, and the word that he may speak shall not be spoken in vain."

The goddess took her dark veil, than which there can be no robe more sombre, and went forth with fleet Iris leading the way before her. The waves of the sea opened them a path, and when they reached the shore they flew up into the heavens, where they found the all-seeing son of Cronus with the blessed gods that live for ever assembled near him. Minerva gave up her seat to her, and she sat down by the side of father Zeus. Hera then placed a fair golden cup in her hand, and spoke to her in words of comfort, whereon Thetis drank and gave her back the cup; and the sire of gods and men was the first to speak.

"So, goddess," said he, "for all your sorrow, and the grief that I well know reigns ever in your heart, you have come hither to Olympus, and I will tell you why I have sent for you. This nine days past the immortals have been quarreling about Achilles waster of cities and the body of Hector. The gods would have Mercury slayer of Argus steal the body, but in furtherance of our peace and amity henceforward, I will concede such honor to your son as I will now tell you. Go, then, to the host and lay these commands upon him; say that the gods are angry with him, and that I am myself more angry than them all, in that he keeps Hector at the ships and will not give him up. He may thus fear me and let the body go. At the same time I will send Iris to great Priam to bid him go to the ships of the Achaeans, and ransom his son, taking with him such gifts for Achilles as may give him satisfaction."

Silver-footed Thetis did as the god had told her, and forthwith down she darted from the topmost summits of Olympus. She went to her son's tents where she found him grieving bitterly, while his trusty comrades round him were busy preparing their morning meal, for which they had killed a great woolly sheep. His mother sat down beside him and caressed him with her hand saying, "My son, how long will you keep on thus grieving and making moan? You are gnawing at your own heart, and think neither of food nor of woman's embraces; and yet these too were well, for you have no long time to live, and death with the strong hand of fate are already close beside you. Now, therefore, heed what I say, for I come as a messenger from Zeus; he says that the gods are angry with you, and himself more angry than them all, in that you keep Hector at the ships and will not give him up. Therefore let him go, and accept a ransom for his body."

And Achilles answered, "So be it. If Olympian Zeus of his own motion thus commands me, let him that brings the ransom bear the body away."

Thus did mother and son talk together at the ships in long discourse with one another. Meanwhile the son of Cronus sent Iris to the strong city of Ilius. "Go," said he, "fleet Iris, from the mansions of Olympus, and tell King Priam in Ilius, that he is to go to the ships of the Achaeans and free the body of his dear son. He is to take such gifts with him as shall give satisfaction to Achilles, and he is to go alone, with no other Trojan, save only some honored servant who may drive his mules and wagon, and bring back the body of him whom noble Achilles has slain. Let him have no thought nor fear of death in his heart, for we will send the slayer of Argus to escort him, and bring him within the tent of Achilles. Achilles will not kill him nor let another do so, for he will take heed to his ways and sin not, and he will entreat a suppliant with all honorable courtesy."

On this Iris, fleet as the wind, sped forth to deliver her message. She went to Priam's house, and found weeping and lamentation therein. His sons were seated round their father in the outer courtyard, and their raiment was wet with tears: the old man sat in the midst of them with his mantle wrapped close about his body, and his head and neck all covered with the filth which he had clutched as he lay groveling in the mire. His daughters and his sons' wives went wailing about the house, as they thought of the many and brave men who lay dead, slain by the Argives. The messenger of Zeus stood by Priam and spoke softly to him, but fear fell upon him as she did so. "Take heart," she said, "Priam offspring of Dardanus, take heart and fear not. I bring no evil tidings, but am minded well towards you. I come as a messenger from Zeus, who though he be not near, takes thought for you and pities you. The lord of Olympus bids you go and ransom noble Hector, and take with you such gifts as shall give satisfaction to Achilles. You are to go alone, with no Trojan, save only some honored servant who may drive your mules and wagon, and bring back to the city the body of him whom noble Achilles has slain. You are to have no thought, nor fear of death, for Zeus will send the slayer of Argus to escort you. When he has brought you within Achilles' tent, Achilles will not kill you nor let another do so, for he will take heed to his ways and sin not, and he will treat a suppliant with all honorable courtesy."

• • •

And Priam said, "Who are you, my friend, and who are your parents, that you speak so truly about the fate of my unhappy son?"

The slayer of Argus, guide and guardian, answered him, "Sir, you would prove me, that you question me about noble Hector. Many a time have I set eyes upon him in battle when he was driving the Argives to their ships and putting them to the sword. We stood still and marveled, for Achilles in his anger with the son of Atreus suffered us not to fight. I am his squire, and came with him in the same ship. I am a Myrmidon, and my father's name is Polyctor: he is a rich man and about as old as you are; he has six sons besides myself, and I am the seventh. We cast lots, and it fell upon me to sail hither with Achilles. I am now come from the ships on to the plain, for with daybreak the Achaeans will set battle in array about the city. They chafe at doing nothing, and are so eager that their princes cannot hold them back."

Then answered Priam, "If you are indeed the squire of Achilles son of Peleus, tell me now the whole truth. Is my son still at the ships, or has Achilles hewn him limb from limb, and given him to his hounds?"

"Sir," replied the slayer of Argus, guide and guardian, "neither hounds nor vultures have yet devoured him; he is still just lying at the tents by the ship of Achilles, and though it is now twelve days that he has lain there, his flesh is not wasted nor have the worms eaten him although they feed on warriors. At daybreak Achilles drags him cruelly round the sepulchre of his dear comrade, but it does him no hurt. You should come yourself and see how he lies fresh as dew, with the blood all washed away, and his wounds every one of them closed though many pierced him with their spears. Such care have the blessed gods taken of your brave son, for he was dear to them beyond all measure."

The old man was comforted as he heard him and said, "My son, see what a good thing it is to have made due offerings to the immortals; for as sure as that he was born my son never forgot the gods that hold Olympus, and now they requite it to him even in death. Accept therefore at my hands this goodly chalice; guard me and with heaven's help guide me till I come to the tent of the son of Peleus."

Then answered the slayer of Argus, guide and guardian, "Sir, you are tempting me and playing upon my youth, but you shall not move me, for you are offering me presents without the knowledge of Achilles whom I fear and hold it great guilt to defraud, lest some evil presently befall me; but as your guide I would go with you even to Argos itself, and would guard you so carefully whether by sea or land, that no one should attack you through making light of him who was with you."

The bringer of good luck then sprang on to the chariot, and seizing the whip and reins he breathed fresh spirit into the mules and horses. When they reached the trench and the wall that was before the ships, those who were on guard had just been getting their suppers, and the slayer of Argus threw them all into a deep sleep. Then he drew back the bolts to open the gates, and took Priam inside with the treasure he had upon his wagon. Ere long they came to the lofty dwelling of the son of Peleus for which the Myrmidons had cut pine and which they had built for their king; when they had built it they thatched it with coarse tussock-grass which they had mown out on the plain, and all round it they made a large courtyard, which was fenced with stakes set close together. The gate was barred with a single bolt of pine which it took three men to force into its place, and three to draw back so as to open the gate, but Achilles could draw it by himself. Mercury opened the gate for the old man, and brought in the treasure that he was taking with him for the son of Peleus. Then he sprang from the chariot on to the ground and said, "Sir, it is I, immortal Mercury, that am come with you, for my father sent me to escort you. I will now leave you, and will not enter into the presence of Achilles, for it might anger him that a god should befriend mortal men thus openly. Go you within, and embrace the knees of the son of Peleus: beseech him by his father, his lovely mother, and his son; thus you may move him."

With these words Mercury went back to high Olympus. Priam sprang from his chariot to the ground, leaving Idaeus where he was, in charge of the mules and horses. The old man went straight into the house where Achilles, loved of the gods, was sitting. There he found him with his men seated at a distance from him: only two, the hero Automedon, and Alcimus of the race of Mars, were busy in attendance about his person, for he had but just done eating and drinking, and the table was still there. King Priam entered without their seeing him, and going right up to Achilles he clasped his knees and kissed the dread murderous hands that had slain so many of his sons.

As when some cruel spite has befallen a man that he should have killed some one in his own country, and must fly to a great man's protection in a land of strangers, and all marvel who see him, even so did Achilles marvel as he beheld Priam. The others looked one to another and marvelled also, but Priam besought Achilles saying, "Think of your father, O Achilles like unto the gods, who is such even as I am, on the sad threshold of old age. It may be that those who dwell near him harass him, and there is none to keep war and ruin from him. Yet when he hears of you being still alive, he is glad, and his days are full of hope that he shall see his dear son come home to him from Troy; but I, wretched man that I am, had the bravest in all Troy for my sons, and there is not one of them left. I had fifty sons when the Achaeans came here; nineteen of them were from a single womb, and the others were borne to me by the women of my household. The greater part of them has fierce Mars laid low, and Hector, him who was alone left, him who was the guardian of the city and ourselves, him have you lately slain; therefore I am now come to the ships of the Achaeans to ransom his body from you with a great ransom. Fear, O Achilles, the wrath of heaven; think on your own father and have compassion upon me, who am the more pitiable, for I have steeled myself as no man yet has ever steeled himself before me, and have raised to my lips the hand of him who slew my son."

Thus spoke Priam, and the heart of Achilles yearned as he bethought him of his father. He took the old man's hand and moved him gently away. The two wept bitterly—Priam, as he lay at Achilles' feet, weeping for Hector, and Achilles now for his father and now for Patroclus, till the house was filled with their lamentation. But when Achilles was now sated with grief and had unburdened the bitterness of his sorrow, he left his seat and raised the old man by the hand, in pity for his white hair and beard; then he said, "Unhappy man, you have indeed been greatly daring; how could you venture to come alone to the ships of the Achaeans, and enter the presence of him who has slain so many of your brave sons? You must have iron courage: sit now upon this seat, and for all our grief we will hide our sorrows in our hearts, for weeping will not avail us. The immortals know no care, yet the lot they spin for man is full of sorrow; on the floor of Zeus's palace there stand two urns, the one filled with evil gifts, and the other with good ones. He for whom Zeus the lord of thunder mixes the gifts he sends, will meet now with good and now with evil fortune; but he to whom Zeus sends none but evil gifts will be pointed at by the finger of scorn, the hand of famine will pursue him to the ends of the world, and he will go up and down the face of the earth, respected neither by gods nor men. Even so did it befall Peleus; the gods endowed him with all good things from his birth upwards, for he reigned over the Myrmidons excelling all men in prosperity and wealth, and mortal though he was they gave him a goddess for his bride. But even on him too did heaven send misfortune, for there is no race of royal children born to him in his house, save one son who is doomed to die all untimely; nor may I take care of him now that he is growing old, for I must stay here at Troy to be the bane of you and your children. And you too, O Priam, I have heard that you were aforetime happy. They say that in wealth and plenitude of offspring you surpassed all that is in Lesbos, the realm of Makar to the northward, Phrygia that is more inland, and those that dwell upon the great Hellespont; but from the day when the dwellers in heaven sent this evil upon you, war and slaughter have been about your city continually. Bear up against it, and let there be some intervals in your sorrow. Mourn as you may for your brave son, you will take nothing by it. You cannot raise him from the dead, ere you do so yet another sorrow shall befall you."

And Priam answered, "O king, bid me not be seated, while Hector is still lying uncared for in your tents, but accept the great ransom which I have brought you, and give him to me at once that I may look upon him. May you prosper with the ransom and reach your own land in safety, seeing that you have suffered me to live and to look upon the light of the sun."

Achilles looked at him sternly and said, "Vex me, sir, no longer; I am of myself minded to give up the body of Hector. My mother, daughter of the old man of the sea, came to me from Zeus to bid me deliver it to you. Moreover I know well, O Priam, and you cannot hide it, that some god has brought you to the ships of the Achaeans, for else, no man however strong and in his prime would dare to come to our host; he could neither pass our guard unseen, nor draw the bolt of my gates thus easily; therefore, provoke me no further, lest I sin against the word of Zeus, and suffer you not, suppliant though you are, within my tents."

The old man feared him and obeyed. Then the son of Peleus sprang like a lion through the door of his house, not alone, but with him went his two squires Automedon and Alcimus who were closer to him than any others of his comrades now that Patroclus was no more. These unyoked the horses and mules, and bade Priam's herald and attendant be seated within the house. They lifted the ransom for Hector's body from the wagon, but they left two mantles and a goodly shirt, that Achilles might wrap the body in them when he gave it to be taken home. Then he called to his servants and ordered them to wash the body and anoint it, but he first took it to a place where Priam should not see it, lest if he did so, he should break out in the bitterness of his grief, and enrage Achilles, who might then kill him and sin against the word of Zeus. When the servants had washed the body and anointed it, and had wrapped it in a fair shirt and mantle, Achilles himself lifted it on to a bier, and he and his men then laid it on the wagon. He cried aloud as he did so and called on the name of his dear comrade, "Be not angry with me, Patroclus," he said, "if you hear even in the house of Hades that I have given Hector to his father for a ransom. It has been no unworthy one, and I will share it equitably with you."

Achilles then went back into the tent and took his place on the richly inlaid seat from which he had risen, by the wall that was at right angles to the one against which Priam was sitting. "Sir," he said, "your son is now laid upon his bier and is ransomed according to desire; you shall look upon him when you take him away at daybreak; for the present let us prepare our supper. Even lovely Niobe had to think about eating, though her twelve children—six daughters and six lusty sons—had been all slain in her house. Apollo killed the sons with arrows from his silver bow, to punish Niobe, and Diana slew the daughters, because Niobe had vaunted herself against Leto; she said Leto had borne two children only, whereas she had herself borne many—whereon the two killed the many. Nine days did they lie weltering, and there was none to bury them, for the son of Cronus turned the people into stone; but on the tenth day the gods in heaven themselves buried them, and Niobe then took food, being worn out with weeping. They say that somewhere among the rocks on the mountain pastures of Sipylus, where the nymphs live that haunt the river Achelous, there, they say, she lives in stone and still nurses the sorrows sent upon her by the hand of heaven. Therefore, noble sir, let us two now take food; you can weep for your dear son hereafter as you are bearing him back to Ilius—and many a tear will he cost you."

With this Achilles sprang from his seat and killed a sheep of silvery whiteness, which his followers skinned and made ready all in due order. They cut the meat carefully up into smaller pieces, spitted them, and drew them off again when they were well roasted. Automedon brought bread in fair baskets and served it round the table, while Achilles dealt out the meat, and they laid their hands on the good things that were before them. As soon as they had had enough to eat and drink, Priam, descendant of Dardanus, marveled at the strength and beauty of Achilles for he was as a god to see, and Achilles marveled at Priam as he listened to him and looked upon his noble presence. When they had gazed their fill Priam spoke first. "And now, O king," he said, "take me to my couch that we may lie down and enjoy the blessed boon of sleep. Never once have my eyes been closed from the day your hands took the life of my son; I have groveled without ceasing in the mire of my stable-yard, making moan and brooding over my countless sorrows. Now, moreover, I have eaten bread and drunk wine; hitherto I have tasted nothing."

As he spoke Achilles told his men and the women-servants to set beds in the room that was in the gatehouse, and make them with good red rugs, and spread coverlets on the top of them with woollen cloaks for Priam and Idaeus to wear. So the maids went out carrying a torch and got the two beds ready in all haste. Then Achilles said laughingly to Priam, "Dear sir, you shall lie outside, lest some counsellor of those who in due course keep coming to advise with me should see you here in the darkness of the flying night, and tell it to Agamemnon. This might cause delay in the delivery of the body. And now tell me and tell me true, for how many days would you celebrate the funeral rites of noble Hector? Tell me, that I may hold aloof from war and restrain the host."

And Priam answered, "Since, then, you suffer me to bury my noble son with all due rites, do thus, Achilles, and I shall be grateful. You know how we are pent up within our city; it is far for us to fetch wood from the mountain, and the people live in fear. Nine days, therefore, will we mourn Hector in my house; on the tenth day we will bury him and there shall be a public feast in his honor; on the eleventh we will build a mound over his ashes, and on the twelfth, if there be need, we will fight."

And Achilles answered, "All, King Priam, shall be as you have said. I will stay our fighting for as long a time as you have named."

As he spoke he laid his hand on the old man's right wrist, in token that he should have no fear; thus then did Priam and his attendant sleep there in the forecourt, full of thought, while Achilles lay in an inner room of the house, with fair Briseis by his side.

And now both gods and mortals were fast asleep through the livelong night, but upon Hermes alone, the bringer of good luck, sleep could take no hold for he was thinking all the time how to get King Priam away from the ships without his being seen by the strong force of sentinels. He hovered therefore over Priam's head and said, "Sir, now that Achilles has spared your life, you seem to have no fear about sleeping in the thick of your foes. You have paid a great ransom, and have received the body of your son; were you still alive and a prisoner the sons whom you have left at home would have to give three times as much to free you; and so it would be if Agamemnon and the other Achaeans were to know of your being here."

When he heard this the old man was afraid and roused his servant. Hermes then yoked their horses and mules, and drove them quickly through the host so that no man perceived them. When they came to the ford of eddying Xanthus, begotten of immortal Zeus, Hermes went back to high Olympus, and dawn in robe of saffron began to break over all the land. Priam and Idaeus then drove on toward the city lamenting and making moan, and the mules drew the body of Hector. No one neither man nor woman saw them, till Cassandra, fair as golden Venus standing on Pergamus, caught sight of her dear father in his chariot, and his servant that was the city's herald with him. Then she saw him that was lying upon the bier, drawn by the mules, and with a loud cry she went about the city saying, "Come hither Trojans, men and women, and look on Hector; if ever you rejoiced to see him coming from battle when he was alive, look now on him that was the glory of our city and all our people."

At this there was not man nor woman left in the city, so great a sorrow had possessed them. Hard by the gates they met Priam as he was bringing in the body. Hector's wife and his mother were the first to mourn him: they flew towards the wagon and laid their hands upon his head, while the crowd stood weeping round them. They would have stayed before the gates, weeping and lamenting the livelong day to the going down of the sun, had not Priam spoken to them from the chariot and said, "Make way for the mules to pass you. Afterwards when I have taken the body home you shall have your fill of weeping."

On this the people stood asunder, and made a way for the wagon. When they had borne the body within the house they laid it upon a bed and seated minstrels round it to lead the dirge, whereon the women joined in the sad music of their lament. Foremost among them all Andromache led their wailing as she clasped the head of mighty Hector in her embrace. "Husband," she cried, "you have died young, and leave me in your house a widow; he of whom we are the ill-starred parents is still a mere child, and I fear he may not reach manhood. Ere he can do so our city will be razed and overthrown, for you who watched over it are no more —you who were its savior, the guardian of our wives and children. Our women will be carried away captives to the ships, and I among them; while you, my child, who will be with me will be put to some unseemly tasks, working for a cruel master. Or, may be, some Achaean will hurl you (O miserable death) from our walls, to avenge some brother, son, or father whom Hector slew; many of them have indeed bitten the dust at his hands, for your father's hand in battle was no light one. Therefore do the people mourn him. You have left, O Hector, sorrow unutterable to your parents, and my own grief is greatest of all, for you did not stretch forth your arms and embrace me as you lay dying, nor say to me any words that might have lived with me in my tears night and day for evermore."

Bitterly did she weep the while, and the women joined in her lament. Hecuba in her turn took up the strains of woe. "Hector," she cried, "dearest to me of all my children. So long as you were alive the gods loved you well, and even in death they have not been utterly unmindful of you; for when Achilles took any other of my sons, he would sell him beyond the seas, to Samos Imbrus or rugged Lemnos; and when he had slain you too with his sword, many a time did he drag you round the sepulcher of his comrade—though this could not give him life—yet here you lie all fresh as dew, and comely as one whom Apollo has slain with his painless shafts."

Thus did she too speak through her tears with bitter moan, and then Helen for a third time took up the strain of lamentation. "Hector," said she, "dearest of all my brothers-in-law—for I am wife to Alexandrus who brought me hither to Troy—would that I had died ere he did so—twenty years are come and gone since I left my home and came from over the sea, but I have never heard one word of insult or unkindness from you. When another would chide with me, as it might be one of your brothers or sisters or of your brothers' wives, or my mother-in-law—for Priam was as kind to me as though he were my own father—you would rebuke and check them with words of gentleness and goodwill. Therefore my tears flow both for you and for my unhappy self, for there is no one else in Troy who is kind to me, but all shrink and shudder as they go by me."

She wept as she spoke and the vast crowd that was gathered round her joined in her lament. Then King Priam spoke to them saying, "Bring wood, O Trojans, to the city, and fear no cunning ambush of the Argives, for Achilles when he dismissed me from the ships gave me his word that they should not attack us until the morning of the twelfth day."

Forthwith they yoked their oxen and mules and gathered together before the city. Nine days long did they bring in great heaps of wood, and on the morning of the tenth day with many tears they took brave Hector forth, laid his dead body upon the summit of the pile, and set the fire thereto. Then when the child of morning, rosy-fingered dawn, appeared on the eleventh day, the people again assembled, round the pyre of mighty Hector. When they were got together, they first quenched the fire with wine wherever it was burning, and then his brothers and comrades with many a bitter tear gathered his white bones, wrapped them in soft robes of purple, and laid them in a golden urn, which they placed in a grave and covered over with large stones set close together. Then they built a barrow hurriedly over it keeping guard on every side lest the Achaeans should attack them before they had finished. When they had heaped up the barrow they went back again into the city, and being well assembled they held high feast in the house of Priam their king.

Thus, then, did they celebrate the funeral of Hector tamer of horses.

History of the Peloponnesian War: The Funeral Oration of Pericles

Thucydides

Thucydides (c. 461–c. 395 BCE) is the first and perhaps the greatest historian in the Western tradition. His history records, as "a possession for all time," a detailed description and analysis of the conflict between Athens and Sparta and their respective allies, which took place between 431 and 404 BCE. The fifth century in ancient Athens had seen one of the greatest flowerings of the arts of philosophy, mathematics, warfare, politics, law, architecture, sculpture, seamanship, and horsemanship in world history, a flowering that gave birth to the classical intellectual and cultural tradition which, together with the Jewish biblical tradition and Christianity, has formed Western Civilization.

Thucydides treats the Peloponnesian War as a great tragedy, the apparently inevitable result of many complex free will decisions. The war brought an end to the hegemony of Athens and its experiment in democratic government. Though Athens continued to play a role in Greek politics, it never regained its past success and prosperity. Thus, with famine, disease, and destruction, the Peloponnesian War marked the end of the seminal period of ancient Greek civilization.

In this excerpt, Pericles, the first citizen of Athens, delivers a public eulogy for the first Athenian soldiers to fall in the war. He employs antithesis, a common figure in the ancient Greek language and in many ways a theme of Greek civilization, visible too in the Parthenon, the tragedy Oedipus Rex, *and other works of the Greek imagination. Pericles addresses the difficulty of giving this eulogy by noting two opposing potential responses of the audience, and later contrasts some of the "points in which our city is worthy of admiration." Success in a one-dimensional struggle is less impressive than success in balancing opposing forces, and the funeral oration, as did Athens itself for a time, finds that success.*

Above: Bust of Thucydides, artist unknown, ca. 430 BCE, marble.

Published 431 BCE; translated by Richard Crawley, 1903, revised by Robert B. Strassler, 1998

In the same winter the Athenians gave a funeral at the public cost to those who had first fallen in this war. It was a custom of their ancestors, and the manner of it is as follows. Three days before the ceremony, the bones of the dead are laid out in a tent which has been erected; and their friends bring to their relatives such offerings as they please. In the funeral procession cypress coffins are borne in carts, one for each tribe; the bones of the deceased being placed in the coffin of their tribe. Among these is carried one empty bier decked for the missing, that is, for those whose bodies could not be recovered. Any citizen or stranger who pleases joins in the procession: and the female relatives are there to wail at the burial. The dead are laid in the public sepulcher in the most beautiful suburb of the city, in which those who fall in war are always buried; with the exception of those slain at Marathon, who for their singular and extraordinary valor were interred on the spot where they fell. After the bodies have been laid in the earth, a man chosen by the state, of approved wisdom and eminent reputation, pronounces over them an appropriate eulogy; after which all retire. Such is the manner of the burying; and throughout the whole of the war, whenever the occasion arose, the established custom was observed. Meanwhile these were the first that had fallen, and Pericles son of Xanthippus was chosen to pronounce their eulogy. When the proper time arrived, he advanced from the sepulcher to an elevated platform in order to be heard by as many of the crowd as possible, and spoke as follows:

"Most of my predecessors in this place have commended him who made this speech part of the law, telling us that it is well that it should be delivered at the burial of those who fall in battle. For myself, I should have thought that the worth which had displayed itself in deeds would be sufficiently rewarded by honors also shown by deeds; such as you now see in this funeral prepared at the people's cost. And I could have wished that the reputations of many brave men were not to be imperiled in the mouth of a single individual, to stand or fall according as he spoke well or ill. For it is hard to speak properly on a subject where it is even difficult to convince your hearers that you are speaking the truth. On the one hand, the friend who is familiar with every fact of the story may think that some point has not been set forth with that fullness which he wishes and knows it to deserve; on the other, he who is a stranger to the matter may be led by envy to suspect exaggeration if he hears anything above his own nature. For men can endure to hear others praised only so long as they can severally persuade themselves of their own ability to equal the actions recounted: when this point is passed, envy comes in and with it incredulity. However, since our ancestors have stamped this custom with their approval, it becomes my duty to obey the law and to try to satisfy your several wishes and opinions as best I may.

"I shall begin with our ancestors: it is both just and proper that they should have the honor of the first mention on an occasion like the present. They dwelt in the country without break in the succession from generation to generation, and handed it down free to the present time by their valor. And if our more remote ancestors deserve praise, much more do our own fathers, who added to their inheritance the empire which we now possess, and spared no pains to be able to leave their acquisitions to us of the present generation. Lastly, there are few parts of our dominions that have not been augmented by those of us here, who are still more or less in the vigor of life; while the mother country has been furnished by us with everything that can enable her to depend on her own resources whether for war or for peace. That part of our history which tells of the military achievements which gave us our several possessions, or of the ready valor with which either we or our fathers stemmed the tide of Hellenic or foreign aggression, is a theme too familiar to my hearers for me to dwell upon, and I shall therefore pass it by. But what was the road by which we reached our position, what the form of government under which our greatness grew, what the national habits out of which it sprang; these are questions which I may try to solve before I proceed to my eulogy upon these men; since I think this to be a subject upon which on the present occasion a speaker may properly dwell, and to which the whole assemblage, whether citizens or foreigners, may listen with advantage.

"Our constitution does not copy the laws of neighboring states; we are rather a pattern to others than imitators ourselves. Its administration favors the many instead of the few; this is why it is called a democracy. If we look to the laws, they afford equal justice to all in their private differences; if to social standing, advancement in public life falls to reputation for capacity, class considerations not being allowed to interfere with merit; nor again does poverty bar the way, if a man is able to serve the state, he is not hindered by the obscurity of his condition. The freedom which we enjoy in our government extends also to our ordinary life. There, far from exercising a jealous surveillance over each other, we do not feel called upon to be angry with our neighbor for doing what he likes, or even to indulge in those injurious looks which cannot fail to be offensive, although they inflict no real harm. But all this ease in our private relations does not make us lawless as citizens. Against this fear is our chief safeguard, teaching us to obey the magistrates and the laws, particularly such as regard the protection of the injured, whether they are actually on the statute book, or belong to that code which, although unwritten, yet cannot be broken without acknowledged disgrace.

"Further, we provide plenty of means for the mind to refresh itself from business. We celebrate games and sacrifices all the year round, and the elegance of our private establishments forms a daily source of pleasure and helps to distract us from what causes us distress; while the magnitude of our city draws the world into our harbor, so that to the Athenian the fruits of other countries are as familiar a luxury as those of his own.

"If we turn to our military policy, there also we differ from our antagonists. We throw open our city to the world, and never by alien acts exclude foreigners from any opportunity of learning or observing, although the eyes of an enemy may occasionally profit by our liberality; trusting less in system and policy than to the native spirit of our citizens; while in education, where our rivals from their very cradles by a painful discipline seek after manliness, at Athens we live exactly as we please, and yet are just as ready to encounter every legitimate danger. In proof of this it may be noticed that the Spartans do not invade our country alone, but bring with them all their confederates; while we Athenians advance unsupported into the territory of a neighbor, and fighting upon a foreign soil usually vanquish with ease men who are defending their homes. Our united force was never yet encountered by any enemy, because we have at once to attend to our marine and to despatch our citizens by land upon a hundred different services; so that, wherever they engage with some such fraction of our strength, a success against a detachment is magnified into a victory over the nation, and a defeat into a reverse suffered at the hands of our entire people. And yet if with habits not of labor but of ease, and courage not of art but of nature, we are still willing to encounter danger, we have the double advantage of not suffering hardships before we need to, and of facing them in the hour of need as fearlessly as those who are never free from them.

"Nor are these the only points in which our city is worthy of admiration.

"We cultivate refinement without extravagance and knowledge without effeminacy; wealth we employ more for use than for show, and place the real disgrace of poverty not in owning to the fact but in declining the struggle against it. Our public men have, besides politics, their private affairs to attend to, and our ordinary citizens, though occupied with the pursuits of industry, are still fair judges of public matters; for, unlike any other nation, we regard the citizen who takes no part in these duties not as unambitious, but as useless, and we are able to judge proposals even if we cannot originate them; instead of looking on discussion as a stumbling-block in the way of action, we think it an indispensable preliminary to any wise action at all. Again, in our enterprises we present the singular spectacle of daring and deliberation, each carried to its highest point, and both united in the same persons; although with the rest of mankind decision is the fruit of ignorance, hesitation of reflection. But the prize for courage will surely be awarded most justly to those who know the difference between hardship and pleasure and yet are never tempted to shrink from danger. In generosity we are equally singular, acquiring our friends by conferring not by receiving favors. Yet, of course, the doer of the favor is the firmer friend of the two, in order by continued kindness to keep the recipient in his debt; while the debtor feels less keenly from the very consciousness that the return he makes will be a payment, not a free gift. And it is only the Athenians who, fearless of consequences, confer their benefits not from calculations of expediency, but in the confidence of liberality.

"In short, I say that as a city we are the school of Hellas; while I doubt if the world can produce a man, who where he has only himself to depend upon, is equal to so many emergencies, and graced by so happy a versatility as the Athenian. And that this is no mere boast thrown out for the occasion, but plain matter of fact, is proved by the power of the state acquired by these habits. For Athens alone of her contemporaries is found when tested to be greater than her reputation, and alone gives no occasion to her assailants to blush at the antagonist by whom they have been worsted, or to her subjects to question her title by rule of merit. Rather, the admiration of the present and succeeding ages will be ours, since we have not left our power without witness, but have shown it by mighty proofs; and far from needing a Homer for our eulogist, or other of his craft whose verses might charm for the moment only for the impression which they gave to melt at the touch of fact, we have forced every sea and land to be the highway of our daring, and everywhere, whether for evil or for good, have left imperishable monuments behind us. Such is the Athens for which these men, in the assertion of their resolve not to lose her, nobly fought and died; and well may every one of their survivors be ready to suffer in her cause.

"Indeed if I have dwelt at some length upon the character of our country, it has been to show that our stake in the struggle is not the same as theirs who have no such blessings to lose, and also that the eulogy of the men over whom I am now speaking might be by definite proofs established. That eulogy is now in a great measure complete; for the Athens that I have celebrated is only what the heroism of these and their like have made her, men whose fame, unlike that of most Hellenes, will be found to be no greater than what they deserve. And if a test of worth be wanted, it is to be found in their closing scene, and this not only in the cases in which it set the final seal upon their merit, but also in those in which it gave the first intimation of their having any. For there is justice in the claim that steadfastness in his country's battles should be as a cloak to cover a man's other imperfections; since the good action has blotted out the bad, and his merit as a citizen more than outweighed his demerits as an individual. But none of these allowed either wealth with its prospect of future enjoyment to unnerve his spirit, or poverty with its hope of a day of freedom and riches to tempt him to shrink from danger. No, holding that vengeance upon their enemies was more to be desired than any personal blessings, and reckoning this to be the most glorious of hazards, they joyfully determined to accept the risk, to make sure of their vengeance and to let their wishes wait; and while committing to hope the uncertainty of final success, in the business before them they thought fit to act boldly and trust in themselves. Thus choosing to die resisting, rather than to live submitting, they fled only from dishonor, but met danger face to face, and after one brief moment, while at the summit of their fortune, left behind them not their fear, but their glory.

"So died these men as became Athenians. You, their survivors, must determine to have as unaltering a resolution in the field, though you may pray that it may have a happier outcome. And not contented with ideas derived only from words of the advantages which are bound up with the defense of your country, though these would furnish a valuable text to a speaker even before an audience so alive to them as the present, you must yourselves realize the power of Athens, and feed your eyes upon her from day to day, till love of her fills your hearts; and then when all her greatness shall break upon you, you must reflect that it was by courage, sense of duty, and a keen feeling of honor in action that men were enabled to win all this, and that no personal failure in an enterprise could make them consent to deprive their country of their valor, but they laid it at her feet as the most glorious contribution that they could offer. For this offering of their lives, made in common by them all, they each of them individually received that renown which never grows old, and for a tomb, not so much that in which their bones have been deposited, but that noblest of shrines wherein their glory is laid up to be eternally remembered upon every occasion on which deed or story shall be commemorated. For heroes have the whole earth for their tomb; and in lands far from their own, where the column with its epitaph declares it, there is enshrined in every breast a record unwritten with no monument to preserve it, except that of the heart. These take as your model, and judging happiness to be the fruit of freedom and freedom of valor, never decline the dangers of war. For it is not the miserable that would most justly be unsparing of their lives; these have nothing to hope for: it is rather they to whom continued life may bring reverses as yet unknown, and to whom a fall, if it came, would be most tremendous in its consequences. And surely, to a man of spirit, the degradation of cowardice must be immeasurably more grievous than the unfelt death which strikes him in the midst of his strength and patriotism!

"Comfort, therefore, not condolence, is what I have to offer the parents of the dead who may be here. Numberless are the chances to which, as they know, the life of man is subject; but fortunate indeed are they who draw for their lot a death so glorious as that which has caused your mourning, and to whom life has been so exactly measured as to terminate in the happiness in which it has been passed. Still I know that this is a hard saying, especially when you will constantly be reminded by seeing in the homes of others blessings of which once you also enjoyed; for grief is felt not so much for the want of what we have never known, as for the loss of that to which we have been long accustomed. Yet you who are still of an age to beget children must bear up in the hope of having others in their stead; not only will they help you to forget those whom you have lost, but will be to the state at once a reinforcement and a security, for never can a fair or just policy be expected of a citizen who does not, like his fellows, bring to the decision the interests and apprehensions of a father. While those of you who have passed your prime must congratulate yourselves with the thought that the best part of your life was fortunate, and that the brief span that remains will be cheered by the fame of the departed. For it is only the love of honor that never grows old; and honor it is, not gain, as some would have it, that rejoices the heart of age and helplessness.

"Turning to the sons or brothers of the dead, I see an arduous struggle before you. When a man is gone, all are wont to praise him, and should your merit be ever so transcendent, you will still find it difficult not merely to overtake, but even to approach their renown. The living have envy to contend with, while those who are no longer in our path are honored with a goodwill into which rivalry does not enter. On the other hand if I must say anything on the subject of female excellence to those of you who will now be in widowhood, it will be all comprised in this brief exhortation. Great will be your glory in not falling short of your natural character; and greatest will be hers who is least talked of among the men whether for good or for bad.

"My task is now finished. I have performed it to the best of my ability, and in words, at least, the requirements of the law are now satisfied. If deeds be in question, those who are here interred have received part of their honors already, and for the rest, their children will be brought up till manhood at the public expense: the state thus offers a valuable prize, as the garland of victory in this race of valor, for the reward both of those who have fallen and their survivors. And where the rewards for merit are greatest, there are found the best citizens.

"And now that you have brought to a close your lamentations for your relatives, you may depart."

Apology
Plato

Apology, *which scholars believe to be one of the earliest of Plato's dialogues, is widely thought to be as close to a historical account of the trial of Socrates as exists.*

The original definition of its title, apology, *was a speech given in one's own defense. Over time, the definition changed to its current meaning of acknowledging a fault or failure, which Plato did not intend.*

In recording Socrates' speech of defense, Plato immortalizes both the founder of Western philosophical thought and some of the West's most fundamental ideas about man and the meaning of life.

Above: *The Death of Socrates,* Jacques-Louis David, 1787, oil on canvas.

ca. 399 BCE; translated by Benjamin Jowett, 1871.

Socrates' Defense

17a　　How you have felt, O men of Athens, at hearing the speeches of my accusers, I cannot tell; but I know that their persuasive words almost made me forget who I was—such was the effect of them; and yet they have hardly spoken a word of truth. But many as their falsehoods were, there was one of them which quite amazed me; I mean when they told you to be upon your guard, and not to let yourselves be deceived by the force of my eloquence. They ought to

17b　have been ashamed of saying this, because they were sure to be detected as soon as I opened my lips and displayed my deficiency; they certainly did appear to be most shameless in saying this, unless by the force of eloquence they mean the force of truth; for then I do indeed admit that I am eloquent. But in how different a way from theirs! Well, as I was saying, they have hardly uttered a word, or not more than a word, of truth; but you shall hear from me the whole truth: not, however, delivered after their manner,

17c　in a set oration duly ornamented with words and phrases. No indeed! but I shall use the words and arguments which occur to me at the moment; for I am certain that this is right, and that at my time of life I ought not to be appearing before you, O men of Athens, in the character of a juvenile orator—let no one expect this of me. And I must beg of you to grant me one favor, which is this: If you hear me using the same words in my defense which I have been in the habit of using, and which most of you may have heard in the agora, and at the tables of the money-changers, or

17d　anywhere else, I would ask you not to be surprised at this, and not to interrupt me. For I am more than seventy years of age, and this is the first time that I have ever appeared in a court of law, and I am quite a stranger to the ways of the place; and therefore I would have you regard me as if I were really a stranger, whom you would excuse if he spoke in his

18a　native tongue, and after the fashion of his country; that I think is not an unfair request. Never mind the manner, which may or may not be good; but think only of the justice of my cause, and give heed to that: let the judge decide justly and the speaker speak truly.

And first, I have to reply to the older charges and to my first accusers, and then I will go to the later ones. For I 18b have had many accusers, who accused me of old, and their false charges have continued during many years; and I am more afraid of them than of Anytus and his associates, who are dangerous, too, in their own way. But far more dangerous are these, who began when you were children, and took possession of your minds with their falsehoods, telling of one Socrates, a wise man, who speculated about the heaven above, and searched into the earth beneath, and made the worse appear the better cause. These are the 18c accusers whom I dread; for they are the circulators of this rumor, and their hearers are too apt to fancy that speculators of this sort do not believe in the gods. And they are many, and their charges against me are of ancient date, and they made them in days when you were impressible—in childhood, or perhaps in youth—and the cause when heard 18d went by default, for there was none to answer. And, hardest of all, their names I do not know and cannot tell; unless in the chance case of a comic poet. But the main body of these slanderers who from envy and malice have wrought upon you—and there are some of them who are convinced themselves, and impart their convictions to others—all these, I say, are most difficult to deal with; for I cannot have them up here, and examine them, and therefore I must simply fight with shadows in my own defense, and examine when there is no one who answers. I will ask you then to assume with me, as I was saying, that my opponents are of 18e two kinds—one recent, the other ancient; and I hope that you will see the propriety of my answering the latter first, for these accusations you heard long before the others, and much oftener.

Well, then, I will make my defense, and I will endeavor 19a in the short time which is allowed to do away with this evil opinion of me which you have held for such a long time; and I hope I may succeed, if this be well for you and me, and that my words may find favor with you. But I know that to accomplish this is not easy—I quite see the nature of the task. Let the event be as God wills: in obedience to the law I make my defense.

I will begin at the beginning, and ask what the accusation is which has given rise to this slander of me, and which has encouraged Meletus to proceed against me. What do the slanderers say? They shall be my prosecutors, and I will sum up their words in an affidavit. "Socrates is an evil-doer, and a curious person, who searches into things under the earth and in heaven, and he makes the worse appear the better cause; and he teaches the aforesaid doctrines to others." That is the nature of the accusation, and that is what you have seen yourselves in the comedy of Aristophanes; who has introduced a man whom he calls Socrates, going about and saying that he can walk in the air, and talking a deal of nonsense concerning matters of which I do not pretend to know either much or little—not that I mean to say anything disparaging of anyone who is a student of natural philosophy. I should be very sorry if Meletus could lay that to my charge. But the simple truth is, O Athenians, that I have nothing to do with these studies. Very many of those here present are witnesses to the truth of this, and to them I appeal. Speak then, you who have heard me, and tell your neighbors whether any of you have ever known me hold forth in few words or in many upon matters of this sort. . . . You hear their answer. And from what they say of this you will be able to judge of the truth of the rest.

As little foundation is there for the report that I am a teacher, and take money; that is no more true than the other. Although, if a man is able to teach, I honor him for being paid. There is Gorgias of Leontium, and Prodicus of Ceos, and Hippias of Elis, who go the round of the cities, and are able to persuade the young men to leave their own citizens, by whom they might be taught for nothing, and come to them, whom they not only pay, but are thankful if they may be allowed to pay them. There is actually a Parian philosopher residing in Athens, of whom I have heard; and I came to hear of him in this way: I met a man who has

19b

19c

19d

19e

20a

spent a world of money on the Sophists, Callias the son of Hipponicus, and knowing that he had sons, I asked him: "Callias," I said, "if your two sons were foals or calves, there would be no difficulty in finding someone to put over them; we should hire a trainer of horses or a farmer

20b probably who would improve and perfect them in their own proper virtue and excellence; but as they are human beings, whom are you thinking of placing over them? Is there anyone who understands human and political virtue? You must have thought about this as you have sons; is there anyone?" "There is," he said. "Who is he?" said I, "and of what country? and what does he charge?" "Evenus the Parian," he replied; "he is the man, and his charge is five

20c minae." Happy is Evenus, I said to myself, if he really has this wisdom, and teaches at such a modest charge. Had I the same, I should have been very proud and conceited; but the truth is that I have no knowledge of the kind.

I dare say, Athenians, that someone among you will reply, "Why is this, Socrates, and what is the origin of these accusations of you: for there must have been something strange which you have been doing? All this great fame and talk about you would never have arisen if you had been like

20d other men: tell us, then, why this is, as we should be sorry to judge hastily of you." Now I regard this as a fair challenge, and I will endeavor to explain to you the origin of this name of "wise," and of this evil fame. Please to attend then. And although some of you may think I am joking, I declare that I will tell you the entire truth. Men of Athens, this reputation of mine has come of a certain sort of wisdom which I possess. If you ask me what kind of wisdom, I reply, such wisdom as is attainable by man, for to

20e that extent I am inclined to believe that I am wise; whereas the persons of whom I was speaking have a superhuman wisdom, which I may fail to describe, because I have it not myself; and he who says that I have, speaks falsely, and is taking away my character. And here, O men of Athens, I must beg you not to interrupt me, even if I seem to say something extravagant. For the word which I will speak is not mine. I will refer you to a witness who is worthy of credit, and will tell you about my wisdom—whether I have any, and of what sort—and that witness shall be the god of

21a Delphi. You must have known Chaerephon; he was early a friend of mine, and also a friend of yours, for he shared in the exile of the people, and returned with you. Well, Chaerephon, as you know, was very impetuous in all his doings, and he went to Delphi and boldly asked the oracle to tell him whether—as I was saying, I must beg you not to interrupt—he asked the oracle to tell him whether there was anyone wiser than I was, and the Pythian prophetess answered that there was no man wiser. Chaerephon is dead himself, but his brother, who is in court, will confirm the truth of this story.

Why do I mention this? Because I am going to explain

21b to you why I have such an evil name. When I heard the answer, I said to myself, What can the god mean? and what is the interpretation of this riddle? for I know that I have no wisdom, small or great. What can he mean when he says that I am the wisest of men? And yet he is a god and cannot lie; that would be against his nature. After a long consideration, I at last thought of a method of trying the question. I reflected that if I could only find a man wiser than myself, then I might go to the god with a refutation in

21c my hand. I should say to him, "Here is a man who is wiser than I am; but you said that I was the wisest." Accordingly I went to one who had the reputation of wisdom, and observed to him— his name I need not mention; he was a politician whom I selected for examination— and the result was as follows: When I began to talk with him, I could not help thinking that he was not really wise, although he was thought wise by many, and wiser still by himself; and I went and tried to explain to him that he thought himself wise, but was not really wise; and the consequence was that

21d he hated me, and his enmity was shared by several who were present and heard me. So I left him, saying to myself, as I went away: Well, although I do not suppose that either of us knows anything really beautiful and good, I am better off than he is—for he knows nothing, and thinks that he knows. I neither know nor think that I know. In this latter particular, then, I seem to have slightly the advantage of him. Then I went to another, who had still higher

21e philosophical pretensions, and my conclusion was exactly the same. I made another enemy of him, and of many others besides him.

After this I went to one man after another, being not unconscious of the enmity which I provoked, and I lamented and feared this: but necessity was laid upon me—the word of God, I thought, ought to be considered first. And I said to myself, Go I must to all who appear to know, and find out the meaning of the oracle. And I swear to you,

22a Athenians, by the dog I swear!—for I must tell you the truth—the result of my mission was just this: I found that the men most in repute were all but the most foolish; and that some inferior men were really wiser and better. I will tell you the tale of my wanderings and of the "Herculean" labors, as I may call them, which I endured only to find at last the oracle irrefutable. When I left the politicians, I

22b went to the poets; tragic, dithyrambic, and all sorts. And there, I said to myself, you will be detected; now you will find out that you are more ignorant than they are. Accordingly, I took them some of the most elaborate passages in their own writings, and asked what was the meaning of them—thinking that they would teach me something. Will you believe me? I am almost ashamed to speak of this, but still I must say that there is hardly a person present who would not have talked better about their poetry than they did themselves. That showed me in

22c an instant that not by wisdom do poets write poetry, but by a sort of genius and inspiration; they are like diviners or soothsayers who also say many fine things, but do not understand the meaning of them. And the poets appeared to me to be much in the same case; and I further observed that upon the strength of their poetry they believed themselves to be the wisest of men in other things in which they were not wise. So I departed, conceiving myself to be superior to them for the same reason that I was superior to the politicians.

22d At last I went to the artisans, for I was conscious that I knew nothing at all, as I may say, and I was sure that they knew many fine things; and in this I was not mistaken, for they did know many things of which I was ignorant, and in this they certainly were wiser than I was. But I observed that even the good artisans fell into the same error as the poets; because they were good workmen they thought that they also knew all sorts of high matters, and this defect in them overshadowed their wisdom—therefore I asked

22e myself on behalf of the oracle, whether I would like to be as I was, neither having their knowledge nor their ignorance, or like them in both; and I made answer to myself and the oracle that I was better off as I was.

23a This investigation has led to my having many enemies of the worst and most dangerous kind, and has given occasion also to many calumnies, and I am called wise, for my hearers always imagine that I myself possess the wisdom which I find wanting in others: but the truth is, O men of Athens, that God only is wise; and in this oracle he means to say that the wisdom of men is little or nothing;

23b he is not speaking of Socrates, he is only using my name as an illustration, as if he said, He, O men, is the wisest, who, like Socrates, knows that his wisdom is in truth worth nothing. And so I go my way, obedient to the god, and make inquisition into the wisdom of anyone, whether citizen or stranger, who appears to be wise; and if he is not wise, then in vindication of the oracle I show him that he is not wise; and this occupation quite absorbs me, and I have no time to give either to any public matter of interest or to

23c any concern of my own, but I am in utter poverty by reason of my devotion to the god.

There is another thing: young men of the richer classes, who have not much to do, come about me of their own accord; they like to hear the pretenders examined, and they often imitate me, and examine others themselves; there are plenty of persons, as they soon enough discover, who think that they know something, but really know little or nothing: and then those who are examined by them instead of being angry with themselves are angry with me: This confounded Socrates, they say; this villainous misleader

23d of youth! and then if somebody asks them, Why, what evil does he practice or teach? they do not know, and cannot tell; but in order that they may not appear to be at a loss, they repeat the ready-made charges which are used against all philosophers about teaching things up in the clouds and under the earth, and having no gods, and making the worse appear the better cause; for they do not like to confess that their pretense of knowledge has been detected, which is the

23e truth: and as they are numerous and ambitious and energetic, and are all in battle array and have persuasive tongues, they have filled your ears with their loud and inveterate calumnies. And this is the reason why my three accusers, Meletus and Anytus and Lycon, have set upon me; Meletus, who has a quarrel with me on behalf of the poets; Anytus, on behalf of the craftsmen; Lycon, on

24a behalf of the rhetoricians: and as I said at the beginning, I cannot expect to get rid of this mass of calumny all in a moment. And this, O men of Athens, is the truth and the whole truth; I have concealed nothing, I have dissembled nothing. And yet I know that this plainness of speech makes them hate me, and what is their hatred but a proof that I am speaking the truth? This is the occasion and

24b reason of their slander of me, as you will find out either in this or in any future inquiry.

I have said enough in my defense against the first class of my accusers; I turn to the second class, who are headed by Meletus, that good and patriotic man, as he calls himself. And now I will try to defend myself against them: these new accusers must also have their affidavit read. What do they say? Something of this sort: that Socrates is a doer of evil, and corrupter of the youth, and he does not believe in the gods of the state, and has other new divinities of his

24c own. That is the sort of charge; and now let us examine the particular counts. He says that I am a doer of evil, who corrupt the youth; but I say, O men of Athens, that Meletus is a doer of evil, and the evil is that he makes a joke of a serious matter, and is too ready at bringing other men to trial from a pretended zeal and interest about matters in which he really never had the smallest interest. And the truth of this I will endeavor to prove.

24d   Come hither, Meletus, and let me ask a question of you. You think a great deal about the improvement of youth?

Yes, I do.

Tell the judges, then, who is their improver; for you must know, as you have taken the pains to discover their corrupter, and are citing and accusing me before them. Speak, then, and tell the judges who their improver is. Observe, Meletus, that you are silent, and have nothing to say. But is not this rather disgraceful, and a very considerable proof of what I was saying, that you have no

24e   interest in the matter? Speak up, friend, and tell us who their improver is.

The laws.

But that, my good sir, is not my meaning. I want to know who the person is, who, in the first place, knows the laws.

The judges, Socrates, who are present in court.

What do you mean to say, Meletus, that they are able to instruct and improve youth?

Certainly they are.

What, all of them, or some only and not others?

All of them.

By the goddess Hera, that is good news! There are

25a   plenty of improvers, then. And what do you say of the audience, do they improve them?

Yes, they do.

And the senators?

Yes, the senators improve them.

But perhaps the members of the citizen assembly corrupt them? or do they too improve them?

They improve them.

Then every Athenian improves and elevates them; all with the exception of myself; and I alone am their corrupter? Is that what you affirm?

That is what I stoutly affirm.

I am very unfortunate if that is true. But suppose I ask you a question: Would you say that this also holds true in 25b the case of horses? Does one man do them harm and all the world good? Is not the exact opposite of this true? One man is able to do them good, or at least not many; the trainer of horses, that is to say, does them good, and others who have to do with them rather injure them? Is not that true, Meletus, of horses, or any other animals? Yes, certainly. Whether you and Anytus say yes or no, that is no matter. Happy indeed would be the condition of youth if they had one corrupter only, and all the rest of the world 25c were their improvers. And you, Meletus, have sufficiently shown that you never had a thought about the young: your carelessness is seen in your not caring about matters spoken of in this very indictment.

And now, Meletus, I must ask you another question: Which is better, to live among bad citizens, or among good ones? Answer, friend, I say; for that is a question which may be easily answered. Do not the good do their neighbors good, and the bad do them evil?

Certainly.

25d And is there anyone who would rather be injured than benefited by those who live with him? Answer, my good friend; the law requires you to answer: does anyone like to be injured?

Certainly not.

And when you accuse me of corrupting and deteriorating the youth, do you allege that I corrupt them intentionally or unintentionally?

Intentionally, I say.

But you have just admitted that the good do their neighbors good, and the evil do them evil. Now is that a truth which your superior wisdom has recognized thus

25e early in life, and am I, at my age, in such darkness and ignorance as not to know that if a man with whom I have to live is corrupted by me, I am very likely to be harmed by him, and yet I corrupt him, and intentionally, too; that is what you are saying, and of that you will never persuade me or any other human being. But either I do not corrupt

26a them, or I corrupt them unintentionally, so that on either view of the case you lie. If my offense is unintentional, the law has no cognizance of unintentional offenses: you ought to have taken me privately, and warned and admonished me; for if I had been better advised, I should have left off doing what I only did unintentionally—no doubt I should; whereas you hated to converse with me or teach me, but you indicted me in this court, which is a place not of instruction, but of punishment.

26b I have shown, Athenians, as I was saying, that Meletus has no care at all, great or small, about the matter. But still I should like to know, Meletus, in what I am affirmed to corrupt the young. I suppose you mean, as I infer from your indictment, that I teach them not to acknowledge the gods which the state acknowledges, but some other new divinities or spiritual agencies in their stead. These are the lessons which corrupt the youth, as you say.

Yes, that I say emphatically.

26c Then, by the gods, Meletus, of whom we are speaking, tell me and the court, in somewhat plainer terms, what you mean! for I do not as yet understand whether you affirm that I teach others to acknowledge some gods, and therefore do believe in gods and am not an entire atheist— this you do not lay to my charge; but only that they are not the same gods which the city recognizes—the charge is that they are different gods. Or, do you mean to say that I am an atheist simply, and a teacher of atheism?

I mean the latter—that you are a complete atheist.

That is an extraordinary statement, Meletus. Why do

26d you say that? Do you mean that I do not believe in the godhead of the sun or moon, which is the common creed of all men?

I assure you, judges, that he does not believe in them; for he says that the sun is stone, and the moon earth.

Friend Meletus, you think that you are accusing Anaxagoras; and you have but a bad opinion of the judges, if you fancy them ignorant to such a degree as not to know that those doctrines are found in the books of Anaxagoras the Clazomenian, who is full of them. And these are the doctrines which the youth are said to learn of Socrates,

26e when there are not unfrequently exhibitions of them at the theatre (price of admission one drachma at the most); and they might cheaply purchase them, and laugh at Socrates if he pretends to father such eccentricities. And so, Meletus, you really think that I do not believe in any god?

I swear by Zeus that you believe absolutely in none at all.

You are a liar, Meletus, not believed even by yourself. For I cannot help thinking, O men of Athens, that Meletus is reckless and impudent, and that he has written this indictment in a spirit of mere wantonness and youthful

27a bravado. Has he not compounded a riddle, thinking to try me? He said to himself: I shall see whether this wise Socrates will discover my ingenious contradiction, or whether I shall be able to deceive him and the rest of them. For he certainly does appear to me to contradict himself in the indictment as much as if he said that Socrates is guilty of not believing in the gods, and yet of believing in them—but this surely is a piece of fun.

I should like you, O men of Athens, to join me in examining what I conceive to be his inconsistency; and do

27b you, Meletus, answer. And I must remind you that you are not to interrupt me if I speak in my accustomed manner.

Did ever man, Meletus, believe in the existence of human things, and not of human beings? . . . I wish, men of Athens, that he would answer, and not be always trying to get up an interruption. Did ever any man believe in horsemanship, and not in horses? or in flute-playing, and not in flute-players? No, my friend; I will answer to you and to the court, as you refuse to answer for yourself. There is no man who ever did. But now please to answer

27c   the next question: Can a man believe in spiritual and divine agencies, and not in spirits or demigods?

He cannot.

I am glad that I have extracted that answer, by the assistance of the court; nevertheless you swear in the indictment that I teach and believe in divine or spiritual agencies (new or old, no matter for that); at any rate, I believe in spiritual agencies, as you say and swear in the

27d   affidavit; but if I believe in divine beings, I must believe in spirits or demigods; is not that true? Yes, that is true, for I may assume that your silence gives assent to that. Now what are spirits or demigods? are they not either gods or the sons of gods? Is that true?

Yes, that is true.

But this is just the ingenious riddle of which I was speaking: the demigods or spirits are gods, and you say first that I don't believe in gods, and then again that I do believe in gods; that is, if I believe in demigods. For if the demigods are the illegitimate sons of gods, whether by the Nymphs or by any other mothers, as is thought, that, as all men will allow, necessarily implies the existence of their

27e   parents. You might as well affirm the existence of mules, and deny that of horses and asses. Such nonsense, Meletus, could only have been intended by you as a trial of me. You have put this into the indictment because you had nothing real of which to accuse me. But no one who has a particle of understanding will ever be convinced by you that the same man can believe in divine and superhuman things, and yet

28a   not believe that there are gods and demigods and heroes.

I have said enough in answer to the charge of Meletus: any elaborate defense is unnecessary; but as I was saying before, I certainly have many enemies, and this is what will be my destruction if I am destroyed; of that I am certain;

not Meletus, nor yet Anytus, but the envy and detraction of the world, which has been the death of many good men,

28b   and will probably be the death of many more; there is no danger of my being the last of them.

Someone will say: And are you not ashamed, Socrates, of a course of life which is likely to bring you to an untimely end? To him I may fairly answer: There you are mistaken: a man who is good for anything ought not to calculate the chance of living or dying; he ought only to consider whether in doing anything he is doing right or wrong—acting the part of a good man or of a bad. Whereas, according to your view, the heroes who fell at

28c   Troy were not good for much, and the son of Thetis above all, who altogether despised danger in comparison with disgrace; and when his goddess mother said to him, in his eagerness to slay Hector, that if he avenged his companion Patroclus, and slew Hector, he would die himself. "Fate," as she said, "waits upon you next after Hector"; he, hearing this, utterly despised danger and death, and instead of

28d   fearing them, feared rather to live in dishonor, and not to avenge his friend. "Let me die next," he replies, "and be avenged of my enemy, rather than abide here by the beaked ships, a scorn and a burden of the earth." Had Achilles any thought of death and danger? For wherever a man's place is, whether the place which he has chosen or that in which he has been placed by a commander, there he ought to remain in the hour of danger; he should not think of death or of anything, but of disgrace. And this, O men of Athens, is a true saying.

Strange, indeed, would be my conduct, O men of

28e   Athens, if I who, when I was ordered by the generals whom you chose to command me at Potidaea and Amphipolis and Delium, remained where they placed me, like any other man, facing death; if, I say, now, when, as I conceive and imagine, God orders me to fulfill the philosopher's mission of searching into myself and other men, I were to desert my

29a   post through fear of death, or any other fear; that would indeed be strange, and I might justly be arraigned in court for denying the existence of the gods, if I disobeyed the oracle because I was afraid of death: then I should be fancying that I was wise when I was not wise. For this fear of death is indeed the pretense of wisdom, and not real wisdom, being the appearance of knowing the unknown; since no one knows whether death, which they in their fear apprehend to be the greatest evil, may not be the greatest

29b good. Is there not here conceit of knowledge, which is a disgraceful sort of ignorance? And this is the point in which, as I think, I am superior to men in general, and in which I might perhaps fancy myself wiser than other men, that whereas I know but little of the world below, I do not suppose that I know: but I do know that injustice and disobedience to a better, whether God or man, is evil and dishonorable, and I will never fear or avoid a possible good rather than a certain evil. And therefore if you let me go

29c now, and reject the counsels of Anytus, who said that if I were not put to death I ought not to have been prosecuted, and that if I escape now, your sons will all be utterly ruined by listening to my words—if you say to me, Socrates, this time we will not mind Anytus, and will let you off, but upon one condition, that are to inquire and speculate in this way any more, and that if you are caught doing this

29d again you shall die—if this was the condition on which you let me go, I should reply: Men of Athens, I honor and love you; but I shall obey God rather than you, and while I have life and strength I shall never cease from the practice and teaching of philosophy, exhorting anyone whom I meet after my manner, and convincing him, saying: O my friend, why do you who are a citizen of the great and mighty and wise city of Athens, care so much about laying up the greatest amount of money and honor and reputation, and

29e so little about wisdom and truth and the greatest improvement of the soul, which you never regard or heed at all? Are you not ashamed of this? And if the person with whom I am arguing says: Yes, but I do care; I do not depart or let him go at once; I interrogate and examine and cross-examine him, and if I think that he has no virtue, but only says that he has, I reproach him with undervaluing the

30a greater, and overvaluing the less. And this I should say to everyone whom I meet, young and old, citizen and alien, but especially to the citizens, inasmuch as they are my brethren. For this is the command of God, as I would have you know; and I believe that to this day no greater good has ever happened in the state than my service to the God. For I do nothing but go about persuading you all, old and young alike, not to take thought for your persons and your properties, but first and chiefly to care about the greatest

30b improvement of the soul. I tell you that virtue is not given by money, but that from virtue come money and every other good of man, public as well as private. This is my teaching, and if this is the doctrine which corrupts the youth, my influence is ruinous indeed. But if anyone says that this is not my teaching, he is speaking an untruth. Wherefore, O men of Athens, I say to you, do as Anytus bids or not as Anytus bids, and either acquit me or not; but

30c whatever you do, know that I shall never alter my ways, not even if I have to die many times.

Men of Athens, do not interrupt, but hear me; there was an agreement between us that you should hear me out. And I think that what I am going to say will do you good: for I have something more to say, at which you may be inclined to cry out; but I beg that you will not do this. I would have you know that, if you kill such a one as I am, you will injure yourselves more than you will injure me. Meletus and Anytus will not injure me: they cannot; for it

30d is not in the nature of things that a bad man should injure a better than himself. I do not deny that he may, perhaps, kill him, or drive him into exile, or deprive him of civil rights; and he may imagine, and others may imagine, that he is doing him a great injury: but in that I do not agree with him; for the evil of doing as Anytus is doing—of unjustly taking away another man's life—is greater far. And now, Athenians, I am not going to argue for my own sake, as you may think, but for yours, that you may not sin against the God, or lightly reject his boon by condemning me. For if

30e you kill me you will not easily find another like me, who, if I may use such a ludicrous figure of speech, am a sort of gadfly, given to the state by the God; and the state is like a great and noble steed who is tardy in his motions owing to his very size, and requires to be stirred into life. I am that gadfly which God has given the state and all day long and in all places am always fastening upon you, arousing and

31a persuading and reproaching you. And as you will not easily find another like me, I would advise you to spare me. I dare say that you may feel irritated at being suddenly awakened when you are caught napping; and you may think that if you were to strike me dead, as Anytus advises, which you easily might, then you would sleep on for the remainder of your lives, unless God in his care of you gives you another gadfly. And that I am given to you by God is proved by

31b this: that if I had been like other men, I should not have neglected all my own concerns, or patiently seen the neglect of them during all these years, and have been doing yours, coming to you individually, like a father or elder brother, exhorting you to regard virtue; this I say, would not be like human nature. And had I gained anything, or if my exhortations had been paid, there would have been some sense in that: but now, as you will perceive, not even the impudence of my accusers dares to say that I have ever

31c exacted or sought pay of anyone; they have no witness of that. And I have a witness of the truth of what I say; my poverty is a sufficient witness.

Someone may wonder why I go about in private, giving advice and busying myself with the concerns of others, but do not venture to come forward in public and advise the state. I will tell you the reason of this. You have often heard

31d me speak of an oracle or sign which comes to me, and is the divinity which Meletus ridicules in the indictment. This sign I have had ever since I was a child. The sign is a voice which comes to me and always forbids me to do something which I am going to do, but never commands me to do anything, and this is what stands in the way of my being a politician. And rightly, as I think. For I am certain, O men of Athens, that if I had engaged in politics, I should have

31e perished long ago and done no good either to you or to myself. And don't be offended at my telling you the truth: for the truth is that no man who goes to war with you or any other multitude, honestly struggling against the commission of unrighteousness and wrong in the state, will

32a save his life; he who will really fight for the right, if he would live even for a little while, must have a private station and not a public one.

I can give you as proofs of this, not words only, but deeds, which you value more than words. Let me tell you a passage of my own life, which will prove to you that I should never have yielded to injustice from any fear of death, and that if I had not yielded I should have died at once. I will tell you a story—tasteless, perhaps, and commonplace, but nevertheless true. The only office of

32b state which I ever held, O men of Athens, was that of senator; the tribe Antiochis, which is my tribe, had the presidency at the trial of the generals who had not taken up the bodies of the slain after the battle of Arginusae; and you proposed to try them all together, which was illegal, as you all thought afterwards; but at the time I was the only one of the Prytanes who was opposed to the illegality, and I gave my vote against you; and when the orators threatened to impeach and arrest me, and have me taken away, and you called and shouted, I made up my mind that I would run

32c the risk, having law and justice with me, rather than take part in your injustice because I feared imprisonment and death. This happened in the days of the democracy. But when the oligarchy of the Thirty was in power, they sent for me and four others into the rotunda, and bade us bring Leon the Salaminian from Salamis, as they wanted to execute him. This was a specimen of the sort of commands which they were always giving with the view of implicating as many as possible in their crimes; and then I showed, not

32d in words only, but in deed, that, if I may be allowed to use such an expression, I cared not a straw for death, and that my only fear was the fear of doing an unrighteous or unholy thing. For the strong arm of that oppressive power did not frighten me into doing wrong; and when we came out of the rotunda the other four went to Salamis and fetched Leon, but I went quietly home. For which I might have lost my life, had not the power of the government shortly

32e   afterwards come to an end. And to this many will witness.

Now do you really imagine that I could have survived all these years, if I had led a public life, supposing that like a good man I had always supported the right and had made justice, as I ought, the first thing? No, indeed, men of

33a   Athens, neither I nor any other. But I have been always the same in all my actions, public as well as private, and never have I yielded any base compliance to those who are slanderously termed my disciples or to any other. For the truth is that I have no regular disciples: but if anyone likes to come and hear me while I am pursuing my mission, whether he be young or old, he may freely come. Nor do I

33b   converse with those who pay only, and not with those who do not pay; but anyone, whether he be rich or poor, may ask and answer me and listen to my words; and whether he turns out to be a bad man or a good one, that cannot be justly laid to my charge, as I never taught him anything. And if anyone says that he has ever learned or heard anything from me in private which all the world has not heard, I should like you to know that he is speaking an untruth.

But I shall be asked, Why do people delight in

33c   continually conversing with you? I have told you already, Athenians, the whole truth about this: they like to hear the cross-examination of the pretenders to wisdom; there is amusement in this. And this is a duty which the God has imposed upon me, as I am assured by oracles, visions, and in every sort of way in which the will of divine power was ever signified to anyone. This is true, O Athenians; or, if not true, would be soon refuted. For if I am really corrupting

33d   the youth, and have corrupted some of them already, those of them who have grown up and have become sensible that I gave them bad advice in the days of their youth should come forward as accusers and take their revenge; and if they do not like to come themselves, some of their relatives, fathers, brothers, or other kinsmen, should say what evil their families suffered at my hands. Now is their time. Many of them I see in the court. There is Crito, who

33e   is of the same age and of the same deme with myself; and there is Critobulus his son, whom I also see. Then again

there is Lysanias of Sphettus, who is the father of Aeschines
—he is present; and also there is Antiphon of Cephisus,
who is the father of Epignes; and there are the brothers of
several who have associated with me. There is Nicostratus
the son of Theosdotides, and the brother of Theodotus
(now Theodotus himself is dead, and therefore he, at any
rate, will not seek to stop him); and there is Paralus the son
of Demodocus, who had a brother Theages; and

34a   Adeimantus the son of Ariston, whose brother Plato is
present; and Aeantodorus, who is the brother of
Apollodorus, whom I also see. I might mention a great
many others, any of whom Meletus should have produced
as witnesses in the course of his speech; and let him still
produce them, if he has forgotten—I will make way for
him. And let him say, if he has any testimony of the sort
which he can produce. Nay, Athenians, the very opposite is
the truth. For all these are ready to witness on behalf of the
corrupter, of the destroyer of their kindred, as Meletus and

34b   Anytus call me; not the corrupted youth only—there might
have been a motive for that—but their uncorrupted elder
relatives. Why should they too support me with their
testimony? Why, indeed, except for the sake of truth and
justice, and because they know that I am speaking the
truth, and that Meletus is lying.

Well, Athenians, this and the like of this is nearly all the
defense which I have to offer. Yet a word more. Perhaps
there may be someone who is offended at me, when he calls

34c   to mind how he himself, on a similar or even a less serious
occasion, had recourse to prayers and supplications with
many tears, and how he produced his children in court,
which was a moving spectacle, together with a posse of his
relations and friends; whereas I, who am probably in
danger of my life, will do none of these things. Perhaps this
may come into his mind, and he may be set against me, and
vote in anger because he is displeased at this. Now if there

34d   be such a person among you, which I am far from affirming,
I may fairly reply to him: My friend, I am a man, and like
other men, a creature of flesh and blood, and not of wood
or stone, as Homer says; and I have a family, yes, and sons.

O Athenians, three in number, one of whom is growing up, and the two others are still young; and yet I will not bring any of them hither in order to petition you for an acquittal. And why not? Not from any self-will or disregard of you.

34e Whether I am or am not afraid of death is another question, of which I will not now speak. But my reason simply is that I feel such conduct to be discreditable to myself, and you, and the whole state. One who has reached my years, and who has a name for wisdom, whether deserved or not, ought not to debase himself. At any rate, the world has decided that Socrates is in some way superior

35a to other men. And if those among you who are said to be superior in wisdom and courage, and any other virtue, demean themselves in this way, how shameful is their conduct! I have seen men of reputation, when they have been condemned, behaving in the strangest manner: they seemed to fancy that they were going to suffer something dreadful if they died, and that they could be immortal if you only allowed them to live; and I think that they were a dishonor to the state, and that any stranger coming in would say of them that the most eminent men of Athens, to

35b whom the Athenians themselves give honor and command, are no better than women. And I say that these things ought not to be done by those of us who are of reputation; and if they are done, you ought not to permit them; you ought rather to show that you are more inclined to condemn, not the man who is quiet, but the man who gets up a doleful scene, and makes the city ridiculous.

But, setting aside the question of dishonor, there
35c seems to be something wrong in petitioning a judge, and thus procuring an acquittal instead of informing and convincing him. For his duty is, not to make a present of justice, but to give judgment; and he has sworn that he will judge according to the laws, and not according to his own good pleasure; and neither he nor we should get into the habit of perjuring ourselves—there can be no piety in that. Do not then require me to do what I consider dishonorable
35d and impious and wrong, especially now, when I am being tried for impiety on the indictment of Meletus. For if, O

men of Athens, by force of persuasion and entreaty, I could overpower your oaths, then I should be teaching you to believe that there are no gods, and convict myself, in my own defense, of not believing in them. But that is not the case; for I do believe that there are gods, and in a far higher sense than that in which any of my accusers believe in them. And to you and to God I commit my cause, to be determined by you as is best for you and me.

The jury finds Socrates guilty.

Socrates' Proposal for His Sentence

35e
36a
There are many reasons why I am not grieved, O men of Athens, at the vote of condemnation. I expected it, and am only surprised that the votes are so nearly equal; for I had thought that the majority against me would have been far larger; but now, had thirty votes gone over to the other side, I should have been acquitted. And I may say that I have escaped Meletus. And I may say more; for without the assistance of Anytus and Lycon, he would not have had a fifth part of the votes, as the law requires, in which case he

36b
would have incurred a fine of a thousand drachmae, as is evident.

And so he proposes death as the penalty. And what shall I propose on my part, O men of Athens? Clearly that which is my due. And what is that which I ought to pay or to receive? What shall be done to the man who has never had the wit to be idle during his whole life; but has been careless of what the many care about—wealth, and family interests, and military offices, and speaking in the assembly, and magistracies, and plots, and parties. Reflecting that I was really too honest a man to follow in this way and live, I

36c
did not go where I could do no good to you or to myself; but where I could do the greatest good privately to everyone of you, thither I went, and sought to persuade every man among you that he must look to himself, and seek virtue and wisdom before he looks to his private interests, and look to the state before he looks to the interests of the state; and that this should be the order which he observes in all his actions. What shall be done to

36d   such a one? Doubtless some good thing, O men of Athens, if he has his reward; and the good should be of a kind suitable to him. What would be a reward suitable to a poor man who is your benefactor, who desires leisure that he may instruct you? There can be no more fitting reward than maintenance in the Prytaneum, O men of Athens, a reward which he deserves far more than the citizen who has won the prize at Olympia in the horse or chariot race, whether the chariots were drawn by two horses or by many. For I

36e   am in want, and he has enough; and he only gives you the appearance of happiness, and I give you the reality. And if I

37a   am to estimate the penalty justly, I say that maintenance in the Prytaneum is the just return.

    Perhaps you may think that I am braving you in saying this, as in what I said before about the tears and prayers. But that is not the case. I speak rather because I am convinced that I never intentionally wronged anyone, although I cannot convince you of that—for we have had a short conversation only; but if there were a law at Athens,

37b   such as there is in other cities, that a capital cause should not be decided in one day, then I believe that I should have convinced you; but now the time is too short. I cannot in a moment refute great slanders; and, as I am convinced that I never wronged another, I will assuredly not wrong myself. I will not say of myself that I deserve any evil, or propose any penalty. Why should I? Because I am afraid of the penalty of death which Meletus proposes? When I do not know whether death is a good or an evil, why should I propose a penalty which would certainly be an evil? Shall I say

37c   imprisonment? And why should I live in prison, and be the slave of the magistrates of the year—of the Eleven? Or shall the penalty be a fine, and imprisonment until the fine is paid? There is the same objection. I should have to lie in prison, for money I have none, and I cannot pay. And if I say exile (and this may possibly be the penalty which you will affix), I must indeed be blinded by the love of life if I were to consider that when you, who are my own citizens,

37d   cannot endure my discourses and words, and have found them so grievous and odious that you would fain have done with them, others are likely to endure me. No, indeed, men of Athens, that is not very likely. And what a life should I lead, at my age, wandering from city to city, living in ever-changing exile, and always being driven out! For I am quite sure that into whatever place I go, as here so also there, the young men will come to me; and if I drive them away, their elders will drive me out at their desire: and if I let them

37e come, their fathers and friends will drive me out for their sakes.

Someone will say: Yes, Socrates, but cannot you hold your tongue, and then you may go into a foreign city, and no one will interfere with you? Now I have great difficulty in making you understand my answer to this. For if I tell you that this would be a disobedience to a divine command, and therefore that I cannot hold my tongue, you will not believe that I am serious; and if I say again that the greatest

38a good of man is daily to converse about virtue, and all that concerning which you hear me examining myself and others, and that the life which is unexamined is not worth living—that you are still less likely to believe. And yet what I say is true, although a thing of which it is hard for me to persuade you. Moreover, I am not accustomed to think that

38b I deserve any punishment. Had I money I might have proposed to give you what I had, and have been none the worse. But you see that I have none, and can only ask you to proportion the fine to my means. However, I think that I could afford a minae, and therefore I propose that penalty; Plato, Crito, Critobulus, and Apollodorus, my friends here, bid me say thirty minae, and they will be the sureties. Well then, say thirty minae, let that be the penalty; for that they will be ample security to you.

The jury condemns Socrates to death.

Socrates' Comments on His Sentence

38c   Not much time will be gained, O Athenians, in return for the evil name which you will get from the detractors of the city, who will say that you killed Socrates, a wise man; for they will call me wise even although I am not wise when they want to reproach you. If you had waited a little while, your desire would have been fulfilled in the course of nature. For I am far advanced in years, as you may perceive, and not far from death. I am speaking now only to those of

38d   you who have condemned me to death. And I have another thing to say to them: You think that I was convicted through deficiency of words—I mean, that if I had thought fit to leave nothing undone, nothing unsaid, I might have gained an acquittal. Not so; the deficiency which led to my conviction was not of words—certainly not. But I had not the boldness or impudence or inclination to address you as you would have liked me to address you, weeping and wailing and lamenting, and saying and doing many things which you have been accustomed to hear from others, and

38e   which, as I say, are unworthy of me. But I thought that I ought not to do anything common or mean in the hour of danger: nor do I now repent of the manner of my defense, and I would rather die having spoken after my manner, than speak in your manner and live. For neither in war nor yet at law ought any man to use every way of escaping death. For

39a   often in battle there is no doubt that if a man will throw away his arms, and fall on his knees before his pursuers, he may escape death; and in other dangers there are other ways of escaping death, if a man is willing to say and do anything. The difficulty, my friends, is not in avoiding death, but in avoiding unrighteousness; for that runs faster than death. I am old and move slowly, and the slower

39b   runner has overtaken me, and my accusers are keen and quick, and the faster runner, who is unrighteousness, has overtaken them. And now I depart hence condemned by you to suffer the penalty of death, and they, too, go their ways condemned by the truth to suffer the penalty of villainy and wrong; and I must abide by my award—let them abide by theirs. I suppose that these things may be regarded as fated—and I think that they are well.

39c   And now, O men who have condemned me, I would fain prophesy to you; for I am about to die, and that is the hour in which men are gifted with prophetic power. And I prophesy to you who are my murderers, that immediately after my death punishment far heavier than you have inflicted on me will surely await you. Me you have killed because you wanted to escape the accuser, and not to give an account of your lives. But that will not be as you suppose: far otherwise. For I say that there will be more accusers of you than there are now; accusers whom hitherto

39d I have restrained: and as they are younger they will be more severe with you, and you will be more offended at them. For if you think that by killing men you can avoid the accuser censuring your lives, you are mistaken; that is not a way of escape which is either possible or honorable; the easiest and noblest way is not to be crushing others, but to be improving yourselves. This is the prophecy which I utter

39e before my departure, to the judges who have condemned me.

Friends, who would have acquitted me, I would like also to talk with you about this thing which has happened, while the magistrates are busy, and before I go to the place at which I must die. Stay then awhile, for we may as well

40a talk with one another while there is time. You are my friends, and I should like to show you the meaning of this event which has happened to me. O my judges—for you I may truly call judges—I should like to tell you of a wonderful circumstance. Hitherto the familiar oracle within me has constantly been in the habit of opposing me even about trifles, if I was going to make a slip or error about anything; and now as you see there has come upon me that which may be thought, and is generally believed to be, the last and worst evil. But the oracle made no sign of

40b opposition, either as I was leaving my house and going out in the morning, or when I was going up into this court, or while I was speaking, at anything which I was going to say; and yet I have often been stopped in the middle of a speech; but now in nothing I either said or did touching this matter has the oracle opposed me. What do I take to be the explanation of this? I will tell you. I regard this as a proof that what has happened to me is a good, and that

40c those of us who think that death is an evil are in error. This is a great proof to me of what I am saying, for the customary sign would surely have opposed me had I been going to evil and not to good.

Let us reflect in another way, and we shall see that there is great reason to hope that death is a good, for one of two things: either death is a state of nothingness and utter unconsciousness, or, as men say, there is a change and migration of the soul from this world to another. Now if you suppose that there is no consciousness, but a sleep like

40d   the sleep of him who is undisturbed even by the sight of dreams, death will be an unspeakable gain. For if a person were to select the night in which his sleep was undisturbed even by dreams, and were to compare with this the other days and nights of his life, and then were to tell us how many days and nights he had passed in the course of his life better and more pleasantly than this one, I think that any man, I will not say a private man, but even the great king,

40e   will not find many such days or nights, when compared with the others. Now if death is like this, I say that to die is gain; for eternity is then only a single night. But if death is the journey to another place, and there, as men say, all the dead are, what good, O my friends and judges, can be greater than this? If indeed when the pilgrim arrives in the

41a   world below, he is delivered from the professors of justice in this world, and finds the true judges who are said to give judgment there, Minos and Rhadamanthus and Aeacus and Triptolemus, and other sons of God who were righteous in their own life, that pilgrimage will be worth making. What would not a man give if he might converse with Orpheus and Musaeus and Hesiod and Homer? Nay, if this be true, let me die again and again. I, too, shall have a wonderful

41b   interest in a place where I can converse with Palamedes, and Ajax the son of Telamon, and other heroes of old, who have suffered death through an unjust judgment; and there will be no small pleasure, as I think, in comparing my own sufferings with theirs. Above all, I shall be able to continue my search into true and false knowledge; as in this world, so also in that; I shall find out who is wise, and who pretends to be wise, and is not. What would not a man give, O judges, to be able to examine the leader of the great Trojan

41c   expedition; or Odysseus or Sisyphus, or numberless others, men and women too! What infinite delight would there be in conversing with them and asking them questions! For in that world they do not put a man to death for this; certainly not. For besides being happier in that world than in this, they will be immortal, if what is said is true.

41d   Wherefore, O judges, be of good cheer about death, and know this of a truth—that no evil can happen to a good man, either in life or after death. He and his are not neglected by the gods; nor has my own approaching end happened by mere chance. But I see clearly that to die and be released was better for me; and therefore the oracle gave no sign. For which reason also, I am not angry with my accusers, or my condemners; they have done me no harm,
41e   although neither of them meant to do me any good; and for this I may gently blame them.

Still I have a favor to ask of them. When my sons are grown up, I would ask you, O my friends, to punish them; and I would have you trouble them, as I have troubled you, if they seem to care about riches, or anything, more than about virtue; or if they pretend to be something when they are really nothing, then reprove them, as I have reproved you, for not caring about that for which they ought to care, and thinking that they are something when they are really
42a   nothing. And if you do this, I and my sons will have received justice at your hands.

The hour of departure has arrived, and we go our ways —I to die, and you to live. Which is better God only knows.

The Republic:
Excerpts from Books II and IX

Plato

The Republic *of Plato (c. 427–c. 347 BCE), a ten-book masterpiece of philosophy, begins with the fundamental question "What is justice?" Socrates pursues an understanding of the nature of the just man by looking first at what a just society would be. In the course of the dialogue, Plato touches on almost every other subject of importance: society, government, virtue, goodness, truth, beauty, and more.*

The first excerpt gives the legend of the Ring of Gyges, a ring that renders its wearer invisible. This story is used to raise the question whether there is any good reason for a person to be just if there is no practical downside to being unjust. (In the twentieth century, the concept was adapted by J.R.R. Tolkien in The Lord of the Rings *trilogy.)*

The second excerpt attempts to refute the idea of Thrasymachus that justice should be defined as the advantage of the stronger.

Above: Detail of Plato, from *School of Athens*, Raphael, 1509–1511, fresco.

ca. 380 BCE; translated by G.M.A. Grube, 1974, revised by C.D.C. Reeve, 1992.

Book II

357a   When I said this, I thought I had done with the discussion, but it turned out to have been only a prelude. Glaucon showed his characteristic courage on this occasion too and refused to accept Thrasymachus' abandonment of the argument. Socrates, he said, do you want to seem to have persuaded us that it is better in every way to be just than unjust, or do you want truly to

357b convince us of this?

I want truly to convince you, I said, if I can.

Well, then, you certainly aren't doing what you want. Tell me, do you think there is a kind of good we welcome, not because we desire what comes from it, but because we welcome it for its own sake—joy, for example, and all the harmless pleasures that have no results beyond the joy of having them?

Certainly, I think there are such things.

And is there a kind of good we like for its own sake and

357c also for the sake of what comes from it—knowing, for example, and seeing and being healthy? We welcome such things, I suppose, on both counts.

Yes.

And do you also see a third kind of good, such as physical training, medical treatment when sick, medicine itself, and the other ways of making money? We'd say that these are onerous but beneficial to us, and we wouldn't choose them for their own sakes, but for the sake of the

357d rewards and other things that come from them.

There is also this third kind. But what of it?

Where do you put justice?

358a   I myself put it among the finest goods, as something to be valued by anyone who is going to be blessed with happiness, both because of itself and because of what comes from it.

That isn't most people's opinion. They'd say that justice belongs to the onerous kind, and is to be practiced for the sake of the rewards and popularity that come from a reputation for justice, but is to be avoided because of itself as something burdensome.

I know that's the general opinion. Thrasymachus faulted justice on these grounds a moment ago and praised injustice, but it seems that I'm a slow learner.

358b   Come, then, and listen to me as well, and see whether you still have that problem, for I think that Thrasymachus gave up before he had to, charmed by you as if he were a snake. But I'm not yet satisfied by the argument on either side. I want to know what justice and injustice are and what power each itself has when it's by itself in the soul. I want to leave out of account their rewards and what comes from each of them. So, if you agree, I'll renew the argument of Thrasymachus. First, I'll state what kind of
358c thing people consider justice to be and what its origins are. Second, I'll argue that all who practice it do so unwillingly, as something necessary, not as something good. Third, I'll argue that they have good reason to act as they do, for the life of an unjust person is, they say, much better than that of a just one.

It isn't, Socrates, that I believe any of that myself. I'm perplexed, indeed, and my ears are deafened listening to Thrasymachus and countless others. But I've yet to hear anyone defend justice in the way I want, proving that it is
358d better than injustice. I want to hear it praised *by itself*, and I think that I'm most likely to hear this from you. Therefore, I'm going to speak at length in praise of the unjust life, and in doing so I'll show you the way I want to hear you praising justice and denouncing injustice. But see whether you want me to do that or not.

I want that most of all. Indeed, what subject could someone with my understanding enjoy discussing more often?

358e   Excellent. Then let's discuss the first subject I mentioned—what justice is and what its origins are.

They say that to do injustice is naturally good and to suffer injustice bad, but that the badness of suffering it so far exceeds the goodness of doing it that those who have done and suffered injustice and tasted both, but who lack the power to do it and avoid suffering it, decide that it is
359a profitable to come to an agreement with each other neither to do injustice nor to suffer it. As a result, they begin to make laws and covenants, and what the law commands they call lawful and just. This, they say, is the origin and essence of justice. It is intermediate between the best and the worst. The best is to do injustice without paying the penalty; the worst is to suffer it without being able to take revenge. Justice is a mean between these two extremes. People value it not as a good but because they are too weak
359b to do injustice with impunity. Someone who has the power to do this, however, and is a true man wouldn't make an agreement with anyone not to do injustice in order not to suffer it. For him that would be madness. This is the nature of justice, according to the argument, Socrates, and these are its natural origins.

We can see most clearly that those who practice justice
359c do it unwillingly and because they lack the power to do injustice, if in our thoughts we grant to a just and an unjust person the freedom to do whatever they like. We can then follow both of them and see where their desires would lead. And we'll catch the just person red-handed traveling the same road as the unjust. The reason for this is the desire to outdo others and get more and more. This is what anyone's nature naturally pursues as good, but nature is forced by law into the perversion of treating fairness with respect.

The freedom I mentioned would be most easily realized if both people had the power they say the ancestor of
359d Gyges of Lydia possessed. The story goes that he was a shepherd in the service of the ruler of Lydia. There was a violent thunderstorm, and an earthquake broke open the ground and created a chasm at the place where he was

tending his sheep. Seeing this, he was filled with
amazement and went down into it. And there, in addition
to many other wonders of which we're told, he saw a
hollow bronze horse. There were windowlike openings in
it, and, peeping in, he saw a corpse, which seemed to be of
more than human size, wearing nothing but a gold ring on
359e its finger. He took the ring and came out of the chasm. He
wore the ring at the usual monthly meeting that reported to
the king on the state of the flocks. And as he was sitting
among the others, he happened to turn the setting of the
ring towards himself to the inside of his hand. When he did
this, he became invisible to those sitting near him, and
360a they went on talking as if he had gone. He wondered at
this, and, fingering the ring, he turned the setting outwards
again and became visible. So he experimented with the ring
to test whether it indeed had this power—and it did. If he
turned the setting inward, he became invisible; if he turned
it outward, he became visible again. When he realized this,
he at once arranged to become one of the messengers sent
to report to the king. And when he arrived there, he
seduced the king's wife, attacked the king with
360b her help, killed him, and took over the kingdom.

    Let's suppose, then, that there were two such rings, one
worn by a just and the other by an unjust person. Now, no
one, it seems, would be so incorruptible that he would stay
on the path of justice or stay away from other people's
property, when he could take whatever he wanted from the
marketplace with impunity, go into people's houses and
360c have sex with anyone he wished, kill or release from prison
anyone he wished, and do all the other things that would
make him like a god among humans. Rather his actions
would be in no way different from those of an unjust
person, and both would follow the same path. This, some
would say, is a great proof that one is never just willingly
but only when compelled to be. No one believes justice to
be a good when it is kept private, since, wherever either
person thinks he can do injustice with impunity, he does it.
Indeed, every man believes that injustice is far more
profitable to himself than justice. And any exponent of this

360d argument will say he's right, for someone who didn't want
to do injustice, given this sort of opportunity, and who
didn't touch other people's property would be thought
wretched and stupid by everyone aware of the situation,
though, of course, they'd praise him in public, deceiving
each other for fear of suffering injustice. So much for my
second topic.

Book IX

588b   All right, then. Since we've reached this point in the
argument, let's return to the first things we said, since they
are what led us here. I think someone said at some point
that injustice profits a completely unjust person who is
believed to be just. Isn't that so?

It certainly is.

Now, let's discuss this with him, since we've agreed on
the retrospective powers that injustice and justice have.

How?

By fashioning an image of the soul in words, so that the
person who says this sort of thing will know what he is saying.

588c   What sort of image?

One like those creatures that legends tell us used to
come into being in ancient times, such as the Chimera,
Scylla, Cerberus, or any of the multitude of others in which
many different kinds of things are said to have grown
together naturally into one.

Yes, the legends do tell us of such things.

Well, then, fashion a single kind of multicolored beast
with a ring of many heads that it can grow and change at
will—some from gentle, some from savage animals.

588d   That's work for a clever artist. However, since words are
more malleable than wax and the like, consider it done.

Then fashion one other kind, that of a lion, and another
of a human being. But make the first much the largest and
the other second to it in size.

That's easier—the sculpting is done.

Now join the three of them into one, so that they somehow grow together naturally.

They're joined.

Then, fashion around them the image of one of them, that of a human being, so that anyone who sees only the 588e outer covering and not what's inside will think it's a single creature, a human being.

It's done.

Then, if someone maintains that injustice profits this human being and that doing just things brings no advantage, let's tell him that he is simply saying that it is beneficial for him, first, to feed the multiform beast well and make it strong, and also the lion and all that pertains 589 to him; second, to starve and weaken the human being within, so that he is dragged along wherever either of the other two leads; and, third, to leave the parts to bite and kill one another rather than accustoming them to each other and making them friendly.

Yes, that's absolutely what someone who praises injustice is saying.

But on the other hand, wouldn't someone who maintains that just things are profitable be saying, first, that all our words and deeds should insure that the human being within this human being has the most control; 589b second, that he should take care of the many-headed beast as a farmer does his animals, feeding and domesticating the gentle heads and preventing the savage ones from growing; and, third, that he should make the lion's nature his ally, care for the community of all his parts, and bring them up in such a way that they will be friends with each other and with himself?

Yes, that's exactly what someone who praises justice is saying.

From every point of view, then, anyone who praises justice speaks truly, and anyone who praises injustice speaks falsely. Whether we look at the matter from the point of view of pleasure, good reputation, or advantage, a

589c praiser of justice tells the truth, while one who condemns it has nothing sound to say and condemns without knowing what he is condemning.

In my opinion at least, he knows nothing about it.

Then let's persuade him gently—for he isn't wrong of his own will—by asking him these questions. Should we say that this is the original basis for the conventions about what is fine and what is shameful? Fine things are those that subordinate the beastlike parts of our nature to the

589d human—or better, perhaps, to the divine; shameful ones are those that enslave the gentle to the savage? Will he agree or what?

He will if he takes my advice.

In light of this argument, can it profit anyone to acquire gold unjustly if, by doing so, he enslaves the best part of himself to the most vicious? If he got the gold by enslaving his son or daughter to the savage and evil men, it

589e wouldn't profit him, no matter how much gold he got. How, then, could he fail to be wretched if he pitilessly enslaves the most divine part of himself to the most godless and polluted one and accepts golden gifts in return

590a for a more terrible destruction than Eriphyle's when she took the necklace in return for her husband's soul?[2]

A much more terrible one, Glaucon said. I'll answer for him.

And don't you think that licentiousness has long been condemned for just these reasons, namely, that because of it, that terrible, large, and multiform beast is let loose more than it should be?

Clearly.

---

[2] Eriphyle was bribed with a golden necklace by Polynices to persuade her husband, Amphiaraus, to join the "Seven Against Thebes." He was killed. See Odyssey xi.326–327; Pindar, Nemean, 9.16ff.

And aren't stubbornness and irritability condemned
590b   because they inharmoniously increase and stretch the
lionlike and snakelike part?

Certainly.

And aren't luxury and softness condemned because the
slackening and loosening of this same part produce
cowardice in it?

Of course.

And aren't flattery and slavishness condemned because
they subject the spirited part to the moblike beast,
accustoming it from youth on to being insulted for the sake
of the money needed to satisfy the beast's insatiable
appetites, so that it becomes an ape instead of a lion?

590c   They certainly are.

Why do you think the condition of a manual worker is
despised? Or is it for any other reason than that, when the
best part is naturally weak in someone, it can't rule the
beasts within him but can only serve them and learn to
flatter them?

Probably so.

Therefore, to insure that someone like that is ruled by
something similar to what rules the best person, we say that
he ought to be the slave of that best person who has a
divine ruler within himself. It isn't to harm the slave that
590d   we say he must be ruled, which is what Thrasymachus
thought to be true of all subjects, but because it is better for
everyone to be ruled by divine reason, preferably from
within himself and his own, otherwise imposed from
without, so that as far as possible all will be alike and
friends, governed by the same thing.

Yes, that's right.

Phaedrus

Allegory
of the Charioteer

Plato

Phaedrus is a dialogue whose three main speeches are about the nature of love: specifically the difference between Platonic love and romantic love and their relation to one another. But love also serves as foundation for discussion of the soul, madness, the role of divine inspiration, aesthetic experience, and the mastery of an art.

The portion excerpted here describes the challenges posed to the soul by the desires and motives of different parts of the self. Using the analogy of a charioteer with two horses pulling in opposite manners, Plato describes how people experience conflict between acting morally and rationally while and being driven by irrationality, passion, and appetite.

The elucidation of this conflict within the soul has had a lasting impact on Western views of personality, decision making, and what it means to be human. The concept of having an angel on one shoulder and a devil on the other—often still employed in cartoons—is an analogy illustrating the same principle of conflict, albeit with different components. The Freudian concepts of id, ego, and superego too stem from this sense of conflict within the person.

Above: Charioteer with two horses, bronze, 25.4 cm x 10.16 cm x 15.24 cm, from http://www.emuseum store.com/Roman-Charioteer-with-Two-Horses-Bonded-Bronze-Small_p_882.html.

Written ca. 370 BCE; translated by Harold North Fowler, 1925

For every body which derives motion from without is soulless, but that which has its motion within itself has a soul, since that is the nature of the soul; but if this is true,

246a — that that which moves itself is nothing else than the soul,— then the soul would necessarily be ungenerated and immortal.

Concerning the immortality of the soul this is enough; but about its form we must speak in the following manner. To tell what the soul really is would be a matter for utterly superhuman and long discourse, but it is within human power to describe it more briefly by an analogy; let us therefore speak in that way. We will liken the soul to this composition: a pair of winged horses and a charioteer.

Now the horses and charioteers of the gods are all good and of good descent, but in other beings there are some good and some bad. First, the charioteer of the human soul

246b drives a pair of horses; secondly, one of the horses is noble and of noble breed, but the other quite the opposite in breed and character. Therefore in our case the driving is necessarily difficult and troublesome. Now we must try to tell why a living being is called mortal or immortal. Soul, considered as a whole, has the care of all that which is soulless, and it traverses the whole heaven, appearing sometimes in one form and sometimes in another. Now when it is perfect and fully winged, it mounts upward and

246c governs the whole world; but the soul which has lost its wings is borne along until it gets hold of something solid, when it settles down, taking upon itself an earthly body, which seems to be self-moving, because of the power of the soul within it; and the whole, compounded of soul and body, is called a living being, and is further designated as mortal. It is not immortal by any reasonable supposition, but we, though we have never see or rightly conceived a

246d god, imagine an immortal being which has both a soul and a body which are united for all time.

Let the existence of such beings, however, and our words concerning them, be as is pleasing to God; we will now consider the reason why the soul loses its wings. The natural function of the wing is to soar upwards and carry that which is heavy up to the place where the gods dwell. More than any other thing that pertains to the body it partakes of the nature of the divine. But the divine is beauty,

246e wisdom, goodness, and all such qualities; by these then the wings of the soul are nourished and grow, but by the opposite qualities, such as vileness and evil, they are wasted away and destroyed.

Now the great leader in heaven, Zeus, driving a winged chariot, goes first, arranging all things and caring for all

247a things. He is followed by an army of gods and spirits, arrayed in eleven squadrons; Hestia alone remains in the house of the gods. Of the rest, those who are included among the twelve great gods and are accounted leaders, are assigned each to his place in the army. There are many blessed sights and many ways hither and thither within the heaven, along which the blessed gods go to and fro attending each to his own duties; and whoever wishes, and is able, follows, for jealousy is excluded from the celestial band. But when they go to a feast

247b and a banquet, they proceed steeply upward to the top of the vault of heaven, where the chariots of the gods, whose well matched horses obey the rein, advance easily, but the others with difficulty; for the horse of evil nature weighs the chariot down, making it heavy and pulling toward the earth the charioteer whose horse is not well trained. There the utmost toil and struggle await the soul. For those that are called

247c immortal, when they reach the top, pass outside and take their place on the outer surface of the heaven, and when they have taken their stand, the revolution carries them round and they behold the things outside of the heaven. But the region above the heaven was never worthily sung by any earthly poet, nor will it ever be. It is, however, as I shall tell; for I must dare to speak the truth, especially as truth is my theme. For the colorless, formless, and intangible truly existing essence, with which all true knowledge is concerned, holds this region and is

247d visible only to the mind, the pilot of the soul. Now the divine intelligence, since it is nurtured on mind and pure knowledge, and the intelligence of every soul which is capable of receiving that which befits it, rejoices in seeing reality for a space of time and by gazing upon truth is nourished and made happy until the revolution brings it again to the same place. In the revolution it beholds absolute justice, temperance, and knowledge, not such knowledge as has a beginning and varies as it is associated with one or another of the things we call 247e realities, but that which abides in the real eternal absolute; and in the same way it beholds and feeds upon the other eternal verities, after which, passing down again within the heaven, it goes home, and there the charioteer puts up the horses at the manger and feeds them with ambrosia and then gives them nectar to drink.

Such is the life of the gods; but of the other souls, that 248a which best follows after God and is most like him, raises the head of the charioteer up into the outer region and is carried round in the revolution, troubled by the horses and hardly beholding the realities; and another sometimes rises and sometimes sinks, and, because its horses are unruly, it sees some things and fails to see others. The other souls follow after, all yearning for the upper region but unable to reach it, and are carried round beneath, trampling upon 248b and colliding with one another, each striving to pass its neighbor. So there is the greatest confusion and sweat of rivalry, wherein many are lamed, and many wings are broken through the incompetence of the drivers; and after much toil they all go away without gaining a view of reality, and when they have gone away they feed upon opinion. But the reason of the great eagerness to see where the plain of truth is, lies in the fact that the fitting pasturage for the best part of the soul is in the meadow there, and the wing on which the soul is raised up is nourished by this.

248c   And this is a law of Destiny, that the soul which follows after God and obtains a view of any of the truths is free from harm until the next period, and if it can always attain this, is always unharmed; but when, through inability to follow, it fails to see, and through some mischance is filled with forgetfulness and evil and grows heavy, and when it has grown heavy, loses 248d its wings and falls to the earth, then it is the law that this soul shall never pass into any beast at its first birth, but the soul that has seen the most shall enter into the birth of a man who is to be a philosopher or a lover of beauty, or one of a musical or loving nature, and the second soul into that of a lawful king or a warlike ruler, and the third into that of a politician or a man of business or a financier, the fourth into that of a hardworking

248e gymnast or one who will be concerned with the cure of the body, and the fifth will lead the life of a of a prophet or some one who conducts mystic rites; to the sixth, a poet or some other imitative artist will be united, to the seventh, a craftsman or a husbandman, to the eighth, a sophist or a demagogue, to the ninth, a tyrant.

Now in all these states, whoever lives justly obtains a better lot, and whoever lives unjustly, a worse. For each soul

249a returns to the place whence it came in ten thousand years; for it does not regain its wings before that time has elapsed, except the soul of him who has been a guileless philosopher or a philosophical lover; these, when for three successive periods of a thousand years they have chosen such a life, after the third period of a thousand years become winged in the three thousandth year and go their way; but the rest, when they have finished their first life, receive judgment, and after the judgment some go to the places of correction under the earth

249b and pay their penalty, while the others, made light and raised up into a heavenly place by justice, live in a manner worthy of the life they led in human form. But in the thousandth year both come to draw lots and choose their second life, each choosing whatever it wishes. Then a human soul may pass into the life of a beast, and a soul which was once human, may pass again from a beast into a man. For the soul which has never seen the truth can never pass into human form. For a human being must understand a general conception formed by collecting into a unity by means of reason the many

249c perceptions of the senses; and this is a recollection of those things which our soul once beheld, when it journeyed with God and, lifting its vision above the things which we now say exist, rose up into real being.

And therefore it is just that the mind of the philosopher only has wings, for he is always, so far as he is able, in communion through memory with those things the communion with which causes God to be divine. Now a man

who employs such memories rightly is always being initiated
into perfect mysteries and he alone becomes truly perfect;
249d but since he separates himself from human interests and turns
his attention toward the divine, he is rebuked by the vulgar,
who consider him mad and do not know that he is inspired.

All my discourse so far has been about the fourth kind
of madness, which causes him to be regarded as mad, who,
when he sees the beauty on earth, remembering the true
beauty, feels his wings growing and longs to stretch them
for an upward flight, but cannot do so, and, like a bird,
gazes upward and neglects the things below.

249e   My discourse has shown that this is, of all inspirations,
the best and of the highest origin to him who has it or who
shares in it, and that he who loves the beautiful, partaking
in this madness, is called a lover. For, as has been said,
every soul of man has by the law of nature beheld the
realities, otherwise it would not have entered into a human
250a being, but it is not easy for all souls to gain from earthly things
a recollection of those realities, either for those which had but
a brief view of them at that earlier time, or for those which,
after falling to earth, were so unfortunate as to be turned
toward unrighteousness through some evil communications
and to have forgotten the holy sights they once saw. Few then
are left which retain an adequate recollection of them; but
these when they see here any likeness of the things of that
other world, are stricken with amazement and can no longer
control themselves; but they do not understand their
condition, because they do not clearly perceive.

250b   Now in the earthly copies of justice and temperance and
the other ideas which are precious to souls there is no light,
but only a few, approaching the images through the darkling
organs of sense, behold in them the nature of that which they
imitate, and these few do this with difficulty. But at that
former time they saw beauty shining in brightness, when, with
a blessed company—we following in the train of Zeus, and
others in that of some other god—they saw the blessed sight
and vision and were initiated into that which is rightly called

250c   the most blessed of mysteries, which we celebrated in a state of perfection, when we were without experience of the evils which awaited us in the time to come, being permitted as initiates to the sight of perfect and simple and calm and happy apparitions, which we saw in the pure light, being ourselves pure and not entombed in this which we carry about with us and call the body, in which we are imprisoned like an oyster in its shell. So much, then, in honor of memory, on account of which I have now spoken at some length, through yearning for the joys of that other time.

250d   But beauty, as I said before, shone in brilliance among those visions; and since we came to earth we have found it shining most clearly through the clearest of our senses; for sight is the sharpest of the physical senses, though wisdom is not seen by it, for wisdom would arouse terrible love, if such a clear image of it were granted as would come through sight, and the same is true of the other lovely realities; but beauty alone has this privilege, and therefore

250e   it is most clearly seen and loveliest.

Now he who is not newly initiated, or has been corrupted, does not quickly rise from this world to that other world and to absolute beauty when he sees its namesake here, and so he does not revere it when he looks upon it, but gives himself up to pleasure and like a beast proceeds to lust and begetting; he makes license his companion and is not afraid or ashamed to

251a   pursue pleasure in violation of nature. But he who is newly initiated, who beheld many of those realities, when he sees a godlike face or form which is a good image of beauty, shudders at first, and something of the old awe comes over him, then, as he gazes, he reveres the beautiful one as a god, and if he did not fear to be thought stark mad, he would offer sacrifice to his beloved as to an idol or a god. And as he looks upon him, a reaction from his shuddering comes over him, with sweat and unwonted heat; for as the effluence of beauty enters him

251b   through the eyes, he is warmed; the effluence moistens the germ of the feathers, and as he grows warm, the parts from which the feathers grow, which were before hard and choked, and prevented the feathers from sprouting, become soft, and as the nourishment streams upon him, the quills of the feathers swell and begin to grow from the roots over all the form of the soul; for it was once all feathered. Now in this process the whole soul throbs and palpitates, and as in those

251c who are cutting teeth there is an irritation and discomfort in the gums, when the teeth begin to grow, just so the soul suffers when the growth of the feathers begins; it is feverish and is uncomfortable and itches when they begin to grow. Then when it gazes upon the beauty of the boy and receives the particles which flow thence to it (for which reason they are

251d called yearning), it is moistened and warmed, ceases from its pain and is filled with joy; but when it is alone and grows dry, the mouths of the passages in which the feathers begin to grow become dry and close up, shutting in the sprouting feathers, and the sprouts within, shut in with the yearning, throb like pulsing arteries, and each sprout pricks the passage in which it is, so that the whole soul, stung in every part, rages with pain; and then again, remembering the beautiful one, it rejoices. So, because of these two mingled sensations, it is greatly troubled

251e by its strange condition; it is perplexed and maddened, and in its madness it cannot sleep at night or stay in any one place by day, but it is filled with longing and hastens wherever it hopes to see the beautiful one. And when it sees him and is bathed with the waters of yearning, the passages that were sealed are opened, the soul has respite from the stings and is eased of its

252a pain, and this pleasure which it enjoys is the sweetest of pleasures at the time. Therefore the soul will not, if it can help it, be left alone by the beautiful one, but esteems him above all others, forgets for him mother and brothers and all friends, neglects property and cares not for its loss, and despising all the customs and proprieties in which it formerly took pride, it is ready to be a slave and to sleep wherever it is allowed, as near as possible to the beloved; for it not only reveres him who

252b possesses beauty, but finds in him the only healer of its greatest woes.

Now this condition, fair boy, about which I am speaking, is called Love by men, but when you hear what the gods call it, perhaps because of your youth you will laugh. But some of the Homeridae, I believe, repeat two verses on Love from the spurious poems of Homer, one of which is very outrageous and not perfectly metrical. They sing them as follows: "Mortals call him winged Love, but the immortals call him the winged One, because he must needs grow wings."

252c You may believe this, or not; but the condition of lovers and the cause of it are just as I have said. Now he who is a follower of Zeus, when seized by love can bear a heavier burden of the winged god; but those who are servants of Ares and followed in his train, when they have been seized by Love and think they have been wronged in any way by the beloved, become murderous and are ready to sacrifice themselves and
252d the beloved. And so it is with the follower of each of the other gods; he lives, so far as he is able, honoring and imitating that god, so long as he is uncorrupted, and is living his first life on earth, and in that way he behaves and conducts himself toward his beloved and toward all others. Now each one chooses his love from the ranks of the beautiful according to his character,
252e and he fashions him and adorns him like a statue, as though he were his god, to honor and worship him.

The followers of Zeus desire that the soul of him whom they love be like Zeus; so they seek for one of philosophical and lordly nature, and when they find him and love him, they do all they can to give him such a character. If they have not previously had experience, they learn then from all who can
253a teach them anything; they seek after information themselves, and when they search eagerly within themselves to find the nature of their god, they are successful, because they have been compelled to keep their eyes fixed upon the god, and as they reach and grasp him by memory they are inspired and receive from him character and habits, so far as it is possible for a man to have part in God. Now they consider the beloved the cause of all this, so they love him more than before, and if they draw the waters of their inspiration from Zeus, like the bacchantes, they pour it out upon the beloved and make him,
253b so far as possible, like their god.

And those who followed after Hera seek a kingly nature, and when they have found such an one, they act in a corresponding manner toward him in all respects; and likewise the followers of Apollo, and of each of the gods, go out and seek for their beloved a youth whose nature accords with that of the god, and when they have gained his affection, by imitating the god themselves and by persuasion and education they lead the beloved to the conduct and nature of the god, so far as each of them can do so; they exhibit no jealousy or meanness toward the loved one, but endeavor by every means in their power to lead him to the

253c likeness of the god whom they honor.

Thus the desire of the true lovers, and the initiation into the mysteries of love, which they teach, if they accomplish what they desire in the way I describe, is beautiful and brings happiness from the inspired lover to the loved one, if he be captured; and the fair one who is captured is caught in the following manner:— In the beginning of this tale I divided

253d each soul into three parts, two of which had the form of horses, the third that of a charioteer. Let us retain this division. Now of the horses we say one is good and the other bad; but we did not define what the goodness of the one and the badness of the other was. That we must now do. The horse that stands at the right hand is upright and has clean limbs; he carries his neck high, has an aquiline nose, is white in color, and has dark eyes; he is a friend of honor joined with temperance and modesty, and a follower of true glory; he needs no whip, but is guided only by the word of command

253e and by reason. The other, however, is crooked, heavy, ill put together, his neck is short and thick, his nose flat, his color dark, his eyes grey and bloodshot; he is the friend of insolence and pride, is shaggy-eared and deaf, hardly obedient to whip and spurs.

Now when the charioteer beholds the love-inspiring vision, and his whole soul is warmed by the sight, and is

254a full of the tickling and prickings of yearning, the horse that is obedient the charioteer, constrained then as always by modesty, controls himself and does not leap upon the beloved; but the other no longer heeds the pricks or the whip of the charioteer, but springs wildly forward, causing all possible trouble to his mate and to the charioteer, and forcing them to approach the beloved and propose the joys of love. And they at first pull back indignantly and will not be forced to do

254b terrible and unlawful deeds; but finally, as the trouble has no end, they go forward with him, yielding and agreeing to do his bidding. And they come to the beloved and behold his radiant face. And as the charioteer looks upon him, his memory is borne back to the true nature of beauty, and he sees it standing with modesty upon a pedestal of chastity, and when he sees this he is afraid and falls backward in reverence, and in falling

254c he is forced to pull the reins so violently backward as to bring both horses upon their haunches, the one quite willing, since he does not oppose him, but the unruly beast very unwilling. And as they go away, one horse in his shame and wonder wets all the soul with sweat, but the other, as soon as he is recovered from the pain of the bit and the fail, before he has fairly taken breath, breaks forth into angry reproaches, bitterly

254d reviling his mate and the charioteer for their cowardice and lack of manhood in deserting their post and breaking their agreement; and again, in spite of their unwillingness, he urges them forward and hardly yields to their prayer that he postpone the matter to another time. Then when the time comes which they have agreed upon, they pretend that they have forgotten it, but he reminds them; struggling, and neighing, and pulling he forces them again with the same purpose to approach the beloved one, and when they are near him, he lowers his head, raises his tail, takes the bit in his

254e teeth, and pulls shamelessly. The effect upon the charioteer is the same as before, but more pronounced; he falls back like a racer from the starting-rope, pulls the bit backward even more violently than before from the teeth of the unruly horse, covers his scurrilous tongue and jaws with blood, and forces his legs and haunches to the ground, causing him much pain. Now when the bad horse has gone through the same experience many times and has ceased from his unruliness, he is humbled and follows henceforth the wisdom of the charioteer, and when he sees the beautiful one, he is overwhelmed with fear; and so from that time on the soul of the lover follows the beloved in reverence and awe.

Katha Upanishad
Allegory of the
Charioteer

The Upanishads are Sanskrit texts that address important concepts in Hinduism. Over 200 Upanishads are known to exist, but the first eleven comprise the mukhya, *or main, Upanishads. Of these eleven, the Katha Upanishad is one of the oldest. It recounts the story of Nâkiketa and his encounter with Yama, the god of death in Vedic mythology. Excerpted here is an allegory of a charioteer that dates very close in time to the allegory of the charioteer in Plato's* Phaedrus. *While this allegory treats the nature of human beings as more complex than Plato's does— considering body, mind, intellect, and the five senses—in the role of the horses (here the five senses, not good or bad desires) it shares the overarching goal of controlling the horses as a means to a good life or truth.*

The purpose of the Upanishad's analogy is to instruct human beings in how to live. The simple structure of the sentences stands in stark contrast to their complex content about right and wrong, the nature of the soul, and the interdependence of controlling one's senses and attaining truth.

> *Note: in the following text, the verse numbers are given in Roman numerals while footnotes about specific concepts are given in Arabic numerals. The annotations are those of the editors.*

Above: the symbol for *Om* (or *Aum*) in Devanagari, an abugida alphabet in India and Nepal. When spoken out loud, it is a sacred incantation in Sanskrit. In the Upanishads, Om is described as being an all-encompassing form of consciousness, a vibration, that existed at the beginning of the creation of the universe.

339

ca. 4ᵗʰ Century BCE; translated by Max Müller, 1879

First Adhâya, Third Vallî

ᴵ There are two, drinking the reward of their own good works in the world, having entered into the cave of the heart, dwelling on the highest summit there. They are the higher self and the lower self. Those who know Brahman[1] —the Seers of Truth—call the lower self "shade" and the higher self "light." Likewise are they called by those who perform the Trinâkiketa[2] sacrifice. ᴵᴵ May we be able to master that Nâkiketa rite[3] which is a bridge for sacrificers; may we also know that which is the highest, imperishable Brahman for those who wish to cross over to the shore beyond fear.

ᴵᴵᴵ Know the Atman[4] (Self) to be the lord of the chariot, the body to be the chariot, the buddhi (intellect) to be the charioteer, and the mind to be the reins. ᴵⱽ The senses are the horses, the objects of the senses are their roads. When the Atman is in union with the body, the senses, and the mind, then wise people call him the Enjoyer.

ⱽ He who has no understanding of right and wrong, of real and unreal, and whose mind is never firmly held, his senses are unmanageable. He is carried away by his passions and desires, just as the charioteer is carried away by vicious horses over which control has been lost. ⱽᴵ But he who has understanding of right and wrong, of what is good versus what is merely pleasant, his mind is always firmly held, and his senses are manageable. He can control himself from running after brief pleasure, his senses serve him as good horses that obey the charioteer.

ⱽᴵᴵ He who has no understanding of these things, who is unmindful and always impure, never reaches that place, but falls again into Samsara, the realm of births and deaths.[5] ⱽᴵᴵᴵ But he

---

[1] A level of reality that stretches beyond the known world; described in some places as the highest level of reality.

[2] Sacrifice involving five sacred fires. See note 3 for more detail.

[3] Nâkiketa is a character in the Katha Upanishad. Earlier in the story, he goes to the house of Yama, who in turn, grants Nâkiketa three wishes. Nâkiketa's second wish is to know the proper procedure for a Vedic fire sacrifice. Yama imparts this knowledge and states that the fire sacrifice will be named after Nâkiketa (1.1.15–19).

[4] Atman is the inner self, or soul. As opposed to the external self apparent to all, the inner self is the underlying essence of an individual.

[5] Samsara is the cycle of reincarnation. Traditionally, people who remain ignorant of their true selves or who accrue bad karma (via bad deeds) are reborn again and again in an endless cycle.

who has understanding, who is mindful and always pure, he indeed reaches that place, from whence he is not born again. IX He who has understanding for his charioteer, and who holds the reins of his mind, he reaches the end of his journey, that highest place of Vishnu, the place of truth.[6]

X Beyond the senses there are the objects, beyond the objects there is the mind, beyond the mind there is the intellect, and beyond the intellect there is the Great Atman. XI Beyond the Great there is the Undeveloped, beyond the Undeveloped there is the Purusha.[7] Beyond the Person there is nothing. This end is the final goal, the highest road. XII That Atman is hidden in all beings and does not shine forth, but it is seen by subtle seers through their sharp and subtle intellect.

XIII A wise man should control his speech by his mind; he should keep them within the Self which is knowledge; he should keep knowledge within the Self which is the Great; and he should keep the Great within the Self which is the Quiet.

XIV Rise! Awaken from the slumber of ignorance! Having obtained your Great Ones, understand them! The sharp edge of a razor is difficult to pass over; thus the wise say the path (to the Self) is hard.

XV He who has perceived that which is without sound, without touch, without form, without decay, without taste, eternal, without smell, without beginning, without end, beyond the Great, and unchangeable, he who knows that is liberated from the jaws of death. XVI A wise man who has repeated or heard the ancient story of Nâkiketa told by Death, is glorified in the world of Brahman.

XVII And he who repeats this greatest mystery in an assembly of Brahmans, or full of devotion at the time of the Śrāddha[8] sacrifice, obtains thereby everlasting rewards.

---

[6] The Trimurti is the Hindu trinity of creation, preservation, and destruction. Vishnu is the god of preservation and protection. "Highest place of Vishnu" can be interpreted in many different ways, but it is often discussed as being a place of greater clarity, closer to Brahman.

[7] Purusha is a concept with many different interpretations, dependent on time, place, and school of thought. Max Müller translates it to mean "person."

[8] Shraddha is a funeral ceremony, often performed for one's deceased ancestors, especially parents.

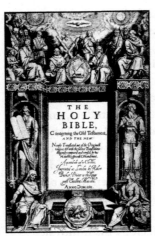

from the
New Testament
Sermon on the Mount
(two versions)
Parable of the Prodigal Son
Parable of the Talents
I Corinthians 13
King James Version

For an introduction to the King James Version of the Bible, see p. 207.

Christianity did not repudiate the Hebrew Scriptures but embraced them as revelation and preparation for the Christian message. To be understood fully, Jesus' teachings must be seen in the context of that older biblical tradition and of the Greco-Roman political and cultural influences that threatened it.

The Sermon on the Mount presents the teachings of Jesus in the form of a series of apparent contradictions to express his revision of the religious and cultural assumptions of his time. Extending the principles of behavior of the Hebrew Scriptures, Jesus holds man to an idealistic standard by asserting principles of thought. Moses says it is wrong to kill a person; Jesus (echoing other parts of Hebrew Scripture) says it is wrong even to hate a person. The sermon also replaces the Greco-Roman values of triumph, success, and power with the values of patience and love: Jesus proclaims that not the winners but the meek shall inherit the earth.

The Parables provide us experiences of realities that are impervious to argumentation and proof. Because their truth can be revealed only by faith, they need more than assertion and evidence to be conveyed. They need story. In the two parables given here Jesus upsets the assumptions of his followers. The message of the parable of the Prodigal Son is that God's love for the found among his children is as great as his love for those who have not been lost. In the parable of the talents, the King James Version makes wonderful use of the English pun on the word talent *as a measure of silver and as a God-given ability. Jesus asserts that God expects human beings to put their God-given talents to use, however great or small those talents may be, and that not to do so is to be wicked and slothful. We are given abilities for a divine purpose that we may not perceive, but that lack of perception is no excuse for not fulfilling the purpose.*

In I Corinthians 13, Saint Paul articulates the doctrine of love in its most spiritual sense (charity or love in English; caritas, in Latin; agape, in Greek). In creating human beings and revealing Himself to them, God challenges them to love as He loves, with pure participation in the divinely bestowed value in whatever is not the self.

Above: Frontispiece to the *King James Bible*, Cornelis Boel, engraving, 1611.

Sermon on the Mount (Matthew 5–7)

Chapter 5

¹ And seeing the multitudes, [Jesus] went up into a mountain: and when he was set, his disciples came unto him: ² And he opened his mouth, and taught them, saying,

³ Blessed are the poor in spirit: for theirs is the kingdom of heaven. ⁴ Blessed are they that mourn: for they shall be comforted. ⁵ Blessed are the meek: for they shall inherit the earth. ⁶ Blessed are they which do hunger and thirst after righteousness: for they shall be filled. ⁷ Blessed are the merciful: for they shall obtain mercy. ⁸ Blessed are the pure in heart: for they shall see God. ⁹ Blessed are the peacemakers: for they shall be called the children of God. ¹⁰ Blessed are they which are persecuted for righteousness' sake: for theirs is the kingdom of heaven. ¹¹ Blessed are ye, when men shall revile you, and persecute you, and shall say all manner of evil against you falsely, for my sake. ¹² Rejoice, and be exceeding glad: for great is your reward in heaven: for so persecuted they the prophets which were before you.

¹³ Ye are the salt of the earth: but if the salt have lost his savour, wherewith shall it be salted? it is thenceforth good for nothing, but to be cast out, and to be trodden under foot of men.

¹⁴ Ye are the light of the world. A city that is set on an hill cannot be hid. ¹⁵ Neither do men light a candle, and put it under a bushel, but on a candlestick; and it giveth light unto all that are in the house. ¹⁶ Let your light so shine before men, that they may see your good works, and glorify your Father which is in heaven.

¹⁷ Think not that I am come to destroy the law, or the prophets: I am not come to destroy, but to fulfil. ¹⁸ For verily I say unto you, Till heaven and earth pass, one jot or one tittle shall in no wise pass from the law, till all be fulfilled. ¹⁹ Whosoever therefore shall break one of these least commandments, and shall teach men so, he shall be called the least in the kingdom of heaven: but whosoever shall do and teach them, the same shall be called great in the kingdom of heaven. ²⁰ For I say unto you, That except your righteousness shall exceed the righteousness of the scribes and Pharisees, ye shall in no case enter into the kingdom of heaven.

21 Ye have heard that it was said of them of old time, Thou shalt not kill; and whosoever shall kill shall be in danger of the judgment: 22 But I say unto you, That whosoever is angry with his brother without a cause shall be in danger of the judgment: and whosoever shall say to his brother, Raca, shall be in danger of the council: but whosoever shall say, Thou fool, shall be in danger of hell fire. 23 Therefore if thou bring thy gift to the altar, and there rememberest that thy brother hath ought against thee; 24 Leave there thy gift before the altar, and go thy way; first be reconciled to thy brother, and then come and offer thy gift. 25 Agree with thine adversary quickly, whiles thou art in the way with him; lest at any time the adversary deliver thee to the judge, and the judge deliver thee to the officer, and thou be cast into prison. 26 Verily I say unto thee, Thou shalt by no means come out thence, till thou hast paid the uttermost farthing.

27 Ye have heard that it was said by them of old time, Thou shalt not commit adultery: 28 But I say unto you, That whosoever looketh on a woman to lust after her hath committed adultery with her already in his heart. 29 And if thy right eye offend thee, pluck it out, and cast it from thee: for it is profitable for thee that one of thy members should perish, and not that thy whole body should be cast into hell. 30 And if thy right hand offend thee, cut it off, and cast it from thee: for it is profitable for thee that one of thy members should perish, and not that thy whole body should be cast into hell.

31 It hath been said, Whosoever shall put away his wife, let him give her a writing of divorcement: 32 But I say unto you, That whosoever shall put away his wife, saving for the cause of fornication, causeth her to commit adultery: and whosoever shall marry her that is divorced committeth adultery.

33 Again, ye have heard that it hath been said by them of old time, Thou shalt not forswear thyself, but shalt perform unto the Lord thine oaths: 34 But I say unto you, Swear not at all; neither by heaven; for it is God's throne: 35 Nor by the earth; for it is his footstool: neither by Jerusalem; for it is the city of the great King. 36 Neither shalt thou swear by thy head, because thou canst not make one hair white or black. 37 But let your communication be, Yea, yea; Nay, nay: for whatsoever is more than these cometh of evil.

38 Ye have heard that it hath been said, An eye for an eye, and a tooth for a tooth: 39 But I say unto you, That ye resist not evil: but whosoever shall smite thee on thy right cheek, turn to him the other also. 40 And if any man will sue thee at the law, and take away thy coat, let him have thy cloak also. 41 And whosoever shall compel thee to go a mile, go with him twain. 42 Give to him that asketh thee, and from him that would borrow of thee turn not thou away.

43 Ye have heard that it hath been said, Thou shalt love thy neighbour, and hate thine enemy. 44 But I say unto you, Love your enemies, bless them that curse you, do good to them that hate you, and pray for them which despitefully use you, and persecute you; 45 That ye may be the children of your Father which is in heaven: for he maketh his sun to rise on the evil and on the good, and sendeth rain on the just and on the unjust. 46 For if ye love them which love you, what reward have ye? do not even the publicans the same? 47 And if ye salute your brethren only, what do ye more than others? do not even the publicans so? 48 Be ye therefore perfect, even as your Father which is in heaven is perfect.

Chapter 6

1 Take heed that ye do not your alms before men, to be seen of them: otherwise ye have no reward of your Father which is in heaven. 2 Therefore when thou doest thine alms, do not sound a trumpet before thee, as the hypocrites do in the synagogues and in the streets, that they may have glory of men. Verily I say unto you, They have their reward. 3 But when thou doest alms, let not thy left hand know what thy right hand doeth: 4 That thine alms may be in secret: and thy Father which seeth in secret himself shall reward thee openly.

5 And when thou prayest, thou shalt not be as the hypocrites are: for they love to pray standing in the synagogues and in the corners of the streets, that they may be seen of men. Verily I say unto you, They have their reward. 6 But thou, when thou prayest, enter into thy closet, and when thou hast shut thy door, pray to thy Father which is in secret; and thy Father which seeth in secret shall reward thee openly. 7 But when ye pray, use not vain repetitions, as the heathen do: for they think that they shall be

heard for their much speaking. 8 Be not ye therefore like unto them: for your Father knoweth what things ye have need of, before ye ask him.

9 After this manner therefore pray ye: Our Father which art in heaven, Hallowed be thy name. 10 Thy kingdom come, Thy will be done in earth, as it is in heaven. 11 Give us this day our daily bread. 12 And forgive us our debts, as we forgive our debtors. 13 And lead us not into temptation, but deliver us from evil: For thine is the kingdom, and the power, and the glory, for ever. Amen. 14 For if ye forgive men their trespasses, your heavenly Father will also forgive you: 15 But if ye forgive not men their trespasses, neither will your Father forgive your trespasses.

16 Moreover when ye fast, be not, as the hypocrites, of a sad countenance: for they disfigure their faces, that they may appear unto men to fast. Verily I say unto you, They have their reward. 17 But thou, when thou fastest, anoint thine head, and wash thy face; 18 That thou appear not unto men to fast, but unto thy Father which is in secret: and thy Father, which seeth in secret, shall reward thee openly.

19 Lay not up for yourselves treasures upon earth, where moth and rust doth corrupt, and where thieves break through and steal: 20 But lay up for yourselves treasures in heaven, where neither moth nor rust doth corrupt, and where thieves do not break through nor steal: 21 For where your treasure is, there will your heart be also.

22 The light of the body is the eye: if therefore thine eye be single, thy whole body shall be full of light. 23 But if thine eye be evil, thy whole body shall be full of darkness. If therefore the light that is in thee be darkness, how great is that darkness!

24 No man can serve two masters: for either he will hate the one, and love the other; or else he will hold to the one, and despise the other. Ye cannot serve God and mammon.

25 Therefore I say unto you, Take no thought for your life, what ye shall eat, or what ye shall drink; nor yet for your body, what ye shall put on. Is not the life more than meat, and the body than raiment? 26 Behold the fowls of the air: for they sow not, neither do they reap, nor gather into barns; yet your heavenly Father feedeth them. Are ye not much better than they? 27 Which

of you by taking thought can add one cubit unto his stature? 28 And why take ye thought for raiment? Consider the lilies of the field, how they grow; they toil not, neither do they spin: 29 And yet I say unto you, That even Solomon in all his glory was not arrayed like one of these. 30 Wherefore, if God so clothe the grass of the field, which to day is, and to morrow is cast into the oven, shall he not much more clothe you, O ye of little faith? 31 Therefore take no thought, saying, What shall we eat? or, What shall we drink? or, Wherewithal shall we be clothed? 32 (For after all these things do the Gentiles seek:) for your heavenly Father knoweth that ye have need of all these things. 33 But seek ye first the kingdom of God, and his righteousness; and all these things shall be added unto you. 34 Take therefore no thought for the morrow: for the morrow shall take thought for the things of itself. Sufficient unto the day is the evil thereof.

Chapter 7

1 Judge not, that ye be not judged. 2 For with what judgment ye judge, ye shall be judged: and with what measure ye mete, it shall be measured to you again. 3 And why beholdest thou the mote that is in thy brother's eye, but considerest not the beam that is in thine own eye? 4 Or how wilt thou say to thy brother, Let me pull out the mote out of thine eye; and, behold, a beam is in thine own eye? 5 Thou hypocrite, first cast out the beam out of thine own eye; and then shalt thou see clearly to cast out the mote out of thy brother's eye. 6 Give not that which is holy unto the dogs, neither cast ye your pearls before swine, lest they trample them under their feet, and turn again and rend you.

7 Ask, and it shall be given you; seek, and ye shall find; knock, and it shall be opened unto you: 8 For every one that asketh receiveth; and he that seeketh findeth; and to him that knocketh it shall be opened. 9 Or what man is there of you, whom if his son ask bread, will he give him a stone? 10 Or if he ask a fish, will he give him a serpent? 11 If ye then, being evil, know how to give good gifts unto your children, how much more shall your Father which is in heaven give good things to them that ask him?

12 Therefore all things whatsoever ye would that men should do to you, do ye even so to them: for this is the law and the prophets.

13 Enter ye in at the strait gate: for wide is the gate, and broad is the way, that leadeth to destruction, and many there be which go in thereat: 14 Because strait is the gate, and narrow is the way, which leadeth unto life, and few there be that find it.

15 Beware of false prophets, which come to you in sheep's clothing, but inwardly they are ravening wolves. 16 Ye shall know them by their fruits. Do men gather grapes of thorns, or figs of thistles? 17 Even so every good tree bringeth forth good fruit; but a corrupt tree bringeth forth evil fruit. 18 A good tree cannot bring forth evil fruit, neither can a corrupt tree bring forth good fruit. 19 Every tree that bringeth not forth good fruit is hewn down, and cast into the fire. 20 Wherefore by their fruits ye shall know them.

21 Not every one that saith unto me, Lord, Lord, shall enter into the kingdom of heaven; but he that doeth the will of my Father which is in heaven. 22 Many will say to me in that day, Lord, Lord, have we not prophesied in thy name? and in thy name have cast out devils? and in thy name done many wonderful works? 23 And then will I profess unto them, I never knew you: depart from me, ye that work iniquity.

24 Therefore whosoever heareth these sayings of mine, and doeth them, I will liken him unto a wise man, which built his house upon a rock: 25 And the rain descended, and the floods came, and the winds blew, and beat upon that house; and it fell not: for it was founded upon a rock. 26 And every one that heareth these sayings of mine, and doeth them not, shall be likened unto a foolish man, which built his house upon the sand: 27 And the rain descended, and the floods came, and the winds blew, and beat upon that house; and it fell: and great was the fall of it. 28 And it came to pass, when Jesus had ended these sayings, the people were astonished at his doctrine: 29 For he taught them as one having authority, and not as the scribes.

Sermon on the Mount (Luke 6:17–49)

¹⁷ And [Jesus] came down with them, and stood in the plain, and the company of his disciples, and a great multitude of people out of all Judaea and Jerusalem, and from the sea coast of Tyre and Sidon, which came to hear him, and to be healed of their diseases; ¹⁸ And they that were vexed with unclean spirits: and they were healed. ¹⁹ And the whole multitude sought to touch him: for there went virtue out of him, and healed them all.

²⁰ And he lifted up his eyes on his disciples, and said, Blessed be ye poor: for yours is the kingdom of God. ²¹ Blessed are ye that hunger now: for ye shall be filled. Blessed are ye that weep now: for ye shall laugh. ²² Blessed are ye, when men shall hate you, and when they shall separate you from their company, and shall reproach you, and cast out your name as evil, for the Son of man's sake. ²³ Rejoice ye in that day, and leap for joy: for, behold, your reward is great in heaven: for in the like manner did their fathers unto the prophets. ²⁴ But woe unto you that are rich! for ye have received your consolation. ²⁵ Woe unto you that are full! for ye shall hunger. Woe unto you that laugh now! for ye shall mourn and weep. ²⁶ Woe unto you, when all men shall speak well of you! for so did their fathers to the false prophets.

²⁷ But I say unto you which hear, Love your enemies, do good to them which hate you, ²⁸ Bless them that curse you, and pray for them which despitefully use you. ²⁹ And unto him that smiteth thee on the one cheek offer also the other; and him that taketh away thy cloak forbid not to take thy coat also. ³⁰ Give to every man that asketh of thee; and of him that taketh away thy goods ask them not again. ³¹ And as ye would that men should do to you, do ye also to them likewise. ³² For if ye love them which love you, what thank have ye? for sinners also love those that love them. ³³ And if ye do good to them which do good to you, what thank have ye? for sinners also do even the same. ³⁴ And if ye lend to them of whom ye hope to receive, what thank have ye? for sinners also lend to sinners, to receive as much again. ³⁵ But love ye your enemies, and do good, and lend, hoping for nothing again; and your reward shall be great, and ye shall be the children of the Highest: for he is kind unto the unthankful and to the evil. ³⁶ Be ye therefore merciful, as your Father also is merciful.

37 Judge not, and ye shall not be judged: condemn not, and ye shall not be condemned: forgive, and ye shall be forgiven: 38 Give, and it shall be given unto you; good measure, pressed down, and shaken together, and running over, shall men give into your bosom. For with the same measure that ye mete withal it shall be measured to you again. 39 And he spake a parable unto them, Can the blind lead the blind? shall they not both fall into the ditch? 40 The disciple is not above his master: but every one that is perfect shall be as his master. 41 And why beholdest thou the mote that is in thy brother's eye, but perceivest not the beam that is in thine own eye? 42 Either how canst thou say to thy brother, Brother, let me pull out the mote that is in thine eye, when thou thyself beholdest not the beam that is in thine own eye? Thou hypocrite, cast out first the beam out of thine own eye, and then shalt thou see clearly to pull out the mote that is in thy brother's eye.

43 For a good tree bringeth not forth corrupt fruit; neither doth a corrupt tree bring forth good fruit. 44 For every tree is known by his own fruit. For of thorns men do not gather figs, nor of a bramble bush gather they grapes. 45 A good man out of the good treasure of his heart bringeth forth that which is good; and an evil man out of the evil treasure of his heart bringeth forth that which is evil: for of the abundance of the heart his mouth speaketh.

46 And why call ye me, Lord, Lord, and do not the things which I say? 47 Whosoever cometh to me, and heareth my sayings, and doeth them, I will shew you to whom he is like: 48 He is like a man which built an house, and digged deep, and laid the foundation on a rock: and when the flood arose, the stream beat vehemently upon that house, and could not shake it: for it was founded upon a rock. 49 But he that heareth, and doeth not, is like a man that without a foundation built an house upon the earth; against which the stream did beat vehemently, and immediately it fell; and the ruin of that house was great.

Parable of the Talents (Matthew 25:14–30)

14 For the kingdom of heaven is as a man travelling into a far country, who called his own servants, and delivered unto them his goods. 15 And unto one he gave five talents, to another two, and to another one; to every man according to his several ability; and straightway took his journey. 16 Then he that had received the five talents went and traded with the same, and made them other five talents. 17 And likewise he that had received two, he also gained other two. 18 But he that had received one went and digged in the earth, and hid his lord's money. 19 After a long time the lord of those servants cometh, and reckoneth with them. 20 And so he that had received five talents came and brought other five talents, saying, Lord, thou deliveredst unto me five talents: behold, I have gained beside them five talents more. 21 His lord said unto him, Well done, thou good and faithful servant: thou hast been faithful over a few things, I will make thee ruler over many things: enter thou into the joy of thy lord. 22 He also that had received two talents came and said, Lord, thou deliveredst unto me two talents: behold, I have gained two other talents beside them. 23 His lord said unto him, Well done, good and faithful servant; thou hast been faithful over a few things, I will make thee ruler over many things: enter thou into the joy of thy lord. 24 Then he which had received the one talent came and said, Lord, I knew thee that thou art an hard man, reaping where thou hast not sown, and gathering where thou hast not strawed: 25 And I was afraid, and went and hid thy talent in the earth: lo, there thou hast that is thine. 26 His lord answered and said unto him, Thou wicked and slothful servant, thou knewest that I reap where I sowed not, and gather where I have not strawed: 27 Thou oughtest therefore to have put my money to the exchangers, and then at my coming I should have received mine own with usury. 28 Take therefore the talent from him, and give it unto him which hath ten talents. 29 For unto every one that hath shall be given, and he shall have abundance: but from him that hath not shall be taken away even that which he hath. 30 And cast ye the unprofitable servant into outer darkness: there shall be weeping and gnashing of teeth.

Parable of the Prodigal Son (Luke 15:11–32)

11 And [Jesus] said, A certain man had two sons: 12 And the younger of them said to his father, Father, give me the portion of goods that falleth to me. And he divided unto them his living. 13 And not many days after the younger son gathered all together, and took his journey into a far country, and there wasted his substance with riotous living. 14 And when he had spent all, there arose a mighty famine in that land; and he began to be in want. 15 And he went and joined himself to a citizen of that country; and he sent him into his fields to feed swine. 16 And he would fain have filled his belly with the husks that the swine did eat: and no man gave unto him. 17 And when he came to himself, he said, How many hired servants of my father's have bread enough and to spare, and I perish with hunger! 18 I will arise and go to my father, and will say unto him, Father, I have sinned against heaven, and before thee, 19 And am no more worthy to be called thy son: make me as one of thy hired servants. 20 And he arose, and came to his father. But when he was yet a great way off, his father saw him, and had compassion, and ran, and fell on his neck, and kissed him. 21 And the son said unto him, Father, I have sinned against heaven, and in thy sight, and am no more worthy to be called thy son. 22 But the father said to his servants, Bring forth the best robe, and put it on him; and put a ring on his hand, and shoes on his feet: 23 And bring hither the fatted calf, and kill it; and let us eat, and be merry: 24 For this my son was dead, and is alive again; he was lost, and is found. And they began to be merry. 25 Now his elder son was in the field: and as he came and drew nigh to the house, he heard musick and dancing. 26 And he called one of the servants, and asked what these things meant. 27 And he said unto him, Thy brother is come; and thy father hath killed the fatted calf, because he hath received him safe and sound. 28 And he was angry, and would not go in: therefore came his father out, and intreated him. 29 And he answering said to his father, Lo, these many years do I serve thee, neither transgressed I at any time thy commandment: and yet thou never gavest me a kid, that I might make merry with my friends: 30 But as soon as this thy son was come, which hath devoured thy living with harlots, thou hast killed for him the fatted calf. 31 And he said unto him, Son, thou art ever with me, and all that I have is thine. 32 It was meet that we should make merry, and be glad: for this thy brother was dead, and is alive again; and was lost, and is found.

I Corinthians 13

[1] Though I speak with the tongues of men and of angels, and have not love, I am become as sounding brass, or a tinkling cymbal. [2] And though I have the gift of prophecy, and understand all mysteries, and all knowledge; and though I have all faith, so that I could remove mountains, and have not love, I am nothing. [3] And though I bestow all my goods to feed the poor, and though I give my body to be burned, and have not love, it profiteth me nothing.

[4] Love suffereth long, and is kind; love envieth not; love vaunteth not itself, is not puffed up, [5] Doth not behave itself unseemly, seeketh not her own, is not easily provoked, thinketh no evil; [6] Rejoiceth not in iniquity, but rejoiceth in the truth; [7] Beareth all things, believeth all things, hopeth all things, endureth all things.

[8] Love never faileth: but whether there be prophecies, they shall fail; whether there be tongues, they shall cease; whether there be knowledge, it shall vanish away. [9] For we know in part, and we prophesy in part. [10] But when that which is perfect is come, then that which is in part shall be done away.

[11] When I was a child, I spake as a child, I understood as a child, I thought as a child: but when I became a man, I put away childish things. [12] For now we see through a glass, darkly; but then face to face: now I know in part; but then shall I know even as also I am known.

[13] And now abideth faith, hope, love, these three; but the greatest of these is love.

Editors' note: In this selection we have replaced the word "charity" with the word "love," an equally common translation of the Greek *agape* in early and later English versions, because in modern usage "charity" (from the Latin *caritas*) has the reduced sense of donation to the needy rather than the sense of selfless care and beneficence for others intended here, a sense it retained in religious contexts well into the 20th century because of its use in the KJV. Similarly, the word "love" here is to be taken in its selfless and spiritual rather than in its affectionate, romantic, or erotic senses.

Confessions
Book II

St. Augustine of Hippo

*Saint Augustine of Hippo (354–430) was born in Numidia, part of Roman
Africa (now Algeria). His Christian mother (Saint Monica) and pagan father
were of the upper class. He was a hedonistic teenager who also studied Latin
literature and later taught grammar and rhetoric. Having left his mother's faith, he
studied Manicheism, neo-Platonism, and other doctrines and for many years lived
with a woman who bore him a son (Adeodatus) out of wedlock. In 386 he
experienced a dramatic conversion, was baptized by St. Ambrose, after the deaths
of his mother and his son gave all his wealth to the poor, and in 391 was ordained
a priest, becoming a famous preacher and later Bishop of Hippo. Through his
teachings and many writings, Augustine became one of the greatest and most
influential of Christian philosophers.*

The excerpt is the second book of his autobiography, called Confessions. *In it,
Augustine describes his adolescence and the conflicts that he experienced in his
actions, desires, and goals. He enters deeply into an analysis of his own youthful
motives to discover the true nature of evil.*

Above: *St. Augustine in His Study,* Sandro Botticelli, ca. 1480, fresco.

Written between 397 and 400; translated and annotated by Albert C. Outler, 1955

I: The Depths of Vice

I wish now to call to mind my past wickedness and the carnal corruptions of my soul—not because I still love them, but that I may love you, my God. For love of your love I do this, recalling in the bitterness of self-examination my wicked ways, that you may grow sweet to me. O, sweetness without deception! Sweetness happy and assured! Thus you may gather me up out of those fragments in which I was torn to pieces, while I turned away from you, O Unity, and lost myself among "the many."[1] For as I became a youth, I longed to be satisfied with worldly things, and I dared to grow wild in a succession of various and shadowy loves. My form wasted away, and I became corrupt in your eyes, yet I was still pleasing to my own eyes—and eager to please the eyes of men.

II: Love and Lust

But what was it that delighted me save to love and to be loved? Still I did not keep the moderate way of the love of mind to mind—the bright path of friendship. Instead, the mists of passion steamed up out of the slimy desires of the flesh, and the hot imagination of puberty, and they so obscured and overcast my heart that I was unable to distinguish pure affection from unholy desire. Both boiled confusedly within me, and dragged my unstable youth down over the cliffs of unchaste desires and plunged me into a gulf of shameful deeds. Your anger had come upon me, and I knew it not. I had been deafened by the clanking of the chains of my mortality, the punishment for my soul's pride, and I wandered farther from you, and you did permit me to do so. I was tossed to and fro, and wasted, and poured out, and I boiled over in my fornications—and yet you remained silent, O my late-found Joy! You still remained silent, and I wandered still farther from you into more and yet more barren fields of sorrow, in proud dejection and restless weariness.

If only there had been someone to regulate my disorder and turn to my profit the fleeting beauties of the things around me, and to fix a bound to their sweetness, so that the tides of my youth might have spent themselves upon the shore of marriage! Then they might have

---

[1] A Plotinian phrase; cf. Enneads, I, 6, 9:1–2.

been tranquilized and satisfied with having children, as your law prescribes, O Lord—you who forms the offspring of our death and are able also with a tender hand to blunt the thorns which were excluded from your paradise![2] For your omnipotence is not far from us even when we are far from you. Now, on the other hand, I might have given more vigilant heed to the voice from the clouds: "Nevertheless, such shall have trouble in the flesh, but I spare you,"[3] and, "It is good for a man not to touch a woman,"[4] and, "He that is unmarried cares for the things that belong to the Lord, how he may please the Lord; but he that is married cares for the things that are of the world, how he may please his wife."[5] I should have listened more attentively to these words, and, thus having been "made a eunuch for the Kingdom of Heaven's sake,"[6] I would have looked with greater happiness to your embraces.

But, fool that I was, I foamed in my wickedness as the sea and, forsaking you, followed the rushing of my own tide, and broke all of your laws. But I did not escape your scourges. For what mortal can do so? You were always by me, mercifully angry and flavoring all my unlawful pleasures with bitter discontent, in order that I might seek pleasures free from discontent. But where could I find such pleasure save in you, O Lord—save in you, who teaches us by sorrow, who wounds us to heal us, and kills us that we may not die apart from you.

Where was I, and how far was I exiled from the delights of your house, in that sixteenth year of the age of my flesh, when the madness of lust held full sway in me—that madness which grants indulgence to human shamelessness, even though it is forbidden by your laws—and I gave myself entirely to it? Meanwhile, my family took no care to save me from ruin by marriage, for their sole care was that I should learn how to make a powerful speech and become a persuasive orator.

---

[2] Cf. Genesis 3:18 and Augustine's *De Bono Conjugali*, 8–9, 35–39 (Nicene and Post-Nicene Fathers, volume III, 396–413).

[3] 1 Corinthians 7:28.

[4] 1 Corinthians 7:1.

[5] 1 Corinthians 7:32, 33.

[6] Cf. Matthew 19:12.

III: A Year of Idleness

Now, in that year my studies were interrupted. I had come back from Madaura, a neighboring city[7] where I had gone to study grammar and rhetoric; and the money for a further term at Carthage was being got together for me. This project was more a matter of my father's ambition than of his means, for he was only a poor citizen of Tagaste.

To whom am I narrating all this? Not to you, O my God, but to my own kind, to humankind, in your presence—to that small part of the human race who may chance to come upon these writings. And to what end? That I and all who read them may understand what depths there are from which we are to cry unto you.[8] For what is more surely heard in your ear than a confessing heart and a faithful life?

Who did not extol and praise my father, because he went quite beyond his means to supply his son with the necessary expenses for a far journey in the interest of his education? For many far richer citizens did not do so much for their children. Still, this same father troubled himself not at all as to how I was progressing toward you nor how chaste I was, just so long as I was skillful in speaking—though I was left a desert, uncultivated for you, O God, who are the one true and good Lord of my heart, which is your field.[9]

During that sixteenth year of my age, I lived with my parents, having a holiday from school for a time—this idleness imposed upon me by my parents' lack of money. The thornbushes of lust grew rank about my head, and there was no hand to root them out. Indeed, when my father saw me one day at the baths and perceived that I was becoming a man, and was showing the signs of adolescence, he joyfully told my mother about it as if already looking forward to grandchildren, rejoicing in that sort of inebriation in which the world so often forgets you, its Creator, and falls in love with your creature instead of you—the

---

[7] Twenty miles from Tagaste, famed as the birthplace of Apuleius, the only notable classical author produced by the province of Africa.

[8] Another echo of the *de profundis* (Psalms 130:1)—and the most explicit statement we have from Augustine of his motive and aim in writing these "confessions."

[9] Cf. 1 Corinthians 3:9.

inebriation of that invisible wine of a perverted will which turns and bows down to infamy. But in my mother's breast you had already begun to build your temple and the foundation of your holy habitation—whereas my father was only a catechumen, and that but recently. She was, therefore, startled with a holy fear and trembling: for though I had not yet been baptized, she feared those crooked ways in which they walk who turn their backs to you and not their faces toward you.

Woe is me! Do I dare affirm that you did remain silent, O my God, while I wandered farther away from you? Did you really then remain silent? Then whose words were they but yours which by my mother, your faithful handmaid, you did pour into my ears? None of them, however, sank into my heart to make me do anything. She deplored and, as I remember, warned me privately with great solicitude, "not to commit fornication; but above all things never to defile another man's wife." These appeared to me but womanish counsels, which I would have blushed to obey. Yet they were from you, and I knew it not. I thought that you were silent and that it was only she who spoke. Yet it was through her that you did not keep silence toward me; and in rejecting her counsel I was rejecting you—I, her son, "the son of your handmaid, your servant."[10]

But I did not realize this, and rushed on headlong with such blindness that, among my friends, I was ashamed to be less shameless than they, when I heard them boasting of their disgraceful exploits—yes, and glorying all the more the worse their baseness was. What is worse, I took pleasure in such exploits, not for the pleasure's sake only but mostly for praise. What is worthy of condemnation except vice itself? Yet I made myself out worse than I was, in order that I might not go lacking for praise. And when in anything I had not sinned as the worst ones in the group, I would still say that I had done what I had not done, in order not to appear contemptible because I was more innocent than they; and not to drop in their esteem because I was more chaste.

Behold with what companions I walked the streets of Babylon! I rolled in its mire and lolled about on it, as if on a bed of spices and precious ointments. And, drawing me more closely

---

[10] Psalms 116:16.

to the very center of that city, my invisible enemy trod me down and seduced me, for I was easy to seduce. My mother had already fled out of the midst of Babylon[11] and was progressing, albeit slowly, toward its outskirts. For in counseling me to chastity, she did not bear in mind what her husband had told her about me. And although she knew that my passions were destructive even then and dangerous for the future, she did not think they should be restrained by the bonds of conjugal affection—if, indeed, they could not be cut away to the quick. She took no heed of this, for she was afraid lest a wife should prove a hindrance and a burden to my hopes. These were not her hopes of the world to come, which my mother had in you, but the hope of learning, which both my parents were too anxious that I should acquire—my father, because he had little or no thought of you, and only vain thoughts for me; my mother, because she thought that the usual course of study would not only be no hindrance but actually a furtherance toward my eventual return to you. This much I conjecture, recalling as well as I can the temperaments of my parents. Meantime, the reins of discipline were slackened on me, so that without the restraint of due severity, I might play at whatsoever I fancied, even to the point of dissoluteness. And in all this there was that mist which shut out from my sight the brightness of your truth, O my God; and my iniquity bulged out, as it were, with fatness![12]

IV: The Stolen Fruit

Theft is punished by your law, O Lord, and by the law written in men's hearts, which not even ingrained wickedness can erase. For what thief will tolerate another thief stealing from him? Even a rich thief will not tolerate a poor thief who is driven to theft by want. Yet I had a desire to commit robbery, and did so, compelled to it by neither hunger nor poverty, but through a contempt for well-doing and a strong impulse to iniquity. For I pilfered something which I already had in sufficient measure, and of much better quality. I did not desire to enjoy what I stole, but only the theft and the sin itself.

---

[11] Cf. Jeremiah 51:6; 50:8.

[12] Cf. Psalms 73:7.

There was a pear tree close to our own vineyard, heavily laden with fruit, which was not tempting either for its color or for its flavor. Late one night—having prolonged our games in the streets until then, as our bad habit was—a group of young scoundrels, and I among them, went to shake and rob this tree. We carried off a huge load of pears, not to eat ourselves, but to dump out to the hogs, after barely tasting some of them ourselves. Doing this pleased us all the more because it was forbidden. Such was my heart, O God, such was my heart—which you did pity even in that bottomless pit. Behold, now let my heart confess to you what it was seeking there, when I was being gratuitously wanton, having no inducement to evil but the evil itself. It was foul, and I loved it. I loved my own undoing. I loved my error—not that for which I erred but the error itself. A depraved soul, falling away from your secure grasp to destruction in itself, seeking nothing from the shameful deed but shame itself.

V: Why Men Sin

Now there is a splendor in all beautiful bodies, and in gold and silver and all things. The sense of touch has its own power to please and the other senses find their proper objects in physical sensation. Worldly honor also has its own glory, and so do the powers to command and to overcome: and from these there springs up the desire for revenge. Yet, in seeking these pleasures, we must not depart from you, O Lord, nor deviate from your law. The life which we live here has its own peculiar attractiveness because it has a certain measure of comeliness of its own and a harmony with all these inferior values. The bond of human friendship has a sweetness of its own, binding many souls together as one. Yet because of these values, sin is committed, because we have an inordinate preference for these goods of a lower order and neglect the better and the higher good— neglecting you, O our Lord God, and your truth and your law. For these inferior values have their delights, but not at all equal to my God, who has created them all. For in him do the righteous delight and he is the sweetness of the upright in heart.

When, therefore, we inquire why a crime was committed, we do not accept the explanation unless it appears that there was the desire to obtain some of those goods which we designate inferior, or else a fear of losing them. For truly they are beautiful and fitting, though in comparison with the superior and celestial goods they are base and contemptible. A man has murdered another man—what was his motive? Either he desired his wife or his property or else he would steal to support himself; or else he was afraid of losing something to him; or else, having been injured, he was burning to be revenged. Would a man commit murder without a motive, taking delight simply in the act of murder? Who would believe such a thing? Even for that savage and brutal man [Catiline], of whom it was said that he was gratuitously wicked and cruel, there is still a motive assigned to his deeds. "Lest through idleness," he says, "hand or heart should grow inactive."[13] And to what purpose? Why, even this: that, having once got possession of the city through his practice of his wicked ways, he might gain honors, empire, and wealth, and thus be exempt from the fear of the laws and from financial difficulties in supplying the needs of his family—and from the consciousness of his own wickedness. So it seems that not even Catiline himself loved his own villainies, but something else, and it was this that gave him the motive for his crimes.

VI: The Anatomy of Evil

What was it in you, O theft of mine, that I, poor wretch, doted on—you deed of darkness—in that sixteenth year of my age? Beautiful you were not, for you were a theft. But are you anything at all, so that I could analyze the case with you? Those pears that we stole were fair to the sight because they were your creation, O Beauty beyond compare, O Creator of all, O thou good God—God the highest good and my true good.[14] Those pears were truly pleasant to the sight, but it was not for them that my miserable soul lusted, for I had an abundance of better pears. I stole those simply that I might steal, for, having stolen them, I threw them away. My sole gratification in them was my own sin, which I was pleased to enjoy; for, if any one of these pears entered my mouth, the only good flavor it had was my sin in eating it. And now, O Lord my God, I ask what it was in that theft of mine that caused me such delight; for behold it had no beauty

---

[13] Cicero, *De Catiline*, 16.

[14] *Deus summum bonum et bonum verum meum.*

of its own—certainly not the sort of beauty that exists in justice and wisdom, nor such as is in the mind, memory senses, and the animal life of man; nor yet the kind that is the glory and beauty of the stars in their courses; nor the beauty of the earth, or the sea— teeming with spawning life, replacing in birth that which dies and decays. Indeed, it did not have that false and shadowy beauty which attends the deceptions of vice.

For thus we see pride wearing the mask of high-spiritedness, although only thou, O God, art high above all. Ambition seeks honor and glory, whereas only thou shouldst be honored above all, and glorified forever. The powerful man seeks to be feared, because of his cruelty; but who ought really to be feared but God only? What can be forced away or withdrawn out of his power— when or where or whither or by whom? The enticements of the wanton claim the name of love; and yet nothing is more enticing than your love, nor is anything loved more healthfully than your truth, bright and beautiful above all. Curiosity prompts a desire for knowledge, whereas it is only you who know all things supremely. Indeed, ignorance and foolishness themselves go masked under the names of simplicity and innocence; yet there is no being that has true simplicity like thine, and none is innocent as thou art. Thus it is that by a sinner's own deeds he is himself harmed. Human sloth pretends to long for rest, but what sure rest is there save in the Lord? Luxury would fain be called plenty and abundance; but thou art the fullness and unfailing abundance of unfading joy. Prodigality presents a show of liberality; but thou art the most lavish giver of all good things. Covetousness desires to possess much; but thou art already the possessor of all things. Envy contends that its aim is for excellence; but what is so excellent as thou? Anger seeks revenge; but who avenges more justly than you? Fear recoils at the unfamiliar and the sudden changes which threaten things beloved, and is wary for its own security; but what can happen that is unfamiliar or sudden to you? Or who can deprive you of what you love? Where, really, is there unshaken security save with you? Grief languishes for things lost in which desire had taken delight, because it wills to have nothing taken from it, just as nothing can be taken from you.

Thus the soul commits fornication when she is turned from you,[15] and seeks apart from you what she cannot find pure and untainted until she returns to you. All things thus imitate you— but pervertedly—when they separate themselves far from you and raise themselves up against you. But, even in this act of perverse imitation, they acknowledge you to be the Creator of all nature, and recognize that there is no place where they can altogether separate themselves from you. What was it, then, that I loved in that theft? And wherein was I imitating my Lord, even in a corrupted and perverted way? Did I wish, if only by gesture, to rebel against your law, even though I had no power to do so actually—so that, even as a captive, I might produce a sort of counterfeit liberty, by doing with impunity deeds that were forbidden, in a deluded sense of omnipotence? Behold this servant of thine, fleeing from his Lord and following a shadow! O rottenness! O monstrousness of life and abyss of death! Could I find pleasure only in what was unlawful, and only because it was unlawful?

VII: Grace That Keeps and Heals

"What shall I render unto the Lord"[16] for the fact that while my memory recalls these things my soul no longer fears them? I will love you, O Lord, and thank you, and confess to your name, because you have forgiven me such wicked and evil deeds. To your grace I attribute it and to your mercy, that thou hast melted away my sin as if it were ice. To your grace also I attribute whatsoever of evil I did *not* commit—for what might I not have done, loving sin as I did, just for the sake of sinning? Yea, all the sins that I confess now to have been forgiven me, both those which I committed willfully and those which, by your providence, I did not commit. What man is there who, when reflecting upon his own infirmity, dares to ascribe his chastity and innocence to his own powers, so that he should love you less—as if he were in less need of your mercy by which you forgive the transgressions of those that return to you? As for that man who, when called by you, obeyed your voice and shunned those things which he here reads of me as I

---

[15] *Avertitur*, the opposite of *convertitur*: the evil will turns the soul away from God; this is sin. By grace it is turned toward God; this is conversion.

[16] Psalms 116:12.

recall and confess them of myself, let him not despise me—for I, who was sick, have been healed by the same Physician by whose aid it was that he did not fall sick, or rather was less sick than I. And for this let him love you just as much—indeed, all the more—since he sees me restored from such a great weakness of sin by him who, as he also sees, has saved him from a similar weakness.

VIII: Comrades in Crime

What profit did I, a wretched one, receive from those things which, when I remember them now, cause me shame—above all, from that theft, which I loved only for the theft's sake? And, as the theft itself was nothing, I was all the more wretched in that I loved it so. Yet by myself alone I would not have done it—I still recall how I felt about this then—I could not have done it alone. I loved it then because of the companionship of my accomplices with whom I did it. I did not, therefore, love the theft alone—yet, indeed, it was only the theft that I loved, for the companionship was nothing. What is this paradox? Who is it that can explain it to me but God, who illumines my heart and searches out the dark corners thereof? What is it that has prompted my mind to inquire about it, to discuss and to reflect upon all this? For had I at that time loved the pears that I stole and wished to enjoy them, I might have done so alone, if I could have been satisfied with the mere act of theft by which my pleasure was served. Nor did I need to have that itching of my own passions inflamed by the encouragement of my accomplices. But since the pleasure I got was not from the pears, it was in the crime itself, enhanced by the companionship of my fellow sinners.

IX: Evil Communications

What passion moved me? It was undoubtedly depraved and a great misfortune for me to feel it. But still, what was it? "Who can understand his errors?"[17]

We laughed because our hearts were tickled at the thought of deceiving the owners, who had no idea of what we were doing and would have strenuously objected. Yet, again, why did I find such delight in doing this which I would not have done alone? Is

---

[17] Psalms 19:12.

it that no one readily laughs alone? No one does so readily; but still sometimes, when men are by themselves and no one else is about, a fit of laughter will overcome them when something very droll presents itself to their sense or mind. Yet alone I would not have done it—alone I could not have done it at all.

Behold, my God, the lively review of my soul's career is laid bare before you. I would not have committed that theft alone. My pleasure in it was not what I stole but, rather, the act of stealing. Nor would I have enjoyed doing it alone—indeed I would not have done it! O friendship all unfriendly! You strange seducer of the soul, who hungers for mischief from impulses of mirth and wantonness, who craves another's loss without any desire for one's own profit or revenge—so that, when they say, "Let's go, let's do it," we are ashamed not to be shameless.

X: A Soul in Waste

Who can unravel such a twisted and tangled knottiness? It is unclean. I hate to reflect upon it. I hate to look on it. But I desire you, O Righteousness and Innocence, so beautiful and comely to all virtuous eyes—I long for you with a satiety that is never satiated. With you there is perfect rest, and life unchanging. He who enters into you enters into the joy of his Lord,[18] and shall have no fear and shall achieve excellence in the Excellent. I fell away from you, O my God, and in my youth I wandered too far from you, my true support. And I became to myself a wasteland.

---

[18] Cf. Matthew 25:21

from *Essays*

Of Idleness

On the Uncertainty
of Our Judgement

Of Democritus and
Heraclitus

On the Vanity of Words

Michel de Montaigne

*Michel de Montaigne (1533–1592) is a complete representative of the age of the
Renaissance. His father was a Catholic soldier, lawyer, landowner, and mayor of
Bordeaux; his mother, from a Sephardic Jewish family, was a convert to Protestantism.
Montaigne studied philosophy and law, had a prodigious memory for the classics,
experienced the Catholic-Huguenot civil wars first-hand, though a Catholic supported
tolerance for the Protestant Huguenots, served two terms as mayor of Bordeaux, and
was admired by both Catholic and Protestant contenders for the French throne. He
traveled through Europe, in one period (not trusting doctors or medicines) looking for
a cure for kidney stones, in another avoiding the plague and civil unrest. He had an
audience with the Pope and came under the threat of Vatican censorship. He had
been married under family pressure and had six daughters, only one of whom lived
past childhood, and had a variety of amorous relationships. His most intimate
relationship was with his dear friend Étienne de la Boétie, about whom he wrote,
"there is no more sign of the seam by which [our souls] were first conjoined" and that
"If a man should importune me to give a reason why I loved him, I find it could no
otherwise be expressed than by making answer: because it was he, because it was I."*

*Montaigne's greatest interest was in conversation and contemplation. His essays,
written and revised during the last twenty years of his life, record the most intimate,
penetrating, wide-ranging, and candid portrait we have of a Renaissance man
contemplating himself, human nature, and the world. He had a medal struck in
1576 which included his age, the Greek term for "I abstain" and, most famously, the
phrase* Que sçay-je? *("What do I know?"). But Montaigne's skepticism was far
from the nihilistic skepticism of some modern existentialists. Rather, it was a
rationally administered antidote to the easy self-delusions to which he knew human
beings are prone. Behind the skepticism stand Montaigne's trust in the truth available
to us through the honest observation of the nature of man and the world, through the
authority of ancient custom, and through the mutual tempering of faith and reason.*

Above: *Portrait de Michel Eyquem, seigneur de Montaigne,* artist unknown, ca. 1578.

Written 1572–1592, translated by Charles Cotton, 17th Century, edited by William Carew Hazlitt, 1877

Book I, Essay 8: Of Idleness

As we see some grounds that have long lain idle and untilled, when grown rich and fertile by rest, to abound with and spend their virtue in the product of innumerable sorts of weeds and wild herbs that are unprofitable, and that to make them perform their true office, we are to cultivate and prepare them for such seeds as are proper for our service; and as we see women that, without knowledge of man, do sometimes of themselves bring forth inanimate and formless lumps of flesh, but that to cause a natural and perfect generation they are to be husbanded with another kind of seed: even so it is with minds, which if not applied to some certain study that may fix and restrain them, run into a thousand extravagances, eternally roving here and there in the vague expanse of the imagination—

Sicut aqua tremulum labris ubi lumen ahenis,
Sole repercussum, aut radiantis imagine lunae,
Omnia pervolitat late loca; jamque sub auras
Erigitur, summique ferit laquearia tecti.

[As when in brazen vats of water the trembling beams of light, reflected from the sun, or from the image of the radiant moon, swiftly float over every place around, and now are darted up on high, and strike the ceilings of the upmost roof . . .—Virgil, *Aeneid*, viii. 22.]

—in which wild agitation there is no folly, nor idle fancy they do not light upon:—

Velut aegri somnia, vanae
Finguntur species.

[As a sick man's dreams, creating vain phantasms—Horace, *De Arte Poetica*, 7.]

The soul that has no established aim loses itself, for, as it is said—

Quisquis ubique habitat, Maxime, nusquam habitat.

[He who lives everywhere, lives nowhere.—Martial, vii. 73.]

When I lately retired to my own house, with a resolution, as much as possibly I could, to avoid all manner of concern in affairs, and to spend in privacy and repose the little remainder of

time I have to live, I fancied I could not more oblige my mind
than to suffer it at full leisure to entertain and divert itself, which
I now hoped it might henceforth do, as being by time become
more settled and mature; but I find—

Variam semper dant otia mentem,

[Leisure ever creates varied thought.—Lucan, iv. 704]

that, quite contrary, it is like a horse that has broke from his rider,
who voluntarily runs into a much more violent career than any
horseman would put him to, and creates me so many chimaeras
and fantastic monsters, one upon another, without order or
design, that, the better at leisure to contemplate their strangeness
and absurdity, I have begun to commit them to writing, hoping in
time to make it ashamed of itself.

Book I, Essay 26 (Cotton/Hazlitt)/Essay 27 (Villey): On the Uncertainty of Our Judgment

[Original title: *C'est folie de rapporter le vray et le faux à nostre suffisance;* That it is folly to measure truth and error by our own capacity—Cotton/Hazlitt; literally, it is folly to gauge the true and the false by our self-sufficiency/ self-importance/capacity.]

'Tis not, perhaps, without reason, that we attribute facility of belief and easiness of persuasion to simplicity and ignorance: for I fancy I have heard belief compared to the impression of a seal upon the soul, which by how much softer and of less resistance it is, is the more easy to be impressed upon.

Ut necesse est, lancem in Libra, ponderibus impositis,
deprimi, sic animum perspicuis cedere.

[As the scale of the balance must give way to the weight that presses it down, so the mind yields to demonstration.—Cicero, *Academica*, ii. 12.]

By how much the soul is more empty and without counterpoise, with so much greater facility it yields under the weight of the first persuasion. And this is the reason that children, the common people, women, and sick folks, are most apt to be led by the ears. But then, on the other hand, 'tis a foolish presumption to slight and condemn all things for false that do not appear to us probable; which is the ordinary vice of such as fancy themselves wiser than their neighbors. I was myself once one of those; and if I heard talk of dead folks walking, of prophecies, enchantments, witchcrafts, or any other story I had no mind to believe:

Somnia, terrores magicos, miracula, sagas,
Nocturnos lemures, portentaque Thessala,

[Dreams, magic terrors, marvels, sorceries, Thessalian prodigies. —Horace, *Epistle* ii. 3, 208.]

I presently pitied the poor people that were abused by these follies. Whereas I now find, that I myself was to be pitied as much, at least, as they; not that experience has taught me anything to alter my former opinions, though my curiosity has endeavoured that way; but reason has instructed me, that thus resolutely to condemn anything for false and impossible, is arrogantly and impiously to circumscribe and limit the will of God, and the power of our mother nature, within the bounds of my own capacity, than which no folly can be greater. If we give the names of monster and miracle to everything our reason cannot comprehend, how many are continually presented before our eyes? Let us but consider through what clouds, and as it were groping in the dark, our teachers lead us to the knowledge of most of the things about us; assuredly we shall find that it is rather custom than knowledge that takes away their strangeness—

Jam nemo, fessus saturusque videndi,
Suspicere in coeli dignatur lucida templa;

[Weary of the sight, now no one deigns to look up to heaven's lucid temples.—Lucretius, ii. 1037. For *saturusque videndi* the original text of Lucretius has '*statiate videnai.*']

and that if those things were now newly presented to us, we should think them as incredible, if not more, than any others.

Si nunc primum mortalibus adsint
Ex improviso, si sint objecta repente,
Nil magis his rebus poterat mirabile dici,
Aute minus ante quod auderent fore credere gentes.

[—Lucretius, ii. 1032. The sense of the passage is in the preceding sentence.]

He that had never seen a river, imagined the first he met with to be the sea; and the greatest things that have fallen within our knowledge, we conclude the extremes that nature makes of the kind.

Scilicet et fluvius qui non est maximus, ei'st
Qui non ante aliquem majorem vidit; et ingens
Arbor, homoque videtur, et omnia de genere omni
Maxima quae vidit quisque, haec ingentia fingit.

[A little river seems to him, who has never seen a larger river, a mighty stream; and so with other things—a tree, a man—anything appears greatest to him that never knew a greater.—Lucretius, vi. 674.]

Consuetudine oculorum assuescunt animi, neque admirantur,
neque requirunt rationes earum rerum, quas semper vident.

[Things grow familiar to men's minds by being often seen; so that they neither admire nor are they inquisitive about things they daily see.—Cicero, *De Natura Deorum*, lib. ii. 38.]

The novelty, rather than the greatness of things, tempts us to inquire into their causes. We are to judge with more reverence, and with greater acknowledgment of our own ignorance and infirmity, of the infinite power of nature. How many unlikely things are there testified by people worthy of faith, which, if we cannot persuade ourselves absolutely to believe, we ought at least to leave them in suspense; for, to condemn them as impossible, is by a temerarious presumption to pretend to know the utmost bounds of possibility. Did we rightly understand the difference betwixt the impossible and the unusual, and betwixt that which is contrary to the order and course of nature and contrary to the common opinion of men, in not believing rashly, and on the other hand, in not being too incredulous, we should observe the rule of 'Ne quid nimis' enjoined by Chilo.

When we find in Froissart, that the Comte de Foix knew in Bearn the defeat of John, king of Castile, at Jubera the next day after it happened, and the means by which he tells us he came to do so, we may be allowed to be a little merry at it, as also at what our annals report, that Pope Honorius, the same day that King Philip Augustus died at Mantes, performed his public obsequies at Rome, and commanded the like throughout Italy, the testimony of these authors not being, perhaps, of authority enough to restrain us. But what if Plutarch, besides several examples that he produces out of antiquity, tells us, he knows of certain knowledge, that in the time of Domitian, the news of the battle lost by Antony in Germany was published at Rome, many days' journey from thence, and dispersed throughout the whole world, the same day it was fought; and if Caesar was of opinion, that it has often happened, that the report has preceded the incident, shall we not say, that these simple people have suffered themselves to be deceived with the vulgar, for not having been so clear-sighted as we? Is there anything more delicate, more clear, more sprightly; than Pliny's judgment, when he is pleased to set it to work? Anything more remote from vanity? Setting aside his learning, of which I make less account, in which of these excellences do any of us excel him? And yet there is scarce a young schoolboy that does not convict him of untruth, and that pretends not to instruct him in the progress of the works of nature. When we read in Bouchet the miracles of St. Hilary's relics, away with them: his authority is not sufficient to deprive us of the liberty of contradicting him; but generally and offhand to condemn all suchlike stories, seems to me a singular impudence. That great St. Augustin' testifies to have seen a blind child recover sight upon the relics of St. Gervasius and St. Protasius at Milan; a woman at Carthage cured of a cancer, by the sign of the cross made upon her by a woman newly baptized; Hesperius, a familiar friend of his, to have driven away the spirits that haunted his house, with a little earth of the sepulcher of our Lord; which earth, being also transported thence into the church, a paralytic to have there been suddenly cured by it; a woman in a procession, having touched St. Stephen's shrine with a nosegay, and rubbing her eyes with it, to have recovered her sight, lost many years before; with several other miracles of which he professes himself to have been an eyewitness: of what shall we excuse him and the two holy bishops, Aurelius and Maximinus, both of whom he attests to the truth of these things? Shall it be of ignorance, simplicity, and facility; or of malice and imposture? Is any man now living so impudent as to think himself comparable to them in virtue, piety, learning, judgment, or any kind of perfection?

> *Qui, ut rationem nullam afferrent,*
> *ipsa auctoritate me frangerent.*

[Who, though they should adduce no reason, would convince me with their authority alone.—Cicero, *Tusculanae Quaestiones* (*Tusculan Disputations*), i. 21.]

'Tis a presumption of great danger and consequence, besides the absurd temerity it draws after it, to contemn what we do not comprehend. For after, according to your fine understanding, you have established the limits of truth and error, and that, afterwards, there appears a necessity upon you of believing stranger things than those you have contradicted, you are already obliged to quit your limits. Now, that which seems to me so much to disorder our consciences in the commotions we are now in concerning religion, is the Catholics dispensing so much with their belief. They fancy they appear moderate, and wise, when they grant to their opponents some of the articles in question; but, besides that they do not discern what advantage it is to those with whom we contend, to begin to give ground and to retire, and how much this animates our enemy to follow his blow: these articles which they select as things indifferent, are sometimes of very great importance. We are either wholly and absolutely to submit ourselves to the authority of our ecclesiastical polity, or totally throw off all obedience to it: 'tis not for us to determine what and how much obedience we owe to it. And this I can say, as having myself made trial of it, that having formerly taken the liberty of my own swing and fancy, and omitted or neglected certain rules of the discipline of our Church, which seemed to me vain and strange coming afterwards to discourse of it with learned men, I have found those same things to be built upon very good and solid ground and strong foundation; and that nothing but stupidity and ignorance makes us receive them with less reverence than the rest. Why do we not consider what contradictions we find in our own judgments; how many things were yesterday articles of our faith, that to-day appear no other than fables? Glory and curiosity are the scourges of the soul; the last prompts us to thrust our noses into everything, the other forbids us to leave anything doubtful and undecided.

Book I, Essay 50: Of Democritus and Heraclitus

The judgment is an utensil proper for all subjects, and will have an oar in everything: which is the reason, that in these Essays I take hold of all occasions where, though it happen to be a subject I do not very well understand, I try, however, sounding it at a distance, and finding it too deep for my stature, I keep me on the shore; and this knowledge that a man can proceed no further, is one effect of its virtue, yes, one of those of which it is most proud. One while in an idle and frivolous subject, I try to find out matter whereof to compose a body, and then to prop and support it; another while, I employ it in a noble subject, one that has been tossed and tumbled by a thousand hands, wherein a man can scarce possibly introduce anything of his own, the way being so beaten on every side that he must of necessity walk in the steps of another: in such a case, 'tis the work of the judgment to take the way that seems best, and of a thousand paths, to determine that this or that is the best. I leave the choice of my arguments to fortune, and take that she first presents to me; they are all alike to me, I never design to go through any of them; for I never see all of anything: neither do they who so largely promise to show it others. Of a hundred members and faces that everything has, I take one, onewhile to look it over only, another while to ripple up the skin, and sometimes to pinch it to the bones: I give a stab, not so wide but as deep as I can, and am for the most part tempted to take it in hand by some new light I discover in it. Did I know myself less, I might perhaps venture to handle something or other to the bottom, and to be deceived in my own inability; but sprinkling here one word and there another, patterns cut from several pieces and scattered without design and without engaging myself too far, I am not responsible for them, or obliged to keep close to my subject, without varying at my own liberty and pleasure, and giving up myself to doubt and uncertainty, and to my own governing method, ignorance.

All motion discovers us: the very same soul of Caesar, that made itself so conspicuous in marshaling and commanding the battle of Pharsalia, was also seen as solicitous and busy in the softer affairs of love and leisure. A man makes a judgment of a horse, not only by seeing him when he is showing off his paces, but by his very walk, nay, and by seeing him stand in the stable.

Amongst the functions of the soul, there are some of a lower and meaner form; he who does not see her in those inferior offices as well as in those of nobler note, never fully discovers her; and, peradventure, she is best shown where she moves her simpler pace. The winds of passions take most hold of her in her highest flights; and the rather by reason that she wholly applies herself to, and exercises her whole virtue upon, every particular subject, and never handles more than one thing at a time, and that not according to it, but according to herself. Things in respect to themselves have, peradventure, their weight, measures, and conditions; but when we once take them into us, the soul forms them as she pleases. Death is terrible to Cicero, coveted by Cato, indifferent to Socrates. Health, conscience, authority, knowledge, riches, beauty, and their contraries, all strip themselves at their entering into us, and receive a new robe, and of another fashion, from the soul; and of what color, brown, bright, green, dark, and of what quality, sharp, sweet, deep, or superficial, as best pleases each of them, for they are not agreed upon any common standard of forms, rules, or proceedings; every one is a queen in her own dominions. Let us, therefore, no more excuse ourselves upon the external qualities of things; it belongs to us to give ourselves an account of them. Our good or ill has no other dependence but on ourselves. 'Tis there that our offerings and our vows are due, and not to fortune she has no power over our manners; on the contrary, they draw and make her follow in their train, and cast her in their own mould. Why should not I judge of Alexander at table, ranting and drinking at the prodigious rate he sometimes used to do?

Or, if he played at chess? what string of his soul was not touched by this idle and childish game? I hate and avoid it, because it is not play enough, that it is too grave and serious a diversion, and I am ashamed to lay out as much thought and study upon it as would serve to much better uses. He did not more pump his brains about his glorious expedition into the Indies, nor than another in unravelling a passage upon which depends the safety of mankind. To what a degree does this ridiculous diversion molest the soul, when all her faculties are summoned together upon this trivial account! and how fair an opportunity she herein gives every one to know and to make a right judgment of himself? I do not more thoroughly sift myself in any other posture than this: what passion are we exempted from in it? Anger, spite, malice, impatience, and a vehement desire of getting the better in a concern wherein it were more excusable to be ambitious of being overcome; for to be eminent, to excel above the common rate in frivolous things, nowise befits a man of honor. What I say in this example may be said in all others. Every particle, every employment of man manifests him equally with any other.

Democritus and Heraclitus were two philosophers, of whom the first, finding human condition ridiculous and vain, never appeared abroad but with a jeering and laughing countenance; whereas Heraclitus commiserating that same condition of ours, appeared always with a sorrowful look, and tears in his eyes:

> *Alter*
> *Ridebat, quoties a limine moverat unum*
> *Protuleratque pedem; flebat contrarius alter.*

> [The one always, as often as he had stepped one pace from his threshold, laughed, the other always wept.—Juvenal, Satires, x. 28.]

I am clearly for the first humour; not because it is more pleasant to laugh than to weep, but because it expresses more contempt and condemnation than the other, and I think we can never be despised according to our full desert. Compassion and bewailing seem to imply some esteem of and value for the thing bemoaned; whereas the things we laugh at are by that expressed to be of no moment. I do not think that we are so unhappy as we are vain, or have in us so much malice as folly; we are not so full of mischief as inanity; nor so miserable as we are vile and mean. And therefore Diogenes, who passed away his time in rolling himself in his tub, and made nothing of the great Alexander, esteeming us no better than flies or bladders puffed up with wind, was a sharper and more penetrating, and, consequently in my opinion, a juster judge than Timon, surnamed the Man-hater; for what a man hates he lays to heart. This last was an enemy to all mankind, who passionately desired our ruin, and avoided our conversation as dangerous, proceeding from wicked and depraved natures: the other valued us so little that we could neither trouble nor infect him by our example; and left us to herd one with another, not out of fear, but from contempt of our society: concluding us as incapable of doing good as evil.

Of the same strain was Statilius' answer, when Brutus courted him into the conspiracy against Caesar; he was satisfied that the enterprise was just, but he did not think mankind worthy of a wise man's concern; according to the doctrine of Hegesias, who said, that a wise man ought to do nothing but for himself, forasmuch as he only was worthy of it: and to the saying of Theodorus, that it was not reasonable a wise man should hazard himself for his country, and endanger wisdom for a company of fools. Our condition is as ridiculous as risible.

Book I, Essay 51: On the Vanity of Words

A rhetorician of times past said, that to make little things appear great was his profession. This was a shoemaker, who can make a great shoe for a little foot.—[A saying of Agesilaus.]—They would in Sparta have sent such a fellow to be whipped for making profession of a tricky and deceitful act; and I fancy that Archidamus, who was king of that country, was a little surprised at the answer of Thucydides, when inquiring of him, which was the better wrestler, Pericles, or he, he replied, that it was hard to affirm; for when I have thrown him, said he, he always persuades the spectators that he had no fall and carries away the prize.— [Quintilian, ii. 15.]—The women who paint, pounce, and plaster up their ruins, filling up their wrinkles and deformities, are less to blame, because it is no great matter whether we see them in their natural complexions; whereas these make it their business to deceive not our sight only but our judgments, and to adulterate and corrupt the very essence of things. The republics that have maintained themselves in a regular and well-modeled government, such as those of Lacedaemon and Crete, had orators in no very great esteem. Aristo wisely defined rhetoric to be "a science to persuade the people;" Socrates and Plato "an art to flatter and deceive." And those who deny it in the general description, verify it throughout in their precepts. The Mohammedans will not suffer their children to be instructed in it, as being useless, and the Athenians, perceiving of how pernicious consequence the practice of it was, it being in their city of universal esteem, ordered the principal part, which is to move the affections, with their exordiums and perorations, to be taken away. 'Tis an engine invented to manage and govern a disorderly and tumultuous rabble, and that never is made use of, but like physic to the sick, in a discomposed state. In those where the vulgar or the ignorant, or both together, have been all-powerful and able to give the law, as in those of Athens, Rhodes, and Rome, and where the public affairs have been in a continual tempest of commotion, to such places have the orators always repaired. And in truth, we shall find few persons in those republics who have pushed their fortunes to any great degree of eminence without the assistance of eloquence.

Pompey, Caesar, Crassus, Lucullus, Lentulus, Metellus, thence took their chiefest spring, to mount to that degree of authority at which they at last arrived, making it of greater use to them than arms, contrary to the opinion of better times; for, L. Volumnius speaking publicly in favor of the election of Q. Fabius and Pub. Decius, to the consular dignity: "These are men," said he, "born for war and great in execution; in the combat of the tongue altogether wanting; spirits truly consular. The subtle, eloquent, and learned are only good for the city, to make praetors of, to administer justice."—[Livy, x. 22.]

Eloquence most flourished at Rome when the public affairs were in the worst condition and most disquieted with intestine commotions; as a free and untilled soil bears the worst weeds. By which it should seem that a monarchical government has less need of it than any other: for the stupidity and facility natural to the common people, and that render them subject to be turned and twined and, led by the ears by this charming harmony of words, without weighing or considering the truth and reality of things by the force of reason: this facility, I say, is not easily found in a single person, and it is also more easy by good education and advice to secure him from the impression of this poison. There was never any famous orator known to come out of Persia or Macedon.

I have entered into this discourse upon the occasion of an Italian I lately received into my service, and who was clerk of the kitchen to the late Cardinal Caraffa till his death. I put this fellow upon an account of his office: when he fell to discourse of this palate-science, with such a settled countenance and magisterial gravity, as if he had been handling some profound point of divinity. He made a learned distinction of the several sorts of appetites; of that a man has before he begins to eat, and of those after the second and third service; the means simply to satisfy the first, and then to raise and actuate the other two; the ordering of the sauces, first in general, and then proceeded to the qualities of the ingredients and their effects; the differences of salads according to their seasons, those which ought to be served up hot, and which cold; the manner of their garnishment and decoration to render them acceptable to the eye. After which he entered upon the order of the whole service, full of weighty and important considerations:

Nec minimo sane discrimine refert,
Quo gestu lepores, et quo gallina secetur;

[Nor with less discrimination observes how we should carve a hare, and how a hen. (Or: Nor with the least discrimination relates how we should carve hares, and how cut up a hen.)—Juvenal, *Satires*, v. 123.]

and all this set out with lofty and magnificent words, the very same we make use of when we discourse of the government of an empire. Which learned lecture of my man brought this of Terence into my memory:

Hoc salsum est, hoc adustum est, hoc lautum est, parum:
Illud recte: iterum sic memento: sedulo
Moneo, qux possum, pro mea sapientia.
Postremo, tanquam in speculum, in patinas,
Demea, Inspicere jubeo, et moneo, quid facto usus sit.

[This is too salt, that's burnt, that's not washed enough; that's well; remember to do so another time. Thus do I ever advise them to have things done properly, according to my capacity; and lastly, Demea, I command my cooks to look into every dish as if it were a mirror, and tell them what they should do.—Terence, *Adelphoe* (*The Brothers*), iii. 3, 71.]

And yet even the Greeks themselves very much admired and highly applauded the order and disposition that Paulus AEmilius observed in the feast he gave them at his return from Macedon. But I do not here speak of effects, I speak of words only.

I do not know whether it may have the same operation upon other men that it has upon me, but when I hear our architects thunder out their bombast words of pilasters, architraves, and cornices, of the Corinthian and Doric orders, and suchlike jargon, my imagination is presently possessed with the palace of Apollidon; when, after all, I find them but the paltry pieces of my own kitchen door.

To hear men talk of metonomies, metaphors, and allegories, and other grammar words, would not one think they signified some rare and exotic form of speaking? And yet they are phrases that come near to the babble of my chambermaid.

And this other is a gullery of the same stamp, to call the offices of our kingdom by the lofty titles of the Romans, though they have no similitude of function, and still less of authority and power. And this also, which I doubt will one day turn to the reproach of this age of ours, unworthily and indifferently to confer upon any we think fit the most glorious surnames with which antiquity honored but one or two persons in several ages. Plato carried away the surname of Divine, by so universal a consent that never any one repined at it, or attempted to take it from him; and yet the Italians, who pretend, and with good reason, to more sprightly wits and sounder sense than the other nations of their time, have lately bestowed the same title upon Aretin, in whose writings, save tumid phrases set out with smart periods, ingenious indeed but far-fetched and fantastic, and the eloquence, be it what it may, I see nothing in him above the ordinary writers of his time, so far is he from approaching the ancient divinity. And we make nothing of giving the surname of great to princes who have nothing more than ordinary in them.

Good Will, Duty, and the Categorical Imperative

from *Foundations of the Metaphysics of Morals*

Immanuel Kant

Immanuel Kant (1724–1804) was a philosopher whose work has been as influential as that of any philosopher since the Middle Ages, having implications for theology, morality, cognitive science, law, and aesthetics.

Born in Königsberg, Germany, Kant came under the influence of German pietism. He studied at the University of Königsberg, where he earned a doctorate and taught first as a tutor and then as a professor. He turned to philosophy (awakened from what he called his "dogmatic slumber," essentially the philosophy of Leibniz, by an argument of David Hume leading to Kant's question "How are synthetic a priori judgments possible?" from which all his later philosophy arose). Not long after Kant published his Critique of Pure Reason, *his ideas were being discussed in schools throughout Germany. Kant's admirers flocked to Königsberg to see him, forcing him to vary the places where he ate each day to avoid the crowds. Except for that variation, Kant lived a highly regimented life, never failing to rise at 5:00 a.m.; the townspeople reportedly set their clocks by the moment at which he passed their houses on his daily walk.*

Kant's reasoning about human reason led him to believe that reason could be applied to human choice, overruling, as Plato had taught, other parts of the self, like desire or preference or fear, and that moral choice-making is the human being's highest faculty. The moral human being, who has absolute value, is one who does the right thing not out of need, desire, or advantage, but out of the will to do the right thing for its own sake, which Kant calls duty. Only such a person can be called a moral being. Kant then argues that human beings can discern what is the right thing to do in any situation. The method for discerning the right thing to do is to apply the categorical imperative: act in such a way that you could will the principle of your action to be a universal principle. This principle is categorical because it is universal; there is no situation in which it does not apply (as distinct from a hypothetical imperative, which depends on particular conditions). To the categorical, Kant adds the practical imperative: treat human beings not only as means but as ends in themselves. These imperatives form the universal moral duty of the rational being.

Above: *Portrait of Immanuel Kant*, Rosmäsler, 1822, engraving.

Published 1785; translated by T.K. Abbott, 1898

Nothing can possibly be conceived in the world, or even out of it, which can be called good, without qualification, except a Good Will. Intelligence, wit, judgment, and the other *talents* of the mind, however they may be named, or courage, resolution, perseverance, as qualities of temperament, are undoubtedly good and desirable in many respects; but these gifts of nature may also become extremely bad and mischievous if the will which is to make use of them, and which, therefore, constitutes what is called *character*, is not good. It is the same with the *gifts of fortune*. Power, riches, honor, even health, and the general well-being and contentment with one's condition which is called *happiness*, inspire pride, and often presumption, if there is not a good will to correct the influence of these on the mind, and with this also to rectify the whole principle of acting, and adapt it to its end. The sight of a being who is not adorned with a single feature of a pure and good will enjoying unbroken prosperity can never give pleasure to an impartial rational spectator. Thus a good will appears to constitute the indispensable condition even of being worthy of happiness.

There are even some qualities which are of service to this good will itself, and may facilitate its action, yet which have no intrinsic unconditional value but always presuppose a good will and this qualifies the esteem that we justly have for them, and does not permit us to regard them as absolutely good. Moderation in the affections and passions, self-control, and calm deliberation are not only good in many respects, but even seem to constitute part of the intrinsic worth of the person; but they are far from deserving to be called good without qualification, although they have been so unconditionally praised by the ancients. For without the principles of a good will they may become extremely bad; and the coolness of a villain not only makes him far more dangerous, but also directly makes him more abominable in our eyes than he would have been without it.

A good will is good not because of what it performs or effects, not by its aptness for the attainment of some proposed end, but simply by virtue of volition, that is, it is good in itself, and considered by itself is to be esteemed much higher than all that can be brought about by it in favor of any inclination, nay, even of the sum-total of all inclinations. Even if it should happen that, owing to special disfavor of fortune, or the niggardly provision of a step-motherly nature, this will should wholly lack power to accomplish its purpose, if with its greatest efforts it should achieve nothing, and there should remain only good (not, to be sure, a mere wish, but the summoning of all means in our power), then, like a jewel, it would still shine by its own light, as a thing which has its whole value in itself. Its usefulness or fruitlessness can neither add to nor take away anything from this value.

Thus the moral worth of an action does not lie in the effect expected from it, nor in any principle of action which requires to borrow its motive from this expected effect. For all these effects —agreeableness of one's condition, and even the promotion of the happiness of others—could have been also brought about by other causes, so that for this there would have been no need of the will of a rational being; whereas it is in this alone that the supreme and unconditional good can be found. The pre-eminent good which we call moral can therefore consist in nothing else than *the conception of law* in itself, *which certainly is only possible in a rational being*, insofar as this conception, and not the expected effect, determines the will. This is a good which is already present in the person who acts accordingly, and we have not to wait for it to appear first in the result.

But what sort of law can that be, the conception of which must determine the will, even without paying any regard to the effect expected from it, in order that this will may be called good absolutely and without qualification? As I have deprived the will of every impulse which could arise to it from obedience to any law, there remains nothing but the universal conformity of its actions to law in general, which alone is to serve the will as a principle, i.e., I am never to act otherwise than *so that I could also will that my maxim should become a universal law*. Here, now, it is the simple conformity to the law in general, without assuming any particular law applicable to certain actions, that serves the will as its principle, and must so serve it, if duty is not to be a vain delusion and a chimerical notion. The common reason of men in its practical judgments perfectly coincides with this and always has in view the principle here suggested. Let the question be, for example: May I when in distress make a promise with the intention not to keep it? I readily distinguish here between the two significations which the question may have: Whether it is prudent, or whether it is right, to make a false promise? The former may undoubtedly be the case. I see clearly indeed that it is not enough to extricate myself from a present difficulty by means of this subterfuge, but it must be well considered whether there may not hereafter spring from this lie much greater inconvenience than that from which I now free myself, and as, with all my supposed *cunning*, the consequences cannot be so easily foreseen but that credit once lost may be much more injurious to me than any mischief which I seek to avoid at present, it should be considered whether it would not be more prudent to act herein according to a universal maxim, and to make it a habit to promise nothing except with the intention of keeping it. But it is soon clear to me that such a maxim will still only be based on the fear of the consequences. Now it is a wholly different thing to be truthful from duty, and to be so from apprehension of injurious consequences. In the first case, the very notion of the action already implies a law for me; in the second case, I must first look about elsewhere to see what results may be combined with it which would affect myself. For to deviate from the principle of duty is beyond all doubt wicked; but to be unfaithful to my maxim of prudence may often be very advantageous to me, although to abide by it is certainly safer. The shortest way, however, and an unerring one, to discover the answer to this question whether a lying promise is consistent with duty, is to ask myself, Should I be content that my maxim (to extricate myself from difficulty by a false promise) should hold good as a universal law, for myself as well as for others? and should I be able to say to myself, "Every one may make a deceitful promise when he finds himself in a difficulty from which he cannot otherwise extricate himself"? Then I presently become aware that while I can will the lie, I can by no means will that lying should be a universal law. For with such a law there would be no promises at all, since it would be in vain to allege my intention in regard to my future actions to those who would not believe this allegation, or if they over-hastily did so, would pay me back in my own coin. Hence my maxim, as soon as it should be made a universal law, would necessarily destroy itself.

I do not, therefore, need any far-reaching penetration to discern what I have to do in order that my will be morally good. Inexperienced in the course of the world, incapable of being prepared for all its contingencies, I ask only myself: Canst thou also will that thy maxim should be a universal law? If not, then it must be rejected, and that not because of a disadvantage accruing from it to myself or even to others, but because it cannot enter as a principle into a possible universal legislation, and reason extorts from me immediate respect for such legislation. I do not indeed as yet *discern* on what this respect is based (this the philosopher may inquire), but at least I understand this, that it is an estimation of the worth which far outweighs all worth of what is recommended by inclination, and that the necessity of acting from *pure* respect for the practical law is what constitutes duty, to which every other motive must give place, because it is the condition of a will being good *in itself*, and the worth of such a will is above everything. . . .

. . . Everything in nature works according to laws. Rational beings alone have the faculty of acting according to the *conception* of laws, that is according to principles, i.e. have a *will*. Since the deduction of actions from principles requires *reason*, the will is nothing but practical reason. If reason infallibly determines the will, then the actions of such a being which are recognized as objectively necessary are subjectively necessary also, i.e. the will is a faculty to choose *that only* which reason independent on inclination recognizes as practically necessary, i.e. as good. But if reason of itself does not sufficiently determine the will, if the latter is subject also to subjective conditions (particular impulses) which do not always coincide with the objective conditions; in a word, if the will does not *in itself* completely accord with reason (which is actually the case with men), then the actions which objectively are recognized as necessary are subjectively contingent, and the determination of such a will according to objective laws is *obligation*, that is to say, the relation of the objective laws to a will that is not thoroughly good is conceived as the determination of the will of a rational being by principles of reason, but which the will from its nature does not of necessity follow.

The conception of an objective principle, in so far as it is obligatory for a will, is called a command (of reason), and the formula of the command is called an Imperative . . . .

Now all *imperatives* command either *hypothetically* or *categorically*. The former represent the practical necessity of a possible action as means to something else that is willed (or at least which one might possibly will). The categorical imperative would be that which represented an action as necessary of itself without reference to another end, i.e. as objectively necessary.

Since every practical law represents a possible action as good, and on this account, for a subject who is practically determinable by reason, necessary, all imperatives are formulae determining an action which is necessary according to the principle of a good will in some respects. If now the action is good only as a means *to something else*, then the imperative is *hypothetical*; if it is conceived as good *in itself* and consequently as being necessarily principle of a will which of itself conforms to reason, then it is *categorical* . . . .

When I conceive a hypothetical imperative, in general I do not know beforehand what it will contain until I am given the condition. But when I conceive a categorical imperative, I know at once what it contains. For as the imperative contains besides the law only the necessity that the maxims shall conform to this law, while the law contains no conditions restricting it, there remains nothing but the general statement that the maxim of the action should conform to a universal law, and it is this conformity alone that the imperative properly represents as necessary.

There is . . . but one categorical imperative, namely, this: *Act only on that maxim whereby thou canst at the same time will that it should become a universal law.*

Now if all imperatives of duty can be deduced from this one imperative as from their principle, then, although it should remain undecided whether what is called duty is not merely a vain notion, yet at least we shall be able to show what we understand by it and what this notion means.

Since the universality of the law according to which effects are produced constitutes what is properly called *nature* in the most general sense (as to form), that is the existence of things so far as it is determined by general laws, the imperative of duty may be expressed thus: *Act as if the maxim of thy action were to become by thy will a universal law of nature.*

We will now enumerate a few duties, adopting the usual division of them into duties to ourselves and to others, and into perfect and imperfect duties.

1. A man reduced to despair by a series of misfortunes feels wearied of life, but is still so far in possession of his reason that he can ask himself whether it would not be contrary to his duty to himself to take his own life. Now he inquires whether the maxim of his action could become a universal law of nature. His maxim is: From self-love I adopt it as a principle to shorten my life when its longer duration is likely to bring more evil than satisfaction. It is asked then simply whether this principle founded on self-love can become a universal law of nature. Now we see at once that a system of nature of which it should be a law to destroy life by means of the very feeling whose special nature it is to impel to the improvement of life would contradict itself, and therefore could not exist as a system of nature; hence that maxim cannot possibly exist as a universal law of nature, and consequently would be wholly inconsistent with the supreme principle of all duty.

2. Another finds himself forced by necessity to borrow money. He knows that he will not be able to repay it, but sees also that nothing will be lent to him unless he promises stoutly to repay it in a definite time. He desires to make this promise, but he has still so much conscience as to ask himself: Is it not unlawful and inconsistent with duty to get out of a difficulty in this way? Suppose, however, that he resolves to do so, then the maxim of his action would be expressed thus: When I think myself in want of money, I will borrow money and promise to repay it, although I know that I never can do so. Now this principle of self-love or of one's own advantage may perhaps be consistent with my whole future welfare; but the question now is, Is it right? I change then suggestion of self-love into a universal law, and state the question thus: How would it be if my maxim were a universal law? Then I see at once that it could never hold as a universal law of nature,

but would necessarily contradict itself. For supposing it to be a universal law that everyone when he thinks himself in a difficulty should be able to promise whatever he pleases, with the purpose of not keeping his promise, the promise itself would become impossible, as well as the end that one might have in view in it, since no one would consider that anything was promised to him, but would ridicule all such statements as vain pretenses.

3. A third finds in himself a talent which with the help of some culture might make him a useful man in many respects. But he finds himself in comfortable circumstances, and prefers to indulge in pleasure rather than to take pains in enlarging and improving his happy natural capacities. He asks, however, whether his maxim of neglect of his natural gifts, besides agreeing with his inclination to indulgence, agrees also with what is called duty. He sees then that a system of nature could indeed subsist with such a universal law although men (like the South Sea Islanders) should let their talents rest, and resolve to devote their lives merely to idleness, amusement, and propagation of their species—in a word, to enjoyment; but he cannot possibly *will* that this should be a universal law of nature, or be implanted in us as such by a natural instinct. For, as a rational being, he necessarily wills that his faculties be developed since they serve him, and have been given him, for all sorts of possible purposes.

4. A fourth, who is in prosperity, while he sees that others have to contend with great wretchedness and that he could help them, thinks: What concern is it of mine? Let everyone be as happy as Heaven pleases, or as he can make himself; I will take nothing from him nor even envy him, only I do not wish to contribute anything to his welfare or to his assistance in distress! Now no doubt if such a mode of thinking were a universal law, the human race might very well subsist, and doubtless even better than in a state in which everyone talks of sympathy and good-will, or even takes care occasionally to put it into practice, but, on the other side, also cheats when he can, betrays the rights of men, or otherwise violates them. But although it is possible that a universal law of nature might exist in accordance with that maxim, it is impossible to will that such a principle should have the universal validity of a law of nature. For a will which resolved this would contradict itself, inasmuch as many cases might occur in which one

would have need of the love and sympathy of others, and in which, by such a law of nature, sprung from his own will, he would deprive himself of all hope of the aid he desires . . . .

We have thus established at least this much, that if duty is a conception which is to have any import and real legislative authority for our actions, it can only be expressed in categorical, and not at all in hypothetical imperatives. We have also, which is of great importance, exhibited clearly and definitely for every practical application the content of the categorical imperative, which must contain the principle of all duty if there is such a thing at all. We have not yet, however, advanced so far as to prove *a priori* that there actually is such an imperative, that there is a practical law which commands absolutely of itself, and without any other impulse, and that the following of this law is duty...

Now I say: man and generally any rational being *exists* as an end in himself, *not merely as a means* to be arbitrarily used by this or that will, but in all his actions, whether they concern himself or other rational beings, must be always regarded at the same time as an end. All objects of the inclinations have only a conditional worth; for if the inclinations and the wants founded on them did not exist, then their object would be without value. But the inclinations themselves being sources of want are so far from having an absolute worth for which they should be desired, that, on the contrary, it must be the universal wish of every rational being to be wholly free from them.

Thus the worth of any object which is *to be acquired* by our action is always conditional. Beings whose existence depends not on our will but on nature's, have nevertheless, if they are non-rational beings, only a relative value as means, and are therefore called *things*; rational beings, on the contrary, are called *persons*, because their very nature points them out as ends in themselves, that is as something which must not be used merely as means, and so far therefore restricts freedom of action (and is an object of respect). These, therefore, are not merely subjective ends whose existence has a worth *for us* as an effort of our action, but *objective ends*, that is things whose existence is an end in itself: an end moreover for which no other can be substituted, which they should subserve *merely* as means, for otherwise nothing whatever would possess *absolute worth*; but if all worth were conditioned and therefore contingent, then there would be no supreme practical principle of reason whatever.

If then there is a supreme practical principle or, in respect of the human will, a categorical imperative, it must be one which, being drawn from the conception of that which is necessarily an end for everyone because it is *an end in itself*, constitutes an *objective* principle of will, and can therefore serve as a universal practical law. The foundation of this principle is: *rational nature exists as an end in itself*. Man necessarily conceives his own existence as being so: so far then this is a *subjective* principle of human actions. But every other rational being regards its existence similarly, just on the same rational principle that holds for me: so that it is at the same time an objective principle, from which as a supreme practical law all laws of the will must be capable of being deduced. Accordingly the practical imperative will be as follows: *So act as to treat humanity, whether in thine own person or in that of any other, in every case as an end withal, never as means only . . . .*

The conception of every rational being as one which must consider itself as giving all the maxims of its will universal laws, so as to judge itself and its actions from this point of view—this conception leads to another which depends on it and is very fruitful, namely, that of a *kingdom of ends...*

By a *kingdom* I understand the union of different rational beings in a system by common laws. Now since it is by laws that ends are determined as regards their universal validity, hence, if we abstract from the personal differences of rational beings, and likewise from all the content of their private ends, we shall be able to conceive all ends combined in a systematic whole (including both rational beings as ends in themselves, and also the special ends which each may propose of himself), that is to say, we can conceive a kingdom of ends, which on the preceding principles is possible.

For all rational beings come under the *law* that each of them must treat itself and all others *never merely as means*, but in every case *at the same time as ends in themselves*. Hence results a systematic union of rational beings by common objective laws, i.e. a kingdom which may be called a kingdom of ends...

Declaration of Independence

Thomas Jefferson, et al.

Voting for independence from Britain on July 2, the Continental Congress approved and signed the Declaration on July 4, 1776. In seeking to justify the reasons for the colonies' choice to declare themselves sovereign states, independent of England and its monarch, the signers articulated the underlying principles of that choice, made literally at the risk of their lives. Those principles in turn became the foundation of the new government of the United States that they would establish thirteen years later after winning the Revolutionary War.

The principles of the Declaration included the "self-evident" truth that every human being, by virtue of being a rational creature, is in possession of certain rights— including the right to life and to liberty. The source of these rights is not government but nature itself and God, nature's creator. Bestowed by powers beyond man, these basic rights cannot be taken away by any man or government, hence they are "unalienable." That all men are created equal in having these rights is derived from the long philosophical tradition, from Aristotle through John Locke, which asserts that a human being, by virtue of possessing rationality (which permits him or her to rule non-rational animals), may not be ruled by another human being without his or her consent. Sovereignty therefore lies not with government or rulers but with the people, each of whom is equal to all others in possessing the right to govern himself or herself and to be governed by others only by consent. Since these rights pre-exist and are not subject to government, the purpose of government is not to bestow them—all men have them already—but to protect these universal rights from infringement by anyone, including by government itself.

The long list of the depravities of King George in relation to the colonies justifies their declaring independence from him precisely because he has infringed upon these newly articulated rights of man. For the first time in human history, a polity is being proclaimed whose foundation of authority over its people is not the past or custom or status or power, not arbitrary will or inherited position, but rather the intellectual principle of the sovereignty of the individual human being.

Above: *Declaration of Independence,* John Trumbull, 1817–1819, oil on canvas.

The unanimous Declaration of the thirteen united States of America,

When in the Course of human events, it becomes necessary for one people to dissolve the political bands which have connected them with another, and to assume among the powers of the earth, the separate and equal station to which the Laws of Nature and of Nature's God entitle them, a decent respect to the opinions of mankind requires that they should declare the causes which impel them to the separation.

We hold these truths to be self-evident, that all men are created equal, that they are endowed by their Creator with certain unalienable Rights, that among these are Life, Liberty and the pursuit of Happiness.—That to secure these rights, Governments are instituted among Men, deriving their just powers from the consent of the governed, —That whenever any Form of Government becomes destructive of these ends, it is the Right of the People to alter or to abolish it, and to institute new Government, laying its foundation on such principles and organizing its powers in such form, as to them shall seem most likely to effect their Safety and Happiness. Prudence, indeed, will dictate that Governments long established should not be changed for light and transient causes; and accordingly all experience hath shewn, that mankind are more disposed to suffer, while evils are sufferable, than to right themselves by abolishing the forms to which they are accustomed. But when a long train of abuses and usurpations, pursuing invariably the same Object evinces a design to reduce them under absolute Despotism, it is their right, it is their duty, to throw off such Government, and to provide new Guards for their future security.—Such has been the patient sufferance of these Colonies; and such is now the necessity which constrains them to alter their former Systems of Government. The history of the present King of Great Britain is a history of repeated injuries and usurpations, all having in direct object the establishment of an absolute Tyranny over these States. To prove this, let Facts be submitted to a candid world.

He has refused his Assent to Laws, the most wholesome and necessary for the public good.

He has forbidden his Governors to pass Laws of immediate and pressing importance, unless suspended in their operation till his Assent should be obtained; and when so suspended, he has utterly neglected to attend to them.

He has refused to pass other Laws for the accommodation of large districts of people, unless those people would relinquish the right of Representation in the Legislature, a right inestimable to them and formidable to tyrants only.

He has called together legislative bodies at places unusual, uncomfortable, and distant from the depository of their public Records, for the sole purpose of fatiguing them into compliance with his measures.

He has dissolved Representative Houses repeatedly, for opposing with manly firmness his invasions on the rights of the people.

He has refused for a long time, after such dissolutions, to cause others to be elected; whereby the Legislative powers, incapable of Annihilation, have returned to the People at large for their exercise; the State remaining in the mean time exposed to all the dangers of invasion from without, and convulsions within.

He has endeavoured to prevent the population of these States; for that purpose obstructing the Laws for Naturalization of Foreigners; refusing to pass others to encourage their migrations hither, and raising the conditions of new Appropriations of Lands.

He has obstructed the Administration of Justice, by refusing his Assent to Laws for establishing Judiciary powers.

He has made Judges dependent on his Will alone, for the tenure of their offices, and the amount and payment of their salaries.

He has erected a multitude of New Offices, and sent hither swarms of Officers to harrass our people, and eat out their substance.

He has kept among us, in times of peace, Standing Armies without the Consent of our legislatures.

He has affected to render the Military independent of and superior to the Civil power.

He has combined with others to subject us to a jurisdiction foreign to our constitution, and unacknowledged by our laws, giving his Assent to their Acts of pretended Legislation:

For Quartering large bodies of armed troops among us;

For protecting them, by a mock Trial, from punishment for any Murders which they should commit on the Inhabitants of these States;

For cutting off our Trade with all parts of the world;

For imposing Taxes on us without our Consent;

For depriving us in many cases, of the benefits of Trial by Jury;

For transporting us beyond Seas to be tried for pretended offences;

For abolishing the free System of English Laws in a neighbouring Province, establishing therein an Arbitrary government, and enlarging its Boundaries so as to render it at once an example and fit instrument for introducing the same absolute rule into these Colonies;

For taking away our Charters, abolishing our most valuable Laws, and altering fundamentally the Forms of our Governments;

For suspending our own Legislatures, and declaring themselves invested with power to legislate for us in all cases whatsoever.

He has abdicated Government here, by declaring us out of his Protection and waging War against us.

He has plundered our seas, ravaged our Coasts, burnt our towns, and destroyed the lives of our people.

He is at this time transporting large Armies of foreign Mercenaries to compleat the works of death, desolation and tyranny, already begun with circumstances of Cruelty & perfidy scarcely paralleled in the most barbarous ages, and totally unworthy the Head of a civilized nation.

He has constrained our fellow Citizens taken Captive on the high Seas to bear Arms against their Country, to become the executioners of their friends and Brethren, or to fall themselves by their Hands.

He has excited domestic insurrections amongst us, and has endeavoured to bring on the inhabitants of our frontiers, the merciless Indian Savages, whose known rule of warfare, is an undistinguished destruction of all ages, sexes and conditions.

In every stage of these Oppressions We have Petitioned for Redress in the most humble terms: Our repeated Petitions have been answered only by repeated injury. A Prince whose character is thus marked by every act which may define a Tyrant, is unfit to be the ruler of a free people.

Nor have We been wanting in attentions to our Brittish brethren. We have warned them from time to time of attempts by their legislature to extend an unwarrantable jurisdiction over us. We have reminded them of the circumstances of our emigration and settlement here. We have appealed to their native justice and magnanimity, and we have conjured them by the ties of our common kindred to disavow these usurpations, which, would inevitably interrupt our connections and correspondence. They too have been deaf to the voice of justice and of consanguinity. We must, therefore, acquiesce in the necessity, which denounces our Separation, and hold them, as we hold the rest of mankind, Enemies in War, in Peace Friends.

We, therefore, the Representatives of the united States of America, in General Congress, Assembled, appealing to the Supreme Judge of the world for the rectitude of our intentions, do, in the Name, and by Authority of the good People of these Colonies, solemnly publish and declare, That these United Colonies are, and of Right ought to be Free and Independent States; that they are Absolved from all Allegiance to the British

Crown, and that all political connection between them and the State of Great Britain, is and ought to be totally dissolved; and that as Free and Independent States, they have full Power to levy War, conclude Peace, contract Alliances, establish Commerce, and to do all other Acts and Things which Independent States may of right do. And for the support of this Declaration, with a firm reliance on the protection of divine Providence, we mutually pledge to each other our Lives, our Fortunes and our sacred Honor.

Signatures:

Georgia:
Button Gwinnett
Lyman Hall
George Walton'

North Carolina:
William Hooper
Joseph Hewes
John Penn

South Carolina:
Edward Rutledge
Thomas Heyward, Jr.
Thomas Lynch, Jr.
Arthur Middleton

Massachusetts:
John Hancock

Virginia:
George Wythe
Richard Henry Lee
Thomas Jefferson
Benjamin Harrison
Thomas Nelson, Jr.
Francis Lightfoot Lee
Carter Braxton

Maryland:
Samuel Chase
William Paca
Thomas Stone
Charles Carroll of Carollton

Pennsylvania:
Robert Morris
Benjamin Rush
Benjamin Franklin
John Morton
George Clymer
James Smith
George Taylor
James Wilson
George Ross

Delaware:
Caesar Rodney
George Read
Thomas McKean

New York:
William Floyd
Philip Livingston
Francis Lewis
Lewis Morris

New Jersey:
Richard Stockton
John Witherspoon
Francis Hopkinson
John Hart
Abraham Clark

New Hampshire:
Josiah Bartlett
William Whipple

Massachusetts:
Samuel Adams
John Adams
Robert Treat Paine
Elbridge Gerry

Rhode Island:
Stephen Hopkins
William Ellery

Connecticut:
Roger Sherman
Samuel Huntington
William Williams
Oliver Wolcott

New Hampshire:
Matthew Thornton

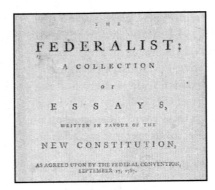

Federalist Papers
Selections:
6, 10, 51, and 84

Alexander Hamilton
James Madison
John Jay

The Federalist Papers are a collection of eighty-five essays written in support of the ratification of the United States Constitution. All of them were published under the pseudonym "Publius," though the authors are known to have been Alexander Hamilton (who authored fifty-one essays), John Jay (who authored five essays), and James Madison (who authored twenty-six essays). The pseudonym was chosen in honor of Publius Valerius Publicola (nicknamed "Poplicola," meaning "friend of the people"), one of the founders of the Roman Republic.

In Federalist 6, Hamilton warns against evils that could arise if the states are not united to one other. He argues that nations that are neighbors often become mutual enemies and that a federal government could prevent such an outcome from happening to the States.

In Federalist 10, Madison continues an argument about factions and their potential harm to the States. He points out that liberty is what will permit factions to form, but that removing liberty to prevent faction would be like removing air to prevent fire. As air is necessary for life, Madison views liberty as necessary for political life.

In Federalist 51, Madison sets forth the specific means by which checks and balances ought to be built into the different branches of the government.

In Federalist 84, Hamilton argues that the Bill of Rights is unnecessary to include in the Constitution because there is no means in the Constitution to curtail any of the rights that such a bill would guarantee. Additionally, he did not want anyone to assume that the list of rights in the Bill of Rights was exhaustive.

Rhetorically, the Federalist Papers engaged in the kind of persuasive argumentation in favor of the Constitution that would have been inappropriate for the Constitution itself. Their authors aimed to disarm the opponents of the Constitution, and they succeeded. On June 21, 1788, the Constitution was ratified. The Bill of Rights, containing the first ten amendments to the Constitution, was ratified in 1791.

Note: Footnotes are those of Alexander Hamilton.

Federalist 6: Concerning Dangers from Dissensions Between the States

Written by Alexander Hamilton; Published in the Independent Journal, November 14, 1787

To the People of the State of New York:

The three last numbers of this paper have been dedicated to an enumeration of the dangers to which we should be exposed, in a state of disunion, from the arms and arts of foreign nations. I shall now proceed to delineate dangers of a different and, perhaps, still more alarming kind—those which will in all probability flow from dissensions between the States themselves, and from domestic factions and convulsions. These have been already in some instances slightly anticipated; but they deserve a more particular and more full investigation.

A man must be far gone in Utopian speculations who can seriously doubt that, if these States should either be wholly disunited, or only united in partial confederacies, the subdivisions into which they might be thrown would have frequent and violent contests with each other. To presume a want of motives for such contests as an argument against their existence, would be to forget that men are ambitious, vindictive, and rapacious. To look for a continuation of harmony between a number of independent, unconnected sovereignties in the same neighborhood, would be to disregard the uniform course of human events, and to set at defiance the accumulated experience of ages.

The causes of hostility among nations are innumerable. There are some which have a general and almost constant operation upon the collective bodies of society. Of this description are the love of power or the desire of pre-eminence and dominion—the jealousy of power, or the desire of equality and safety. There are others which have a more circumscribed though an equally operative influence within their spheres. Such are the rivalships and competitions of commerce between commercial nations. And there are others, not less numerous than either of the former, which take their origin entirely in private passions; in the attachments, enmities, interests, hopes, and fears of leading individuals in the communities of which they are members. Men of this class, whether the favorites of a king or of a people, have in too many instances abused the confidence they possessed; and assuming the pretext of some public motive, have not scrupled to sacrifice the national tranquillity to personal advantage or personal gratification.

The celebrated Pericles, in compliance with the resentment of a prostitute,[1] at the expense of much of the blood and treasure of his countrymen, attacked, vanquished, and destroyed the city of the Samnians. The same man, stimulated by private pique against the Megarensians,[2] another nation of Greece, or to avoid a prosecution with which he was threatened as an accomplice of a supposed theft of the statuary Phidias,[3] or to get rid of the accusations prepared to be brought against him for dissipating the funds of the state in the purchase of popularity,[4] or from a combination of all these causes, was the primitive author of that famous and fatal war, distinguished in the Grecian annals by the name of the Peloponnesian war; which, after various vicissitudes, intermissions, and renewals, terminated in the ruin of the Athenian commonwealth.

The ambitious cardinal, who was prime minister to Henry VIII., permitting his vanity to aspire to the triple crown,[5] entertained hopes of succeeding in the acquisition of that splendid prize by the influence of the Emperor Charles V. To secure the favor and interest of this enterprising and powerful monarch, he precipitated England into a war with France, contrary to the plainest dictates of policy, and at the hazard of the safety and independence, as well of the kingdom over which he presided by his counsels, as of Europe in general. For if there ever was a sovereign who bid fair to realize the project of universal monarchy, it was the Emperor Charles V., of whose intrigues Wolsey was at once the instrument and the dupe.

The influence which the bigotry of one female,[6] the petulance

---

[1] Aspasia, vide Plutarch's Life of Pericles.

[2] Ibid.

[3] Ibid.

[4] Ibid. Phidias was supposed to have stolen some public gold, with the connivance of Pericles, for the embellishment of the statue of Minerva.

[5] Worn by the popes.

[6] Madame de Maintenon.

of another,[7] and the cabals of a third,[8] had in the contemporary policy, ferments, and pacifications, of a considerable part of Europe, are topics that have been too often descanted upon not to be generally known.

To multiply examples of the agency of personal considerations in the production of great national events, either foreign or domestic, according to their direction, would be an unnecessary waste of time. Those who have but a superficial acquaintance with the sources from which they are to be drawn, will themselves recollect a variety of instances; and those who have a tolerable knowledge of human nature will not stand in need of such lights to form their opinion either of the reality or extent of that agency. Perhaps, however, a reference, tending to illustrate the general principle, may with propriety be made to a case which has lately happened among ourselves. If Shays had not been a desperate debtor, it is much to be doubted whether Massachusetts would have been plunged into a civil war.

But notwithstanding the concurring testimony of experience, in this particular, there are still to be found visionary or designing men, who stand ready to advocate the paradox of perpetual peace between the States, though dismembered and alienated from each other. The genius of republics (say they) is pacific; the spirit of commerce has a tendency to soften the manners of men, and to extinguish those inflammable humors which have so often kindled into wars. Commercial republics, like ours, will never be disposed to waste themselves in ruinous contentions with each other. They will be governed by mutual interest, and will cultivate a spirit of mutual amity and concord.

Is it not (we may ask these projectors in politics) the true interest of all nations to cultivate the same benevolent and philosophic spirit? If this be their true interest, have they in fact pursued it? Has it not, on the contrary, invariably been found that momentary passions, and immediate interest, have a more active and imperious control over human conduct than general or remote considerations of policy, utility or justice? Have republics in practice been less addicted to war than monarchies? Are not the

[7] Duchess of Marlborough.

[8] Madame de Pompadour.

former administered by men as well as the latter? Are there not aversions, predilections, rivalships, and desires of unjust acquisitions, that affect nations as well as kings? Are not popular assemblies frequently subject to the impulses of rage, resentment, jealousy, avarice, and of other irregular and violent propensities? Is it not well known that their determinations are often governed by a few individuals in whom they place confidence, and are, of course, liable to be tinctured by the passions and views of those individuals? Has commerce hitherto done anything more than change the objects of war? Is not the love of wealth as domineering and enterprising a passion as that of power or glory? Have there not been as many wars founded upon commercial motives since that has become the prevailing system of nations, as were before occasioned by the cupidity of territory or dominion? Has not the spirit of commerce, in many instances, administered new incentives to the appetite, both for the one and for the other? Let experience, the least fallible guide of human opinions, be appealed to for an answer to these inquiries.

Sparta, Athens, Rome, and Carthage were all republics; two of them, Athens and Carthage, of the commercial kind. Yet were they as often engaged in wars, offensive and defensive, as the neighboring monarchies of the same times. Sparta was little better than a well-regulated camp; and Rome was never sated of carnage and conquest.

Carthage, though a commercial republic, was the aggressor in the very war that ended in her destruction. Hannibal had carried her arms into the heart of Italy and to the gates of Rome, before Scipio, in turn, gave him an overthrow in the territories of Carthage, and made a conquest of the commonwealth.

Venice, in later times, figured more than once in wars of ambition, till, becoming an object to the other Italian states, Pope Julius II. found means to accomplish that formidable league,[9] which gave a deadly blow to the power and pride of this haughty republic.

The provinces of Holland, till they were overwhelmed in debts and taxes, took a leading and conspicuous part in the wars of Europe. They had furious contests with England for the dominion of the sea, and were among the most persevering and most implacable of the opponents of Louis XIV.

---

[9] The League of Cambray, comprehending the Emperor, the King of France, the King of Aragon, and most of the Italian princes and states.

In the government of Britain the representatives of the people compose one branch of the national legislature. Commerce has been for ages the predominant pursuit of that country. Few nations, nevertheless, have been more frequently engaged in war; and the wars in which that kingdom has been engaged have, in numerous instances, proceeded from the people.

There have been, if I may so express it, almost as many popular as royal wars. The cries of the nation and the importunities of their representatives have, upon various occasions, dragged their monarchs into war, or continued them in it, contrary to their inclinations, and sometimes contrary to the real interests of the State. In that memorable struggle for superiority between the rival houses of Austria and Bourbon, which so long kept Europe in a flame, it is well known that the antipathies of the English against the French, seconding the ambition, or rather the avarice, of a favorite leader,[10] protracted the war beyond the limits marked out by sound policy, and for a considerable time in opposition to the views of the court.

The wars of these two last-mentioned nations have in a great measure grown out of commercial considerations, the desire of supplanting and the fear of being supplanted, either in particular branches of traffic or in the general advantages of trade and navigation, and sometimes even the more culpable desire of sharing in the commerce of other nations without their consent.

The last war but between Britain and Spain sprang from the attempts of the British merchants to prosecute an illicit trade with the Spanish main. These unjustifiable practices on their part produced severity on the part of the Spaniards toward the subjects of Great Britain which were not more justifiable, because they exceeded the bounds of a just retaliation and were chargeable with inhumanity and cruelty. Many of the English who were taken on the Spanish coast were sent to dig in the mines of Potosi; and by the usual progress of a spirit of resentment, the innocent were, after a while, confounded with the guilty in indiscriminate punishment. The complaints of the merchants kindled a violent flame throughout the nation, which soon after broke out in the House of Commons, and was communicated from that body to the ministry. Letters of reprisal

---

[10] The Duke of Marlborough.

were granted, and a war ensued, which in its consequences overthrew all the alliances that but twenty years before had been formed with sanguine expectations of the most beneficial fruits.

From this summary of what has taken place in other countries, whose situations have borne the nearest resemblance to our own, what reason can we have to confide in those reveries which would seduce us into an expectation of peace and cordiality between the members of the present confederacy, in a state of separation? Have we not already seen enough of the fallacy and extravagance of those idle theories which have amused us with promises of an exemption from the imperfections, weaknesses and evils incident to society in every shape? Is it not time to awake from the deceitful dream of a golden age, and to adopt as a practical maxim for the direction of our political conduct that we, as well as the other inhabitants of the globe, are yet remote from the happy empire of perfect wisdom and perfect virtue?

Let the point of extreme depression to which our national dignity and credit have sunk, let the inconveniences felt everywhere from a lax and ill administration of government, let the revolt of a part of the State of North Carolina, the late menacing disturbances in Pennsylvania, and the actual insurrections and rebellions in Massachusetts, declare!

So far is the general sense of mankind from corresponding with the tenets of those who endeavor to lull asleep our apprehensions of discord and hostility between the States, in the event of disunion, that it has from long observation of the progress of society become a sort of axiom in politics, that vicinity or nearness of situation, constitutes nations natural enemies. An intelligent writer expresses himself on this subject to this effect: "NEIGHBORING NATIONS (says he) are naturally enemies of each other unless their common weakness forces them to league in a CONFEDERATE REPUBLIC, and their constitution prevents the differences that neighborhood occasions, extinguishing that secret jealousy which disposes all states to aggrandize themselves at the expense of their neighbors."[11] This passage, at the same time, points out the EVIL and suggests the REMEDY.

— PUBLIUS

---

[11] Vide Principes des Negociations par l'Abbé de Mably.

Federalist 10: The Utility of the Union as a Safeguard Against Domestic Faction and Insurrection (continued)

Written by James Madison; Published in The Daily Advertiser, November 22, 1787

To the People of the State of New York:

Among the numerous advantages promised by a well constructed Union, none deserves to be more accurately developed than its tendency to break and control the violence of faction. The friend of popular governments never finds himself so much alarmed for their character and fate, as when he contemplates their propensity to this dangerous vice. He will not fail, therefore, to set a due value on any plan which, without violating the principles to which he is attached, provides a proper cure for it. The instability, injustice, and confusion introduced into the public councils, have, in truth, been the mortal diseases under which popular governments have everywhere perished; as they continue to be the favorite and fruitful topics from which the adversaries to liberty derive their most specious declamations. The valuable improvements made by the American constitutions on the popular models, both ancient and modern, cannot certainly be too much admired; but it would be an unwarrantable partiality, to contend that they have as effectually obviated the danger on this side, as was wished and expected. Complaints are everywhere heard from our most considerate and virtuous citizens, equally the friends of public and private faith, and of public and personal liberty, that our governments are too unstable, that the public good is disregarded in the conflicts of rival parties, and that measures are too often decided, not according to the rules of justice and the rights of the minor party, but by the superior force of an interested and overbearing majority. However anxiously we may wish that these complaints had no foundation, the evidence, of known facts will not permit us to deny that they are in some degree true. It will be found, indeed, on a candid review of our situation, that some of the distresses under which we labor have been erroneously charged on the operation of our governments; but it will be found, at the same time, that other causes will not alone account for many of our heaviest misfortunes; and, particularly, for that prevailing and increasing distrust of public engagements, and alarm for private rights, which are echoed from one end of the continent to the other. These must be chiefly, if not wholly, effects of the unsteadiness and injustice with which a factious spirit has tainted our public administrations.

By a faction, I understand a number of citizens, whether amounting to a majority or a minority of the whole, who are united and actuated by some common impulse of passion, or of interest, adversed to the rights of other citizens, or to the permanent and aggregate interests of the community.

There are two methods of curing the mischiefs of faction: the one, by removing its causes; the other, by controlling its effects.

There are again two methods of removing the causes of faction: the one, by destroying the liberty which is essential to its existence; the other, by giving to every citizen the same opinions, the same passions, and the same interests.

It could never be more truly said than of the first remedy, that it was worse than the disease. Liberty is to faction what air is to fire, an aliment without which it instantly expires. But it could not be less folly to abolish liberty, which is essential to political life, because it nourishes faction, than it would be to wish the annihilation of air, which is essential to animal life, because it imparts to fire its destructive agency.

The second expedient is as impracticable as the first would be unwise. As long as the reason of man continues fallible, and he is at liberty to exercise it, different opinions will be formed. As long as the connection subsists between his reason and his self-love, his opinions and his passions will have a reciprocal influence on each other; and the former will be objects to which the latter will attach themselves. The diversity in the faculties of men, from which the rights of property originate, is not less an insuperable obstacle to a uniformity of interests. The protection of these faculties is the first object of government. From the protection of different and unequal faculties of acquiring property, the possession of different degrees and kinds of property immediately results; and from the influence of these on the sentiments and views of the respective proprietors, ensues a division of the society into different interests and parties.

The latent causes of faction are thus sown in the nature of man; and we see them everywhere brought into different degrees of activity, according to the different circumstances of civil society. A zeal for different opinions concerning religion, concerning government, and many other points, as well of speculation as of practice; an attachment to different leaders ambitiously contending for pre-eminence and power; or to persons of other descriptions whose fortunes have been interesting to the human passions, have, in turn, divided mankind into parties, inflamed them with mutual animosity, and rendered them much more disposed to vex and oppress each other than to co-operate for their common good. So strong is this propensity of mankind to fall into mutual animosities, that where no substantial occasion presents itself, the most frivolous and fanciful distinctions have been sufficient to kindle their unfriendly passions and excite their most violent conflicts. But the most common and durable source of factions has been the various and unequal distribution of property. Those who hold and those who are without property have ever formed distinct interests in society. Those who are creditors, and those who are debtors, fall under a like discrimination. A landed interest, a manufacturing interest, a mercantile interest, a moneyed interest, with many lesser interests, grow up of necessity in civilized nations, and divide them into different classes, actuated by different sentiments and views. The regulation of these various and interfering interests forms the principal task of modern legislation, and involves the spirit of party and faction in the necessary and ordinary operations of the government.

No man is allowed to be a judge in his own cause, because his interest would certainly bias his judgment, and, not improbably, corrupt his integrity. With equal, nay with greater reason, a body of men are unfit to be both judges and parties at the same time; yet what are many of the most important acts of legislation, but so many judicial determinations, not indeed concerning the rights of single persons, but concerning the rights of large bodies of citizens? And what are the different classes of legislators but advocates and parties to the causes which they determine? Is a law proposed concerning private debts? It is a question to which the creditors are parties on one side and the debtors on the other. Justice ought to hold the balance between them. Yet the parties are, and must be, themselves the judges; and the most numerous party, or, in other words, the most powerful faction must be expected to prevail. Shall domestic manufactures be encouraged, and in what degree, by restrictions on foreign manufactures? are questions which would be differently decided by the landed and the manufacturing classes, and probably by neither with a sole regard to justice and the public good. The apportionment of taxes on the various descriptions of property is an act which seems to require the most exact impartiality; yet there is, perhaps, no legislative act in which greater opportunity and temptation are given to a predominant party to trample on the rules of justice. Every shilling with which they overburden the inferior number, is a shilling saved to their own pockets.

It is in vain to say that enlightened statesmen will be able to adjust these clashing interests, and render them all subservient to the public good. Enlightened statesmen will not always be at the helm. Nor, in many cases, can such an adjustment be made at all without taking into view indirect and remote considerations, which will rarely prevail over the immediate interest which one party may find in disregarding the rights of another or the good of the whole.

The inference to which we are brought is, that the causes of faction cannot be removed, and that relief is only to be sought in the means of controlling its effects.

If a faction consists of less than a majority, relief is supplied by the republican principle, which enables the majority to defeat its sinister views by regular vote. It may clog the administration, it may convulse the society; but it will be unable to execute and mask its violence under the forms of the Constitution. When a majority is included in a faction, the form of popular government, on the other hand, enables it to sacrifice to its ruling passion or interest both the public good and the rights of other citizens. To secure the public good and private rights against the danger of such a faction, and at the same time to preserve the spirit and the form of popular government, is then the great object to which our inquiries are directed. Let me add that it is the great desideratum by which this form of government can be rescued from the opprobrium under which it has so long labored, and be recommended to the esteem and adoption of mankind.

By what means is this object attainable? Evidently by one of two only. Either the existence of the same passion or interest in a majority at the same time must be prevented, or the majority, having such coexistent passion or interest, must be rendered, by their number and local situation, unable to concert and carry into effect schemes of oppression. If the impulse and the opportunity be suffered to coincide, we well know that neither moral nor religious motives can be relied on as an adequate control. They are not found to be such on the injustice and violence of individuals, and lose their efficacy in proportion to the number combined together, that is, in proportion as their efficacy becomes needful.

From this view of the subject it may be concluded that a pure democracy, by which I mean a society consisting of a small number of citizens, who assemble and administer the government in person, can admit of no cure for the mischiefs of faction. A common passion or interest will, in almost every case, be felt by a majority of the whole; a communication and concert result from the form of government itself; and there is nothing to check the inducements to sacrifice the weaker party or an obnoxious individual. Hence it is that such democracies have ever been spectacles of turbulence and contention; have ever been found incompatible with personal security or the rights of property; and have in general been as short in their lives as they have been violent in their deaths. Theoretic politicians, who have patronized this species of government, have erroneously supposed that by reducing mankind to a perfect equality in their political rights, they would, at the same time, be perfectly equalized and assimilated in their possessions, their opinions, and their passions.

A republic, by which I mean a government in which the scheme of representation takes place, opens a different prospect, and promises the cure for which we are seeking. Let us examine the points in which it varies from pure democracy, and we shall comprehend both the nature of the cure and the efficacy which it must derive from the Union.

The two great points of difference between a democracy and a republic are: first, the delegation of the government, in the latter, to a small number of citizens elected by the rest; secondly, the greater number of citizens, and greater sphere of country, over which the latter may be extended.

The effect of the first difference is, on the one hand, to refine and enlarge the public views, by passing them through the medium of a chosen body of citizens, whose wisdom may best discern the true interest of their country, and whose patriotism and love of justice will be least likely to sacrifice it to temporary or partial considerations. Under such a regulation, it may well happen that the public voice, pronounced by the representatives of the people, will be more consonant to the public good than if pronounced by the people themselves, convened for the purpose. On the other hand, the effect may be inverted. Men of factious tempers, of local prejudices, or of sinister designs, may, by intrigue, by corruption, or by other means, first obtain the suffrages, and then betray the interests, of the people. The question resulting is, whether small or extensive republics are more favorable to the election of proper guardians of the public weal; and it is clearly decided in favor of the latter by two obvious considerations:

In the first place, it is to be remarked that, however small the republic may be, the representatives must be raised to a certain number, in order to guard against the cabals of a few; and that, however large it may be, they must be limited to a certain number, in order to guard against the confusion of a multitude. Hence, the number of representatives in the two cases not being in proportion to that of the two constituents, and being proportionally greater in the small republic, it follows that, if the proportion of fit characters be not less in the large than in the small republic, the former will present a greater option, and consequently a greater probability of a fit choice.

In the next place, as each representative will be chosen by a greater number of citizens in the large than in the small republic, it will be more difficult for unworthy candidates to practice with success the vicious arts by which elections are too often carried; and the suffrages of the people being more free, will be more likely to centre in men who possess the most attractive merit and the most diffusive and established characters.

It must be confessed that in this, as in most other cases, there is a mean, on both sides of which inconveniences will be found to lie. By enlarging too much the number of electors, you render the representatives too little acquainted with all their local circumstances and lesser interests; as by reducing it too much, you render him unduly attached to these, and too little fit to comprehend and pursue great and national objects. The federal Constitution forms a happy combination in this respect; the great and aggregate interests being referred to the national, the local and particular to the State legislatures.

The other point of difference is, the greater number of citizens and extent of territory which may be brought within the compass of republican than of democratic government; and it is this circumstance principally which renders factious combinations less to be dreaded in the former than in the latter. The smaller the society, the fewer probably will be the distinct parties and interests composing it; the fewer the distinct parties and interests, the more frequently will a majority be found of the same party; and the smaller the number of individuals composing a majority, and the smaller the compass within which they are placed, the more easily will they concert and execute their plans of oppression. Extend the sphere, and you take in a greater variety of parties and interests; you make it less probable that a majority of the whole will have a common motive to invade the rights of other citizens; or if such a common motive exists, it will be more difficult for all who feel it to discover their own strength, and to act in unison with each other. Besides other impediments, it may be remarked that, where there is a consciousness of unjust or dishonorable purposes, communication is always checked by distrust in proportion to the number whose concurrence is necessary.

Hence, it clearly appears, that the same advantage which a republic has over a democracy, in controlling the effects of faction, is enjoyed by a large over a small republic,—is enjoyed by the Union over the States composing it. Does the advantage consist in the substitution of representatives whose enlightened views and virtuous sentiments render them superior to local prejudices and schemes of injustice? It will not be denied that the representation of the Union will be most likely to possess these requisite endowments. Does it consist in the greater security afforded by a greater variety of parties, against the event of any one party being able to outnumber and oppress the rest? In an equal degree does the increased variety of parties comprised within the Union, increase this security. Does it, in fine, consist in the greater obstacles opposed to the concert and accomplishment of the secret wishes of an unjust and interested majority? Here, again, the extent of the Union gives it the most palpable advantage.

The influence of factious leaders may kindle a flame within their particular States, but will be unable to spread a general conflagration through the other States. A religious sect may degenerate into a political faction in a part of the Confederacy; but the variety of sects dispersed over the entire face of it must secure the national councils against any danger from that source. A rage for paper money, for an abolition of debts, for an equal division of property, or for any other improper or wicked project, will be less apt to pervade the whole body of the Union than a particular member of it; in the same proportion as such a malady is more likely to taint a particular county or district, than an entire State.

In the extent and proper structure of the Union, therefore, we behold a republican remedy for the diseases most incident to republican government. And according to the degree of pleasure and pride we feel in being republicans, ought to be our zeal in cherishing the spirit and supporting the character of Federalists.

— PUBLIUS

Federalist 51: The Structure of the Government Must Furnish the Proper Checks and Balances Between the Different Departments

Written by James Madison; Published in Independent Journal, February 6, 1788

To the People of the State of New York:

To what expedient, then, shall we finally resort, for maintaining in practice the necessary partition of power among the several departments, as laid down in the Constitution? The only answer that can be given is, that as all these exterior provisions are found to be inadequate, the defect must be supplied, by so contriving the interior structure of the government as that its several constituent parts may, by their mutual relations, be the means of keeping each other in their proper places. Without presuming to undertake a full development of this important idea, I will hazard a few general observations, which may perhaps place it in a clearer light, and enable us to form a more correct judgment of the principles and structure of the government planned by the convention.

In order to lay a due foundation for that separate and distinct exercise of the different powers of government, which to a certain extent is admitted on all hands to be essential to the preservation of liberty, it is evident that each department should have a will of its own; and consequently should be so constituted that the members of each should have as little agency as possible in the appointment of the members of the others. Were this principle rigorously adhered to, it would require that all the appointments for the supreme executive, legislative, and judiciary magistracies should be drawn from the same fountain of authority, the people, through channels having no communication whatever with one another. Perhaps such a plan of constructing the several departments would be less difficult in practice than it may in contemplation appear. Some difficulties, however, and some additional expense would attend the execution of it. Some deviations, therefore, from the principle must be admitted. In the constitution of the judiciary department in particular, it might be inexpedient to insist rigorously on the principle: first, because peculiar qualifications being essential in the members, the primary consideration ought to be to select that mode of choice which best secures these qualifications; secondly, because the permanent tenure by which the appointments are held in that department, must soon destroy all sense of dependence on the authority conferring them.

It is equally evident, that the members of each department should be as little dependent as possible on those of the others, for the emoluments annexed to their offices. Were the executive magistrate, or the judges, not independent of the legislature in this particular, their independence in every other would be merely nominal.

But the great security against a gradual concentration of the several powers in the same department, consists in giving to those who administer each department the necessary constitutional means and personal motives to resist encroachments of the others. The provision for defense must in this, as in all other cases, be made commensurate to the danger of attack. Ambition must be made to counteract ambition. The interest of the man must be connected with the constitutional rights of the place. It may be a reflection on human nature, that such devices should be necessary to control the abuses of government. But what is government itself, but the greatest of all reflections on human nature? If men were angels, no government would be necessary. If angels were to govern men, neither external nor internal controls on government would be necessary. In framing a government which is to be administered by men over men, the great difficulty lies in this: you must first enable the government to control the governed; and in the next place oblige it to control itself. A dependence on the people is, no doubt, the primary control on the government; but experience has taught mankind the necessity of auxiliary precautions.

This policy of supplying, by opposite and rival interests, the defect of better motives, might be traced through the whole system of human affairs, private as well as public. We see it particularly displayed in all the subordinate distributions of power, where the constant aim is to divide and arrange the several offices in such a manner as that each may be a check on the other —that the private interest of every individual may be a sentinel over the public rights. These inventions of prudence cannot be less requisite in the distribution of the supreme powers of the State.

But it is not possible to give to each department an equal power of self-defense. In republican government, the legislative authority necessarily predominates. The remedy for this inconveniency is to divide the legislature into different branches; and to render them, by different modes of election and different principles of action, as little connected with each other as the nature of their common functions and their common dependence on the society will admit. It may even be necessary to guard against dangerous encroachments by still further precautions. As the weight of the legislative authority requires that it should be thus divided, the weakness of the executive may require, on the other hand, that it should be fortified. An absolute negative on the legislature appears, at first view, to be the natural defense with which the executive magistrate should be armed. But perhaps it would be neither altogether safe nor alone sufficient. On ordinary occasions it might not be exerted with the requisite firmness, and on extraordinary occasions it might be perfidiously abused. May not this defect of an absolute negative be supplied by some qualified connection between this weaker department and the weaker branch of the stronger department, by which the latter may be led to support the constitutional rights of the former, without being too much detached from the rights of its own department?

If the principles on which these observations are founded be just, as I persuade myself they are, and they be applied as a criterion to the several State constitutions, and to the federal Constitution it will be found that if the latter does not perfectly correspond with them, the former are infinitely less able to bear such a test.

There are, moreover, two considerations particularly applicable to the federal system of America, which place that system in a very interesting point of view.

First. In a single republic, all the power surrendered by the people is submitted to the administration of a single government; and the usurpations are guarded against by a division of the government into distinct and separate departments. In the compound republic of America, the power surrendered by the people is first divided between two distinct governments, and then the portion allotted to each subdivided among distinct and separate departments. Hence a double security arises to the rights of the people. The different governments will control each other, at the same time that each will be controlled by itself.

Second. It is of great importance in a republic not only to guard the society against the oppression of its rulers, but to guard one part of the society against the injustice of the other part. Different interests necessarily exist in different classes of citizens. If a majority be united by a common interest, the rights of the minority will be insecure. There are but two methods of providing against this evil: the one by creating a will in the community independent of the majority—that is, of the society itself; the other, by comprehending in the society so many separate descriptions of citizens as will render an unjust combination of a majority of the whole very improbable, if not impracticable. The first method prevails in all governments possessing an hereditary or self-appointed authority. This, at best, is but a precarious security; because a power independent of the society may as well espouse the unjust views of the major, as the rightful interests of the minor party, and may possibly be turned against both parties. The second method will be exemplified in the federal republic of the United States. Whilst all authority in it will be derived from and dependent on the society, the society itself will be broken into so many parts, interests, and classes of citizens, that the rights of individuals, or of the minority, will be in little danger from interested combinations of the majority. In a free government the security for civil rights must be the same as that for religious rights. It consists in the one case in the multiplicity of interests, and in the other in the multiplicity of sects. The degree of security in both cases will depend on the number of interests and sects; and this may be presumed to depend on the extent of country and number of people comprehended under the same government. This view of the subject must particularly recommend a proper federal system to all the sincere and considerate friends of republican government, since it shows that in exact proportion as the territory of the Union may be formed into more circumscribed Confederacies, or States oppressive combinations of a majority will be facilitated:

the best security, under the republican forms, for the rights of every class of citizens, will be diminished: and consequently the stability and independence of some member of the government, the only other security, must be proportionately increased. Justice is the end of government. It is the end of civil society. It ever has been and ever will be pursued until it be obtained, or until liberty be lost in the pursuit. In a society under the forms of which the stronger faction can readily unite and oppress the weaker, anarchy may as truly be said to reign as in a state of nature, where the weaker individual is not secured against the violence of the stronger; and as, in the latter state, even the stronger individuals are prompted, by the uncertainty of their condition, to submit to a government which may protect the weak as well as themselves; so, in the former state, will the more powerful factions or parties be gradnally induced, by a like motive, to wish for a government which will protect all parties, the weaker as well as the more powerful. It can be little doubted that if the State of Rhode Island was separated from the Confederacy and left to itself, the insecurity of rights under the popular form of government within such narrow limits would be displayed by such reiterated oppressions of factious majorities that some power altogether independent of the people would soon be called for by the voice of the very factions whose misrule had proved the necessity of it. In the extended republic of the United States, and among the great variety of interests, parties, and sects which it embraces, a coalition of a majority of the whole society could seldom take place on any other principles than those of justice and the general good; whilst there being thus less danger to a minor from the will of a major party, there must be less pretext, also, to provide for the security of the former, by introducing into the government a will not dependent on the latter, or, in other words, a will independent of the society itself. It is no less certain than it is important, notwithstanding the contrary opinions which have been entertained, that the larger the society, provided it lie within a practical sphere, the more duly capable it will be of self-government. And happily for the republican cause, the practicable sphere may be carried to a very great extent, by a judicious modification and mixture of the federal principle.

    — PUBLIUS

Federalist 84: Certain General and Miscellaneous Objections to the Constitution Considered and Answered

Written by Alexander Hamilton; Published in Independent Journal, July 16, July 26, August 9, 1788

To the People of the State of New York:

In the course of the foregoing review of the Constitution, I have taken notice of, and endeavored to answer most of the objections which have appeared against it. There, however, remain a few which either did not fall naturally under any particular head or were forgotten in their proper places. These shall now be discussed; but as the subject has been drawn into great length, I shall so far consult brevity as to comprise all my observations on these miscellaneous points in a single paper.

The most considerable of the remaining objections is that the plan of the convention contains no bill of rights. Among other answers given to this, it has been upon different occasions remarked that the constitutions of several of the States are in a similar predicament. I add that New York is of the number. And yet the opposers of the new system, in this State, who profess an unlimited admiration for its constitution, are among the most intemperate partisans of a bill of rights. To justify their zeal in this matter, they allege two things: one is that, though the constitution of New York has no bill of rights prefixed to it, yet it contains, in the body of it, various provisions in favor of particular privileges and rights, which, in substance amount to the same thing; the other is, that the Constitution adopts, in their full extent, the common and statute law of Great Britain, by which many other rights, not expressed in it, are equally secured.

To the first I answer, that the Constitution proposed by the convention contains, as well as the constitution of this State, a number of such provisions.

Independent of those which relate to the structure of the government, we find the following: Article 1, section 3, clause 7 "Judgment in cases of impeachment shall not extend further than to removal from office, and disqualification to hold and enjoy any office of honor, trust, or profit under the United States; but the party convicted shall, nevertheless, be liable and subject to indictment, trial, judgment, and punishment according to law." Section 9, of the same article, clause 2 "The privilege of the writ of habeas corpus shall not be suspended, unless when in cases of rebellion or invasion the public safety may require it." Clause 3 "No bill of attainder or ex-post-facto law shall be passed." Clause 7 "No title of nobility shall be granted by the United States; and no person holding any office of profit or trust under them, shall, without the consent of the Congress, accept of any present, emolument, office, or title of any kind whatever, from any king, prince, or foreign state." Article 3, section 2, clause 3 "The trial of all crimes, except in cases of impeachment, shall be by jury; and such trial shall be held in the State where the said crimes shall have been committed; but when not committed within any State, the trial shall be at such place or places as the Congress may by law have directed." Section 3, of the same article "Treason against the United States shall consist only in levying war against them, or in adhering to their enemies, giving them aid and comfort. No person shall be convicted of treason, unless on the testimony of two witnesses to the same overt act, or on confession in open court." And clause 3, of the same section "The Congress shall have power to declare the punishment of treason; but no attainder of treason shall work corruption of blood, or forfeiture, except during the life of the person attainted." It may well be a question, whether these are not, upon the whole, of equal importance with any which are to be found in the constitution of this State. The establishment of the writ of habeas corpus, the prohibition of ex-post-facto laws, and of TITLES OF NOBILITY, TO WHICH WE HAVE NO CORRESPONDING PROVISION IN OUR CONSTITUTION, are perhaps greater securities to liberty and republicanism than any it contains. The creation of crimes after the commission of the fact, or, in other words, the subjecting of men to punishment for things which, when they were done, were breaches of no law, and the practice of arbitrary imprisonments, have been, in all ages, the favorite and most formidable instruments of tyranny. The observations of the judicious Blackstone,[1] in reference to the latter, are well worthy of recital: "To bereave a man of life, [says he] or by violence to confiscate his estate,

---

[1] Vide Blackstone's *Commentaries*, Vol. 1, p. 136.

without accusation or trial, would be so gross and notorious an act of despotism, as must at once convey the alarm of tyranny throughout the whole nation; but confinement of the person, by secretly hurrying him to jail, where his sufferings are unknown or forgotten, is a less public, a less striking, and therefore A MORE DANGEROUS ENGINE of arbitrary government." And as a remedy for this fatal evil he is everywhere peculiarly emphatical in his encomiums on the habeas-corpus act, which in one place he calls "the BULWARK of the British Constitution."[2]

Nothing need be said to illustrate the importance of the prohibition of titles of nobility. This may truly be denominated the corner-stone of republican government; for so long as they are excluded, there can never be serious danger that the government will be any other than that of the people.

To the second that is, to the pretended establishment of the common and state law by the Constitution, I answer, that they are expressly made subject "to such alterations and provisions as the legislature shall from time to time make concerning the same." They are therefore at any moment liable to repeal by the ordinary legislative power, and of course have no constitutional sanction. The only use of the declaration was to recognize the ancient law and to remove doubts which might have been occasioned by the Revolution. This consequently can be considered as no part of a declaration of rights, which under our constitutions must be intended as limitations of the power of the government itself.

It has been several times truly remarked that bills of rights are, in their origin, stipulations between kings and their subjects, abridgements of prerogative in favor of privilege, reservations of rights not surrendered to the prince. Such was MAGNA CHARTA, obtained by the barons, sword in hand, from King John. Such were the subsequent confirmations of that charter by succeeding princes. Such was the PETITION OF RIGHT assented to by Charles I., in the beginning of his reign. Such, also, was the Declaration of Right presented by the Lords and Commons to the Prince of Orange in 1688, and afterwards thrown into the form of an act of parliament called the Bill of Rights. It is evident, therefore, that, according to their primitive

---

[2] Idem, Vol. 4, p. 438.

signification, they have no application to constitutions professedly founded upon the power of the people, and executed by their immediate representatives and servants. Here, in strictness, the people surrender nothing; and as they retain every thing they have no need of particular reservations. "WE, THE PEOPLE of the United States, to secure the blessings of liberty to ourselves and our posterity, do ORDAIN and ESTABLISH this Constitution for the United States of America." Here is a better recognition of popular rights, than volumes of those aphorisms which make the principal figure in several of our State bills of rights, and which would sound much better in a treatise of ethics than in a constitution of government.

But a minute detail of particular rights is certainly far less applicable to a Constitution like that under consideration, which is merely intended to regulate the general political interests of the nation, than to a constitution which has the regulation of every species of personal and private concerns. If, therefore, the loud clamors against the plan of the convention, on this score, are well founded, no epithets of reprobation will be too strong for the constitution of this State. But the truth is, that both of them contain all which, in relation to their objects, is reasonably to be desired.

I go further, and affirm that bills of rights, in the sense and to the extent in which they are contended for, are not only unnecessary in the proposed Constitution, but would even be dangerous. They would contain various exceptions to powers not granted; and, on this very account, would afford a colorable pretext to claim more than were granted. For why declare that things shall not be done which there is no power to do? Why, for instance, should it be said that the liberty of the press shall not be restrained, when no power is given by which restrictions may be imposed? I will not contend that such a provision would confer a regulating power; but it is evident that it would furnish, to men disposed to usurp, a plausible pretense for claiming that power. They might urge with a semblance of reason, that the Constitution ought not to be charged with the absurdity of providing against the abuse of an authority which was not given, and that the provision against restraining the liberty of the press afforded a clear implication, that a power to prescribe proper regulations concerning it was intended to be vested in the national government. This may serve as a specimen of the numerous handles which would be given to the doctrine of constructive powers, by the indulgence of an injudicious zeal for bills of rights.

On the subject of the liberty of the press, as much as has been said, I cannot forbear adding a remark or two: in the first place, I observe, that there is not a syllable concerning it in the constitution of this State; in the next, I contend, that whatever has been said about it in that of any other State, amounts to nothing. What signifies a declaration, that "the liberty of the press shall be inviolably preserved"? What is the liberty of the press? Who can give it any definition which would not leave the utmost latitude for evasion? I hold it to be impracticable; and from this I infer, that its security, whatever fine declarations may be inserted in any constitution respecting it, must altogether depend on public opinion, and on the general spirit of the people and of the government.[3] And here, after all, as is intimated upon another occasion, must we seek for the only solid basis of all our rights.

There remains but one other view of this matter to conclude the point. The truth is, after all the declamations we have heard, that the Constitution is itself, in every rational sense, and to every useful purpose, A BILL OF RIGHTS. The several bills of rights in Great Britain form its Constitution, and conversely the constitution of each State is its bill of rights. And the proposed Constitution, if adopted, will be the bill of rights of the Union. Is it one object of a bill of rights to declare and specify the political privileges of the citizens in the structure and administration of

---

[3] To show that there is a power in the Constitution by which the liberty of the press may be affected, recourse has been had to the power of taxation. It is said that duties may be laid upon the publications so high as to amount to a prohibition. I know not by what logic it could be maintained, that the declarations in the State constitutions, in favor of the freedom of the press, would be a constitutional impediment to the imposition of duties upon publications by the State legislatures. It cannot certainly be pretended that any degree of duties, however low, would be an abridgment of the liberty of the press. We know that newspapers are taxed in Great Britain, and yet it is notorious that the press nowhere enjoys greater liberty than in that country. And if duties of any kind may be laid without a violation of that liberty, it is evident that the extent must depend on legislative discretion, respecting the liberty of the press, will give it no greater security than it will have without them. The same invasions of it may be effected under the State constitutions which contain those declarations through the means of taxation, as under the proposed Constitution, which has nothing of the kind. It would be quite as significant to declare that government ought to be free, that taxes ought not to be excessive, etc., as that the liberty of the press ought not to be restrained.

the government? This is done in the most ample and precise manner in the plan of the convention; comprehending various precautions for the public security, which are not to be found in any of the State constitutions. Is another object of a bill of rights to define certain immunities and modes of proceeding, which are relative to personal and private concerns? This we have seen has also been attended to, in a variety of cases, in the same plan. Adverting therefore to the substantial meaning of a bill of rights, it is absurd to allege that it is not to be found in the work of the convention. It may be said that it does not go far enough, though it will not be easy to make this appear; but it can with no propriety be contended that there is no such thing. It certainly must be immaterial what mode is observed as to the order of declaring the rights of the citizens, if they are to be found in any part of the instrument which establishes the government. And hence it must be apparent, that much of what has been said on this subject rests merely on verbal and nominal distinctions, entirely foreign from the substance of the thing.

Another objection which has been made, and which, from the frequency of its repetition, it is to be presumed is relied on, is of this nature: "It is improper [say the objectors] to confer such large powers, as are proposed, upon the national government, because the seat of that government must of necessity be too remote from many of the States to admit of a proper knowledge on the part of the constituent, of the conduct of the representative body." This argument, if it proves any thing, proves that there ought to be no general government whatever. For the powers which, it seems to be agreed on all hands, ought to be vested in the Union, cannot be safely intrusted to a body which is not under every requisite control. But there are satisfactory reasons to show that the objection is in reality not well founded. There is in most of the arguments which relate to distance a palpable illusion of the imagination. What are the sources of information by which the people in Montgomery County must regulate their judgment of the conduct of their representatives in the State legislature? Of personal observation they can have no benefit. This is confined to the citizens on the spot. They must therefore depend on the information of intelligent men, in whom they confide; and how must these men obtain their information?

Evidently from the complexion of public measures, from the public prints, from correspondences with their representatives, and with other persons who reside at the place of their deliberations. This does not apply to Montgomery County only, but to all the counties at any considerable distance from the seat of government.

It is equally evident that the same sources of information would be open to the people in relation to the conduct of their representatives in the general government, and the impediments to a prompt communication which distance may be supposed to create, will be overbalanced by the effects of the vigilance of the State governments. The executive and legislative bodies of each State will be so many sentinels over the persons employed in every department of the national administration; and as it will be in their power to adopt and pursue a regular and effectual system of intelligence, they can never be at a loss to know the behavior of those who represent their constituents in the national councils, and can readily communicate the same knowledge to the people. Their disposition to apprise the community of whatever may prejudice its interests from another quarter, may be relied upon, if it were only from the rivalship of power. And we may conclude with the fullest assurance that the people, through that channel, will be better informed of the conduct of their national representatives, than they can be by any means they now possess of that of their State representatives.

It ought also to be remembered that the citizens who inhabit the country at and near the seat of government will, in all questions that affect the general liberty and prosperity, have the same interest with those who are at a distance, and that they will stand ready to sound the alarm when necessary, and to point out the actors in any pernicious project. The public papers will be expeditious messengers of intelligence to the most remote inhabitants of the Union.

Among the many curious objections which have appeared against the proposed Constitution, the most extraordinary and the least colorable is derived from the want of some provision respecting the debts due TO the United States. This has been represented as a tacit relinquishment of those debts, and as a wicked contrivance to screen public defaulters. The newspapers have teemed with the most inflammatory railings on this head; yet there is nothing clearer than that the suggestion is entirely void of foundation, the offspring of extreme ignorance or extreme dishonesty. In addition to the remarks I have made upon the subject in another place, I shall only observe that as it is a plain dictate of common-sense, so it is also an established doctrine of political law, that "STATES NEITHER LOSE ANY OF THEIR RIGHTS, NOR ARE DISCHARGED FROM ANY OF THEIR OBLIGATIONS, BY A CHANGE IN THE FORM OF THEIR CIVIL GOVERNMENT."[4] The last objection of any consequence, which I at present recollect, turns upon the article of expense. If it were even true, that the adoption of the proposed government would occasion a considerable increase of expense, it would be an objection that ought to have no weight against the plan.

The great bulk of the citizens of America are with reason convinced, that Union is the basis of their political happiness. Men of sense of all parties now, with few exceptions, agree that it cannot be preserved under the present system, nor without radical alterations; that new and extensive powers ought to be granted to the national head, and that these require a different organization of the federal government a single body being an unsafe depositary of such ample authorities. In conceding all this, the question of expense must be given up; for it is impossible, with any degree of safety, to narrow the foundation upon which the system is to stand. The two branches of the legislature are, in the first instance, to consist of only sixty-five persons, which is the same number of which Congress, under the existing Confederation, may be composed. It is true that this number is intended to be increased; but this is to keep pace with the progress of the population and resources of the country. It is evident that a less number would, even in the first instance, have been unsafe, and that a continuance of the present number would, in a more advanced stage of population, be a very inadequate representation of the people.

Whence is the dreaded augmentation of expense to spring? One source indicated, is the multiplication of offices under the new government. Let us examine this a little.

It is evident that the principal departments of the administration under the present government, are the same which will be required under the new. There are now a Secretary

---

[4] Vide Rutherford's Institutes, Vol. 2, Book II, Chapter X, Sections XIV and XV. Vide also Grotius, Book II, Chapter IX, Sections VIII and IX.

of War, a Secretary of Foreign Affairs, a Secretary for Domestic Affairs, a Board of Treasury, consisting of three persons, a Treasurer, assistants, clerks, etc. These officers are indispensable under any system, and will suffice under the new as well as the old. As to ambassadors and other ministers and agents in foreign countries, the proposed Constitution can make no other difference than to render their characters, where they reside, more respectable, and their services more useful. As to persons to be employed in the collection of the revenues, it is unquestionably true that these will form a very considerable addition to the number of federal officers; but it will not follow that this will occasion an increase of public expense. It will be in most cases nothing more than an exchange of State for national officers. In the collection of all duties, for instance, the persons employed will be wholly of the latter description. The States individually will stand in no need of any for this purpose. What difference can it make in point of expense to pay officers of the customs appointed by the State or by the United States? There is no good reason to suppose that either the number or the salaries of the latter will be greater than those of the former.

Where then are we to seek for those additional articles of expense which are to swell the account to the enormous size that has been represented to us? The chief item which occurs to me respects the support of the judges of the United States. I do not add the President, because there is now a president of Congress, whose expenses may not be far, if any thing, short of those which will be incurred on account of the President of the United States. The support of the judges will clearly be an extra expense, but to what extent will depend on the particular plan which may be adopted in regard to this matter. But upon no reasonable plan can it amount to a sum which will be an object of material consequence.

Let us now see what there is to counterbalance any extra expense that may attend the establishment of the proposed government. The first thing which presents itself is that a great part of the business which now keeps Congress sitting through the year will be transacted by the President. Even the management of foreign negotiations will naturally devolve upon him, according to general principles concerted with the Senate, and subject to their final concurrence. Hence it is evident that a portion of the year will suffice for the session of both the Senate and the House of Representatives; we may suppose about a fourth for the latter and a third, or perhaps half, for the former. The extra business of treaties and appointments may give this extra occupation to the Senate. From this circumstance we may infer that, until the House of Representatives shall be increased greatly beyond its present number, there will be a considerable saving of expense from the difference between the constant session of the present and the temporary session of the future Congress.

But there is another circumstance of great importance in the view of economy. The business of the United States has hitherto occupied the State legislatures, as well as Congress. The latter has made requisitions which the former have had to provide for. Hence it has happened that the sessions of the State legislatures have been protracted greatly beyond what was necessary for the execution of the mere local business of the States. More than half their time has been frequently employed in matters which related to the United States. Now the members who compose the legislatures of the several States amount to two thousand and upwards, which number has hitherto performed what under the new system will be done in the first instance by sixty-five persons, and probably at no future period by above a fourth or fifth of that number. The Congress under the proposed government will do all the business of the United States themselves, without the intervention of the State legislatures, who thenceforth will have only to attend to the affairs of their particular States, and will not have to sit in any proportion as long as they have heretofore done. This difference in the time of the sessions of the State legislatures will be clear gain, and will alone form an article of saving, which may be regarded as an equivalent for any additional objects of expense that may be occasioned by the adoption of the new system.

The result from these observations is that the sources of additional expense from the establishment of the proposed Constitution are much fewer than may have been imagined; that they are counterbalanced by considerable objects of saving; and that while it is questionable on which side the scale will preponderate, it is certain that a government less expensive would be incompetent to the purposes of the Union.

— PUBLIUS

Constitution of the United States

Philadelphia Convention

The Constitution of the United States of America was written in 1787, ratified by the colonies in 1788, and came into force in 1789. Founded upon the principles of the Declaration of Independence—that the people are sovereign, that they have unalienable rights to life, liberty, and the pursuit of happiness, and that government exists to secure those rights—the Constitution established a federal political union of the several sovereign states. It enshrines in its articles the following principles: limited government under specifically enumerated powers; separation of powers of the legislative, executive, and judiciary branches, with checks and balances among those separated branches; and federalism, the specific rights and responsibilities of the states in relation to the federal government and of the federal government in relation to the states. The first ten amendments to the Constitution, called the Bill of Rights, enumerated specific individual rights which the federal government could not infringe and must protect, like the right to freedom of speech, of the press, of religion, of assembly, and others.

In fairly stark rhetorical contrast with the Declaration of Independence and the Federalist Papers, the language of the Constitution does not aim to persuade; it aims to establish laws. Whereas the Declaration of Independence sought to argue that a new government, separate from Britain, should be founded on specific philosophical and political principles, the Constitution set up the laws of operation for that government on the foundation of those principles. The forceful argumentation of the Declaration became the specific practical rules of the Constitution. However, in spite of its specificity and practicality, it is efficient: even at its present length with twenty seven amendments, it is the shortest written constitution in force.

Historical Note

The Delegates who convened at the Federal Convention on May 25, 1787, quickly rejected the idea of revising the Articles of Confederation and agreed to construct a new framework for a national government. Throughout the summer months at the Convention in Philadelphia, delegates from 12 States debated the proper form such a government should take, but few questioned the need to establish a more vigorous government to preside over the union of States. The 39 delegates who signed the Constitution on September 17, 1787, expected the new charter to provide a permanent guarantee of the political liberties achieved in the Revolution.

Prior to the adoption of the Federal Constitution, the Articles of Confederation, drafted by the Continental Congress and approved by 13 States, provided for a union of the former British colonies. Even before Maryland became the last State to accede to the Articles in 1781, a number of Americans, particularly those involved in the prosecution of the Revolutionary War, recognized the inadequacies of the Articles as a national government. In the 1780s these nationally-minded Americans became increasingly disturbed by the Articles' failure to provide the central government with authority to raise revenue, regulate commerce, or enforce treaties.

Despite repeated proposals that the Continental Congress revise the Articles, the movement for a new national government began outside the Congress. Representatives of Maryland and Virginia, meeting at Mt. Vernon to discuss trade problems between the two States, agreed to invite delegates from all States to discuss commercial affairs at a meeting in Annapolis, Maryland, in September 1786. Although delegates from only five States reached the Annapolis Convention, that group issued a call for a meeting of all States to discuss necessary revisions of the Articles of Confederation. Responding to this call and the endorsement of the Continental Congress, every State except Rhode Island selected delegates for the meeting in the State House at Philadelphia.

The document printed here was the product of nearly four months of deliberations in the Federal Convention at Philadelphia. The challenging task before the delegates was to create a republican

---

This section, the following section on the text of the Constitution, and all internal footnotes for the Constitution are taken from: The Constitution of the United States, As Amended (US Government Printing Office, Doc. 110-50, 2007), retrieved from http://www.gpo.gov/fdsys/pkg/CDOC-110hdoc50/pdf/CDOC-110hdoc50.pdf.

form of government that could encompass the 13 States and accommodate the anticipated expansion to the West. The distribution of authority between legislative, executive, and judicial branches was a boldly original attempt to create an energetic central government at the same time that the sovereignty of the people was preserved.

The longest debate of the Convention centered on the proper form of representation and election for the Congress. The division between small States that wished to perpetuate the equal representation of States in the Continental Congress and the large States that proposed representation proportional to population threatened to bring the Convention proceedings to a halt. Over several weeks the delegates developed a complicated compromise that provided for equal representation of the States in a Senate elected by State legislature and proportional representation in a popularly-elected House of Representatives.

The conflict between large and small States disappeared in the early years of the republic. More lasting was the division between slave and free States that had been a disturbing undercurrent in the Convention debates. The Convention's strained attempt to avoid using the word slavery in the articles granting recognition and protection to that institution scarcely hid the regional divisions that would remain unresolved under the terms of union agreed to in 1787.

The debates in the State ratification conventions of 1787 and 1788 made clear the need to provide amendments to the basic framework drafted in Philadelphia. Beginning with Massachusetts, a number of State conventions ratified the Constitution with the request that a bill of rights be added to protect certain liberties at the core of English and American political traditions. The First Congress approved a set of amendments which became the Bill of Rights when ratified by the States in 1791. The continuing process of amendment, clearly described in the note of the following text, has enabled the Constitution to accommodate changing conditions in American society at the same time that the Founders' basic outline of national government remains intact.

Note on the Text of the Constitution

This text of the Constitution follows the engrossed copy signed by Gen. Washington and the deputies from 12 States. The small superior figures preceding the paragraphs designate clauses, and were not in the original and have no reference to footnotes.

The Constitution was adopted by a convention of the States on September 17, 1787, and was subsequently ratified by the several States, on the following dates: Delaware, December 7, 1787; Pennsylvania, December 12, 1787; New Jersey, December 18, 1787; Georgia, January 2, 1788; Connecticut, January 9, 1788; Massachusetts, February 6, 1788; Maryland, April 28, 1788; South Carolina, May 23, 1788; New Hampshire, June 21, 1788.

Ratification was completed on June 21, 1788.

The Constitution was subsequently ratified by Virginia, June 25, 1788; New York, July 26, 1788; North Carolina, November 21, 1789; Rhode Island, May 29, 1790; and Vermont, January 10, 1791.

In May 1785, a committee of Congress made a report recommending an alteration in the Articles of Confederation, but no action was taken on it, and it was left to the State Legislatures to proceed in the matter. In January 1786, the Legislature of Virginia passed a resolution providing for the appointment of five commissioners, who, or any three of them, should meet such commissioners as might be appointed in the other States of the Union, at a time and place to be agreed upon, to take into consideration the trade of the United States; to consider how far a uniform system in their commercial regulations may be necessary to their common interest and their permanent harmony; and to report to the several States such an act, relative to this great object, as, when ratified by them, will enable the United States in Congress effectually to provide for the same. The Virginia commissioners, after some correspondence, fixed the first Monday in September as the time, and the city of Annapolis as the place for the meeting, but only four other States were represented, viz: Delaware, New York, New Jersey, and Pennsylvania; the commissioners appointed by Massachusetts, New Hampshire, North Carolina, and Rhode Island failed to attend. Under the circumstances of so partial a representation, the commissioners present agreed upon a report (drawn by Mr.

Hamilton, of New York) expressing their unanimous conviction that it might essentially tend to advance the interests of the Union if the States by which they were respectively delegated would concur, and use their endeavors to procure the concurrence of the other States, in the appointment of commissioners to meet at Philadelphia on the second Monday of May following, to take into consideration the situation of the United States; to devise such further provisions as should appear to them necessary to render the Constitution of the Federal Government adequate to the exigencies of the Union; and to report such an act for that purpose to the United States in Congress assembled as, when agreed to by them and afterwards confirmed by the Legislatures of every State, would effectually provide for the same.

Congress, on the 21st of February, 1787, adopted a resolution in favor of a convention, and the Legislatures of those States which had not already done so (with the exception of Rhode Island) promptly appointed delegates. On the 25th of May, seven States having convened, George Washington, of Virginia, was unanimously elected President, and the consideration of the proposed constitution was commenced. On the 17th of September, 1787, the Constitution as engrossed and agreed upon was signed by all the members present, except Mr. Gerry of Massachusetts, and Messrs. Mason and Randolph, of Virginia. The president of the convention transmitted it to Congress, with a resolution stating how the proposed Federal Government should be put in operation, and an explanatory letter. Congress, on the 28th of September, 1787, directed the Constitution so framed, with the resolutions and letter concerning the same, to "be transmitted to the several Legislatures in order to be submitted to a convention of delegates chosen in each State by the people thereof, in conformity to the resolves of the convention."

On the 4th of March, 1789, the day which had been fixed for commencing the operations of Government under the new Constitution, it had been ratified by the conventions chosen in each State to consider it, as follows: Delaware, December 7, 1787; Pennsylvania, December 12, 1787; New Jersey, December 18, 1787; Georgia, January 2, 1788; Connecticut, January 9, 1788;

Massachusetts, February 6, 1788; Maryland, April 28, 1788; South Carolina, May 23, 1788; New Hampshire, June 21, 1788; Virginia, June 25, 1788; and New York, July 26, 1788.

The President informed Congress, on the 28th of January, 1790, that North Carolina had ratified the Constitution November 21, 1789; and he informed Congress on the 1st of June, 1790, that Rhode Island had ratified the Constitution May 29, 1790. Vermont, in convention, ratified the Constitution January 10, 1791, and was, by an act of Congress approved February 18, 1791, "received and admitted into this Union as a new and entire member of the United States."

Constitution of the United States, Original Text

Completed on September 17, 1787.

WE THE PEOPLE of the United States, in Order to form a more perfect Union, establish Justice, insure domestic Tranquility, provide for the common defense, promote the general Welfare, and secure the Blessings of Liberty to ourselves and our Posterity, do ordain and establish this Constitution for the United States of America.

Article I

SECTION 1. All legislative Powers herein granted shall be vested in a Congress of the United States, which shall consist of a Senate and House of Representatives.

SECTION 2. The House of Representatives shall be composed of Members chosen every second Year by the People of the several States, and the Electors in each State shall have the Qualifications requisite for Electors of the most numerous Branch of the State Legislature.

No Person shall be a Representative who shall not have attained to the Age of twenty five Years, and been seven Years a Citizen of the United States, and who shall not, when elected, be an Inhabitant of that State in which he shall be chosen.

Representatives and direct Taxes shall be apportioned among the several States which may be included within this Union, according to their respective Numbers, which shall be determined by adding to the whole Number of free Persons, including those bound to Service for a Term of Years, and excluding Indians not taxed, three fifths of all other Persons.[1] The actual Enumeration shall be made within three Years after the first Meeting of the Congress of the United States, and within every subsequent Term of ten Years, in such Manner as they shall by Law direct. The Number of Representatives shall not exceed one for every thirty Thousand, but each State shall have at Least one Representative; and until such enumeration shall be made,

---

[1] The part of this clause relating to the mode of apportionment of representatives among the several States has been affected by section 2 of amendment XIV, and as to taxes on incomes without apportionment by amendment XVI.

the State of New Hampshire shall be entitled to chuse three, Massachusetts eight, Rhode-Island and Providence Plantations one, Connecticut five, New-York six, New Jersey four, Pennsylvania eight, Delaware one, Maryland six, Virginia ten, North Carolina five, South Carolina five, and Georgia three.

When vacancies happen in the Representation from any State, the Executive Authority thereof shall issue Writs of Election to fill such Vacancies.

The House of Representatives shall chuse their Speaker and other Officers; and shall have the sole Power of Impeachment.

SECTION 3. The Senate of the United States shall be composed of two Senators from each State, chosen by the Legislature thereof[2] for six Years; and each Senator shall have one Vote.

Immediately after they shall be assembled in Consequence of the first Election, they shall be divided as equally as may be into three Classes. The Seats of the Senators of the first Class shall be vacated at the Expiration of the second Year, of the second Class at the Expiration of the fourth Year, and of the third Class at the Expiration of the sixth Year, so that one third may be chosen every second Year; and if Vacancies happen by Resignation, or otherwise, during the Recess of the Legislature of any State, the Executive thereof may make temporary Appointments until the next Meeting of the Legislature, which shall then fill such Vacancies.[3]

No Person shall be a Senator who shall not have attained to the Age of thirty Years, and been nine Years a Citizen of the United States, and who shall not, when elected, be an Inhabitant of that State for which he shall be chosen.

The Vice President of the United States shall be President of the Senate, but shall have no Vote, unless they be equally divided.

The Senate shall chuse their other Officers, and also a President pro tempore, in the Absence of the Vice President, or when he shall exercise the Office of President of the United States.

The Senate shall have the sole Power to try all Impeachments. When sitting for that Purpose, they shall be on Oath or Affirmation.

---

[2] This clause has been affected by clause 1 of amendment XVII.

[3] This clause has been affected by clause 2 of amendment XVIII.

When the President of the United States is tried, the Chief Justice shall preside: And no Person shall be convicted without the Concurrence of two thirds of the Members present.

Judgment in Cases of Impeachment shall not extend further than to removal from Office, and disqualification to hold and enjoy any Office of honor, Trust or Profit under the United States: but the Party convicted shall nevertheless be liable and subject to Indictment, Trial, Judgment and Punishment, according to Law.

SECTION 4. The Times, Places and Manner of holding Elections for Senators and Representatives, shall be prescribed in each State by the Legislature thereof; but the Congress may at any time by Law make or alter such Regulations, except as to the Places of chusing Senators.

The Congress shall assemble at least once in every Year, and such Meeting shall be on the first Monday in December,[4] unless they shall by Law appoint a different Day.

SECTION 5. Each House shall be the Judge of the Elections, Returns and Qualifications of its own Members, and a Majority of each shall constitute a Quorum to do Business; but a smaller Number may adjourn from day to day, and may be authorized to compel the Attendance of absent Members, in such Manner, and under such Penalties as each House may provide.

Each House may determine the Rules of its Proceedings, punish its Members for disorderly Behaviour, and, with the Concurrence of two thirds, expel a Member.

Each House shall keep a Journal of its Proceedings, and from time to time publish the same, excepting such Parts as may in their Judgment require Secrecy; and the Yeas and Nays of the Members of either House on any question shall, at the Desire of one fifth of those Present, be entered on the Journal.

Neither House, during the Session of Congress, shall, without the Consent of the other, adjourn for more than three days, nor to any other Place than that in which the two Houses shall be sitting.

---

[4] This clause has been affected by amendment XX.

SECTION 6. The Senators and Representatives shall receive a Compensation for their Services, to be ascertained by Law, and paid out of the Treasury of the United States.[5] They shall in all Cases, except Treason, Felony and Breach of the Peace, be privileged from Arrest during their Attendance at the Session of their respective Houses, and in going to and returning from the same; and for any Speech or Debate in either House, they shall not be questioned in any other Place.

No Senator or Representative shall, during the Time for which he was elected, be appointed to any civil Office under the Authority of the United States, which shall have been created, or the Emoluments whereof shall have been encreased during such time; and no Person holding any Office under the United States, shall be a Member of either House during his Continuance in Office.

SECTION 7. All Bills for raising Revenue shall originate in the House of Representatives; but the Senate may propose or concur with Amendments as on other Bills.

Every Bill which shall have passed the House of Representatives and the Senate, shall, before it become a Law, be presented to the President of the United States: If he approve he shall sign it, but if not he shall return it, with his Objections to that House in which it shall have originated, who shall enter the Objections at large on their Journal, and proceed to reconsider it.If after such Reconsideration two thirds of that House shall agree to pass the Bill, it shall be sent, together with the Objections, to the other House, by which it shall likewise be reconsidered, and if approved by two thirds of that House, it shall become a Law. But in all such Cases the Votes of both Houses shall be determined by yeas and Nays, and the Names of the Persons voting for and against the Bill shall be entered on the Journal of each House respectively. If any Bill shall not be returned by the President within ten Days (Sundays excepted) after it shall have been presented to him, the Same shall be a Law, in like Manner as if he had signed it, unless the Congress by their Adjournment prevent its Return, in which Case it shall not be a Law.

Every Order, Resolution, or Vote to which the Concurrence of the Senate and House of Representatives may be necessary

---

[5] This clause has been affected by amendment XXVII.

(except on a question of Adjournment) shall be presented to the President of the United States; and before the Same shall take Effect, shall be approved by him, or being disapproved by him, shall be repassed by two thirds of the Senate and House of Representatives, according to the Rules and Limitations prescribed in the Case of a Bill.

SECTION 8. The Congress shall have Power To lay and collect Taxes, Duties, Imposts and Excises, to pay the Debts and provide for the common Defence and general Welfare of the United States; but all Duties, Imposts and Excises shall be uniform throughout the United States;

To borrow Money on the credit of the United States;

To regulate Commerce with foreign Nations, and among the several States, and with the Indian Tribes;

To establish an uniform Rule of Naturalization, and uniform Laws on the subject of Bankruptcies throughout the United States;

To coin Money, regulate the Value thereof, and of foreign Coin, and fix the Standard of Weights and Measures;

To provide for the Punishment of counterfeiting the Securities and current Coin of the United States;

To establish Post Offices and post Roads;

To promote the Progress of Science and useful Arts, by securing for limited Times to Authors and Inventors the exclusive Right to their respective Writings and Discoveries;

To constitute Tribunals inferior to the supreme Court;

To define and punish Piracies and Felonies committed on the high Seas, and Offences against the Law of Nations;

To declare War, grant Letters of Marque and Reprisal, and make Rules concerning Captures on Land and Water;

To raise and support Armies, but no Appropriation of Money to that Use shall be for a longer Term than two Years;

To provide and maintain a Navy;

To make Rules for the Government and Regulation of the land and naval Forces;

To provide for calling forth the Militia to execute the Laws of the Union, suppress Insurrections and repel Invasions;

To provide for organizing, arming, and disciplining, the Militia, and for governing such Part of them as may be employed in the Service of the United States, reserving to the States respectively, the Appointment of the Officers, and the Authority of training the Militia according to the discipline prescribed by Congress;

To exercise exclusive Legislation in all Cases whatsoever, over such District (not exceeding ten Miles square) as may, by Cession of particular States, and the Acceptance of Congress, become the Seat of the Government of the United States, and to exercise like Authority over all Places purchased by the Consent of the Legislature of the State in which the Same shall be, for the Erection of Forts, Magazines, Arsenals, dock-Yards, and other needful Buildings;—And

To make all Laws which shall be necessary and proper for carrying into Execution the foregoing Powers, and all other Powers vested by this Constitution in the Government of the United States, or in any Department or Officer thereof.

SECTION 9. The Migration or Importation of such Persons as any of the States now existing shall think proper to admit, shall not be prohibited by the Congress prior to the Year one thousand eight hundred and eight, but a Tax or duty may be imposed on such Importation, not exceeding ten dollars for each Person.

The Privilege of the Writ of Habeas Corpus shall not be suspended, unless when in Cases of Rebellion or Invasion the public Safety may require it.

No Bill of Attainder or ex post facto Law shall be passed.

No Capitation, or other direct, Tax shall be laid, unless in Proportion to the Census or enumeration herein before directed to be taken.[6]

No Tax or Duty shall be laid on Articles exported from any State.

No Preference shall be given by any Regulation of Commerce or Revenue to the Ports of one State over those of another; nor

---

[6] This clause has been affected by amendment XVI.

shall Vessels bound to, or from, one State, be obliged to enter, clear, or pay Duties in another.

No Money shall be drawn from the Treasury, but in Consequence of Appropriations made by Law; and a regular Statement and Account of the Receipts and Expenditures of all public Money shall be published from time to time.

No Title of Nobility shall be granted by the United States: And no Person holding any Office of Profit or Trust under them, shall, without the Consent of the Congress, accept of any present, Emolument, Office, or Title, of any kind whatever, from any King, Prince, or foreign State.

SECTION 10. No State shall enter into any Treaty, Alliance, or Confederation; grant Letters of Marque and Reprisal; coin Money; emit Bills of Credit; make any Thing but gold and silver Coin a Tender in Payment of Debts; pass any Bill of Attainder, ex post facto Law, or Law impairing the Obligation of Contracts, or grant any Title of Nobility.

No State shall, without the Consent of the Congress, lay any Imposts or Duties on Imports or Exports, except what may be absolutely necessary for executing it's inspection Laws: and the net Produce of all Duties and Imposts, laid by any State on Imports or Exports, shall be for the Use of the Treasury of the United States; and all such Laws shall be subject to the Revision and Controul of the Congress.

No State shall, without the Consent of Congress, lay any Duty of Tonnage, keep Troops, or Ships of War in time of Peace, enter into any Agreement or Compact with another State, or with a foreign Power, or engage in War, unless actually invaded, or in such imminent Danger as will not admit of delay.

Article II

SECTION 1. The executive Power shall be vested in a President of the United States of America. He shall hold his Office during the Term of four Years, and, together with the Vice President, chosen for the same Term, be elected, as follows:

Each State shall appoint, in such Manner as the Legislature thereof may direct, a Number of Electors, equal to the whole

Number of Senators and Representatives to which the State may be entitled in the Congress: but no Senator or Representative, or Person holding an Office of Trust or Profit under the United States, shall be appointed an Elector.

The Electors shall meet in their respective States, and vote by Ballot for two Persons, of whom one at least shall not be an Inhabitant of the same State with themselves. And they shall make a List of all the Persons voted for, and of the Number of Votes for each; which List they shall sign and certify, and transmit sealed to the Seat of the Government of the United States, directed to the President of the Senate. The President of the Senate shall, in the Presence of the Senate and House of Representatives, open all the Certificates, and the Votes shall then be counted. The Person having the greatest Number of Votes shall be the President, if such Number be a Majority of the whole Number of Electors appointed; and if there be more than one who have such Majority, and have an equal Number of Votes, then the House of Representatives shall immediately chuse by Ballot one of them for President; and if no Person have a Majority, then from the five highest on the List the said House shall in like Manner chuse the President. But in chusing the President, the Votes shall be taken by States, the Representation from each State having one Vote; A quorum for this purpose shall consist of a Member or Members from two thirds of the States, and a Majority of all the States shall be necessary to a Choice. In every Case, after the Choice of the President, the Person having the greatest Number of Votes of the Electors shall be the Vice President. But if there should remain two or more who have equal Votes, the Senate shall chuse from them by Ballot the Vice President.[7]

The Congress may determine the Time of chusing the Electors, and the Day on which they shall give their Votes; which Day shall be the same throughout the United States.

No Person except a natural born Citizen, or a Citizen of the United States, at the time of the Adoption of this Constitution, shall be eligible to the Office of President; neither shall any Person be eligible to that Office who shall not have attained to the

---

[7] This clause has been superseded by amendment XII.

Age of thirty five Years, and been fourteen Years a Resident within the United States.

In Case of the Removal of the President from Office, or of his Death, Resignation, or Inability to discharge the Powers and Duties of the said Office,[8] the Same shall devolve on the Vice President, and the Congress may by Law provide for the Case of Removal, Death, Resignation or Inability, both of the President and Vice President, declaring what Officer shall then act as President, and such Officer shall act accordingly, until the Disability be removed, or a President shall be elected.

The President shall, at stated Times, receive for his Services, a Compensation, which shall neither be increased nor diminished during the Period for which he shall have been elected, and he shall not receive within that Period any other Emolument from the United States, or any of them.

Before he enter on the Execution of his Office, he shall take the following Oath or Affirmation:"I do solemnly swear (or affirm) that I will faithfully execute the Office of President of the United States, and will to the best of my Ability, preserve, protect and defend the Constitution of the United States."

SECTION 2. The President shall be Commander in Chief of the Army and Navy of the United States, and of the Militia of the several States, when called into the actual Service of the United States; he may require the Opinion, in writing, of the principal Officer in each of the executive Departments, upon any Subject relating to the Duties of their respective Offices, and he shall have Power to grant Reprieves and Pardons for Offences against the United States, except in Cases of Impeachment.

He shall have Power, by and with the Advice and Consent of the Senate, to make Treaties, provided two thirds of the Senators present concur; and he shall nominate, and by and with the Advice and Consent of the Senate, shall appoint Ambassadors, other public Ministers and Consuls, Judges of the supreme Court, and all other Officers of the United States, whose Appointments are not herein otherwise provided for, and which shall be established by Law: but the Congress may by Law vest the Appointment of

---

[8] This clause has been affected by amendment XXV.

such inferior Officers, as they think proper, in the President alone, in the Courts of Law, or in the Heads of Departments.

The President shall have Power to fill up all Vacancies that may happen during the Recess of the Senate, by granting Commissions which shall expire at the End of their next Session.

SECTION 3. He shall from time to time give to the Congress Information of the State of the Union, and recommend to their Consideration such Measures as he shall judge necessary and expedient; he may, on extraordinary Occasions, convene both Houses, or either of them, and in Case of Disagreement between them, with Respect to the Time of Adjournment, he may adjourn them to such Time as he shall think proper; he shall receive Ambassadors and other public Ministers; he shall take Care that the Laws be faithfully executed, and shall Commission all the Officers of the United States.

SECTION 4. The President, Vice President and all civil Officers of the United States, shall be removed from Office on Impeachment for, and Conviction of, Treason, Bribery, or other high Crimes and Misdemeanors.

Article III

SECTION 1. The judicial Power of the United States shall be vested in one supreme Court, and in such inferior Courts as the Congress may from time to time ordain and establish. The Judges, both of the supreme and inferior Courts, shall hold their Offices during good Behaviour, and shall, at stated Times, receive for their Services a Compensation, which shall not be diminished during their Continuance in Office.

SECTION 2. The judicial Power shall extend to all Cases, in Law and Equity, arising under this Constitution, the Laws of the United States, and Treaties made, or which shall be made, under their Authority;—to all Cases affecting Ambassadors, other public Ministers and Consuls;—to all Cases of admiralty and maritime Jurisdiction;—to Controversies to which the United States shall be a Party;—to Controversies between two or more States;—between a State and Citizens of another State,[9]—between Citizens of

---

[9] This clause has been affected by amendment XI.

different States,—between Citizens of the same State claiming Lands under Grants of different States, and between a State, or the Citizens thereof, and foreign States, Citizens or Subjects.

In all Cases affecting Ambassadors, other public Ministers and Consuls, and those in which a State shall be Party, the supreme Court shall have original Jurisdiction. In all the other Cases before mentioned, the supreme Court shall have appellate Jurisdiction, both as to Law and Fact, with such Exceptions, and under such Regulations as the Congress shall make.

The Trial of all Crimes, except in Cases of Impeachment, shall be by Jury; and such Trial shall be held in the State where the said Crimes shall have been committed; but when not committed within any State, the Trial shall be at such Place or Places as the Congress may by Law have directed.

SECTION 3. Treason against the United States, shall consist only in levying War against them, or in adhering to their Enemies, giving them Aid and Comfort. No Person shall be convicted of Treason unless on the Testimony of two Witnesses to the same overt Act, or on Confession in open Court.

The Congress shall have Power to declare the Punishment of Treason, but no Attainder of Treason shall work Corruption of Blood, or Forfeiture except during the Life of the Person attainted.

Article IV

SECTION 1. Full Faith and Credit shall be given in each State to the public Acts, Records, and judicial Proceedings of every other State. And the Congress may by general Laws prescribe the Manner in which such Acts, Records and Proceedings shall be proved, and the Effect thereof.

SECTION 2. The Citizens of each State shall be entitled to all Privileges and Immunities of Citizens in the several States.

A Person charged in any State with Treason, Felony, or other Crime, who shall flee from Justice, and be found in another State, shall on Demand of the executive Authority of the State from which he fled, be delivered up, to be removed to the State having Jurisdiction of the Crime.

No Person held to Service or Labour in one State, under the Laws thereof, escaping into another, shall, in Consequence of any Law or Regulation therein, be discharged from such Service or Labour, but shall be delivered up on Claim of the Party to whom such Service or Labour may be due.[10]

SECTION 3. New States may be admitted by the Congress into this Union; but no new State shall be formed or erected within the Jurisdiction of any other State; nor any State be formed by the Junction of two or more States, or Parts of States, without the Consent of the Legislatures of the States concerned as well as of the Congress.

The Congress shall have Power to dispose of and make all needful Rules and Regulations respecting the Territory or other Property belonging to the United States; and nothing in this Constitution shall be so construed as to Prejudice any Claims of the United States, or of any particular State.

SECTION 4. The United States shall guarantee to every State in this Union a Republican Form of Government, and shall protect each of them against Invasion; and on Application of the Legislature, or of the Executive (when the Legislature cannot be convened), against domestic Violence.

Article V

The Congress, whenever two thirds of both Houses shall deem it necessary, shall propose Amendments to this Constitution, or, on the Application of the Legislatures of two thirds of the several States, shall call a Convention for proposing Amendments, which, in either Case, shall be valid to all Intents and Purposes, as Part of this Constitution, when ratified by the Legislatures of three fourths of the several States, or by Conventions in three fourths thereof, as the one or the other Mode of Ratification may be proposed by the Congress; Provided that no Amendment which may be made prior to the Year One thousand eight hundred and eight shall in any Manner affect the first and fourth Clauses in the Ninth Section of the first Article; and that no State, without its Consent, shall be deprived of its equal Suffrage in the Senate.

---

[10] This clause has been affected by amendment XIII.

Article VI

All Debts contracted and Engagements entered into, before the Adoption of this Constitution, shall be as valid against the United States under this Constitution, as under the Confederation.

This Constitution, and the Laws of the United States which shall be made in Pursuance thereof; and all Treaties made, or which shall be made, under the Authority of the United States, shall be the supreme Law of the Land; and the Judges in every State shall be bound thereby, any Thing in the Constitution or Laws of any State to the Contrary notwithstanding.

The Senators and Representatives before mentioned, and the Members of the several State Legislatures, and all executive and judicial Officers, both of the United States and of the several States, shall be bound by Oath or Affirmation, to support this Constitution; but no religious Test shall ever be required as a Qualification to any Office or public Trust under the United States.

Article VII

The Ratification of the Conventions of nine States, shall be sufficient for the Establishment of this Constitution between the States so ratifying the Same.

The Word, "the," being interlined between the seventh and eighth Lines of the first Page, the Word "Thirty" being partly written on an Erazure in the fifteenth Line of the first Page, The Words "is tried" being interlined between the thirty second and thirty third Lines of the first Page and the Word "the" being interlined between the forty third and forty fourth Lines of the second Page.

Attest William Jackson Secretary

Done in Convention by the Unanimous Consent of the States present the Seventeenth Day of September in the Year of our Lord one thousand seven hundred and Eighty seven and of the Independence of the United States of America the Twelfth In witness whereof We have hereunto subscribed our Names,

[Signed also by the deputies of twelve States]

Delaware
Geo. Read
Gunning Bedford jun
John Dickinson
Richard Bassett
Jaco Broom

Maryland
James McHenry
Dan of St Thos. Jenifer
Danl. Carroll

Virginia
John Blair
James Madison Jr.

North Carolina
Wm. Blount
Richd. Dobbs Spaight
Hu Williamson

South Carolina
J. Rutledge
Charles Cotesworth Pinckney
Charles Pinckney
Pierce Butler

Georgia
William Few
Abr Baldwin

New Hampshire
John Langdon
Nicholas Gilman

Massachusetts
Nathaniel Gorham
Rufus King

Connecticut
Wm. Saml. Johnson
Roger Sherman

New York
Alexander Hamilton

New Jersey
Wil: Livingston
David Brearley
Wm. Paterson
Jona Dayton

Pennsylvania
B Franklin
Thomas Mifflin
Robt. Morris
Geo. Clymer
Thos. FitzSimons
Jared Ingersoll
James Wilson
Gouv Morris

Above: *Scene at the Signing of the Constitution of the United States,* Howard Chandler Christy, 1940, oil on canvas.

Following page: Key to identifying figures.

1. Washington, George, Va.
2. Franklin, Benjamin, Pa.
3. Madison, James, Va.
4. Hamilton, Alexander, N.Y.
5. Morris, Gouverneur, Pa.
6. Morris, Robert, Pa.
7. Wilson, James, Pa.
8. Pinckney, Charles Cotesworth, S.C.
9. Pinckney, Charles, S.C.
10. Rutledge, John, S.C.

11. Butler, Pierce, S.C.
12. Sherman, Roger, Conn.
13. Johnson, William Samuel, Conn.
14. McHenry, James, Md.
15. Read, George, Del.
16. Bassett, Richard, Del.
17. Spaight, Richard Dobbs, N.C.
18. Blount, William, N.C.
19. Williamson, Hugh, N.C.
20. Jenifer, Daniel of St. Thomas, Md.

21. King, Rufus, Mass.
22. Gorham, Nathaniel, Mass.
23. Dayton, Jonathan, N.J.
24. Carroll, Daniel, Md.
25. Few, William, Ga.
26. Baldwin, Abraham, Ga.
27. Langdon, John, N.H.
28. Gilman, Nicholas, N.H.
29. Livingston, William, N.J.
30. Paterson, William, N.J.

31. Mifflin, Thomas, Pa.
32. Clymer, George, Pa.
33. FitzSimons, Thomas, Pa.
34. Ingersoll, Jared, Pa.
35. Bedford, Gunning, Jr., Del.
36. Brearley, David, N.J.
37. Dickinson, John, Del.
38. Blair, John, Va.
39. Broom, Jacob, Del.
40. Jackson, William, Secretary

Constitution of the United States

Articles in Addition to, and Amendment of, the Constitution of the United States of America, Proposed by Congress, and Ratified by the Legislatures of the Several States, Pursuant to the Fifth Article of the Original Constitution[1]

Article [I][2]

Congress shall make no law respecting an establishment of religion, or prohibiting the free exercise thereof; or abridging the freedom of speech, or of the press; of the right of the people peaceably to assemble, and to petition the Government for a redress of grievances.

Article [II]

A well regulated Militia, being necessary to the security of a free State, the right of the people to keep and bear Arms, shall not be infringed.

Article [III]

No Soldier shall, in time of peace be quartered in any house, without the consent of the Owner, nor in time of war, but in a manner to be prescribed by law.

Article [IV]

The right of the people to be secure in their persons, houses, papers, and effects, against unreasonable searches and seizures,

---

[1] The first ten amendments of the Constitution of the United States (and two others, one of which failed of ratification and the other which later became the 27th amendment) were proposed to the legislatures of the several States by the First Congress on September 25, 1789. The first ten amendments were ratified by the following States, and the notifications of ratification by the Governors thereof were successively communicated by the President to Congress: New Jersey, November 20, 1789; Maryland, December 19, 1789; North Carolina, December 22, 1789; South Carolina, January 19, 1790; New Hampshire, January 25, 1790; Delaware, January 28, 1790; New York, February 24, 1790; Pennsylvania, March 10, 1790; Rhode Island, June 7, 1790; Vermont, November 3, 1791; and Virginia, December 15, 1791. Ratification was completed on December 15, 1791. The amendments were subsequently ratified by the legislatures of Massachusetts, March 2, 1939; Georgia, March 18, 1939; and Connecticut, April 19, 1939.

[2] Only the 13th, 14th, 15th, and 16th articles of amendment had numbers assigned to them at the time of ratification.

shall not be violated, and no Warrants shall issue, but upon probable cause, supported by Oath or affirmation, and particularly describing the place to be searched, and the persons or things to be seized.

Article [V]

No person shall be held to answer for a capital, or otherwise infamous crime, unless on a presentment or indictment of a Grand Jury, except in cases arising in the land or naval forces, or in the Militia, when in actual service in time of War or public danger; nor shall any person be subject for the same offence to be twice put in jeopardy of life or limb; nor shall be compelled in any criminal case to be a witness against himself, nor be deprived of life, liberty, or property, without due process of law; nor shall private property be taken for public use, without just compensation.

Article [VI]

In all criminal prosecutions, the accused shall enjoy the right to a speedy and public trial, by an impartial jury of the State and district wherein the crime shall have been committed, which district shall have been previously ascertained by law, and to be informed of the nature and cause of the accusation; to be confronted with the witnesses against him; to have compulsory process for obtaining witnesses in his favor, and to have the Assistance of Counsel for his defense.

Article [VII]

In Suits at common law, where the value in controversy shall exceed twenty dollars, the right of trial by jury shall be preserved, and no fact tried by a jury, shall be otherwise re-examined in any Court of the United States, than according to the rules of the common law.

Article [VIII]

Excessive bail shall not be required, nor excessive fines imposed, nor cruel and unusual punishments inflicted.

Article [IX]

The enumeration in the Constitution, of certain rights, shall not be construed to deny or disparage others retained by the people.

Article [X]

The powers not delegated to the United States by the Constitution, nor prohibited by it to the States, are reserved to the States respectively, or to the people.

Article [XI]

The Judicial power of the United States shall not be construed to extend to any suit in law or equity, commenced or prosecuted against one of the United States by Citizens of another State, or by Citizens or Subjects of any Foreign State.

Article [XII]

The Electors shall meet in their respective states, and vote by ballot for President and Vice-President, one of whom, at least, shall not be an inhabitant of the same state with themselves; they shall name in their ballots the person voted for as President, and in distinct ballots the person voted for as Vice-President, and they shall make distinct lists of all persons voted for as President, and of all persons voted for as Vice-President, and of the number of votes for each, which lists they shall sign and certify, and transmit sealed to the seat of the government of the United States, directed to the President of the Senate;—The President of the Senate shall, in the presence of the Senate and House of Representatives, open all the certificates and the votes shall then be counted;—The person having the greatest number of votes for President, shall be the President, if such number be a majority of the whole number of Electors appointed; and if no person have such majority, then from the persons having the highest numbers not exceeding three on the list of those voted for as President, the House of Representatives shall choose immediately, by ballot, the President. But in choosing the President, the votes shall be taken by states, the representation from each state having one vote; a quorum for this purpose shall consist of a member or members from two-thirds of the states, and a majority of all the states shall be necessary to a choice. And if the House of Representatives shall not choose a President whenever the right of choice shall devolve upon them, before the fourth day of March next following, then the Vice-President shall act as President, as in the case of the death or other constitutional disability of the

President.[3]—The person having the greatest number of votes as Vice-President, shall be the Vice-President, if such number be a majority of the whole number of Electors appointed, and if no person have a majority, then from the two highest numbers on the list, the Senate shall choose the Vice-President; a quorum for the purpose shall consist of two-thirds of the whole number of Senators, and a majority of the whole number shall be necessary to a choice. But no person constitutionally ineligible to the office of President shall be eligible to that of Vice-President of the United States.

Article XIII

SECTION 1. Neither slavery nor involuntary servitude, except as a punishment for crime whereof the party shall have been duly convicted, shall exist within the United States, or any place subject to their jurisdiction.

SECTION 2. Congress shall have power to enforce this article by appropriate legislation.

Article XIV

SECTION 1. All persons born or naturalized in the United States, and subject to the jurisdiction thereof, are citizens of the United States and of the State wherein they reside. No State shall make or enforce any law which shall abridge the privileges or immunities of citizens of the United States; nor shall any State deprive any person of life, liberty, or property, without due process of law; nor deny to any person within its jurisdiction the equal protection of the laws.

SECTION 2. Representatives shall be apportioned among the several States according to their respective numbers, counting the whole number of persons in each State, excluding Indians not taxed. But when the right to vote at any election for the choice of electors for President and Vice President of the United States, Representatives in Congress, the Executive and Judicial officers of a State, or the members of the Legislature thereof, is denied to any of the male inhabitants of such State, being twenty-one years of age,[4] and citizens of the United States, or in any way abridged, except for participation in rebellion, or other crime, the basis of

---

[3] This sentence has been superseded by section 3 of amendment XX.

[4] See amendment XIX and section 1 of amendment XXVI.

representation therein shall be reduced in the proportion which the number of such male citizens shall bear to the whole number of male citizens twenty-one years of age in such State.

SECTION 3. No person shall be a Senator or Representative in Congress, or elector of President and Vice President, or hold any office, civil or military, under the United States, or under any State, who, having previously taken an oath, as a member of Congress, or as an officer of the United States, or as a member of any State legislature, or as an executive or judicial officer of any State, to support the Constitution of the United States, shall have engaged in insurrection or rebellion against the same, or given aid or comfort to the enemies thereof. But Congress may by a vote of two-thirds of each House, remove such disability.

SECTION 4. The validity of the public debt of the United States, authorized by law, including debts incurred for payment of pensions and bounties for services in suppressing insurrection or rebellion, shall not be questioned. But neither the United States nor any State shall assume or pay any debt or obligation incurred in aid of insurrection or rebellion against the United States, or any claim for the loss or emancipation of any slave; but all such debts, obligations and claims shall be held illegal and void.

SECTION 5. The Congress shall have power to enforce, by appropriate legislation, the provisions of this article.

Article XV

SECTION 1. The right of citizens of the United States to vote shall not be denied or abridged by the United States or by any State on account of race, color, or previous condition of servitude.

SECTION 2. The Congress shall have power to enforce this article by appropriate legislation.

Article XVI

The Congress shall have power to lay and collect taxes on incomes, from whatever source derived, without apportionment among the several States, and without regard to any census or enumeration.

Article [XVII]

The Senate of the United States shall be composed of two Senators from each State, elected by the people thereof, for six years; and each Senator shall have one vote. The electors in each State shall have the qualifications requisite for electors of the most numerous branch of the State legislatures.

When vacancies happen in the representation of any State in the Senate, the executive authority of such State shall issue writs of election to fill such vacancies: Provided, That the legislature of any State may empower the executive thereof to make temporary appointments until the people fill the vacancies by election as the legislature may direct.

This amendment shall not be so construed as to affect the election or term of any Senator chosen before it becomes valid as part of the Constitution.

Article [XVIII][5]

SECTION 1. After one year from the ratification of this article the manufacture, sale, or transportation of intoxicating liquors within, the importation thereof into, or the exportation thereof from the United States and all territory subject to the jurisdiction thereof for beverage purposes is hereby prohibited.

SECTION 2. The Congress and the several States shall have concurrent power to enforce this article by appropriate legislation.

SECTION 3. This article shall be inoperative unless it shall have been ratified as an amendment to the Constitution by the legislatures of the several States, as provided in the Constitution, within seven years from the date of the submission hereof to the States by the Congress.

Article [XIX]

The right of citizens of the United States to vote shall not be denied or abridged by the United States or by any State on account of sex.

Congress shall have power to enforce this article by appropriate legislation.

---

[5] Repealed by section 1 of amendment XXI.

Article [XX]

SECTION 1. The terms of the President and Vice President shall end at noon on the 20th day of January, and the terms of Senators and Representatives at noon on the 3d day of January, of the years in which such terms would have ended if this article had not been ratified; and the terms of their successors shall then begin.

SECTION 2. The Congress shall assemble at least once in every year, and such meeting shall begin at noon on the 3d day of January, unless they shall by law appoint a different day.

SECTION 3. If, at the time fixed for the beginning of the term of the President, the President elect shall have died, the Vice President elect shall become President. If a President shall not have been chosen before the time fixed for the beginning of his term, or if the President elect shall have failed to qualify, then the Vice President elect shall act as President until a President shall have qualified; and the Congress may by law provide for the case wherein neither a President elect nor a Vice President elect shall have qualified, declaring who shall then act as President, or the manner in which one who is to act shall be selected, and such person shall act accordingly until a President or Vice President shall have qualified.

SECTION 4. The Congress may by law provide for the case of the death of any of the persons from whom the House of Representatives may choose a President whenever the right of choice shall have devolved upon them, and for the case of the death of any of the persons from whom the Senate may choose a Vice President whenever the right of choice shall have devolved upon them.

SECTION 5. Sections 1 and 2 shall take effect on the 15th day of October following the ratification of this article.

SECTION 6. This article shall be inoperative unless it shall have been ratified as an amendment to the Constitution by the legislatures of three-fourths of the several States within seven years from the date of its submission.

Article [XXI]

SECTION 1. The eighteenth article of amendment to the Constitution of the United States is hereby repealed.

SECTION 2. The transportation or importation into any State, Territory, or possession of the United States for delivery or use therein of intoxicating liquors, in violation of the laws thereof, is hereby prohibited.

SECTION 3. This article shall be inoperative unless it shall have been ratified as an amendment to the Constitution by conventions in the several States, as provided in the Constitution, within seven years from the date of the submission hereof to the States by the Congress.

Article [XXII]

SECTION 1. No person shall be elected to the office of the President more than twice, and no person who has held the office of President, or acted as President, for more than two years of a term of which some other person was elected President shall be elected to the office of the President more than once. But this Article shall not apply to any person holding the office of President when this Article was proposed by the Congress, and shall not prevent any person who may be holding the office of President, or acting as President, during the term within which this Article becomes operative from holding the office of President or acting as President during the remainder of such term.

SECTION 2. This article shall be inoperative unless it shall have been ratified as an amendment to the Constitution by the legislatures of three-fourths of the several States within seven years from the date of its submission to the States by the Congress.

Article [XXIII]

SECTION 1. The District constituting the seat of Government of the United States shall appoint in such manner as the Congress may direct:

A number of electors of President and Vice President equal to the whole number of Senators and Representatives in Congress to which the District would be entitled if it were a State, but in no event more than the least populous State; they shall be in addition to those appointed by the States, but they shall be considered, for the purposes of the election of President and Vice President, to be electors appointed by a State; and they shall meet in the District and perform such duties as provided by the twelfth article of amendment.

SECTION 2. The Congress shall have power to enforce this article by appropriate legislation.

Article [XXIV]

SECTION 1. The right of citizens of the United States to vote in any primary or other election for President or Vice President, for electors for President or Vice President, or for Senator or Representative in Congress, shall not be denied or abridged by the United States or any State by reason of failure to pay any poll tax or other tax.

SECTION 2. The Congress shall have power to enforce this article by appropriate legislation.

Article [XXV]

SECTION 1. In case of the removal of the President from office or of his death or resignation, the Vice President shall become President.

SECTION 2. Whenever there is a vacancy in the office of the Vice President, the President shall nominate a Vice President who shall take office upon confirmation by a majority vote of both Houses of Congress.

SECTION 3. Whenever the President transmits to the President pro tempore of the Senate and the Speaker of the House of Representatives his written declaration that he is unable to discharge the powers and duties of his office, and until he transmits to them a written declaration to the contrary, such powers and duties shall be discharged by the Vice President as Acting President.

SECTION 4. Whenever the Vice President and a majority of either the principal officers of the executive departments or of such other body as Congress may by law provide, transmit to the President pro tempore of the Senate and the Speaker of the House of Representatives their written declaration that the President is unable to discharge the powers and duties of his office, the Vice President shall immediately assume the powers and duties of the office as Acting President.

Thereafter, when the President transmits to the President pro tempore of the Senate and the Speaker of the House of

Representatives his written declaration that no inability exists, he shall resume the powers and duties of his office unless the Vice President and a majority of either the principal officers of the executive department[6] or of such other body as Congress may by law provide, transmit within four days to the President pro tempore of the Senate and the Speaker of the House of Representatives their written declaration that the President is unable to discharge the powers and duties of his office. Thereupon Congress shall decide the issue, assembling within forty-eight hours for that purpose if not in session. If the Congress, within twenty-one days after receipt of the latter written declaration, or, if Congress is not in session, within twenty-one days after Congress is required to assemble, determines by two-thirds vote of both Houses that the President is unable to discharge the powers and duties of his office, the Vice President shall continue to discharge the same as Acting President; otherwise, the President shall resume the powers and duties of his office.

Article [XXVI]

SECTION 1. The right of citizens of the United States, who are eighteen years of age or older, to vote shall not be denied or abridged by the United States or by any State on account of age.

SECTION 2. The Congress shall have power to enforce this article by appropriate legislation.

Article [XXVII]

No law, varying the compensation for the services of the Senators and Representatives, shall take effect, until an election of Representatives shall have intervened.

---

[6] So in original. Probably should be "departments".

Declaration of the Rights of Man and of the Citizen

Marquis de Lafayette

The Declaration of the Rights of Man and of the Citizen (Déclaration des droits de l'homme et du citoyen, *in French) was largely the work of the Marquis de Lafayette (1757–1834). Lafayette came from a wealthy French land-holding and military family, was commissioned as an officer at the age of thirteen, and came to America for idealistic reasons to support the American Revolution. He served in various positions of command in the Revolutionary War and eventually helped hold off the forces of Cornwallis until reinforcements could arrive to win at Yorktown. He became a friend of Washington, Hamilton, and Jefferson. Elected to the Estates General in 1789, he fled the reign of terror, was captured by Austria, and spent five years in prison there until released by Napoleon, in whose regime Lafayette chose not to serve. He later became a member of the Chamber of Deputies under the Bourbon restoration. In 1824, invited to the U.S. by President Monroe, Lafayette visited all the states in the union and was lionized as a hero of the American Revolution and reminder of why the Revolutionary War had been fought. In the July Revolution of 1830 Lafayette refused the offer to become the dictator of France.*

In 1789 Lafayette drafted the "Declaration of the Rights of Man and of the Citizen" with the help of his friend Thomas Jefferson, who was serving as a U.S. diplomat in France at the time, and of Honoré Mirabeau, a moderate leader of the French Revolution in favor of constitutional monarchy. The Declaration is heavily influenced by the ideas on the natural rights of man enshrined in the American Declaration of Independence, by various enlightenment ideas of Rousseau (individualism, social contract, general will) and Montesquieu (separation of powers), and possibly by Madison's proposed amendments to the U.S. Constitution, which became our Bill of Rights, which had been presented eleven weeks before the adoption of the French Declaration. The Declaration has been referred to by French governments ever since, up to and including the present Fifth French Republic, and has helped to spread ideas of democracy and the natural rights of man to many other nations of the world.

Above: *Declaration of the Rights of Man and of the Citizen in 1789,* Jean-Jacques-François Le Barbier, ca. 1789, oil on canvas.

Approved by the National Assembly of France, August 26, 1789.

The representatives of the French people, organized as a National Assembly, believing that the ignorance, neglect, or contempt of the rights of man are the sole cause of public calamities and of the corruption of governments, have determined to set forth in a solemn declaration the natural, unalienable, and sacred rights of man, in order that this declaration, being constantly before all the members of the Social body, shall remind them continually of their rights and duties; in order that the acts of the legislative power, as well as those of the executive power, may be compared at any moment with the objects and purposes of all political institutions and may thus be more respected, and, lastly, in order that the grievances of the citizens, based hereafter upon simple and incontestable principles, shall tend to the maintenance of the constitution and redound to the happiness of all. Therefore the National Assembly recognizes and proclaims, in the presence and under the auspices of the Supreme Being, the following rights of man and of the citizen:

Articles:

1. Men are born and remain free and equal in rights. Social distinctions may be founded only upon the general good.

2. The aim of all political association is the preservation of the natural and imprescriptible rights of man. These rights are liberty, property, security, and resistance to oppression.

3. The principle of all sovereignty resides essentially in the nation. No body nor individual may exercise any authority which does not proceed directly from the nation.

4. Liberty consists in the freedom to do everything which injures no one else; hence the exercise of the natural rights of each man has no limits except those which assure to the other members of the society the enjoyment of the same rights. These limits can only be determined by law.

5. Law can only prohibit such actions as are hurtful to society. Nothing may be prevented which is not forbidden by law, and no one may be forced to do anything not provided for by law.

6. Law is the expression of the general will. Every citizen has a right to participate personally, or through his representative, in its foundation. It must be the same for all, whether it protects or punishes. All citizens, being equal in the eyes of the law, are equally eligible to all dignities and to all public positions and occupations, according to their abilities, and without distinction except that of their virtues and talents.

7. No person shall be accused, arrested, or imprisoned except in the cases and according to the forms prescribed by law. Any one soliciting, transmitting, executing, or causing to be executed, any arbitrary order, shall be punished. But any citizen summoned or arrested in virtue of the law shall submit without delay, as resistance constitutes an offense.

8. The law shall provide for such punishments only as are strictly and obviously necessary, and no one shall suffer punishment except it be legally inflicted in virtue of a law passed and promulgated before the commission of the offense.

9. As all persons are held innocent until they shall have been declared guilty, if arrest shall be deemed indispensable, all harshness not essential to the securing of the prisoner's person shall be severely repressed by law.

10. No one shall be disquieted on account of his opinions, including his religious views, provided their manifestation does not disturb the public order established by law.

11. The free communication of ideas and opinions is one of the most precious of the rights of man. Every citizen may, accordingly, speak, write, and print with freedom, but shall be responsible for such abuses of this freedom as shall be defined by law.

12. The security of the rights of man and of the citizen requires public military forces. These forces are, therefore, established for the good of all and not for the personal advantage of those to whom they shall be entrusted.

13. A common contribution is essential for the maintenance of the public forces and for the cost of administration. This should be equitably distributed among all the citizens in proportion to their means.

14. All the citizens have a right to decide, either personally or by their representatives, as to the necessity of the public contribution; to grant this freely; to know to what uses it is put; and to fix the proportion, the mode of assessment and of collection and the duration of the taxes.

15. Society has the right to require of every public agent an account of his administration.

16. A society in which the observance of the law is not assured, nor the separation of powers defined, has no constitution at all.

17. Since property is an inviolable and sacred right, no one shall be deprived thereof except where public necessity, legally determined, shall clearly demand it, and then only on condition that the owner shall have been previously and equitably indemnified.

Farewell Address

George Washington

George Washington (1732–1799) commanded the Continental Army during the Revolutionary War and is considered one of the founding fathers of the United States. Having served as the commander in chief of the Continental Army during the Revolutionary War, his popularity was second to no one else in the nation. Washington was profoundly beloved both by all of the soldiers he had led and by all of the other inhabitants of the colonies. He was universally thought the best qualified person to lead the country. From December 15, 1788, through January 10, 1789, the United States held its first presidential election under the Constitution. George Washington was elected president having received the unanimous support of the electors. John Adams was elected the Vice President.

This address was written by Washington when his second term as President of the United States was coming to an end. The address was first published on September 19, 1796, subsequently reprinted in nearly every newspaper in the country, and circulated as a pamphlet. The address was never delivered orally.

By talking to his audience in the second person, Washington made his suggestions both more immediate and more personal. He was thoughtful, clear, and thorough, taking advantage of the written form of his address to present arguments more detailed and support more complete than could easily be offered in a public speech, where time limits the opportunity for listeners to digest ideas and relate later statements to earlier ones.

Above: Portrait of George Washington on the dollar bill, 1869, engraving, after Gilbert Stuart's *Athenaeum Portrait*, 1796, unfinished oil on canvas.

Published September 19, 1796.

Friends and Citizens,

The period for a new election of a citizen to administer the executive government of the United States being not far distant, and the time actually arrived when your thoughts must be employed in designating the person who is to be clothed with that important trust, it appears to me proper, especially as it may conduce to a more distinct expression of the public voice, that I should now apprise you of the resolution I have formed, to decline being considered among the number of those out of whom a choice is to be made.

I beg you, at the same time, to do me the justice to be assured that this resolution has not been taken without a strict regard to all the considerations appertaining to the relation which binds a dutiful citizen to his country; and that in withdrawing the tender of service, which silence in my situation might imply, I am influenced by no diminution of zeal for your future interest, no deficiency of grateful respect for your past kindness, but am supported by a full conviction that the step is compatible with both.

The acceptance of, and continuance hitherto in, the office to which your suffrages have twice called me have been a uniform sacrifice of inclination to the opinion of duty and to a deference for what appeared to be your desire. I constantly hoped that it would have been much earlier in my power, consistently with motives which I was not at liberty to disregard, to return to that retirement from which I had been reluctantly drawn. The strength of my inclination to do this, previous to the last election, had even led to the preparation of an address to declare it to you; but mature reflection on the then perplexed and critical posture of our affairs with foreign nations, and the unanimous advice of persons entitled to my confidence, impelled me to abandon the idea.

I rejoice that the state of your concerns, external as well as internal, no longer renders the pursuit of inclination incompatible with the sentiment of duty or propriety, and am persuaded, whatever partiality may be retained for my services, that, in the present circumstances of our country, you will not disapprove my determination to retire.

The impressions with which I first undertook the arduous trust were explained on the proper occasion. In the discharge of this trust, I will only say that I have, with good intentions, contributed towards the organization and administration of the government the best exertions of which a very fallible judgment was capable. Not unconscious in the outset of the inferiority of my qualifications, experience in my own eyes, perhaps still more in the eyes of others, has strengthened the motives to diffidence of myself; and every day the increasing weight of years admonishes me more and more that the shade of retirement is as necessary to me as it will be welcome. Satisfied that if any circumstances have given peculiar value to my services, they were temporary, I have the consolation to believe that, while choice and prudence invite me to quit the political scene, patriotism does not forbid it.

In looking forward to the moment which is intended to terminate the career of my public life, my feelings do not permit me to suspend the deep acknowledgment of that debt of gratitude which I owe to my beloved country for the many honors it has conferred upon me; still more for the steadfast confidence with which it has supported me; and for the opportunities I have thence enjoyed of manifesting my inviolable attachment, by services faithful and persevering, though in usefulness unequal to my zeal. If benefits have resulted to our country from these services, let it always be remembered to your praise, and as an instructive example in our annals, that under circumstances in which the passions, agitated in every direction, were liable to mislead, amidst appearances sometimes dubious, vicissitudes of fortune often discouraging, in situations in which not unfrequently want of success has countenanced the spirit of criticism, the constancy of your support was the essential prop of the efforts, and a guarantee of the plans by which they were effected. Profoundly penetrated with this idea, I shall carry it with me to my grave, as a strong incitement to unceasing vows that heaven may continue to you the choicest tokens of its beneficence; that your union and brotherly affection may be perpetual; that the free Constitution, which is the work of your hands, may be sacredly maintained; that its administration in every department may be stamped with wisdom and virtue; that, in fine, the happiness of the people of these States, under the auspices of liberty, may be made complete by so careful a preservation and so prudent a use of this blessing as will acquire to them the glory of recommending it to the applause, the affection, and adoption of every nation which is yet a stranger to it.

Here, perhaps, I ought to stop. But a solicitude for your welfare, which cannot end but with my life, and the apprehension of danger, natural to that solicitude, urge me, on an occasion like the present, to offer to your solemn contemplation, and to recommend to your frequent review, some sentiments which are the result of much reflection, of no inconsiderable observation, and which appear to me all-important to the permanency of your felicity as a people. These will be offered to you with the more freedom, as you can only see in them the disinterested warnings of a parting friend, who can possibly have no personal motive to bias his counsel. Nor can I forget, as an encouragement to it, your indulgent reception of my sentiments on a former and not dissimilar occasion.

Interwoven as is the love of liberty with every ligament of your hearts, no recommendation of mine is necessary to fortify or confirm the attachment.

The unity of government which constitutes you one people is also now dear to you. It is justly so, for it is a main pillar in the edifice of your real independence, the support of your tranquility at home, your peace abroad; of your safety; of your prosperity; of that very liberty which you so highly prize. But as it is easy to foresee that, from different causes and from different quarters, much pains will be taken, many artifices employed to weaken in your minds the conviction of this truth; as this is the point in your political fortress against which the batteries of internal and external enemies will be most constantly and actively (though often covertly and insidiously) directed, it is of infinite moment that you should properly estimate the immense value of your national union to your collective and individual happiness; that you should cherish a cordial, habitual, and immovable attachment to it; accustoming yourselves to think and speak of it as of the palladium of your political safety and prosperity; watching for its preservation with jealous anxiety; discountenancing whatever may suggest even a suspicion that it can in any event be abandoned; and indignantly frowning upon the first dawning of every attempt to alienate any portion of our country from the rest, or to enfeeble the sacred ties which now link together the various parts.

For this you have every inducement of sympathy and interest. Citizens, by birth or choice, of a common country, that country has a right to concentrate your affections. The name of American, which belongs to you in your national capacity, must always exalt the just pride of patriotism more than any appellation derived from local discriminations. With slight shades of difference, you have the same religion, manners, habits, and political principles. You have in a common cause fought and triumphed together; the independence and liberty you possess are the work of joint counsels, and joint efforts of common dangers, sufferings, and successes.

But these considerations, however powerfully they address themselves to your sensibility, are greatly outweighed by those which apply more immediately to your interest. Here every portion of our country finds the most commanding motives for carefully guarding and preserving the union of the whole.

The North, in an unrestrained intercourse with the South, protected by the equal laws of a common government, finds in the productions of the latter great additional resources of maritime and commercial enterprise and precious materials of manufacturing industry. The South, in the same intercourse, benefiting by the agency of the North, sees its agriculture grow and its commerce expand. Turning partly into its own channels the seamen of the North, it finds its particular navigation invigorated; and, while it contributes, in different ways, to nourish and increase the general mass of the national navigation, it looks forward to the protection of a maritime strength, to which itself is unequally adapted. The East, in a like intercourse with the West, already finds, and in the progressive improvement of interior communications by land and water, will more and more find a valuable vent for the commodities which it brings from abroad, or manufactures at home. The West derives from the East supplies requisite to its growth and comfort, and, what is perhaps of still greater consequence, it must of necessity owe the secure enjoyment of indispensable outlets for its own productions to the weight, influence, and the future maritime strength of the Atlantic side of the Union, directed by an indissoluble community of interest as one nation. Any other tenure by which the West can hold this essential advantage, whether derived from its own separate strength, or from an apostate and unnatural connection with any foreign power, must be intrinsically precarious.

While, then, every part of our country thus feels an immediate and particular interest in union, all the parts combined cannot fail to find in the united mass of means and efforts greater strength, greater resource, proportionably greater security from external danger, a less frequent interruption of their peace by foreign nations; and, what is of inestimable value, they must derive from union an exemption from those broils and wars between themselves, which so frequently afflict neighboring countries not tied together by the same governments, which their own rival ships alone would be sufficient to produce, but which opposite foreign alliances, attachments, and intrigues would stimulate and embitter. Hence, likewise, they will avoid the necessity of those overgrown military establishments which, under any form of government, are inauspicious to liberty, and which are to be regarded as particularly hostile to republican liberty. In this sense it is that your union ought to be considered as a main prop of your liberty, and that the love of the one ought to endear to you the preservation of the other.

These considerations speak a persuasive language to every reflecting and virtuous mind, and exhibit the continuance of the Union as a primary object of patriotic desire. Is there a doubt whether a common government can embrace so large a sphere? Let experience solve it. To listen to mere speculation in such a case were criminal. We are authorized to hope that a proper organization of the whole with the auxiliary agency of governments for the respective subdivisions, will afford a happy issue to the experiment. It is well worth a fair and full experiment. With such powerful and obvious motives to union, affecting all parts of our country, while experience shall not have demonstrated its impracticability, there will always be reason to distrust the patriotism of those who in any quarter may endeavor to weaken its bands.

In contemplating the causes which may disturb our Union, it occurs as matter of serious concern that any ground should have been furnished for characterizing parties by geographical discriminations, Northern and Southern, Atlantic and Western; whence designing men may endeavor to excite a belief that there is a real difference of local interests and views. One of the expedients of party to acquire influence within particular districts is to misrepresent the opinions and aims of other districts. You cannot shield yourselves too much against the jealousies and heartburnings which spring from these misrepresentations; they tend to render alien to each other those who ought to be bound together by fraternal affection. The inhabitants of our Western country have lately had a useful lesson on this head; they have seen, in the negotiation by the Executive, and in the unanimous ratification by the Senate, of the treaty with Spain, and in the universal satisfaction at that event, throughout the United States, a decisive proof how unfounded were the suspicions propagated among them of a policy in the General Government and in the Atlantic States unfriendly to their interests in regard to the Mississippi; they have been witnesses to the formation of two treaties, that with Great Britain, and that with Spain, which secure to them everything they could desire, in respect to our foreign relations, towards confirming their prosperity. Will it not be their wisdom to rely for the preservation of these advantages on the Union by which they were procured? Will they not henceforth be deaf to those advisers, if such there are, who would sever them from their brethren and connect them with aliens?

To the efficacy and permanency of your Union, a government for the whole is indispensable. No alliance, however strict, between the parts can be an adequate substitute; they must inevitably experience the infractions and interruptions which all alliances in all times have experienced. Sensible of this momentous truth, you have improved upon your first essay, by the adoption of a constitution of government better calculated than your former for an intimate union, and for the efficacious management of your common concerns. This government, the offspring of our own choice, uninfluenced and unawed, adopted upon full investigation and mature deliberation, completely free in its principles, in the distribution of its powers, uniting security with energy, and containing within itself a provision for its own amendment, has a just claim to your confidence and your support. Respect for its authority, compliance with its laws, acquiescence in its measures, are duties enjoined by the fundamental maxims of true liberty. The basis of our political systems is the right of the people to make and to alter their constitutions of government. But the Constitution which at any time exists, till changed by an explicit and authentic act of the whole people, is sacredly obligatory upon all. The very idea of the power and the right of the people to establish government presupposes the duty of every individual to obey the established government.

All obstructions to the execution of the laws, all combinations and associations, under whatever plausible character, with the real design to direct, control, counteract, or awe the regular deliberation and action of the constituted authorities, are destructive of this fundamental principle, and of fatal tendency. They serve to organize faction, to give it an artificial and extraordinary force; to put, in the place of the delegated will of the nation the will of a party, often a small but artful and enterprising minority of the community; and, according to the alternate triumphs of different parties, to make the public administration the mirror of the ill-concerted and incongruous projects of faction, rather than the organ of consistent and wholesome plans digested by common counsels and modified by mutual interests.

However combinations or associations of the above description may now and then answer popular ends, they are likely, in the course of time and things, to become potent engines, by which cunning, ambitious, and unprincipled men will be enabled to subvert the power of the people and to usurp for themselves the reins of government, destroying afterwards the very engines which have lifted them to unjust dominion.

Towards the preservation of your government, and the permanency of your present happy state, it is requisite, not only that you steadily discountenance irregular oppositions to its acknowledged authority, but also that you resist with care the spirit of innovation upon its principles, however specious the pretexts. One method of assault may be to effect, in the forms of the Constitution, alterations which will impair the energy of the system, and thus to undermine what cannot be directly overthrown. In all the changes to which you may be invited, remember that time and habit are at least as necessary to fix the true character of governments as of other human institutions; that experience is the surest standard by which to test the real tendency of the existing constitution of a country; that facility in changes, upon the credit of mere hypothesis and opinion, exposes to perpetual change, from the endless variety of hypothesis and opinion; and remember, especially, that for the efficient management of your common interests, in a country so extensive as ours, a government of as much vigor as is consistent with the perfect security of liberty is indispensable. Liberty itself will find in such a government, with powers properly distributed and adjusted, its surest guardian. It is, indeed, little else than a name, where the government is too feeble to withstand the enterprises of faction, to confine each member of the society within the limits prescribed by the laws, and to maintain all in the secure and tranquil enjoyment of the rights of person and property.

I have already intimated to you the danger of parties in the State, with particular reference to the founding of them on geographical discriminations. Let me now take a more comprehensive view, and warn you in the most solemn manner against the baneful effects of the spirit of party generally.

This spirit, unfortunately, is inseparable from our nature, having its root in the strongest passions of the human mind. It exists under different shapes in all governments, more or less stifled, controlled, or repressed; but, in those of the popular form, it is seen in its greatest rankness, and is truly their worst enemy.

The alternate domination of one faction over another, sharpened by the spirit of revenge, natural to party dissension, which in different ages and countries has perpetrated the most horrid enormities, is itself a frightful despotism. But this leads at length to a more formal and permanent despotism. The disorders and miseries which result gradually incline the minds of men to seek security and repose in the absolute power of an individual; and sooner or later the chief of some prevailing faction, more able or more fortunate than his competitors, turns this disposition to the purposes of his own elevation, on the ruins of public liberty.

Without looking forward to an extremity of this kind (which nevertheless ought not to be entirely out of sight), the common and continual mischiefs of the spirit of party are sufficient to make it the interest and duty of a wise people to discourage and restrain it.

It serves always to distract the public councils and enfeeble the public administration. It agitates the community with ill-founded jealousies and false alarms, kindles the animosity of one part against another, foments occasionally riot and insurrection. It opens the door to foreign influence and corruption, which finds a facilitated access to the government itself through the channels of party passions. Thus the policy and the will of one country are subjected to the policy and will of another.

There is an opinion that parties in free countries are useful checks upon the administration of the government and serve to keep alive the spirit of liberty. This within certain limits is probably true; and in governments of a monarchical cast, patriotism may look with indulgence, if not with favor, upon the spirit of party. But in those of the popular character, in governments purely elective, it is a spirit not to be encouraged. From their natural tendency, it is certain there will always be enough of that spirit for every salutary purpose. And there being constant danger of excess, the effort ought to be by force of public opinion, to mitigate and assuage it. A fire not to be quenched, it demands a uniform vigilance to prevent its bursting into a flame, lest, instead of warming, it should consume.

It is important, likewise, that the habits of thinking in a free country should inspire caution in those entrusted with its administration, to confine themselves within their respective constitutional spheres, avoiding in the exercise of the powers of one department to encroach upon another. The spirit of encroachment tends to consolidate the powers of all the departments in one, and thus to create, whatever the form of government, a real despotism. A just estimate of that love of power, and proneness to abuse it, which predominates in the human heart, is sufficient to satisfy us of the truth of this position. The necessity of reciprocal checks in the exercise of political power, by dividing and distributing it into different depositaries, and constituting each the guardian of the public weal against invasions by the others, has been evinced by experiments ancient and modern; some of them in our country and under our own eyes. To preserve them must be as necessary as to institute them. If, in the opinion of the people, the distribution or modification of the constitutional powers be in any particular wrong, let it be corrected by an amendment in the way which the Constitution designates. But let there be no change by usurpation; for though this, in one instance, may be the instrument of good, it is the customary weapon by which free governments are destroyed. The precedent must always greatly overbalance in permanent evil any partial or transient benefit, which the use can at any time yield.

Of all the dispositions and habits which lead to political prosperity, religion and morality are indispensable supports. In vain would that man claim the tribute of patriotism, who should labor to subvert these great pillars of human happiness, these firmest props of the duties of men and citizens. The mere politician, equally with the pious man, ought to respect and to cherish them. A volume could not trace all their connections with private and public felicity. Let it simply be asked: Where is the security for property, for reputation, for life, if the sense of religious obligation desert the oaths which are the instruments of investigation in courts of justice ? And let us with caution indulge the supposition that morality can be maintained without religion. Whatever may be conceded to the influence of refined education on minds of peculiar structure, reason and experience both forbid us to expect that national morality can prevail in exclusion of religious principle.

It is substantially true that virtue or morality is a necessary spring of popular government. The rule, indeed, extends with more or less force to every species of free government. Who that is a sincere friend to it can look with indifference upon attempts to shake the foundation of the fabric?

Promote then, as an object of primary importance, institutions for the general diffusion of knowledge. In proportion as the structure of a government gives force to public opinion, it is essential that public opinion should be enlightened.

As a very important source of strength and security, cherish public credit. One method of preserving it is to use it as sparingly as possible, avoiding occasions of expense by cultivating peace, but remembering also that timely disbursements to prepare for danger frequently prevent much greater disbursements to repel it, avoiding likewise the accumulation of debt, not only by shunning occasions of expense, but by vigorous exertion in time of peace to discharge the debts which unavoidable wars may have occasioned, not ungenerously throwing upon posterity the burden which we ourselves ought to bear. The execution of these maxims belongs to your representatives, but it is necessary that public opinion should co-operate. To facilitate to them the performance of their duty, it is essential that you should practically bear in mind that towards the payment of debts there must be revenue; that to have revenue there must be taxes; that no taxes can be devised which are not more or less inconvenient and unpleasant; that the intrinsic embarrassment, inseparable from the selection of the proper objects (which is always a choice of difficulties), ought to be a decisive motive for a candid construction of the conduct of the government in making it, and for a spirit of acquiescence in the measures for obtaining revenue, which the public exigencies may at any time dictate.

Observe good faith and justice towards all nations; cultivate peace and harmony with all. Religion and morality enjoin this conduct; and can it be, that good policy does not equally enjoin it —it will be worthy of a free, enlightened, and at no distant period, a great nation, to give to mankind the magnanimous and too novel example of a people always guided by an exalted justice and benevolence. Who can doubt that, in the course of time and things, the fruits of such a plan would richly repay any temporary advantages which might be lost by a steady adherence to it ? Can it be that Providence has not connected the permanent felicity of a nation with its virtue? The experiment, at least, is recommended by every sentiment which ennobles human nature. Alas! is it rendered impossible by its vices?

In the execution of such a plan, nothing is more essential than that permanent, inveterate antipathies against particular nations, and passionate attachments for others, should be excluded; and that, in place of them, just and amicable feelings towards all should be cultivated. The nation which indulges towards another a habitual hatred or a habitual fondness is in some degree a slave. It is a slave to its animosity or to its affection, either of which is sufficient to lead it astray from its duty and its interest. Antipathy in one nation against another disposes each more readily to offer insult and injury, to lay hold of slight causes of umbrage, and to be haughty and intractable, when accidental or trifling occasions of dispute occur. Hence, frequent collisions, obstinate, envenomed, and bloody contests. The nation, prompted by ill-will and resentment, sometimes impels to war the government, contrary to the best calculations of policy. The government sometimes participates in the national propensity, and adopts through passion what reason would reject; at other times it makes the animosity of the nation subservient to projects of hostility instigated by pride, ambition, and other sinister and pernicious motives. The peace often, sometimes perhaps the liberty, of nations, has been the victim.

So likewise, a passionate attachment of one nation for another produces a variety of evils. Sympathy for the favorite nation, facilitating the illusion of an imaginary common interest in cases where no real common interest exists, and infusing into one the enmities of the other, betrays the former into a participation in the quarrels and wars of the latter without adequate inducement or justification. It leads also to concessions to the favorite nation of privileges denied to others which is apt doubly to injure the nation making the concessions; by unnecessarily parting with what ought to have been retained, and by exciting jealousy, ill-will, and a disposition to retaliate, in the parties from whom equal privileges are withheld. And it gives to ambitious, corrupted, or deluded citizens (who devote themselves to the favorite nation), facility to betray or sacrifice the interests of their own country, without odium, sometimes even with popularity; gilding, with the appearances of a virtuous sense of obligation, a commendable deference for public opinion, or a laudable zeal for public good, the base or foolish compliances of ambition, corruption, or infatuation.

As avenues to foreign influence in innumerable ways, such attachments are particularly alarming to the truly enlightened and independent patriot. How many opportunities do they afford to tamper with domestic factions, to practice the arts of seduction, to mislead public opinion, to influence or awe the public councils.

Such an attachment of a small or weak towards a great and powerful nation dooms the former to be the satellite of the latter.

Against the insidious wiles of foreign influence (I conjure you to believe me, fellow-citizens) the jealousy of a free people ought to be constantly awake, since history and experience prove that foreign influence is one of the most baneful foes of republican government. But that jealousy to be useful must be impartial; else it becomes the instrument of the very influence to be avoided, instead of a defense against it. Excessive partiality for one foreign nation and excessive dislike of another cause those whom they actuate to see danger only on one side, and serve to veil and even second the arts of influence on the other. Real patriots who may resist the intrigues of the favorite are liable to become suspected and odious, while its tools and dupes usurp the applause and confidence of the people, to surrender their interests.

The great rule of conduct for us in regard to foreign nations is in extending our commercial relations, to have with them as little political connection as possible. So far as we have already formed engagements, let them be fulfilled with perfect good faith. Here let us stop. Europe has a set of primary interests which to us have none; or a very remote relation. Hence she must be engaged in frequent controversies, the causes of which are essentially foreign to our concerns. Hence, therefore, it must be unwise in us to implicate ourselves by artificial ties in the ordinary vicissitudes of her politics, or the ordinary combinations and collisions of her friendships or enmities.

Our detached and distant situation invites and enables us to pursue a different course. If we remain one people under an efficient government. the period is not far off when we may defy material injury from external annoyance; when we may take such an attitude as will cause the neutrality we may at any time resolve upon to be scrupulously respected; when belligerent nations, under the impossibility of making acquisitions upon us, will not lightly hazard the giving us provocation; when we may choose peace or war, as our interest, guided by justice, shall counsel.

Why forego the advantages of so peculiar a situation? Why quit our own to stand upon foreign ground? Why, by interweaving our destiny with that of any part of Europe, entangle our peace and prosperity in the toils of European ambition, rivalship, interest, humor or caprice?

It is our true policy to steer clear of permanent alliances with any portion of the foreign world; so far, I mean, as we are now at liberty to do it; for let me not be understood as capable of patronizing infidelity to existing engagements. I hold the maxim no less applicable to public than to private affairs, that honesty is always the best policy. I repeat it, therefore, let those engagements be observed in their genuine sense. But, in my opinion, it is unnecessary and would be unwise to extend them.

Taking care always to keep ourselves by suitable establishments on a respectable defensive posture, we may safely trust to temporary alliances for extraordinary emergencies.

Harmony, liberal intercourse with all nations, are recommended by policy, humanity, and interest. But even our commercial policy should hold an equal and impartial hand; neither seeking nor granting exclusive favors or preferences; consulting the natural course of things; diffusing and diversifying by gentle means the streams of commerce, but forcing nothing; establishing (with powers so disposed, in order to give trade a stable course, to define the rights of our merchants, and to enable the government to support them) conventional rules of intercourse, the best that present circumstances and mutual opinion will permit, but temporary, and liable to be from time to time abandoned or varied, as experience and circumstances shall dictate; constantly keeping in view that it is folly in one nation to look for disinterested favors from another; that it must pay with a portion of its independence for whatever it may accept under that character; that, by such acceptance, it may place itself in the condition of having given equivalents for nominal favors, and yet of being reproached with ingratitude for not giving more. There can be no greater error than to expect or calculate upon real favors from nation to nation. It is an illusion, which experience must cure, which a just pride ought to discard.

In offering to you, my countrymen, these counsels of an old and affectionate friend, I dare not hope they will make the strong and lasting impression I could wish; that they will control the usual current of the passions, or prevent our nation from running the course which has hitherto marked the destiny of nations. But, if I may even flatter myself that they may be productive of some partial benefit, some occasional good; that they may now and then recur to moderate the fury of party spirit, to warn against the mischiefs of foreign intrigue, to guard against the impostures of pretended patriotism; this hope will be a full recompense for the solicitude for your welfare, by which they have been dictated.

How far in the discharge of my official duties I have been guided by the principles which have been delineated, the public records and other evidences of my conduct must witness to you and to the world. To myself, the assurance of my own conscience is, that I have at least believed myself to be guided by them.

In relation to the still subsisting war in Europe, my proclamation of the twenty-second of April, 1793, is the index of my plan. Sanctioned by your approving voice, and by that of your representatives in both houses of Congress, the spirit of that measure has continually governed me, uninfluenced by any attempts to deter or divert me from it.

After deliberate examination, with the aid of the best lights I could obtain, I was well satisfied that our country, under all the circumstances of the case, had a right to take, and was bound in duty and interest to take, a neutral position. Having taken it, I determined, as far as should depend upon me, to maintain it, with moderation, perseverance, and firmness.

The considerations which respect the right to hold this conduct, it is not necessary on this occasion to detail. I will only observe that, according to my understanding of the matter, that right, so far from being denied by any of the belligerent powers, has been virtually admitted by all.

The duty of holding a neutral conduct may be inferred, without anything more, from the obligation which justice and humanity impose on every nation, in cases in which it is free to act, to maintain inviolate the relations of peace and amity towards other nations.

The inducements of interest for observing that conduct will best be referred to your own reflections and experience. With me a predominant motive has been to endeavor to gain time to our country to settle and mature its yet recent institutions, and to progress without interruption to that degree of strength and consistency which is necessary to give it, humanly speaking, the command of its own fortunes.

Though, in reviewing the incidents of my administration, I am unconscious of intentional error, I am nevertheless too sensible of my defects not to think it probable that I may have committed many errors. Whatever they may be, I fervently beseech the Almighty to avert or mitigate the evils to which they may tend. I shall also carry with me the hope that my country will never cease to view them with indulgence; and that, after forty five years of my life dedicated to its service with an upright zeal, the faults of incompetent abilities will be consigned to oblivion, as myself must soon be to the mansions of rest.

Relying on its kindness in this as in other things, and actuated by that fervent love towards it, which is so natural to a man who views in it the native soil of himself and his progenitors for several generations, I anticipate with pleasing expectation that retreat in which I promise myself to realize, without alloy, the sweet enjoyment of partaking, in the midst of my fellow-citizens, the benign influence of good laws under a free government, the ever-favorite object of my heart, and the happy reward, as I trust, of our mutual cares, labors, and dangers.

—George Washington

Declaration of Sentiments
and
We Now Demand Our Right to Vote

Elizabeth Cady Stanton

Elizabeth Cady Stanton (1815–1902) was a lifelong advocate for the rights of women. She was formally educated (in Latin, Greek, mathematics, science, and French, as well as in religion) at Johnstown Academy, where she competed intellectually with boys in co-educational classes and won several academic awards, and at the Troy Female Seminary (later called the Emma Willard School). She was active in support of the abolitionist and temperance movements and, along with Lucretia Mott, organized the Seneca Falls Women's Rights Convention, which initiated the women's suffrage movement. Her lifetime of impassioned arguments, along with those of her friend and co-suffragist Susan B. Anthony, significantly influenced the ultimate passage (eighteen years after her death) of the 19th Amendment to the U.S. Constitution, giving women the right to vote.

At 11AM on the morning of July 19, 1848, the Seneca Falls Women's Rights Convention met. The first event at the convention was Elizabeth Cady Stanton's reading of the "Declaration of Sentiments" that she offered for the acceptance of the convention. The style of this declaration might remind you of another famous declaration from seventy two years prior. Later in the day, she offered a defense of the resolutions calling for women's suffrage that the assembly had passed. Her defense is entitled "We Now Demand Our Right to Vote."

Both speeches delivered July 19, 1848, in Seneca Falls, New York

Declaration of Sentiments

When, in the course of human events, it becomes necessary for one portion of the family of man to assume among the people of the earth a position different from that which they have hitherto occupied, but one to which the laws of nature and of nature's God entitle them, a decent respect to the opinions of mankind requires that they should declare the causes that impel them to such a course.

We hold these truths to be self-evident: that all men and women are created equal; that they are endowed by their Creator with certain inalienable rights; that among these are life, liberty, and the pursuit of happiness; that to secure these rights governments are instituted, deriving their just powers from the consent of the governed. Whenever any form of government becomes destructive of these ends, it is the right of those who suffer from it to refuse allegiance to it, and to insist upon the institution of a new government, laying its foundation on such principles, and organizing its powers in such form, as to them shall seem most likely to effect their safety and happiness.

Prudence, indeed, will dictate that governments long established should not be changed for light and transient causes; and, accordingly, all experience has shown that mankind are more disposed to suffer, while evils are sufferable, than to right themselves by abolishing the forms to which they were accustomed. But when a long train of abuses and usurpations, pursuing invariably the same object, evinces a design to reduce them under absolute despotism, it is their duty to throw off such government and to provide new guards for their future security. Such has been the patient sufferance of the women under this government, and such is now the necessity which constrains them to demand the equal station to which they are entitled.

The history of mankind is a history of repeated injuries and usurpations on the part of man toward woman, having in direct object the establishment of an absolute tyranny over her. To prove this, let facts be submitted to a candid world.

He has never permitted her to exercise her inalienable right to the elective franchise.

He has compelled her to submit to law in the formation of which she had no voice.

He has withheld from her rights which are given to the most ignorant and degraded men, both natives and foreigners. Having deprived her of this first right as a citizen, the elective franchise, thereby leaving her without representation in the halls of legislation, he has oppressed her on all sides.

He has made her, if married, in the eye of the law, civilly dead.

He has taken from her all right in property, even to the wages she earns.

He has made her morally, an irresponsible being, as she can commit many crimes with impunity, provided they be done in the presence of her husband.

In the covenant of marriage, she is compelled to promise obedience to her husband, he becoming, to all intents and purposes, her master—the law giving him power to deprive her of her liberty and to administer chastisement.

He has so framed the laws of divorce, as to what shall be the proper causes and, in case of separation, to whom the guardianship of the children shall be given, as to be wholly regardless of the happiness of the women—the law, in all cases, going upon a false supposition of the supremacy of man and giving all power into his hands.

After depriving her of all rights as a married woman, if single and the owner of property, he has taxed her to support a government which recognizes her only when her property can be made profitable to it.

He has monopolized nearly all the profitable employments, and from those she is permitted to follow, she receives but a scanty remuneration. He closes against her all the avenues to wealth and distinction which he considers most honorable to himself. As a teacher of theology, medicine, or law, she is not known.

He has denied her the facilities for obtaining a thorough education, all colleges being closed against her.

He allows her in church, as well as state, but a subordinate position, claiming apostolic authority for her exclusion from the ministry, and, with some exceptions, from any public participation in the affairs of the church.

He has created a false public sentiment by giving to the world a different code of morals for men and women, by which moral delinquencies which exclude women from society are not only tolerated but deemed of little account in man.

He has usurped the prerogative of Jehovah himself, claiming it as his right to assign for her a sphere of action, when that belongs to her conscience and to her God.

He has endeavored, in every way that he could, to destroy her confidence in her own powers, to lessen her self-respect, and to make her willing to lead a dependent and abject life. Now, in view of this entire disfranchisement of one-half the people of this country, their social and religious degradation, in view of the unjust laws above mentioned, and because women do feel themselves aggrieved, oppressed, and fraudulently deprived of their most sacred rights, we insist that they have immediate admission to all the rights and privileges which belong to them as citizens of the United States.

In entering upon the great work before us, we anticipate no small amount of misconception, misrepresentation, and ridicule; but we shall use every instrumentality within our power to effect our object. We shall employ agents, circulate tracts, petition the state and national legislatures, and endeavor to enlist the pulpit and the press in our behalf. We hope this Convention will be followed by a series of conventions embracing every part of the country.

[after the Declaration was read, the following resolutions were read]

Whereas, the great precept of nature is conceded to be that "man shall pursue his own true and substantial happiness." Blackstone in his Commentaries remarks that this law of nature, being coeval with mankind and dictated by God himself, is, of course, superior in obligation to any other. It is binding over all the globe, in all countries and at all times; no human laws are of any validity if contrary to this, and such of them as are valid derive all their force, and all their validity, and all their authority, mediately and immediately, from this original; therefore,

Resolved, that such laws as conflict, in any way, with the true and substantial happiness of woman, are contrary to the great precept of nature and of no validity, for this is "superior in obligation to any other."

Resolved, that all laws which prevent woman from occupying such a station in society as her conscience shall dictate, or which place her in a position inferior to that of man, are contrary to the great precept of nature and therefore of no force or authority.

Resolved, that woman is man's equal, was intended to be so by the Creator, and the highest good of the race demands that she should be recognized as such.

Resolved, that the women of this country ought to be enlightened in regard to the laws under which they live, that they may no longer publish their degradation by declaring themselves satisfied with their present position, nor their ignorance, by asserting that they have all the rights they want.

Resolved, that inasmuch as man, while claiming for himself intellectual superiority, does accord to woman moral superiority, it is preeminently his duty to encourage her to speak and teach, as she has an opportunity, in all religious assemblies.

Resolved, that the same amount of virtue, delicacy, and refinement of behavior that is required of woman in the social state also be required of man, and the same transgressions should be visited with equal severity on both man and woman.

Resolved, that the objection of indelicacy and impropriety, which is so often brought against woman when she addresses a public audience, comes with a very ill grace from those who encourage, by their attendance, her appearance on the stage, in the concert, or in feats of the circus.

Resolved, that woman has too long rested satisfied in the circumscribed limits which corrupt customs and a perverted application of the Scriptures have marked out for her, and that it is time she should move in the enlarged sphere which her great Creator has assigned her.

Resolved, that it is the duty of the women of this country to secure to themselves their sacred right to the elective franchise.

Resolved, that the equality of human rights results necessarily from the fact of the identity of the race in capabilities and responsibilities.

Resolved, that the speedy success of our cause depends upon the zealous and untiring efforts of both men and women for the overthrow of the monopoly of the pulpit, and for the securing to woman an equal participation with men in the various trades, professions, and commerce.

Resolved, therefore, that, being invested by the Creator with the same capabilities and same consciousness of responsibility for their exercise, it is demonstrably the right and duty of woman, equally with man, to promote every righteous cause by every righteous means; and especially in regard to the great subjects of morals and religion, it is self-evidently her right to participate with her brother in teaching them, both in private and in public, by writing and by speaking, by any instrumentalities proper to be used, and in any assemblies proper to be held; and this being a self-evident truth growing out of the divinely implanted principles of human nature, any custom or authority adverse to it, whether modern or wearing the hoary sanction of antiquity, is to be regarded as a self-evident falsehood, and at war with mankind.

We Now Demand Our Right to Vote

We have met here today to discuss our rights and wrongs, civil and political, and not, as some have supposed, to go into the detail of social life alone. We do not propose to petition the legislature to make our husbands just, generous, and courteous, to seat every man at the head of a cradle, and to clothe every woman in male attire. None of these points, however important they may be considered by leading men, will be touched in this convention. As to their costume, the gentlemen need feel no fear of our imitating that, for we think it in violation of every principle of taste, beauty, and dignity; notwithstanding all the contempt cast upon our loose, flowing garments, we still admire the graceful folds, and consider our costume far more artistic than theirs. Many of the nobler sex seem to agree with us in this opinion, for the bishops, priests, judges, barristers, and lord mayors of the first nation on the globe, and the Pope of Rome, with his cardinals, too, all wear the loose flowing robes, thus tacitly acknowledging that the male attire is neither dignified nor imposing. No, we shall not molest you in your philosophical experiments with stocks, pants, high-heeled boots, and Russian belts. Yours be the glory to discover, by personal experience, how long the kneepan can resist the terrible strapping down which you impose, in how short time the well-developed muscles of the throat can be reduced to mere threads by the constant pressure of the stock, how high the heel of a boot must be to make a short man tall, and how tight the Russian belt may be drawn and yet have wind enough left to sustain life.

But we are assembled to protest against a form of government existing without the consent of the governed—to declare our right to be free as man is free, to be represented in the government which we are taxed to support, to have such disgraceful laws as give man the power to chastise and imprison his wife, to take the wages which she earns, the property which she inherits, and, in case of separation, the children of her love; laws which make her the mere dependent on his bounty. It is to protest against such unjust laws as these that we are assembled today, and to have them, if possible, forever erased from our statute books, deeming them a shame and a disgrace to a Christian republic in the nineteenth century.

We have met "To uplift woman's fallen divinity / Upon an even pedestal with man's."[1]

And, strange as it may seem to many, we now demand our right to vote according to the declaration of the government under which we live. This right no one pretends to deny. We need not prove ourselves equal to Daniel Webster to enjoy this privilege, for the ignorant Irishman in the ditch has all the civil rights he has. We need not prove our muscular power equal to this same Irishman to enjoy this privilege, for the most tiny, weak, ill-shaped stripling of twenty-one has all the civil rights of the Irishman. We have no objection to discuss the question of equality, for we feel that the weight of argument lies wholly with us, but we wish the question of equality kept distinct from the question of rights, for the proof of the one does not determine the truth of the other. All white men in this country have the same rights, however they may differ in mind, body, or estate.

The right is ours. The question now is: how shall we get possession of what rightfully belongs to us? We should not feel so sorely grieved if no man who had not attained the full stature of a Webster, Clay, Van Buren, or Gerrit Smith could claim the right of the elective franchise. But to have drunkards, idiots, horse-racing, rum-selling rowdies, ignorant foreigners, and silly boys fully recognized, while we ourselves are thrust out from all the rights that belong to citizens, it is too grossly insulting to the dignity of woman to be longer quietly submitted to. The right is ours. Have it, we must. Use it, we will. The pens, the tongues, the fortunes, the indomitable wills of many women are already pledged to secure this right. The great truth that no just government can be formed without the consent of the governed we shall echo and re-echo in the ears of the unjust judge, until by continual coming we shall weary him.

There seems now to be a kind of moral stagnation in our midst. Philanthropists have done their utmost to rouse the nation to a sense of its sins. War, slavery, drunkenness, licentiousness, gluttony, have been dragged naked before the people, and all their abominations and deformities fully brought to light, yet with idiotic laugh we hug those monsters to our breasts and rush on to

---

[1] A reference to Alfred Lord Tennyson, The Princess, 1847, ll. 207–208.

destruction. Our churches are multiplying on all sides, our missionary societies, Sunday schools, and prayer meetings and innumerable charitable and reform organizations are all in operation, but still the tide of vice is swelling, and threatens the destruction of everything, and the battlements of righteousness are weak against the raging elements of sin and death. Verily, the world waits the coming of some new element, some purifying power, some spirit of mercy and love. The voice of woman has been silenced in the state, the church, and the home, but man cannot fulfill his destiny alone, he cannot redeem his race unaided. There are deep and tender chords of sympathy and love in the hearts of the downfallen and oppressed that woman can touch more skillfully than man.

The world has never yet seen a truly great and virtuous nation, because in the degradation of woman the very fountains of life are poisoned at their source. It is vain to look for silver and gold from mines of copper and lead. It is the wise mother that has the wise son. So long as your women are slaves you may throw your colleges and churches to the winds. You can't have scholars and saints so long as your mothers are ground to powder between the upper and nether millstone of tyranny and lust. How seldom, now, is a father's pride gratified, his fond hopes realized, in the budding genius of his son! The wife is degraded, made the mere creature of caprice, and the foolish son is heaviness to his heart. Truly are the sins of the fathers visited upon the children to the third and fourth generation. God, in His wisdom, has so linked the whole human family together that any violence done at one end of the chain is felt throughout its length, and here, too, is the law of restoration, as in woman all have fallen, so in her elevation shall the race be recreated.

"Voices" were the visitors and advisers of Joan of Arc. Do not "voices" come to us daily from the haunts of poverty, sorrow, degradation, and despair, already too long unheeded. Now is the time for the women of this country, if they would save our free institutions, to defend the right, to buckle on the armor that can best resist the keenest weapons of the enemy—contempt and ridicule. The same religious enthusiasm that nerved Joan of Arc to her work nerves us to ours. In every generation God calls some men and women for the utterance of truth, a heroic action, and our work today is the fulfilling of what has long since been foretold by the Prophet—Joel 2:28: "And it shall come to pass afterward, that I will pour out my spirit upon all flesh; and your sons and your daughters shall prophesy." We do not expect our path will be strewn with the flowers of popular applause, but over the thorns of bigotry and prejudice will be our way, and on our banners will beat the dark storm clouds of opposition from those who have entrenched themselves behind the stormy bulwarks of custom and authority, and who have fortified their position by every means, holy and unholy. But we will steadfastly abide the result. Unmoved we will bear it aloft. Undauntedly we will unfurl it to the gale, for we know that the storm cannot rend from it a shred, that the electric flash will but more clearly show to us the glorious words inscribed upon it, "Equality of Rights."

Second Inaugural Address

Abraham Lincoln

Five weeks before his assassination, Abraham Lincoln (1809–1865) delivered his second inaugural address from the steps of the Capitol.

In less than a thousand words, Lincoln gives a complete narrative of the previous four years and sets forth his goals for the next four. In his first sentence he states that in this, his second inaugural address, "there is less occasion for an extended address than there was at the first." He knew that the Civil War was coming to an end and that the Union would be the victor.

In the speech Lincoln reiterates his condemnation of slavery, but his rebuke ends there. Instead of taking a triumphalist approach, describing the events of the Civil War in detail and trumpeting the victory of the North, a stance that many people may have expected, Lincoln opts for a public call for reconciliation, exemplified in one of the most oft-quoted lines from the speech: "with malice toward none; with charity for all." Highlighting the need for the North and the South to focus on their similarities, not their differences, he reminds his divided audience of the characteristics they hold in common: "Neither party expected for the war the magnitude or the duration which it has already attained. . . . Both read the same Bible, and pray to the same God . . . ." Both sides having suffered in the war, he exhorts his audience to achieve a true reunification by striving together for "a just and lasting peace among ourselves and with all nations."

Just over a month later, on April 9, 1865, Robert E. Lee surrendered his Army of Northern Virginia, ending the Civil War. Five days after that, Abraham Lincoln was assassinated by John Wilkes Booth, a Southern sympathizer. A funeral train carried Lincoln's body back to Springfield, Illinois, through all the states Lincoln had visited on his way to Washington, DC, as president-elect. Crowds of mourners lined the route and many thousands turned out at every stop to honor the beloved fallen leader.

Delivered March 4, 1865, at the United States Capitol, Washington, DC.

Fellow-countrymen: At this second appearing to take the oath of the presidential office, there is less occasion for an extended address than there was at the first. Then a statement, somewhat in detail, of a course to be pursued, seemed fitting and proper. Now, at the expiration of four years, during which public declarations have been constantly called forth on every point and phase of the great contest which still absorbs the attention and engrosses the energies of the nation, little that is new could be presented. The progress of our arms, upon which all else chiefly depends, is as well known to the public as to myself; and it is, I trust, reasonably satisfactory and encouraging to all. With high hope for the future, no prediction in regard to it is ventured.

On the occasion corresponding to this four years ago, all thoughts were anxiously directed to an impending civil war. All dreaded it—all sought to avert it. While the inaugural address was being delivered from this place, devoted altogether to saving the Union without war, insurgent agents were in the city seeking to destroy it without war—seeking to dissolve the Union, and divide effects, by negotiation. Both parties deprecated war; but one of them would make war rather than let the nation survive; and the other would accept war rather than let it perish. And the war came.

One-eighth of the whole population were colored slaves, not distributed generally over the Union, but localized in the Southern part of it. These slaves constituted a peculiar and powerful interest. All knew that this interest was, somehow, the cause of the war. To strengthen, perpetuate, and extend this interest was the object for which the insurgents would rend the Union, even by war; while the government claimed no right to do more than to restrict the territorial enlargement of it.

Neither party expected for the war the magnitude or the duration which it has already attained. Neither anticipated that the cause of the conflict might cease with, or even before, the conflict itself should cease. Each looked for an easier triumph, and a result less fundamental and astounding. Both read the same Bible, and pray to the same God; and each invokes his aid against the other. It may seem strange that any men should dare to ask a just God's assistance in wringing their bread from the sweat of other men's faces; but let us judge not, that we be not judged. The prayers of both could not be answered—that of neither has been answered fully.

The Almighty has his own purposes. "Woe unto the world because of offenses! for it must needs be that offenses come; but woe to that man by whom the offense cometh." If we shall suppose that American slavery is one of those offenses which, in the providence of God, must needs come, but which, having continued through his appointed time, he now wills to remove, and that he gives to both North and South this terrible war, as the woe due to those by whom the offense came, shall we discern therein any departure from those divine attributes which the believers in a living God always ascribe to him? Fondly do we hope—fervently do we pray—that this mighty scourge of war may speedily pass away. Yet, if God wills that it continue until all the wealth piled by the bondman's two hundred and fifty years of unrequited toil shall be sunk, and until every drop of blood drawn with the lash shall be paid by another drawn with the sword, as was said three thousand years ago, so still it must be said, "The judgments of the Lord are true and righteous altogether."

With malice toward none; with charity for all; with firmness in the right, as God gives us to see the right, let us strive on to finish the work we are in; to bind up the nation's wounds; to care for him who shall have borne the battle, and for his widow, and his orphan—to do all which may achieve and cherish a just and lasting peace among ourselves, and with all nations.

On Liberty
Excerpt from Book II,
Of the Liberty of Thought
and Discussion
John Stuart Mill

John Stuart Mill (1806–1873) was one of the most influential British thinkers of the 19th Century. Political philosopher, economic philosopher, civil servant, Rector of the University of Saint Andrews, Mill was also a Member of Parliament and the first to call for the right to vote to be given to women. A precocious child, raised by his father in a strict and demanding regimen that later led to a temporary mental breakdown, Mill was taught Greek at three years old and Latin at eight. He studied the classics, as well as mathematics, and could read Plato and Aristotle in Greek by the age of ten. At twelve he studied the logic of the Scholastic philosophers of the Middle Ages. He also composed an addition to the Iliad of Homer. Early a follower of the utilitarianism of his father's friend Jeremy Bentham, Mill later would distinguish, as Bentham did not, between lower and higher pleasures in seeking the greatest pleasure for the greatest number. He wrote on logic, political economy, representative government, the subjection of women, and religion, and he composed an autobiography.

Mill's book On Liberty, *published in 1859, discusses the relation between authority and individual liberty in light of his commitment to his version of utilitarianism, whose goal was the individual's achievement of what he called the "higher pleasures." That goal could be achieved only under conditions of individual liberty, which is limited only by the requirement to prevent harm to others. "Over himself, over his body and mind, the individual is sovereign," though Mill made exceptions for children and "barbarians," who are benefitted by some limitation of their freedom. Mill was especially concerned about the "tyranny of the majority," which could suppress individual liberty not necessarily by potentially reversible government action but by the subtle and more powerful pressure of majority opinion and culture.*

In our excerpt Mill argues that the expression of individual opinions—no matter how much they differ from received ideas, the opinions of the majority, or the moral codes of society and religion—ought never to be suppressed.

Published in 1859

...Let us suppose, therefore, that the government is entirely at one with the people, and never thinks of exerting any power of coercion unless in agreement with what it conceives to be their voice. But I deny the right of the people to exercise such coercion, either by themselves or by their government. The power itself is illegitimate. The best government has no more title to it than the worst. It is as noxious, or more noxious, when exerted in accordance with public opinion, than when in or opposition to it. If all mankind minus one, were of one opinion, and only one person were of the contrary opinion, mankind would be no more justified in silencing that one person, than he, if he had the power, would be justified in silencing mankind. Were an opinion a personal possession of no value except to the owner; if to be obstructed in the enjoyment of it were simply a private injury, it would make some difference whether the injury was inflicted only on a few persons or on many. But the peculiar evil of silencing the expression of an opinion is, that it is robbing the human race; posterity as well as the existing generation; those who dissent from the opinion, still more than those who hold it. If the opinion is right, they are deprived of the opportunity of exchanging error for truth: if wrong, they lose, what is almost as great a benefit, the clearer perception and livelier impression of truth, produced by its collision with error.

It is necessary to consider separately these two hypotheses, each of which has a distinct branch of the argument corresponding to it. We can never be sure that the opinion we are endeavouring to stifle is a false opinion; and if we were sure, stifling it would be an evil still.

First: the opinion which it is attempted to suppress by authority may possibly be true. Those who desire to suppress it, of course deny its truth; but they are not infallible. They have no authority to decide the question for all mankind, and exclude every other person from the means of judging. To refuse a hearing to an opinion, because they are sure that it is false, is to assume that *their* certainty is the same thing as *absolute* certainty. All silencing of discussion is an assumption of infallibility. Its condemnation may be allowed to rest on this common argument, not the worse for being common.

Unfortunately for the good sense of mankind, the fact of their fallibility is far from carrying the weight in their practical judgment, which is always allowed to it in theory; for while every one well knows himself to be fallible, few think it necessary to take any precautions against their own fallibility, or admit the supposition that any opinion, of which they feel very certain, may be one of the examples of the error to which they acknowledge themselves to be liable. Absolute princes, or others who are accustomed to unlimited deference, usually feel this complete confidence in their own opinions on nearly all subjects. People more happily situated, who sometimes hear their opinions disputed, and are not wholly unused to be set right when they are wrong, place the same unbounded reliance only on such of their opinions as are shared by all who surround them, or to whom they habitually defer: for in proportion to a man's want of confidence in his own solitary judgment, does he usually repose, with implicit trust, on the infallibility of "the world" in general. And the world, to each individual, means the part of it with which he comes in contact; his party, his sect, his church, his class of society: the man may be called, by comparison, almost liberal and large-minded to whom it means anything so comprehensive as his own country or his own age. Nor is his faith in this collective authority at all shaken by his being aware that other ages, countries, sects, churches, classes, and parties have thought, and even now think, the exact reverse. He devolves upon his own world the responsibility of being in the right against the dissentient worlds of other people; and it never troubles him that mere accident has decided which of these numerous worlds is the object of his reliance, and that the same causes which make him a Churchman in London, would have made him a Buddhist or a Confucian in Pekin. Yet it is as evident in itself as any amount of argument can make it, that ages are no more infallible than individuals; every age having held many opinions which subsequent ages have deemed not only false but absurd; and it is as certain that many opinions, now general, will be rejected by future ages, as it is that many, once general, are rejected by the present.

The objection likely to be made to this argument, would probably take some such form as the following. There is no greater assumption of infallibility in forbidding the propagation of error, than in any other thing which is done by public authority on its own judgment and responsibility. Judgment is given to men that they may use it. Because it may be used erroneously, are men to be told that they ought not to use it at all? To prohibit what they think pernicious, is not claiming exemption from error, but fulfilling the duty incumbent on them, although fallible, of acting on their conscientious conviction. If we were never to act on our opinions, because those opinions may be wrong, we should leave all our interests uncared for, and all our duties unperformed. An objection which applies to all conduct, can be no valid objection to any conduct in particular. It is the duty of governments, and of individuals, to form the truest opinions they can; to form them carefully, and never impose them upon others unless they are quite sure of being right. But when they are sure (such reasoners may say), it is not conscientiousness but cowardice to shrink from acting on their opinions, and allow doctrines which they honestly think dangerous to the welfare of mankind, either in this life or in another, to be scattered abroad without restraint, because other people, in less enlightened times, have persecuted opinions now believed to be true. Let us take care, it may be said, not to make the same mistake: but governments and nations have made mistakes in other things, which are not denied to be fit subjects for the exercise of authority: they have laid on bad taxes, made unjust wars. Ought we therefore to lay on no taxes, and, under whatever provocation, make no wars? Men, and governments, must act to the best of their ability. There is no such thing as absolute certainty, but there is assurance sufficient for the purposes of human life. We may, and must, assume our opinion to be true for the guidance of our own conduct: and it is assuming no more when we forbid bad men to pervert society by the propagation of opinions which we regard as false and pernicious.

I answer that it is assuming very much more. There is the greatest difference between presuming an opinion to be true, because, with every opportunity for contesting it, it has not been refuted, and assuming its truth for the purpose of not permitting its refutation. Complete liberty of contradicting and disproving our opinion, is the very condition which justifies us in assuming its truth for purposes of action; and on no other terms can a being with human faculties have any rational assurance of being right. . . .

The Death of
Ivan Ilych
Leo Tolstoy

The Death of Ivan Ilych is a study of the meaning of suffering and death. What does it mean to die? What is the meaning of life if it must end in death? What is the meaning of the suffering that the prospect of death forces upon us? Leo Tolstoy, one of the greatest of modern writers and seekers of meaning, aims to address these questions through this work.

The story was occasioned by the actual death from cancer of a local magistrate, about whom Tolstoy heard that in his last days he had "lamented the fruitlessness of his life."[1] But Tolstoy had been contemplating for years how he could find meaning in Christianity while avoiding superstition and retaining the reason and science that modern life imposes upon us all.

The narrative technique is to give us the end of the story first, or rather the end of the objective story. Ivan Ilych dies. Once we know that ending, Tolstoy tells us the same story from within, giving us the subjective details. It is through the narration of the character's unfolding first-person experience that we discover the meaning of that ending. The outer world is represented in the story by the superficial life Ivan has lived among the Russian upper classes of the late nineteenth century. It is a world that, like ours, strives at all costs to avoid contemplation of man's mortality. The story shows us that world invaded by the inescapable facts of pain, disease, and the prospect of death. These force upon Ivan questions that he has never before tried or wanted to address.

By depicting Ivan's inner life in the context of his death, which we know from the title and the first page is inevitable, and by contrasting Ivan's inner questioning with the conventional society around him, Tolstoy is able to depict man within society, an inner life within an outer, a soul within a body, an experience of meaning within the events leading to death. Thus the meaning of life as Tolstoy sees it and the meaning of the story become one, embodied in the form of the telling itself. By allowing us to discover this meaning as we read the story, Tolstoy grants us a moment of enlightenment similar to that of Ivan Ilych himself.

---

[1] Hugh McLean, "Afterword" to Leo Tolstoy, The Death of Ivan Ilych and Other Stories (New York: Signet Classic, 2003), p. 292.

published 1886; translated by Aylmer and Louise Maude, 1934

Chapter I

During an interval in the Melvinski trial in the large building of the Law Courts the members and public prosecutor met in Ivan Egorovich Shebek's private room, where the conversation turned on the celebrated Krasovski case. Fedor Vasilievich warmly maintained that it was not subject to their jurisdiction, Ivan Egorovich maintained the contrary, while Peter Ivanovich, not having entered into the discussion at the start, took no part in it but looked through the Gazette, which had just been handed in.

"Gentlemen," he said, "Ivan Ilych has died!"

"You don't say so!"

"Here, read it yourself," replied Peter Ivanovich, handing Fedor Vasilievich the paper still damp from the press. Surrounded by a black border were the words: "Praskovya Fedorovna Golovina, with profound sorrow, informs relatives and friends of the demise of her beloved husband Ivan Ilych Golovin, Member of the Court of Justice, which occurred on February the 4th of this year 1882. The funeral will take place on Friday at one o'clock in the afternoon."

Ivan Ilych had been a colleague of the gentlemen present and was liked by them all. He had been ill for some weeks with an illness said to be incurable. His post had been kept open for him, but there had been conjectures that in case of his death Alexeev might receive his appointment, and that either Vinnikov or Shtabel would succeed Alexeev. So on receiving the news of Ivan Ilych's death the first thought of each of the gentlemen in that private room was of the changes and promotions it might occasion among themselves or their acquaintances.

"I shall be sure to get Shtabel's place or Vinnikov's," thought Fedor Vasilievich. "I was promised that long ago, and the promotion means an extra eight hundred rubles a year for me besides the allowance."

"Now I must apply for my brother-in-law's transfer from Kaluga," thought Peter Ivanovich. "My wife will be very glad, and then she won't be able to say that I never do anything for her relations."

"I thought he would never leave his bed again," said Peter Ivanovich aloud. "It's very sad."

"But what really was the matter with him?"

"The doctors couldn't say—at least they could, but each of them said something different. When last I saw him I thought he was getting better."

"And I haven't been to see him since the holidays. I always meant to go."

"Had he any property?"

"I think his wife had a little—but something quite trifling."

"We shall have to go to see her, but they live so terribly far away."

"Far away from you, you mean. Everything's far away from your place."

"You see, he never can forgive my living on the other side of the river," said Peter Ivanovich, smiling at Shebek. Then, still talking of the distances between different parts of the city, they returned to the Court.

Besides considerations as to the possible transfers and promotions likely to result from Ivan Ilych's death, the mere fact of the death of a near acquaintance aroused, as usual, in all who heard of it the complacent feeling that, "it is he who is dead and not I."

Each one thought or felt, "Well, he's dead but I'm alive!" But the more intimate of Ivan Ilych's acquaintances, his so-called friends, could not help thinking also that they would now have to fulfill the very tiresome demands of propriety by attending the funeral service and paying a visit of condolence to the widow.

Fedor Vasilievich and Peter Ivanovich had been his nearest acquaintances.

Peter Ivanovich had studied law with Ivan Ilych and had considered himself to be under obligations to him.

Having told his wife at dinnertime of Ivan Ilych's death, and of his conjecture that it might be possible to get her brother transferred to their circuit, Peter Ivanovich sacrificed his usual nap, put on his evening clothes, and drove to Ivan Ilych's house.

At the entrance stood a carriage and two cabs. Leaning against the wall in the hall downstairs near the cloak stand was a coffin lid covered with cloth of gold, ornamented with gold cord and tassels, which had been polished up with metal powder. Two ladies in black were taking off their fur cloaks. Peter Ivanovich recognized one of them as Ivan Ilych's sister, but the other was a stranger to him. His colleague Schwartz was just coming downstairs, but on seeing Peter Ivanovich enter he stopped and winked at him, as if to say: "Ivan Ilych has made a mess of things —not like you and me."

Schwartz's face with his Piccadilly whiskers, and his slim figure in evening dress, had as usual an air of elegant solemnity which contrasted with the playfulness of his character and had a special piquancy here, or so it seemed to Peter Ivanovich.

Peter Ivanovich allowed the ladies to precede him and slowly followed them upstairs. Schwartz did not come down but remained where he was, and Peter Ivanovich understood that he wanted to arrange where they should play bridge that evening. The ladies went upstairs to the widow's room, and Schwartz with seriously compressed lips but a playful look in his eyes, indicated by a twist of his eyebrows the room to the right where the body lay.

Peter Ivanovich, like everyone else on such occasions, entered feeling uncertain what he would have to do. All he knew was that at such times it is always safe to cross oneself. But he was not quite sure whether one should make obeisance while doing so. He therefore adopted a middle course. On entering the room he began crossing himself and made a slight movement resembling a bow. At the same time, as far as the motion of his head and arm allowed, he surveyed the room. Two young men—apparently nephews, one of whom was a high-school pupil—were leaving the room, crossing themselves as they did so. An old woman was standing motionless, and a lady with strangely arched eyebrows was saying something to her in a whisper. A vigorous, resolute Church Reader, in a frock coat, was reading something in a loud voice with an expression that precluded any contradiction. The butler's assistant, Gerasim, stepping lightly in front of Peter Ivanovich, was strewing something on the floor. Noticing this, Peter Ivanovich was immediately aware of a faint odor of a decomposing body. The last time he had called on Ivan Ilych,

Peter Ivanovich had seen Gerasim in the study. Ivan Ilych had been particularly fond of him and he was performing the duty of a sick nurse.

Peter Ivanovich continued to make the sign of the cross slightly inclining his head in an intermediate direction between the coffin, the Reader, and the icons on the table in a corner of the room. Afterwards, when it seemed to him that this movement of his arm in crossing himself had gone on too long, he stopped and began to look at the corpse.

The dead man lay, as dead men always lie, in a specially heavy way, his rigid limbs sunk in the soft cushions of the coffin, with the head forever bowed on the pillow. His yellow waxen brow with bald patches over his sunken temples was thrust up in the way peculiar to the dead, the protruding nose seeming to press on the upper lip. He was much changed and grown even thinner since Peter Ivanovich had last seen him, but, as is always the case with the dead, his face was handsomer and above all more dignified than when he was alive. The expression on the face said that what was necessary had been accomplished, and accomplished rightly. Besides this there was in that expression a reproach and a warning to the living. This warning seemed to Peter Ivanovich out of place, or at least not applicable to him. He felt a certain discomfort and so he hurriedly crossed himself once more and turned and went out of the door—too hurriedly and too regardless of propriety, as he himself was aware.

Schwartz was waiting for him in the adjoining room with legs spread wide apart and both hands toying with his top hat behind his back. The mere sight of that playful, well-groomed, and elegant figure refreshed Peter Ivanovich. He felt that Schwartz was above all these happenings and would not surrender to any depressing influences. His very look said that this incident of a church service for Ivan Ilych could not be a sufficient reason for infringing the order of the session—in other words, that it would certainly not prevent his unwrapping a new pack of cards and shuffling them that evening while a footman placed fresh candles on the table: in fact, that there was no reason for supposing that this incident would hinder their spending the evening agreeably. Indeed he said this in a whisper as Peter Ivanovich passed him, proposing that they should meet for a game at Fedor Vasilievich's.

But apparently Peter Ivanovich was not destined to play bridge that evening. Praskovya Fedorovna (a short, fat woman who despite all efforts to the contrary had continued to broaden steadily from her shoulders downwards and who had the same extraordinarily arched eyebrows as the lady who had been standing by the coffin), dressed all in black, her head covered with lace, came out of her own room with some other ladies, conducted them to the room where the dead body lay, and said: "The service will begin immediately. Please go in."

Schwartz, making an indefinite bow, stood still, evidently neither accepting nor declining this invitation. Praskovya Fedorovna recognizing Peter Ivanovich, sighed, went close up to him, took his hand, and said: "I know you were a true friend to Ivan Ilych . . ." and looked at him awaiting some suitable response. And Peter Ivanovich knew that, just as it had been the right thing to cross himself in that room, so what he had to do here was to press her hand, sigh, and say, "Believe me . . ." So he did all this and as he did it felt that the desired result had been achieved: that both he and she were touched.

"Come with me. I want to speak to you before it begins," said the widow. "Give me your arm."

Peter Ivanovich gave her his arm and they went to the inner rooms, passing Schwartz who winked at Peter Ivanovich compassionately.

"That does for our bridge! Don't object if we find another player. Perhaps you can cut in when you do escape," said his playful look.

Peter Ivanovich sighed still more deeply and despondently, and Praskovya Fedorovna pressed his arm gratefully. When they reached the drawing room, upholstered in pink cretonne and lighted by a dim lamp, they sat down at the table—she on a sofa and Peter Ivanovich on a low pouf, the springs of which yielded spasmodically under his weight. Praskovya Fedorovna had been on the point of warning him to take another seat, but felt that such a warning was out of keeping with her present condition and so changed her mind. As he sat down on the pouf Peter Ivanovich recalled how Ivan Ilych had arranged this room and had consulted him regarding this pink cretonne with green leaves. The whole room was full of furniture and knick-knacks, and on her way to the sofa the lace of the widow's black shawl caught on the edge of the table. Peter Ivanovich rose to detach it, and the springs of the pouf, relieved of his weight, rose also and gave him a push. The widow began detaching her shawl herself, and Peter Ivanovich again sat down, suppressing the rebellious springs of the pouf under him. But the widow had not quite freed herself and Peter Ivanovich got up again, and again the pouf rebelled and even creaked. When this was all over she took out a clean cambric handkerchief and began to weep. The episode with the shawl and the struggle with the pouf had cooled Peter Ivanovich's emotions and he sat there with a sullen look on his face. This awkward situation was interrupted by Sokolov, Ivan Ilych's butler, who came to report that the plot in the cemetery that Praskovya Fedorovna had chosen would cost two hundred rubles. She stopped weeping and, looking at Peter Ivanovich with the air of a victim, remarked in French that it was very hard for her. Peter Ivanovich made a silent gesture signifying his full conviction that it must indeed be so.

"Please smoke," she said in a magnanimous yet crushed voice, and turned to discuss with Sokolov the price of the plot for the grave.

Peter Ivanovich while lighting his cigarette heard her inquiring very circumstantially into the prices of different plots in the cemetery and finally decide which she would take. When that was done she gave instructions about engaging the choir. Sokolov then left the room.

"I look after everything myself," she told Peter Ivanovich, shifting the albums that lay on the table; and noticing that the table was endangered by his cigarette ash, she immediately passed him an ash tray, saying as she did so: "I consider it an affectation to say that my grief prevents my attending to practical affairs. On the contrary, if anything can—I won't say console me, but—distract me, it is seeing to everything concerning him." She again took out her handkerchief as if preparing to cry, but suddenly, as if mastering her feeling, she shook herself and began to speak calmly. "But there is something I want to talk to you about." Peter Ivanovich bowed, keeping control of the springs of the pouf, which immediately began quivering under him.

"He suffered terribly the last few days."

"Did he?" said Peter Ivanovich.

"Oh, terribly! He screamed unceasingly, not for minutes but for hours. For the last three days he screamed incessantly. It was unendurable. I cannot understand how I bore it; you could hear him three rooms off. Oh, what I have suffered!"

"Is it possible that he was conscious all that time?" asked Peter Ivanovich.

"Yes," she whispered. "To the last moment. He took leave of us a quarter of an hour before he died, and asked us to take Volodya away."

The thought of the suffering of this man he had known so intimately, first as a merry little boy, then as a schoolmate, and later as a grown-up colleague, suddenly struck Peter Ivanovich with horror, despite an unpleasant consciousness of his own and this woman's dissimulation. He again saw that brow, and that nose pressing down on the lip, and felt afraid for himself.

"Three days of frightful suffering and the death! Why, that might suddenly, at any time, happen to me," he thought, and for a moment felt terrified. But—he did not himself know how—the customary reflection at once occurred to him that this had happened to Ivan Ilych and not to him, and that it should not and could not happen to him, and that to think that it could would be yielding to depression which he ought not to do, as Schwartz's expression plainly showed. After which reflection Peter Ivanovich felt reassured, and began to ask with interest about the details of Ivan Ilych's death, as though death was an accident natural to Ivan Ilych but certainly not to himself. After many details of the really dreadful physical sufferings Ivan Ilych had endured (which details he learnt only from the effect those sufferings had produced on Praskovya Fedorovna's nerves) the widow apparently found it necessary to get to business.

"Oh, Peter Ivanovich, how hard it is! How terribly, terribly hard!" and she again began to weep.

Peter Ivanovich sighed and waited for her to finish blowing her nose. When she had done so he said, "Believe me . . ." and she again began talking and brought out what was evidently her chief concern with him—namely, to question him as to how she could obtain a grant of money from the government on the occasion of her husband's death. She made it appear that she was asking Peter Ivanovich's advice about her pension, but he soon saw that she already knew about that to the minutest detail, more even than he did himself. She knew how much could be got out of the government in consequence of her husband's death, but wanted to find out whether she could not possibly extract something more. Peter Ivanovich tried to think of some means of doing so, but after reflecting for a while and, out of propriety, condemning the government for its niggardliness, he said he thought that nothing more could be got. Then she sighed and evidently began to devise means of getting rid of her visitor. Noticing this, he put out his cigarette, rose, pressed her hand, and went out into the anteroom.

In the dining room where the clock stood that Ivan Ilych had liked so much and had bought at an antique shop, Peter Ivanovich met a priest and a few acquaintances who had come to attend the service, and he recognized Ivan Ilych's daughter, a handsome young woman. She was in black and her slim figure appeared slimmer than ever. She had a gloomy, determined, almost angry expression, and bowed to Peter Ivanovich as though he were in some way to blame. Behind her, with the same offended look, stood a wealthy young man, an examining magistrate, whom Peter Ivanovich also knew and who was her fiancé, as he had heard. He bowed mournfully to them and was about to pass into the death-chamber, when from under the stairs appeared the figure of Ivan Ilych's schoolboy son, who was extremely like his father. He seemed a little Ivan Ilych, such as Peter Ivanovich remembered when they studied law together. His tear-stained eyes had in them the look that is seen in the eyes of boys of thirteen or fourteen who are not pure-minded.

When he saw Peter Ivanovich he scowled morosely and shamefacedly. Peter Ivanovich nodded to him and entered the death-chamber. The service began: candles, groans, incense, tears, and sobs. Peter Ivanovich stood looking gloomily down at his feet. He did not look once at the dead man, did not yield to any depressing influence, and was one of the first to leave the room. There was no one in the anteroom, but Gerasim darted out of the dead man's room, rummaged with his strong hands among the fur coats to find Peter Ivanovich's and helped him on with it.

"Well, friend Gerasim," said Peter Ivanovich, so as to say something. "It's a sad affair, isn't it?"

"It's God will. We shall all come to it some day," said Gerasim, displaying his teeth—the even white teeth of a healthy peasant—and, like a man in the thick of urgent work, he briskly opened the front door, called the coachman, helped Peter Ivanovich into the sledge, and sprang back to the porch as if in readiness for what he had to do next.

Peter Ivanovich found the fresh air particularly pleasant after the smell of incense, the dead body, and carbolic acid.

"Where to sir?" asked the coachman.

"It's not too late even now . . . . I'll call round on Fedor Vasilievich."

He accordingly drove there and found them just finishing the first rubber, so that it was quite convenient for him to cut in.

Chapter II

Ivan Ilych's life had been most simple and most ordinary and therefore most terrible.

He had been a member of the Court of Justice, and died at the age of forty-five. His father had been an official who after serving in various ministries and departments in Petersburg had made the sort of career which brings men to positions from which by reason of their long service they cannot be dismissed, though they are obviously unfit to hold any responsible position, and for whom therefore posts are specially created, which though fictitious carry salaries of from six to ten thousand rubles that are not fictitious, and in receipt of which they live on to a great age.

Such was the Privy Councilor and superfluous member of various superfluous institutions, Ilya Epimovich Golovin.

He had three sons, of whom Ivan Ilych was the second. The eldest son was following in his father's footsteps only in another department, and was already approaching that stage in the service at which a similar sinecure would be reached. The third son was a failure. He had ruined his prospects in a number of positions and was not serving in the railway department. His father and brothers, and still more their wives, not merely disliked meeting him, but avoided remembering his existence unless compelled to do so. His sister had married Baron Greff, a Petersburg official of her father's type. Ivan Ilych was *le phenix de la famille* as people said. He was neither as cold and formal as his elder brother nor as wild as the younger, but was a happy mean between them—an intelligent polished, lively and agreeable man. He had studied with his younger brother at the School of Law, but the latter had failed to complete the course and was expelled when he was in the fifth class. Ivan Ilych finished the course well. Even when he was at the School of Law he was just what he remained for the rest of his life: a capable, cheerful, good-natured, and sociable man, though strict in the fulfillment of what he considered to be his duty: and he considered his duty to be what was so considered by those in authority. Neither as a boy nor as a man was he a toady, but from early youth was by nature attracted to people of high station as a fly is drawn to the light, assimilating their ways and views of life and establishing friendly relations with them. All the enthusiasms of childhood and youth passed without leaving much trace on him; he succumbed to sensuality, to vanity, and latterly among the highest classes to liberalism, but always within limits which his instinct unfailingly indicated to him as correct.

At school he had done things which had formerly seemed to him very horrid and made him feel disgusted with himself when he did them; but when later on he saw that such actions were done by people of good position and that they did not regard them as wrong, he was able not exactly to regard them as right, but to forget about them entirely or not be at all troubled at remembering them. Having graduated from the School of Law and qualified for the tenth rank of the civil service, and having received money from his father for his equipment, Ivan Ilych ordered himself clothes at Scharmer's, the fashionable tailor, hung a medallion inscribed *respice finem* on his watch-chain, took leave of his professor and the prince who was patron of the school, had a farewell dinner with his comrades at Donon's first-class restaurant, and with his new and fashionable portmanteau, linen, clothes, shaving and other toilet appliances, and a traveling rug, all purchased at the best shops, he set off for one of the provinces where through his father's influence, he had been attached to the governor as an official for special service.

In the province Ivan Ilych soon arranged as easy and agreeable a position for himself as he had had at the School of Law. He performed his official task, made his career, and at the same time amused himself pleasantly and decorously. Occasionally he paid official visits to country districts where he behaved with dignity both to his superiors and inferiors, and performed the duties entrusted to him, which related chiefly to the sectarians, with an exactness and incorruptible honesty of which he could not but feel proud.

In official matters, despite his youth and taste for frivolous gaiety, he was exceedingly reserved, punctilious, and even severe; but in society he was often amusing and witty, and always good-natured, correct in his manner, and *bon enfant,* as the governor and his wife— with whom he was like one of the family—used to say of him.

In the province he had an affair with a lady who made advances to the elegant young lawyer, and there was also a milliner; and there were carousals with aides-de-camp who visited the district, and after-supper visits to a certain outlying street of doubtful reputation; and there was too some obsequiousness to his chief and even to his chief's wife, but all this was done with such a tone of good breeding that no hard names could be applied to it. It all came under the heading of the French saying: "*Il faut que jeunesse se passe.*" It was all done with clean hands, in clean linen, with French phrases, and above all among people of the best society and consequently with the approval of people of rank.

So Ivan Ilych served for five years and then came a change in his official life. The new and reformed judicial institutions were introduced, and new men were needed. Ivan Ilych became such a new man. He was offered the post of examining magistrate, and he accepted it though the post was in another province and obliged him to give up the connections he had formed and to make new ones. His friends met to give him a send-off; they had a group photograph taken and presented him with a silver cigarette case, and he set off to his new post.

As examining magistrate Ivan Ilych was just as *comme il faut* and decorous a man, inspiring general respect and capable of separating his official duties from his private life, as he had been when acting as an official on special service. His duties now as examining magistrate were far more interesting and attractive than before. In his former position it had been pleasant to wear an undress uniform made by Scharmer, and to pass through the crowd of petitioners and officials who were timorously awaiting an audience with the governor, and who envied him as with free and easy gait he went straight into his chief's private room to have a cup of tea and a cigarette with him. But not many people had then been directly dependent on him—only police officials and the sectarians when he went on special missions —and he liked to treat them politely, almost as comrades, as if he were letting them feel that he who had the power to crush them was treating them in this simple, friendly way. There were then but few such people. But now, as an examining magistrate, Ivan Ilych felt that everyone without exception, even the most important and self-satisfied, was in his power, and that he need only write a few words on a sheet of paper with a certain heading, and this or that important, self-satisfied person would be brought before him in the role of an accused person or a witness, and if he did not choose to allow him to sit down, would have to stand before him and answer his questions. Ivan Ilych never abused his power; he tried on the contrary to soften its expression, but the consciousness of it and the possibility of softening its effect, supplied the chief interest and attraction of his office. In his work itself, especially in his examinations, he very soon acquired a method of eliminating all considerations irrelevant to the legal aspect of the case, and reducing even the most complicated case to a form in which it would be presented on paper only in its externals, completely excluding his personal opinion of the matter, while above all observing every prescribed formality. The work was new and Ivan Ilych was one of the first men to apply the new Code of 1864.

On taking up the post of examining magistrate in a new town, he made new acquaintances and connections, placed himself on a new footing and assumed a somewhat different tone. He took up an attitude of rather dignified aloofness towards the provincial authorities, but picked out the best circle of legal gentlemen and wealthy gentry living in the town and assumed a tone of slight dissatisfaction with the government, of moderate liberalism, and of enlightened citizenship. At the same time, without at all altering the elegance of his toilet, he ceased shaving his chin and allowed his beard to grow as it pleased.

Ivan Ilych settled down very pleasantly in this new town. The society there, which inclined towards opposition to the governor was friendly, his salary was larger, and he began to play vint [a form of bridge], which he found added not a little to the pleasure of life, for he had a capacity for cards, played good-humoredly, and calculated rapidly and astutely, so that he usually won.

After living there for two years he met his future wife, Praskovya Fedorovna Mikhel, who was the most attractive, clever, and brilliant girl of the set in which he moved, and among other amusements and relaxations from his labors as examining magistrate, Ivan Ilych established light and playful relations with her.

While he had been an official on special service he had been accustomed to dance, but now as an examining magistrate it was exceptional for him to do so. If he danced now, he did it as if to show that though he served under the reformed order of things, and had reached the fifth official rank, yet when it came to dancing he could do it better than most people. So at the end of an evening he sometimes danced with Praskovya Fedorovna, and it was chiefly during these dances that he captivated her. She fell in love with him. Ivan Ilych had at first no definite intention of marrying, but when the girl fell in love with him he said to himself: "Really, why shouldn't I marry?

"Praskovya Fedorovna came of a good family, was not bad looking, and had some little property. Ivan Ilych might have aspired to a more brilliant match, but even this was good. He had his salary, and she, he hoped, would have an equal income. She was well connected, and was a sweet, pretty, and thoroughly correct young woman. To say that Ivan Ilych married because he fell in love with Praskovya Fedorovna and found that she sympathized with his views of life would be as incorrect as to say that he married because his social circle approved of the match. He was swayed by both these considerations: the marriage gave him personal satisfaction, and at the same time it was considered the right thing by the most highly placed of his associates.

So Ivan Ilych got married.

The preparations for marriage and the beginning of married life, with its conjugal caresses, the new furniture, new crockery, and new linen, were very pleasant until his wife became pregnant—so that Ivan Ilych had begun to think that marriage would not impair the easy, agreeable, gay and always decorous character of his life, approved of by society and regarded by himself as natural, but would even improve it. But from the first months of his wife's pregnancy, something new, unpleasant, depressing, and unseemly, and from which there was no way of escape, unexpectedly showed itself.

His wife, without any reason—*de gaiete de coeur* as Ivan Ilych expressed it to himself—began to disturb the pleasure and propriety of their life. She began to be jealous without any cause, expected him to devote his whole attention to her, found fault with everything, and made coarse and ill-mannered scenes.

At first Ivan Ilych hoped to escape from the unpleasantness of this state of affairs by the same easy and decorous relation to life that had served him heretofore: he tried to ignore his wife's disagreeable moods, continued to live in his usual easy and pleasant way, invited friends to his house for a game of cards, and also tried going out to his club or spending his evenings with friends. But one day his wife began upbraiding him so vigorously, using such coarse words, and continued to abuse him every time he did not fulfill her demands, so resolutely and with such evident determination not to give way till he submitted—that is, till he stayed at home and was bored just as she was—that he became alarmed. He now realized that matrimony—at any rate with Praskovya Fedorovna—was not always conducive to the pleasures and amenities of life, but on the contrary often infringed both comfort and propriety, and that he must therefore entrench himself against such infringement. And Ivan Ilych began to seek for means of doing so. His official duties were the one thing that imposed upon Praskovya Fedorovna, and by means of his official work and the duties attached to it he began struggling with his wife to secure his own independence.

With the birth of their child, the attempts to feed it and the various failures in doing so, and with the real and imaginary illnesses of mother and child, in which Ivan Ilych's sympathy was demanded but about which he understood nothing, the need of securing for himself an existence outside his family life became still more imperative.

As his wife grew more irritable and exacting and Ivan Ilych transferred the center of gravity of his life more and more to his official work, so did he grow to like his work better and became more ambitious than before.

Very soon, within a year of his wedding, Ivan Ilych had realized that marriage, though it may add some comforts to life, is in fact a very intricate and difficult affair towards which in order to perform one's duty, that is, to lead a decorous life approved of by society, one must adopt a definite attitude just as towards one's official duties.

And Ivan Ilych evolved such an attitude towards married life. He only required of it those conveniences—dinner at home, housewife, and bed—which it could give him, and above all that propriety of external forms required by public opinion. For the rest he looked for lighthearted pleasure and propriety, and was very thankful when he found them, but if he met with antagonism and querulous ness he at once retired into his separate fenced-off world of official duties, where he found satisfaction.

Ivan Ilych was esteemed a good official, and after three years was made Assistant Public Prosecutor. His new duties, their importance, the possibility of indicting and imprisoning anyone he chose, the publicity his speeches received, and the success he had in all these things, made his work still more attractive. More children came. His wife became more and more querulous and ill tempered, but the attitude Ivan Ilych had adopted towards his home life rendered him almost impervious to her grumbling.

After seven years' service in that town he was transferred to another province as Public Prosecutor. They moved, but were short of money and his wife did not like the place they moved to. Though the salary was higher the cost of living was greater, besides which two of their children died and family life became still more unpleasant for him.

Praskovya Fedorovna blamed her husband for every inconvenience they encountered in their new home. Most of the conversations between husband and wife, especially as to the children's education, led to topics that recalled former disputes, and these disputes were apt to flare up again at any moment. There remained only those rare periods of amorousness, which still came to them at times but did not last long. These were islets at which they anchored for a while and then again set out upon that ocean of veiled hostility which showed itself in their aloofness from one another. This aloofness might have grieved Ivan Ilych had he considered that it ought not to exist, but he now regarded the position as normal, and even made it the goal at which he aimed in family life. His aim was to free himself more and more from those unpleasantnesses and to give them a semblance of harmlessness and propriety. He attained this by spending less and less time with his family, and when obliged to be at home he tried to safeguard his position by the presence of outsiders. The chief thing however was that he had his official duties. The whole interest of his life now centered in the official world and that interest absorbed him. The consciousness of his power, being able to ruin anybody he wished to ruin, the importance, even the external dignity of his entry into court, or meetings with his subordinates, his success with superiors and inferiors, and above all his masterly handling of cases, of which he was conscious—all this gave him pleasure and filled his life, together with chats with his colleagues, dinners, and bridge. So that on the whole Ivan Ilych's life continued to flow as he considered it should do—pleasantly and properly.

So things continued for another seven years. His eldest daughter was already sixteen, another child had died, and only one son was left, a schoolboy and a subject of dissension. Ivan Ilych wanted to put him in the School of Law, but to spite him Praskovya Fedorovna entered him at the High School. The daughter had been educated at home and had turned out well: the boy did not learn badly either.

Chapter III

So Ivan Ilych lived for seventeen years after his marriage. He was already a Public Prosecutor of long standing, and had declined several proposed transfers while awaiting a more desirable post, when an unanticipated and unpleasant occurrence quite upset the peaceful course of his life. He was expecting to be offered the post of presiding judge in a University town, but Happe somehow came to the front and obtained the appointment instead. Ivan Ilych became irritable, reproached Happe, and quarreled both him and with his immediate superiors—who became colder to him and again passed him over when other appointments were made.

This was in 1880, the hardest year of Ivan Ilych's life. It was then that it became evident on the one hand that his salary was insufficient for them to live on, and on the other that he had been forgotten, and not only this, but that what was for him the greatest and most cruel injustice appeared to others a quite ordinary occurrence. Even his father did not consider it his duty to help him. Ivan Ilych felt himself abandoned by everyone, and that they regarded his position with a salary of 3,500 rubles as quite normal and even fortunate. He alone knew that with the consciousness of the injustices done him, with his wife's incessant nagging, and with the debts he had contracted by living beyond his means, his position was far from normal.

In order to save money that summer he obtained leave of absence and went with his wife to live in the country at her brother's place. In the country, without his work, he experienced ennui for the first time in his life, and not only ennui but intolerable depression, and he decided that it was impossible to go on living like that, and that it was necessary to take energetic measures.

Having passed a sleepless night pacing up and down the veranda, he decided to go to Petersburg and bestir himself, in order to punish those who had failed to appreciate him and to get transferred to another ministry.

Next day, despite many protests from his wife and her brother, he started for Petersburg with the sole object of obtaining a post with a salary of five thousand rubles a year. He was no longer bent on any particular department, or tendency, or kind of activity. All he now wanted was an appointment to another post with a salary of five thousand rubles, either in the administration, in the banks, with the railways in one of the Empress Marya's Institutions, or even in the customs—but it had to carry with it a salary of five thousand rubles and be in a ministry other than that in which they had failed to appreciate him.

And this quest of Ivan Ilych's was crowned with remarkable and unexpected success. At Kursk an acquaintance of his, F. I. Ilyin, got into the first-class carriage, sat down beside Ivan Ilych, and told him of a telegram just received by the governor of Kursk announcing that a change was about to take place in the ministry: Peter Ivanovich was to be superseded by Ivan Semonovich.

The proposed change, apart from its significance for Russia, had a special significance for Ivan Ilych, because by bringing forward a new man, Peter Petrovich, and consequently his friend Zachar Ivanovich, it was highly favorable for Ivan Ilych, since Sachar Ivanovich was a friend and colleague of his.

In Moscow this news was confirmed, and on reaching Petersburg Ivan Ilych found Zachar Ivanovich and received a definite promise of an appointment in his former Department of Justice.

A week later he telegraphed to his wife: "Zachar in Miller's place. I shall receive appointment on presentation of report."

Thanks to this change of personnel, Ivan Ilych had unexpectedly obtained an appointment in his former ministry which placed him two states above his former colleagues besides giving him five thousand rubles salary and three thousand five hundred rubles for expenses connected with his removal. All his ill humor towards his former enemies and the whole department vanished, and Ivan Ilych was completely happy.

He returned to the country more cheerful and contented than he had been for a long time. Praskovya Fedorovna also cheered up and a truce was arranged between them. Ivan Ilych told of how he had been feted by everybody in Petersburg, how all those who had been his enemies were put to shame and now fawned on him, how envious they were of his appointment, and how much everybody in Petersburg had liked him.

Praskovya Fedorovna listened to all this and appeared to believe it. She did not contradict anything, but only made plans for their life in the town to which they were going. Ivan Ilych saw with delight that these plans were his plans, that he and his wife agreed, and that, after a stumble, his life was regaining its due and natural character of pleasant lightheartedness and decorum.

Ivan Ilych had come back for a short time only, for he had to take up his new duties on the 10th of September. Moreover, he needed time to settle into the new place, to move all his belongings from the province, and to buy and order many additional things: in a word, to make such arrangements as he had resolved on, which were almost exactly what Praskovya Fedorovna too had decided on.

Now that everything had happened so fortunately, and that he and his wife were at one in their aims and moreover saw so little of one another, they got on together better than they had done since the first years of marriage. Ivan Ilych had thought of taking his family away with him at once, but the insistence of his wife's brother and her sister-in-law, who had suddenly become particularly amiable and friendly to him and his family, induced him to depart alone. So he departed, and the cheerful state of mind induced by his success and by the harmony between his wife and himself, the one intensifying the other, did not leave him. He found a delightful house, just the thing both he and his wife had dreamt of. Spacious, lofty reception rooms in the old style, a convenient and dignified study, rooms for his wife and daughter, a study for his son—it might have been specially built for them. Ivan Ilych himself superintended the arrangements, chose the wallpapers, supplemented the furniture (preferably with antiques which he considered particularly *comme il faut*), and supervised the upholstering. Everything progressed and progressed and approached the ideal he had set himself: even when things were only half completed they exceeded his expectations. He saw what a refined and elegant character, free from vulgarity, it would all have when it was ready. On falling asleep he pictured to himself how the reception room would look. Looking at the yet unfinished drawing room he could see the fireplace, the screen, the what-not, the little chairs dotted here and there, the dishes and plates on the walls, and the bronzes, as they would be when everything was in place. He was pleased by the thought of how his wife and daughter, who shared his taste in this matter, would be impressed by it. They were certainly not expecting as much. He had been particularly successful in finding, and buying cheaply, antiques which gave a particularly aristocratic character to the whole place. But in his letters he intentionally understated everything in order to be able to surprise them. All this so absorbed him that his new duties— though he liked his official work—interested him less than he had expected. Sometimes he even had moments of absent-mindedness during the court sessions and would consider whether he should have straight or curved cornices for his curtains. He was so interested in it all that he often did things himself, rearranging the furniture, or rehanging the curtains. Once when mounting a step ladder to show the upholsterer, who did not understand, how he wanted the hangings draped, he made a false step and slipped, but being a strong and agile man he clung on and only knocked his side against the knob of the window frame. The bruised place was painful but the pain soon passed, and he felt particularly bright and well just then. He wrote: "I feel fifteen years younger." He thought he would have everything ready by September, but it dragged on till mid-October. But the result was charming not only in his eyes but to everyone who saw it.

In reality it was just what is usually seen in the houses of people of moderate means who want to appear rich, and therefore succeed only in resembling others like themselves: there are damasks, dark wood, plants, rugs, and dull and polished bronzes —all the things people of a certain class have in order to resemble other people of that class. His house was so like the others that it would never have been noticed, but to him it all seemed to be quite exceptional. He was very happy when he met his family at the station and brought them to the newly furnished house all lit up, where a footman in a white tie opened the door into the hall decorated with plants, and when they went on into the drawing-room and the study uttering exclamations of delight. He conducted them everywhere, drank in their praises eagerly, and beamed with pleasure. At tea that evening, when Praskovya Fedorovna among others things asked him about his fall, he laughed, and showed them how he had gone flying and had frightened the upholsterer.

"It's a good thing I'm a bit of an athlete. Another man might have been killed, but I merely knocked myself, just here; it hurts when it's touched, but it's passing off already—it's only a bruise."

So they began living in their new home—in which, as always happens, when they got thoroughly settled in they found they were just one room short—and with the increased income, which as always was just a little (some five hundred rubles) too little, but it was all very nice.

Things went particularly well at first, before everything was finally arranged and while something had still to be done: this thing bought, that thing ordered, another thing moved, and something else adjusted. Though there were some disputes between husband and wife, they were both so well satisfied and had so much to do that it all passed off without any serious quarrels. When nothing was left to arrange it became rather dull and something seemed to be lacking, but they were then making acquaintances, forming habits, and life was growing fuller.

Ivan Ilych spent his mornings at the law court and came home to diner, and at first he was generally in a good humor, though he occasionally became irritable just on account of his house. (Every spot on the tablecloth or the upholstery, and every broken window-blind string, irritated him. He had devoted so much trouble to arranging it all that every disturbance of it distressed him.) But on the whole his life ran its course as he believed life should do: easily, pleasantly, and decorously.

He got up at nine, drank his coffee, read the paper, and then put on his undress uniform and went to the law courts. There the harness in which he worked had already been stretched to fit him and he donned it without a hitch: petitioners, inquiries at the chancery, the chancery itself, and the sittings public and administrative. In all this the thing was to exclude everything fresh and vital, which always disturbs the regular course of official business, and to admit only official relations with people, and then only on official grounds. A man would come, for instance, wanting some information. Ivan Ilych, as one in whose sphere the matter did not lie, would have nothing to do with him: but if the man had some business with him in his official capacity, something that could be expressed on officially stamped paper, he would do everything, positively everything he could within the limits of such relations, and in doing so would maintain the semblance of friendly human relations, that is, would observe the courtesies of life. As soon as the official relations ended, so did everything else. Ivan Ilych possessed this capacity to separate his real life from the official side of affairs and not mix the two, in the highest degree, and by long practice and natural aptitude had brought it to such a pitch that sometimes, in the manner of a virtuoso, he would even allow himself to let the human and official relations mingle. He let himself do this just because he felt that he could at any time he chose resume the strictly official attitude again and drop the human relation. And he did it all easily, pleasantly, correctly, and even artistically. In the intervals between the sessions he smoked, drank tea, chatted a little about politics, a little about general topics, a little about cards, but most of all about official appointments. Tired, but with the feelings of a virtuoso—one of the first violins who has played his part in an orchestra with precision—he would return home to find that his wife and daughter had been out paying calls, or had a visitor, and that his son had been to school, had done his homework with his tutor, and was surely learning what is taught at High Schools. Everything was as it should be. After dinner, if they had no visitors, Ivan Ilych sometimes read a book that was being much discussed at the time, and in the evening settled down to work, that is, read official papers, compared the depositions of witnesses, and noted paragraphs of the Code applying to them. This was neither dull nor amusing. It was dull when he might have been playing bridge, but if no bridge was available it was at any rate better than doing nothing or sitting with his wife. Ivan Ilych's chief pleasure was giving little dinners to which he invited men and women of good social position, and just as his drawing room resembled all other drawing rooms so did his enjoyable little parties resemble all other such parties.

Once they even gave a dance. Ivan Ilych enjoyed it and everything went off well, except that it led to a violent quarrel with his wife about the cakes and sweets. Praskovya Fedorovna had made her own plans, but Ivan Ilych insisted on getting everything from an expensive confectioner and ordered too many cakes, and the quarrel occurred because some of those cakes were left over and the confectioner's bill came to forty-five rubles. It was a great and disagreeable quarrel. Praskovya Fedorovna called him "a fool and an imbecile," and he clutched at his head and made angry allusions to divorce.

But the dance itself had been enjoyable. The best people were there, and Ivan Ilych had danced with Princess Trufonova, a sister of the distinguished founder of the Society "Bear My Burden."

The pleasures connected with his work were pleasures of ambition; his social pleasures were those of vanity; but Ivan Ilych's greatest pleasure was playing bridge. He acknowledged that whatever disagreeable incident happened in his life, the pleasure that beamed like a ray of light above everything else was to sit down to bridge with good players, not noisy partners, and of course to fourhanded bridge (with five players it was annoying to have to stand out, though one pretended not to mind), to play a clever and serious game (when the cards allowed it) and then to have supper and drink a glass of wine. After a game of bridge, especially if he had won a little (to win a large sum was unpleasant), Ivan Ilych went to bed in an especially good humor.

So they lived. They formed a circle of acquaintances among the best people and were visited by people of importance and by young folk. In their views as to their acquaintances, husband, wife and daughter were entirely agreed, and tacitly and unanimously kept at arm's length and shook off the various shabby friends and relations who, with much show of affection, gushed into the drawing-room with its Japanese plates on the walls. Soon these shabby friends ceased to obtrude themselves and only the best people remained in the Golovins' set.

Young men made up to Lisa, and Petrishchev, an examining magistrate and Dmitri Ivanovich Petrishchev's son and sole heir, began to be so attentive to her that Ivan Ilych had already spoken to Praskovya Fedorovna about it, and considered whether they should not arrange a party for them, or get up some private theatricals.

So they lived, and all went well, without change, and life flowed pleasantly.

Chapter IV

They were all in good health. It could not be called ill health if Ivan Ilych sometimes said that he had a queer taste in his mouth and felt some discomfort in his left side.

But this discomfort increased and, though not exactly painful, grew into a sense of pressure in his side accompanied by ill humor. And his irritability became worse and worse and began to mar the agreeable, easy, and correct life that had established itself in the Golovin family. Quarrels between husband and wife became more and more frequent, and soon the ease and amenity disappeared and even the decorum was barely maintained. Scenes again became frequent, and very few of those islets remained on which husband and wife could meet without an explosion. Praskovya Fedorovna now had good reason to say that her husband's temper was trying. With characteristic exaggeration she said he had always had a dreadful temper, and that it had needed all her good nature to put up with it for twenty years. It was true that now the quarrels were started by him. His bursts of temper always came just before dinner, often just as he began to eat his soup. Sometimes he noticed that a plate or dish was chipped, or the food was not right, or his son put his elbow on the table, or his daughter's hair was not done as he liked it, and for all this he blamed Praskovya Fedorovna. At first she retorted and said disagreeable things to him, but once or twice he fell into such a rage at the beginning of dinner that she realized it was due to some physical derangement brought on by taking food, and so she restrained herself and did not answer, but only hurried to get the dinner over. She regarded this self-restraint as highly praiseworthy. Having come to the conclusion that her husband had a dreadful temper and made her life miserable, she began to feel sorry for herself, and the more she pitied herself the more she hated her husband. She began to wish he would die; yet she did not want him to die because then his salary would cease. And this irritated her against him still more. She considered herself dreadfully unhappy just because not even his death could save her, and though she concealed her exasperation, that hidden exasperation of hers increased his irritation also.

After one scene in which Ivan Ilych had been particularly unfair and after which he had said in explanation that he certainly was irritable but that it was due to his not being well, she said that he was ill it should be attended to, and insisted on his going to see a celebrated doctor.

He went. Everything took place as he had expected and as it always does. There was the usual waiting and the important air assumed by the doctor, with which he was so familiar (resembling that which he himself assumed in court), and the sounding and listening, and the questions which called for answers that were foregone conclusions and were evidently unnecessary, and the look of importance which implied that "if only you put yourself in our hands we will arrange everything—we know indubitably how it has to be done, always in the same way for everybody alike." It was all just as it was in the law courts. The doctor put on just the same air towards him as he himself put on towards an accused person.

The doctor said that so-and-so indicated that there was so-and-so inside the patient, but if the investigation of so-and-so did not confirm this, then he must assume that and that. If he assumed that and that, then ... and so on. To Ivan Ilych only one question was important: was his case serious or not? But the doctor ignored that inappropriate question. From his point of view it was not the one under consideration, the real question was to decide between a floating kidney, chronic catarrh, or appendicitis. It was not a question the doctor solved brilliantly, as it seemed to Ivan Ilych, in favor of the appendix, with the reservation that should an examination of the urine give fresh indications the matter would be reconsidered. All this was just what Ivan Ilych had himself brilliantly accomplished a thousand times in dealing with men on trial. The doctor summed up just as brilliantly, looking over his spectacles triumphantly and even gaily at the accused. From the doctor's summing up Ivan Ilych concluded that things were bad, but that for the doctor, and perhaps for everybody else, it was a matter of indifference, though for him it was bad. And this conclusion struck him painfully, arousing in him a great feeling of pity for himself and of bitterness towards the doctor's indifference to a matter of such importance.

He said nothing of this, but rose, placed the doctor's fee on the table, and remarked with a sigh: "We sick people probably often put inappropriate questions. But tell me, in general, is this complaint dangerous, or not?"

The doctor looked at him sternly over his spectacles with one eye, as if to say: "Prisoner, if you will not keep to the questions put to you, I shall be obliged to have you removed from the court."

"I have already told you what I consider necessary and proper. The analysis may show something more." And the doctor bowed.

Ivan Ilych went out slowly, seated himself disconsolately in his sledge, and drove home. All the way home he was going over what the doctor had said, trying to translate those complicated, obscure, scientific phrases into plain language and find in them an answer to the question: "Is my condition bad? Is it very bad? Or is there as yet nothing much wrong?" And it seemed to him that the meaning of what the doctor had said was that it was very bad. Everything in the streets seemed depressing. The cabmen, the houses, the passers-by, and the shops, were dismal. His ache, this dull gnawing ache that never ceased for a moment, seemed to have acquired a new and more serious significance from the doctor's dubious remarks. Ivan Ilych now watched it with a new and oppressive feeling.

He reached home and began to tell his wife about it. She listened, but in the middle of his account his daughter came in with her hat on, ready to go out with her mother. She sat down reluctantly to listen to this tedious story, but could not stand it long, and her mother too did not hear him to the end.

"Well, I am very glad," she said. "Mind now to take your medicine regularly. Give me the prescription and I'll send Gerasim to the chemist's." And she went to get ready to go out.

While she was in the room Ivan Ilych had hardly taken time to breathe, but he sighed deeply when she left it.

"Well," he thought, "perhaps it isn't so bad after all."

He began taking his medicine and following the doctor's directions, which had been altered after the examination of the urine. But then it happened that there was a contradiction between the indications drawn from the examination of the urine and the symptoms that showed themselves. It turned out that what was happening differed from what the doctor had told him, and that he had either forgotten or blundered, or hidden something from him. He could not, however, be blamed for that, and Ivan Ilych still obeyed his orders implicitly and at first derived some comfort from doing so.

From the time of his visit to the doctor, Ivan Ilych's chief occupation was the exact fulfillment of the doctor's instructions regarding hygiene and the taking of medicine, and the observation of his pain and his excretions. His chief interest came to be people's ailments and people's health. When sickness, deaths, or recoveries were mentioned in his presence, especially when the illness resembled his own, he listened with agitation that he tried to hide, asked questions, and applied what he heard to his own case.

The pain did not grow less, but Ivan Ilych made efforts to force himself to think that he was better. And he could do this so long as nothing agitated him. But as soon as he had any unpleasantness with his wife, any lack of success in his official work, or held bad cards at bridge, he was at once acutely sensible of his disease. He had formerly borne such mischances, hoping soon to adjust what was wrong, to master it and attain success, or make a grand slam. But now every mischance upset him and plunged him into despair. He would say to himself: "There now, just as I was beginning to get better and the medicine had begun to take effect, comes this accursed misfortune, or unpleasantness . . . ." And he was furious with the mishap, or with the people who were causing the unpleasantness and killing him, for he felt that this fury was killing him but he could not restrain it. One would have thought that it should have been clear to him that this exasperation with circumstances and people aggravated his illness, and that he ought therefore to ignore unpleasant occurrences. But he drew the very opposite conclusion: he said that he needed peace, and he watched for everything that might disturb it and became irritable at the slightest infringement of it. His condition was rendered worse by the fact that he read medical books and consulted doctors. The progress of his disease was so gradual that he could deceive himself when comparing one day with another—the difference was so slight. But when he consulted the doctors it seemed to him that he was getting worse, and even very rapidly. Yet despite this he was continually consulting them.

That month he went to see another celebrity, who told him almost the same as the first had done but put his questions rather differently, and the interview with this celebrity only increased Ivan Ilych's doubts and fears. A friend of a friend of his, a very good doctor, diagnosed his illness again quite differently from the others, and though he predicted recovery, his questions and suppositions bewildered Ivan Ilych still more and increased his doubts. A homoeopathist diagnosed the disease in yet another way, and prescribed medicine that Ivan Ilych took secretly for a week. But after a week, not feeling any improvement and having lost confidence both in the former doctor's treatment and in this one's, he became still more despondent. One day a lady acquaintance mentioned a cure affected by a wonder-working icon. Ivan Ilych caught himself listening attentively and beginning to believe that it had occurred. This incident alarmed him. "Has my mind really weakened to such an extent?" he asked himself. "Nonsense! It's all rubbish. I mustn't give way to nervous fears but having chosen a doctor must keep strictly to his treatment. That is what I will do. Now it's all settled. I won't think about it, but will follow the treatment seriously till summer, and then we shall see. From now there must be no more of this wavering!" this was easy to say but impossible to carry out. The pain in his side oppressed him and seemed to grow worse and more incessant, while the taste in his mouth grew stranger and stranger. It seemed to him that his breath had a disgusting smell, and he was conscious of a loss of appetite and strength. There was no deceiving himself: something terrible, new, and more important than anything before in his life, was taking place within him of which he alone was aware. Those about him did not understand or would not understand it, but thought everything in the world was going on as usual. That tormented Ivan Ilych more than anything. He saw that his household, especially his wife and daughter who were in a perfect whirl of visiting, did not understand anything of it and were annoyed that he was so depressed and so exacting, as if he were to blame for it. Though they tried to disguise it he saw that he was an obstacle in their path, and that his wife had adopted a definite line in regard to his illness and kept to it regardless of anything he said or did. Her attitude was this: "You know," she would say to her friends, "Ivan Ilych can't do as other people do, and keep to the treatment prescribed for him. One day he'll take his drops and keep strictly to his diet and go to bed in good time, but the next day unless I watch him he'll suddenly forget his medicine, eat sturgeon—which is forbidden—and sit up playing cards till one o'clock in the morning."

"Oh, come, when was that?" Ivan Ilych would ask in vexation. "Only once at Peter Ivanovich's."

"And yesterday with Shebek."

"Well, even if I hadn't stayed up, this pain would have kept me awake."

"Be that as it may you'll never get well like that, but will always make us wretched."

Praskovya Fedorovna's attitude to Ivan Ilych's illness, as she expressed it both to others and to him, was that it was his own fault and was another of the annoyances he caused her. Ivan Ilych felt that this opinion escaped her involuntarily—but that did not make it easier for him.

At the law courts too, Ivan Ilych noticed, or thought he noticed, a strange attitude towards himself. It sometimes seemed to him that people were watching him inquisitively as a man whose place might soon be vacant. Then again, his friends would suddenly begin to chaff him in a friendly way about his low spirits, as if the awful, horrible, and unheard-of thing that was going on within him, incessantly gnawing at him and irresistibly drawing him away, was a very agreeable subject for jests. Schwartz in particular irritated him by his jocularity, vivacity, and *savoir-faire*, which reminded him of what he himself had been ten years ago.

Friends came to make up a set and they sat down to cards. They dealt, bending the new cards to soften them, and he sorted the diamonds in his hand and found he had seven. His partner said "No trumps" and supported him with two diamonds. What more could be wished for? It ought to be jolly and lively. They would make a grand slam. But suddenly Ivan Ilych was conscious of that gnawing pain, that taste in his mouth, and it seemed ridiculous that in such circumstances he should be pleased to make a grand slam.

He looked at his partner Mikhail Mikhaylovich, who rapped the table with his strong hand and instead of snatching up the tricks pushed the cards courteously and indulgently towards Ivan Ilych that he might have the pleasure of gathering them up without the trouble of stretching out his hand for them. "Does he think I am too weak to stretch out my arm?" thought Ivan Ilych, and forgetting what he was doing he over-trumped his partner, missing the grand slam by three tricks. And what was most awful of all was that he saw how upset Mikhail Mikhaylovich was about it but did not himself care. And it was dreadful to realize why he did not care.

They all saw that he was suffering, and said: "We can stop if you are tired. Take a rest." Lie down? No, he was not at all tired, and he finished the rubber. All were gloomy and silent. Ivan Ilych felt that he had diffused this gloom over them and could not dispel it. They had supper and went away, and Ivan Ilych was left alone with the consciousness that his life was poisoned and was poisoning the lives of others, and that this poison did not weaken but penetrated more and more deeply into his whole being.

With this consciousness, and with physical pain besides the terror, he must go to bed, often to lie awake the greater part of the night. Next morning he had to get up again, dress, go to the law courts, speak, and write; or if he did not go out, spend at home those twenty-four hours a day each of which was a torture. And he had to live thus all alone on the brink of an abyss, with no one who understood or pitied him.

Chapter V

So one month passed and then another. Just before the New Year his brother-in-law came to town and stayed at their house. Ivan Ilych was at the law courts and Praskovya Fedorovna had gone shopping. When Ivan Ilych came home and entered his study he found his brother-in-law there—a healthy, florid man—unpacking his portmanteau himself. He raised his head on hearing Ivan Ilych's footsteps and looked up at him for a moment without a word. That stare told Ivan Ilych everything. His brother-in-law opened his mouth to utter an exclamation of surprise but checked himself, and that action confirmed it all.

"I have changed, eh?"

"Yes, there is a change."

And after that, try as he would to get his brother-in-law to return to the subject of his looks, the latter would say nothing about it. Praskovya Fedorovna came home and her brother went out to her. Ivan Ilych locked to door and began to examine himself in the glass, first full face, then in profile. He took up a portrait of himself taken with his wife, and compared it with what he saw in the glass. The change in him was immense. Then he bared his arms to the elbow, looked at them, drew the sleeves down again, sat down on an ottoman, and grew blacker than night.

"No, no, this won't do!" he said to himself, and jumped up, went to the table, took up some law papers and began to read them, but could not continue. He unlocked the door and went into the reception-room. The door leading to the drawing room was shut. He approached it on tiptoe and listened.

"No, you are exaggerating!" Praskovya Fedorovna was saying.

"Exaggerating! Don't you see it? Why, he's a dead man! Look at his eyes—there's no life in them. But what is it that is wrong with him?" "No one knows. Nikolaevich [that was another doctor] said something, but I don't know what. And Seshchetitsky [this was the celebrated specialist] said quite the contrary . . ."

Ivan Ilych walked away, went to his own room, lay down, and began musing; "The kidney, a floating kidney." He recalled all the doctors had told him of how it detached itself and swayed about. And by an effort of imagination he tried to catch that kidney and arrest it and support it. So little was needed for this, it seemed to him. "No, I'll go to see Peter Ivanovich again." [That was the friend whose friend was a doctor.] He rang, ordered the carriage, and got ready to go.

"Where are you going, Jean?" asked his wife with an especially sad and exceptionally kind look.

This exceptionally kind look irritated him. He looked morosely at her.

"I must go to see Peter Ivanovich."

He went to see Peter Ivanovich, and together they went to see his friend, the doctor. He was in, and Ivan Ilych had a long talk with him.

Reviewing the anatomical and physiological details of what in the doctor's opinion was going on inside him, he understood it all.

There was something, a small thing, in the vermiform appendix. It might all come right. Only stimulate the energy of one organ and check the activity of another, then absorption would take place and everything would come right. He got home rather late for dinner, ate his dinner, and conversed cheerfully, but could not for a long time bring himself to go back to work in his room. At last, however, he went to his study and did what was necessary, but the consciousness that he had put something aside—an important, intimate matter which he would revert to when his work was done —never left him. When he had finished his work he remembered that this intimate matter was the thought of his vermiform appendix. But he did not give himself up to it, and went to the drawing room for tea. There were callers there, including the examining magistrate who was a desirable match for his daughter, and they were conversing, playing the piano, and singing. Ivan Ilych, as Praskovya Fedorovna remarked, spent that evening more cheerfully than usual, but he never for a moment forgot that he had postponed the important matter of the appendix. At eleven o'clock he said goodnight and went to his bedroom. Since his illness he had slept alone in a small room next to his study. He undressed and took up a novel by Zola, but instead of reading it he fell into thought, and in his imagination that desired improvement in the vermiform appendix occurred. There was the absorption and evacuation and the re-establishment of normal activity. "Yes, that's it!" he said to himself. "One need only assist nature, that's all." He remembered his medicine, rose, took it, and lay down on his back watching for the beneficent action of the medicine and for it to lessen the pain. "I need only take it regularly and avoid all injurious influences. I am already feeling better, much better." He began touching his side: it was not painful to the touch. "There, I really don't feel it. It's much better already." He put out the light and turned on his side. . . . "The appendix is getting better, absorption is occurring." Suddenly he felt the old, familiar, dull, gnawing pain, stubborn and serious. There was the same familiar loathsome taste in his mouth. His heart sand and he felt dazed. "My God! My God!" he muttered. "Again, again! And it will never cease." And suddenly the matter presented itself in a quite different aspect. "Vermiform appendix! Kidney!" he said to himself. "It's not a question of appendix or kidney, but of life and . . . death. Yes, life was there and now it is going, going and I cannot stop it. Yes. Why deceive myself? Isn't it obvious to everyone but me that I'm dying, and that it's only a question of weeks, days . . . it may happen this moment. There was light and now there is darkness. I was here and now I'm going there! Where?" A chill came over him, his breathing ceased, and he felt only the throbbing of his heart.

"When I am not, what will there be? There will be nothing. Then where shall I be when I am no more? Can this be dying? No, I don't want to!" He jumped up and tried to light the candle, felt for it with trembling hands, dropped candle and candlestick on the floor, and fell back on his pillow.

"What's the use? It makes no difference," he said to himself, staring with wide open eyes into the darkness. "Death. Yes, death. And none of them knows or wishes to know it, and they have no pity for me. Now they are playing." (He heard through the door the distant sound of a song and its accompaniment.) "It's all the same to them, but they will die too! Fools! I first, and they later, but it will be the same for them. And now they are merry . . . the beasts!"

Anger choked him and he was agonizingly, unbearably miserable. "It is impossible that all men have been doomed to suffer this awful horror!" He raised himself.

"Something must be wrong. I must calm myself—must think it all over from the beginning." And he again began thinking. "Yes, the beginning of my illness: I knocked my side, but I was still quite well that day and the next. It hurt a little, then rather more. I saw the doctors, and then followed despondency and anguish, more doctors, and I drew nearer to the abyss. My strength grew less and I kept coming nearer and nearer, and now I have wasted away and there is no light in my eyes. I think of the appendix— but this is death! I think of mending the appendix, and all the while here is death! Can it really be death?" Again terror seized him and he gasped for breath. He leant down and began feeling for the matches, pressing with his elbow on the stand beside the bed. It was in his way and hurt him, he grew furious with it, pressed on it still harder, and upset it. Breathless and in despair he fell on his back, expecting death to come immediately.

Meanwhile the visitors were leaving. Praskovya Fedorovna was seeing them off. She heard something fall and came in.

"What has happened?"

"Nothing. I knocked it over accidentally."

She went out and returned with a candle. He lay there panting heavily, like a man who has run a thousand yards, and stared upwards at her with a fixed look.

"What is it, Jean?"

"No . . . o . . . thing. I upset it." ("Why speak of it? She won't understand," he thought.) And in truth she did not understand. She picked up the stand, lit his candle, and hurried away to see another visitor off. When she came back he still lay on his back, looking upwards.

"What is it? Do you feel worse?"

"Yes."

She shook her head and sat down.

"Do you know, Jean, I think we must ask Leshchetitsky to come and see you here."

This meant calling in the famous specialist, regardless of expense. He smiled malignantly and said "No." She remained a little longer and then went up to him and kissed his forehead.

While she was kissing him he hated her from the bottom of his soul and with difficulty refrained from pushing her away.

"Good night. Please God you'll sleep."

"Yes."

Chapter VI

Ivan Ilych saw that he was dying, and he was in continual despair.

In the depth of his heart he knew he was dying, but not only was he not accustomed to the thought, he simply did not and could not grasp it.

The syllogism he had learnt from Kiesewetter's Logic: "Caius is a man, men are mortal, therefore Caius is mortal," had always seemed to him correct as applied to Caius, but certainly not as applied to himself. That Caius—man in the abstract—was mortal, was perfectly correct, but he was not Caius, not an abstract man, but a creature quite, quite separate from all others. He had been little Vanya, with a mamma and a papa, with Mitya and Volodya, with the toys, a coachman and a nurse, afterwards with Katenka and with all the joys, griefs, and delights of childhood, boyhood, and youth. What did Caius know of the smell of that striped leather ball Vanya had been so fond of? Had Caius kissed his mother's hand like that, and did the silk of her dress rustle so for Caius? Had he rioted like that at school when the pastry was bad? Had Caius been in love like that? Could Caius preside at a session as he did? "Caius really was mortal, and it was right for him to die; but for me, little Vanya, Ivan Ilych, with all my thoughts and emotions, it's altogether a different matter. It cannot be that I ought to die. That would be too terrible."

Such was his feeling.

"If I had to die like Caius I would have known it was so. An inner voice would have told me so, but there was nothing of the sort in me and I and all my friends felt that our case was quite different from that of Caius. And now here it is!" he said to himself. "It can't be. It's impossible! But here it is. How is this? How is one to understand it?"

He could not understand it, and tried to drive this false, incorrect, morbid thought away and to replace it by other proper and healthy thoughts. But that thought, and not the thought only but the reality itself, seemed to come and confront him.

And to replace that thought he called up a succession of others, hoping to find in them some support. He tried to get back into the former current of thoughts that had once screened the thought of death from him. But strange to say, all that had formerly shut off, hidden, and destroyed his consciousness of death, no longer had that effect. Ivan Ilych now spent most of his time in attempting to reestablish that old current. He would say to himself: "I will take up my duties again—after all I used to live by them." And banishing all doubts he would go to the law courts, enter into conversation with his colleagues, and sit carelessly as was his wont, scanning the crowd with a thoughtful look and leaning both his emaciated arms on the arms of his oak chair; bending over as usual to a colleague and drawing his papers nearer he would interchange whispers with him, and then suddenly raising his eyes and sitting erect would pronounce certain words and open the proceedings. But suddenly in the midst of those proceedings the pain in his side, regardless of the stage the proceedings had reached, would begin its own gnawing work. Ivan Ilych would turn his attention to it and try to drive the thought of it away, but without success. It would come and stand before him and look at him, and he would be petrified and the light would die out of his eyes, and he would again begin asking himself whether It alone was true. And his colleagues and subordinates would see with surprise and distress that he, the brilliant and subtle judge, was becoming confused and making mistakes. He would shake himself, try to pull himself together, manage somehow to bring the sitting to a close, and return home with the sorrowful consciousness that his judicial labors could not as formerly hide from him what he wanted them to hide, and could not deliver him from It. And what was worst of all was that It drew his attention to itself not in order to make him take some action but only that he should look at It, look it straight in the face: look at it and without doing anything, suffer inexpressibly.

And to save himself from this condition Ivan Ilych looked for consolations—new screens—and new screens were found and for a while seemed to save him, but then they immediately fell to pieces or rather became transparent, as if It penetrated them and nothing could veil It.

In these latter days he would go into the drawing room he had arranged—that drawing room where he had fallen and for the sake of which (how bitterly ridiculous it seemed) he had sacrificed his life—for he knew that his illness originated with that knock. He would enter and see that something had scratched the polished table. He would look for the cause of this and find that it was the bronze ornamentation of an album, which had got bent. He would take up the expensive album which he had lovingly arranged, and feel vexed with his daughter and her friends for their untidiness—for the album was torn here and there and some of the photographs turned upside down. He would put it carefully in order and bend the ornamentation back into position. Then it would occur to him to place all those things in another corner of the room, near the plants. He would call the footman, but his daughter or wife would come to help him. They would not agree, and his wife would contradict him, and he would dispute and grow angry. But that was all right, for then he did not think about It. It was invisible.

But then, when he was moving something himself, his wife would say: "Let the servants do it. You will hurt yourself again." And suddenly It would flash through the screen and he would see it. It was just a flash, and he hoped it would disappear, but he would involuntarily pay attention to his side. "It sits there as before, gnawing just the same!" And he could no longer forget It, but could distinctly see it looking at him from behind the flowers. "What is it all for?" "It really is so! I lost my life over that curtain as I might have done when storming a fort. Is that possible? How terrible and how stupid. It can't be true! It can't, but it is."

He would go to his study, lie down, and again be alone with It: face to face with It.

And nothing could be done with It except to look at it and shudder.

Chapter VII

How it happened it is impossible to say because it came about step by step, unnoticed, but in the third month of Ivan Ilych's illness, his wife, his daughter, his son, his acquaintances, the doctors, the servants, and above all he himself, were aware that the whole interest he had for other people was whether he would soon vacate his place, and at last release the living from the discomfort caused by his presence and be himself released from his sufferings.

He slept less and less. He was given opium and hypodermic injections of morphine, but this did not relieve him. The dull depression he experienced in a somnolent condition at first gave him a little relief, but only as something new, afterwards it became as distressing as the pain itself or even more so. Special foods were prepared for him by the doctors' orders, but all those foods became increasingly distasteful and disgusting to him.

For his excretions also special arrangements had to be made, and this was a torment to him every time—a torment from the uncleanliness, the unseemliness, and the smell, and from knowing that another person had to take part in it.

But just through his most unpleasant matter, Ivan Ilych obtained comfort. Gerasim, the butler's young assistant, always came in to carry the things out. Gerasim was a clean, fresh peasant lad, grown stout on town food and always cheerful and bright. At first the sight of him, in his clean Russian peasant costume, engaged on that disgusting task embarrassed Ivan Ilych.

Once when he got up from the commode too weak to draw up his trousers, he dropped into a soft armchair and looked with horror at his bare, enfeebled thighs with the muscles so sharply marked on them.

Gerasim with a firm light tread, his heavy boots emitting a pleasant smell of tar and fresh winter air, came in wearing a clean Hessian apron, the sleeves of his print shirt tucked up over his strong bare young arms; and refraining from looking at his sick master out of consideration for his feelings, and restraining the joy of life that beamed from his face, he went up to the commode.

"Gerasim!" said Ivan Ilych in a weak voice.

Gerasim started, evidently afraid he might have committed some blunder, and with a rapid movement turned his fresh, kind, simple young face which just showed the first downy signs of a beard.

"Yes, sir?"

"That must be very unpleasant for you. You must forgive me. I am helpless."

"Oh, why, sir," and Gerasim's eyes beamed and he showed his glistening white teeth, "what's a little trouble? It's a case of illness with you, sir."

And his deft strong hands did their accustomed task, and he went out of the room stepping lightly. Five minutes later he as lightly returned.

Ivan Ilych was still sitting in the same position in the armchair.

"Gerasim," he said when the latter had replaced the freshly-washed utensil. "Please come here and help me." Gerasim went up to him. "Lift me up. It is hard for me to get up, and I have sent Dmitri away."

Gerasim went up to him, grasped his master with his strong arms deftly but gently, in the same way that he stepped—lifted him, supported him with one hand, and with the other drew up his trousers and would have set him down again, but Ivan Ilych asked to be led to the sofa. Gerasim, without an effort and without apparent pressure, led him, almost lifting him, to the sofa and placed him on it.

"Thank you. How easily and well you do it all!"

Gerasim smiled again and turned to leave the room. But Ivan Ilych felt his presence such a comfort that he did not want to let him go.

"One thing more, please move up that chair. No, the other one—under my feet. It is easier for me when my feet are raised."

Gerasim brought the chair, set it down gently in place, and raised Ivan Ilych's legs on it. It seemed to Ivan Ilych that he felt better while Gerasim was holding up his legs.

"It's better when my legs are higher," he said. "Place that cushion under them." Gerasim did so. He again lifted the legs and placed them, and again Ivan Ilych felt better while Gerasim held his legs. When he set them down Ivan Ilych fancied he felt worse.

"Gerasim," he said. "Are you busy now?"

"Not at all, sir," said Gerasim, who had learnt from the townsfolk how to speak to gentlefolk.

"What have you still to do?"

"What have I to do? I've done everything except chopping the logs for tomorrow."

"Then hold my legs up a bit higher, can you?"

"Of course I can. Why not?" and Gerasim raised his master's legs higher and Ivan Ilych thought that in that position he did not feel any pain at all.

"And how about the logs?"

"Don't trouble about that, sir. There's plenty of time." Ivan Ilych told Gerasim to sit down and hold his legs, and began to talk to him. And strange to say it seemed to him that he felt better while Gerasim held his legs up.

After that Ivan Ilych would sometimes call Gerasim and get him to hold his legs on his shoulders, and he liked talking to him. Gerasim did it all easily, willingly, simply, and with a good nature that touched Ivan Ilych. Health, strength, and vitality in other people were offensive to him, but Gerasim's strength and vitality did not mortify but soothed him.

What tormented Ivan Ilych most was the deception, the lie, which for some reason they all accepted, that he was not dying but was simply ill, and they only need keep quiet and undergo a treatment and then something very good would result. He however knew that do what they would nothing would come of it, only still more agonizing suffering and death. This deception tortured him—their not wishing to admit what they all knew and what he knew, but wanting to lie to him concerning his terrible condition, and wishing and forcing him to participate in that lie. Those lies—lies enacted over him on the eve of his death and destined to degrade this awful, solemn act to the level of their visiting, their curtains, their sturgeon for dinner—were a terrible agony for Ivan Ilych. And strangely enough, many times when they were going through their antics over him he had been within a hairbreadth of calling out to them: "Stop lying! You know and I know that I am dying. Then at least stop lying about it!" But he had never had the spirit to do it. The awful, terrible act of his dying was, he could see, reduced by those about him to the level of a casual, unpleasant, and almost indecorous incident (as if someone entered a drawing room defusing an unpleasant odor) and this was done by that very decorum which he had served all his life long. He saw that no one felt for him, because no one even wished to grasp his position. Only Gerasim recognized it and pitied him. And so Ivan Ilych felt at ease only with him. He felt comforted when Gerasim supported his legs (sometimes all night long) and refused to go to bed, saying: "Don't you worry, Ivan Ilych. I'll get sleep enough later on," or when he suddenly became familiar and exclaimed: "If you weren't sick it would be another matter, but as it is, why should I grudge a little trouble?" Gerasim alone did not lie; everything showed that he alone understood the facts of the case and did not consider it necessary to disguise them, but simply felt sorry for his emaciated and enfeebled master. Once when Ivan Ilych was sending him away he even said straight out: "We shall all of us die, so why should I grudge a little trouble?"—expressing the fact that he did not think his work burdensome, because he was doing it for a dying man and hoped someone would do the same for him when his time came.

Apart from this lying, or because of it, what most tormented Ivan Ilych was that no one pitied him as he wished to be pitied. At certain moments after prolonged suffering he wished most of all (though he would have been ashamed to confess it) for someone to pity him as a sick child is pitied. He longed to be petted and comforted. He knew he was an important functionary, that he had a beard turning gray, and that therefore what he longed for was impossible, but still he longed for it. And in Gerasim's attitude towards him there was something akin to what he wished for, and so that attitude comforted him. Ivan Ilych wanted to weep, wanted to be petted and cried over, and then his colleague Shebek would come, and instead of weeping and being petted, Ivan Ilych would assume a serious, severe, and profound air, and by force of habit would express his opinion on a decision of the Court of Cassation and would stubbornly insist on that view. This falsity around him and within him did more than anything else to poison his last days.

Chapter VIII

It was morning. He knew it was morning because Gerasim had gone, and Peter the footman had come and put out the candles, drawn back one of the curtains, and begun quietly to tidy up. Whether it was morning or evening, Friday or Sunday, made no difference, it was all just the same: the gnawing, unmitigated, agonizing pain, never ceasing for an instant, the consciousness of life inexorably waning but not yet extinguished, the approach of that ever dreaded and hateful Death which was the only reality, and always the same falsity. What were days, weeks, hours, in such a case?

"Will you have some tea, sir?"

"He wants things to be regular, and wishes the gentlefolk to drink tea in the morning," thought Ivan Ilych, and only said "No."

"Wouldn't you like to move onto the sofa, sir?"

"He wants to tidy up the room, and I'm in the way. I am uncleanliness and disorder," he thought, and said only:

"No, leave me alone."

The man went on bustling about. Ivan Ilych stretched out his hand. Peter came up, ready to help.

"What is it, sir?"

"My watch."

Peter took the watch which was close at hand and gave it to his master.

"Half-past eight. Are they up?"

"No sir, except Vladimir Ivanovich" (the son) "who has gone to school. Praskovya Fedorovna ordered me to wake her if you asked for her. Shall I do so?"

"No, there's no need to." "Perhaps I'd better have some tea," he thought, and added aloud: "Yes, bring me some tea."

Peter went to the door, but Ivan Ilych dreaded being left alone. "How can I keep him here? Oh yes, my medicine." "Peter, give me my medicine." "Why not? Perhaps it may still do some good." He took a spoonful and swallowed it. "No, it won't help. It's all tomfoolery, all deception," he decided as soon as he became aware of the familiar, sickly, hopeless taste. "No, I can't believe in it any longer. But the pain, why this pain? If it would only cease just for a moment!" And he moaned. Peter turned towards him. "It's all right. Go and fetch me some tea."

Peter went out. Left alone Ivan Ilych groaned not so much with pain, terrible thought that was, as from mental anguish. Always and forever the same, always these endless days and nights. If only it would come quicker! If only what would come quicker? Death, darkness? . . . No, no! Anything rather than death!

When Peter returned with the tea on a tray, Ivan Ilych stared at him for a time in perplexity, not realizing who and what he was. Peter was disconcerted by that look and his embarrassment brought Ivan Ilych to himself.

"Oh, tea! All right, put it down. Only help me to wash and put on a clean shirt."

And Ivan Ilych began to wash. With pauses for rest, he washed his hands and then his face, cleaned his teeth, brushed his hair, and looked in the glass. He was terrified by what he saw, especially by the limp way in which his hair clung to his pallid forehead.

While his shirt was being changed he knew that he would be still more frightened at the sight of his body, so he avoided looking at it. Finally he was ready. He drew on a dressing gown, wrapped himself in a plaid, and sat down in the armchair to take his tea. For a moment he felt refreshed, but as soon as he began to drink the tea he was again aware of the same taste, and the pain also returned. He finished it with an effort, and then lay down stretching out his legs, and dismissed Peter.

Always the same. Now a spark of hope flashes up, then a sea of despair rages, and always pain; always pain, always despair, and always the same. When alone he had a dreadful and distressing desire to call someone, but he knew beforehand that with others present it would be still worse. "Another dose of morphine—to lose consciousness. I will tell him, the doctor, that he must think of something else. It's impossible, impossible, to go on like this."

An hour and another pass like that. But now there is a ring at the doorbell. Perhaps it's the doctor? It is. He comes in fresh, hearty, plump, and cheerful, with that look on his face that seems to say: "There now, you're in a panic about something, but we'll arrange it all for you directly!" The doctor knows this expression is out of place here, but he has put it on once for all and can't take it off—like a man who has put on a frock coat in the morning to pay a round of calls.

The doctor rubs his hands vigorously and reassuringly.

"Brr! How cold it is! There's such a sharp frost; just let me warm myself!" he says, as if it were only a matter of waiting till he was warm, and then he would put everything right.

"Well now, how are you?"

Ivan Ilych feels that the doctor would like to say: "Well, how are our affairs?" but that even he feels that this would not do, and says instead: "What sort of a night have you had?"

Ivan Ilych looks at him as much as to say: "Are you really never ashamed of lying?" But the doctor does not wish to understand this question, and Ivan Ilych says: "Just as terrible as ever. The pain never leaves me and never subsides. If only something . . ."

"Yes, you sick people are always like that. . . . There, now I think I am warm enough. Even Praskovya Fedorovna, who is so particular, could find no fault with my temperature. Well, now I can say good morning," and the doctor presses his patient's hand.

Then dropping his former playfulness, he begins with a most serious face to examine the patient, feeling his pulse and taking his temperature, and then begins the sounding and auscultation.

Ivan Ilych knows quite well and definitely that all this is nonsense and pure deception, but when the doctor, getting down on his knee, leans over him, putting his ear first higher then lower, and performs various gymnastic movements over him with a significant expression on his face, Ivan Ilych submits to it all as he used to submit to the speeches of the lawyers, though he knew very well that they were all lying and why they were lying.

The doctor, kneeling on the sofa, is still sounding him when Praskovya Fedorovna's silk dress rustles at the door and she is heard scolding Peter for not having let her know of the doctor's arrival.

She comes in, kisses her husband, and at once proceeds to prove that she has been up a long time already, and only owing to a misunderstanding failed to be there when the doctor arrived.

Ivan Ilych looks at her, scans her all over, sets against her the whiteness and plumpness and cleanness of her hands and neck, the gloss of her hair, and the sparkle of her vivacious eyes. He hates her with his whole soul. And the thrill of hatred he feels for her makes him suffer from her touch.

Her attitude towards him and his diseases is still the same. Just as the doctor had adopted a certain relation to his patient which he could not abandon, so had she formed one towards him —that he was not doing something he ought to do and was himself to blame, and that she reproached him lovingly for this— and she could not now change that attitude.

"You see he doesn't listen to me and doesn't take his medicine at the proper time. And above all he lies in a position that is no doubt bad for him—with his legs up."

She described how he made Gerasim hold his legs up.

The doctor smiled with a contemptuous affability that said: "What's to be done? These sick people do have foolish fancies of that kind, but we must forgive them."

When the examination was over the doctor looked at his watch, and then Praskovya Fedorovna announced to Ivan Ilych that it was of course as he pleased, but she had sent today for a celebrated specialist who would examine him and have a consultation with Michael Danilovich (their regular doctor).

"Please don't raise any objections. I am doing this for my own sake," she said ironically, letting it be felt that she was doing it all for his sake and only said this to leave him no right to refuse. He remained silent, knitting his brows. He felt that he was surrounded and involved in a mesh of falsity that it was hard to unravel anything.

Everything she did for him was entirely for her own sake, and she told him she was doing for herself what she actually was doing for herself, as if that was so incredible that he must understand the opposite.

At half-past eleven the celebrated specialist arrived. Again the sounding began and the significant conversations in his presence and in another room, about the kidneys and the appendix, and the questions and answers, with such an air of importance that again, instead of the real question of life and death which now alone confronted him, the question arose of the kidney and appendix which were not behaving as they ought to and would now be attached by Michael Danilovich and the specialist and forced to amend their ways.

The celebrated specialist took leave of him with a serious though not hopeless look, and in reply to the timid question Ivan Ilych, with eyes glistening with fear and hope, put to him as to whether there was a chance of recovery, said that he could not vouch for it but there was a possibility. The look of hope with which Ivan Ilych watched the doctor out was so pathetic that Praskovya Fedorovna, seeing it, even wept as she left the room to hand the doctor his fee.

The gleam of hope kindled by the doctor's encouragement did not last long. The same room, the same pictures, curtains, wallpaper, medicine bottles, were all there, and the same aching suffering body, and Ivan Ilych began to moan. They gave him a subcutaneous injection and he sank into oblivion.

It was twilight when he came to. They brought him his dinner and he swallowed some beef tea with difficulty, and then everything was the same again and night was coming on.

After dinner, at seven o'clock, Praskovya Fedorovna came into the room in evening dress, her full bosom pushed up by her corset, and with traces of powder on her face. She had reminded him in the morning that they were going to the theatre. Sarah Bernhardt was visiting the town and they had a box, which he had insisted on their taking. Now he had forgotten about it and her toilet offended him, but he concealed his vexation when he remembered that he had himself insisted on their securing a box and going because it would be an instructive and aesthetic pleasure for the children.

Praskovya Fedorovna came in, self-satisfied but yet with a rather guilty air. She sat down and asked how he was, but, as he saw, only for the sake of asking and not in order to learn about it, knowing that there was nothing to learn—and then went on to what she really wanted to say: that she would not on any account have gone but that the box had been taken and Helen and their daughter were going, as well as Petrishchev (the examining magistrate, their daughter's fiancé) and that it was out of the question to let them go alone; but that she would have much preferred to sit with him for a while; and he must be sure to follow the doctor's orders while she was away.

"Oh, and Fedor Petrovich" (the fiancé) "would like to come in. May he? And Lisa?"

"All right."

Their daughter came in in full evening dress, her fresh young flesh exposed (making a show of that very flesh which in his own case caused so much suffering), strong, healthy, evidently in love, and impatient with illness, suffering, and death, because they interfered with her happiness.

Fedor Petrovich came in too, in evening dress, his hair curled a la Capoul, a tight stiff collar round his long sinewy neck, an enormous white shirt-front and narrow black trousers tightly stretched over his strong thighs. He had one white glove tightly drawn on, and was holding his opera hat in his hand.

Following him the schoolboy crept in unnoticed, in a new uniform, poor little fellow, and wearing gloves. Terribly dark shadows showed under his eyes, the meaning of which Ivan Ilych knew well.

His son had always seemed pathetic to him, and now it was dreadful to see the boy's frightened look of pity. It seemed to Ivan Ilych that Vasya was the only one besides Gerasim who understood and pitied him.

They all sat down and again asked how he was. A silence followed. Lisa asked her mother about the opera glasses, and there was an altercation between mother and daughter as to who had taken them and where they had been put. This occasioned some unpleasantness.

Fedor Petrovich inquired of Ivan Ilych whether he had ever seen Sarah Bernhardt. Ivan Ilych did not at first catch the question, but then replied: "No, have you seen her before?"

"Yes, in Adrienne Lecouvreur."

Praskovya Fedorovna mentioned some roles in which Sarah Bernhardt was particularly good. Her daughter disagreed. Conversation sprang up as to the elegance and realism of her acting—the sort of conversation that is always repeated and is always the same.

In the midst of the conversation Fedor Petrovich glanced at Ivan Ilych and became silent. The others also looked at him and grew silent. Ivan Ilych was staring with glittering eyes straight before him, evidently indignant with them. This had to be rectified, but it was impossible to do so. The silence had to be broken, but for a time no one dared to break it and they all became afraid that the conventional deception would suddenly become obvious and the truth become plain to all. Lisa was the first to pluck up courage and break that silence, but by trying to hide what everybody was feeling, she betrayed it.

"Well, if we are going it's time to start," she said, looking at her watch, a present from her father, and with a faint and significant smile at Fedor Petrovich relating to something known only to them. She got up with a rustle of her dress.

They all rose, said goodnight, and went away.

When they had gone it seemed to Ivan Ilych that he felt better; the falsity had gone with them. But the pain remained—that same pain and that same fear that made everything monotonously alike, nothing harder and nothing easier. Everything was worse.

Again minute followed minute and hour followed hour. Everything remained the same and there was no cessation. And the inevitable end of it all became more and more terrible.

"Yes, send Gerasim here," he replied to a question Peter asked.

Chapter IX

His wife returned late at night. She came in on tiptoe, but he heard her, opened his eyes, and made haste to close them again. She wished to send Gerasim away and to sit with him herself, but he opened his eyes and said: "No, go away."

"Are you in great pain?"

"Always the same."

"Take some opium."

He agreed and took some. She went away.

Till about three in the morning he was in a state of stupefied misery. It seemed to him that he and his pain were being thrust into a narrow, deep black sack, but though they were pushed further and further in they could not be pushed to the bottom. And this, terrible enough in itself, was accompanied by suffering. He was frightened yet wanted to fall through the sack, he struggled but yet cooperated. And suddenly he broke through, fell, and regained consciousness. Gerasim was sitting at the foot of the bed dozing quietly and patiently, while he himself lay with his emaciated stockinged legs resting on Gerasim's shoulders; the same shaded candle was there and the same unceasing pain.

"Go away, Gerasim," he whispered.

"It's all right, sir. I'll stay a while."

"No. Go away."

He removed his legs from Gerasim's shoulders, turned sideways onto his arm, and felt sorry for himself. He only waited till Gerasim had gone into the next room and then restrained himself no longer but wept like a child. He wept on account of his helplessness, his terrible loneliness, the cruelty of man, the cruelty of God, and the absence of God.

"Why hast Thou done all this? Why hast Thou brought me here? Why, why dost Thou torment me so terribly?"

He did not expect an answer and yet wept because there was no answer and could be none. The pain again grew more acute, but he did not stir and did not call. He said to himself: "Go on! Strike me! But what is it for? What have I done to Thee? What is it for?"

Then he grew quiet and not only ceased weeping but even held his breath and became all attention. It was as though he were listening not to an audible voice but to the voice of his soul, to the current of thoughts arising within him.

"What is it you want?" was the first clear conception capable of expression in words that he heard.

"What do you want? What do you want?" he repeated to himself.

"What do I want? To live and not to suffer," he answered.

And again he listened with such concentrated attention that even his pain did not distract him.

"To live? How?" asked his inner voice.

"Why, to live as I used to—well and pleasantly."

"As you lived before, well and pleasantly?" the voice repeated.

And in imagination he began to recall the best moments of his pleasant life. But strange to say none of those best moments of his pleasant life now seemed at all what they had then seemed—none of them except the first recollections of childhood. There, in childhood, there had been something really pleasant with which it would be possible to live if it could return. But the child who had experienced that happiness existed no longer; it was like a reminiscence of somebody else.

As soon as the period began which had produced the present Ivan Ilych, all that had then seemed joys now melted before his sight and turned into something trivial and often nasty.

And the further he departed from childhood and the nearer he came to the present the more worthless and doubtful were the joys. This began with the School of Law. A little that was really good was still found there—there was lightheartedness, friendship, and hope. But in the upper classes there had already been fewer of such good moments. Then during the first years of his official career, when he was in the service of the governor, some pleasant moments again occurred: they were the memories of love for a woman. Then all became confused and there was still less of what was good; later on again there was still less that was good, and the further he went the less there was. His marriage, a mere accident, then the disenchantment that followed it, his wife's bad breath and the sensuality and hypocrisy: then that deadly official life and those preoccupations about money, a year of it, and two, and ten, and twenty, and always the same thing. And the longer it lasted the more deadly it became. "It is as if I had been going downhill while I imagined I was going up. And that is really what it was. I was going up in public opinion, but to the same extent life was ebbing away from me. And now it is all done and there is only death.

"Then what does it mean? Why? It can't be that life is so senseless and horrible. But if it really has been so horrible and senseless, why must I die and die in agony? There is something wrong!

"Maybe I did not live as I ought to have done," it suddenly occurred to him. "But how could that be, when I did everything properly?" he replied, and immediately dismissed from his mind this, the sole solution of all the riddles of life and death, as something quite impossible.

"Then what do you want now? To live? Live how? Live as you lived in the law courts when the usher proclaimed 'The judge is coming!' The judge is coming, the judge!" he repeated to himself. "Here he is, the judge. But I am not guilty!" he exclaimed angrily. "What is it for?" And he ceased crying, but turning his face to the wall continued to ponder on the same question: Why, and for what purpose, is there all this horror? But however much he pondered he found no answer. And whenever the thought occurred to him, as it often did, that it all resulted from his not having lived as he ought to have done, he at once recalled the correctness of his whole life and dismissed so strange an idea.

Chapter X

Another fortnight passed. Ivan Ilych now no longer left his
sofa. He would not lie in bed but lay on the sofa, facing the wall
nearly all the time. He suffered ever the same unceasing agonies
and in his loneliness pondered always on the same insoluble
question: "What is this? Can it be that it is Death?" And the inner
voice answered: "Yes, it is Death."

"Why these sufferings?" And the voice answered, "For no
reason—they just are so." Beyond and besides this there was
nothing.

From the very beginning of his illness, ever since he had first
been to see the doctor, Ivan Ilych's life had been divided between
two contrary and alternating moods: now it was despair and the
expectation of this uncomprehended and terrible death, and now
hope and an intently interested observation of the functioning of
his organs. Now before his eyes there was only a kidney or an
intestine that temporarily evaded its duty, and now only that
incomprehensible and dreadful death from which it was
impossible to escape.

These two states of mind had alternated from the very
beginning of his illness, but the further it progressed the more
doubtful and fantastic became the conception of the kidney, and
the more real the sense of impending death. He had but to call to
mind what he had been three months before and what he was
now, to call to mind with what regularity he had been going
downhill, for every possibility of hope to be shattered.

Latterly during the loneliness in which he found himself as he
lay facing the back of the sofa, a loneliness in the midst of a
populous town and surrounded by numerous acquaintances and
relations but that yet could not have been more complete
anywhere—either at the bottom of the sea or under the earth—
during that terrible loneliness Ivan Ilych had lived only in
memories of the past. Pictures of his past rose before him one
after another. They always began with what was nearest in time
and then went back to what was most remote—to his childhood
—and rested there. If he thought of the stewed prunes that had
been offered him that day, his mind went back to the raw
shriveled French plums of his childhood, their peculiar flavor and

the flow of saliva when he sucked their stones, and along with the memory of that taste came a whole series of memories of those days: his nurse, his brother, and their toys. "No, I mustn't think of that. . . . It is too painful," Ivan Ilych said to himself, and brought himself back to the present—to the button on the back of the sofa and the creases in its morocco. "Morocco is expensive, but it does not wear well: there had been a quarrel about it. It was a different kind of quarrel and a different kind of morocco that time when we tore father's portfolio and were punished, and mamma brought us some tarts. . . ." And again his thoughts dwelt on his childhood, and again it was painful and he tried to banish them and fix his mind on something else.

Then again together with that chain of memories another series passed through his mind—of how his illness had progressed and grown worse. There also the further back he looked the more life there had been. There had been more of what was good in life and more of life itself. The two merged together. "Just as the pain went on getting worse and worse, so my life grew worse and worse," he thought. "There is one bright spot there at the back, at the beginning of life, and afterwards all becomes blacker and blacker and proceeds more and more rapidly —in inverse ratio to the square of the distance from death," thought Ivan Ilych. And the example of a stone falling downwards with increasing velocity entered his mind. Life, a series of increasing sufferings, flies further and further towards its end—the most terrible suffering. "I am flying. . . ." He shuddered, shifted himself, and tried to resist, but was already aware that resistance was impossible, and again with eyes weary of gazing but unable to cease seeing what was before them, he stared at the back of the sofa and waited—awaiting that dreadful fall and shock and destruction.

"Resistance is impossible!" he said to himself. "If I could only understand what it is all for! But that too is impossible. An explanation would be possible if it could be said that I have not lived as I ought to. But it is impossible to say that," and he remembered all the legality, correctitude, and propriety of his life. "That at any rate can certainly not be admitted," he thought, and his lips smiled ironically as if someone could see that smile and be taken in by it. "There is no explanation! Agony, death . . . . What for?"

Chapter XI

Another two weeks went by in this way and during that fortnight an event occurred that Ivan Ilych and his wife had desired. Petrishchev formally proposed. It happened in the evening. The next day Praskovya Fedorovna came into her husband's room considering how best to inform him of it, but that very night there had been a fresh change for the worse in his condition. She found him still lying on the sofa but in a different position. He lay on his back, groaning and staring fixedly straight in front of him.

She began to remind him of his medicines, but he turned his eyes towards her with such a look that she did not finish what she was saying; so great an animosity, to her in particular, did that look express.

"For Christ's sake let me die in peace!" he said.

She would have gone away, but just then their daughter came in and went up to say good morning. He looked at her as he had done at his wife, and in reply to her inquiry about his health said dryly that he would soon free them all of himself. They were both silent and after sitting with him for a while went away.

"Is it our fault?" Lisa said to her mother. "It's as if we were to blame! I am sorry for papa, but why should we be tortured?"

The doctor came at his usual time. Ivan Ilych answered "Yes" and "No," never taking his angry eyes from him, and at last said: "You know you can do nothing for me, so leave me alone."

"We can ease your sufferings."

"You can't even do that. Let me be."

The doctor went into the drawing room and told Praskovya Fedorovna that the case was very serious and that the only resource left was opium to allay her husband's sufferings, which must be terrible.

It was true, as the doctor said, that Ivan Ilych's physical sufferings were terrible, but worse than the physical sufferings were his mental sufferings which were his chief torture.

His mental sufferings were due to the fact that that night, as he looked at Gerasim's sleepy, good-natured face with it prominent cheek-bones, the question suddenly occurred to him: "What if my whole life has been wrong?"

It occurred to him that what had appeared perfectly impossible before, namely that he had not spent his life as he should have done, might after all be true. It occurred to him that his scarcely perceptible attempts to struggle against what was considered good by the most highly placed people, those scarcely noticeable impulses which he had immediately suppressed, might have been the real thing, and all the rest false. And his professional duties and the whole arrangement of his life and of his family, and all his social and official interests, might all have been false. He tried to defend all those things to himself and suddenly felt the weakness of what he was defending. There was nothing to defend.

"But if that is so," he said to himself, "and I am leaving this life with the consciousness that I have lost all that was given me and it is impossible to rectify it—what then?"

He lay on his back and began to pass his life in review in quite a new way. In the morning when he saw first his footman, then his wife, then his daughter, and then the doctor, their every word and movement confirmed to him the awful truth that had been revealed to him during the night. In them he saw himself—all that for which he had lived—and saw clearly that it was not real at all, but a terrible and huge deception which had hidden both life and death. This consciousness intensified his physical suffering tenfold. He groaned and tossed about, and pulled at his clothing, which choked and stifled him. And he hated them on that account.

He was given a large dose of opium and became unconscious, but at noon his sufferings began again. He drove everybody away and tossed from side to side.

His wife came to him and said:

"Jean, my dear, do this for me. It can't do any harm and often helps. Healthy people often do it."

He opened his eyes wide.

"What? Take communion? Why? It's unnecessary! However . . ."

She began to cry.

"Yes, do, my dear. I'll send for our priest. He is such a nice man."

"All right. Very well," he muttered.

When the priest came and heard his confession, Ivan Ilych was softened and seemed to feel a relief from his doubts and consequently from his sufferings, and for a moment there came a ray of hope. He again began to think of the vermiform appendix and the possibility of correcting it. He received the sacrament with tears in his eyes.

When they laid him down again afterwards he felt a moment's ease, and the hope that he might live awoke in him again. He began to think of the operation that had been suggested to him. "To live! I want to live!" he said to himself. His wife came in to congratulate him after his communion, and when uttering the usual conventional words she added:

"You feel better, don't you?"

Without looking at her he said, "Yes."

Her dress, her figure, the expression of her face, the tone of her voice, all revealed the same thing. "This is wrong, it is not as it should be. All you have lived for and still live for is falsehood and deception, hiding life and death from you." And as soon as he admitted that thought, his hatred and his agonizing physical suffering again sprang up, and with that suffering a consciousness of the unavoidable, approaching end. And to this was added a new sensation of grinding shooting pain and a feeling of suffocation.

The expression of his face when he uttered that "Yes" was dreadful. Having uttered it, he looked her straight in the eyes, turned on his face with a rapidity extraordinary in his weak state and shouted:

"Go away! Go away and leave me alone!"

Chapter XII

From that moment the screaming began that continued for three days, and was so terrible that one could not hear it through two closed doors without horror. At the moment he answered his wife he realized that he was lost, that there was no return, that the end had come, the very end, and his doubts were still unsolved and remained doubts.

"Oh! Oh! Oh!" he cried in various intonations. He had begun by screaming, "I won't!" and continued screaming on the letter "O."

For three whole days, during which time did not exist for him, he struggled in that black sack into which he was being thrust by an invisible, resistless force. He struggled as a man condemned to death struggles in the hands of the executioner, knowing that he cannot save himself. And every moment he felt that despite all his efforts he was drawing nearer and nearer to what terrified him. He felt that his agony was due to his being thrust into that black hole and still more to his not being able to get right into it. He was hindered from getting into it by his conviction that his life had been a good one. That very justification of his life held him fast and prevented his moving forward, and it caused him most torment of all.

Suddenly some force struck him in the chest and side, making it still harder to breathe, and he fell through the hole and there at the bottom was a light. What had happened to him was like the sensation one sometimes experiences in a railway carriage when one thinks one is going backwards while one is really going forwards and suddenly becomes aware of the real direction.

"Yes, it was not the right thing," he said to himself, "but that's no matter. It can be done. But what is the right thing?" He asked himself, and suddenly grew quiet. This occurred at the end of the third day, two hours before his death. Just then his schoolboy son had crept softly in and gone up to the bedside. The dying man was still screaming desperately and waving his arms. His hand fell on the boy's head, and the boy caught it, pressed it to his lips, and began to cry.

At that very moment Ivan Ilych fell through and caught sight of the light, and it was revealed to him that though his life had not been what it should have been, this could still be rectified. He asked himself, "What is the right thing?" and grew still, listening.

Then he felt that someone was kissing his hand. He opened his eyes, looked at his son, and felt sorry for him. His wife came up to him and he glanced at her. She was gazing at him open-mouthed, with undried tears on her nose and cheek and a despairing look on her face. He felt sorry for her too.

"Yes, I am making them wretched," he thought. "They are sorry, but it will be better for them when I die." He wished to say this but had not the strength to utter it. "Besides, why speak? I must act," he thought. With a look at his wife he indicated his son and said: "Take him away . . . sorry for him . . . sorry for you too. . . ." He tried to add, "Forgive me," but said "Forego" and waved his hand, knowing that He whose understanding mattered would understand.

And suddenly it grew clear to him that what had been oppressing him and would not leave him was all dropping away at once from two sides, from ten sides, and from all sides. He was sorry for them, he must act so as not to hurt them: release them and free himself from these sufferings. "How good and how simple!" he thought. "And the pain?" he asked himself. "What has become of it? Where are you, pain?"

He turned his attention to it.

"Yes, here it is. Well, what of it? Let the pain be."

"And death . . . where is it?"

He sought his former accustomed fear of death and did not find it. "Where is it? What death?" There was no fear because there was no death.

In place of death there was light.

"So that's what it is!" he suddenly exclaimed aloud. "What joy!"

To him all this happened in a single instant, and the meaning of that instant did not change. For those present his agony continued for another two hours. Something rattled in his throat, his emaciated body twitched, then the gasping and rattle became less and less frequent.

"It is finished!" said someone near him.

He heard these words and repeated them in his soul.

"Death is finished," he said to himself. "It is no more!"

He drew in a breath, stopped in the midst of a sigh, stretched out, and died.

Freedom or Death

Emmeline Pankhurst

Emmeline Pankhurst (née Goulden, 1858–1928) was the leader of the British suffragette movement. Her parents were very interested in women's rights, and at the age of eight, Pankhurst was introduced to the idea of women's suffrage. She was educated at École Normale de Neuilly in Paris, where women were offered classes in chemistry and bookkeeping, which was unusual for the time, as well as more traditional offerings related to housekeeping and textiles. In 1889, she founded the Women's Franchise League with her husband Richard. Here, she befriended Harriot Eaton Stanton Blatch, daughter of Elizabeth Cady Stanton. Though the league was short-lived, Pankhurst joined the Independent Labour Party (ILP) and later founded the Women's Social and Political Union, a militant but non-violent organization open only to women (much as the ILP had been open only to men when she had applied to be a member). On the subject of their militancy, Pankhurst remarked, "The condition of our sex is so deplorable that it is our duty to break the law in order to call attention to the reasons why we do."

Speech delivered November 13, 1913, in Hartford Connecticut

Mrs. Hepburn, ladies and gentlemen: Many people come to Hartford to address meetings as advocates of some reform. Tonight it is not to advocate a reform that I address a meeting in Hartford. I do not come here as an advocate, because whatever position the suffrage movement may occupy in the United States of America, in England it has passed beyond the realm of advocacy and it has entered into the sphere of practical politics. It has become the subject of revolution and civil war, and so tonight I am not here to advocate woman suffrage. American suffragists can do that very well for themselves.

I am here as a soldier who has temporarily left the field of battle in order to explain—it seems strange it should have to be explained—what civil war is like when civil war is waged by women. I am not only here as a soldier temporarily absent from the field at battle; I am here—and that, I think, is the strangest part of my coming—I am here as a person who, according to the law courts of my country, it has been decided, is of no value to the community at all: and I am adjudged because of my life to be a dangerous person, under sentence of penal servitude in a convict prison. So you see there is some special interest in hearing so unusual a person address you. I dare say, in the minds of many of you—you will perhaps forgive me this personal touch —that I do not look either very like a soldier or very like a convict, and yet I am both.

Now, first of all I want to make you understand the inevitableness of revolution and civil war, even on the part of women, when you reach a certain stage in the development of a community's life. It is not at all difficult if revolutionaries come to you from Russia, if they come to you from China, or from any other part of the world, if they are men, to make you understand revolution in five minutes, every man and every woman to understand revolutionary methods when they are adopted by men.

Many of you have expressed sympathy, probably even practical sympathy, with revolutionaries in Russia. I dare say you have followed with considerable interest the story of how the Chinese revolutionary, Sun Yat-sen, conducted the Chinese revolution from England. And yet I find in American newspapers there is a great deal of misunderstanding of the fact that one of the chief minds engaged in conducting the women's revolution is, for purposes of convenience, located in Paris. It is quite easy for you to understand—it would not be necessary for me to enter into explanations at all—the desirability of revolution if I were a man, in any of these countries, even in a part of the British Empire known to you as Ireland. If an Irish revolutionary had addressed this meeting, and many have addressed meetings all over the United States during the last twenty or thirty years, it would not be necessary for that revolutionary to explain the need of revolution beyond saying that the people of his country were denied—and by people, meaning men—were denied the right of self-government. That would explain the whole situation. If I were a man and I said to you, "I come from a country which professes to have representative institutions and yet denies me, a taxpayer, an inhabitant of the country, representative rights," you would at once understand that that human being, being a man, was justified in the adoption of revolutionary methods to get representative institutions. But since I am a woman it is necessary in the twentieth century to explain why women have adopted revolutionary methods in order to win the rights of citizenship.

You see, in spite of a good deal that we hear about revolutionary methods not being necessary for American women, because American women are so well off, most of the men of the United States quite calmly acquiesce in the fact that half of the community are deprived absolutely of citizen rights, and we women, in trying to make our case clear, always have to make as part of our argument, and urge upon men in our audience the fact —a very simple fact—that women are human beings. It is quite evident you do not all realize we are human beings or it would not be necessary to argue with you that women may, suffering from intolerable injustice, be driven to adopt revolutionary methods. We have, first of all to convince you we are human beings, and I hope to be able to do that in the course of the evening before I sit down, but before doing that, I want to put a few political arguments before you—not arguments for the suffrage, because I said when I opened, I didn't mean to do that—

but arguments for the adoption of militant methods in order to win political rights.

A great many of you have been led to believe, from the somewhat meagre accounts you get in the newspapers, that in England there is a strange manifestation taking place, a new form of hysteria being swept across part of the feminist population of those Isles, and this manifestation takes the shape of irresponsible breaking of windows, burning of letters, general inconvenience to respectable, honest business people who want to attend to their business. It is very irrational you say: even if these women had sufficient intelligence to understand what they were doing, and really did want the vote, they have adopted very irrational means for getting the vote. "How are they going to persuade people that they ought to have the vote by breaking their windows?" you say. Now, if you say that, it shows you do not understand the meaning of our revolution at all, and I want to show you that when damage is done to property it is not done in order to convert people to woman suffrage at all. It is a practical political means, the only means we consider open to voteless persons to bring about a political situation, which can only be solved by giving women the vote.

Suppose the men of Hartford had a grievance, and they laid that grievance before their legislature, and the legislature obstinately refused to listen to them, or to remove their grievance, what would be the proper and the constitutional and the practical way of getting their grievance removed? Well, it is perfectly obvious at the next general election, when the legislature is elected, the men of Hartford in sufficient numbers would turn out that legislature and elect a new one: entirely change the personnel of an obstinate legislature which would not remove their grievance. It is perfectly simple and perfectly easy for voting communities to get their grievances removed if they act in combination and make an example of the legislature by changing the composition of the legislature and sending better people to take the place of those who have failed to do justice.

But let the men of Hartford imagine that they were not in the position of being voters at all, that they were governed without their consent being obtained, that the legislature turned an absolutely deaf ear to their demands, what would the men of

Hartford do then? They couldn't vote the legislature out. They would have to choose; they would have to make a choice of two evils: they would either have to submit indefinitely to an unjust state of affairs, or they would have to rise up and adopt some of the antiquated means by which men in the past got their grievances remedied. We know what happened when your forefathers decided that they must have representation for taxation, many, many years ago. When they felt they couldn't wait any longer, when they laid all the arguments before an obstinate British government that they could think of, and when their arguments were absolutely disregarded, when every other means had failed, they began by the tea party at Boston, and they went on until they had won the independence of the United States of America. That is what happened in the old days.

It is perfectly evident to any logical mind that when you have got the vote, by the proper use of the vote in sufficient numbers, by combination, you can get out of any legislature whatever you want, or, if you cannot get it, you can send them about their business and choose other people who will be more attentive to your demands, But, it is clear to the meanest intelligence that if you have not got the vote, you must either submit to laws just or unjust, administration just or unjust, or the time inevitably comes when you will revolt against that injustice and use violent means to put an end to it, That is so logically correct that we hear politicians today talk about the inherent right of revolution and rebellion on the part of human beings suffering from an intolerable injustice, and in England today we are having a situation brought about by men which exactly illustrates the case. We have got in Ireland today a very serious situation. I refer to the fact that for generations Irish agitators, Irish lawbreakers, Irish criminals, who have been sentenced to long terms of imprisonment in English convict prisons, have come over to America and have asked the people of the United States to give them money, to send them help in various forms to fight the Irish rebellion.

The Irish rebellion has at last, during the past few years, come into practical politics, and it has found shape in a measure which has now passed through the House of Commons and through the House of Lords, giving what the Irishmen so long wanted, home rule to Ireland. That is to say, next June, a parliament is going to be set up in Dublin, an Irish parliament, for the management of Irish affairs quite distinct from the government in London. The majority of men in Ireland desired it; presumably the majority of women acquiesced in their desire, but they were not asked whether they wished it or not. It is certain that in the course of the Irish rebellion women have taken a very prominent part; and it is rather a notable point to which I should like to call your attention, that when the imprisonments of Irishmen took place in the course of their political rebellion they were put almost invariably, after a certain amount of struggle, in the first division, and were treated as political offenders; but when women, helping the men, got into the coils of the law, all those women in Ireland who were helping the men to get home rule, were invariably treated as ordinary criminals and got ordinary criminals' treatment. You see, ladies, even in a rebellion, there is an advantage in being a voter, and if you are not a voter you are liable to get very much worse treatment than the voters, even the law-breaking voters, get. Now, the situation today then is, that home rule for Ireland is to take effect early next year, or in the course of next year.

But there is a part of Ireland which does not want home rule. There is a part of Ireland which prefers to be governed from London. That is the north of Ireland, in the County of Ulster. For racial reasons, for religious reasons, for economic reasons, the majority of the people there do not want home rule at all. They call themselves Loyalists, Unionists, and they want to maintain the union with Great Britain in its present form. Directly the home rule bill passed, directly it was perfectly clear that Home Rule was to be granted, these people began to revolt. They had a leader, a man who formed a part of the last Conservative administration, Sir Edward Carson. A distinguished lawyer, a distinguished statesman: he is an Irishman. Sir Edward Carson came to be the leader of the Ulster rebellion. He has advocated civil war: he has not only advocated civil war, he has urged the men of Ulster to drill and prepare to fight if civil war comes to pass. The first stage in this rebellion was the signing of a great declaration on behalf of the Union. It is rather notable that not only men signed that declaration, but women signed it also; the women of Ulster were invited to sign the declaration along with the men. And to those people who say that the province of woman is quite apart from politics, and that women by nature take no interest in politics, I would like to say that more women signed that declaration than did men, considerably more.

Well, the last stage of this struggle, and the struggle is coming to a head, is this; that Sir Edward Carson has been making speeches in which he has gloried in having broken the law; he has challenged the British government to arrest him; arms have been shipped to Ireland; and there is not a club, a young men's club, a workingman's club, or the middle class or the upper class men's club, where they are not drilling and preparing for civil war. The law has already been broken, because there has been considerable riot in the streets of Belfast, and lives even have been lost, and I want to say to you in this meeting how much have you heard of all this in the American newspapers? Have you heard loud condemnation from English newspapers echoed in your own papers? No; the newspapers and you have accepted quite calmly the fact that revolution is preparing in Ireland, and not one of you, whether you are a newspaper editor writing leading articles in your sanctum, or whether you are a business man or a professional man, not one of you has questioned the right of those men in Ulster, although they are voters and have a constitutional means for getting redress for their grievances, the right of those men to resort to revolution if everything else fails.

Well, there is another picture, another contrast I want to draw. We have Sir Edward Carson preaching revolution and justifying bloodshed in defense of what he calls the rights of the manhood of Ulster, the right of having themselves governed in the way they prefer. He has not hesitated to advocate the shedding of blood because be says it is quite worthwhile to shed blood, of your own and other people's, in defense of your citizen rights, in the defense of your having the right to choose the form of government you wish. Sir Edward Carson has not been arrested; Sir Edward Carson has not been charged with conspiracy; Sir Edward Carson has not been sent to jail. He has been making precisely the same kind of speeches that I made up to the month of March last, with this difference: that while he has justified the shedding of human blood in a revolution, I have always said that nothing would bring me to the point of claiming that we should destroy human life in the course of our woman's agitation. That is the only distinction between his speeches and mine, that he has advocated and justified the taking of life where I have always stopped short in my justification, at property, at inanimate objects. I have always said human life is sacred, and in a woman's revolution we respect human life, and we stop short of injury to human life.

Now, to those people who say that women are better treated than men when they break the laws, to those people who say that there is no need for women to take to methods of revolution, I want to draw this contrast; here is Sir Edward Carson, a man who presumably by his education and training, ought to be more respectful of the law than persons who are not either fit to understand the laws or to vote for those who make them. You have Sir Edward Carson, a chartered libertine, going to and fro in England and in Ireland, making these speeches; whereas you have me, a woman arrested and charged and sentenced to a long term of penal servitude for doing precisely what he has done, although he has not had the justification that I have, because, again I want to call your attention to the point, that Sir Edward Carson and his friends have the vote, and therefore have the legitimate and proper way of getting redress for their grievances, whereas neither I nor any of the women have any constitutional means whatever and no legitimate, recognized methods of getting redress or our grievances except the methods of revolution and violence.

Well now, I want to argue with you as to whether our way is the right one: I want to explain all these things that you have not understood: I want to make you understand exactly what our plan of campaign has been because I have always felt that if you could only make people understand most people's hearts are in the right place and most people's understandings are sound and most people are more or less logical—if you could only make them understand.

Now, I want to come back to the point where I said, if the men of Hartford had a grievance and had no vote to get their redress, if they felt that grievance sufficiently, they would be forced to adopt other methods. That brings me to an explanation of these methods that you have not been able to understand. I am going to talk later on about the grievances, but I want to first of all make you understand that this civil war carried on by women is not the hysterical manifestation which you thought it was, but was carefully and logically thought out, and I think when I have finished you will say, admitted the grievance, admitted the strength of the cause, that we could not do anything else, that there was no other way, that we had either to submit to intolerable injustice and let the woman's movement go back and remain in a worse position than it was before we began, or we had to go on with these methods until victory was secured; and I want also to convince you that these methods are going to win, because when you adopt the methods of revolution there are two justifications which I feel are necessary or to be desired. The first is, that you have good cause for adopting your methods in the beginning, and secondly that you have adopted methods which when pursued with sufficient courage and determination are bound, in the long run, to win.

Now, it would take too long to trace the course of militant methods as adopted by women, because it is about eight years since the word militant was first used to describe what we were doing; it is about eight years since the first militant action was taken by women. It was not militant at all, except that it provoked militancy on the part of those who were opposed to it. When women asked questions in political meetings and failed to get answers, they were not doing anything militant. To ask questions at political meetings is an acknowledged right of all people who attend public meetings; certainly in my country, men have always done it, and I hope they do it in America, because it seems to me that if you allow people to enter your legislatures without asking them any questions as to what they are going to do when they get there you are not exercising your citizen rights and your citizen duties as you ought. At any rate in Great Britain it is a custom, a time-honored one, to ask questions of candidates for parliament and ask questions of members of the government. No man was ever put out of a public meeting for asking a question until Votes for Women came onto the political horizon. The first people who were put out of a political meeting for asking questions, were women; they were brutally ill-used; they found themselves in jail before twenty-four hours had expired.

But instead of the newspapers, which are largely inspired by the politicians, putting militancy and the reproach of militancy, if reproach there is, on the people who had assaulted the women, they actually said it was the women who were militant and very much to blame. How different the reasoning is that men adopt when they are discussing the cases of men and those of women. Had they been men who asked the questions, and had those men been brutally ill-used, you would have heard a chorus of reprobation on the part of the people toward those who refused to answer those questions. But as they were women who asked the questions, it was not the speakers on the platform who would not answer them, who were to blame, or the ushers at the meeting; it was the poor women who had had their bruises and their knocks and scratches, and who were put into prison for doing precisely nothing but holding a protest meeting in the street after it was all over. However, we were called militant for doing that, and we were quite willing to accept the name, because militancy for us is time-honored; you have the church militant, and in the sense of spiritual militancy we were very militant indeed. We were determined to press this question of the enfranchisement of women to the point where we were no longer to be ignored by the politicians as had been the case for about fifty years, during which time women had patiently used every means open to them to win their political enfranchisement.

We found that all the fine phrases about freedom and liberty were entirely for male consumption, and that they did not in any way apply to women. When it was said taxation without representation is tyranny, when it was "Taxation of men without representation is tyranny," everybody quite calmly accepted the fact that women had to pay taxes and even were sent to prison if they failed to pay them—quite right. We found that "Government of the people, by the people and for the people," which is also a time-honored Liberal principle, was again only for male consumption; half of the people were entirely ignored; it was the duty of women to pay their taxes and obey the laws and look as pleasant as they could under the circumstances. In fact, every principle of liberty enunciated in any civilized country on earth, with very few exceptions, was intended entirely for men, and when women tried to force the putting into practice of these principles, for women, then they discovered they had come into a very, very unpleasant situation indeed.

Now, I am going to pass rapidly over all the incidents that happened after the two first women went to prison for asking questions of cabinet ministers, and come right up to the time when our militancy became real militancy, when we organized ourselves on an army basis, when we determined, if necessary, to fight for our rights just as our forefathers had fought for their rights. Then people began to say that while they believed they had no criticism of militancy, as militancy, while they thought it was quite justifiable for people to revolt against intolerable injustice, it was absurd and ridiculous for women to attempt it because women could not succeed. After all the most practical criticism of our militancy coming from men has been the argument that it could not succeed. They would say, "We would be with you if you could succeed but it is absurd for women who are the weaker sex, for women who have not got the control of any large interests, for women who have got very little money, who have peculiar duties as women, which handicaps them extremely—for example, the duty of caring for children—it is absurd for women to think they can ever win their rights by fighting; you had far better give it up and submit because there it is, you have always been subject and you always will be." Well now, that really became the testing time. Then we women determined to show the world, that women, handicapped as women are, can still fight and can still win, and now I want to show you how this plan of ours was carefully thought out, even our attacks on private property, which has been so much misunderstood. I have managed in London to make audiences of business men who came into the meetings very, very angry with us indeed, some of whom had their telephonic communication cut off for several hours and had not been able to even get telegrams from their stock-brokers in cities far distant, who naturally came to our meetings in a very angry frame of mind, understand the situation: and if it has been possible to make them understand, if some of them even get fairly enthusiastic about our methods, it ought to be possible, Mrs Hepburn, for me to explain the situation to an audience in Hartford, who, after all, are far enough off to be able to see, unlike men in our own country who are not able to see wood for trees.

I would like to suggest that if later on, while I am explaining these matters to you, there comes into the mind of any man or woman in the audience some better plan for getting what we want out of an obstinate government, I would be thankful and grateful if that person, man or woman, would tell me of some better plan than ours for dealing with the situation.

Here we have a political system where no reforms can get onto the statute book of the old country unless it is initiated by the government of the country, by the cabinet, by the handful of people who really govern the country. It doesn't matter whether you have practically every member of parliament on your side, you cannot get what you want unless the cabinet initiate legislation, a situation by which the private member has become almost of no account at all, the ordinary private member of parliament. He may introduce bills, but he knows himself that he is only registering a pious opinion of a certain number of electors in his constituency; it may be his own; but that pious opinion will never find its way onto the statute book of his country until the government in power, the prime minister and his colleagues, introduces a government measure to carry that reform. Well then, the whole problem of people who want reform is, to bring enough political pressure to bear upon the government to lead them to initiate, to draft a bill, and introduce it in the first instance, into the House of Commons, force it through the House of Commons, press it through the House of Lords, and finally land it safely, having passed through the shoals and rapids of the parliamentary river, safely on the statute book as an Act of Parliament. Well, combinations of voters have tried for generations, even with the power of the vote, to get their reforms registered in legislation, and have failed. You have to get your cause made a first class measure; you have to make the situation in the country so urgent and so pressing that it has become politically dangerous for the government to neglect that question any longer, so politically expedient for them to do it that they realize they cannot present themselves to the country at the next general election unless it has been done.

Well, that was the problem we had to face, and we faced it, a mere handful of women. Well, whether you like our methods or not, we have succeeded in making woman suffrage one of the questions which even cabinet ministers now admit cannot indefinitely be neglected. It must be dealt with within a very short period of time. No other methods than ours would have brought about that result. You may have sentimental articles in magazines by the chancellor of the exchequer who seems to be able to spare time from his ordinary avocations to write magazine articles telling you that militancy is a drag on the movement for woman suffrage. But our answer to that is, methinks our gentlemen doth protest too much, because until militancy became to be known neither Mr Lloyd George nor any statesman, no, nor any member of parliament, ever thought it was necessary to mention the subject of woman suffrage at all. Now they mention it constantly, to tell us what damage we have done to our cause. They are all urging us to consider the serious position into which we have brought the cause of woman suffrage.

Well now, let me come to the situation as we find it. We felt we had to rouse the public to such a point that they would say to the government, you must give women the vote. We had to get the electors, we had to get the business interests, we had to get the professional interests, we had to get the men of leisure all unitedly saying to the government, relieve the strain of this situation and give women the vote; and that is a problem that I think the most astute politician in this meeting would find very difficult. We have done it; we are doing it every day; and I think when you take that fact into consideration you will realize why we have been attacking private property, why we have been attacking the property of men so absorbed in their business that they generally forget to vote in ordinary elections, why we have attacked the pleasures of men whose whole life is spent in a round of pleasure, and who think politics so dull and so beneath their distinguished ossification that they hardly know which party is in power. All these people have had to be moved in order to bring enough pressure to bear upon the government to compel them to deal with the question of woman suffrage. And now that in itself is an explanation. There is a homely English proverb which may help to clear the situation which is this: "You cannot rouse the Britisher unless you touch his pocket." That is literally true. Perhaps you now can understand why we women thought we must attack the thing that was of most value in modem life in order to make these people wake up and realize that women wanted the vote, and that things were going to be very uncomfortable until women got the vote, because it is not by making people comfortable you get things in practical life, it is by making them uncomfortable. That is a homely truth that all of us have to learn.

I don't know, Mrs. Hepburn, whether I have used the domestic illustration in Hartford, but it is a very good one: it is quite worth using again. You have two babies very hungry and wanting to be fed. One baby is a patient baby, and waits indefinitely until its mother is ready to feed it. The other baby is an impatient baby and cries lustily, screams and kicks and makes everybody unpleasant until it is fed. Well, we know perfectly well which baby is attended to first. That is the whole history of politics. Putting sentiment aside, people who really want reforms learn that lesson very quickly. It is only the people who are quite content to go on advocating them indefinitely who play the part of the patient baby in politics. You have to make more noise than anybody else, you have to make yourself more obtrusive than anybody else, you have to fill all the papers more than anybody else, in fact you have to be there all the time and see that they do not snow you under, if you are really going to get your reform realized.

That is what we women have been doing, and in the course of our desperate struggle we have had to make a great many people very uncomfortable. Now, one woman was arrested on an occasion when a great many windows were broken in London, as a protest against a piece of trickery on the part of the government, which will be incredible in fifty years, when the history of the movement is read. Women broke some windows as a protest: they broke a good many shopkeepers' windows: they broke the windows of shopkeepers where they spent most of their money when they bought their hats and their clothing. They also broke the windows of many of the clubs, the smart clubs in Piccadilly.

One of the clubs was the Guard Club. Well, the ordinary army man is not much in politics, but he very often, because of his aristocratic and social connections, has considerable influence if he would use it. One woman broke the windows of the Guard Club, and when she broke those windows she stood there quietly until the Guard hall porter came out and seized her and held her until the policemen came to take her to prison. A number of the guards came out to see the kind of woman it was who had broken their windows, and they saw there a quiet little woman. She happened to be an actress, a woman who had come into our militant movement because she knew of the difficulties and dangers and temptations of the actress's life, of how badly paid she is, what her private sorrows are and her difficulties, and so she had come into the militant movement to get votes for actresses as quickly as possible, so that through the vote they could secure better conditions. Some of the guards—I think men who had never known what it was to earn a living, who knew nothing of the difficulties of a man's life, let alone the difficulties of a woman's life—came out, and they said: "Why did you break our windows? We have done nothing." She said: "It is because you have done nothing I have broken your windows." And perhaps out of that woman's breaking of windows has come this new movement of men of my country, where we find distinguished men who fought through the Boer war are drilling now like Sir Edward Carson in Belfast, drilling men in order to form a bodyguard to protect the militant women. Probably that broken window of the Guard Club did a good deal to rouse men to the defense of women and to the injustice of their situation.

Well, then the shopkeepers who could not understand why we should break the shopkeepers' windows. Why should we alienate the sympathy of the shopkeepers? Well, there is the other side of the question, gentlemen—why should the shopkeepers alienate the sympathy of their customers by refusing to help them to get political power, some power to make the condition of the woman who helps to earn the shopkeepers money by serving in his shop, easier than it is at the present time? Those women broke shopkeepers' windows, and what was the situation? Just at the beginning of the winter season when all the new winter hats and coats were being shown, the shopkeepers had to barricade all their windows with wood and nobody could see the new winter fashions. Well, there again is an impossible situation. The shopkeeper cannot afford to quarrel with his customers, and we have today far more practical sympathy amongst the shopkeepers of London than we ever had when we were quiet, gentle, ladylike suffragists asking nicely for a vote.

Well then, there were the men of pleasure, or the businessmen who were so busy earning money during the week that all they could think of when the week came to an end was recreation, and the great recreation in England today is playing golf. Everywhere on Saturday you see men streaming away into the country for the weekend to play golf. They so monopolize the golf links that they have made a rule that although the ladies may play golf all the week, the golf links are entirely reserved for men on Saturday and Sunday: and you have this spectacle of the exodus of men from London into the country to fill up the week-end with playing golf. They are not, ladies, putting their heads together thinking how best they can govern the country for you, what good laws they can make for you and for the world: they are there, all of them, getting their health, and I do not blame them for it, at the week-end. Well, we attacked the golf links; we wanted to make them think, and if you had been in London and taken a Sunday paper you would have read, especially if you played golf, with consternation, that all the beautiful greens that had taken years to make, had been cut up or destroyed with an acid or made almost impossible to play upon on the Friday night, and in many cases there were going to be important matches on the Saturday afternoon and Sunday.

Just to give you an illustration of the effectiveness of these methods in waking the Britisher up, in conveying to him that women want the vote and are going to get it even if we do not adopt quite the men's methods in order to do so. I was staying at a little house in the country on a golf links, a house that had been loaned to me to use whenever I could get away from my work, and several times in the course of that Sunday morning I got telephone calls from gentlemen who were prominent members of golf clubs in that vicinity. It so happened that the golf links where I was spending the weekend, had not been touched. Those links had been respected because some of the prominent women suffragettes happened to be members of the club, and those women who destroyed the greens—I don't know who they were, but it was no doubt done by women—spared the links where these women, whom they admired and respected, played. Well, then that morning I was rung up over and over again by excited gentlemen who begged that those golf links should be spared, saying: "I don't know whether your followers know that we are all suffragists, on our committee, we are entirely in favor of woman suffrage." And I said: "Well, don't you think you had better tell Mr Asquith so, because if you are suffragists and do nothing, naturally you will only add to the indignation of the women. If you really want your golf links spared you had better intimate to Mr. Asquith that you think it is high time he put his principles into practice and gave the women the vote." There was another gentleman who rang up and said: "The members of our committee, who are all suffragists, are seriously considering turning all the women members out of the club if this sort of thing goes on." "Well," I said, "don't you think your greater safety is to keep the women in the club as a sort of insurance policy against anything happening to your links?"

But this experience will show you that if you really want to get anything done, it is not so much a matter of whether you alienate sympathy; sympathy is a very unsatisfactory thing if it is not practical sympathy. It does not matter to the practical suffragist whether she alienates sympathy that was never of any use to her. What she wants is to get something practical done, and whether it is done out of sympathy or whether it is done out of fear, or whether it is done because you want to be comfortable again and not be worried in this way, doesn't particularly matter so long as you get it. We had enough of sympathy for fifty years; it never brought us anything, and we would rather have an angry man going to the government and saying, my business is interfered with and I won't submit to its being interfered with any longer because you won't give women the vote, than to have a gentleman come onto our platforms year in and year out and talk about his ardent sympathy with woman suffrage.

Now then, let me come to the more serious matters and to some of the more recent happenings. You know when you have war, many things happen that all of us deplore. We fought a great war not very long ago, in South Africa. Women were expected to face with equanimity the loss of those dearest to them in warfare; they were expected to submit to being impoverished; they were expected to pay the war tax exactly like the men for a war about which the women were never consulted at all. When you think of the object of that war it really makes some of us feel very indignant at the hypocrisy of some of our critics. That war was fought ostensibly to get equal rights for all whites in South Africa. The whole country went wild. We had a disease which was called Mafeka, because when the victory of Mafeking was declared everybody in the country, except a few people who tried to keep their heads steady, went absolutely mad with gratification at the sacrifice of thousands of human beings in the carrying on of that war. That war was fought to get votes for white men in South Africa, a few years sooner than they would have had them under existing conditions, and it was justified on those grounds, to get a voice in the government of South Africa for men who would have had that voice in five or six years if they had waited. That was considered ample justification for one of the most costly and bloody wars of modern times.

Very well, then when you have warfare things happen; people suffer; the noncombatants suffer as well as the combatants. And so it happens in civil war. When your forefathers threw the tea into Boston harbor, a good many women had to go without their tea. It has always seemed to me an extraordinary thing that you did not follow it up by throwing the whiskey overboard; you sacrificed the women; and there is a good deal of warfare for which men take a great deal of glorification which has involved more practical sacrifice on women than it has on any man. It always has been so. The grievances of those who have got power, the influence of those who have got power commands a great deal of attention; but the wrongs and the grievances of those people who have no power at all are apt to be absolutely ignored. That is the history of humanity right from the beginning.

Well, in our civil war people have suffered, but you cannot make omelets without breaking eggs; you cannot have civil war without damage to something. The great thing is to see that no more damage is done than is absolutely necessary, that you do just as much as will arouse enough feeling to bring about peace, to bring about an honorable peace for the combatants, and that is what we have been doing. Within the last few days you have read —I don't know how accurate the news cables are to America. I always take them with a grain of salt—but you have read within the last few days that some more empty houses have been burned, that a cactus house has been destroyed and some valuable plants have suffered in that house, that some pavilion at a pleasure ground has also been burned. Well, it is quite possible that it has happened.

I knew before I came here that for one whole day telegraphic and telephonic communication between Glasgow and London was entirely suspended. We do more in England in our civil war without the sacrifice of a single life than they did in the war of the Balkan States when they had the siege of Adrianople, because during the whole of that siege, in the course of which thousands of people were killed and houses were shelled and destroyed, telegraphic communication was continuous the whole time. If there had been a stock broker in Adrianople who wanted to communicate with a customer in London, he could have done it; there might have been a little delay, but he was able to do it, but we, without the loss of a single life in our war, in this effort to rouse business men to compel the government to give us the vote, because they are the people who can do it in the last resort, we entirely prevented stock brokers in London from telegraphing to stock brokers in Glasgow and vice versa: for one whole day telegraphic and telephonic communication was entirely stopped. I am not going to tell you how it was done. I am not going to tell you how the women got to the mains and cut the wires; but it was done. It was done, and it was proved to the authorities that weak women, suffrage women, as we are supposed to be, had enough ingenuity to create a situation of that kind. Now, I ask you, if women can do that, is there any limit to what we can do except the limit we put upon ourselves?

If you are dealing with an industrial revolution, if you get the men and women of one class to rising up against the men and women of another class, you can locate the difficulty; if there is a great industrial strike, you know exactly where the violence is, and every man knows exactly how the warfare is going to be waged; but in our war against the government you can't locate it. You can take Mrs Hepburn and myself on this platform, and now, without being told, how could you tell that Mrs Hepburn is a non-militant and that I am a militant? Absolutely impossible. If any gentleman who is the father of daughters in this meeting went into his home and looked around at his wife and daughters, if he lived in England and was an Englishman, he couldn't tell whether some of his daughters were militants or non-militants. When his daughters went out to post a letter, he couldn't tell if they went harmlessly out to make a tennis engagement at that pillarbox by posting a letter, or whether they went to put some corrosive matter in that would burn all the letters up inside of that box. We wear no mark; we belong to every class; we permeate every class of the community from the highest to the lowest; and so you see in the woman's civil war the dear men of my country are discovering it is absolutely impossible to deal with it: you cannot locate it, and you cannot stop it.

"Put them in prison," they said, "that will stop it." But it didn't stop it. They put women in prison for long terms of imprisonment, for making a nuisance of themselves—that was the expression when they took petitions in their hands to the door of the House of Commons; and they thought that by sending them to prison, giving them a day's imprisonment, would cause them to all settle down again and there would be no further trouble. But it didn't happen so at all: instead of the women giving it up, more women did it, and more and more and more women did it until there were three hundred women at a time, who had not broken a single law, only "made a nuisance of themselves" as the politicians say. Well then they thought they must go a little farther, and so then they began imposing punishments of a very serious kind. The judge who sentenced me last May to three years penal servitude for certain speeches in which I had accepted responsibility for acts of violence done by other women, said that if I could say I was sorry, if I could promise not to do it again, that he would revise the sentence and shorten it, because he admitted that it was a very heavy sentence, especially as the jury recommended me to mercy because of the purity of my motives; and he said he was giving me a determinate sentence, a sentence that would convince me that I would give up my "evil ways" and would also deter other women from imitating me. But it hadn't that effect at all. So far from it having that effect more and more women have been doing these things and I had incited them to do, and were more determined in doing them: so that the long determinate sentence had no effect in crushing the agitation.

Well then they felt they must do something else, and they began to legislate. I want to tell men in this meeting that the British government, which is not remarkable for having very mild laws to administer, has passed more stringent laws to deal with this agitation than it ever found it necessary during all the history of political agitation in my country. They were able to deal with the revolutionaries of the Chartists' time; they were able to deal with the trades union agitation; they were able to deal with the revolutionaries later on when the Reform Acts of 1867 and 1884 were passed: but the ordinary law has not sufficed to curb insurgent women. They have had to pass special legislation, and now they are on the point of admitting that that special legislation has absolutely failed. They had to dip back into the middle ages to find a means of repressing the women in revolt, and the whole history shows how futile it is for men who have been considered able statesmen to deal with dissatisfied women who are determined to win their citizenship and who will not submit to government until their consent is obtained. That is the whole point of our agitation. The whole argument with the anti-suffragists, or even the critical suffragist man, is this: that you can govern human beings without their consent.

They have said to us government rests upon force, the women haven't force so they must submit. Well, we are showing them that government does not rest upon force at all: it rests upon consent. As long as women consent to be unjustly governed, they can be, but directly women say: "We withhold our consent, we will not be governed any longer so long as that government is unjust." Not by the forces of civil war can you govern the very weakest woman. You can kill that woman, but she escapes you then; you cannot govern her. And that is, I think, a most valuable demonstration we have been making to the world. We have been proving in our own person that government does not rest upon force; it rests upon consent; as long as people consent to government, it is perfectly easy to govern, but directly they refuse then no power on earth can govern a human being, however feeble, who withholds his or her consent: and all of the strange happenings that you have read about over here, have been manifestations of a refusal to consent on the part of the women.

When they put us in prison at first, simply for taking petitions, we submitted; we allowed them to dress us in prison clothes; we allowed them to put us in solitary confinement; we allowed them to treat us as ordinary criminals, and put us amongst the most degraded of those criminals: and we were very glad of the experience, because out of that experience we learned of the need for prison reform; we learned of the fearful mistakes that men of all nations have made when it is a question of dealing with human beings; we learned of some of the appalling evils of our so-called civilization that we could not have learned in any other way except by going through the police courts of our country, in the prison vans that take you up to prison and right through that prison experience. It was valuable experience, and we were glad to get it. But there came a time when we said: "It is unjust to send political agitators to prison in this way for merely asking for justice, and we will not submit any longer."

And I am always glad to remind American audiences that two of the first women that came to the conclusion that they would not submit to unjust imprisonment any longer were two American girls who are doing some of the most splendid suffrage work in America today up in Washington. I think they are making things extremely lively for the politicians up there, and I don't know whether every American woman knows what those two women, working in conjunction with others, are doing for the enfranchisement of American women at this moment. I am always proud to think that Miss Lucy Burns and Miss Alice Paul served their suffrage apprenticeship in the militant ranks in England, and they were not slow about it either because one of them came, I believe it was, from Heidelberg, traveling all night, to take part in one of those little processions to Parliament with a petition. She was arrested and thrown into prison with about twenty others, and that group of twenty women were the first women who decided they would not submit themselves to the degradation of wearing prison clothes; and they refused, and they were almost the first to adopt the "hunger strike" as a protest against the criminal treatment. They forced their way out of prison. Well, then it was that women began to withhold their consent.

I have been in audiences where I have seen men smile when they heard the words "hunger strike", and yet I think there are very few men today who would be prepared to adopt a "hunger strike" for any cause. It is only people who feel an intolerable sense of oppression who would adopt a means of that kind. I know of no people who did it before us except revolutionaries in Russia—who adopted the hunger strike against intolerable prison conditions. Well, our women decided to terminate those unjust sentences at the earliest possible moment by the terrible means of the hunger strike. It means, you refuse food until you are at death's door, and then the authorities have to choose between letting you die, and letting you go; and then they let the women go.

Now, that went on so long that the government felt they had lost their power, and that they were unable to cope with the situation. Then it was that, to the shame of the British government, they set the example to authorities all over the world of feeding sane, resisting human beings by force. There may be doctors in this meeting: if so, they know it is one thing to treat an insane person, to feed by force an insane person, or a patient who has some form of illness which makes it necessary; but it is quite another thing to feed a sane, resisting human being who resists with every nerve and with every fibre of her body the indignity and the outrage of forcible feeding. Now, that was done in England, and the government thought they had crushed us. But they found that it did not quell the agitation, that more and more women came in and even passed that terrible ordeal, and that they were not able with all their forcible feeding to make women serve out their unjust sentences. They were obliged to let them go.

Then came the legislation to which I have referred, the legislation which is known in England as the "Cat and Mouse Act". It got through the British House of Commons because the home secretary assured the House of Commons that he wanted the bill passed in the interests of humanity. He said he was a humane man and he did not like having to resort to forcible feeding; he wanted the House of Commons to give him some way of disposing of them, and this was his way: he said, "Give me the power to let these women go when they are at death's door, and leave them at liberty under license until they have recovered their health again and then bring them back; leave it to me to fix the time of their licenses: leave it in my hands altogether to deal with this intolerable situation, because the laws must be obeyed and people who are sentenced for breaking the law must he compelled to serve their sentences." Well, the House of Commons passed the law. They said: "As soon as the women get a taste of this they will give it up." In fact, it was passed to repress the agitation, to make the women yield—because that is what it has really come to, ladies and gentlemen. It has come to a battle between the women and the government as to who shall yield first, whether they will yield and give us the vote, or whether we will give up our agitation.

Well, they little know what women are. Women are very slow to rouse, but once they are aroused, once they are determined, nothing on earth and nothing in heaven will make women give way; it is impossible. And so this "Cat and Mouse Act" which is being used against women today has failed: and the home secretary has taken advantage of the fact that parliament is not sitting, to revive and use alongside of it the forcible feeding. At the present time there are women lying at death's door, recovering enough strength to undergo operations, who have had both systems applied to them, and have not given in and won't give in, and who will be prepared, as soon as they get up from their sick beds, to go on as before. There are women who are being carried from their sick beds on stretchers into meetings. They are too weak to speak, but they go amongst their fellow workers just to show that their spirits are unquenched, and that their spirit is alive, and they mean to go on as long as life lasts.

Now, I want to say to you who think women cannot succeed, we have brought the government of England to this position, that it has to face this alternative: either women are to be killed or women are to have the vote. I ask American men in this meeting, what would you say if in your state you were faced with that alternative, that you must either kill them or give them their citizenship—women, many of whom you respect, women whom you know have lived useful lives, women whom you know, even If you do not know them personally, are animated with the highest motives, women who are in pursuit of liberty and the power to do useful public service? Well, there is only one answer to that alternative; there is only one way out of it, unless you are prepared to put back civilization two or three generations: you must give those women the vote. Now that is the outcome of our civil war.

You won your freedom in America when you had the revolution, by bloodshed, by sacrificing human life. You won the civil war by the sacrifice of human life when you decided to emancipate the negro. You have left it to women in your land, the men of all civilized countries have left it to women, to work out their own salvation. That is the way in which we women of England are doing. Human life for us is sacred, but we say if any life is to be sacrificed it shall be ours; we won't do it ourselves, but we will put the enemy in the position where they will have to choose between giving us freedom or giving us death.

Now whether you approve of us or whether you do not, you must see that we have brought the question of women's suffrage into a position where it is of first rate importance, where it can be ignored no longer. Even the most hardened politician will hesitate to take upon himself directly the responsibility of sacrificing the lives of women of undoubted honor, of undoubted earnestness of purpose. That is the political situation as I lay it before you today.

Now then, let me say something about what has brought it about because you must realize that only the very strongest of motives would lead women to do what we have done. Life is sweet to all of us. Every human being loves life and loves to enjoy the good things and the happiness that life gives: and yet we have a state of things in England that has made not two or three women but thousands of women quite prepared to face these terrible situations that I have been trying without any kind of passion or exaggeration to lay before you.

Well, I might spend two or three nights dealing with the industrial situation as it affects women, with the legal position of women, with the social position of women. I want very briefly to say a few words about all. First of all there is the condition of the working woman. One of the things which gives strength to our agitation is that the women who are taking an active part in it are not the poorest women, are not the overworked women; they are the women who are held to be fortunate, the women who have no special personal grievance of their own. Those women have taken up this fight for their own sake, it is true, because they wish to be free, but chiefly for the sake of the women less fortunate than themselves. The industrial workers of Great Britain have an average wage, mind you, not a minimum wage, an average wage, of less than two dollars a week. Think what would happen in any country if the men in industry of that country had to subsist on a wage like that. Thousands upon thousands of these women— because there are over five million wage earners in my country— thousands of these women have dependents; they are women with children dependent upon them, deserted wives with children dependent on them, or wives with sick husbands; they are unmarried mothers, or they are unmarried women who have old parents or younger brothers and sisters, or sick relatives dependent upon them. Their average income, taking the highly skilled woman teacher and averaging her wage with the unskilled home worker, the average income is less than two dollars a week. There you have in itself an explanation of an uprising of a very determined kind to secure better conditions; and when you know that the government is the largest employer of all the employers and sets a horribly bad example to the private employer in the wages that it pays to women, there you have another explanation. Constant economies are being affected in government departments by the substitution of women's labour for men's, and there is always a reduction in wages whenever women are employed. That is the industrial situation. To speak of the sweated home-worker would take too long, but there are women, women even with dependents, only able to earn three or four shillings a week, thousands of them, and having to pay with the increased cost of living, exorbitant rents in our great cities for single rooms, so that you get several families in one room: they cannot afford even to have a room for themselves. So much for the industrial situation.

Then there is the legal situation. The marriage laws of our country are bringing hundreds and hundreds of women into the militant ranks because we cannot get reform, the kind of reform that women want, of our marriage laws. First of all, a girl is held marriageable by English law, at the age of twelve years. When I was on trial they produced a little girl as a witness, a little girl who had found something in the neighborhood of the house of the chancellor of the exchequer, which was destroyed by some women, and this little girl was produced as a witness. It was said that it was a terrible thing to bring a little girl of twelve years of age and put her in the witness box in a court of law. I agreed, but I pointed out to the judge and the jury that one of the reasons why women were in revolt was because that little girl, whose head just appeared over the top of the witness box, was considered old enough by the laws of her country to take upon herself the terrible responsibilities of wifehood and motherhood, and women could not get it altered, no politicians would listen to us, when we asked to have the marriage law altered in that particular.

Then, the position of the wife. It is very frequently said that every woman who wants a vote, wants a vote because she has been disappointed, because she has not been chosen to be a wife. Well, I can assure you that if most women made a study of the laws before they decided to get married, a great many women would seriously consider whether it was worthwhile, whether the price was not too heavy, because, according to English law, a woman may toil all her life for her husband and her family, she may work in her husband's business, she may help him to build up the family income, and if he chooses at the end of a long life to take every penny of the money that woman has helped to earn away from her and her children, he can do it, and she has no redress. She may at the end of a long, hard life find herself and her children absolutely penniless because her husband has chosen to will the money away from her. So that you see when you look at it from the legal point of view, it is not such a very, very great gain to become a wife in my country. There are a great many risks that go along with it.

Then take her as a mother. If the child of two parents has any property inherited from relatives, and that child dies before it is of age to make a will, or without making a will, the only person who inherits the property of that child is the child's father; the mother does not exist as her child's heir at all; and during the father's lifetime she not only cannot inherit from her child but she has no voice whatever in deciding the life of her child. Her husband can give the child away to be educated somewhere else or he can bring whomever he pleases into the house to educate the child. He decides absolutely the conditions in which that child is to live; he decides how it is to be educated; he can even decide what religion it is to profess, and the mother's consent is not obtained to any of these decisions. Women are trying to alter it, have tried for generations, but they cannot because the legislatures have no time to listen to the opinions and the desires of people who have no votes.

Well then, when it comes to the question of how people are to get out of marriage, if they are unhappy, under the laws of divorce, the English law of divorce is the most scandalous divorce law in the civilized world. There may be a few states in America, and I believe in Canada, where the same law obtains, but the English divorce law is in itself such a stigma upon women, such a degradation to women, such an invitation to immorality on the part of the married man, that I think that divorce law in itself would justify a rebellion on the part of the women. You get registered in law unequal standards of morals in marriage, and a married man is encouraged by law to think that he can make as many lapses as he thinks fit in marital fidelity; whereas, if one act of infidelity is proved against her the husband can get rid of her by divorce, can take her children away from her and make her an outcast. Women who have been clamoring for an equal divorce law for generations cannot get any attention. Well now, we have had a royal commission on divorce and we have had a report, but there is no security for women that they are to have justice under a new law so long as men are chosen by men to legislate and those men are likely to register the moral opinions of men, not the moral opinions of women, in legislation.

We have to look facts in the face. Part of the militant movement for woman suffrage has had that effect, that women have learned to look facts in the face; they have got rid of sentimentalities; they are looking at actual facts: and when anti-suffragists talk about chivalry, and when they talk about putting women on pedestals and guarding them from all the difficulties and dangers of life, we look to the facts in life as we see them and we say: "Women have every reason to distrust that kind of thing, every reason to be dissatisfied; we want to know the truth however bad it is, and we face that truth because it is only through knowing the truth that you ever will get to anything better." We are determined to have these things faced and cleared up, and it is absolutely ridiculous to say to women that they can safely trust their interests in the hands of men who have already registered in the legislation of their country a standard of morals so unequal for both sexes as we find on the statute books of England today.

When the divorce commission sat, evidence was given by all kinds of people, and women had the experience of reading in the newspapers the evidence of the man who had been chosen by other men to preside over the divorce court, the judge whose duty it was to decide what was legal cruelty and decide whether women were to continue to be bound to their husbands or not. What did he say? I am glad to think that he is not in a position to give effect to his ideas any more; he now adorns the House of Lords: but he was still judge of the divorce court when he said, that in his opinion the wise wife was the woman who closed her eyes to the moral failings of her husband; and that was the man, women in this meeting, who had for years decided what was legal cruelty and what women were to endure or what they were not to endure in that relationship of husband and wife.

Well, can you wonder that all these things make us more militant? It seems to me that once you look at things from the woman's point of view, once you cease to listen to politicians, once you cease to allow yourself to look at the facts of life through men's spectacles but look at them through your own, every day that passes you are having fresh illustrations of the need there is for women to refuse to wait any longer for their enfranchisement.

Then, the latest manifestation, the latest cause of militancy has been the breaking of the great conspiracy of silence with regard to moral questions and the question of social disease that we have had during the last few years. I want to offer my testimony of gratitude to women like the lady who presides over us today and to the many of the medical men of the United States in making a lead in that direction. Before some of the suffragists had the courage even to study the question, these people spoke out; the medical profession in America has led the way, and through Dr Prince Morrow, and other men whose names we honor, we are at last beginning to know the real facts of the situation. We know this, that whatever women's wishes might be, it is their duty for the sake of the race, itself, to save the race, to insist upon having this question of the moral health of the nation approached from the women's point of view and settled by women in cooperation with men. It is our business to show the close relationship there is between the appalling state of social health and the political degradation of women. The two things go hand in hand. I have been reading a great many articles by very profound thinkers lately, and I see that somehow or other when you get men writing about them, even the best of men, they do evade the real issue, and that is, the status of women.

We women see so clearly the fact that the only way to deal with this thing is to raise the status of women; first the political status, then the industrial and the social status of women. You must make women count as much as men; you must have an equal standard of morals; and the only way to enforce that is through giving women political power so that you can get that equal moral standard registered in the laws of the country. It is the only way. I

585

don't know whether men sufficiently realize it, but we women do realize it: we more and more realize it, and so women have nerved themselves to speak out on this question. First of all, we feel that what is most important is that women should know it. Ten years ago it would have been impossible for any woman or any man to speak openly upon that question on any platform, because women had been taught that they must keep their eyes closed to all these things; women had been taught that they must ignore the fact even that a large section of their sex were living lives of degradation and outlawry. If they knew of it at all, they were told in vague terms that it was in order to make the lives of the rest of the women safe; they were told it was a necessary evil; they were told it was something that the good woman does not understand and must not know anything about. All that is now at an end. Women are refusing, men in this meeting, even if that were true, to have their lives made safe at the expense of their sisters. The women are determined. A good deal of the opposition to woman suffrage is coming from the very worst element in the population, who realize that once you get woman suffrage, a great many places that are tolerated today will have to disappear. It is perhaps a hard saying for many men that there will have to be self-control and an equal standard of morals, but the best men now, the scientists of every country, are supporting the woman's point of view.

It was thirty years ago in England that a splendid woman named Josephine Butler fought to establish an equal moral code for both sexes. She fought all her life; she was stoned; she was hooted; her meetings were broken up; her life was made absolutely dangerous; and yet that woman persisted and she secured the repeal of certain laws relating to prostitution which disgraced the statute books of our country. In those days the doctors were against her; practically everybody was against her. Men were told that it was necessary for their health that we should have an unequal moral code. Now that is all done away with and the foremost medical men and the foremost scientists are agreeing with the women; they are agreeing with the women that it is quite possible, and it is necessary for the sake of the race itself, that this equal moral code shall be established. Well, it is probably difficult; it is perhaps going to be difficult for generations; but it is to come, and it is out of the woman's movement that it is coming, because women today who have had the benefits of education, who have had the benefit of medical training and who have had the benefit of legal training, are informing their sex upon this question, and there is a good deal of opposition coming to it from strange directions; even people who have self-appointed themselves as the custodians of public morals are opposing the facts being told.

One of the strangest things that I have experienced for years is the fact that in New York, quite recently, copies of our paper, The Suffragette, in which were articles written by my daughter, quoting the opinions of medical men all over the world on this question, and relying on those quotations as a statement of fact, were offered for sale, and an attempt, a successful attempt temporarily, was made to prevent that paper being sold because it contained these articles telling the truth: and a book containing the articles in collected form prefaced with an article telling why this book was written, has also had an attack made upon it by that self-constituted guardian of public morals, Mr Comstock, supported by certain sections of the American press. Well, that book is here tonight: that book is here on sale. That book was written, not for people of my age, not for people who if there are dangers to be faced have either escaped or suffered from them: that book was written for young people. That book was written so that women should know. What is the use of locking the stable after the horse is stolen? Prevention is better than cure. This book was written to convince everybody of the danger, to point out the plain facts of the situation, and to convince thoughtful people that only through the emancipation of women, only through the uplifting of women, can you ever effectively deal with the situation. We have tried, we women, for generations to undo some of this evil; we have had our rescue societies; we have made all kinds of efforts; we have taken the poor unfortunate children who have been the outcome of this unequal code of morals between men and women, and what has happened? Matters have become sadly worse; we have scratched on the surface instead of cutting out the root of the evil. All that is changed. Today women are working in my country, are sacrificing and suffering to win the political enfranchisement of their sex, so that we may get better laws and better administration of the laws.

I could go on tonight pointing out to you how in my country small crimes against property, small thefts, small injuries to property are punished more severely than are any crimes committed against the physical and the moral integrity of members of my sex. I think I have said enough at least to make you understand that this uprising on the part of the British women has as much justification and as much provocation as any uprising on the part of men in their desire for political liberty in the past. We are not working to get the vote. We are not going to prison to get the vote, merely to say we have the vote. We are going through all this to get the vote so that by means of the vote we can bring about better conditions not only for ourselves but for the community as a whole.

Men have done splendid things in this world; they have made great achievements in engineering; they have done splendid organization work; but they have failed, they have miserably failed, when it has come to dealing with the lives of human beings. They stand self-confessed failures, because the problems that perplex civilization are absolutely appalling today. Well, that is the function of women in life: it is our business to care for human beings, and we are determined that we must come without delay to the saving of the race. The race must be saved, and it can only be saved through the emancipation of women.

Well, ladies and gentlemen, I want to say that I am very thankful to you for listening to me here tonight; I am glad if I have been able even to a small extent to explain to you something of the English situation. I want to say that I am not here to apologize. I do not care very much even whether you really understand, because when you are in a fighting movement, a movement which every fibre of your being has forced you to enter, it is not the approval of other human beings that you want; you are so concentrated on your object that you mean to achieve that object even if the whole world was up in arms against you. So I am not here tonight to apologize or to win very much your approbation. People have said: "Why does Mrs Pankhurst come to America? Has she come to America to rouse American women to be militant?" No, I have not come to America to arouse American women to be militant. I believe that American women, as their earnestness increases, as they realize the need for the enfranchisement of their sex, will find out for themselves the best way to secure that object. Each nation must work out its own salvation, and so the American women will find their own way and use their own methods capably.

Other people have said: "What right has Mrs Pankhurst to come to America and ask for American dollars?" Well, I think I have the right that all oppressed people have to ask for practical sympathy of others freer than themselves. Your right to send to France and ask for help was never questioned. You did it, and you got that help. Men of all nationalities have come to America, and they have not gone away empty-handed, because American sympathy has been extended to struggling peoples all over the world.

In England, if you could understand it, there is the most pathetic and the most courageous fight going on, because you find the people whom you have been accustomed to look upon as weak and reliant, the people you have always thought leaned upon other people for protection, have stood up and are fighting for themselves. Women have found a new kind of self-respect, a new kind of energy, a new kind of strength: and I think that of all oppressed peoples who might claim your sympathy and support, women who are fighting this fight unknown in the history of humanity before, fighting this fight in the twentieth century for greater powers of self-development, self-expression and self-government, might very well attract the sympathy and the practical help of American people.

There hasn't been a victory the women of America have won that we have not rejoiced in. I think as we have read month by month of the new States that have been added to the list of fully enfranchised states, perhaps we who know how hard the fight is, have rejoiced even more than American women themselves.

I have heard cheers ring out in a meeting in London when the news of some new state being added to the list was given, cheers louder and more enthusiastic than I have ever heard for any victory in an American meeting. It is very true that those who are fighting a hard battle, those who are sacrificing greatly in order to win a victory, appreciate victories and are more enthusiastic when victories are won. We have rejoiced wholeheartedly in your victories. We feel that those victories have been easier perhaps because of the hard times that we were having, because out of our militant movement in the storm centre of the suffrage movement have gone waves that have helped to rouse women all over the world. You could only explain the strange phenomena in that way. Ten years ago there was hardly any woman suffrage movement at all. Now even in China and Japan, in India, in Turkey, everywhere women are rising up and asking for these larger opportunities, which modern conditions demand that women should have: and we women think that we have helped. Well, if we have helped at all, if, as has been said from the chair tonight, we have even helped to rouse suffrage enthusiasm in Connecticut, can you blame me very much if I come and tell you of the desperate struggle we are having, of how the government is trying to break us down in every possible way, even by involving us in lawsuits, and trying to frighten our subscribers by threatening to prosecute even people who help us by subscribing money? Can you wonder I come over to America? Have you read about American dollars that have been given the Irish law-breakers?

So here am I. I come in the intervals of prison appearance: I come after having been four times imprisoned under the "Cat and Mouse Act", probably going back to be rearrested as soon as I set my foot on British soil. I come to ask you to help to win this fight. If we win it, this hardest of all fights, then, to be sure, in the future it is going to be made easier for women all over the world to win their fight when their time comes. So I make no apologies for coming, and I make no apologies, Mrs Hepburn, for asking this audience if any of them feel inclined to help me to take back some money from America and put it with the money that I know our women are raising by desperate personal sacrifice at home, so that when we begin our next year's campaign, facing a general election, as probably we shall face next year, our anxieties on the money side will not be so heavy as they would have been if I had not found strength and health enough to come and carry out this somewhat arduous tour in the United States of America.

On the Discovery
of Radium

Marie Sklowdowska Curie

*Marie Sklowdowska Curie (1867–1934) was a chemist and physicist who
remains the only person to win Nobel Prizes in two different sciences: She won in
Physics in 1903 for the discovery of radioactivity, sharing the prize with her
husband, Pierre Curie, and with Antoine Henri Becquerel; eight years later, she
won in Chemistry for isolating radium. She was also the first woman to receive a
Nobel prize. In this speech, she turns a very technical topic—the discovery of
radium—into a narrative that is as accessible to non-scientists as to other chemists
and physicists. She tells a story about a somewhat anthropomorphized element
("Radium is no more a baby," she says early on) that leads to a much broader
message very warmly received by her audience. That message was that scientific
research can be important for the sake of pure knowledge.*

Delivered May 14, 1921, at Vassar College

I could tell you many things about radium and radioactivity and it would take a long time. But as we cannot do that, I shall only give you a short account of my early work about radium. Radium is no more a baby, it is more than twenty years old, but the conditions of the discovery were somewhat peculiar, and so it is always of interest to remember them and to explain them.

We must go back to the year 1897. Professor Curie and I worked at that time in the laboratory of the school of Physics and Chemistry where Professor Curie held his lectures. I was engaged in some work on uranium rays which had been discovered two years before by Professor Becquerel. I spent some time in studying the way of making good measurements of the uranium rays, and then I wanted to know if there were other elements, giving out rays of the same kind. So I took up a work about all known elements, and their compounds and found that uranium compounds are active and also all thorium compounds, but other elements were not found active, nor were their compounds. As for the uranium and thorium compounds, I found that they were active in proportion to their uranium or thorium content. The more uranium or thorium, the greater the activity, the activity being an atomic property of the elements, uranium and thorium. Then I took up measurements of minerals and I found that several of those which contain uranium or thorium or both were active. But then the activity was not what I could expect, it was greater than for uranium or thorium compounds like the oxides which are almost entirely composed of these elements. Then I thought that there should be in the minerals some unknown element having a much greater radioactivity than uranium or thorium. And I wanted to find and to separate that element, and I settled to that work with Professor Curie. We thought it would be done in several weeks or months, but it was not so. It took many years of hard work to finish that task. There was not one new element, there were several of them. But the most important is radium, which could be separated in a pure state. Now, the special interest of radium is in the intensity of its rays which is several million times greater than the uranium rays. And the effects of the rays make the radium so important. If we take a practical point of view, then the most important property of the rays is the production of physiological effects on the cells of the human organism. These effects may be used for the cure of several diseases. Good results have been obtained in many cases. What is considered particularly important is the treatment of cancer. The medical utilization of radium makes it necessary to get that element in sufficient quantities. And so a factory of radium was started to begin with in France, and later in America where a big quantity of ore named carnotite is available. America does produce many grams of radium every year, but the price is still very high because the quantity of radium contained in the ore is so small. The radium is more than a hundred thousand times dearer than gold. But we must not forget that when radium was discovered no one knew that it would prove useful in hospitals. The work was one of pure science. And this is a proof that scientific work must not be considered from the point of view of the direct usefulness of it. It must be done for itself, for the beauty of science, and then there is always the chance that a scientific discovery may become like the radium a benefit for humanity. The scientific history of radium is beautiful. The properties of the rays have been studied very closely. We know that particles are expelled from radium with a very great velocity near to that of the light. We know that the atoms of radium are destroyed by expulsion of these particles, some of which are atoms of helium. And in that way it has been proved that the radioactive elements are constantly disintegrating and that they produce at the end ordinary elements, principally helium and lead. That is, as you see, a theory of transformation of atoms which are not stable, as was believed before, but may undergo spontaneous changes.

Radium is not alone in having these properties. Many having other radio-elements are known already, the polonium, the mesothorium, the radiothorium, the actinium. We know also radioactive gases, named emanations. There is a great variety of substances and effects in radioactivity. There is always a vast field left to experimentation and I hope that we may have some beautiful progress in the following years. It is my earnest desire that some of you should carry on this scientific work and keep for your ambition the determination to make a permanent contribution to science.

Anthropology and the Abnormal
Excerpts

Ruth Benedict

Ruth Fulton Benedict (1887–1948) was an American anthropologist. She taught at Columbia University after earning her Ph.D. in anthropology there.

In 1934 Benedict wrote "Anthropology and the Abnormal" and published Patterns of Culture, *her most influential book. Today we are very familiar and at ease with the concept of culture. We speak of the culture of a place as effortlessly as we discuss its location and time period. This familiarity is due in great part to Benedict and her book.*

In the article excerpted here Benedict makes the case that normality and abnormality are culturally defined concepts, and that applying those terms to human behavior can take place only within a cultural context. That is, nothing is abnormal in the absolute sense; the abnormal is that which is uncommon in a particular culture. Toward the end of the article she asserts that as it is with human behavior, so it is with judgments of morality: "all our local conventions of moral behavior and of immoral are without absolute validity." "Yet" she says, with more data from other cultures "it is quite possible that a modicum of what is considered right and what wrong could be disentangled that is shared by the whole human race." However, from her viewpoint it is highly likely that such a "shared modicum" would have little in common with ideas of absolute morality prevalent in our culture today.

Published in 1934 in *Journal of General Psychology*, *10 (1)*, pp. 59–80.

Modern social anthropology has become more and more a study of the varieties and common elements of cultural environment and the consequences of these in human behavior. For such a study of diverse social orders primitive peoples fortunately provide a laboratory not yet entirely vitiated by the spread of a standardized worldwide civilization. Dyaks and Hopis, Fijians and Yakuts are significant for psychological and sociological study because only among these simpler peoples has there been sufficient isolation to give opportunity for the development of localized social forms. In the higher cultures the standardization of custom and belief over a couple of continents has given a false sense of the inevitability of the particular forms that have gained currency, and we need to turn to a wider survey in order to check the conclusions we hastily base upon this near-universality of familiar customs. Most of the simpler cultures did not gain the wide currency of the one which, out of our experience, we identify with human nature, but this was for various historical reasons, and certainly not for any that gives us as its carriers a monopoly of social good or of social sanity. Modern civilization, from this point of view, becomes not a necessary pinnacle of human achievement but one entry in a long series of possible adjustments.

These adjustments, whether they are in mannerisms like the ways of showing anger, or joy, or grief in any society, or in major human drives like those of sex, prove to be far more variable than experience in any one culture would suggest. In certain fields, such as that of religion or of formal marriage arrangements, these wide limits of variability are well known and can be fairly described. In others it is not yet possible to give a generalized account, but that does not absolve us of the task of indicating the significance of the work that has been done and of die problems that have arisen.

One of these problems relates to the customary modern normal/abnormal categories and our conclusions regarding them. In how far are such categories culturally determined, or in how far can we with assurance regard them as absolute? In how far can we regard inability to function socially as abnormality, or in how far is it necessary to regard this as a function of the culture?

As a matter of fact, one of the most striking facts that emerge from a study of widely varying cultures is the ease with which our abnormals function in other cultures. It does not matter what kind of "abnormality" we choose for illustration, those which indicate extreme instability, or those which are more in the nature of character traits like sadism or delusions of grandeur or of persecution; there are well-described cultures in which these abnormals function at ease and with honor, and apparently without danger or difficulty to the society. . . .

The most notorious of these is trance and catalepsy. Even a very mild mystic is aberrant in our culture. But most peoples have regarded even extreme psychic manifestations not only as normal and desirable, but even as characteristic of highly valued and gifted individuals. This was true even in our own cultural background in that period when Catholicism made the ecstatic experience the mark of sainthood. It is hard for us, born and brought up in a culture that makes no use of the experience, to realize how important a role it may play and how many individuals are capable of it, once it has been given an honorable place in any society . . . .

It is clear that culture may value and make socially available even highly unstable human types. If it chooses to treat their peculiarities as the most valued variants of human behavior, the individuals in question will rise to the occasion and perform their social roles without reference to our usual ideas of the types who can make social adjustments and those who cannot.

Cataleptic and trance phenomena are, of course, only one illustration of the fact that those whom we regard as abnormals may function adequately in other cultures. Many of our culturally discarded traits are selected for elaboration in different societies. Homosexuality is an excellent example, for in this case our attention is not constantly diverted, as in the consideration of trance, to the interruption of routine activity which it implies. Homosexuality poses the problem very simply. A tendency toward this trait in our culture exposes an individual to all the conflicts to which all aberrants are always exposed, and we tend to identify the consequences of this conflict with homosexuality. But these consequences are obviously local and cultural. Homosexuals in many societies are not incompetent, but they may be such if the culture asks adjustments of them that would strain any man's vitality. Wherever homosexuality has been given an honorable place in any society, those to whom it is congenial have filled adequately the honorable roles society assigns to them. Plato's *Republic* is, of course, the most convincing statement of such a reading of homosexuality. It is presented as one of the major means to the good life, and it was generally so regarded in Greece at that time.

The cultural attitude toward homosexuals has not always been on such a high ethical plane, but it has been very varied. Among many American Indian tribes there exists the institution of the berdache, as the French called them. These men-women were men who at puberty or thereafter took the dress and the occupations of women. Sometimes they married other men and lived with them. Sometimes they were men with no inversion, persons of weak sexual endowment who chose this role to avoid the jeers of the women. The berdaches were never regarded as of first-rate supernatural power, as similar men-women were in Siberia, but rather as leaders in women's occupations, good healers in certain diseases, or, among certain tribes, as the genial organizers of social affairs. In any case, they were socially placed. They were not left exposed to the conflicts that visit the deviant who is excluded from participation in the recognized patterns of his society.

The most spectacular illustrations of the extent to which normality may be culturally defined are those cultures where an abnormality of our culture is the cornerstone of their social structure. It is not possible to do justice to these possibilities in a short discussion. A recent study of an island of northwest Melanesia by Fortune describes a society built upon traits which we regard as beyond the border of paranoia. In this tribe the exogamic groups look upon each other as prime manipulators of black magic, so that one marries always into an enemy group which remains for life one's deadly and unappeasable foes. They look upon a good garden crop as a confession of theft, for everyone is engaged in making magic to induce into his garden the productiveness of his neighbors'; therefore no secrecy in the island is so rigidly insisted upon as the secrecy of a man's harvesting of his yams. Their polite phrase at the acceptance of a gift is, "And if you now poison me, how shall I repay you this present?" Their preoccupation with poisoning is constant; no woman ever leaves her cooking pot for a moment unattended. Even the great affinal economic exchanges that are characteristic of this Melanesian culture area are quite altered in Dobu since they are incompatible with this fear and distrust that pervades the culture. They go farther and people the whole world outside their own quarters with such malignant spirits that all-night feasts and ceremonials simply do not occur here. They have even rigorous religiously enforced customs that forbid the sharing of seed even in one family group. Anyone else's food is deadly poison to you, so that communality of stores is out of the question. For some months before harvest the whole society is on the verge of starvation, but if one falls to the temptation and eats up one's seed yams, one is an outcast and a beachcomber for life. There is no coming back. It involves, as a matter of course, divorce and the breaking of all social ties.

Now in this society where no one may work with another and no one may share with another, Fortune describes the individual who was regarded by all his fellows as crazy. He was not one of those who periodically ran amok and, beside himself and frothing at the mouth, fell with a knife upon anyone he could reach. Such behavior they did not regard as putting anyone outside the pale. They did not even put the individuals who were known to be liable to these attacks under any kind of control. They merely fled when they saw the attack coming on and kept out of the way. "He would be all right tomorrow." But there was one man of sunny, kindly disposition who liked work and liked to be helpful. The compulsion was too strong for him to repress it in favor of the opposite tendencies of his culture. Men and women never spoke of him without laughing; he was silly and simple and definitely crazy. Nevertheless, to the ethnologist used to a culture that has, in Christianity, made his type the model of all virtue, he seemed a pleasant fellow . . . .

. . . Among the Kwakiutl it did not matter whether a relative had died in bed of disease, or by the hand of an enemy, in either case death was an affront to be wiped out by the death of another person. The fact that one had been caused to mourn was proof that one had been put upon. A chief's sister and her daughter had gone up to Victoria, and either because they drank bad whiskey or because their boat capsized they never came back. The chief called together his warriors, "Now I ask you, tribes, who shall wail? Shall I do it or shall another?" The spokesman answered, of course, "Not you, Chief. Let some other of the tribes." Immediately they set up the war pole to announce their intention of wiping out the injury, and gathered a war party. They set out, and found seven men and two children asleep and killed them. "Then they felt good when they arrived at Sebaa in the evening."

The point which is of interest to us is that in our society those who on that occasion would feel good when they arrived at Sebaa that evening would be the definitely abnormal. There would be some, even in our society, but it is not a recognized and approved mood under the circumstance. On the Northwest Coast those are favored and fortunate to whom that mood under those circumstances is congenial, and those to whom it is repugnant are unlucky. This latter minority can register in their own culture only by doing violence to their congenial responses and acquiring others that are difficult for them. The person, for instance, who, like a Plains Indian whose wife has been taken from him, is too proud to fight, can deal with the Northwest Coast civilization only by ignoring its strongest bents. If he cannot achieve it, he is the deviant in that culture, their instance of abnormality.

This head-hunting that takes place on the Northwest Coast after a death is no matter of blood revenge or of organized vengeance. There is no effort to tie up the subsequent killing with any responsibility on the part of the victim for the death of the person who is being mourned. A chief whose son has died goes visiting wherever his fancy dictates, and he says to his host, "My prince has died today, and you go with him." Then he kills him. In this, according to their interpretation, he acts nobly because he has not been downed. He has thrust back in return. The whole procedure is meaningless without the fundamental paranoid reading of bereavement. Death, like all the other untoward accidents of existence, confounds man's pride and can only be handled in the category of insults.

The behavior honored upon the Northwest Coast is one which is recognized as abnormal in our civilization, and yet it is sufficiently close to the attitudes of our own culture to be intelligible to us and to have a definite vocabulary with which we may discuss it. The megalomaniac paranoid trend is a definite danger in our society. It is encouraged by some of our major preoccupations, and it confronts us with a choice of two possible attitudes. One is to brand it as abnormal and reprehensible, and it is the attitude we have chosen in our civilization. The other is to make it an essential attribute of ideal man, and this is the solution in the culture of the Northwest Coast.

These illustrations, which it has been possible to indicate only in the briefest manner, force upon us the fact that normality is culturally defined. An adult shaped to the drives and standards of either of these cultures, if he were transported into our civilization, would fall into our categories of abnormality. He would be faced with the psychic dilemmas of the socially unavailable. In his own culture, however, he is the pillar of society, the end result of socially inculcated mores, and the problem of personal instability in his case simply does not arise.

No one civilization can possibly utilize in its mores the whole potential range of human behavior. Just as there are great numbers of possible phonetic articulations, and the possibility of language depends on a selection and standardization of a few of these in order that speech communication may be possible at all, so the possibility of organized behavior of every sort, from the fashions of local dress and houses to the dicta of a people's ethics and religion, depends upon a similar selection among the possible behavior traits. In the field of recognized economic obligations or sex tabus this selection is as nonrational and subconscious a process as it is in the field of phonetics. It is a process which goes on in the group for long periods of time and is historically conditioned by innumerable accidents of isolation or of contact of peoples. In any comprehensive study of psychology, the selection that different cultures have made in the course of history within the great circumference of potential behavior is of great significance.

Every society, beginning with some slight inclination in one direction or another, carries its preference farther and farther, integrating itself more and more completely upon its chosen basis, and discarding those types of behavior that are uncongenial. Most of those organizations of personality that seem to us most uncontrovertibly abnormal have been used by different civilizations in the very foundations of their institutional life. Conversely the most valued traits of our normal individuals have been looked on in differently organized cultures as aberrant. Normality, in short, within a very wide range, is culturally defined. It is primarily a term for the socially elaborated segment of human behavior in any culture; and abnormality, a term for the segment that particular civilization does not use. The very eyes with which we see the problem are conditioned by the long traditional habits of our own society.

It is a point that has been made more often in relation to ethics than in relation to psychiatry. We do not any longer make the mistake of deriving the morality of our locality and decade directly from the inevitable constitution of human nature. We do not elevate it to the dignity of a first principle. We recognize that morality differs in every society, and is a convenient term for socially approved habits. Mankind has always preferred to say, "It is morally good," rather than "It is habitual," and the fact of this preference is matter enough for a critical science of ethics. But historically the two phrases are synonymous.

The concept of the normal is properly a variant of the concept of the good. It is that which society has approved. A normal action is one which falls well within the limits of expected behavior for a particular society. Its variability among different peoples is essentially a function of the variability of the behavior patterns that different societies have created for themselves, and can never be wholly divorced from a consideration of culturally institutionalized types of behavior.

Each culture is a more or less elaborate working-out of the potentialities of the segment it has chosen. In so far as a civilization is well integrated and consistent within itself, it will tend to carry farther and farther, according to its nature, its initial impulse toward a particular type of action, and from the point of view of any other culture those elaborations will include more and more extreme and aberrant traits.

Each of these traits, in proportion as it reinforces the chosen behavior patterns of that culture, is for that culture normal. Those individuals to whom it is congenial either congenitally, or as the result of childhood sets, are accorded prestige in that culture, and are not visited with the social contempt or disapproval which their traits would call down upon them in a society that was differently organized. On the other hand, those individuals whose characteristics are not congenial to the selected type of human behavior in that community are the deviants, no matter how valued their personality traits may be in a contrasted civilization.

The Dobuan who is not easily susceptible to fear of treachery, who enjoys work and likes to be helpful, is their neurotic and regarded as silly. On the Northwest Coast the person who finds it difficult to read life in terms of an insult contest will be the person upon whom fall all the difficulties of the culturally unprovided for. The person who does not find it easy to humiliate a neighbor, nor to see humiliation in his own experience, who is genial and loving, may, of course, find some unstandardized way of achieving satisfactions in his society, but not in the major patterned responses that his culture requires of him. If he is born to play an important role in a family with many hereditary privileges, he can succeed only by doing violence to his whole personality. If he does not succeed, he has betrayed his culture; that is, he is abnormal.

I have spoken of individuals as having sets toward certain types of behavior, and of these sets as running sometimes counter to the types of behavior which are institutionalized in the culture to which they belong. From all that we know of contrasting cultures it seems clear that differences of temperament occur in every society. The matter has never been made the subject of investigation, but from the available material it would appear that these temperament types are very likely of universal recurrence. That is, there is an ascertainable range of human behavior that is found wherever a sufficiently large series of individuals is observed. But the proportion in which behavior types stand to one another in different societies is not universal. The vast majority of individuals in any group are shaped to the fashion of that culture. In other words, most individuals are plastic to the moulding force of the society into which they are born. In a society that values trance, as in India, they will have supernormal experience. In a society that institutionalizes homosexuality, they will be homosexual. In a society that sets the gathering of possessions as the chief human objective, they will amass property. The deviants, whatever the type of behavior the culture has institutionalized, will remain few in number, and there seems no more difficulty in moulding the vast malleable majority to the "normality" of what we consider an aberrant trait, such as delusions of reference, than to the normality of such accepted behavior patterns as acquisitiveness. The small proportion of the number of the deviants in any culture is not a function of the sure instinct with which that society has built itself upon the fundamental sanities, but of the universal fact that, happily, the majority of mankind quite readily take any shape that is presented to them . . . .

The problem of understanding abnormal human behavior in any absolute sense independent of cultural factors is still far in the future. The categories of borderline behavior which we derive from the study of the neuroses and psychoses of our civilization are categories of prevailing local types of instability. They give much information about the stresses and strains of Western civilization, but no final picture of inevitable human behavior. Any conclusions about such behavior must await the collection by trained observers of psychiatric data from other cultures. Since no adequate work of the kind has been done at the present time, it is impossible to say what core of definition of abnormality may be found valid from the comparative material. It is as it is in ethics; all our local conventions of moral behavior and of immoral are without absolute validity, and yet it is quite possible that a modicum of what is considered right and what wrong could be disentangled that is shared by the whole human race. When data are available in psychiatry, this minimum definition of abnormal human tendencies will be probably quite unlike our culturally conditioned, highly elaborated psychoses such as those that are described, for instance, under the terms of schizophrenia and manic-depressive.

The Rhetoric of Hitler's "Battle"

Kenneth Burke

Kenneth Burke (1897–1993) was an American literary theorist with a prolific career. During his life, he published twelve nonfiction books on literary criticism, a book of fiction, and another of essays. He developed dramatism as a theory of human communication and relationships, a theory that is still widely used in literary analyses.

In 1925 and 1926 Adolf Hitler published a two-volume autobiography, Mein Kampf *(literally, "my struggle" in German). This work served as a manifesto for the National Socialist (Nazi) Party in Germany. In 1933 Hitler was appointed Chancellor of Germany by Paul von Hindenberg, and he quickly established a totalitarian regime.*

In March of 1939 Mein Kampf *was published in English unabridged (it had been translated and published in several abridged versions previously). Three months later, Kenneth Burke published the following article detailing the mechanisms he saw at work in Hitler's words. He wrote that his desire was not only to discover what would likely happen in Germany but also to prevent similar things from happening in America. Three months after his review was published, Germany invaded Poland, beginning World War II.*

> *Note: Footnotes were added by Burke when he reprinted this article in his* Philosophy of Literary Form. *The footnotes included here appear as they are in the second edition of this text in 1967 by Louisiana State University Press, which first published this article in* The Southern Review.

Published in The Southern Review, 5; 1-21.

The appearance of *Mein Kampf* in unexpurgated translation has called forth far too many vandalistic comments. There are other ways of burning books than on the pyre—and the favorite method of the hasty reviewer is to deprive himself and his readers by inattention. I maintain that it is thoroughly vandalistic for the reviewer to content himself with the mere inflicting of a few symbolic wounds upon this book and its author, of an intensity varying with the resources of the reviewer and the time at his disposal. Hitler's "Battle" is exasperating, even nauseating. Yet the fact remains: If the reviewer but knocks off a few adverse attitudinizings and calls it a day, with a guaranty, in advance, that his article will have a favorable reception among the decent members of our population, he is contributing more to our gratification than to our enlightenment.

Here is the testament of a man who swung a great people into his wake. Let us watch it carefully; and let us watch it, not merely to discover some grounds for prophesying what political move is to follow Munich, and what move is to follow that move, etc.; let us try also to discover what kind of "medicine" this medicine-man has concocted, that we may know, with greater accuracy, exactly what to guard against if we are to forestall the concocting of similar medicine in America.

Already, in many quarters of our country, we are "beyond" the stage where we are being saved from Nazism by our *virtues.* And fascist integration is being staved off, rather by the *conflicts among our vices.* Our vices cannot get together in a grand united front of prejudices; and the result of this frustration, if or until they succeed in surmounting it, speaks, as the Bible might say, "in the name of" democracy. Hitler found a "cure for what ails you," a "snakeoil," that made such sinister unifying possible within his own nation. And he was helpful enough to put his cards face up on the table, that we might examine his hands. Let us, then, for God's sake, examine them. This book is the well of Nazi magic; crude magic, but effective. A people trained in pragmatism should want to inspect this magic.

I

Every movement that would recruit its followers from among many discordant and divergent bands, must have some spot towards which all roads lead. Each man may get there in his own way, but it must be the one unifying center of reference for all. Hitler considered this matter carefully, and decided that this center must be not merely a centralizing hub of *ideas,* but a mecca geographically located, towards which all eyes could turn at the appointed hours of prayer (or, in this case, the appointed hours of prayer-in-reverse, the hours of vituperation). So he selected Munich, as the *materialization* of his unifying panacea. As he puts it:

> The geo-political importance of a center of a movement cannot be overrated. Only the presence of such a center and of a place, bathed in the magic of a Mecca or a Rome, can at length give a movement that force which is rooted in the inner unity and in the recognition of a hand that represents this unity.*

If a movement must have its Rome, it must also have its devil. For as Russell pointed out years ago, an important ingredient of unity in the Middle Ages (an ingredient that long did its unifying work despite the many factors driving towards disunity) was the symbol of a *common enemy,* the Prince of Evil himself. Men who can unite on nothing else can unite on the basis of a foe shared by all. Hitler himself states the case very succinctly:

> As a whole, and at all times, the efficiency of the truly national leader consists primarily in preventing the division of the attention of a people, and always in concentrating it on a single enemy. The more uniformly the fighting will of a people is put into action, the greater will be the magnetic force of the movement and the more powerful the impetus of the blow. It is part of the genius of a great leader to make adversaries of different fields appear as always belonging to one category only, because to weak and unstable characters the knowledge that there are various enemies will lead only too easily to incipient doubts as to their own cause.
>
> As soon as the wavering masses find themselves confronted with too many enemies, objectivity at once steps in, and the question is raised whether actually all the others are wrong and their own nation or their own movement alone is right.
>
> Also with this comes the first paralysis of their own strength.

---

* The quotations are from the Reynal & Hitchcock edition ($3.00).

> Therefore, a number of essentially different enemies must always
> be regarded as one in such a way that in the opinion of the mass of
> one's own adherents the war is being waged against one enemy
> alone. This strengthens the belief in one's own cause and increases
> one's bitterness against the attacker.

As everyone knows, this policy was exemplified in his
selection of an "international" devil, the "international Jew" (the
Prince was international, universal, "catholic"). This *materialization*
of a religious pattern is, I think, one terrifically effective weapon
of propaganda in a period where religion has been progressively
weakened by many centuries of capitalist materialism. You need
but go back to the sermonizing of centuries to be reminded that
religion had a powerful enemy long before organized atheism
came upon the scene. Religion is based upon the "prosperity of
poverty," upon the use of ways for converting our sufferings and
handicaps into a good—but capitalism is based upon the
prosperity of acquisitions, the only scheme of value, in fact, by
which its proliferating store of gadgets could be sold, assuming
for the moment that capitalism had not got so drastically in its
own way that it can't sell its gadgets even after it has trained
people to feel that human dignity, the "higher standard of living,"
could be attained only by their vast private accumulation.

So, we have, as unifying step number 1, the international devil
materialized, in the visible, point-to-able form of people with a
certain kind of "blood," a burlesque of contemporary neo-
positivism's ideal of meaning, which insists upon a *material* reference.

Once Hitler has thus essentialized his enemy, all "proof"
henceforth is automatic. If you point out the enormous amount
of evidence to show that the Jewish worker is at odds with the
"international Jew stock exchange capitalist," Hitler replies with one
hundred per cent regularity: That is one more indication of the
cunning with which the "Jewish plot" is being engineered. Or would
you point to "Aryans" who do the same as his conspiratorial Jews?
Very well; it is proof that the "Aryan" has been "seduced" by the Jew.

The sexual symbolism that runs through Hitler's book, lying
in wait to draw upon the responses of contemporary sexual
values, is easily characterized: Germany in dispersion is the
"dehorned Siegfried." The masses are "feminine." As such, they
desire to be led by a dominating male. This male, as orator, woos

them—and, when he has won them, he commands them. The rival male, the villainous Jew, would on the contrary "seduce" them. If he succeeds, he poisons their blood by intermingling with them. Whereupon, by purely associative connections of ideas, we are moved into attacks upon syphilis, prostitution, incest, and other similar misfortunes, which are introduced as a kind of "musical" argument when he is on the subject of "blood-poisoning" by intermarriage or, in its "spiritual" equivalent, by the infection of "Jewish" ideas, such as democracy.[1]

The "medicinal" appeal of the Jew as scapegoat operates from another angle. The middle class contains, within the mind of each member, a duality: its members simultaneously have a cult of money and a detestation of this cult. When capitalism is going well, this conflict is left more or less in abeyance. But when capitalism is balked, it comes to the fore. Hence, there is "medicine" for the "Aryan" members of the middle class in the projective device of the scapegoat, whereby the "bad" features can be allocated to the "devil," and one can "respect himself" by a distinction between "good" capitalism and "bad" capitalism, with those of a different lodge being the vessels of the "bad" capitalism. It is doubtless the "relief" of this solution that spared Hitler the necessity of explaining just how the "Jewish plot" was to work out. Nowhere does this book, which is so full of war plans, make the slightest attempt to explain the steps whereby the triumph of "Jewish Bolshevism," which destroys *all* finance, will be the triumph of *"Jewish"* finance. Hitler well knows the point at which his "elucidations" should rely upon the lurid alone.

The question arises, in those trying to gauge Hitler: Was his selection of the Jew, as his unifying devil-function, a purely calculating act? Despite the quotation I have already given, I believe that it was *not.* The vigor with which he utilized it, I think, derives from a much more complex state of affairs. It seems that, when Hitler went to Vienna, in a state close to total poverty, he genuinely suffered. He lived among the impoverished; and he describes his misery at the spectacle. He was *sensitive* to it; and his

---

[1] Hitler also strongly insists upon the total identification between leader and people. Thus, in wooing the people, he would in a roundabout way be wooing himself. The thought might suggest how the Führer. dominating the feminine masses by his diction, would have an incentive to remain unmarried.

way of manifesting this sensitiveness impresses me that he is, at this point, wholly genuine, as with his wincing at the broken family relationships caused by alcoholism, which he in turn relates to impoverishment. During this time he began his attempts at political theorizing; and his disturbance was considerably increased by the skill with which Marxists tied him into knots. One passage in particular gives you reason, reading between the lines, to believe that the dialecticians of the class struggle, in their still at blasting his muddled speculations, put him into a state of uncertainty that was finally "solved" by rage:

> The more I argued with them, the more I got to know their dialectics. First they counted on the ignorance of their adversary; then, when there was no way out, they themselves pretended stupidity. If all this was of no avail, they refused to understand or they changed the subject when driven into a corner; they brought up truisms, but they immediately transferred their acceptance to quite different subjects, and, if attacked again, they gave way and pretended to know nothing exactly. Wherever one attacked one of these prophets, one's hands seized slimy jelly; it slipped through one's fingers only to collect again in the next moment. If one smote one of them so thoroughly that, with the bystanders watching, he could but agree, and if one thus thought he had advanced at least one step, one was greatly astonished the following day. The Jew did not in the least remember the day before, he continued to talk in the same old strain as if nothing had happened, and if indignantly confronted, he pretended to be astonished and could not remember anything except that his assertions had already been proved true the day before.

> Often I was stunned.

> One did not know what to admire more: their glibness of tongue or their skill in lying.

> I gradually began to hate them.

At this point, I think, he is tracing the *spontaneous* rise of his anti-Semitism. He tells how, once he had discovered the "cause" of the misery about him, he could *confront it.* Where he had had to avert his eyes, he could now *positively welcome* the scene. Here his drastic structure of *acceptance* was being formed. He tells of the "internal happiness" that descended upon him.

> This was the time in which the greatest change I was ever to experience took place in me.

> From a feeble cosmopolite I turned into a fanatical anti-Semite. . . .

609

And thence we move, by one of those associational tricks which he brings forth at all strategic moments, into a vision of the end of the world—out of which in turn he emerges with his slogan: "I am acting in the sense of the Almighty Creator: *By warding off Jews I am fighting for the Lord's work*" (italics his).

He talks of this transition as a period of "double life," a struggle of "reason" and "reality" against his "heart."[2] It was as "bitter" as it was "blissful." And finally, it was "reason" that won! Which prompts us to note that those who attack Hitlerism as a cult of the irrational should emend their statements to this extent: irrational it is, but it is carried on under the *slogan* of "reason." Similarly, his cult of war is developed "in the name of" humility love, and peace. Judged on a quantitative basis, Hitler's book certainly falls under the classification of hate. Its venom is everywhere, its charity is sparse. But the rationalized family tree for this hate situates it in "Aryan love." Some deep-probing German poets, whose work adumbrated the Nazi movement did gravitate towards thinking *in the name of* war, irrationality, and hate. But Hitler was not among them. After all, when it is so easy to draw a doctrine of war out of a doctrine of peace, why should

---

[2] Other aspects of the career symbolism: Hitler's book begins: "Today I consider it my good fortune that Fate designated Braunau on the Inn as the place of my birth. For this small town is situated on the border between those two German States, the reunion of which seems, at least to us of the younger generation, a task to be furthered with every means our lives long," an indication of his "transitional" mind, what Wordsworth might have called the "borderer." He neglects to give the date of his birth, 1889, which is supplied by the editors. Again there is a certain "correctness" here, as Hitler was not "born" until many years later—but he does give the exact date of his war wounds, which were indeed formative. During his early years in Vienna and Munich, he foregoes protest, on the grounds that he is "nameless." And when his party is finally organized and effective, he stresses the fact that his "nameless" period is over (i. e., he has shaped himself an identity). When reading in an earlier passage of his book some generalizations to the effect that one should not crystallize his political views until he is thirty, I made a note: "See what Hitler does at thirty." I felt sure that, though such generalizations may be dubious as applied to people as a whole, they must, given the Hitler type of mind (with his complete identification between himself and his followers), be valid statements about himself. One should do what he did. The hunch was verified: about the age of thirty Hitler, in a group of seven, began working with the party that was to conquer Germany. I trace these steps particularly because I believe that the orator who has a strong sense of his own "rebirth" has this to draw upon when persuading his audiences that his is offering them the way to a "new life." However, I see no categorical objection to this attitude; its menace derives solely from the values in which it is exemplified. They may be wholesome or unwholesome. If they are unwholesome, but backed by conviction, the basic sincerity of the conviction acts as a sound virtue to reinforce a vice—and this combination is the most disastrous one that a people can encounter in a demagogue.

the astute politician do otherwise, particularly when Hitler has slung together his doctrines, without the slightest effort at logical symmetry? Furthermore, church thinking always got to its wars in Hitler's "sounder" manner; and the patterns of Hitler's thought are a bastardized or caricatured version of religious thought.

I spoke of Hitler's fury at the dialectics of those who opposed him when his structure was in the stage of scaffolding. From this we may move to another tremendously important section of his theory: his attack upon the *parliamentary*. For it is, again, I. submit, an important aspect of his medicine, in its function as medicine for him personally and as medicine for those who were later to identify themselves with him.

There is a problem in the parliament—and nowhere was this problem more acutely in evidence than in the prewar Vienna that was to serve as Hitler's political schooling. For the parliament, at its best, is a "babel" of voices. There is the wrangle of men representing interests lying awkwardly on the bias across one another, sometimes opposing, sometimes vaguely divergent. Morton Prince's psychiatric study of "Miss Beauchamp," the case of a woman split into several sub-personalities at odds with one another, variously combining under hypnosis, and frequently in turmoil, is the allegory of a democracy fallen upon evil days. The parliament of the Hapsburg Empire just prior to its collapse was an especially drastic instance of such disruption, such vocal diaspora, with movements that would reduce one to a disintegrated mass of fragments if he attempted to encompass the totality of its discordancies. So Hitler, suffering under the alienation of poverty and confusion, yearning for some integrative core, came to take this parliament as the basic symbol of all that he would move away from. He damned the tottering Hapsburg Empire as a "State of Nationalities." The many conflicting voices of the spokesmen of the many political blocs arose from the fact that various separationist movements of a nationalistic sort had arisen within a Catholic imperial structure formed prior to the nationalistic emphasis and slowly breaking apart under its development. So, you had this Babel of voices; and, by the method of associative mergers, *using ideas as imagery,* it became tied up, in the Hitler rhetoric, with "Babylon," Vienna as the city of poverty, prostitution, immorality, coalitions, half-measures, incest, democracy (i.e., majority-rule leading to "lack of personal responsibility"), death, internationalism, seduction, and anything else of thumbs-down sort the associative enterprise cared to add on this side of the balance.

Hitler's way of treating the parliamentary babel, I am sorry to say, was at one important point not much different from that of the customary editorial in our own newspapers. Every conflict among the parliamentary spokesmen represents a corresponding conflict among the material interests of the groups for whom they are speaking. But Hitler did not discuss the babel from this angle. He discussed it on a purely *symptomatic* basis. The strategy of our orthodox press, in thus ridiculing the cacophonous verbal output of Congress, is obvious: by thus centering attack upon the *symptoms* of business conflict, as they reveal themselves on the dial of political wrangling, and leaving the underlying cause, the business conflicts themselves, out of the case, they can gratify the very public they would otherwise alienate: namely, the businessmen who are the activating members of their reading public. Hitler, however, went them one better. For not only did he stress the purely *symptomatic* attack here. He proceeded to search for the "cause." And this "cause," of course, he derived from his medicine, his racial theory by which he could give a noneconomic interpretation of a phenomenon economically engendered.

Here again is where Hitler's corrupt use of religious patterns comes to the fore. Church thought, being primarily concerned with matters of the "personality," with problems of moral betterment, naturally, and I think rightly, stresses as a necessary feature, the act of will upon the part of the individual. Hence its resistance to a purely "environmental" account of human ills. Hence its emphasis upon the "person." Hence its proneness to seek a noneconomic explanation of economic phenomena. Hitler's proposal of a noneconomic "cause" for the disturbances thus had much to recommend it from this angle. And, as a matter of fact, it was Lueger's Christian-Social Party in Vienna that taught Hitler the tactics of tying up a program of social betterment with an anti-Semitic "unifier." The two parties that he carefully studied at that time were this Catholic faction and Schoenerer's Pan-German group. And his analysis of their attainments and shortcomings, from the standpoint of demagogic efficacy, is an extremely astute piece of work, revealing how carefully this man used the current situation in Vienna as an experimental laboratory for the maturing of his plans.

His unification device, we may summarize, had the following important features:

(1) Inborn dignity. In both religious and humanistic patterns of thought, a "natural born" dignity of man is stressed. And this categorical dignity is considered to be an attribute , of *all men*, if they will but avail themselves of it, by right thinking and right living. But Hitler gives this ennobling attitude an ominous twist by his theories of race and nation, whereby the "Aryan" is elevated above all others by the innate endowment of his blood, while other "races," in particular Jews and Negroes, are innately inferior. This sinister secularized revision of Christian theology thus puts the sense of dignity upon a fighting basis, requiring the conquest of "inferior races." After the defeat of Germany in the World War, there were especially strong emotional needs that this compensatory doctrine of an *inborn* superiority could gratify.

(2) *Projection* device. The "curative" process that comes with the ability to hand over one's ills to a scapegoat, thereby getting purification by dissociation. This was especially medicinal, since the sense of frustration leads to a self-questioning. Hence if one can hand over his infirmities to a vessel, or "cause," outside the self, one can battle an external enemy instead of battling an enemy within. And the greater one's internal inadequacies, the greater the amount of evils one can load upon the back of "the enemy." This device is furthermore given a semblance of reason because the individual properly realizes that he is not alone responsible for his condition. There *are* inimical factors in the scene itself. And he wants to have them "placed," preferably in a way that would require a minimum change in the ways of thinking to which he had been accustomed. This was especially appealing to the middle class, who were encouraged to feel that they could conduct their businesses without any basic change whatever, once the businessmen of a different "race" were eliminated.

(3) Symbolic rebirth. Another aspect of the two features already noted. The projective device of the scapegoat, coupled with the Hitlerite doctrine of inborn racial superiority, provides

its followers with a "positive" view of life. They can again get the feel of *moving forward,* towards a *goal* (a promissory feature of which Hitler makes much). In Hitler, as the group's prophet, such rebirth involved a symbolic change of lineage. Here, above all, we see Hitler giving a malign twist to a benign aspect of Christian thought. For whereas the Pope, in the familistic pattern of thought basic to the Church, stated that the Hebrew prophets were the *spiritual ancestors* of Christianity, Hitler uses this same mode of thinking in reverse. He renounces this "ancestry" in a "materialistic" way by voting himself and the members of his lodge a different "blood stream" from that of the Jews.

(4) Commercial use. Hitler obviously here had something to sell—and it was but a question of time until he sold it (i.e., got financial backers for his movement). For it provided a *noneconomic interpretation of economic ills.* As such, it served with maximum efficiency in deflecting the attention from the economic factors involved in modern conflict; hence by attacking "Jew finance" instead of *finance,* it could stimulate an enthusiastic movement that left "Aryan" finance in control.

Never once, throughout his book, does Hitler deviate from the above formula. Invariably, he ends his diatribes against contemporary economic ills by a shift into an insistence that we must get to the "true" cause, which is centered in "race." The "Aryan" is "constructive"; the Jew is "destructive"; and the "Aryan," to continue his *construction,* must *destroy* the Jewish *destruction.* The Aryan, as the vessel of *love,* must *hate* the Jewish *hate.*

Perhaps the most enterprising use of his method is in his chapter, "The Causes of the Collapse," where he refuses to consider Germany's plight as in any basic way connected with the consequences of war. Economic factors, he insists, are "only of second or even third importance," but "political, ethical-moral, as well as factors of blood and race, are of the first importance." His rhetorical steps are especially interesting here, in that he begins by seeming to flout the national susceptibilities: "The military defeat of the German people is not an undeserved catastrophe, but rather a deserved punishment by eternal retribution." He then proceeds to present the military collapse as but a "consequence of moral poisoning, visible to all, the consequence of a decrease in the instinct of self-preservation . . . which had already begun to undermine the foundations of the people and the Reich many years before." This moral decay derived from "a sin against the blood and the degradation of the race," so its innerness was an outerness after all: the Jew, who thereupon gets saddled with a vast amalgamation of evils, among them being capitalism, democracy, pacifism, journalism, poor housing, modernism, big cities, loss of religion, half measures, ill health, and weakness of the monarch.

II

Hitler had here another important psychological ingredient to play upon. If a State is in economic collapse (and his theories, tentatively taking shape in the pre-war Vienna, were but developed with greater efficiency in post-war Munich), you cannot possibly derive dignity from economic stability. Dignity must come first— and if you possess it, and implement it, from it may follow its economic counterpart. There is much justice to this line of reasoning, so far as it goes. A people in collapse, suffering under economic frustration and the defeat of nationalistic aspirations, with the very midrib of their integrative efforts (the army) in a state of dispersion, have little other than some "spiritual" basis to which they could refer their nationalistic dignity. Hence, the categorical dignity of superior race was a perfect recipe for the situation.

Furthermore, you had the desire for unity, such as a discussion of class conflict, on the basis of conflicting interests, could not satisfy. The yearning for unity is so great that people are always willing to meet you halfway if you will give it to them by fiat, by flat statement, regardless of the facts. Hence, Hitler consistently refused to consider internal political conflict on the basis of conflicting interests. Here again, he could draw upon a religious pattern, by insisting upon a *personal* statement of the relation between classes, the relation between leaders and followers, each group in its way fulfilling the same commonalty of interests, as the soldiers and captains of an army share a common interest in victory. People so dislike the idea of internal division that, where there is a real internal division, their dislike can easily be turned against the man or group who would so much as *name* it, let alone proposing to act upon it. Their natural and justified resentment against internal division itself, is turned against the diagnostician who states it as a *fact*. This diagnostician, it is felt, is the *cause* of the disunity he named.

Cutting in from another angle, therefore, we note how two sets of equations were built up, with Hitler combining or coalescing *ideas* the way a poet combines or coalesces *images*. On the one side, were the ideas, or images, of disunity, centering in the parliamentary wrangle of the Hapsburg "State of Nationalities." This was offered as the antithesis of German nationality, which was presented in the curative imagery of unity, focused upon the glories of the Prussian Reich, with its Mecca now moved to "folkish" Vienna. For though Hitler at first attacked the many "folkish" movements, with their hankerings after a kind of Wagnerian mythology of Germanic origins, he subsequently took "folkish" as a basic word by which to conjure. It was, after all, another noneconomic basis of reference. At first we find him objecting to "those who drift about with the word 'folkish' on their caps," and asserting that "such a Babel of opinions cannot serve as the basis of a political fighting movement." But later he seems to have realized, as he well should, that its vagueness was a major point in its favor. So it was incorporated in the grand coalition of his ideational imagery, or imagistic ideation; and Chapter XI ends with the vision of "a State which represents not a mechanism of economic considerations and interests, alien to the people, but a folkish organism."

So, as against the disunity equations, already listed briefly in our discussion of his attacks upon the parliamentary, we get a contrary purifying set; the wrangle of the parliamentary is to be stilled by the giving of *one* voice to the whole people, this to be the "inner voice" of Hitler, made uniform throughout the German boundaries, as leader and people were completely identified with each other. In sum: Hitler's inner voice, equals leader-people identification, equals unity, equals Reich, equals the Mecca of Munich, equals plow, equals sword, equals work, equals war, equals army as midrib, equals responsibility (the personal responsibility of the absolute ruler), equals sacrifice, equals the theory of "German democracy" (the free popular choice of the leader, who then accepts the responsibility, and demands absolute obedience in exchange for his sacrifice), equals love (with the masses as feminine), equals idealism, equals obedience to nature, equals race, nation.[3]

And, of course, the two keystones of these opposite equations were Aryan "heroism" and "sacrifice" vs. Jewish "cunning" and "arrogance." Here again we get an astounding caricature of religious thought. For Hitler presents the concept of "Aryan" superiority, of all ways, in terms of "Aryan humility." This "humility" is extracted by a very delicate process that requires, I am afraid, considerable "good will" on the part of the reader who would follow it:

The Church, we may recall, had proclaimed an integral relationship between Divine Law and Natural Law. Natural Law was the expression of the Will of God. Thus, in the Middle Ages, it was a result of natural law, working through tradition, that some people were serfs and other people nobles. And every good member of the Church was "obedient" to this law. Everybody resigned himself to it. Hence, the serf resigned himself to his poverty, and the noble resigned himself to his riches. The monarch resigned himself to his position as representative of the people. And at times the Churchmen resigned themselves to the need of trying to represent the people instead. And the pattern was made symmetrical by the consideration that each traditional "right" had its corresponding "obligations." Similarly, the Aryan doctrine is a doctrine of resignation, hence of humility. It is in accordance with the laws of nature that the "Aryan blood" is superior to all other bloods. Also, the "law of the survival of the fittest" is God's law, working through natural law. Hence, if the

---

[3] One could carry out the equations further, on both the disunity and unity side. In the aesthetic field, for instance. we have expressionism on the thumbs-down side, as against aesthetic hygiene on the thumbs-up side. This again is a particularly ironic moment in Hitler's strategy. For the expressionist movement was unquestionably a symptom of unhealthiness. It reflected the increasing alienation that went with the movement towards world war and the disorganization after the world war. It was "lost," vague in identity, a drastically accurate reflection of the response to material confusion, a pathetic attempt by sincere artists to make their wretchedness bearable at least to the extent that comes of giving it expression. And it attained its height during the period of wild inflation, when the capitalist world, which bases its morality of work and savings upon the soundness of its money structure, had this last prop of stability removed. The anguish, in short. reflected precisely the kind of disruption that made people ripe for a Hitler. It was the antecedent in a phrase of which Hitlerism was the consequent. But by thundering against his symptom he could gain persuasiveness, though attacking the very foreshadowings of hImself.

Aryan blood has been vested with the awful responsibility of its inborn superiority, the bearers of this "culture-creating" blood must resign themselves to struggle in behalf of its triumph. Otherwise, the laws of God have been disobeyed, with human decadence as a result. We must fight, he says, in order to "deserve to be alive." The Aryan "obeys" nature. It is only "Jewish arrogance" that thinks of "conquering" nature by democratic ideals of equality.

This picture has some nice distinctions worth following. The major virtue of the Aryan race was its instinct for self-preservation (in obedience to natural law). But the major vice of the Jew was his instinct for self-preservation; for, if he did not have this instinct to a maximum degree, he would not be the "perfect" enemy—that is, he wouldn't be strong enough to account for the ubiquitousness and omnipotence of his conspiracy in destroying the world to become its master.

How, then, are we to distinguish between the benign instinct of self-preservation at the roots of Aryanism, and the malign instinct of self-preservation at the roots of Semitism? We shall distinguish thus: The Aryan self-preservation is based upon *sacrifice*, the sacrifice of the individual to the group, hence, militarism, army discipline, and one big company union. But Jewish self-preservation is based upon individualism, which attains its cunning ends by the exploitation of peace. How, then, can such arrant individualists concoct the world-wide plot? By the help of their "herd instinct." By their sheer "herd instinct" individualists can band together for a common end. They have no real solidarity, but unite opportunistically to seduce the Aryan. Still, that brings up another technical problem, For we have been hearing much about the importance of the *person*. We have been told how, by the "law of the survival of the fittest," there is a sifting of people on the basis of their individual capacities. We even have a special chapter of pure Aryanism: "The Strong Man is Mightiest Alone." Hence, another distinction is necessary: The Jew represents individualism; the Aryan represents "super-individualism."

I had thought, when coming upon the "Strong Man is Mightiest Alone" chapter, that I was going to find Hitler at his weakest. Instead, I found him at his strongest. (I am not referring to *quality*, but to *demagogic effectiveness*.) For the chapter is not at all, as you might infer from the title, done in a "rise of Adolph

Hitler" manner. Instead, it deals with the Nazis' gradual absorption of the many disrelated "folkish" groups. And it is managed throughout by means of a spontaneous identification between leader and people. Hence, the Strong Man's "aloneness" is presented as a *public* attribute, in terms of tactics for the struggle against the *Party's* dismemberment under the pressure of rival saviors. There is no explicit talk of Hitler at all. And it is simply *taken for granted* that *his* leadership is the norm, and all other leaderships the abnorm. There is no "philosophy of the superman," in Nietzschean cast. Instead, Hitler's blandishments so integrate leader and people, commingling them so inextricably, that the politician does not even present himself as candidate. Somehow, the battle is over already, the decision has been made. "German democracy" has chosen. And the deployments of politics are, you might say, the chartings of Hitler's private mind translated into the vocabulary of nationalistic events. He says *what he thought* in terms of *what parties did*.

Here, I think, we see the distinguishing quality of Hitler's method as an instrument of persuasion, with reference to the question whether Hitler is sincere or deliberate, whether his vision of the omnipotent conspirator has the drastic honesty of paranoia or the sheer shrewdness of a demagogue trained in *Realpolitik* of the Machiavellian sort.[4] Must we choose? Or may we not, rather, replace the "either-or" with a "both-and"? Have we not by now offered grounds enough for our contention that Hitler's sinister powers of persuasion derive from the fact that he spontaneously evolved his "cure-all" in response to inner necessities?

---

[4] I should not want to use the word "Machiavellian," however, without offering a kind of apology to Machiavelli. It seems to me that Machiavelli's Prince has more to be said in extenuation than is usually said of it. Machiavelli's strategy, as I see it, was something like this: He accepted the values of the Renaissance rule as a fact. That is: whether you like these values or not, they were there and operating, and it was useless to try persuading the ambitious ruler to adopt other values, such as those of the Church. These men believed in the cult of material power, and they had the power to implement their beliefs. With so much as "the given," could anything in the way of benefits for the people be salvaged? Machiavelli evolved a typical "Machiavellian" argument in favor of popular benefits, on the basis of the prince's own scheme of values. That is: the ruler, to attain the maximum strength requires the backing of the populace. That this backing be as effective as possible, the populace should be made as strong as possible. And that the populace be as strong as possible, they should be well treated. Their gratitude would further repay itself in the form of increased loyalty. It was Machiavelli's hope that, for this roundabout project, he would be rewarded with a well-paying office in the prince's administrative bureaucracy.

III

So much, then, was "spontaneous." It was further channelized into the anti-Semitic pattern by the incentives he derived from the Catholic Christian-Social Party in Vienna itself. Add, now, the step into *criticism*. Not criticism in the "parliamentary" sense of doubt, of hearkening to the opposition and attempting to mature a policy in the light of counter-policies; but the "unified" kind of criticism that simply seeks for conscious ways of making one's position more "efficient," more thoroughly itself. This is the kind of criticism at which Hitler was an adept. As a result, he could *spontaneously* turn to a scapegoat mechanism, and he could be conscious planning, perfect the symmetry of the solution towards which he had spontaneously turned.

This is the meaning of Hitler's diatribes against "objectivity." "Objectivity" is interference-criticism. What Hitler wanted was the kind of criticism that would be a pure and simple coefficient of power, enabling him to go most effectively in the direction he had chosen. And the "inner voice" of which he speaks would henceforth dictate to him the greatest amount of realism, as regards the tactics of efficiency. For instance, having decided that the masses required certainty, and simple certainty, quite as he did himself, he later worked out a 25-point program as the platform of his National Socialist German Workers Party. And he resolutely refused to change one single item in this program, even for purposes of "improvement." He felt that the *fixity* of the platform was more important for propagandistic purposes than any revision of his slogans could be, even though the revisions in themselves had much to be said in their favor. The astounding thing is that, although such an attitude gave good cause to doubt the Hitlerite promises, he could explicitly explain his tactics in his book and still employ them without loss of effectiveness.[5]

---

[5] On this point, Hitler reasons as follows:
"Here, too, one can learn from the Catholic Church. Although its structure of doctrines in many instances collides, quite unnecessarily, with exact science and research, yet it is unwilling to sacrifice even one little syllable of its dogmas. It has rightly recognized that its resistibility does not lie in a more or less great adjustment to the scientific results of the moment, which in reality are always changing, but rather in a strict adherence to dogmas, once laid down, which alone give the entire structure the character of creed. Today, therefore, the Catholic Church stands firmer than ever. One can prophesy that in the same measure in which the appearances flee, the Church itself, as the resting pole in the flight of appearances, will gain more and more blind adherence."

Hitler also tells of his technique in speaking, once the Nazi party had become effectively organized, and had its army of guards, or bouncers, to maltreat hecklers and throw them from the hall. He would, he recounts, fill his speech with *provocative* remarks, whereat his bouncers would promptly swoop down in flying formation, with swinging fists, upon anyone whom these provocative remarks provoked to answer. The efficiency of Hitlerism is the efficiency of the one voice, implemented throughout a total organization. The trinity of government which he finally offers is: *popularity* of the leader, *force* to back the popularity, and popularity and force maintained together long enough to become backed by a *tradition.* Is such thinking spontaneous or deliberate—or is it not rather both?[6]

Freud has given us a succinct paragraph that bears upon the spontaneous aspect of Hitler's persecution mania. (A persecution mania, I should add, different from the pure product in that it was constructed of *public* materials; all the ingredients Hitler stirred into his brew were already rife, with spokesmen and bands of followers, before Hitler "took them over." Both the pre-war and post-war periods were dotted with saviors, of nationalistic and "folkish" cast. This proliferation was analogous to the swarm of barter schemes and currency-tinkering that burst loose upon the United States after the crash of 1929. Also, the commercial availability of Hitler's politics was, in a low sense of the term, a *public* qualification, removing it from the realm of "pure" paranoia, where the sufferer develops a wholly *private* structure of interpretations.)

---

[6] [editors' note: In addition to the footnotes, this sentence was added by Burke in his Philosophy of Literary Form.] Hitler also paid great attention to the conditions under which political oratory is most effective. He sums up thus:

"All these cases involve encroachments upon man's freedom of will. This applies, of course, most of all to meetings to which people with a contrary orientation of will are coming, and who now have to be won for new intentions. It seems that in the morning and even during the day men's will power revolts with highest energy against an attempt at being forced under another's will and another's opinion. In the evening, however, they succumb more easily to the dominating force of a stronger will. For truly every such meeting presents a wrestling match between two opposed forces. The superior oratorical talent of a domineering apostolic nature will now succeed more easily in winning for the new will people who themselves have in turn experienced a weakening of their force of resistance in the most natural way. than people who still have full command of the energies of their minds and their will power.

"The same purpose serves also the artificially created and yet mysterious dusk of the Catholic churches, the burning candles, incense. censers, etc."

I cite from Freud's *Totem and Taboo*:

Another trait in the attitude of primitive races towards their rulers recalls a mechanism which is universally present in mental disturbances, and is openly revealed in the so-called delusions of persecution. Here the importance of a particular person is extraordinarily heightened and his omnipotence is raised to the improbable in order to make it easier to attribute to him responsibility for everything painful which happens to the patient. Savages really do not act differently towards their rulers when they ascribe to them power over rain and shine, wind and weather, and then dethrone them or kill them because nature has disappointed their expectation of a good hunt or a ripe harvest. The prototype which the paranoiac reconstructs in his persecution mania is found in the relation of the child to its father. Such omnipotence is regularly attributed to the father in the imagination or the son, and distrust of the father has been shown to be intimately connected with the heightened esteem for him. When a paranoiac names a person of his acquaintance as his "persecutor," he thereby elevates him to the paternal succession and brings him under conditions which enable him to make him responsible for all the, misfortune which he experiences.

I have already proposed my modifications of this account when discussing the symbolic change of lineage connected with Hitler's project of a "new way of life." He is voting himself a new identity (something contrary to the wrangles of the Habsburg Babylon, a soothing national unity); whereupon the vessels of the old identity become a "bad" father, i.e., the persecutor. It is not hard to see how, as his enmity becomes implemented by the backing of an organization, the role of "persecutor" is transformed into the role of persecuted, as he sets out with his like-minded band to "destroy the destroyer."

Were Hitler simply a poet, he might have written a work with an anti-Semitic turn, and let it go at that. But Hitler, who began as a student of painting, and later shifted to architecture, himself treats his political activities as an extension of his artistic ambitions. He remained, in his own eyes, an "architect," building a "folkish" State that was to match, in political materials, the "folkish" architecture of Munich.

We might consider the matter this way (still trying, that is, to make precise the relationship between the drastically sincere and the deliberately scheming): Do we not know of many authors who seem, as they turn from the role of citizen to the role of spokesman, to leave one room and enter another? Or who has not, on occasion, talked with a man in private conversation, and then been almost startled at the transformation this man undergoes when addressing a public audience? And I know persons today, who shift between the writing of items in the class of academic, philosophic speculation to items of political pamphleteering, and whose entire style and method change with this change of role. In their academic manner, they are cautious, painstaking, eager to present all significant aspects of the case they are considering; but when they turn to political pamphleteering, they hammer forth with vituperation, they systematically misrepresent the position of their opponent, they go into a kind of political trance, in which, during its throes, they throb like a locomotive; and behold, a moment later, the mediumistic state is abandoned, and they are the most moderate of men.

Now, one will find few pages in Hitler that one could call "moderate." But there are many pages in which he gauges resistances and opportunities with the "rationality" of a skilled advertising man planning a new sales campaign. Politics, he says, must be sold like soap—and soap is not sold in a trance. But he did have the experience of his trance, in the "exaltation" of his anti-Semitism. And later, as he became a successful orator (he insists that revolutions are made solely by the power of the spoken word), he had this "poetic" role to draw upon, plus the great relief it provided as a way of slipping from the burden of logical analysis into the pure "spirituality" of vituperative prophecy. What more natural, therefore, than that a man so insistent upon unification would integrate this mood with less ecstatic moments, particularly when he had found the followers and the backers that put a price, both spiritual and material, upon such unification?

Once this happy "unity" is under way, one has a "logic" for the development of a method. One knows when to "spiritualize" a material issue, and when to "materialize" a spiritual one. Thus, when it is a matter of materialistic interests that cause a conflict between employer and employee, Hitler here disdainfully shifts to a high moral plane. He is "above" such low concerns. Everything becomes a matter of "sacrifices" and "personality." It becomes crass to treat employers and employees as different *classes* with a corresponding difference in the classification of their interests. Instead, relations between employer and employee must be on the "personal" basis of leader and follower, and "whatever may have a divisive effect in national life should be given a unifying effect through the army." When talking of national rivalries, however, he makes a very shrewd materialistic gauging of Britain and France with relation to Germany. France, he says, desires the "Balkanization of Germany" (i.e., its breakup into separationist movements—the "disunity" theme again) in order to maintain commercial hegemony on the continent. But Britain desires the "Balkanization of *Europe,*" hence would favor a fairly strong and unified Germany, to use as a counter-weight against French hegemony. *German* nationality, however, is unified by the *spiritual* quality of Aryanism (that would produce the national organization via the Party) while this in turn is *materialized* in the myth of the blood-stream.

IV

What are we to learn from Hitler's book? For one thing, I believe that he has shown, to a very disturbing degree, the power of repetition. Every circular advertising a Nazi meeting had, at the bottom, two slogans: "Jews not admitted" and "War victims free." And the substance of Nazi propaganda was built about these two "complementary" themes. He describes the power of spectacle; insists that mass meetings are the fundamental way of giving the individual the sense of being protectively surrounded by a movement, the sense of "community." He also drops one wise hint that I wish the American authorities would take in treating Nazi gatherings. He says that the presence of a special Nazi guard, in Nazi uniforms, was of great importance in building up, among the followers, a tendency to place the center of authority in the Nazi party. I believe that we should take him at his word here, but use the advice in reverse, by insisting that, where Nazi meetings are to be permitted, they be policed by the constituted authorities alone, and that uniformed Nazi guards to enforce the law be prohibited.

But is it possible that an equally important feature of appeal was not so much in the repetitiousness *per se*, but in the fact that, by means of it, Hitler provided a "world view" for people who had previously seen the world but piecemeal? Did not much of his lure derive, once more, from the *bad* filling of a *good* need? Are not those who insist upon a purely *planless* working of the market asking people to accept far too slovenly a scheme of human purpose, a slovenly scheme that can be accepted so long as it operates with a fair degree of satisfaction, but becomes abhorrent to the victims of its disarray? Are they not then psychologically ready for a rationale, *any* rationale, if it but offer them some specious "universal" explanation? Hence, I doubt whether the appeal was in the sloganizing element alone (particularly as even slogans can only be hammered home, in speech after speech, and two or three hours at a stretch, by endless *variations* on the themes). And Hitler himself somewhat justifies my interpretation by laying so much stress upon the *half-measures* of the middle-class politicians, and the contrasting certainty of his own methods. He was not offering people a *rival* world view; rather, he was offering a world view to people who had no other to pit against it.

As for the basic Nazi trick: the "curative" unification by a fictitious devil-function, gradually made convincing by the sloganizing repetitiousness of standard advertising technique— the opposition must be as unwearying in the attack upon it. It may well be that people, in their human frailty, require an enemy as well as a goal. Very well: Hitlerism itself has provided us with such an enemy—and the clear example of its operation is guaranty that we have, in him and all he stands for, no purely fictitious "devil-function" made to look like a world menace by rhetorical blandishments, but a reality whose ominousness is clarified by the record of its conduct to date. In selecting his brand of doctrine as our "scapegoat," and in tracking down its equivalents in America, we shall be at the very center of accuracy. The Nazis themselves have made the task of clarification easier. Add to them Japan and Italy, and you have *case histories* of fascism for those who might find it more difficult to approach an understanding of its imperialistic drives by a vigorously economic explanation.

But above all, I believe, we must make it apparent that Hitler appeals by relying upon a bastardization of fundamentally religious patterns of thought. In this, if properly presented, there is no slight to religion. There is nothing in religion proper that requires a fascist state. There is much in religion, when misused, that does lead to a fascist state. There is a Latin proverb,

"Corruptio optimi pessima," the corruption of the best is the worst. And it is the corruptors of religion who are a major menace to the world today, in giving the profound patterns of religious thought a crude and sinister distortion.

Our job, then, our Anti-Hitler Battle, is to find all available ways of making the Hitlerite distortions of religion apparent, in order that politicians of his kind in America be unable to perform a similar swindle. The desire for unity is genuine and admirable. The desire for national unity, in the present state of the world, is genuine and admirable. But this unity, if attained on a deceptive basis, by emotional trickeries that shift our criticism from the accurate locus of our trouble, is no unity at all. For, even if we are among those who happen to be "Aryans," we solve no problems even for ourselves by such solutions, since the factors pressing towards calamity remain. Thus, in Germany, after all the upheaval, we see nothing beyond a drive for ever more and more upheaval, precisely because the "new way of life" was no new way, but the dismally oldest way of sheer deception—hence, after all the "change," the factors driving towards unrest are left intact, and even strengthened. True, the Germans had the resentment of a lost war to increase their susceptibility to Hitler's rhetoric. But in a wider sense, it has repeatedly been observed, the whole world lost the War—and the accumulating ills of the capitalist order were but accelerated in their movements towards confusion. Hence, here too there are the resentments that go with frustration of men's ability to work and earn. At that point a certain kind of industrial or financial monopolist may, annoyed by the contrary voices of our parliament, wish for the momentary peace of one voice, amplified by social organizations, with all the others not merely quieted, but given the quietus. So he might, under Nazi promptings, be tempted to back a group of gangsters who, on becoming the political rulers of the state, would protect him against the necessary demands of the workers. His gangsters, then would be his insurance against his workers. But who would be his insurance against his gangsters?

Their Finest Hour
and
The Few

Winston Churchill

Winston Churchill (1874–1965) was the Prime Minister of the United Kingdom from 1940–1945, and again from 1951–1955. The Battle of Britain (July 10– October 31, 1940), between Germany and the United Kingdom, was the first to be fought entirely by air forces. In it the Royal Air Force (RAF), at great cost, defended the British Isles from the Luftwaffe's bombers and in turn from possible German invasion. The name of that battle comes from Churchill's speech "Their Finest Hour," which he delivered on June 18, 1940: ". . . the Battle of France is over. I expect that the Battle of Britain is about to begin." During that battle, Churchill delivered his speech "The Few" (August 20, 1940), in which he expresses the gratitude of the nation for the sacrifices of the RAF in its defense.

Not only was Churchill adept at and meticulous in the writing of his speeches, he delivered them in a composed and reserved voice that deliberately contrasted with the styles of Hitler and Mussolini. Rather than emphasizing with volume and excitability, he used dramatic pauses and a calm temperament that exuded conviction and clarity .

> *Note: The existing audio recordings of these speeches by Churchill were made after they were actually delivered to Parliament because verbatim recordings were not permitted in the House of Commons at the time. Some spoken recordings were made after the war for Decca/London Records, some were made in broadcasts by the BBC. As a result, you may find many verbal differences between the audio recordings and the actual speeches as given to Parliament and then transcribed for publication. What we have reprinted here are the officially transcribed speeches as originally delivered. [Our gratitude to Richard M. Langworth for clarification of this matter.]*

Their Finest Hour

Delivered June 18, 1940

I spoke the other day of the colossal military disaster which occurred when the French High Command failed to withdraw the Northern Armies from Belgium at the moment when they knew that the French front was decisively broken at Sedan and on the Meuse. This delay entailed the loss of fifteen or sixteen French divisions and threw out of action for the critical period the whole of the British Expeditionary Force. Our Army and 120,000 French troops were indeed rescued by the British Navy from Dunkirk but only with the loss of their cannon, vehicles and modem equipment. This loss inevitably took some weeks to repair, and in the first two of those weeks the battle in France has been lost. When we consider the heroic resistance made by the French Army against heavy odds in this battle, the enormous losses inflicted upon the enemy and the evident exhaustion of the enemy, it may well be thought that these twenty-five divisions of the best-trained and best-equipped troops might have turned the scale. However, General Weygand had to fight without them. Only three British divisions or their equivalent were able to stand in the line with their French comrades. They had suffered severely, but they had fought well. We sent every man we could to France as fast as we could re-equip and transport their formations.

I am not reciting these facts for the purpose of recrimination. That I judge to be utterly futile and even harmful. We cannot afford it. I recite them in order to explain why it was we did not have, as we could have had, between twelve and fourteen British divisions fighting in the line in this great battle instead of only three. Now I put all this aside. I put it on the shelf, from which the historians, when they have time, will select their documents to tell their stories. We have to think of the future and not of the past. This also applies in a small way to our own affairs at home. There are many who would hold an inquest in the House of Commons on the conduct of the Governments—and of Parliaments, for they are in it, too—during the years which led up to this catastrophe. They seek to indict those who were responsible for the guidance of our affairs. This also would be a foolish and pernicious process. There are too many in it. Let each man search his conscience and search his speeches. I frequently search mine.

Of this I am quite sure, that if we open a quarrel between the past and the present, we shall find that we have lost the future. Therefore, I cannot accept the drawing of any distinctions between Members of the present Government. It was formed at a moment of crisis in order to unite all the parties and all sections of opinion. It has received the almost unanimous support of both Houses of Parliament. Its Members are going to stand together, and, subject to the authority of the House of Commons, we are going to govern the country and fight the war. It is absolutely necessary at a time like this that every Minister who tries each day to do his duty shall be respected; and their subordinates must know that their chiefs are not threatened men, men who are here today and gone tomorrow, but that their directions must be punctually and faithfully obeyed. Without this concentrated power we cannot face what lies before us. I should not think it would be very advantageous for the House to prolong this Debate this afternoon under conditions of public stress. Many facts are not clear that will be clear in a short time. We are to have a Secret Session on Thursday, and I should think that would be a better opportunity for the many earnest expressions of opinion which Members will desire to make and for the House to discuss vital matters without having everything read the next morning by our dangerous foes.

The disastrous military events which have happened during the past fortnight have not come to me with any sense of surprise. Indeed, I indicated a fortnight ago as clearly as I could to the House that the worst possibilities were open; and I made it perfectly clear then that whatever happened in France would make no difference to the resolve of Britain and the British Empire to fight on, "if necessary for years, if necessary alone." During the last few days we have successfully brought off the great majority of the troops we had on the lines of communication in France; and seven-eighths of the troops we have sent to France since the beginning of the war—that is to say, about 350,000 out of 400,000 men—are safely back in this country. Others are still fighting with the French, and fighting with considerable success in their local encounters against the enemy. We have also brought back a great mass of stores, rifles and munitions of all kinds which had been accumulated in France during the last nine months.

We have, therefore, in this island today a very large and powerful military force. This force comprises all our best-trained and our finest troops, including scores of thousands of those who have already measured their quality against the Germans and found themselves at no disadvantage. We have under arms at the present time in this island over a million and a quarter men. Behind these we have the Local Defense Volunteers, numbering half a million, only a portion of whom, however, are yet armed with rifles or other firearms. We have incorporated into our Defense Forces every man for whom we have a weapon. We expect very large additions to our weapons in the near future, and in preparation for this we intend forthwith to call up, drill and train further large numbers. Those who are not called up, or else are employed upon the vast business of munitions production in all its branches—and their ramifications are innumerable—will serve their country best by remaining at their ordinary work until they receive their summons. We have also over here Dominions armies. The Canadians had actually landed in France, but have now been safely withdrawn, much disappointed, but in perfect order, with all their artillery and equipment. And these very high-class forces from the Dominions will now take part in the defense of the Mother Country.

Lest the account which I have given of these large forces should raise the question: Why did they not take part in the great battle in France? I must make it clear that, apart from the divisions training and organizing at home, only twelve divisions were equipped to fight upon a scale which justified their being sent abroad. And this was fully up to the number which the French had been led to expect would be available in France at the ninth month of the war. The rest of our forces at home have fighting value for home defense which will, of course, steadily increase every week that passes. Thus, the invasion of Great Britain would at this time require the transportation across the sea of hostile armies on a very large scale, and after they been so transported they would have to be continually maintained with all the masses of munitions and supplies which are required for continuous battle—as continuous battle it will surely be.

Here is where we come to the Navy—and after all, we have a Navy. Some people seem to forget that we have a Navy. We must remind them. For the last thirty years I have been concerned in discussions about the possibilities of overseas invasion, and I took the responsibility on behalf of the Admiralty, at the beginning of the last war, of allowing all regular troops to be sent out of the country. That was a very serious step to take, because our Territorials had only just been called up and were quite untrained. Therefore, this island was for several months practically denuded of fighting troops. The Admiralty had confidence at that time in their ability to prevent a mass invasion even though at that time the Germans had a magnificent battle fleet the proportion of ten to sixteen, even though they were capable of fighting a general engagement every day and any day, whereas now they have only a couple of heavy ships worth speaking of—the *Scharnhorst* and the *Gneisenau*. We are also told that the Italian Navy is to come out and gain sea superiority in these waters. If they seriously intend it, 1 shall only say that we shall be delighted to offer Signor Mussolini a free and safeguarded passage through the Straits of Gibraltar in order that he may play the part to which he aspires. There is a general curiosity in the British Fleet to find out whether the Italians are up to the level they were at in the last war or whether they have fallen off at all.

Therefore, it seems to me that as far as seaborne invasion on a great scale is concerned, we are far more capable of meeting it today than we were at many periods in the last war and during the early months of this war, before our other troops were trained, and while the BEF [*British Expeditionary Force*] had proceeded abroad. Now, the Navy have never pretended to be able to prevent raids by bodies of 5,000 or 10,000 men flung suddenly across and thrown ashore at several points on the coast some dark night or foggy morning. The efficacy of sea-power, especially under modern conditions, depends upon the invading force being of large size. It has to be of large size, in view of our military strength, to be of any use. If it is of large size, then the Navy have something they can find and meet and, as it were, bite on. Now we must remember that even five divisions, however lightly equipped, would require 200 to 250 ships, and with modern air reconnaissance and photography it would not be easy to collect such an armada, marshal it and conduct it across the sea without any powerful naval forces to escort it; and there would be very great possibilities, to put it mildly, that this armada would be intercepted long before it reached the coast, and all the men drowned in the sea or, at the worst, blown to pieces with their equipment while they were trying to land. We also have a great system of minefields, recently strongly reinforced, through which we alone know the channels. If the enemy tries to sweep passages through these minefields, it will be the task of the Navy to destroy the minesweepers and any other forces employed to protect them. There should be no difficulty in this, owing to our great superiority at sea.

Those are the regular, well-tested, well-proved arguments on which we have relied during many years in peace and war. But the question is whether there are any new methods by which those solid assurances can be circumvented. Odd as it may seem, some attention has been given to this by the Admiralty, whose prime duty and responsibility it is to destroy any large seaborne expedition before it reaches, or at the moment when it reaches these shores. It would not be a good thing for me to go into details of this. It might suggest ideas to other people which they have not thought of, and they would not be likely to give us any of their ideas in exchange. All I will say is that untiring vigilance and mind-searching must be devoted to the subject, because the enemy is crafty and cunning and full of novel treacheries and stratagems. The House may be assured that the utmost ingenuity is being displayed and imagination is being evoked from large numbers of competent officers, well trained in tactics and thoroughly up to date, to measure and counterwork novel possibilities. Untiring vigilance and untiring searching of the mind is being, and must be, devoted to the subject, because, remember, the enemy is crafty and there is no dirty trick he will not do.

Some people will ask why, then, was it that the British Navy was not able to prevent the movement of a large army from Germany into Norway across the Skaggerak? But the conditions in the Channel and in the North Sea are in no way like those which prevail in the Skaggerak. In the Skaggerak, because of the distance, we could give no air support to our surface ships, and consequently, lying as we did close to the enemy's main air power, we were compelled to use only our submarines. We could not enforce the decisive blockade or interruption which is possible from surface vessels. Our submarines took a heavy toll but could not, by themselves, prevent the invasion of Norway. In the Channel and in the North Sea, on the other hand, our superior naval surface forces, aided by our submarines, will operate with close and effective air assistance.

This brings me, naturally, to the great question of invasion from the air, and of the impending struggle between the British and

German Air Forces. It seems quite clear that no invasion on a scale beyond the capacity of our land forces to crush speedily is likely to take place from the air until our Air Force has been definitely overpowered. In the meantime, there may be raids by parachute troops and attempted descents of airborne soldiers. We should be able to give those gentry a warm reception, both in the air and on the ground, if they reach it in any condition to continue the dispute. But the great question is: Can we break Hitler's air weapon? Now, of course, it is a very great pity that we have not got an Air Force at least equal to that of the most powerful enemy within striking distance of these shores. But we have a very powerful Air Force which has proved itself far superior in. quality, both in men and in many types of machine, to what we have met so far in the numerous and fierce air battles which have been fought with the Germans. In France, where we were at a considerable disadvantage and lost many machines on the ground when they were standing round the aerodromes, we were accustomed to inflict in the air losses of as much as two to two-and-a-half to one. In the fighting over Dunkirk, which was a sort of no-man's land, we undoubtedly beat the German Air Force, and gained the mastery of the local air, inflicting here a loss of three or four to one day after day. Anyone who looks at the photographs which were published a week or so ago of the re-embarkation, showing the masses of troops assembled on the beach and forming an ideal target for hours at a time, must realize that this re-embarkation would not have been possible unless the enemy had resigned all hope of recovering air superiority at that time and at that place.

In the defense of this island the advantages to the defenders will be much greater than they were in the fighting around Dunkirk. We hope to improve on the rate of three or four to one which was realized at Dunkirk; and in addition all our injured machines and their crews which get down safe—and, surprisingly, a very great many injured machines and men do get down safely in modern air fighting—all of these will fall, in an attack upon these islands, on friendly soil and live to fight another day; whereas all the injured enemy machines and their complements will be total losses as far as the war is concerned.

During the great battle in France, we gave very powerful and continuous aid to the French Army, both by fighters and bombers; but in spite of every kind of pressure we never would allow the entire metropolitan fighter strength of the Air Force to be consumed. This decision was painful, but it was also right, because the fortunes of the battle in France could not have been decisively affected even if we had thrown in our entire fighter force. That battle was lost by the unfortunate strategical opening, by the extraordinary and unforeseen power of the armored columns and by the great preponderance of the German Army in numbers. Our fighter Air Force might easily have been exhausted as a mere accident in that great struggle, and then we should have found ourselves at the present time in a very serious plight. But as it is, 1 am happy to inform the House that our fighter strength is stronger at the present time relatively to the Germans, who have suffered terrible losses, than it has ever been; and consequently we believe ourselves possessed of the capacity to continue the war in the air under better conditions than we have ever experienced before. 1 look forward confidently to the exploits of our fighter pilots—these splendid men, this brilliant youth—who will have the glory of saving their native land, their island home, and all they love, from the most deadly of all attacks.

There remains, of course, the danger of bombing attacks, which will certainly be made very soon upon us by the bomber forces of the enemy. It is true that the German bomber force is superior in numbers to ours; but we have a very large bomber force also, which we shall use to strike at military targets in Germany without intermission. 1 do not at all underrate the severity of the ordeal which lies before us; but 1 believe our countrymen will show themselves capable of standing up to it, like the brave men of Barcelona, and will be able to stand up to it, and carry on in spite of it, at least as well as any other people in the world. Much will depend upon this; every man and every woman will have the chance to show the finest qualities of their race, and render the highest service to their cause. For all of us, at this time, whatever our sphere, our station, our occupation or our duties, it will be a help to remember the famous lines:

> He nothing common did or mean,
> Upon that memorable scene.[1]

---

[1] From "An Horatian Ode upon Cromwell's Return from Ireland," Andrew Marvell. Written 1650, published 1681.

I have thought it right upon this occasion to give the House and the country some indication of the solid, practical grounds upon which we base our inflexible resolve to continue the war. There are a good many people who say, 'Never mind. Win or lose, sink or swim, better die than submit to tyranny—and such a tyranny.' And I do not dissociate myself from them. But I can assure them that our professional advisers of the three Services unitedly advise that we should carry on the war, and that there are good and reasonable hopes of final victory. We have fully informed and consulted all the self-governing Dominions, these great communities far beyond the oceans who have been built up on our laws and on our civilization, and who are absolutely free to choose their course, but are absolutely devoted to the ancient Motherland, and who feel themselves inspired by the same emotions which lead me to stake our all upon duty and honor. We have fully consulted them, and I have received from their Prime Ministers, Mr Mackenzie King of Canada, Mr Menzies of Australia, Mr Fraser of New Zealand, and General Smuts of South Africa—that wonderful man, with his immense profound mind, and his eye watching from a distance the whole panorama of European affairs—I have received from all these eminent men, who all have Governments behind them elected on wide franchises, who are all there because they represent the will of their people, messages couched in the most moving terms in which they endorse our decision to fight on, and declare themselves ready to share our fortunes and to persevere to the end. That is what we are going to do.

We may now ask ourselves: In what way has our position worsened since the beginning of the war? It has worsened by the fact that the Germans have conquered a large part of the coastline of Western Europe, and many small countries have been overrun by them. This aggravates the possibilities of air attack and adds to our naval preoccupations. It in no way diminishes, but on the contrary definitely increases, the power of our long distance blockade. Similarly, the entrance of Italy into the war increases the power of our long-distance blockade. We have stopped the worst leak by that. We do not know whether military resistance will come to an end in France or not, but should it do so, then of course, the Germans will be able to concentrate their forces, both military and industrial, upon us. But for the reasons I have given to the House these will not be found so easy to apply. If invasion has become more imminent, as no doubt it has, we, being relieved from the task of maintaining a large army in France, have far larger and more efficient forces to meet it.

If Hitler can bring under his despotic control the industries of the countries he has conquered, this will add greatly to his already vast armament output. On the other hand, this will not happen immediately, and we are now assured of immense, continuous and increasing support in supplies and munitions of all kinds from the United States; and especially of airplanes and pilots from the Dominions and across the oceans, coming from regions which are beyond the reach of enemy bombers.

I do not see how any of these factors can operate to our detriment on balance before the winter comes; and the winter will impose a strain upon the Nazi regime, with almost all Europe writhing and starving under its cruel heel, which, for all their ruthlessness, will run them very hard. We must not forget that from the moment when we declared war on the 3 September it was always possible for Germany to turn all her air force upon this country, together with any other devices of invasion she might conceive, and that France could have done little or nothing to prevent her doing so. We have, therefore, lived under this danger, in principle and in a slightly modified form, during all these months. In the meanwhile, however, we have enormously improved our methods of defense, and we have learned, what we had no right to assume at the beginning, namely, that the individual aircraft and the individual British pilot have a sure and definite superiority. Therefore, in casting up this dread balance sheet and contemplating our dangers with a disillusioned eye, I see great reason for intense vigilance and exertion but none whatever for panic or despair.

During the first four years of the last war the Allies experienced nothing but disaster and disappointment. That was our constant fear: one blow after another, terrible losses, frightful dangers. Everything miscarried. And yet at the end of those four years the morale of the Allies was higher than that of the Germans, who had moved from one aggressive triumph to another, and who stood everywhere triumph?int invaders of the lands into which they had broken. During that war we repeatedly asked ourselves the question: How are we going to win? And no one was able ever to answer it with much precision, until at the end, quite suddenly, quite unexpectedly, our terrible foe collapsed before us, and we were so glutted with victory that in our folly we threw it away.

We do not yet know what will happen in France or whether the French resistance will be prolonged, both in France and in the French Empire overseas. The French Government will be throwing away great opportunities and casting adrift their future if they do not continue the war in accordance with their Treaty obligations, from which we have not felt able to release them. The House will have read the historic declaration in which, at the desire of many Frenchmen—and of our own hearts—we have proclaimed our willingness at the darkest hour in French history to conclude a union of common citizenship in this struggle. However matters may go in France or with the French Government, or other French Governments, we in this island and in the British Empire will never lose our sense of comradeship with the French people. If we are now called upon to endure what they have been suffering, we shall emulate their courage, and if final victory rewards our toils they shall share the gains, aye, and freedom shall be restored to all. We abate nothing of our just demands; not one jot or tittle do we recede. Czechs, Poles, Norwegians, Dutch, Belgians have joined their causes to our own. All these shall be restored.

What General Weygand called the Battle of France is over. I expect that the Battle of Britain is about to begin. Upon this battle depends the survival of Christian civilization. Upon it depends our own British life, and the long continuity of our institutions and our Empire. The whole fury and might of the enemy must very soon be turned on us. Hitler knows that he will have to break us in this island or lose the war. If we can stand up to him, all Europe may be free and the life of the world may move forward into broad, sunlit uplands. But if we fail, then the whole world, including the United States, including all that we have known and cared for, will sink into the abyss of a new Dark Age made more sinister, and perhaps more protracted, by the lights of perverted science. Let us therefore brace ourselves to our duties and so bear ourselves that, if the British Empire and its Commonwealth last for a thousand years, men will still say, "This was their finest hour."

The Few

Speech delivered August 20, 1940

Almost a year has passed since the war began, and it is natural for us, I think, to pause on our journey at this milestone and survey the dark, wide field. It is also useful to compare the first year of this second war against German aggression with its forerunner a quarter of a century ago. Although this war is in fact only a continuation of the last, very great differences in its character are apparent. In the last war millions of men fought by hurling enormous masses of steel at one another. "Men and shells" was the cry, and prodigious slaughter was the consequence.

In this war nothing of this kind has yet appeared. It is a conflict of strategy, of organization, of technical apparatus, of science, mechanics, and morale. The British casualties in the first 12 months of the Great War amounted to 365,000. In this war, I am thankful to say, British killed, wounded, prisoners, and missing, including civilians, do not exceed 92,000, and of these a large proportion are alive as prisoners of war. Looking more widely around, one may say that throughout all Europe for one man killed or wounded in the first year perhaps five were killed or wounded in 1914–15.

The slaughter is only a small fraction, but the consequences to the belligerents have been even more deadly. We have seen great countries with powerful armies dashed out of coherent existence in a few weeks. We have seen the French Republic and the renowned French Army beaten into complete and total submission with less than the casualties which they suffered in any one of half a dozen of the battles of 1914–18.

The entire body—it might almost seem at times the soul—of France has succumbed to physical effects incomparably less terrible than those which were sustained with fortitude and undaunted will power 25 years ago. Although up to the present the loss of life has been mercifully diminished, the decisions reached in the course of the struggle are even more profound upon the fate of nations than anything that has ever happened since barbaric times. Moves are made upon the scientific and strategic boards, advantages are gained by mechanical means, as a result of which scores of millions of men become incapable of further resistance, or judge themselves incapable of further resistance, and a fearful game of chess proceeds from check to mate by which the unhappy players seem to be inexorably bound.

There is another more obvious difference from 1914. The whole of the warring nations are engaged, not only soldiers, but the entire population, men, women, and children. The fronts are everywhere. The trenches are dug in the towns and streets. Every village is fortified. Every road is barred. The front line runs through the factories. The workmen are soldiers with different weapons but the same courage. These are great and distinctive changes from what many of us saw in the struggle of a quarter of a century ago.

There seems to be every reason to believe that this new kind of war is well suited to the genius and the resources of the British nation and the British Empire and that, once we get properly equipped and properly started, a war of this kind will be more favorable to us than the somber mass slaughters of the Somme and Passchendaele. If it is a case of the whole nation fighting and suffering together, that ought to suit us, because we are the most united of all the nations, because we entered the war upon the national will and with our eyes open, and because we have been nurtured in freedom and individual responsibility and are the products, not of totalitarian uniformity but of tolerance and variety.

If all these qualities are turned, as they are being turned, to the arts of war, we may be able to show the enemy quite a lot of things that they have not thought of yet. Since the Germans drove the Jews out and lowered their technical standards, our science is definitely ahead of theirs. Our geographical position, the command of the sea, and the friendship of the United States enable us to draw resources from the whole world and to manufacture weapons of war of every kind, but especially of the superfine kinds, on a scale hitherto practiced only by Nazi Germany.

Hitler is now sprawled over Europe. Our offensive springs are being slowly compressed, and we must resolutely and methodically prepare ourselves for the campaigns of 1941 and 1942. Two or three years are not a long time, even in our short, precarious lives. They are nothing in the history of the nation, and when we are doing the finest thing in the world, and have the honor to be the sole champion of the liberties of all Europe, we must not grudge these years of weary as we toil and struggle through them. It does not follow that our energies in future years will be exclusively confined to defending ourselves and our possessions. Many opportunities may lie open to amphibious power, and we must be ready to take advantage of them.

One of the ways to bring this war to a speedy end is to convince the enemy, not by words, but by deeds, that we have both the will and the means, not only to go on indefinitely but to strike heavy and unexpected blows. The road to victory may not be so long as we expect. But we have no right to count upon this. Be it long or short, rough or smooth, we mean to reach our journey's end.

It is our intention to maintain and enforce a strict blockade not only of Germany but of Italy, France, and all the other countries that have fallen into the German power. I read in the papers that Herr Hitler has also proclaimed a strict blockade of the British Islands. No one can complain of that. I remember the Kaiser doing it in the last war. What indeed would be a matter of general complaint would be if we were to prolong the agony of all Europe by allowing food to come in to nourish the Nazis and aid their war effort, or to allow food to go in to the subjugated peoples, which certainly would be pillaged off them by their Nazi conquerors.

There have been many proposals, founded on the highest motives, that food should be allowed to pass the blockade for the relief of these populations. I regret that we must refuse these requests. The Nazis declare that they have created a new unified economy in Europe. They have repeatedly stated that they possess ample reserves of food and that they can feed their captive peoples.

In a German broadcast of 27th June it was said that while Mr. Hoover's plan for relieving France, Belgium, and Holland deserved commendation, the German forces had already taken the necessary steps. We know that in Norway when the German troops went in, there were food supplies to last for a year. We know that Poland, though not a rich country, usually produces sufficient food for her people. Moreover, the other countries which Herr Hitler has invaded all held considerable stocks when the Germans entered and are themselves, in many cases, very substantial food producers. If all this food is not available now, it can only be because it has been removed to feed the people of Germany and to give them increased rations—for a change—during the last few months.

At this season of the year and for some months to come, there is the least chance of scarcity as the harvest has just been gathered in. The only agencies which can create famine in any part of Europe now and during the coming winter, will be German exactions or German failure to distribute the supplies which they command.

There is another aspect. Many of the most valuable foods are essential to the manufacture of vital war material. Fats are used to make explosives. Potatoes make the alcohol for motor spirit. The plastic materials now so largely used in the construction of aircraft are made of milk. If the Germans use these commodities to help them to bomb our women and children, rather than to feed the populations who produce them, we may be sure that imported foods would go the same way, directly or indirectly, or be employed to relieve the enemy of the responsibilities he has so wantonly assumed.

Let Hitler bear his responsibilities to the full and let the peoples of Europe who groan beneath his yoke aid in every way the coming of the day when that yoke will be broken. Meanwhile, we can and we will arrange in advance for the speedy entry of food into any part of the enslaved area, when this part has been wholly cleared of German forces, and has genuinely regained its freedom. We shall do our best to encourage the building up of reserves of food all over the world, so that there will always be held up before the eyes of the peoples of Europe, including—I say deliberately—the German and Austrian peoples, the certainty that the shattering of the Nazi power will bring to them all immediate food, freedom and peace.

Rather more than a quarter of a year has passed since the new Government came into power in this country. What a cataract of disaster has poured out upon us since then. The trustful Dutch overwhelmed; their beloved and respected Sovereign driven into exile; the peaceful city of Rotterdam the scene of a massacre as hideous and brutal as anything in the Thirty Years' War. Belgium invaded and beaten down; our own fine Expeditionary Force, which King Leopold called to his rescue, cut off and almost captured, escaping as it seemed only by a miracle and with the loss of all its equipment; our Ally, France, out; Italy in against us; all France in the power of the enemy, all its arsenals and vast masses of military material converted or convertible to the enemy's use; a puppet Government set up at Vichy which may at any moment be forced to become our foe; the whole Western seaboard of Europe from the

North Cape to the Spanish frontier in German hands; all the ports, all the air-fields on this immense front, employed against us as potential springboards of invasion. Moreover, the German air power, numerically so far outstripping ours, has been brought so close to our Island that what we used to dread greatly has come to pass and the hostile bombers not only reach our shores in a few minutes and from many directions, but can be escorted by their fighting aircraft.

Why, Sir, if we had been confronted at the beginning of May with such a prospect, it would have seemed incredible that at the end of a period of horror and disaster, or at this point in a period of horror and disaster, we should stand erect, sure of ourselves, masters of our fate and with the conviction of final victory burning unquenchable in our hearts. Few would have believed we could survive; none would have believed that we should today not only feel stronger but should actually be stronger than we have ever been before.

Let us see what has happened on the other side of the scales. The British nation and the British Empire finding themselves alone, stood undismayed against disaster. No one flinched or wavered; nay, some who formerly thought of peace, now think only of war. Our people are united and resolved, as they have never been before. Death and ruin have become small things compared with the shame of defeat or failure in duty.

We cannot tell what lies ahead. It may be that even greater ordeals lie before us. We shall face whatever is coming to us. We are sure of ourselves and of our cause and that is the supreme fact which has emerged in these months of trial.

Meanwhile, we have not only fortified our hearts but our Island. We have rearmed and rebuilt our armies in a degree which would have been deemed impossible a few months ago. We have ferried across the Atlantic, in the month of July, thanks to our friends over there, an immense mass of munitions of all kinds, cannon, rifles, machine-guns, cartridges, and shell, all safely landed without the loss of a gun or a round. The output of our own factories, working as they have never worked before, has poured forth to the troops. The whole British Army is at home. More than 2,000,000 determined men have rifles and bayonets in their hands tonight and three-quarters of them are in regular military formations. We have never had armies like this in our Island in time of war. The whole Island bristles against invaders, from the sea or from the air.

As I explained to the House in the middle of June, the stronger our Army at home, the larger must the invading expedition be, and the larger the invading expedition, the less difficult will be the task of the Navy in detecting its assembly and in intercepting and destroying it on passage; and the greater also would be the difficulty of feeding and supplying the invaders if ever they landed, in the teeth of continuous naval and air attack on their communications. All this is classical and venerable doctrine. As in Nelson's day, the maxim holds, "Our first line of defense is the enemy's ports." Now air reconnaissance and photography have brought to an old principle a new and potent aid.

Our Navy is far stronger than it was at the beginning of the war. The great flow of new construction set on foot at the outbreak is now beginning to come in. We hope our friends across the ocean will send us a timely reinforcement to bridge the gap between the peace flotillas of 1939 and the war flotillas of 1941. There is no difficulty in sending such aid. The seas and oceans are open. The U-boats are contained. The magnetic mine is, up to the present time, effectively mastered. The merchant tonnage under the British flag, after a year of unlimited U-boat war, after eight months of intensive mining attack, is larger than when we began. We have, in addition, under our control at least 4,000,000 tons of shipping from the captive countries which has taken refuge here or in the harbors of the Empire. Our stocks of food of all kinds are far more abundant than in the days of peace and a large and growing program of food production is on foot.

Why do I say all this? Not assuredly to boast; not assuredly to give the slightest countenance to complacency. The dangers we face are still enormous, but so are our advantages and resources.

I recount them because the people have a right to know that there are solid grounds for the confidence which we feel, and that we have good reason to believe ourselves capable, as I said in a very dark hour two months ago, of continuing the war "if necessary alone, if necessary for years." I say it also because the fact that the British Empire stands invincible, and that Nazidom is still being resisted, will kindle again the spark of hope in the breasts of hundreds of millions of downtrodden or despairing men and women throughout

Europe, and far beyond its bounds, and that from these sparks there will presently come cleansing and devouring flame.

The great air battle which has been in progress over this Island for the last few weeks has recently attained a high intensity. It is too soon to attempt to assign limits either to its scale or to its duration. We must certainly expect that greater efforts will be made by the enemy than any he has so far put forth. Hostile air fields are still being developed in France and the Low Countries, and the movement of squadrons and material for attacking us is still proceeding.

It is quite plain that Herr Hitler could not admit defeat in his air attack on Great Britain without sustaining most serious injury. If, after all his boastings and blood-curdling threats and lurid accounts trumpeted round the world of the damage he has inflicted, of the vast numbers of our Air Force he has shot down, so he says, with so little loss to himself; if after tales of the panic-stricken British crushed in their holes cursing the plutocratic Parliament which has led them to such a plight; if after all this his whole air onslaught were forced after a while tamely to peter out, the Führer's reputation for veracity of statement might be seriously impugned. We may be sure, therefore, that he will continue as long as he has the strength to do so, and as long as any preoccupations he may have in respect of the Russian Air Force allow him to do so.

On the other hand, the conditions and course of the fighting have so far been favorable to us. I told the House two months ago that whereas in France our fighter aircraft were wont to inflict a loss of two or three to one upon the Germans, and in the fighting at Dunkirk, which was a kind of no-man's-land, a loss of about three or four to one, we expected that in an attack on this Island we should achieve a larger ratio. This has certainly come true. It must also be remembered that all the enemy machines and pilots which are shot down over our Island, or over the seas which surround it, are either destroyed or captured; whereas a considerable proportion of our machines, and also of our pilots, are saved, and soon again in many cases come into action.

A vast and admirable system of salvage, directed by the Ministry of Aircraft Production, ensures the speediest return to the fighting line of damaged machines, and the most provident and speedy use of all the spare parts and material. At the same time the splendid, nay, astounding increase in the output and repair of British aircraft and engines which Lord Beaverbrook has achieved by a genius of organization and drive, which looks like magic, has given us overflowing reserves of every type of aircraft, and an ever-mounting stream of production both in quantity and quality.

The enemy is, of course, far more numerous than we are. But our new production already, as I am advised, largely exceeds his, and the American production is only just beginning to flow in. It is a fact, as I see from my daily returns, that our bomber and fighter strength now, after all this fighting, are larger than they have ever been. We believe that we shall be able to continue the air struggle indefinitely and as long as the enemy pleases, and the longer it continues the more rapid will be our approach, first towards that parity, and then into that superiority in the air, upon which in a large measure the decision of the war depends.

The gratitude of every home in our Island, in our Empire, and indeed throughout the world, except in the abodes of the guilty, goes out to the British airmen who, undaunted by odds, unwearied in their constant challenge and mortal danger, are turning the tide of the world war by their prowess and by their devotion. Never in the field of human conflict was so much owed by so many to so few.

All hearts go out to the fighter pilots, whose brilliant actions we see with our own eyes day after day; but we must never forget that all the time, night after night, month after month, our bomber squadrons travel far into Germany, find their targets in the darkness by the highest navigational skill, aim their attacks, often under the heaviest fire, often with serious loss, with deliberate careful discrimination, and inflict shattering blows upon the whole of the technical and war-making structure of the Nazi power. On no part of the Royal Air Force does the weight of the war fall more heavily than on the daylight bombers who will play an invaluable part in the case of invasion and whose unflinching zeal it has been necessary in the meanwhile on numerous occasions to restrain.

We are able to verify the results of bombing military targets in Germany, not only by reports which reach us through many sources, but also, of course, by photography. I have no hesitation in saying that this process of bombing the military industries and communications of Germany and the air bases and storage depots from which we are attacked, which process will continue upon an ever-increasing scale until the end of the war, and may in another year attain dimensions hitherto undreamed of, affords one at least of the most certain, if not the shortest of all the roads to victory. Even if the Nazi legions stood triumphant on the Black Sea, or indeed upon the Caspian, even if Hitler was at the gates of India, it would profit him nothing if at the same time the entire economic and scientific apparatus of German war power lay shattered and pulverized at home.

The fact that the invasion of this Island upon a large scale has become a far more difficult operation with every week that has passed since we saved our Army at Dunkirk, and our very great preponderance of sea-power enable us to turn our eyes and to turn our strength increasingly towards the Mediterranean and against that other enemy who, without the slightest provocation, coldly and deliberately, for greed and gain, stabbed France in the back in the moment of her agony, and is now marching against us in Africa.

The defection of France has, of course, been deeply damaging to our position in what is called, somewhat oddly, the Middle East. In the defense of Somaliland, for instance, we had counted upon strong French forces attacking the Italians from Djibouti. We had counted also upon the use of the French naval and air bases in the Mediterranean, and particularly upon the North African shore. We had counted upon the French Fleet. Even though metropolitan France was temporarily overrun, there was no reason why the French Navy, substantial parts of the French Army, the French Air Force and the French Empire overseas should not have continued the struggle at our side.

Shielded by overwhelming sea-power, possessed of invaluable strategic bases and of ample funds, France might have remained one of the great combatants in the struggle. By so doing, France would have preserved the continuity of her life, and the French Empire might have advanced with the British Empire to the rescue of the independence and integrity of the French Motherland.

In our own case, if we had been put in the terrible position of France, a contingency now happily impossible, although, of course, it would have been the duty of all war leaders to fight on here to the end, it would also have been their duty, as I indicated in my speech of 4th June, to provide as far as possible for the Naval security of Canada and our Dominions and to make sure they had the means to carry the struggle from beyond the oceans. Most of the other countries that have been overrun by Germany for the time being have preserved valiantly and faithfully. The Czechs, the Poles, the Norwegians, the Dutch, the Belgians are still in the field, sword in hand, recognized by Great Britain and the United States as the sole representative authorities and lawful Governments of their respective States.

That France alone should lie prostrate at this moment, is the crime, not of a great and noble nation, but of what are called "the men of Vichy." We have profound sympathy with the French people. Our old comradeship with France is not dead. In General de Gaulle and his gallant band, that comradeship takes an effective form. These free Frenchmen have been condemned to death by Vichy, but the day will come, as surely as the sun will rise tomorrow, when their names will be held in honor, and their names will be graven in stone in the streets and villages of a France restored in a liberated Europe to its full freedom and its ancient fame.

But this conviction which I feel of the future cannot affect the immediate problems which confront us in the Mediterranean and in Africa. It had been decided some time before the beginning of the war not to defend the Protectorate of Somaliland. That policy was changed when the French gave in, and when our small forces there, a few battalions, a few guns, were attacked by all the Italian troops, nearly two divisions, which had formerly faced the French at Djibouti, it was right to withdraw our detachments, virtually intact, for action elsewhere. Far larger operations no doubt impend in the Middle East theatre, and I shall certainly not attempt to discuss or prophesy about their probable course. We have large armies and many means of reinforcing them. We have the complete sea command of the Eastern Mediterranean. We intend to do our best to give a good account of ourselves, and to discharge faithfully and resolutely all our obligations and duties in that quarter of the world. More than that I do not think the House would wish me to say at the present time.

A good many people have written to me to ask me to make on this occasion a fuller statement of our war aims, and of the kind of peace we wish to make after the war, than is contained in the very considerable declaration which was made early in the Autumn. Since then we have made common cause with Norway, Holland, and Belgium. We have recognized the Czech Government of Dr. Benes, and we have told General de Gaulle that our success will carry with it the restoration of France.

I do not think it would be wise at this moment, while the battle rages and the war is still perhaps only in its earlier stage, to embark upon elaborate speculations about the future shape which should be given to Europe or the new securities which must be arranged to spare mankind the miseries of a third World War. The ground is not new, it has been frequently traversed and explored, and many ideas are held about it in common by all good men, and all free men. But before we can undertake the task of rebuilding we have not only to be convinced ourselves, but we have to convince all other countries that the Nazi tyranny is going to be finally broken.

The right to guide the course of world history is the noblest prize of victory. We are still toiling up the hill; we have not yet reached the crest-line of it; we cannot survey the landscape or even imagine what its condition will be when that longed-for morning comes. The task which lies before us immediately is at once more practical, more simple and more stern. I hope— indeed I pray—that we shall not be found unworthy of our victory if after toil and tribulation it is granted to us. For the rest, we have to gain the victory. That is our task.

There is, however, one direction in which we can see a little more clearly ahead. We have to think not only for ourselves but for the lasting security of the cause and principles for which we are fighting and of the long future of the British Commonwealth of Nations.

Some months ago we came to the conclusion that the interests of the United States and of the British Empire both required that the United States should have facilities for the naval and air defense of the Western hemisphere against the attack of a Nazi power which might have acquired temporary but lengthy control of a large part of Western Europe and its formidable resources.

We had therefore decided spontaneously, and without being asked or offered any inducement, to inform the Government of the United States that we would be glad to place such defense facilities at their disposal by leasing suitable sites in our Transatlantic possessions for their greater security against the unmeasured dangers of the future.

The principle of association of interests for common purposes between Great Britain and the United States had developed even before the war. Various agreements had been reached about certain small islands in the Pacific Ocean which had become important as air fuelling points. In all this line of thought we found ourselves in very close harmony with the Government of Canada.

Presently we learned that anxiety was also felt in the United States about the air and naval defense of their Atlantic seaboard, and President Roosevelt has recently made it clear that he would like to discuss with us, and with the Dominion of Canada and with Newfoundland, the development of American naval and air facilities in Newfoundland and in the West Indies. There is, of course, no question of any transference of sovereignty—that has never been suggested—or of any action being taken, without the consent or against the wishes of the various Colonies concerned, but for our part, His Majesty's Government are entirely willing to accord defense facilities to the United States on a 99 years' leasehold basis, and we feel sure that our interests no less than theirs, and the interests of the Colonies themselves and of Canada and Newfoundland will be served thereby.

These are important steps. Undoubtedly this process means that these two great organizations of the English-speaking democracies, the British Empire and the United States, will have to be somewhat mixed up together in some of their affairs for mutual and general advantage.

For my own part, looking out upon the future, I do not view the process with any misgivings. I could not stop it if I wished; no one can stop it. Like the Mississippi, it just keeps rolling along. Let it roll. Let it roll on full flood, inexorable, irresistible, benignant, to broader lands and better days.

The *Iliad,* or
Poem of Force
Simone Weil

Simone Weil (1909–1943) was born in Paris, France, to Jewish parents who had moved to Paris after Germany annexed Alsace-Lorraine. Fluent in Ancient Greek by the age of 12, she was a dedicated and precocious student. Raised in "complete agnosticism,"[1] she became interested in the existence of God and was fascinated by Greek and Egyptian mystery religions, Hinduism, Buddhism, and Christianity.

In the summer and autumn of 1940, after France was conquered by the invading Nazi army, Weil wrote about the character of force in Homer's Iliad. She published it under the acrostical pseudonym "Emile Novis" in the December 1940 and January 1941 issues of Cahiers du Sud, *a literary magazine in Marseilles.*

In 1942, Weil traveled to the United States with her parents and, after knowing that they were safe in America, returned to Europe to join the French Resistance. Weakened by her decision to reduce her food intake in sympathy with the European victims of the war, she died in England in 1943.

---

[1] Simone Weil, *What is a Jew,* as cited by George A. Panichas, *Simone Weil Reader* (1977), p.8.

Written in 1940; published in December 1940 and January 1941; translated by Mary McCarthy, 1945

The true hero, the true subject, the center of the *Iliad* is force. Force employed by man, force that enslaves man, force before which man's flesh shrinks away. In this work, at all times, the human spirit is shown as modified by its relations with force, as swept away, blinded by the very force it imagined it could handle, as deformed by the weight of the force it submits to. For those dreamers who considered that force, thanks to progress, would soon be a thing of the past, the *Iliad* could appear as an historical document; for others, whose powers of recognition are more acute and who perceive force, today as yesterday, at the very center of human history, the *Iliad* is the purest and the loveliest of mirrors.

To define force—it is that x that turns anybody who is subjected to it into a thing. Exercised to the limit, it turns man into a thing in the most literal sense: it makes a corpse out of him. Somebody was here, and the next minute there is nobody here at all; this is a spectacle the *Iliad* never wearies of showing us:

> . . . the horses
> *Rattled the empty chariots through the files of battle,*
> *Longing for their noble drivers. But they on the ground*
> *Lay, dearer to the vultures than to their wives.*

The hero becomes a thing dragged behind a chariot in the dust:

> All around, his black hair
> Was spread; in the dust his whole head lay,
> That once-charming head; now Zeus had let his enemies
> Defile it on his native soil.

The bitterness of such a spectacle is offered us absolutely undiluted. No comforting fiction intervenes; no consoling prospect of immortality; and on the hero's head no washed-out halo of patriotism descends.

> His soul, fleeing his limbs, passed to Hades,
> Mourning its fate, forsaking its youth and its vigor.

Still more poignant—so painful is the contrast—is the sudden evocation, as quickly rubbed out, of another world: the far-away precarious, touching world of peace, of the family, the world in which each man counts more than anything else to those about him.

> She ordered her bright-haired maids in the palace
> To place on the fire a large tripod, preparing
> A hot bath for Hector, returning from battle.
> Foolish woman! Already he lay, far from hot baths,
> Slain by grey-eyed Athena, who guided Achilles' arm.

Far from hot baths he was indeed, poor man. And not he alone. Nearly all the *Iliad* takes place far from hot baths. Nearly all of human life, then and now, takes place far from hot baths.

Here we see force in its grossest and most summary form—the force that kills. How much more varied in its processes, how much more surprising in its effects is the other force, the force that does not kill, i.e., that does not kill just yet. It will surely kill, it will possibly kill, or perhaps it merely hangs, poised and ready, over the head of the creature it can kill, at any moment, which is to say at every moment. In whatever aspect, it effect is the same: it turns a man into a stone. From its first property (the ability to turn a human being into a thing by the simple method of killing him) flows another, quite prodigious too in its own way, the ability to turn a human being into a thing while he is still alive. He is alive; he has a soul; and yet—he is a thing. An extraordinary entity this—a thing that has a soul. And as for the soul, what an extraordinary house it finds itself in! Who can say what it costs it, moment by moment, to accommodate itself to this residence, how much writhing and bending, folding and pleating are required of it? It was not made to live inside a thing; if it does so, under pressure of necessity, there is not a single element of its nature to which violence is not done.

A man stands disarmed and naked with a weapon pointing at him; this person becomes a corpse before anybody or anything touches him. Just a minute ago, he was thinking, acting, hoping:

> Motionless, he pondered. And the other drew near,
> Terrified, anxious to touch his knees, hoping in his heart
> To escape evil death and black destiny . . .
> With one hand he clasped, suppliant, his knees,
> While the other clung to the sharp spear, not letting go . . .

Soon, however, he grasps the fact that the weapon which is pointing at him will not be diverted; and now, still breathing, he is simply matter; still thinking, he can think no longer:

> Thus spoke the brilliant son of Priam
> In begging words. But he heard a harsh reply:

> He spoke. And the other's knees and heart failed him.
> Dropping his spear, he knelt down, holding out his arms.
> Achilles, drawing his sharp sword, struck
> Through the neck and breastbone. The two-edged sword
> Sunk home its full length. The other, face down,
> Lay still, and the black blood ran out, wetting the ground.

If a stranger, completely disabled, disarmed, strengthless, throws himself on the mercy of a warrior, he is not, by this very act, condemned to death; but a moment of impatience on the warrior's part will suffice to relieve him of his life. In any case, his flesh has lost that very important property which in the laboratory distinguishes living flesh from dead—the galvanic response. If you give a frog's leg an electric shock, it twitches. If you confront a human being with the touch or sight of something horrible or terrifying, this bundle of muscles, nerves, and flesh likewise twitches. Alone of all living things, the supplicant we have just described neither quivers nor trembles. He has lost the right to do so. As his lips advance to touch the object that is for him of all things most charged with horror, they do not draw back on his teeth—they cannot:

> No one saw great Priam enter. He stopped,
> Clasped the knees of Achilles, kissed his hands,
> Those terrible man-killing hands that had slaughtered so many of his
> sons.

The sight of a human being pushed to such an extreme of suffering chills us like the sight of a dead body:

> As when harsh misfortune strikes a man if in his own country
> He has killed a man, and arrives at last at someone else's door,
> The door of a rich man; a shudder seizes those who see him.
> So Achilles shuddered to see divine Priam;
> The others shuddered too, looking one at the other.

But this feeling lasts only a moment. Soon the very presence of the suffering creature is forgotten:

> He spoke. The other, remembering his own father, longed to weep;
> Taking the old man's arm, he pushed him away.
> Both were remembering. Thinking of Hector, killer of men,
> Priam wept, abased at the feet of Achilles.
> But Achilles wept, now for his father,
> Now for Patroclus. And their sobs resounded through the house.

It was not insensibility that made Achilles with a single movement of his hand push away the old man who had been clinging to his knees; Priam's words, recalling his own old father, had moved him to tears. It was merely a question of his being as free in his attitudes and movements as if, clasping his knees, there were not a suppliant but an inert object. Anybody who is in our vicinity exercises a certain power over us by his very presence, and a power that belongs to him alone, that is, the power of halting, repressing, modifying each movement that our body sketches out. If we step aside for a passer-by on the road, it is not the same thing as stepping aside to avoid a billboard; alone in our rooms, we get up, walk about, sit down again quite differently from the way we do when we have a visitor. But this indefinable influence that the presence of another human being has on us is not exercised by men whom a moment of impatience can deprive of life, who can die before even thought has a chance to pass sentence on them. In their presence, people move about as if they were not there; they, on their side, running the risk of being reduced to nothing in a single instant, imitate nothingness in their own persons. Pushed, they fall. Fallen, they lie where they are, unless chance gives somebody the idea of raising them up again. But supposing that at long last they have been picked up, honored with cordial remarks, they still do not venture to take this resurrection seriously; they dare not express a wish lest an irritated voice return them forever to silence:

He spoke; the old man trembled and obeyed.

At least a suppliant, once his prayer is answered, becomes a human being again, like everybody else. But there are other, more unfortunate creatures who have become things for the rest of their lives. Their days hold no pastimes, no free spaces, no room in them for any impulse of their own. It is not that their life is harder than other men's nor that they occupy a lower place in the social hierarchy; no, they are another human species, a compromise between a man and a corpse. The idea of a person's being a thing is a logical contradiction. Yet what is impossible in logic becomes true in life, and the contradiction lodged within the soul tears it to shreds. This thing is constantly aspiring to be a man or a woman, and never achieving it—here, surely, is death but death strung out over a whole lifetime; here, surely is life, but life that death congeals before abolishing.

This strange fate awaits the virgin, the priest's daughter:

I will not give her up. Sooner shall old age come upon her

In our house in Argos, far from her native land,
Tending the loom and sharing my bed.

It awaits the young wife, the young mother, the prince's bride:

And perhaps one day, in Argos, you will weave cloth for another,
And the Messeian or Hyperian water you will fetch,
Much against your will, yielding to a harsh necessity.

It awaits the baby, heir to the royal scepter:

Soon they will be carried off in the hollow ships,
I with them. And you, my child, will either go with me,
To a land where you will work at wretched tasks,
Laboring for a pitiless master . . .

In the mother's eyes, such a fate is, for her child, as terrible as death; the husband would rather die than see his wife reduced to it; all the plagues of heaven are invoked by the father against the army that subjects his daughter to it. Yet the victims themselves are beyond all this. Curses, feelings of rebellion, comparisons, reflections on the future and the past, are obliterated from the mind of the captive; and memory itself barely lingers on. Fidelity to his city and his dead is not the slave's privilege.

And what does it take to make the slave weep? The misfortune of his master, his oppressor, despoiler, pillager, of the man who laid waste his town and killed his dear ones under his very eyes. This man suffers or dies; then the slave's tears come. And really why not? This is for him the only occasion on which tears are permitted, are, indeed, required. A slave will always cry whenever he can do so with impunity his situation keeps tears on tap for him.

She spoke, weeping, and the women groaned,
Using the pretext of Patroclus to bewail their own torments.

Since the slave has no license to express anything except what is pleasing to his master, it follows that the only emotion that can touch or enliven him a little, that can reach him in the desolation of his life, is the emotion of love for his master. There is no place else to send the gift of love; all other outlets are barred, just as, with the horse in harness, bit, shafts, reins bar every way but one. And if, by some miracle, in the slave's breast a hope is born, the hope of becoming, some day, through somebody's influence, someone once again, how far won't these captives go to show love and thankfulness, even though these emotions are addressed to the very men who should, considering the very recent past, still reek with horror for them:

> My husband, to whom my father and respected mother gave me,
> I saw before the city transfixed by the sharp bronze.
> My three brothers, children, with me, of a single mother,
> So dear to me! They all met their fatal day.
> But you did not allow me to weep, when swift Achilles
> Slaughtered my husband and laid waste the city of Mynes.
> You promised me that I would be taken by divine Achilles,
> For his legitimate wife, that he would carry me away in his ships,
> To Pythia, where our marriage would be celebrated among the
>   Myrmidons,
> So without respite I mourn for you, you who have always been gentle.

To lose more than the slave does is impossible, for he loses his whole inner life. A fragment of it he may get back if he sees the possibility of changing his fate, but this is his only hope. Such is the empire of force, as extensive as the empire of nature. Nature, too, when vital needs are at stake, can erase the whole inner life, even the grief of a mother:

> But the thought of eating came to her, when she was tired of tears.

Force, in the hands of another, exercises over the soul the same tyranny that extreme hunger does; for it possesses, and *in perpetuo*, the power of life and death. Its rule, moreover, is as cold and hard as the rule of inert matter. The man who knows himself weaker than another is more alone in the heart of a city than a man lost in the desert.

> Two casks are placed before Zeus's doorsill,
> Containing the gifts he gives, the bad in one, the good in the other . . .
> The man to whom he gives baneful gifts, he exposes to outrage;
> A frightful need drives across the divine earth;
> He is a wanderer, and gets no respect from gods or men.

Force is as pitiless to the man who possesses it, or thinks he does, as it is to its victims; the second it crushes, the first it intoxicates. The truth is, nobody really possesses it. The human race is not divided up, in the *Iliad*, into conquered persons, slaves, suppliants, on the one hand, and conquerors and chiefs on the other. In this poem there is not a single man who does not at one time or another have to bow his neck to force. The common soldier in the *Iliad* is free and has right to bear arms; nevertheless he is subject to the indignity of orders and abuse:

> But whenever he came upon a commoner shouting out,
> He struck him with his scepter and spoke sharply:
> "Good for nothing! Be still and listen to your betters,
> You are weak and cowardly and unwarlike,
> You count for nothing, neither in battle nor in council."

Thersites pays dear for the perfectly reasonable comments he makes, comments not at all different, moreover, from those made by Achilles:

> He hit him with his scepter on back and shoulders,
> So that he doubled over, and a great tear welled up,
> And a bloody welt appeared on his back
> Under the golden scepter. Frightened, he sat down,
> Wiping away his tears, bewildered and in pain.
> Troubled though they were, the others laughed long at him.

Achilles himself, that proud hero, the undefeated, is shown us at the outset of the poem, weeping with humiliation and helpless grief—the woman he wanted for his bride has been taken from under his nose, and he has not dared to oppose it:

> ... But Achilles
> Weeping, sat apart from his companions,
> By the white-capped waves, staring over the boundless ocean.

What has happened is that Agamemnon has deliberately humiliated Achilles, to show that he himself is the master:

> ... So you will learn
> That I am greater than you, and anyone else will hesitate
> To treat me as an equal and set himself against me.

But a few days pass and now the supreme commander is weeping in his turn. He must humble himself, he must plead, and have, moreover, the added misery of doing it all in vain.

In the same way, there is not a single one of the combatants who is spared the shameful experience of fear. The heroes quake like everybody else. It only needs a challenge from Hector to throw the whole Greek force into consternation—except for Achilles and his men, and they did not happen to be present:

> He spoke and all grew still and held their peace,
> Ashamed to refuse, afraid to accept.

But once Ajax comes forward and offers himself, fear quickly changes sides:

> A shudder of terror ran through the Trojans, making their limbs weak;

> And Hector himself felt his heart leap in his breast.
> But he no longer had the right to tremble, or to run away . . . .

Two days later, it is Ajax's turn to be terrified:

> Zeus the father on high, makes fear rise in Ajax.
> He stops, overcome, puts behind him his buckler made of seven hides,
> Trembles, looks at the crowd around, like a wild beast...

Even to Achilles the moment comes; he too must shake and stammer with fear, though it is a river that has this effect on him, not a man. But, with the exception of Achilles, every man in the Iliad tastes a moment of defeat in battle. Victory is less a matter of valor than of blind destiny, which is symbolized in the poem by Zeus's golden scales:

> Then Zeus the father took his golden scales,
> In them he put the two fates of death that cuts down all men,
> One for the Trojans, tamers of horses, one for the bronze-sheathed Greeks.
> He seized the scales by the middle; it was the fatal day of Greece that sank.

By its very blindness, destiny establishes a kind of justice. Blind also is she who decrees to warriors punishment in kind. He that takes the sword, will perish by the sword. The *Iliad* formulated the principle long before the Gospels did, and in almost the same terms:

> Ares is just, and kills those who kill.

Perhaps all men, by the very act of being born, are destined to suffer violence; yet this is a truth to which circumstance shuts men's eyes. The strong are, as a matter of fact, never absolutely strong, nor are the weak absolutely weak, but neither is aware of this. They have in common a refusal to believe that they both belong to the same species: the weak see no relation between themselves and the strong, and vice versa. The man who is the possessor of force seems to walk through a non-resistant element; in the human substance that surrounds him nothing has the power to interpose, between the impulse and the act, the tiny interval that is reflection. Where there is no room for reflection, there is none either for justice or prudence. Hence we see men in arms behaving harshly and madly. We see their sword bury itself in the breast of a disarmed enemy who is in the very act of pleading at their knees. We see them triumph over a dying man by describing to him the outrages his corpse will endure. We see Achilles cut the throats of twelve Trojan boys on the funeral pyre of Patroclus as naturally as we cut flowers for a grave. These men, wielding power, have no suspicion of the fact that the consequences of their deeds will at length come home to them— they too will bow the neck in their turn. If you can make an old man fall silent, tremble, obey, with a single word of your own, why should it occur to you that the curses of this old man, who is after all a priest, will have their own importance in the gods' eyes? Why should you refrain from taking Achilles' girl away from him if you know that neither he nor she can do anything but obey you? Achilles rejoices over the sight of the Greeks fleeing in misery and confusion. What could possibly suggest to him that this rout, which will last exactly as long as he wants it to and end when his mood indicates it, that this very rout will be the cause of his friend's death, and, for that matter, of his own? Thus it happens that those who have force on loan from fate count on it too much and are destroyed.

But at the time their own destruction seems impossible to them. For they do not see that the force in their possession is only a limited quantity; nor do they see their relations with other human beings as a kind of balance between unequal amounts of force. Since other people do not impose on their movements that halt, that interval of hesitation, wherein lies all our consideration for our brothers in humanity, they conclude that destiny has given complete license to them, and none at all to their inferiors. And at this point they exceed the measure of the force that is actually at their disposal. Inevitably they exceed it, since they are not aware that it is limited. And now we see them committed irretrievably to chance; suddenly things cease to obey them. Sometimes chance is kind to them, sometimes cruel. But in any case there they are, exposed, open to misfortune; gone is the armor of power that formerly protected their naked souls; nothing, no shield, stands between them and tears.

This retribution, which has a geometrical rigor, which operates automatically to penalize the abuse of force, was the main subject of Greek thought. It is the soul of the epic. Under the name of Nemesis, it functions as the mainspring of Aeschylus's tragedies. To the Pythagoreans, to Socrates and Plato, it was the jumping-off point of speculation upon the nature of man and the universe. Wherever Hellenism has penetrated, we find the idea of its familiar. In Oriental countries which are steeped in Buddhism, it is perhaps this Greek idea that has lived on under the name of Kharma. The Occident, however, has lost it, and no longer even has a word to express it in any of its languages: conceptions of limit, measure, equilibrium, which ought to determine the conduct of life are, in the West, restricted to a servile function in the vocabulary of technics. We are only geometricians of matter; the Greeks were, first of all, geometricians in their apprenticeship to virtue.

The progress of the war in the *Iliad* is simply a continual game of seesaw. The victor of the moment feels himself invincible, even though, only a few hours before, he may have experienced defeat; he forgets to treat victory as a transitory thing. At the end of the first day of combat described in the *Iliad*, the victorious Greeks were in a position to obtain the object of all their efforts, i.e., Helen and her riches assuming of course as Homer did, that the Greeks had reason to believe that Helen was in Troy. Actually, the Egyptian priests, who ought to have known, affirmed later on to Herodotus that she was in Egypt. In any case, that evening the Greeks are no longer interested in her or her possessions:

> "For the present, let us not accept the riches of Paris;
> Nor Helen; everybody sees, even the most ignorant,
> That Troy stands on the verge of ruin."
> He spoke, and all the Achaeans acclaimed him.

What they want is, in fact, everything. For booty, all the riches of Troy; for their bonfires, all the palaces, temples, houses; for slaves, all the women and children; for corpses, all the men. They forget one detail, that everything is not within their power, for they are not in Troy. Perhaps they will be there tomorrow; perhaps not. Hector, the same day, makes the same mistake:

> For I know well in my entrails and in my hearts,
> A day will come when Holy Troy will perish,
> And Priam, and the nation of Priam of the good lance.
> But I think less of the grief that is in store for the Trojans,
> And of Hecuba herself, and of Priam the king,
> And of my brothers, so numerous and so brave,
> Who will fall in the dust under the blows of the enemy,
> Than of you that day when a Greek in his bronze breastplate
> Will drag you away weeping and deprive you of your liberty.

> But as for me, may I be dead, and may the earth have covered me
> Before I hear you cry out or see you dragged away!

At this moment what would he not give to turn aside those horrors which he believes to be inevitable? But at this moment nothing he could give would be of any use. The next day but one, however, the Greeks have run away miserably, and Agamemnon himself is in favor of putting to the sea again. And now Hector, by making a very few concessions, could readily secure the enemy's departure; yet now he is even unwilling to let them go empty-handed:

> Set fires everywhere and let the brightness mount the skies
> Lest in the night the long-haired Greeks,
> Escaping, sail over the broad back of ocean . . .
> Let each of them take home a wound to heal
> . . . thus others will fear
> To bring dolorous war to the Trojans, tamers of horses.

His wish is granted; the Greeks stay; and the next day they reduce Hector and his men to a pitiable condition:

> As for them—they fled across the plain like cattle
> Whom a lion hunts before him in the dark midnight . . .
> Thus the mighty Agamemnon, son of Atreus, pursued them,
> Steadily killing the hindmost; and still they fled.

In the course of the afternoon, Hector regains the ascendancy, withdraws again, then puts the Greeks to flight, then is repulsed by Patroclus, who has come in with his fresh troops. Patroclus, pressing his advantage, ends by finding himself exposed, wounded and without armor, to the sword of Hector. And finally that evening the victorious Hector hears the prudent counsel of Polydamas and repudiates it sharply:

> Now that wily Kronos's son has given me
> Glory at the ships; now that I have driven the Greeks to the sea,
> Do not offer, fool, such counsels to the people.
> No Trojan will listen to you; nor would I permit it . . .
> So Hector spoke, and the Trojans acclaimed him . . . .

The next day Hector is lost. Achilles has harried him across the field and is about to kill him. He has always been the stronger of the two in combat; how much the more so now, after several weeks of rest, ardent for vengeance and victory, against an exhausted enemy? And Hector stands alone, before the walls of Troy, absolutely alone, alone to wait for death and to steady his soul to face it:

> Alas, were I to slip through the gate, behind the rampart,
> Polydamas at once would heap dishonor on me . . .
> And now that through my recklessness I have destroyed my people,

> I fear the Trojans and the long-robed Trojan women,
> I fear to hear from some one far less brave than I:
> "Hector, trusting his own strength too far, has ruined his people." . . .
> Suppose I were to down my bossed shield,
> My massive helmet, and, leaning my spear against the wall,
> Should go to meet renowned Achilles? . . .
> But why spin out these fancies? Why such dreams?
> I would not reach him, nor would he pity me,
> Or respect me. He would kill me like a woman
> If I came naked thus . . . .

Not a jot of the grief and ignominy that fall to the unfortunate is Hector spared. Alone, stripped of the prestige of force, he discovers that the courage that kept him from taking to the shelter of the walls is not enough to save him from flight:

> Seeing him, Hector began to tremble. He had not the heart
> To stay . . . .
> . . . It is not for a ewe nor the skin of an ox,
> That they are striving, not these ordinary rewards of the race;
> It is for a life that they run, the life of Hector, tamer of horses.

Wounded to death, he enhances his conqueror's triumph by vain supplications:

> I implore you, by your soul, by your knees,
> by your parents . . .

But the auditors of the *Iliad* knew that the death of Hector would be but a brief joy to Achilles, and the death of Achilles but a brief joy to the Trojans, and the destruction of Troy but a brief joy to the Achaeans.

Thus violence obliterates anybody who feels its touch. It comes to seem just as external to its employer as to its victim. And from this springs the idea of a destiny before which executioner and victim stand equally innocent, before which conquered and conqueror are brothers in the same distress. The conquered brings misfortune to the conqueror, and vice versa:

> A single son, short-lived, was born to him.
> Neglected by me, he grows old—for far from home
> I camp before Troy, injuring you and your sons.

A moderate use of force, which alone would enable man to escape being enmeshed in its machinery, would require superhuman virtue, which is as rare as dignity in weakness. Moreover, moderation itself is not without its perils, since prestige, from which force derives at least three quarters of its strength, rests principally upon that marvelous indifference that the strong feel toward the weak, an indifference so contagious that it infects the very people who are the objects of it. Yet ordinarily excess is not arrived at through prudence or politic considerations. On the contrary, man dashes to it as to an irresistible temptation. The voice of reason is occasionally heard in the mouths of the characters in the *Iliad*. Thersites' speeches are reasonable to the highest degree; so are the speeches of the angry Achilles:

> Nothing is worth my life, not all the goods
> They say the well-built city of Ilium contains. . . .
> A man can capture steers and fatted sheep
> But, once gone, the soul cannot be captured back.

But words of reason drop into the void. If they come from an inferior, he is punished and shuts up; if from a chief, his actions betray them. And failing everything else, there is always a god handy to advise him to be unreasonable. In the end, the very idea of wanting to escape the role fate has allotted one—the business of killing and dying—disappears from the mind:

> We to whom Zeus
> Has assigned suffering, from the youth to old age,
> Suffering in grievous wars, till we perish to the last man.

Already these warriors, like Craonne's so much later, felt themselves to be "condemned men."

It was the simplest trap that pitched them into this situation. At the outset, at the embarkation, their hearts are light, as hearts always are if you have a large force on your side and nothing but space to oppose you. Their weapons are in their hands; the enemy is absent. Unless your spirit has been conquered in advance by the reputation of the enemy, you always feel yourself to be much stronger than anybody who is not there. An absent man does not impose the yoke of necessity. To the spirits of those embarking no necessity yet presents itself; consequently they go off as though to a game, as though on holiday from the confinement of daily life.

> Where have they gone, those braggadocio boasts
> We proudly flung upon the air at Lemnos,
> Stuffing ourselves with flesh of horned steers,
> Drinking from cups brimming over with wine?

> As for Trojans—a hundred or two each man of us
> Could handle in battle. And now one is too much for us.

But the first contact of war does not immediately destroy the illusion that war is a game. War's necessity is terrible, altogether different in kind from the necessity of peace. So terrible is it that the human spirit will not submit to it so long as it can possibly escape; and whenever it can escape it takes refuge in long days empty of necessity, days of play, of revery, days arbitrary and unreal. Danger then becomes an abstraction; the lives you destroy are like toys broken by a child, and quite as incapable of feeling; heroism is but a theatrical gesture and smirched with boastfulness. This becomes doubly true if a momentary access of vitality comes to reinforce the divine hand that wards off defeat and death. Then war is easy and basely, coarsely loved.

But with the majority of the combatants this state of mind does not persist. Soon there comes a day when fear, or defeat, or the death of beloved comrades touches the warrior's spirit, and it crumbles in the hand of necessity. At that moment war is no more a game or a dream; now at last the warrior cannot doubt the reality of its existence. And this reality, which he perceives, is hard, much too hard to be borne, for it enfolds death. Once you acknowledge death to be a practical possibility, the thought of it becomes unendurable, except in flashes. True enough, all men are fated to die; true enough also, a soldier may grow old in battles; yet for those whose spirits have bent under the yoke of war, the relation between death and the future is different than for other men. For other men death appears as a limit set in advance on the future; for the soldier death is the future, the future his profession assigns him. Yet the idea of man's having death for a future is abhorrent to nature. Once the experience of war makes visible the possibility of death that lie locked up in each moment, our thoughts cannot travel from one day to the next without meeting death's face. The mind is then strung up to a pitch it can stand for only a short time; but each new dawn reintroduces the same necessity; and days piled on days make years. On each one of these days the soul suffers violence. Regularly, every morning, the soul castrates itself of aspiration, for thought cannot journey through time without meeting death on the way. Thus war effaces all conceptions of purpose or goal, including even its own "war aims." It effaces the very notion of war's being brought to an end. To be outside a situation so violent as this is to find it inconceivable; to be inside it is to be unable to conceive its end. Consequently, nobody does anything to bring this end about. In the presence of an armed enemy, what hand can relinquish its weapon? The mind ought to find a way out, but the mind has lost all capacity to so much as look outward. The mind is completely absorbed in doing itself violence. Always in human life, whether war or slavery is in question, intolerable sufferings continue, as it were, by the force of their own specific gravity, and so look to the outsider as though they were easy to bear; actually, they continue because they have deprived the sufferer of the resources which might serve to extricate him.

Nevertheless, the soul that is enslaved to war cries out for deliverance, but deliverance itself appears to it in an extreme and tragic aspect, the aspect of destruction. Any other solution, more moderate, more reasonable in character, would expose the mind to suffering so naked, so violent that it could not be borne, even as memory. Terror, grief, exhaustion, slaughter, the annihilation of comrades—it is credible that these things should not continually tear at the soul, if the intoxication of force had not intervened to drown them? The idea that an unlimited effort should bring in only a limited profit or no profit at all is terribly painful.

> What? Will we let Priam and the Trojans boast
> Of Argive Helen, she for whom so many Greeks
> Died before Troy, far from their native land?
> What? Do you want us to leave the city, wide-streeted Troy,
> Standing, when we have suffered so much for it?

But actually what is Helen to Ulysses? What indeed is Troy, full of riches that will not compensate him for Ithaca's ruin? For the Greeks, Troy and Helen are in reality mere sources of blood and tears; to master them is to master frightful memories. If the existence of an enemy has made a soul destroy in itself the thing nature put there, then the only remedy the soul can imagine is the destruction of the enemy. At the same time the death of dearly loved comrades arouses a spirit of somber emulation, a rivalry in death:

> May I die, then, at once! Since fate has not let me
> Protect my dead friend, who far from home
> Perished, longing for me to defend him from death.

So now I go to seek the murderer of my friend,
Hector. And death shall I find at the moment
Zeus will it—Zeus and the other immortal.

It is the same despair that drives him on toward death, on the one hand, and slaughter on the other:

I know it well, my fate is to perish here,
Far from father and dearly loved mother; but meanwhile
I shall not stop till the Trojans have had their fill of war.

The man possessed by this twofold need for death belongs, so long as he has not become something still different, to a different race from the race of the living.

What echo can the timid hopes of life strike in such a heart? How can it hear the defeated begging for another sight of the light of day? The threatened life has already been relieved of nearly all its consequence by a single, simple distinction: it is now unarmed; its adversary possesses a weapon. Furthermore, how can a man who has rooted out of himself the notion that the light of day is sweet to the eyes respect such a notion when it makes its appearance in some futile and humble lament?

I clasp tight your knees, Achilles. Have a thought, have pity for me.
I stand here, 0 son of Zeus, a suppliant, to be respected.
In your house it was I first tasted Demeter's bread,
That day in my well-pruned vineyard you caught me
And sold me, sending me far from father and friends,
To holy Lemnos; a hundred oxen was my price.
And now I will pay you three hundred for ransom.
This dawn is for me my twelfth day in Troy,
After so many sorrows. See me here, in your hands,
Through some evil fate. Zeus surely must hate me
Who again puts me into your hands. Alas, my poor mother Laothoe,
Daughter of the old man, Altes—a short-lived son you have borne.

What a reception this feeble hope gets!

Come, friend, you too must die. Why make a fuss about it?
Patroclus, he too has died—a far better man than you are.
Don't you see how handsome I am, how mighty?
A noble father begat me, and I have a goddess for mother.
Yet even I, like you, must some day encounter my fate,
Whether the hour strikes at noon, or evening, or sunrise,
The hour that comes when some arms-bearing warrior will kill me.

To respect life in somebody else when you have had to castrate yourself of all yearning for it demands a truly heart-breaking exertion of the powers of generosity. It is impossible to imagine any of Homer's warriors being capable of such an exertion, unless it is that warrior who dwells, in a peculiar way, at the very center of the poem—I mean Patroclus, who "knew how to be sweet to everybody," and who throughout the *Iliad* commits no cruel or brutal act. But then how many men do we know, in several thousand years of human history, who would have displayed such god-like generosity? Two or three ?—even this is doubtful. Lacking this generosity, the conquering soldier is like a scourge of nature. Possessed by war, he, like the slave, becomes a thing, though his manner of doing so is different—over him too, words are as powerless as over matter itself. And both, at the touch of force, experience its inevitable effects: they become deaf and dumb.

Such is the nature of force. Its power of converting a man into a thing is a double one, and in its application double-edged. To the same degree, though in different fashions, those who use it and those who endure it are turned to stone. This property of force achieves its maximum effectiveness during the clash of arms, in battle, when the tide of the day has turned, and everything is rushing toward a decision. It is not the planning man, the man of strategy, the man acting on the resolution taken, who wins or loses a battle; battles are fought and decided by men deprived of these faculties, men who have undergone a transformation, who have dropped either to the level of inert matter, which is pure passivity, or to the level of blind force, which is pure momentum. Here in lies the last secret of war, a secret revealed by the *Iliad* in its similes, which liken the warriors either to fire, flood, wind, wild beasts, or God knows what blind cause of disaster, or else to frightened animals, trees, water, sand, to anything in nature that is set into motion by the violence of external forces. Greeks and Trojans, from one day to the next, sometimes even from one hour to the next, experience, turn and turn about, one or the other of these transmutations:

> As when a lion, murderous, springs among the cattle
> Which by thousands are grazing over some vast marshy field. . . .
> And their flanks heave with terror; even so the Achaians
> Scattered in panic before Hector and Zeus, the great father.
> As when a ravening fire breaks out deep in a bushy wood
> And the wheeling wind scatters sparks far and wide,

> And trees, root and branch, topple over in flames;
> So Atreus' son, Agamemnon, roared through the ranks
> Of the Trojans in flight. . . .

The art of war is simply the art of producing such transformations, and its equipment, its processes, even the casualties it inflicts on the enemy, are only means directed toward this end—its true object is the warrior's soul. Yet these transformations are always a mystery; the gods are their authors, the gods who kindle men's imagination. But however caused, this petrifactive quality of force, two-fold always, is essential to its nature; and a soul which has entered the province of force will not escape this except by a miracle. Such miracles are rare and of brief duration.

The wantonness of the conqueror that knows no respect for any creature or thing that is at its mercy or is imagined to be so, the despair of the soldier that drives him on to destruction, the obliteration of the slave or the conquered man, the wholesale slaughter—all these elements combine in the *Iliad* to make a picture of uniform horror, of which force is the sole hero. A monotonous desolation would result were it not for those few luminous moments, scattered here and there throughout the poem, those brief, celestial moments in which man possesses his soul. The soul that awakes then, to live for an instant only and be lost almost at once in force's vast kingdom, awakes pure and whole; it contains no ambiguities, nothing complicated or turbid; it has no room for anything but courage and love. Sometimes it is in the course of inner deliberations that a man finds his soul: he meets it, like Hector before Troy, as he tries to face destiny on his own terms, without the help of gods or men. At other times, it is in a moment of love that men discover their souls—and there is hardly any form of pure love known to humanity of which the *Iliad* does not treat. The tradition of hospitality persists, even through several generations, to dispel the blindness of combat.

> Thus I am for you a beloved guest in the breast of Argos...
> Let us turn our lances away from each other, even in battle.

The love of the son for the parents, of father for son, of mother for son, is continually described, in a manner as touching as it is curt:

> Thetis answered, shedding tears,
> "You were born to me for a short life, my child, as you say . . . "

Even brotherly love:

> My three brothers whom the same mother bore for me,
> So dear. . . .

Conjugal love, condemned to sorrow, is of an astonishing purity. Imaging the humiliations of slavery which await a beloved wife, the husband passes over the one indignity which even in anticipation would stain their tenderness. What could be simpler than the words spoken by his wife to the man about to die?

> . . . Better for me
> Losing you, to go under the earth. No other comfort
> Will remain, when you have encountered your death-heavy fate,
> Only grief, only sorrow . . . .

Not less touching are the words expressed to a dead husband:

> Dear husband, you died young, and left me your widow
> Alone in the palace. Our child is still tiny,
> The child you and I, crossed by fate, had together.
> I think he will never grow up . . .
> For not in your bed did you die, holding my hand
> And speaking to me prudent words which forever
> Night and day, as I weep, might live in my memory.

The most beautiful friendship of all, the friendship between comrades-at-arms, is the final theme of The Epic:

> . . . But Achilles
> Wept, dreaming of the beloved comrade; sleep, all-prevailing,
> Would not take him; he turned over again and again.

But the purest triumph of love, the crowning grace of war, is the friendship that floods the hearts of mortal enemies. Before it a murdered son or a murdered friend no longer cries out for vengeance. Before it—even more miraculous—the distance between benefactor and suppliant, between victor and vanquished, shrinks to nothing:

> But when thirst and hunger had been appeased,
> Then Dardanian Priam fell to admiring Achilles.
> How tall he was, and handsome; he had the face of a god;
> And in his turn Dardanian Priam was admired by Achilles,
> Who watched his handsome face and listened to his words.
> And when they were satisfied with contemplation of each other ...

These moments of grace are rare in the *Iliad*, but they are enough to make us feel with sharp regret what it is that violence has killed and will kill again.

However, such a heaping-up of violent deeds would have a frigid effect, were it not for the note of incurable bitterness that continually makes itself heard, though often only a single word marks its presence, often a mere stroke of the verse, or a run-on line. It is in this that the *Iliad* is absolutely unique, in this bitterness that proceeds from tenderness and that spreads over the whole human race, impartial as sunlight. Never does the tone lose its coloring of bitterness; yet never does the bitterness drop into lamentation. Justice and love, which have hardly any place in this study of extremes and of unjust acts of violence, nevertheless bathe the work in their light without ever becoming noticeable themselves, except as a kind of accent. Nothing precious is scorned, whether or not death is its destiny; everyone's unhappiness is laid bare without dissimulation or disdain; no man is set above or below the condition common to all men; whatever is destroyed is regretted. Victors and vanquished are brought equally near us; under the same head, both are seen as counterparts of the poet, and the listener as well. If there is any difference, it is that the enemy's misfortunes are possibly more sharply felt.

> So he fell there, put to sleep in the sleep of bronze,
> Unhappy man, far from his wife, defending his own people . ...

And what accents echo the fate of the lad Achilles sold at Lemnos!

> Eleven days he rejoiced his heart among those he loved,
> Returning from Lemnos; the twelfth day, once more,
> God delivered him into the hands of Achilles,
> To him who had to send him, unwilling, to Hades.

And the fate of Euphorbus, who saw only a single day of war,

> Blood soaked his hair, the hair like to the Graces' ...

When Hector is lamented:

> . . . guardian of chaste wives and little children . . . .

In these few words, chastity appears, dirtied by force, and childhood, delivered to the sword. The fountain at the gates of Troy becomes an object of poignant nostalgia when Hector runs by, seeking to elude his doom:

> Close by there stood the great stone tanks,
> Handsomely built, where silk-greaming garments
> Were washed clean by Troy's lovely daughters and housewives

In the old days of peace, long ago, when the Greeks had not come.
Past these did they run their race, pursued and pursuer.

The whole of the *Iliad* lies under the shadow of the greatest calamity the human race can experience—the destruction of a city. This calamity could not tear more at the heart had the poet been born in Troy. But the tone is not different when the Achaeans are dying, far from home.

Insofar as this other life, the life of the living, seems calm and full, the brief evocations of the world of peace are felt as pain:

> With the break of dawn and the rising of the day,
> On both sides arrows flew, men fell.
> But at the very hour that the woodcutter goes home to fix his meal
> In the mountain valleys when his arms have had enough
> Of hacking great trees, and disgust rises in his heart,
> And the desire for sweet food seizes his entrails,
> At that hour, by their valor, the Danaans broke the front.

Whatever is not war, whatever war destroys or threatens, the *Iliad* wraps in poetry; the realities of war, never. No reticence veils the step from life to death:

> Then his teeth flew out; from two sides,
> Blood came to his eyes; the blood that from lips and nostril
> He was spilling, open-mouthed; death enveloped him in its black
>   cloud.

The cold brutality of the deeds of war is left undisguised; neither victors nor vanquished are admired, scorned, or hated. Almost always, fate and the gods decide the changing lot of battle. Within the limits fixed by fate, the gods determine with sovereign authority victory and defeat. It is always they who provoke those fits of madness, those treacheries, which are forever blocking peace; war is their true business; their only motives, caprice and malice. As for the warriors, victors or vanquished, those comparisons which liken them to beasts or things can inspire neither admiration nor contempt, but only regret that men are capable of being so transformed.

There may be, unknown to us, other expressions of the extraordinary sense of equity which breathes through the *Iliad*; certainly it has not been imitated. One is barely aware that the poet is a Greek and not a Trojan. The tone of the poem furnishes a direct clue to the origin of its oldest portions; history perhaps will never be able to tell us more. If one believes with Thucydides that eighty years after the fall of Troy, the Achaeans in their turn were conquered, one may ask whether these songs, with their rare references to iron, are not the songs of a conquered people, of whom a few went into exile. Obliged to live and die, "very far from the homeland," like the Greeks who fell before Troy, having lost their cities like the Trojans, they saw their own image both in the conquerors, who had been their fathers, and in the conquered, whose misery was like their own. They could still see the Trojan war over that brief span of years in its true light, unglossed by pride or shame. They could look at it as conquered and as conquerors simultaneously, and so perceive what neither conqueror nor conquered ever saw, for both were blinded. Of course, this is mere fancy; one can see such distant times only in fancy's light.

In any case, this poem is a miracle. Its bitterness is the only justifiable bitterness, for it springs from the subjections of the human spirit to force, that is, in the last analysis, to matter. This subjection is the common lot, although each spirit will bear it differently, in proportion to its own virtue. No one in the *Iliad* is spared by it, as no one on earth is. No one who succumbs to it is by virtue of this fact regarded with contempt. Whoever, within his own soul and in human relations, escapes the dominion of force is loved but loved sorrowfully because of the threat of destruction that constantly hangs over him.

Such is the spirit of the only true epic the Occident possesses. The *Odyssey* seems merely a good imitation, now of the *Iliad*, now of Oriental poems; the Aeneid is an imitation which, however brilliant, is disfigured by frigidity, bombast, and bad taste. The *chansons de geste*, lacking the sense of equity, could not attain greatness: in the *Chanson de Roland*, the death of an enemy does not come home to either author or reader in the same way as does the death of Roland.

Attic tragedy, or at any rate the tragedy of Aeschylus and Sophocles, is the true continuation of the epic. The conception of justice enlightens it, without ever directly intervening in it; here force appears in its coldness and hardness, always attended by effects from whose fatality neither those who use it nor those who suffer it can escape; here the shame of the coerced spirit is neither disguised, nor enveloped in facile pity, nor held up to scorn; here more than one spirit bruised and degraded by misfortune is offered for our admiration. The Gospels are the last marvelous expression of the Greek genius, as the *Iliad* is the first: here the Greek spirit reveals itself not only in the injunction given mankind to seek above all other goods, "the kingdom and justice of our Heavenly Father," but also in the fact that human suffering is laid bare, and we see it in a being who is at once divine and human. The accounts of the Passion show that a divine spirit, incarnate, is changed by misfortune, trembles before suffering and death, feels itself, in the depths of its agony, to be cut off from man and God. The sense of human misery gives the Gospels that accent of simplicity that is the mark of the Greek genius, and that endows Greek tragedy and the *Iliad* with all their value. Certain phrases have a ring strangely reminiscent of the epic, and it is the Trojan lad dispatched to Hades, though he does not wish to go, who comes to mind when Christ says to Peter: "Another shall gird thee and carry thee whither thou wouldst not." This accent cannot be separated from the idea that inspired the Gospels, for the sense of human misery is a pre-condition of justice and love. He who does not realize to what extent shifting fortune and necessity hold in subjection every human spirit, cannot regard as fellow-creatures nor love as he loves himself those whom chance separated from him by an abyss. The variety of constraints pressing upon man give rise to the illusion of several distinct species that cannot communicate. Only he who has measured the dominion of force, and knows how not to respect it, is capable of love and justice.

The relations between destiny and the human soul, the extent to which each soul creates its own destiny, the question of what elements in the soul are transformed by merciless necessity as it tailors the soul to fit the requirements of shifting fate, and of what elements can on the other hand be preserved, through the exercise of virtue and through grace—this whole question is fraught with temptations to falsehood, temptations that are positively enhanced by pride, by shame, by hatred, contempt, indifference, by the will to oblivion or to ignorance. Moreover, nothing is so rare as to see misfortune fairly portrayed; the tendency is either to treat the unfortunate person as though catastrophe were his natural vocation, or to ignore the effects of misfortune on the soul, to assume, that is, that the soul can suffer and remain unmarked by it, can fail, in fact, to be recast in misfortune's image. The Greeks, generally speaking, were endowed with spiritual force that allowed them to avoid self-deception. The rewards of this were great; they discovered how to achieve in all their acts the greatest lucidity, purity, and simplicity. But the spirit that was transmitted from the *Iliad* to the Gospels by way of the tragic poets never jumped the borders of Greek civilization; once Greece was destroyed, nothing remained of this spirit but pale reflections.

Both the Romans and the Hebrews believed themselves to be exempt from the misery that is the common human lot. The Romans saw their country as the nation chosen by destiny to be mistress of the world; with the Hebrews, it was their God who exalted them and they retained their superior position just as long as they obeyed Him. Strangers, enemies, conquered peoples, subjects, slaves, were objects of contempt to the Romans; and the Romans had no epics, no tragedies. In Rome gladiatorial fights took the place of tragedy. With the Hebrews, misfortune was a sure indication of sin and hence a legitimate object of contempt; to them a vanquished enemy was abhorrent to God himself and condemned to expiate all sorts of crimes—this is a view that makes cruelty permissible and indeed indispensable. And no text of the Old Testament strikes a note comparable to the note heard in the Greek epic, unless it be certain parts of the book of Job. Throughout twenty centuries of Christianity, the Romans and the Hebrews have been admired, read, imitated, both in deed and word; their masterpieces have yielded an appropriate quotation every time anybody had a crime he wanted to justify.

Furthermore, the spirit of the Gospels was not handed down in a pure state from one Christian generation to the next. To undergo suffering and death joyfully was from the very beginning considered a sign of grace in the Christian martyrs—as though grace could do more for a human being than it could for Christ. Those who believe that God himself, once he became man, could not face the harshness of destiny without a long tremor of anguish, should have understood that the only people who can give the impression of having risen to a higher plane, who seem superior to ordinary human misery, are the people who resort to the aids of illusion, exaltation, fanaticism, to conceal the harshness of destiny from their own eyes. The man who does not wear the armor of the lie cannot experience force without being touched by it to the very soul. Grace can prevent this touch from corrupting him, but it cannot spare him the wound. Having forgotten it too well, Christian tradition can only rarely recover that simplicity that renders so poignant every sentence in the story of the Passion. On the other hand, the practice of forcible proselytization threw a veil over the effects of force on the souls of those who used it.

In spite of the brief intoxication induced at the time of the Renaissance by the discovery of Greek literature, there has been, during the course of twenty centuries, no revival of the Greek genius. Something of it was seen in Villon, in Shakespeare, Cervantes, Moliere, and—just once—in Racine. The bones of human suffering are exposed in *L'Ecole des Femmes* and in *Phèdre*, love being the context—a strange century indeed, which took the opposite view from that of the epic period, and would only acknowledge human suffering in the context of love, while it insisted on swathing with glory the effects of force in war and in politics. To the list of writers given above, a few other names might be added. But nothing the peoples of Europe have produced is worth the first known poem that appeared among them. Perhaps they will yet rediscover the epic genius, when they learn that there is no refuge from fate, learn not to admire force, not to hate the enemy, nor to scorn the unfortunate. How soon this will happen is another question.

Address to Congress Requesting a Declaration of War Against Japan

and

Second Bill of Rights

Franklin Delano Roosevelt

Franklin Delano Roosevelt (1882–1945), 32nd President of the United States, led the nation through the years of the Great Depression and World War II with optimism and determination despite his partial paralysis in the aftermath of a bout with polio. He died in office during his fourth term as president, the only president in American history to have served for more than eight years. He was the father of the New Deal, a vast increase in the reach and power of the federal government, which intended to provide relief and recovery for the country's economy and set the agenda for Democratic party liberalism to the present day, for better and for worse.

On the morning of December 7, 1941, Japan sent 353 fighter planes, bombers, and torpedo planes to attack the United States naval base at Pearl Harbor in Hawaii. The strike was intended to prevent the United States from interfering with Japan's plans in Southeast Asia. Prior to the attack the United States had been formally neutral in World War II, though it had been supplying war materials and troop replacements to Britain and other anti-Axis powers. With the attack on Pearl Harbor and Roosevelt's immediate and strong response, American resistance to intervention in the war dissolved, and the United States entered World War II in both the Pacific and European theaters.

In January of 1944, in his State of the Union Address, Roosevelt proposed a list of rights, sometimes called the Second Bill of Rights, sometimes called the Economic Bill of Rights, that he saw as being necessary to ensuring "equality in the pursuit of happiness." Three years later many of the same rights were written into the United Nations' Universal Declaration of Human Rights.

Address to Congress Requesting a Declaration of War Against Japan

Delivered December 8, 1941

Mr. Vice President, Mr. Speaker, Members of the Senate, and of the House of Representatives:

Yesterday, December 7th, 1941—a date which will live in infamy—the United States of America was suddenly and deliberately attacked by naval and air forces of the Empire of Japan.

The United States was at peace with that nation and, at the solicitation of Japan, was still in conversation with its government and its emperor looking toward the maintenance of peace in the Pacific.

Indeed, one hour after Japanese air squadrons had commenced bombing in the American island of Oahu, the Japanese ambassador to the United States and his colleague delivered to our Secretary of State a formal reply to a recent American message. And while this reply stated that it seemed useless to continue the existing diplomatic negotiations, it contained no threat or hint of war or of armed attack. It will be recorded that the distance of Hawaii from Japan makes it obvious that the attack was deliberately planned many days or even weeks ago. During the intervening time, the Japanese government has deliberately sought to deceive the United States by false statements and expressions of hope for continued peace.

The attack yesterday on the Hawaiian islands has caused severe damage to American naval and military forces. I regret to tell you that very many American lives have been lost. In addition, American ships have been reported torpedoed on the high seas between San Francisco and Honolulu.

Yesterday, the Japanese government also launched an attack against Malaya.

Last night, Japanese forces attacked Hong Kong.

Last night, Japanese forces attacked Guam.

Last night, Japanese forces attacked the Philippine Islands.

Last night, the Japanese attacked Wake Island.

And this morning, the Japanese attacked Midway Island.

Japan has, therefore, undertaken a surprise offensive extending throughout the Pacific area. The facts of yesterday and today speak for themselves. The people of the United States have already formed their opinions and well understand the implications to the very life and safety of our nation.

As commander in chief of the Army and Navy, I have directed that all measures be taken for our defense. But always will our whole nation remember the character of the onslaught against us. No matter how long it may take us to overcome this premeditated invasion, the American people in their righteous might will win through to absolute victory. I believe that I interpret the will of the Congress and of the people when I assert that we will not only defend ourselves to the uttermost, but will make it very certain that this form of treachery shall never again endanger us. Hostilities exist. There is no blinking at the fact that our people, our territory, and our interests are in grave danger.

With confidence in our armed forces, with the unbounding determination of our people, we will gain the inevitable triumph —so help us God.

I ask that the Congress declare that since the unprovoked and dastardly attack by Japan on Sunday, December 7th, 1941, a state of war has existed between the United States and the Japanese empire.

Second Bill of Rights (from 1944 State of the Union Address)

Delivered on January 11, 1944

It is our duty now to begin to lay the plans and determine the strategy for the winning of a lasting peace and the establishment of an American standard of living higher than ever before known. We cannot be content, no matter how high that general standard of living may be, if some fraction of our people—whether it be one-third or one-fifth or one-tenth—is ill-fed, ill-clothed, ill-housed, and insecure.

This Republic had its beginning, and grew to its present strength, under the protection of certain inalienable political rights—among them the right of free speech, free press, free worship, trial by jury, freedom from unreasonable searches and seizures. They were our rights to life and liberty.

As our nation has grown in size and stature, however—as our industrial economy expanded—these political rights proved inadequate to assure us equality in the pursuit of happiness.

We have come to a clear realization of the fact that true individual freedom cannot exist without economic security and independence. "Necessitous men are not free men." People who are hungry and out of a job are the stuff of which dictatorships are made.

In our day these economic truths have become accepted as self-evident. We have accepted, so to speak, a second Bill of Rights under which a new basis of security and prosperity can be established for all—regardless of station, race, or creed.

Among these are:

The right to a useful and remunerative job in the industries or shops or farms or mines of the nation;

The right to earn enough to provide adequate food and clothing and recreation;

The right of every farmer to raise and sell his products at a return which will give him and his family a decent living;

The right of every businessman, large and small, to trade in an atmosphere of freedom from unfair competition and domination by monopolies at home or abroad;

The right of every family to a decent home;

The right to adequate medical care and the opportunity to achieve and enjoy good health;

The right to adequate protection from the economic fears of old age, sickness, accident, and unemployment;

The right to a good education.

All of these rights spell security. And after this war is won we must be prepared to move forward, in the implementation of these rights, to new goals of human happiness and well-being.

America's own rightful place in the world depends in large part upon how fully these and similar rights have been carried into practice for all our citizens. For unless there is security here at home there cannot be lasting peace in the world.

Universal Declaration of Human Rights

United Nations Commission on Human Rights

In response to the atrocities of World War II the United Nations founded a Commission on Human Rights in 1946. It met for the first time in January of 1947 and was commissioned to draft a declaration on human rights. That declaration was voted on by the United Nations General Assembly in December of 1948.

Forty-eight countries voted in favor: Afghanistan, Argentina, Australia, Belgium, Bolivia, Brazil, Canada, Chile, China, Colombia, Costa Rica, Cuba, Denmark, Dominican Republic, Ecuador, Egypt, El Salvador, Ethiopia, France, Greece, Guatemala, Haiti, Honduras, Iceland, India, Iran, Iraq, Lebanon, Liberia, Luxembourg, Mexico, Netherlands, New Zealand, Nicaragua, Norway, Pakistan, Panama, Paraguay, Peru, Philippine Republic, Siam, Sweden,Syria, Turkey, United Kingdom, United States, Uruguay, and Venezuela.

No countries voted against it.

Eight countries abstained: Byelorussian Soviet Socialist Republic, Czechoslovakia, People's Republic of Poland, Kingdom of Saudi Arabia, Soviet Union, Union of South Africa, Ukrainian Soviet Socialist Republic, and People's Federal Republic of Yugoslavia.

The declaration is described by the Guinness Book of Records as the most translated document in the world.

Above: Emblem of the United Nations, adopted on December 7, 1946.

Rhetoric

Adopted on December 10, 1948.

PREAMBLE

Whereas recognition of the inherent dignity and of the equal and inalienable rights of all members of the human family is the foundation of freedom, justice and peace in the world,

Whereas disregard and contempt for human rights have resulted in barbarous acts which have outraged the conscience of mankind, and the advent of a world in which human beings shall enjoy freedom of speech and belief and freedom from fear and want has been proclaimed as the highest aspiration of the common people,

Whereas it is essential, if man is not to be compelled to have recourse, as a last resort, to rebellion against tyranny and oppression, that human rights should be protected by the rule of law,

Whereas it is essential to promote the development of friendly relations between nations,

Whereas the peoples of the United Nations have in the Charter reaffirmed their faith in fundamental human rights, in the dignity and worth of the human person and in the equal rights of men and women and have determined to promote social progress and better standards of life in larger freedom,

Whereas Member States have pledged themselves to achieve, in co-operation with the United Nations, the promotion of universal respect for and observance of human rights and fundamental freedoms,

Whereas a common understanding of these rights and freedoms is of the greatest importance for the full realization of this pledge,

Now, Therefore THE GENERAL ASSEMBLY proclaims THIS UNIVERSAL DECLARATION OF HUMAN RIGHTS as a common standard of achievement for all peoples and all nations, to the end that every individual and every organ of society, keeping this Declaration constantly in mind, shall strive by teaching and education to promote respect for these rights and freedoms and by progressive measures, national and international, to secure their universal and effective recognition and observance, both among the peoples of Member States themselves and among the peoples of territories under their jurisdiction.

Article 1

All human beings are born free and equal in dignity and rights. They are endowed with reason and conscience and should act towards one another in a spirit of brotherhood.

Article 2

Everyone is entitled to all the rights and freedoms set forth in this Declaration, without distinction of any kind, such as race, colour, sex, language, religion, political or other opinion, national or social origin, property, birth or other status. Furthermore, no distinction shall be made on the basis of the political, jurisdictional or international status of the country or territory to which a person belongs, whether it be independent, trust, non-self-governing or under any other limitation of sovereignty.

Article 3

Everyone has the right to life, liberty and security of person.

Article 4

No one shall be held in slavery or servitude; slavery and the slave trade shall be prohibited in all their forms.

Article 5

No one shall be subjected to torture or to cruel, inhuman or degrading treatment or punishment.

Article 6

Everyone has the right to recognition everywhere as a person before the law.

Article 7

All are equal before the law and are entitled without any discrimination to equal protection of the law. All are entitled to equal protection against any discrimination in violation of this Declaration and against any incitement to such discrimination.

Article 8

Everyone has the right to an effective remedy by the competent national tribunals for acts violating the fundamental rights granted him by the constitution or by law.

Article 9

No one shall be subjected to arbitrary arrest, detention or exile.

Article 10

Everyone is entitled in full equality to a fair and public hearing by an independent and impartial tribunal, in the determination of his rights and obligations and of any criminal charge against him.

Article 11

(1) Everyone charged with a penal offence has the right to be presumed innocent until proved guilty according to law in a public trial at which he has had all the guarantees necessary for his defence.

(2) No one shall be held guilty of any penal offence on account of any act or omission which did not constitute a penal offence, under national or international law, at the time when it was committed. Nor shall a heavier penalty be imposed than the one that was applicable at the time the penal offence was committed.

Article 12

No one shall be subjected to arbitrary interference with his privacy, family, home or correspondence, nor to attacks upon his honour and reputation. Everyone has the right to the protection of the law against such interference or attacks.

Article 13

(1) Everyone has the right to freedom of movement and residence within the borders of each state.

(2) Everyone has the right to leave any country, including his own, and to return to his country.

Article 14

(1) Everyone has the right to seek and to enjoy in other countries asylum from persecution.

(2) This right may not be invoked in the case of prosecutions genuinely arising from non-political crimes or from acts contrary to the purposes and principles of the United Nations.

Article 15

(1) Everyone has the right to a nationality.

(2) No one shall be arbitrarily deprived of his nationality nor denied the right to change his nationality.

Article 16

(1) Men and women of full age, without any limitation due to race, nationality or religion, have the right to marry and to found a family. They are entitled to equal rights as to marriage, during marriage and at its dissolution.

(2) Marriage shall be entered into only with the free and full consent of the intending spouses.

(3) The family is the natural and fundamental group unit of society and is entitled to protection by society and the State.

Article 17

(1) Everyone has the right to own property alone as well as in association with others.

(2) No one shall be arbitrarily deprived of his property.

Article 18

Everyone has the right to freedom of thought, conscience and religion; this right includes freedom to change his religion or belief, and freedom, either alone or in community with others and in public or private, to manifest his religion or belief in teaching, practice, worship and observance.

Article 19

Everyone has the right to freedom of opinion and expression; this right includes freedom to hold opinions without interference and to seek, receive and impart information and ideas through any media and regardless of frontiers.

Article 20

(1) Everyone has the right to freedom of peaceful assembly and association.

(2) No one may be compelled to belong to an association.

Article 21

(1) Everyone has the right to take part in the government of his country, directly or through freely chosen representatives.

(2) Everyone has the right of equal access to public service in his country.

(3) The will of the people shall be the basis of the authority of government; this will shall be expressed in periodic and genuine elections which shall be by universal and equal suffrage and shall be held by secret vote or by equivalent free voting procedures.

Article 22

Everyone, as a member of society, has the right to social security and is entitled to realization, through national effort and international co-operation and in accordance with the organization and resources of each State, of the economic, social and cultural rights indispensable for his dignity and the free development of his personality.

Article 23

(1) Everyone has the right to work, to free choice of employment, to just and favourable conditions of work and to protection against unemployment.

(2) Everyone, without any discrimination, has the right to equal pay for equal work.

(3) Everyone who works has the right to just and favourable remuneration ensuring for himself and his family an existence worthy of human dignity, and supplemented, if necessary, by other means of social protection.

(4) Everyone has the right to form and to join trade unions for the protection of his interests.

Article 24

Everyone has the right to rest and leisure, including reasonable limitation of working hours and periodic holidays with pay.

Article 25

(1) Everyone has the right to a standard of living adequate for the health and well-being of himself and of his family, including food, clothing, housing and medical care and necessary social services, and the right to security in the event of unemployment, sickness, disability, widowhood, old age or other lack of livelihood in circumstances beyond his control.

(2) Motherhood and childhood are entitled to special care and assistance. All children, whether born in or out of wedlock, shall enjoy the same social protection.

Article 26

(1) Everyone has the right to education. Education shall be free, at least in the elementary and fundamental stages. Elementary education shall be compulsory. Technical and professional education shall be made generally available and higher education shall be equally accessible to all on the basis of merit.

(2) Education shall be directed to the full development of the human personality and to the strengthening of respect for human rights and fundamental freedoms. It shall promote understanding, tolerance and friendship among all nations, racial or religious groups, and shall further the activities of the United Nations for the maintenance of peace.

(3) Parents have a prior right to choose the kind of education that shall be given to their children.

Article 27

(1) Everyone has the right freely to participate in the cultural life of the community, to enjoy the arts and to share in scientific advancement and its benefits.

(2) Everyone has the right to the protection of the moral and material interests resulting from any scientific, literary or artistic production of which he is the author.

Article 28

Everyone is entitled to a social and international order in which the rights and freedoms set forth in this Declaration can be fully realized.

Article 29

(1) Everyone has duties to the community in which alone the free and full development of his personality is possible.

(2) In the exercise of his rights and freedoms, everyone shall be subject only to such limitations as are determined by law solely for the purpose of securing due recognition and respect for the rights and freedoms of others and of meeting the just requirements of morality, public order and the general welfare in a democratic society.

(3) These rights and freedoms may in no case be exercised contrary to the purposes and principles of the United Nations.

Article 30

Nothing in this Declaration may be interpreted as implying for any State, group or person any right to engage in any activity or to perform any act aimed at the destruction of any of the rights and freedoms set forth herein.

Inaugural Address
John Fitzgerald Kennedy

John Fitzgerald Kennedy (1917–1963) was inaugurated as the 35th President of the United States on January 20, 1961. He came into office when the Cold War was at its peak. Having won in a very close election, he sought to unite the nation in its resolve to resist the advances of the Soviet Union and the Communist Bloc. More generally, he promised that the United States would not falter in promoting liberty throughout the world.

This speech is a rhetorical masterpiece of a modern inaugural address

He employs anaphora throughout the speech. Early on, to impart what his pledges would be to each of several important groups, he uses anaphora: "To those old allies . . . to those new states . . . to those people in the huts and villages . . . to our sister republics . . . to that world assembly of sovereign states, the United Nations, . . . to those nations who would make themselves our adversary. . . ."

Chiasmus is used as he describes the new beginning he aimed for with those nations he mentioned in the last group: "Let us never negotiate out of fear, but let us never fear to negotiate." He continued with anaphora once again, starting each main idea with "let both sides," to emphasize the mutual responsibility of America and the Soviet Union in advancing the "freedom of man."

The most famous line is another textbook example of anaphora plus chiasmus: "Ask not what your country can do for you; ask what you can do for your country." He continued with the same structure to address the international world: "My fellow citizens of the world, ask not what America will do for you, but what together we can do for the freedom of man."

With these and other rhetorical devices Kennedy succeeded in using rhetoric as a means of persuasion: after he delivered this speech, Kennedy had a nearly seventy-five percent approval rating in America.

Delivered January 20, 1961, at the United States Capitol, Washington, DC.

Vice President Johnson, Mr. Speaker, Mr. Chief Justice, President Eisenhower, Vice President Nixon, President Truman, reverend clergy, fellow citizens:

We observe today not a victory of party, but a celebration of freedom—symbolizing an end, as well as a beginning—signifying renewal, as well as change. For I have sworn before you and Almighty God the same solemn oath our forebears prescribed nearly a century and three-quarters ago.

The world is very different now. For man holds in his mortal hands the power to abolish all forms of human poverty and all forms of human life. And yet the same revolutionary beliefs for which our forebears fought are still at issue around the globe— the belief that the rights of man come not from the generosity of the state, but from the hand of God.

We dare not forget today that we are the heirs of that first revolution. Let the word go forth from this time and place, to friend and foe alike, that the torch has been passed to a new generation of Americans—born in this century, tempered by war, disciplined by a hard and bitter peace, proud of our ancient heritage, and unwilling to witness or permit the slow undoing of those human rights to which this nation has always been committed, and to which we are committed today at home and around the world.

Let every nation know, whether it wishes us well or ill, that we shall pay any price, bear any burden, meet any hardship, support any friend, oppose any foe, to assure the survival and the success of liberty.

This much we pledge—and more.

To those old allies whose cultural and spiritual origins we share, we pledge the loyalty of faithful friends. United there is little we cannot do in a host of cooperative ventures. Divided there is little we can do—for we dare not meet a powerful challenge at odds and split asunder.

To those new states whom we welcome to the ranks of the free, we pledge our word that one form of colonial control shall not have passed away merely to be replaced by a far more iron tyranny. We shall not always expect to find them supporting our view. But we shall always hope to find them strongly supporting their own freedom—and to remember that, in the past, those who foolishly sought power by riding the back of the tiger ended up inside.

To those people in the huts and villages of half the globe struggling to break the bonds of mass misery, we pledge our best efforts to help them help themselves, for whatever period is required—not because the Communists may be doing it, not because we seek their votes, but because it is right. If a free society cannot help the many who are poor, it cannot save the few who are rich.

To our sister republics south of our border, we offer a special pledge: to convert our good words into good deeds, in a new alliance for progress, to assist free men and free governments in casting off the chains of poverty. But this peaceful revolution of hope cannot become the prey of hostile powers. Let all our neighbors know that we shall join with them to oppose aggression or subversion anywhere in the Americas. And let every other power know that this hemisphere intends to remain the master of its own house.

To that world assembly of sovereign states, the United Nations, our last best hope in an age where the instruments of war have far outpaced the instruments of peace, we renew our pledge of support—to prevent it from becoming merely a forum for invective, to strengthen its shield of the new and the weak, and to enlarge the area in which its writ may run.

Finally, to those nations who would make themselves our adversary, we offer not a pledge but a request: that both sides begin anew the quest for peace, before the dark powers of destruction unleashed by science engulf all humanity in planned or accidental self-destruction.

We dare not tempt them with weakness. For only when our arms are sufficient beyond doubt can we be certain beyond doubt that they will never be employed.

But neither can two great and powerful groups of nations take comfort from our present course—both sides overburdened by the cost of modern weapons, both rightly alarmed by the steady spread of the deadly atom, yet both racing to alter that uncertain balance of terror that stays the hand of mankind's final war.

So let us begin anew—remembering on both sides that civility is not a sign of weakness, and sincerity is always subject to proof. Let us never negotiate out of fear, but let us never fear to negotiate.

Let both sides explore what problems unite us instead of belaboring those problems which divide us.

Let both sides, for the first time, formulate serious and precise proposals for the inspection and control of arms, and bring the absolute power to destroy other nations under the absolute control of all nations.

Let both sides seek to invoke the wonders of science instead of its terrors. Together let us explore the stars, conquer the deserts, eradicate disease, tap the ocean depths, and encourage the arts and commerce.

Let both sides unite to heed, in all corners of the earth, the command of Isaiah—to "undo the heavy burdens, and let the oppressed go free."[1]

And, if a beachhead of cooperation may push back the jungle of suspicion, let both sides join in creating a new endeavor—not a new balance of power, but a new world of law—where the strong are just, and the weak secure, and the peace preserved.

All this will not be finished in the first one hundred days. Nor will it be finished in the first one thousand days; nor in the life of this Administration; nor even perhaps in our lifetime on this planet. But let us begin.

In your hands, my fellow citizens, more than mine, will rest the final success or failure of our course. Since this country was founded, each generation of Americans has been summoned to give testimony to its national loyalty. The graves of young Americans who answered the call to service surround the globe.

---

[1] Isaiah 58:6

Now the trumpet summons us again—not as a call to bear arms, though arms we need—not as a call to battle, though embattled we are—but a call to bear the burden of a long twilight struggle, year in and year out, "rejoicing in hope; patient in tribulation,"[2] a struggle against the common enemies of man: tyranny, poverty, disease, and war itself.

Can we forge against these enemies a grand and global alliance, North and South, East and West, that can assure a more fruitful life for all mankind? Will you join in that historic effort?

In the long history of the world, only a few generations have been granted the role of defending freedom in its hour of maximum danger. I do not shrink from this responsibility—I welcome it. I do not believe that any of us would exchange places with any other people or any other generation. The energy, the faith, the devotion which we bring to this endeavor will light our country and all who serve it. And the glow from that fire can truly light the world.

And so, my fellow Americans, ask not what your country can do for you; ask what you can do for your country.

My fellow citizens of the world, ask not what America will do for you, but what together we can do for the freedom of man.

Finally, whether you are citizens of America or citizens of the world, ask of us here the same high standards of strength and sacrifice which we ask of you. With a good conscience our only sure reward, with history the final judge of our deeds, let us go forth to lead the land we love, asking His blessing and His help, but knowing that here on earth God's work must truly be our own.

---

[2] Romans 12:12

Letter from
Birmingham Jail
and
I Have a Dream
Martin Luther King Jr.

Dr. Martin Luther King Jr. (1929–1968) is one of America's most influential civil-rights activists. On April 3, 1963, his Southern Christian Leadership Conference, together with the Alabama Christian Movement for Human Rights, began the "Birmingham Campaign." This non-violent, direct action protest was intended to highlight racial segregation policies in Birmingham, Alabama. One week later, in response to the protests, Eugene "Bull" Connor, Commissioner of Public Safety in Birmingham, obtained an injunction that outlawed "parading, demonstrating, boycotting, and picketing." Two days later, King and many other participants in the protests were arrested. During his incarceration King wrote the letter reproduced here. Just over four months later, he would deliver his famous "I Have a Dream" speech to several hundred-thousand people who had gathered for the March on Washington for Jobs and Freedom. That march was a demonstration of support for what would become the Civil Rights Act of 1964, introduced by President Kennedy in June, 1963.

Letter from Birmingham Jail

Written April 16, 1963

My Dear Fellow Clergymen:

While confined here in the Birmingham city jail, I came across your recent statement calling my present activities "unwise and untimely." Seldom do I pause to answer criticism of my work and ideas. If I sought to answer all the criticisms that cross my desk, my secretaries would have little time for anything other than such correspondence in the course of the day, and I would have no time for constructive work. But since I feel that you are men of genuine good will and that your criticisms are sincerely set forth, I want to try to answer your statement in what I hope will be patient and reasonable terms.

I think I should indicate why I am here in Birmingham, since you have been influenced by the view which argues against "outsiders coming in." I have the honor of serving as president of the Southern Christian Leadership Conference, an organization operating in every southern state, with headquarters in Atlanta, Georgia. We have some eighty-five affiliated organizations across the South, and one of them is the Alabama Christian Movement for Human Rights. Frequently we share staff, educational and financial resources with our affiliates. Several months ago the affiliate here in Birmingham asked us to be on call to engage in a nonviolent direct action program if such were deemed necessary. We readily consented, and when the hour came we lived up to our promise. So I, along with several members of my staff, am here because I was invited here. I am here because I have organizational ties here.

But more basically, I am in Birmingham because injustice is here. Just as the prophets of the eighth century B.C. left their villages and carried their "thus saith the Lord" far beyond the boundaries of their home towns, and just as the Apostle Paul left his village of Tarsus and carried the gospel of Jesus Christ to the far corners of the Greco Roman world, so am I compelled to carry the gospel of freedom beyond my own home town. Like Paul, I must constantly respond to the Macedonian call for aid.

Moreover, I am cognizant of the interrelatedness of all communities and states. I cannot sit idly by in Atlanta and not be concerned about what happens in Birmingham. Injustice anywhere is a threat to justice everywhere. We are caught in an inescapable network of mutuality, tied in a single garment of destiny. Whatever affects one directly, affects all indirectly. Never again can we afford to live with the narrow, provincial "outside agitator" idea. Anyone who lives inside the United States can never be considered an outsider anywhere within its bounds.

You deplore the demonstrations taking place in Birmingham. But your statement, I am sorry to say, fails to express a similar concern for the conditions that brought about the demonstrations. I am sure that none of you would want to rest content with the superficial kind of social analysis that deals merely with effects and does not grapple with underlying causes. It is unfortunate that demonstrations are taking place in Birmingham, but it is even more unfortunate that the city's white power structure left the Negro community with no alternative.

In any nonviolent campaign there are four basic steps: collection of the facts to determine whether injustices exist; negotiation; self purification; and direct action. We have gone through all these steps in Birmingham. There can be no gainsaying the fact that racial injustice engulfs this community. Birmingham is probably the most thoroughly segregated city in the United States. Its ugly record of brutality is widely known. Negroes have experienced grossly unjust treatment in the courts. There have been more unsolved bombings of Negro homes and churches in Birmingham than in any other city in the nation. These are the hard, brutal facts of the case. On the basis of these conditions, Negro leaders sought to negotiate with the city fathers. But the latter consistently refused to engage in good faith negotiation.

Then, last September, came the opportunity to talk with leaders of Birmingham's economic community. In the course of the negotiations, certain promises were made by the merchants —for example, to remove the stores' humiliating racial signs. On the basis of these promises, the Reverend Fred Shuttlesworth and the leaders of the Alabama Christian Movement for Human Rights agreed to a moratorium on all demonstrations. As the weeks and months went by, we realized that we were the victims of a broken promise. A few signs, briefly removed, returned; the others remained. As in so many past experiences, our hopes had been blasted, and the shadow of deep disappointment settled upon us. We had no alternative except to prepare for direct action, whereby we would present our very bodies as a means of laying our case before the conscience of the local and the national community. Mindful of the difficulties involved, we decided to undertake a process of self purification. We began a series of workshops on nonviolence, and we repeatedly asked ourselves: "Are you able to accept blows without retaliating?" "Are you able to endure the ordeal of jail?" We decided to schedule our direct action program for the Easter season, realizing that except for Christmas, this is the main shopping period of the year. Knowing that a strong economic-withdrawal program would be the by product of direct action, we felt that this would be the best time to bring pressure to bear on the merchants for the needed change.

Then it occurred to us that Birmingham's mayoral election was coming up in March, and we speedily decided to postpone action until after election day. When we discovered that the Commissioner of Public Safety, Eugene "Bull" Connor, had piled up enough votes to be in the run off, we decided again to postpone action until the day after the run off so that the demonstrations could not be used to cloud the issues. Like many others, we waited to see Mr. Connor defeated, and to this end we endured postponement after postponement. Having aided in this community need, we felt that our direct action program could be delayed no longer.

You may well ask: "Why direct action? Why sit ins, marches and so forth? Isn't negotiation a better path?" You are quite right in calling for negotiation. Indeed, this is the very purpose of direct action. Nonviolent direct action seeks to create such a crisis and foster such a tension that a community which has constantly refused to negotiate is forced to confront the issue. It seeks so to dramatize the issue that it can no longer be ignored. My citing the creation of tension as part of the work of the nonviolent resister may sound rather shocking. But I must confess that I am not afraid of the word "tension." I have earnestly opposed violent tension, but there is a type of constructive, nonviolent tension which is necessary for growth. Just as Socrates felt that it was necessary to create a tension in the mind so that individuals could rise from the bondage of myths and half truths to the unfettered realm of creative analysis and objective appraisal, so must we see the need for nonviolent gadflies to create the kind of tension in society that will help men rise from the dark depths of prejudice and racism to the majestic heights of understanding and brotherhood. The purpose of our direct action program is to create a situation so crisis packed that it will inevitably open the door to negotiation. I therefore concur with you in your call for negotiation. Too long has our beloved Southland been bogged down in a tragic effort to live in monologue rather than dialogue.

One of the basic points in your statement is that the action that I and my associates have taken in Birmingham is untimely. Some have asked: "Why didn't you give the new city administration time to act?" The only answer that I can give to this query is that the new Birmingham administration must be prodded about as much as the outgoing one, before it will act. We are sadly mistaken if we feel that the election of Albert Boutwell as mayor will bring the millennium to Birmingham. While Mr. Boutwell is a much more gentle person than Mr. Connor, they are both segregationists, dedicated to maintenance of the status quo. I have hope that Mr. Boutwell will be reasonable enough to see the futility of massive resistance to desegregation. But he will not see this without pressure from devotees of civil rights. My friends, I must say to you that we have not made a single gain in civil rights without determined legal and nonviolent pressure. Lamentably, it is an historical fact that privileged groups seldom give up their privileges voluntarily. Individuals may see the moral light and voluntarily give up their unjust posture; but, as Reinhold Niebuhr has reminded us, groups tend to be more immoral than individuals.

We know through painful experience that freedom is never voluntarily given by the oppressor; it must be demanded by the oppressed. Frankly, I have yet to engage in a direct action campaign that was "well timed" in the view of those who have not suffered unduly from the disease of segregation. For years now I have heard the word "Wait!" It rings in the ear of every Negro with piercing familiarity. This "Wait" has almost always meant "Never." We must come to see, with one of our distinguished jurists, that "justice too long delayed is justice denied."

We have waited for more than 340 years for our constitutional and God given rights. The nations of Asia and Africa are moving with jetlike speed toward gaining political independence, but we still creep at horse and buggy pace toward gaining a cup of coffee at a lunch counter. Perhaps it is easy for those who have never felt the stinging darts of segregation to say, "Wait." But when you have seen vicious mobs lynch your mothers and fathers at will and drown your sisters and brothers at whim; when you have seen hate filled policemen curse, kick and even kill your black brothers and sisters; when you see the vast majority of your twenty million Negro brothers smothering in an airtight cage of poverty in the midst of an affluent society; when you suddenly find your tongue twisted and your speech stammering as you seek to explain to your six year old daughter why she can't go to the public amusement park that has just been advertised on television, and see tears welling up in her eyes when she is told that Funtown is closed to colored children, and see ominous clouds of inferiority beginning to form in her little mental sky, and see her beginning to distort her personality by developing an unconscious bitterness toward white people; when you have to concoct an answer for a five year old son who is asking: "Daddy, why do white people treat colored people so mean?"; when you take a cross county drive and find it necessary to sleep night after night in the uncomfortable corners of your automobile because no motel will accept you; when you are humiliated day in and day out by nagging signs reading "white" and "colored"; when your first name becomes "nigger," your middle name becomes "boy" (however old you are) and your last name becomes "John," and your wife and mother are never given the respected title "Mrs."; when you are harried by day and haunted by night by the fact that you are a Negro, living constantly at tiptoe stance, never quite knowing what to expect next, and are plagued with inner fears and outer resentments; when you are forever fighting a degenerating sense of "nobodiness"—then you will understand why we find it difficult to wait. There comes a time when the cup of endurance runs over, and men are no longer willing to be plunged into the abyss of despair. I hope, sirs, you can understand our legitimate and unavoidable impatience. You express a great deal of anxiety over our willingness to break laws. This is certainly a legitimate concern. Since we so diligently urge people to obey the Supreme Court's decision of 1954 outlawing segregation in the public schools, at first glance it may seem rather paradoxical for us consciously to break laws. One may well ask: "How can you advocate breaking some laws and obeying others?" The answer lies in the fact that there are two types of laws: just and unjust. I would be the first to advocate obeying just laws. One has not only a legal but a moral responsibility to obey just laws. Conversely, one has a moral responsibility to disobey unjust laws. I would agree with St. Augustine that "an unjust law is no law at all."

Now, what is the difference between the two? How does one determine whether a law is just or unjust? A just law is a man-made code that squares with the moral law or the law of God. An unjust law is a code that is out of harmony with the moral law. To put it in the terms of St. Thomas Aquinas: An unjust law is a human law that is not rooted in eternal law and natural law. Any law that uplifts human personality is just. Any law that degrades human personality is unjust. All segregation statutes are unjust because segregation distorts the soul and damages the personality. It gives the segregator a false sense of superiority and the segregated a false sense of inferiority. Segregation, to use the terminology of the Jewish philosopher Martin Buber, substitutes an "I-it" relationship for an "I-thou" relationship and ends up relegating persons to the status of things. Hence segregation is not only politically, economically and sociologically unsound, it is morally wrong and sinful. Paul Tillich has said that sin is separation. Is not segregation an existential expression of man's tragic separation, his awful estrangement, his terrible sinfulness? Thus it is that I can urge men to obey the 1954 decision of the Supreme Court, for it is morally right; and I can urge them to disobey segregation ordinances, for they are morally wrong.

Let us consider a more concrete example of just and unjust laws. An unjust law is a code that a numerical or power majority group compels a minority group to obey but does not make binding on itself. This is difference made legal. By the same token, a just law is a code that a majority compels a minority to follow and that it is willing to follow itself. This is sameness made legal. Let me give another explanation. A law is unjust if it is inflicted on a minority that, as a result of being denied the right to vote, had no part in enacting or devising the law. Who can say that the legislature of Alabama which set up that state's segregation laws was democratically elected? Throughout Alabama all sorts of devious methods are used to prevent Negroes from becoming registered voters, and there are some counties in which, even though Negroes constitute a majority of the population, not a single Negro is registered. Can any law enacted under such circumstances be considered democratically structured?

Sometimes a law is just on its face and unjust in its application. For instance, I have been arrested on a charge of parading without a permit. Now, there is nothing wrong in having an ordinance which requires a permit for a parade. But such an ordinance becomes unjust when it is used to maintain segregation and to deny citizens the First-Amendment privilege of peaceful assembly and protest.

I hope you are able to see the distinction I am trying to point out. In no sense do I advocate evading or defying the law, as would the rabid segregationist. That would lead to anarchy. One who breaks an unjust law must do so openly, lovingly, and with a willingness to accept the penalty. I submit that an individual who breaks a law that conscience tells him is unjust, and who willingly accepts the penalty of imprisonment in order to arouse the conscience of the community over its injustice, is in reality expressing the highest respect for law.

Of course, there is nothing new about this kind of civil disobedience. It was evidenced sublimely in the refusal of Shadrach, Meshach and Abednego to obey the laws of Nebuchadnezzar, on the ground that a higher moral law was at stake. It was practiced superbly by the early Christians, who were willing to face hungry lions and the excruciating pain of chopping blocks rather than submit to certain unjust laws of the Roman Empire. To a degree, academic freedom is a reality today because Socrates practiced civil disobedience. In our own nation, the Boston Tea Party represented a massive act of civil disobedience.

We should never forget that everything Adolf Hitler did in Germany was "legal" and everything the Hungarian freedom fighters did in Hungary was "illegal." It was "illegal" to aid and comfort a Jew in Hitler's Germany. Even so, I am sure that, had I lived in Germany at the time, I would have aided and comforted my Jewish brothers. If today I lived in a Communist country where certain principles dear to the Christian faith are suppressed, I would openly advocate disobeying that country's antireligious laws.

I must make two honest confessions to you, my Christian and Jewish brothers. First, I must confess that over the past few years I have been gravely disappointed with the white moderate. I have almost reached the regrettable conclusion that the Negro's great stumbling block in his stride toward freedom is not the White Citizen's Counciler or the Ku Klux Klanner, but the white moderate, who is more devoted to "order" than to justice; who prefers a negative peace which is the absence of tension to a positive peace which is the presence of justice; who constantly says: "I agree with you in the goal you seek, but I cannot agree with your methods of direct action"; who paternalistically believes he can set the timetable for another man's freedom; who lives by a mythical concept of time and who constantly advises the Negro to wait for a "more convenient season." Shallow understanding from people of good will is more frustrating than absolute misunderstanding from people of ill will. Lukewarm acceptance is much more bewildering than outright rejection.

I had hoped that the white moderate would understand that law and order exist for the purpose of establishing justice and that when they fail in this purpose they become the dangerously structured dams that block the flow of social progress. I had hoped that the white moderate would understand that the present tension in the South is a necessary phase of the transition from an obnoxious negative peace, in which the Negro passively accepted his unjust plight, to a substantive and positive peace, in which all men will respect the dignity and worth of human personality. Actually, we who engage in nonviolent direct action are not the creators of tension. We merely bring to the surface the hidden tension that is already alive. We bring it out in the open, where it can be seen and dealt with. Like a boil that can never be cured so long as it is covered up but must be opened with all its ugliness to the natural medicines of air and light, injustice must be exposed, with all the tension its exposure creates, to the light of human conscience and the air of national opinion before it can be cured.

In your statement you assert that our actions, even though peaceful, must be condemned because they precipitate violence. But is this a logical assertion? Isn't this like condemning a robbed man because his possession of money precipitated the evil act of robbery? Isn't this like condemning Socrates because his unswerving commitment to truth and his philosophical inquiries precipitated the act by the misguided populace in which they made him drink hemlock? Isn't this like condemning Jesus because his unique God consciousness and never ceasing devotion to God's will precipitated the evil act of crucifixion? We must come to see that, as the federal courts have consistently affirmed, it is wrong to urge an individual to cease his efforts to gain his basic constitutional rights because the quest may precipitate violence. Society must protect the robbed and punish the robber. I had also hoped that the white moderate would reject the myth concerning time in relation to the struggle for freedom. I have just received a letter from a white brother in Texas. He writes: "All Christians know that the colored people will receive equal rights eventually, but it is possible that you are in too great a religious hurry. It has taken Christianity almost two thousand years to accomplish what it has. The teachings of Christ take time to come to earth." Such an attitude stems from a tragic misconception of time, from the strangely irrational notion that there is something in the very flow of time that will inevitably cure all ills. Actually, time itself is neutral; it can be used either destructively or constructively. More and more I feel that the people of ill will have used time much more effectively than have the people of good will. We will have to repent in this generation not merely for the hateful words and actions of the bad people but for the appalling silence of the good people. Human progress never rolls in on wheels of inevitability; it comes through the tireless efforts of men willing to be co workers with God, and without this hard work, time itself becomes an ally of the forces of social stagnation. We must use time creatively, in the knowledge that the time is always ripe to do right. Now is the time to make real the promise of democracy and transform our pending national elegy into a creative psalm of brotherhood. Now is the time to lift our national policy from the quicksand of racial injustice to the solid rock of human dignity.

You speak of our activity in Birmingham as extreme. At first I was rather disappointed that fellow clergymen would see my nonviolent efforts as those of an extremist. I began thinking about the fact that I stand in the middle of two opposing forces in the Negro community. One is a force of complacency, made up in part of Negroes who, as a result of long years of oppression, are so drained of self respect and a sense of "somebodiness" that they have adjusted to segregation; and in part of a few middle-class Negroes who, because of a degree of academic and economic security and because in some ways they profit by segregation, have become insensitive to the problems of the masses. The other force is one of bitterness and hatred, and it comes perilously close to advocating violence. It is expressed in the various black nationalist groups that are springing up across the nation, the largest and best known being Elijah Muhammad's Muslim movement. Nourished by the Negro's frustration over the continued existence of racial discrimination, this movement is made up of people who have lost faith in America, who have absolutely repudiated Christianity, and who have concluded that the white man is an incorrigible "devil."

I have tried to stand between these two forces, saying that we need emulate neither the "do nothingism" of the complacent nor the hatred and despair of the black nationalist. For there is the more excellent way of love and nonviolent protest. I am grateful to God that, through the influence of the Negro church, the way of nonviolence became an integral part of our struggle. If this philosophy had not emerged, by now many streets of the South would, I am convinced, be flowing with blood. And I am further convinced that if our white brothers dismiss as "rabble rousers" and "outside agitators" those of us who employ nonviolent direct action, and if they refuse to support our nonviolent efforts, millions of Negroes will, out of frustration and despair, seek solace and security in black nationalist ideologies—a development that would inevitably lead to a frightening racial nightmare.

Oppressed people cannot remain oppressed forever. The yearning for freedom eventually manifests itself, and that is what has happened to the American Negro. Something within has reminded him of his birthright of freedom, and something without has reminded him that it can be gained. Consciously or unconsciously, he has been caught up by the Zeitgeist, and with his black brothers of Africa and his brown and yellow brothers of Asia, South America and the Caribbean, the United States Negro is moving with a sense of great urgency toward the promised land of racial justice. If one recognizes this vital urge that has engulfed the Negro community, one should readily understand why public demonstrations are taking place. The Negro has many pent up resentments and latent frustrations, and he must release them. So let him march; let him make prayer pilgrimages to the city hall; let him go on freedom rides—and try to understand why he must do so. If his repressed emotions are not released in nonviolent ways, they will seek expression through violence; this is not a threat but a fact of history. So I have not said to my people: "Get rid of your discontent." Rather, I have tried to say that this normal and healthy discontent can be channeled into the creative outlet of nonviolent direct action. And now this approach is being termed extremist. But though I was initially disappointed at being categorized as an extremist, as I continued to think about the matter I gradually gained a measure of satisfaction from the label. Was not Jesus an extremist for love: "Love your enemies, bless them that curse you, do good to them that hate you, and pray for them which despitefully use you, and persecute you." Was not Amos an extremist for justice: "Let justice roll down like waters and righteousness like an ever flowing stream." Was not Paul an extremist for the Christian gospel: "I bear in my body the marks of the Lord Jesus." Was not Martin Luther an extremist: "Here I stand; I cannot do otherwise, so help me God." And John Bunyan: "I will stay in jail to the end of my days before I make a butchery of my conscience." And Abraham Lincoln: "This nation cannot survive half slave and half free." And Thomas Jefferson: "We hold these truths to be self evident, that all men are created equal . . ." So the question is not whether we will be extremists, but what kind of extremists we will be. Will we be extremists for hate or for love? Will we be extremists for the preservation of injustice or for the extension of justice? In that dramatic scene on

Calvary's hill three men were crucified. We must never forget that all three were crucified for the same crime—the crime of extremism. Two were extremists for immorality, and thus fell below their environment. The other, Jesus Christ, was an extremist for love, truth and goodness, and thereby rose above his environment. Perhaps the South, the nation and the world are in dire need of creative extremists.

I had hoped that the white moderate would see this need. Perhaps I was too optimistic; perhaps I expected too much. I suppose I should have realized that few members of the oppressor race can understand the deep groans and passionate yearnings of the oppressed race, and still fewer have the vision to see that injustice must be rooted out by strong, persistent and determined action. I am thankful, however, that some of our white brothers in the South have grasped the meaning of this social revolution and committed themselves to it. They are still all too few in quantity, but they are big in quality. Some—such as Ralph McGill, Lillian Smith, Harry Golden, James McBride Dabbs, Ann Braden and Sarah Patton Boyle—have written about our struggle in eloquent and prophetic terms. Others have marched with us down nameless streets of the South. They have languished in filthy, roach infested jails, suffering the abuse and brutality of policemen who view them as "dirty nigger-lovers." Unlike so many of their moderate brothers and sisters, they have recognized the urgency of the moment and sensed the need for powerful "action" antidotes to combat the disease of segregation. Let me take note of my other major disappointment. I have been so greatly disappointed with the white church and its leadership. Of course, there are some notable exceptions. I am not unmindful of the fact that each of you has taken some significant stands on this issue. I commend you, Reverend Stallings, for your Christian stand on this past Sunday, in welcoming Negroes to your worship service on a nonsegregated basis. I commend the Catholic leaders of this state for integrating Spring Hill College several years ago.

But despite these notable exceptions, I must honestly reiterate that I have been disappointed with the church. I do not say this as one of those negative critics who can always find something wrong with the church. I say this as a minister of the gospel, who loves the church; who was nurtured in its bosom;

who has been sustained by its spiritual blessings and who will remain true to it as long as the cord of life shall lengthen.

When I was suddenly catapulted into the leadership of the bus protest in Montgomery, Alabama, a few years ago, I felt we would be supported by the white church. I felt that the white ministers, priests and rabbis of the South would be among our strongest allies. Instead, some have been outright opponents, refusing to understand the freedom movement and misrepresenting its leaders; all too many others have been more cautious than courageous and have remained silent behind the anesthetizing security of stained glass windows.

In spite of my shattered dreams, I came to Birmingham with the hope that the white religious leadership of this community would see the justice of our cause and, with deep moral concern, would serve as the channel through which our just grievances could reach the power structure. I had hoped that each of you would understand. But again I have been disappointed.

I have heard numerous southern religious leaders admonish their worshipers to comply with a desegregation decision because it is the law, but I have longed to hear white ministers declare: "Follow this decree because integration is morally right and because the Negro is your brother." In the midst of blatant injustices inflicted upon the Negro, I have watched white churchmen stand on the sideline and mouth pious irrelevancies and sanctimonious trivialities. In the midst of a mighty struggle to rid our nation of racial and economic injustice, I have heard many ministers say: "Those are social issues, with which the gospel has no real concern." And I have watched many churches commit themselves to a completely other worldly religion which makes a strange, un-Biblical distinction between body and soul, between the sacred and the secular.

I have traveled the length and breadth of Alabama, Mississippi and all the other southern states. On sweltering summer days and crisp autumn mornings I have looked at the South's beautiful churches with their lofty spires pointing heavenward. I have beheld the impressive outlines of her massive religious education buildings. Over and over I have found myself asking: "What kind of people worship here? Who is their God?

Where were their voices when the lips of Governor Barnett dripped with words of interposition and nullification? Where were they when Governor Wallace gave a clarion call for defiance and hatred? Where were their voices of support when bruised and weary Negro men and women decided to rise from the dark dungeons of complacency to the bright hills of creative protest?"

Yes, these questions are still in my mind. In deep disappointment I have wept over the laxity of the church. But be assured that my tears have been tears of love. There can be no deep disappointment where there is not deep love. Yes, I love the church. How could I do otherwise? I am in the rather unique position of being the son, the grandson and the great grandson of preachers. Yes, I see the church as the body of Christ. But, oh! How we have blemished and scarred that body through social neglect and through fear of being nonconformists.

There was a time when the church was very powerful—in the time when the early Christians rejoiced at being deemed worthy to suffer for what they believed. In those days the church was not merely a thermometer that recorded the ideas and principles of popular opinion; it was a thermostat that transformed the mores of society. Whenever the early Christians entered a town, the people in power became disturbed and immediately sought to convict the Christians for being "disturbers of the peace" and "outside agitators."' But the Christians pressed on, in the conviction that they were "a colony of heaven," called to obey God rather than man. Small in number, they were big in commitment. They were too God-intoxicated to be "astronomically intimidated." By their effort and example they brought an end to such ancient evils as infanticide and gladiatorial contests. Things are different now. So often the contemporary church is a weak, ineffectual voice with an uncertain sound. So often it is an archdefender of the status quo. Far from being disturbed by the presence of the church, the power structure of the average community is consoled by the church's silent—and often even vocal—sanction of things as they are.

But the judgment of God is upon the church as never before. If today's church does not recapture the sacrificial spirit of the early church, it will lose its authenticity, forfeit the loyalty of millions, and be dismissed as an irrelevant social club with no meaning for the twentieth century. Every day I meet young people whose disappointment with the church has turned into outright disgust.

Perhaps I have once again been too optimistic. Is organized religion too inextricably bound to the status quo to save our nation and the world? Perhaps I must turn my faith to the inner spiritual church, the church within the church, as the true ekklesia and the hope of the world. But again I am thankful to God that some noble souls from the ranks of organized religion have broken loose from the paralyzing chains of conformity and joined us as active partners in the struggle for freedom. They have left their secure congregations and walked the streets of Albany, Georgia, with us. They have gone down the highways of the South on tortuous rides for freedom. Yes, they have gone to jail with us. Some have been dismissed from their churches, have lost the support of their bishops and fellow ministers. But they have acted in the faith that right defeated is stronger than evil triumphant. Their witness has been the spiritual salt that has preserved the true meaning of the gospel in these troubled times. They have carved a tunnel of hope through the dark mountain of disappointment. I hope the church as a whole will meet the challenge of this decisive hour. But even if the church does not come to the aid of justice, I have no despair about the future. I have no fear about the outcome of our struggle in Birmingham, even if our motives are at present misunderstood. We will reach the goal of freedom in Birmingham and all over the nation, because the goal of America is freedom. Abused and scorned though we may be, our destiny is tied up with America's destiny. Before the pilgrims landed at Plymouth, we were here. Before the pen of Jefferson etched the majestic words of the Declaration of Independence across the pages of history, we were here. For more than two centuries our forebears labored in this country without wages; they made cotton king; they built the homes of their masters while suffering gross injustice and shameful humiliation —and yet out of a bottomless vitality they continued to thrive and develop. If the inexpressible cruelties of slavery could not stop us, the opposition we now face will surely fail. We will win our freedom because the sacred heritage of our nation and the eternal will of God are embodied in our echoing demands. Before closing I feel impelled to mention one other point in your statement that has troubled me profoundly. You warmly commended the Birmingham police force for keeping "order" and "preventing violence." I doubt that you would have so warmly commended the police force if you had seen its dogs sinking their teeth into unarmed, nonviolent Negroes. I doubt that you would so quickly commend the policemen if you were to observe their ugly and inhumane treatment of Negroes here in the city jail; if you were to watch them push and curse old Negro women and young Negro girls; if you were to see them slap and kick old Negro men and young boys; if you were to observe them, as they did on two occasions, refuse to give us food because we wanted to sing our grace together. I cannot join you in your praise of the Birmingham police department.

It is true that the police have exercised a degree of discipline in handling the demonstrators. In this sense they have conducted themselves rather "nonviolently" in public. But for what purpose? To preserve the evil system of segregation. Over the past few years I have consistently preached that nonviolence demands that the means we use must be as pure as the ends we seek. I have tried to make clear that it is wrong to use immoral means to attain moral ends. But now I must affirm that it is just as wrong, or perhaps even more so, to use moral means to preserve immoral ends. Perhaps Mr. Connor and his policemen have been rather nonviolent in public, as was Chief Pritchett in Albany, Georgia, but they have used the moral means of nonviolence to maintain the immoral end of racial injustice. As T. S. Eliot has said: "The last temptation is the greatest treason: To do the right deed for the wrong reason."

I wish you had commended the Negro sit inners and demonstrators of Birmingham for their sublime courage, their willingness to suffer and their amazing discipline in the midst of great provocation. One day the South will recognize its real heroes. They will be the James Merediths, with the noble sense of purpose that enables them to face jeering and hostile mobs, and with the agonizing loneliness that characterizes the life of the pioneer. They will be old, oppressed, battered Negro women, symbolized in a seventy two year old woman in Montgomery,

Alabama, who rose up with a sense of dignity and with her people decided not to ride segregated buses, and who responded with ungrammatical profundity to one who inquired about her weariness: "My feets is tired, but my soul is at rest." They will be the young high school and college students, the young ministers of the gospel and a host of their elders, courageously and nonviolently sitting in at lunch counters and willingly going to jail for conscience' sake. One day the South will know that when these disinherited children of God sat down at lunch counters, they were in reality standing up for what is best in the American dream and for the most sacred values in our Judaeo Christian heritage, thereby bringing our nation back to those great wells of democracy which were dug deep by the founding fathers in their formulation of the Constitution and the Declaration of Independence.

Never before have I written so long a letter. I'm afraid it is much too long to take your precious time. I can assure you that it would have been much shorter if I had been writing from a comfortable desk, but what else can one do when he is alone in a narrow jail cell, other than write long letters, think long thoughts and pray long prayers?

If I have said anything in this letter that overstates the truth and indicates an unreasonable impatience, I beg you to forgive me. If I have said anything that understates the truth and indicates my having a patience that allows me to settle for anything less than brotherhood, I beg God to forgive me.

I hope this letter finds you strong in the faith. I also hope that circumstances will soon make it possible for me to meet each of you, not as an integrationist or a civil-rights leader but as a fellow clergyman and a Christian brother. Let us all hope that the dark clouds of racial prejudice will soon pass away and the deep fog of misunderstanding will be lifted from our fear drenched communities, and in some not too distant tomorrow the radiant stars of love and brotherhood will shine over our great nation with all their scintillating beauty.

Yours for the cause of Peace and Brotherhood,

Martin Luther King Jr.

I Have a Dream

Speech delivered August 28, 1963, at the Lincoln Memorial, Washington, DC.

I am happy to join with you today in what will go down in history as the greatest demonstration for freedom in the history of our nation.

Five score years ago, a great American, in whose symbolic shadow we stand today, signed the Emancipation Proclamation. This momentous decree came as a great beacon light of hope to millions of Negro slaves who had been seared in the flames of withering injustice. It came as a joyous daybreak to end the long night of their captivity.

But one hundred years later, the Negro still is not free. One hundred years later, the life of the Negro is still sadly crippled by the manacles of segregation and the chains of discrimination. One hundred years later, the Negro lives on a lonely island of poverty in the midst of a vast ocean of material prosperity. One hundred years later, the Negro is still languished in the corners of American society and finds himself an exile in his own land. And so we've come here today to dramatize a shameful condition.

In a sense we've come to our nation's capital to cash a check. When the architects of our republic wrote the magnificent words of the Constitution and the Declaration of Independence, they were signing a promissory note to which every American was to fall heir. This note was a promise that all men, yes, black men as well as white men, would be guaranteed the "unalienable Rights" of "Life, Liberty and the pursuit of Happiness." It is obvious today that America has defaulted on this promissory note, insofar as her citizens of color are concerned. Instead of honoring this sacred obligation, America has given the Negro people a bad check, a check which has come back marked "insufficient funds."

But we refuse to believe that the bank of justice is bankrupt. We refuse to believe that there are insufficient funds in the great vaults of opportunity of this nation. And so, we've come to cash this check, a check that will give us upon demand the riches of freedom and the security of justice.

We have also come to this hallowed spot to remind America of the fierce urgency of Now. This is no time to engage in the luxury of cooling off or to take the tranquilizing drug of gradualism. Now is the time to make real the promises of democracy. Now is the time to rise from the dark and desolate valley of segregation to the sunlit path of racial justice. Now is the time to lift our nation from the quicksands of racial injustice to the solid rock of brotherhood. Now is the time to make justice a reality for all of God's children.

It would be fatal for the nation to overlook the urgency of the moment. This sweltering summer of the Negro's legitimate discontent will not pass until there is an invigorating autumn of freedom and equality. Nineteen sixty-three is not an end, but a beginning. And those who hope that the Negro needed to blow off steam and will now be content will have a rude awakening if the nation returns to business as usual. And there will be neither rest nor tranquility in America until the Negro is granted his citizenship rights. The whirlwinds of revolt will continue to shake the foundations of our nation until the bright day of justice emerges.

But there is something that I must say to my people, who stand on the warm threshold which leads into the palace of justice: In the process of gaining our rightful place, we must not be guilty of wrongful deeds. Let us not seek to satisfy our thirst for freedom by drinking from the cup of bitterness and hatred. We must forever conduct our struggle on the high plane of dignity and discipline. We must not allow our creative protest to degenerate into physical violence. Again and again, we must rise to the majestic heights of meeting physical force with soul force.

The marvelous new militancy which has engulfed the Negro community must not lead us to a distrust of all white people, for many of our white brothers, as evidenced by their presence here today, have come to realize that their destiny is tied up with our destiny. And they have come to realize that their freedom is inextricably bound to our freedom.

We cannot walk alone.

And as we walk, we must make the pledge that we shall always march ahead.

We cannot turn back.

There are those who are asking the devotees of civil rights, "When will you be satisfied?" We can never be satisfied as long as the Negro is the victim of the unspeakable horrors of police brutality. We can never be satisfied as long as our bodies, heavy with the fatigue of travel, cannot gain lodging in the motels of the highways and the hotels of the cities. We cannot be satisfied as long as the negro's basic mobility is from a smaller ghetto to a larger one. We can never be satisfied as long as our children are stripped of their self-hood and robbed of their dignity by signs stating: "For Whites Only." We cannot be satisfied as long as a Negro in Mississippi cannot vote and a Negro in New York believes he has nothing for which to vote. No, no, we are not satisfied, and we will not be satisfied until "justice rolls down like waters, and righteousness like a mighty stream."[1]

I am not unmindful that some of you have come here out of great trials and tribulations. Some of you have come fresh from narrow jail cells. And some of you have come from areas where your quest—quest for freedom left you battered by the storms of persecution and staggered by the winds of police brutality. You have been the veterans of creative suffering. Continue to work with the faith that unearned suffering is redemptive. Go back to Mississippi, go back to Alabama, go back to South Carolina, go back to Georgia, go back to Louisiana, go back to the slums and ghettos of our northern cities, knowing that somehow this situation can and will be changed.

Let us not wallow in the valley of despair, I say to you today, my friends.

And so even though we face the difficulties of today and tomorrow, I still have a dream. It is a dream deeply rooted in the American dream.

I have a dream that one day this nation will rise up and live out the true meaning of its creed: "We hold these truths to be self-evident, that all men are created equal."

---

[1] Amos 5:24

I have a dream that one day on the red hills of Georgia, the sons of former slaves and the sons of former slave owners will be able to sit down together at the table of brotherhood.

I have a dream that one day even the state of Mississippi, a state sweltering with the heat of injustice, sweltering with the heat of oppression, will be transformed into an oasis of freedom and justice.

I have a dream that my four little children will one day live in a nation where they will not be judged by the color of their skin but by the content of their character.

I have a *dream* today!

I have a dream that one day, down in Alabama, with its vicious racists, with its governor having his lips dripping with the words of "interposition" and "nullification"—one day right there in Alabama little black boys and black girls will be able to join hands with little white boys and white girls as sisters and brothers.

I have a *dream* today!

I have a dream that one day every valley shall be exalted, and every hill and mountain shall be made low, the rough places will be made plain, and the crooked places will be made straight; "and the glory of the Lord shall be revealed and all flesh shall see it together."[2]

This is our hope, and this is the faith that I go back to the South with.

With this faith, we will be able to hew out of the mountain of despair a stone of hope. With this faith, we will be able to transform the jangling discords of our nation into a beautiful symphony of brotherhood. With this faith, we will be able to work together, to pray together, to struggle together, to go to jail together, to stand up for freedom together, knowing that we will be free one day.

---

[2] Isaiah 40:4–5. Quotation marks are excluded from part of this moment in the text because King's rendering of Isaiah 40:4 does not precisely follow the KJV version from which he quotes (e.g., "hill" and "mountain" are reversed in the KJV). King's rendering of Isaiah 40:5, however, is precisely quoted from the KJV.

And this will be the day—this will be the day when all of God's children will be able to sing with new meaning:

My country 'tis of thee, sweet land of liberty, of thee I sing.

Land where my fathers died, land of the Pilgrim's pride,

From every mountainside, let freedom ring!

And if America is to be a great nation, this must become true.

And so let freedom ring from the prodigious hilltops of New Hampshire.

Let freedom ring from the mighty mountains of New York.

Let freedom ring from the heightening Alleghenies of Pennsylvania.

Let freedom ring from the snow-capped Rockies of Colorado.

Let freedom ring from the curvaceous slopes of California.

But not only that:

Let freedom ring from Stone Mountain of Georgia.

Let freedom ring from Lookout Mountain of Tennessee.

Let freedom ring from every hill and molehill of Mississippi.

From every mountainside, let freedom ring.

And when this happens, and when we allow freedom ring, when we let it ring from every village and every hamlet, from every state and every city, we will be able to speed up that day when *all* of God's children, black men and white men, Jews and Gentiles, Protestants and Catholics, will be able to join hands and sing in the words of the old Negro spiritual:

Free at last! Free at last!

Thank God Almighty, we are free at last!

The Ballot or the Bullet

Malcolm X

Exactly one year after the Birmingham Campaign began, Malcolm X (1925–1965) delivered what would become one of his most famous speeches. In this speech Malcolm X reiterates time and again that he is not "anti-white"; rather he is against some of the actions of those groups: "we're anti-exploitation, we're anti-degradation, we're anti-oppression." This position was in contrast to his earlier rhetoric from the period in which he was a member of the Nation of Islam. One month prior to this speech, he had publicly announced his departure from the Nation of Islam and expressed his desire to create a politically oriented "black nationalist party."

It is clear from the title of this speech alone that Malcolm X did not see eye to eye with Martin Luther King on the appropriate methods for achieving necessary progress. King advocated for non-violence as the only means; Malcolm X advocated for non-violence first, but was always adamant that violence was a perfectly acceptable alternative if it was justified. "I don't even call it violence when it's in self defense; I call it intelligence." Whereas King's most famous speech is in the style of a Protestant sermon, the style of Malcolm X's speech is plain but eloquent, both colloquial and forceful.

Speech delivered April 3, 1964, at the Cory Methodist Church, Cleveland, Ohio

Mr. Moderator, Brother Lomax, brothers and sisters, friends and enemies: I just can't believe everyone in here is a friend, and I don't want to leave anybody out. The question tonight, as I understand it, is "The Negro Revolt, and Where Do We Go From Here?" or "What Next?" In my little humble way of understanding it, it points toward either the ballot or the bullet.

Before we try and explain what is meant by the ballot or the bullet, I would like to clarify something concerning myself. I'm still a Muslim; my religion is still Islam. That's my personal belief. Just as Adam Clayton Powell is a Christian minister who heads the Abyssinian Baptist Church in New York, but at the same time takes part in the political struggles to try and bring about rights to the black people in this country; and Dr. Martin Luther King is a Christian minister down in Atlanta, Georgia, who heads another organization fighting for the civil rights of black people in this country; and Reverend Galamison, I guess you've heard of him, is another Christian minister in New York who has been deeply involved in the school boycotts to eliminate segregated education; well, I myself am a minister, not a Christian minister, but a Muslim minister; and I believe in action on all fronts by whatever means necessary.

Although I'm still a Muslim, I'm not here tonight to discuss my religion. I'm not here to try and change your religion. I'm not here to argue or discuss anything that we differ about, because it's time for us to submerge our differences and realize that it is best for us to first see that we have the same problem, a common problem, a problem that will make you catch hell whether you're a Baptist, or a Methodist, or a Muslim, or a nationalist. Whether you're educated or illiterate, whether you live on the boulevard or in the alley, you're going to catch hell just like I am. We're all in the same boat and we all are going to catch the same hell from the same man. He just happens to be a white man. All of us have suffered here, in this country, political oppression at the hands of the white man, economic exploitation at the hands of the white man, and social degradation at the hands of the white man.

Now in speaking like this, it doesn't mean that we're anti-white, but it does mean we're anti-exploitation, we're anti-degradation, we're anti-oppression. And if the white man doesn't want us to be anti-him, let him stop oppressing and exploiting and degrading us. Whether we are Christians or Muslims or nationalists or agnostics or atheists, we must first learn to forget our differences. If we have differences, let us differ in the closet; when we come out in front, let us not have anything to argue about until we get finished arguing with the man. If the late President Kennedy could get together with Khrushchev and exchange some wheat, we certainly have more in common with each other than Kennedy and Khrushchev had with each other.

If we don't do something real soon, I think you'll have to agree that we're going to be forced either to use the ballot or the bullet. It's one or the other in 1964. It isn't that time is running out—time has run out!

1964 threatens to be the most explosive year America has ever witnessed. The most explosive year. Why? It's also a political year. It's the year when all of the white politicians will be back in the so-called Negro community jiving you and me for some votes. The year when all of the white political crooks will be right back in your and my community with their false promises, building up our hopes for a letdown, with their trickery and their treachery, with their false promises which they don't intend to keep. As they nourish these dissatisfactions, it can only lead to one thing, an explosion; and now we have the type of black man on the scene in America today—I'm sorry, Brother Lomax—who just doesn't intend to turn the other cheek any longer.

Don't let anybody tell you anything about the odds are against you. If they draft you, they send you to Korea and make you face 800 million Chinese. If you can be brave over there, you can be brave right here. These odds aren't as great as those odds. And if you fight here, you will at least know what you're fighting for.

I'm not a politician, not even a student of politics; in fact, I'm not a student of much of anything. I'm not a Democrat. I'm not a Republican, and I don't even consider myself an American. If you and I were Americans, there'd be no problem. Those Honkies that just got off the boat, they're already Americans; Polacks are already Americans; the Italian refugees are already Americans.

Everything that came out of Europe, every blue-eyed thing, is already an American. And as long as you and I have been over here, we aren't Americans yet.

Well, I am one who doesn't believe in deluding myself. I'm not going to sit at your table and watch you eat, with nothing on my plate, and call myself a diner. Sitting at the table doesn't make you a diner, unless you eat some of what's on that plate. Being here in America doesn't make you an American. Being born here in America doesn't make you an American. Why, if birth made you American, you wouldn't need any legislation; you wouldn't need any amendments to the Constitution; you wouldn't be faced with civil-rights filibustering in Washington, DC, right now. They don't have to pass civil-rights legislation to make a Polack an American.

No, I'm not an American. I'm one of the 22 million black people who are the victims of Americanism. One of the 22 million black people who are the victims of democracy, nothing but disguised hypocrisy. So, I'm not standing here speaking to you as an American, or a patriot, or a flag-saluter, or a flag-waver —no, not I. I'm speaking as a victim of this American system. And I see America through the eyes of the victim. I don't see any American dream; I see an American nightmare.

These 22 million victims are waking up. Their eyes are coming open. They're beginning to see what they used to only look at. They're becoming politically mature. They are realizing that there are new political trends from coast to coast. As they see these new political trends, it's possible for them to see that every time there's an election the races are so close that they have to have a recount. They had to recount in Massachusetts to see who was going to be governor, it was so close. It was the same way in Rhode Island, in Minnesota, and in many other parts of the country. And the same with Kennedy and Nixon when they ran for president. It was so close they had to count all over again. Well, what does this mean? It means that when white people are evenly divided, and black people have a bloc of votes of their own, it is left up to them to determine who's going to sit in the White House and who's going to be in the dog house.

It was the black man's vote that put the present administration in Washington, DC. Your vote, your dumb vote, your ignorant vote, your wasted vote put in an administration in Washington, DC, that has seen fit to pass every kind of legislation imaginable, saving you until last, then filibustering on top of that. And your and my leaders have the audacity to run around clapping their hands and talk about how much progress we're making. And what a good president we have. If he wasn't good in Texas, he sure can't be good in Washington, DC. Because Texas is a lynch state. It is in the same breath as Mississippi, no different; only they lynch you in Texas with a Texas accent and lynch you in Mississippi with a Mississippi accent. And these Negro leaders have the audacity to go and have some coffee in the White House with a Texan, a Southern cracker—that's all he is—and then come out and tell you and me that he's going to be better for us because, since he's from the South, he knows how to deal with the Southerners. What kind of logic is that? Let Eastland be president, he's from the South too. He should be better able to deal with them than Johnson.

In this present administration they have in the House of Representatives 257 Democrats to only 177 Republicans. They control two-thirds of the House vote. Why can't they pass something that will help you and me? In the Senate, there are 67 senators who are of the Democratic Party. Only 33 of them are Republicans. Why, the Democrats have got the government sewed up, and you're the one who sewed it up for them. And what have they given you for it? Four years in office, and just now getting around to some civil-rights legislation. Just now, after everything else is gone, out of the way, they're going to sit down now and play with you all summer long—the same old giant con game that they call filibuster. All those are in cahoots together. Don't you ever think they're not in cahoots together, for the man that is heading the civil-rights filibuster is a man from Georgia named Richard Russell. When Johnson became president, the first man he asked for when he got back to Washington, DC, was "Dicky"—that's how tight they are. That's his boy, that's his pal, that's his buddy. But they're playing that old con game. One of them makes believe he's for you, and he's got it fixed where the other one is so tight against you, he never has to keep his promise.

So it's time in 1964 to wake up. And when you see them coming up with that kind of conspiracy, let them know your eyes are open. And let them know you—something else that's wide open too. It's got to be the ballot or the bullet. The ballot or the bullet. If you're afraid to use an expression like that, you should get on out of the country; you should get back in the cotton patch; you should get back in the alley. They get all the Negro vote, and after they get it, the Negro gets nothing in return. All they did when they got to Washington was give a few big Negroes big jobs. Those big Negroes didn't need big jobs, they already had jobs. That's camouflage, that's trickery, that's treachery, window-dressing. I'm not trying to knock out the Democrats for the Republicans. We'll get to them in a minute. But it is true; you put the Democrats first and the Democrats put you last.

Look at it the way it is. What alibis do they use, since they control Congress and the Senate? What alibi do they use when you and I ask, "Well, when are you going to keep your promise?" They blame the Dixiecrats. What is a Dixiecrat? A Democrat. A Dixiecrat is nothing but a Democrat in disguise. The titular head of the Democrats is also the head of the Dixiecrats, because the Dixiecrats are a part of the Democratic Party. The Democrats have never kicked the Dixiecrats out of the party. The Dixiecrats bolted themselves once, but the Democrats didn't put them out. Imagine, these lowdown Southern segregationists put the Northern Democrats down. But the Northern Democrats have never put the Dixiecrats down. No, look at that thing the way it is. They have got a con game going on, a political con game, and you and I are in the middle. It's time for you and me to wake up and start looking at it like it is, and trying to understand it like it is; and then we can deal with it like it is.

The Dixiecrats in Washington, DC, control the key committees that run the government. The only reason the Dixiecrats control these committees is because they have seniority. The only reason they have seniority is because they come from states where Negroes can't vote. This is not even a government that's based on democracy. It is not a government that is made up of representatives of the people. Half of the people in the South can't even vote. Eastland is not even supposed to be in Washington. Half of the senators and congressmen who occupy these key positions in Washington, DC, are there illegally, are there unconstitutionally.

I was in Washington, DC, a week ago Thursday, when they were debating whether or not they should let the bill come onto the floor. And in the back of the room where the Senate meets, there's a huge map of the United States, and on that map it shows the location of Negroes throughout the country. And it shows that the Southern section of the country, the states that are most heavily concentrated with Negroes, are the ones that have senators and congressmen standing up filibustering and doing all other kinds of trickery to keep the Negro from being able to vote. This is pitiful. But it's not pitiful for us any longer; it's actually pitiful for the white man, because soon now, as the Negro awakens a little more and sees the vise that he's in, sees the bag that he's in, sees the real game that he's in, then the Negro's going to develop a new tactic.

These senators and congressmen actually violate the constitutional amendments that guarantee the people of that particular state or county the right to vote. And the Constitution itself has within it the machinery to expel any representative from a state where the voting rights of the people are violated. You don't even need new legislation. Any person in Congress right now, who is there from a state or a district where the voting rights of the people are violated, that particular person should be expelled from Congress. And when you expel him, you've removed one of the obstacles in the path of any real meaningful legislation in this country. In fact, when you expel them, you don't need new legislation, because they will be replaced by black representatives from counties and districts where the black man is in the majority, not in the minority.

If the black man in these Southern states had his full voting rights, the key Dixiecrats in Washington, DC, which means the key Democrats in Washington, DC, would lose their seats. The Democratic Party itself would lose its power. It would cease to be powerful as a party. When you see the amount of power that would be lost by the Democratic Party if it were to lose the Dixiecrat wing, or branch, or element, you can see where it's against the interests of the Democrats to give voting rights to Negroes in states where the Democrats have been in complete power and authority ever since the Civil War. You just can't belong to that Party without analyzing it.

I say again, I'm not anti-Democrat, I'm not anti-Republican, I'm not anti-anything. I'm just questioning their sincerity, and some of the strategy that they've been using on our people by promising them promises that they don't intend to keep. When you keep the Democrats in power, you're keeping the Dixiecrats in power. I doubt that my good Brother Lomax will deny that. A vote for a Democrat is a vote for a Dixiecrat. That's why, in 1964, it's time now for you and me to become more politically mature and realize what the ballot is for; what we're supposed to get when we cast a ballot; and that if we don't cast a ballot, it's going to end up in a situation where we're going to have to cast a bullet. It's either a ballot or a bullet.

In the North, they do it a different way. They have a system that's known as gerrymandering, whatever that means. It means when Negroes become too heavily concentrated in a certain area, and begin to gain too much political power, the white man comes along and changes the district lines. You may say, "Why do you keep saying white man?" Because it's the white man who does it. I haven't ever seen any Negro changing any lines. They don't let him get near the line. It's the white man who does this. And usually, it's the white man who grins at you the most, and pats you on the back, and is supposed to be your friend. He may be friendly, but he's not your friend.

So, what I'm trying to impress upon you, in essence, is this: You and I in America are faced not with a segregationist conspiracy, we're faced with a government conspiracy. Everyone who's filibustering is a senator—that's the government. Everyone who's finagling in Washington, DC, is a congressman—that's the government. You don't have anybody putting blocks in your path but people who are a part of the government. The same government that you go abroad to fight for and die for is the government that is in a conspiracy to deprive you of your voting rights, deprive you of your economic opportunities, deprive you of decent housing, deprive you of decent education. You don't need to go to the employer alone, it is the government itself, the government of America, that is responsible for the oppression and exploitation and degradation of black people in this country. And you should drop it in their lap. This government has failed the Negro. This so-called democracy has failed the Negro. And all these white liberals have definitely failed the Negro.

So, where do we go from here? First, we need some friends. We need some new allies. The entire civil-rights struggle needs a new interpretation, a broader interpretation. We need to look at this civil-rights thing from another angle—from the inside as well as from the outside. To those of us whose philosophy is black nationalism, the only way you can get involved in the civil-rights struggle is give it a new interpretation. That old interpretation excluded us. It kept us out. So, we're giving a new interpretation to the civil-rights struggle, an interpretation that will enable us to come into it, take part in it. And these handkerchief-heads who have been dillydallying and pussy footing and compromising— we don't intend to let them pussyfoot and dillydally and compromise any longer.

How can you thank a man for giving you what's already yours? How then can you thank him for giving you only part of what's already yours? You haven't even made progress, if what's being given to you, you should have had already. That's not progress. And I love my Brother Lomax, the way he pointed out we're right back where we were in 1954. We're not even as far up as we were in 1954. We're behind where we were in 1954. There's more segregation now than there was in 1954. There's more racial animosity, more racial hatred, more racial violence today in 1964, than there was in 1954. Where is the progress?

And now you're facing a situation where the young Negro's coming up. They don't want to hear that "turn-the-other-cheek" stuff, no. In Jacksonville, those were teenagers, they were throwing Molotov cocktails. Negroes have never done that before. But it shows you there's a new deal coming in. There's new thinking coming in. There's new strategy coming in. It'll be Molotov cocktails this month, hand grenades next month, and something else next month. It'll be ballots, or it'll be bullets. It'll be liberty, or it will be death. The only difference about this kind of death—it'll be reciprocal. You know what is meant by "reciprocal"? That's one of Brother Lomax's words. I stole it from him. I don't usually deal with those big words because I don't usually deal with big people. I deal with small people. I find you can get a whole lot of small people and whip hell out of a whole lot of big people. They haven't got anything to lose, and they've got every thing to gain. And they'll let you know in a minute: "It takes two to tango; when I go, you go."

The black nationalists, those whose philosophy is black nationalism, in bringing about this new interpretation of the entire meaning of civil rights, look upon it as meaning, as Brother Lomax has pointed out, equality of opportunity. Well, we're justified in seeking civil rights, if it means equality of opportunity, because all we're doing there is trying to collect for our investment. Our mothers and fathers invested sweat and blood. Three hundred and ten years we worked in this country without a dime in return—I mean without a dime in return. You let the white man walk around here talking about how rich this country is, but you never stop to think how it got rich so quick. It got rich because you made it rich.

You take the people who are in this audience right now. They're poor. We're all poor as individuals. Our weekly salary individually amounts to hardly anything. But if you take the salary of everyone in here collectively, it'll fill up a whole lot of baskets. It's a lot of wealth. If you can collect the wages of just these people right here for a year, you'll be rich—richer than rich. When you look at it like that, think how rich Uncle Sam had to become, not with this handful, but millions of black people. Your and my mother and father, who didn't work an eight-hour shift, but worked from "can't see" in the morning until "can't see" at night, and worked for nothing, making the white man rich, making Uncle Sam rich. This is our investment. This is our contribution, our blood.

Not only did we give of our free labor, we gave of our blood. Every time he had a call to arms, we were the first ones in uniform. We died on every battlefield the white man had. We have made a greater sacrifice than anybody who's standing up in America today. We have made a greater contribution and have collected less. Civil rights, for those of us whose philosophy is black nationalism, means: "Give it to us now. Don't wait for next year. Give it to us yesterday, and that's not fast enough."

I might stop right here to point out one thing. Whenever you're going after something that belongs to you, anyone who's depriving you of the right to have it is a criminal. Understand that. Whenever you are going after something that is yours, you are within your legal rights to lay claim to it. And anyone who puts forth any effort to deprive you of that which is yours, is breaking the law, is a criminal. And this was pointed out by the Supreme Court decision. It outlawed segregation.

Which means segregation is against the law. Which means a segregationist is breaking the law. A segregationist is a criminal. You can't label him as anything other than that. And when you demonstrate against segregation, the law is on your side. The Supreme Court is on your side.

Now, who is it that opposes you in carrying out the law? The police department itself. With police dogs and clubs. Whenever you demonstrate against segregation, whether it is segregated education, segregated housing, or anything else, the law is on your side, and anyone who stands in the way is not the law any longer. They are breaking the law; they are not representatives of the law. Any time you demonstrate against segregation and a man has the audacity to put a police dog on you, kill that dog, kill him, I'm telling you, kill that dog. I say it, if they put me in jail tomorrow, kill that dog. Then you'll put a stop to it. Now, if these white people in here don't want to see that kind of action, get down and tell the mayor to tell the police department to pull the dogs in. That's all you have to do. If you don't do it, someone else will.

If you don't take this kind of stand, your little children will grow up and look at you and think "shame." If you don't take an uncompromising stand, I don't mean go out and get violent; but at the same time you should never be nonviolent unless you run into some nonviolence. I'm nonviolent with those who are nonviolent with me. But when you drop that violence on me, then you've made me go insane, and I'm not responsible for what I do. And that's the way every Negro should get. Any time you know you're within the law, within your legal rights, within your moral rights, in accord with justice, then die for what you believe in. But don't die alone. Let your dying be reciprocal. This is what is meant by equality. What's good for the goose is good for the gander.

When we begin to get in this area, we need new friends, we need new allies. We need to expand the civil-rights struggle to a higher level—to the level of human rights. Whenever you are in a civil-rights struggle, whether you know it or not, you are confining yourself to the jurisdiction of Uncle Sam. No one from the outside world can speak out in your behalf as long as your struggle is a civil-rights struggle. Civil rights comes within the domestic affairs of this country. All of our African brothers and our Asian brothers and our Latin-American brothers cannot open their mouths and interfere in the domestic affairs of the United States. And as long as it's civil rights, this comes under the jurisdiction of Uncle Sam.

But the United Nations has what's known as the charter of human rights; it has a committee that deals in human rights. You may wonder why all of the atrocities that have been committed in Africa and in Hungary and in Asia, and in Latin America are brought before the UN, and the Negro problem is never brought before the UN. This is part of the conspiracy. This old, tricky blue eyed liberal who is supposed to be your and my friend, supposed to be in our corner, supposed to be subsidizing our struggle, and supposed to be acting in the capacity of an adviser, never tells you anything about human rights. They keep you wrapped up in civil rights. And you spend so much time barking up the civil-rights tree, you don't even know there's a human-rights tree on the same floor.

When you expand the civil-rights struggle to the level of human rights, you can then take the case of the black man in this country before the nations in the UN. You can take it before the General Assembly. You can take Uncle Sam before a world court. But the only level you can do it on is the level of human rights. Civil rights keeps you under his restrictions, under his jurisdiction. Civil rights keeps you in his pocket. Civil rights means you're asking Uncle Sam to treat you right. Human rights are something you were born with. Human rights are your God-given rights. Human rights are the rights that are recognized by all nations of this earth. And any time any one violates your human rights, you can take them to the world court.

Uncle Sam's hands are dripping with blood, dripping with the blood of the black man in this country. He's the earth's number-one hypocrite. He has the audacity—yes, he has—imagine him posing as the leader of the free world. The free world! And you over here singing "We Shall Overcome." Expand the civil-rights struggle to the level of human rights. Take it into the United Nations, where our African brothers can throw their weight on our side, where our Asian brothers can throw their weight on our side, where our Latin-American brothers can throw their weight on our side, and where 800 million Chinamen are sitting there waiting to throw their weight on our side.

Let the world know how bloody his hands are. Let the world know the hypocrisy that's practiced over here. Let it be the ballot or the bullet. Let him know that it must be the ballot or the bullet.

When you take your case to Washington, DC, you're taking it to the criminal who's responsible; it's like running from the wolf to the fox. They're all in cahoots together. They all work political chicanery and make you look like a chump before the eyes of the world. Here you are walking around in America, getting ready to be drafted and sent abroad, like a tin soldier, and when you get over there, people ask you what are you fighting for, and you have to stick your tongue in your cheek. No, take Uncle Sam to court, take him before the world.

By ballot I only mean freedom. Don't you know—I disagree with Lomax on this issue—that the ballot is more important than the dollar? Can I prove it? Yes. Look in the UN. There are poor nations in the UN; yet those poor nations can get together with their voting power and keep the rich nations from making a move. They have one nation—one vote, everyone has an equal vote. And when those brothers from Asia, and Africa and the darker parts of this earth get together, their voting power is sufficient to hold Sam in check. Or Russia in check. Or some other section of the earth in check. So, the ballot is most important.

Right now, in this country, if you and I, 22 million African-Americans—that's what we are—Africans who are in America. You're nothing but Africans. Nothing but Africans. In fact, you'd get farther calling yourself African instead of Negro. Africans don't catch hell. You're the only one catching hell. They don't have to pass civil-rights bills for Africans. An African can go anywhere he wants right now. All you've got to do is tie your head up. That's right, go anywhere you want. Just stop being a Negro.

Change your name to Hoogagagooba. That'll show you how silly the white man is. You're dealing with a silly man. A friend of mine who's very dark put a turban on his head and went into a restaurant in Atlanta before they called themselves desegregated. He went into a white restaurant, he sat down, they served him, and he said, "What would happen if a Negro came in here? And there he's sitting, black as night, but because he had his head wrapped up the waitress looked back at him and says, "Why, there wouldn't no nigger dare come in here."

So, you're dealing with a man whose bias and prejudice are making him lose his mind, his intelligence, every day. He's frightened. He looks around and sees what's taking place on this earth, and he sees that the pendulum of time is swinging in your direction. The dark people are waking up. They're losing their fear of the white man. No place where he's fighting right now is he winning. Everywhere he's fighting, he's fighting someone your and my complexion. And they're beating him. He can't win any more. He's won his last battle. He failed to win the Korean War. He couldn't win it. He had to sign a truce. That's a loss.

Any time Uncle Sam, with all his machinery for warfare, is held to a draw by some rice eaters, he's lost the battle. He had to sign a truce. America's not supposed to sign a truce. She's supposed to be bad. But she's not bad any more. She's bad as long as she can use her hydrogen bomb, but she can't use hers for fear Russia might use hers. Russia can't use hers, for fear that Sam might use his. So, both of them are weaponless. They can't use the weapon because each's weapon nullifies the other's. So the only place where action can take place is on the ground. And the white man can't win another war fighting on the ground. Those days are over The black man knows it, the brown man knows it, the red man knows it, and the yellow man knows it. So they engage him in guerrilla warfare. That's not his style. You've got to have heart to be a guerrilla warrior, and he hasn't got any heart. I'm telling you now.

I just want to give you a little briefing on guerrilla warfare because, before you know it, before you know it. It takes heart to be a guerrilla warrior because you're on your own. In conventional warfare you have tanks and a whole lot of other people with you to back you up—planes over your head and all that kind of stuff. But a guerrilla is on his own. All you have is a

rifle, some sneakers and a bowl of rice, and that's all you need—
and a lot of heart. The Japanese on some of those islands in the
Pacific, when the American soldiers landed, one Japanese
sometimes could hold the whole army off. He'd just wait until the
sun went down, and when the sun went down they were all equal.
He would take his little blade and slip from bush to bush, and
from American to American. The white soldiers couldn't cope
with that. Whenever you see a white soldier that fought in the
Pacific, he has the shakes, he has a nervous condition, because
they scared him to death.

The same thing happened to the French up in French
Indochina. People who just a few years previously were rice
farmers got together and ran the heavily-mechanized French
army out of Indochina. You don't need it—modern warfare today
won't work. This is the day of the guerrilla. They did the same
thing in Algeria. Algerians, who were nothing but Bedouins, took
a rifle and sneaked off to the hills, and de Gaulle and all of his
highfalutin' war machinery couldn't defeat those guerrillas.
Nowhere on this earth does the white man win in a guerrilla
warfare. It's not his speed. Just as guerrilla warfare is prevailing in
Asia and in parts of Africa and in parts of Latin America, you've
got to be mighty naive, or you've got to play the black man cheap,
if you don't think some day he's going to wake up and find that it's
got to be the ballot or the bullet.

l would like to say, in closing, a few things concerning the
Muslim Mosque, Inc., which we established recently in New York
City. It's true we're Muslims and our religion is Islam, but we
don't mix our religion with our politics and our economics and
our social and civil activities—not any more We keep our religion
in our mosque. After our religious services are over, then as
Muslims we become involved in political action, economic action
and social and civic action. We become involved with anybody,
anywhere, any time and in any manner that's designed to
eliminate the evils, the political, economic and social evils that
are afflicting the people of our community.

The political philosophy of black nationalism means that the
black man should control the politics and the politicians in his
own community; no more. The black man in the black
community has to be re-educated into the science of politics so

he will know what politics is supposed to bring him in return. Don't be throwing out any ballots. A ballot is like a bullet. You don't throw your ballots until you see a target, and if that target is not within your reach, keep your ballot in your pocket.

The political philosophy of black nationalism is being taught in the Christian church. It's being taught in the NAACP. It's being taught in CORE meetings. It's being taught in SNCC Student Nonviolent Coordinating Committee meetings. It's being taught in Muslim meetings. It's being taught where nothing but atheists and agnostics come together. It's being taught everywhere. Black people are fed up with the dillydallying, pussyfooting, compromising approach that we've been using toward getting our freedom. We want freedom now, but we're not going to get it saying "We Shall Overcome." We've got to fight until we overcome.

The economic philosophy of black nationalism is pure and simple. It only means that we should control the economy of our community. Why should white people be running all the stores in our community? Why should white people be running the banks of our community? Why should the economy of our community be in the hands of the white man? Why? If a black man can't move his store into a white community, you tell me why a white man should move his store into a black community. The philosophy of black nationalism involves a re-education program in the black community in regards to economics. Our people have to be made to see that any time you take your dollar out of your community and spend it in a community where you don't live, the community where you live will get poorer and poorer, and the community where you spend your money will get richer and richer.

Then you wonder why where you live is always a ghetto or a slum area. And where you and I are concerned, not only do we lose it when we spend it out of the community, but the white man has got all our stores in the community tied up; so that though we spend it in the community, at sundown the man who runs the store takes it over across town somewhere. He's got us in a vise. So the economic philosophy of black nationalism means in every church, in every civic organization, in every fraternal order, it's time now for our people to be come conscious of the importance of controlling the economy of our community. If we own the stores, if we operate the businesses, if we try and establish some industry in our own community, then we're developing to the position where we are creating employment for our own kind. Once you gain control of the economy of your own community, then you don't have to picket and boycott and beg some cracker downtown for a job in his business.

The social philosophy of black nationalism only means that we have to get together and remove the evils, the vices, alcoholism, drug addiction, and other evils that are destroying the moral fiber of our community. We our selves have to lift the level of our community, the standard of our community to a higher level, make our own society beautiful so that we will be satisfied in our own social circles and won't be running around here trying to knock our way into a social circle where we're not wanted. So I say, in spreading a gospel such as black nationalism, it is not designed to make the black man re-evaluate the white man—you know him already—but to make the black man re-evaluate himself. Don't change the white man's mind—you can't change his mind, and that whole thing about appealing to the moral conscience of America— America's conscience is bankrupt. She lost all conscience a long time ago. Uncle Sam has no conscience.

They don't know what morals are. They don't try and eliminate an evil because it's evil, or because it's illegal, or because it's immoral; they eliminate it only when it threatens their existence. So you're wasting your time appealing to the moral conscience of a bankrupt man like Uncle Sam. If he had a conscience, he'd straighten this thing out with no more pressure being put upon him. So it is not necessary to change the white man's mind. We have to change our own mind. You can't change his mind about us. We've got to change our own minds about each other. We have to see each other with new eyes. We have to see each other as brothers and sisters. We have to come together with warmth so we can develop unity and harmony that's necessary to get this problem solved ourselves. How can we do this? How can we avoid jealousy? How can we avoid the suspicion and the divisions that exist in the community? I'll tell you how.

I have watched how Billy Graham comes into a city, spreading what he calls the gospel of Christ, which is only white nationalism. That's what he is. Billy Graham is a white nationalist; I'm a black nationalist. But since it's the natural tendency for leaders to be jealous and look upon a powerful figure like Graham with suspicion and envy, how is it possible for him to come into a city and get all the cooperation of the church leaders? Don't think because they're church leaders that they don't have weaknesses that make them envious and jealous—no, everybody's got it. It's not an accident that when they want to choose a cardinal, as Pope I over there in Rome, they get in a closet so you can't hear them cussing and fighting and carrying on.

Billy Graham comes in preaching the gospel of Christ. He evangelizes the gospel. He stirs everybody up, but he never tries to start a church. If he came in trying to start a church, all the churches would be against him. So, he just comes in talking about Christ and tells everybody who gets Christ to go to any church where Christ is; and in this way the church cooperates with him. So we're going to take a page from his book.

Our gospel is black nationalism. We're not trying to threaten the existence of any organization, but we're spreading the gospel of black nationalism. Anywhere there's a church that is also preaching and practicing the gospel of black nationalism, join that church. If the NAACP is preaching and practicing the gospel of black nationalism, join the NAACP. If CORE is spreading and practicing the gospel of black nationalism, join CORE. Join any organization that has a gospel that's for the uplift of the black man. And when you get into it and see them pussyfooting or compromising, pull out of it because that's not black nationalism. We'll find another one.

And in this manner, the organizations will increase in number and in quantity and in quality, and by August, it is then our intention to have a black nationalist convention which will consist of delegates from all over the country who are interested in the political, economic and social philosophy of black nationalism. After these delegates convene, we will hold a seminar; we will hold discussions; we will listen to everyone. We want to hear new ideas and new solutions and new answers. And at that time, if we see fit then to form a black nationalist party, we'll form a black nationalist party. If it's necessary to form a black nationalist army, we'll form a black nationalist army. It'll be the ballot or the bullet. It'll be liberty or it'll be death.

It's time for you and me to stop sitting in this country, letting some cracker senators, Northern crackers and Southern crackers, sit there in Washington, DC, and come to a conclusion in their mind that you and I are supposed to have civil rights. There's no white man going to tell me anything about my rights. Brothers and sisters, always remember, if it doesn't take senators and congressmen and presidential proclamations to give freedom to the white man, it is not necessary for legislation or proclamation or Supreme Court decisions to give freedom to the black man. You let that white man know, if this is a country of freedom, let it be a country of freedom; and if it's not a country of freedom, change it.

We will work with anybody, anywhere, at any time, who is genuinely interested in tackling the problem head-on, nonviolently as long as the enemy is nonviolent, but violent when the enemy gets violent. We'll work with you on the voter-registration drive, we'll work with you on rent strikes, we'll work with you on school boycotts; I don't believe in any kind of integration; I'm not even worried about it, because I know you're not going to get it anyway; you're not going to get it because you're afraid to die; you've got to be ready to die if you try and force yourself on the white man, because he'll get just as violent as those crackers in Mississippi, right here in Cleveland. But we will still work with you on the school boycotts be cause we're against a segregated school system. A segregated school system produces children who, when they graduate, graduate with crippled minds. But this does not mean that a school is segregated because it's all black. A segregated school means a school that is controlled by people who have no real interest in it whatsoever.

Let me explain what I mean. A segregated district or community is a community in which people live, but outsiders control the politics and the economy of that community. They never refer to the white section as a segregated community. It's the all-Negro section that's a segregated community. Why? The white man controls his own school, his own bank, his own economy, his own politics, his own everything, his own community; but he also controls yours. When you're under someone else's control, you're segregated. They'll always give you the lowest or the worst that there is to offer, but it doesn't mean you're segregated just because you have your own. You've got to control your own. Just like the white man has control of his, you need to control yours.

You know the best way to get rid of segregation? The white man is more afraid of separation than he is of integration.

Segregation means that he puts you away from him, but not far enough for you to be out of his jurisdiction; separation means you're gone. And the white man will integrate faster than he'll let you separate. So we will work with you against the segregated school system because it's criminal, because it is absolutely destructive, in every way imaginable, to the minds of the children who have to be exposed to that type of crippling education.

Last but not least, I must say this concerning the great controversy over rifles and shotguns. The only thing that I've ever said is that in areas where the government has proven itself either unwilling or unable to defend the lives and the property of Negroes, it's time for Negroes to defend themselves. Article number two of the constitutional amendments provides you and me the right to own a rifle or a shotgun. It is constitutionally legal to own a shotgun or a rifle. This doesn't mean you're going to get a rifle and form battalions and go out looking for white folks, although you'd be within your rights—I mean, you'd be justified; but that would be illegal and we don't do anything illegal. If the white man doesn't want the black man buying rifles and shotguns, then let the government do its job.

That's all. And don't let the white man come to you and ask you what you think about what Malcolm says—why, you old Uncle Tom. He would never ask you if he thought you were going to say, "Amen!" No, he is making a Tom out of you." So, this doesn't mean forming rifle clubs and going out looking for people, but it is time, in 1964, if you are a man, to let that man know. If he's not going to do his job in running the government and providing you and me with the protection that our taxes are supposed to be for, since he spends all those billions for his defense budget, he certainly can't begrudge you and me spending $12 or $15 for a single-shot, or double-action. I hope you understand. Don't go out shooting people, but any time—brothers and sisters, and especially the men in this audience; some of you wearing Congressional Medals of Honor, with shoulders this wide, chests this big, muscles that big—any time you and I sit around and read where they bomb a church and murder in cold blood, not some grownups, but four little girls while they were praying to the same God the white man taught them to pray to, and you and I see the government go down and can't find who did it.

Why, this man—he can find Eichmann hiding down in Argentina somewhere. Let two or three American soldiers, who are minding somebody else's business way over in South Vietnam, get killed, and he'll send battleships, sticking his nose in their business. He wanted to send troops down to Cuba and make them have what he calls free elections—this old cracker who doesn't have free elections in his own country.

No, if you never see me another time in your life, if I die in the morning, I'll die saying one thing: the ballot or the bullet, the ballot or the bullet.

If a Negro in 1964 has to sit around and wait for some cracker senator to filibuster when it comes to the rights of black people, why, you and I should hang our heads in shame. You talk about a march on Washington in 1963, you haven't seen anything. There's some more going down in '64.

And this time they're not going like they went last year. They're not going singing "We Shall Overcome." They're not going with white friends. They're not going with placards already painted for them. They're not going with round-trip tickets. They're going with one way tickets. And if they don't want that non-nonviolent army going down there, tell them to bring the filibuster to a halt.

The black nationalists aren't going to wait. Lyndon B. Johnson is the head of the Democratic Party. If he's for civil rights, let him go into the Senate next week and declare himself. Let him go in there right now and declare himself. Let him go in there and denounce the Southern branch of his party. Let him go in there right now and take a moral stand—right now, not later. Tell him, don't wait until election time. If he waits too long, brothers and sisters, he will be responsible for letting a condition develop in this country which will create a climate that will bring seeds up out of the ground with vegetation on the end of them looking like something these people never dreamed of. In 1964, it's the ballot or the bullet.

Thank you.

A Time for Choosing

and

We Will Be a City Upon a Hill

Ronald Reagan

Ronald Reagan (1911–2004), the 40th President of the United States, was nicknamed "The Great Communicator" for his ability to convey to all levels of society the most fundamental principles and values of the nation: self-government, limited government, and individual liberty founded on individual responsibility. Allied with Prime Minister Margaret Thatcher of England and Pope John Paul II, Reagan led the free world to a level of strength and resolve that contributed to the disintegration of the Soviet Union and of the worldwide Communist movement. He was the last president in recent memory able to unite a vast majority of Americans of all political persuasions under the shared conviction that America is "the last best hope of man on earth."

We have included here two speeches that Reagan gave prior to becoming President.

He delivered "A Time for Choosing" several times at various speaking engagements. In 1964 he gave the speech on television in support of Barry Goldwater's campaign for president. The version reproduced here is from that television broadcast. While Goldwater did not succeed in his run for the presidency, this speech did establish Reagan's own political visibility.

Three years later, Reagan became the governor of California. In 1974 he decided not to seek re-election as governor. That same year he gave an address at the first Conservative Political Action Conference, "We Will Be a City Upon a Hill." In 1976 he ran for President of the United States. Though his first run was unsuccessful, he ran again in 1980 and was elected twice, serving as President from 1981 to 1989.

A Time for Choosing

Stump speech for the Goldwater Presidential Campaign, delivered several times in 1964

I am going to talk of controversial things. I make no apology for this.

It's time we asked ourselves if we still know the freedoms intended for us by the Founding Fathers. James Madison said, "We base all our experiments on the capacity of mankind for self government."

This idea—that government was beholden to the people, that it had no other source of power—is still the newest, most unique idea in all the long history of man's relation to man. This is the issue of this election: Whether we believe in our capacity for self-government or whether we abandon the American Revolution and confess that a little intellectual elite in a far-distant capital can plan our lives for us better than we can plan them ourselves.

You and I are told we must choose between a left or right, but I suggest there is no such thing as a left or right. There is only an up or down. Up to man's age-old dream—the maximum of individual freedom consistent with order—or down to the ant heap of totalitarianism. Regardless of their sincerity, their humanitarian motives, those who would sacrifice freedom for security have embarked on this downward path. Plutarch warned, "The real destroyer of the liberties of the people is he who spreads among them bounties, donations and benefits."

The Founding Fathers knew a government can't control the economy without controlling people. And they knew when a government sets out to do that, it must use force and coercion to achieve its purpose. So we have come to a time for choosing.

Public servants say, always with the best of intentions, "What greater service we could render if only we had a little more money and a little more power." But the truth is that outside of its legitimate function, government does nothing as well or as economically as the private sector.

Yet any time you and I question the schemes of the do-gooders, we're denounced as being opposed to their humanitarian goals. It seems impossible to legitimately debate their solutions

739

with the assumption that all of us share the desire to help the less fortunate. They tell us we're always "against," never "for" anything.

We are for a provision that destitution should not follow unemployment by reason of old age, and to that end we have accepted Social Security as a step toward meeting the problem. However, we are against those entrusted with this program when they practice deception regarding its fiscal shortcomings, when they charge that any criticism of the program means that we want to end payments. . . .

We are for aiding our allies by sharing our material blessings with nations which share our fundamental beliefs, but we are against doling out money government to government, creating bureaucracy, if not socialism, all over the world.

We need true tax reform that will at least make a start toward restoring for our children the American Dream that wealth is denied to no one, that each individual has the right to fly as high as his strength and ability will take him. . . . But we cannot have such reform while our tax policy is engineered by people who view the tax as a means of achieving changes in our social structure. . . .

Have we the courage and the will to face up to the immorality and discrimination of the progressive tax, and demand a return to traditional proportionate taxation? . . . Today in our country the tax collector's share is 37 cents of every dollar earned. Freedom has never been so fragile, so close to slipping from our grasp.

Are you willing to spend time studying the issues, making yourself aware, and then conveying that information to family and friends? Will you resist the temptation to get a government handout for your community? Realize that the doctor's fight against socialized medicine is your fight. We can't socialize the doctors without socializing the patients. Recognize that government invasion of public power is eventually an assault upon your own business. If some among you fear taking a stand because you are afraid of reprisals from customers, clients, or even government, recognize that you are just feeding the crocodile hoping he'll eat you last.

If all of this seems like a great deal of trouble, think what's at stake. We are faced with the most evil enemy mankind has known in his long climb from the swamp to the stars. There can be no security anywhere in the free world if there is no fiscal and economic stability within the United States. Those who ask us to trade our freedom for the soup kitchen of the welfare state are architects of a policy of accommodation.

They say the world has become too complex for simple answers. They are wrong. There are no easy answers, but there are simple answers. We must have the courage to do what we know is morally right. Winston Churchill said that "the destiny of man is not measured by material computation. When great forces are on the move in the world, we learn we are spirits—not animals." And he said, "There is something going on in time and space, and beyond time and space, which, whether we like it or not, spells duty."

You and I have a rendezvous with destiny. We will preserve for our children this, the last best hope of man on earth, or we will sentence them to take the first step into a thousand years of darkness. If we fail, at least let our children and our children's children say of us we justified our brief moment here. We did all that could be done.

We Will Be a City Upon a Hill

Address at the first Conservative Political Action Conference, delivered January 25, 1974

There are three men here tonight I am very proud to introduce. It was a year ago this coming February when this country had its spirits lifted as they have never been lifted in many years. This happened when planes began landing on American soil and in the Philippines, bringing back men who had lived with honor for many miserable years in North Vietnam prisons. Three of those men are here tonight, John McCain, Bill Lawrence and Ed Martin. It is an honor to be here tonight. I am proud that you asked me and I feel more than a little humble in the presence of this distinguished company.

There are men here tonight who, through their wisdom, their foresight and their courage, have earned the right to be regarded as prophets of our philosophy. Indeed they are prophets of our times. In years past when others were silent or too blind to the facts, they spoke up forcefully and fearlessly for what they believed to be right. A decade has passed since Barry Goldwater walked a lonely path across this land reminding us that even a land as rich as ours can't go on forever borrowing against the future, leaving a legacy of debt for another generation and causing a runaway inflation to erode the savings and reduce the standard of living. Voices have been raised trying to rekindle in our country all of the great ideas and principles which set this nation apart from all the others that preceded it, but louder and more strident voices utter easily sold cliches.

Cartoonists with acid-tipped pens portray some of the reminders of our heritage and our destiny as old-fashioned. They say that we are trying to retreat into a past that actually never existed. Looking to the past in an effort to keep our country from repeating the errors of history is termed by them as "taking the country back to McKinley." Of course, I never found that was so bad—under McKinley we freed Cuba. On the span of history, we are still thought of as a young upstart country celebrating soon only our second century as a nation, and yet we are the oldest continuing republic in the world.

I thought that tonight, rather than talking on the subjects you are discussing, or trying to find something new to say, it might be appropriate to reflect a bit on our heritage.

You can call it mysticism if you want to, but I have always believed that there was some divine plan that placed this great continent between two oceans to be sought out by those who were possessed of an abiding love of freedom and a special kind of courage.

This was true of those who pioneered the great wilderness in the beginning of this country, as it is also true of those later immigrants who were willing to leave the land of their birth and come to a land where even the language was unknown to them. Call it chauvinistic, but our heritage does set us apart. Some years ago a writer, who happened to be an avid student of history, told me a story about that day in the little hall in Philadelphia where honorable men, hard-pressed by a King who was flouting the very law they were willing to obey, debated whether they should take the fateful step of declaring their independence from that king. I was told by this man that the story could be found in the writings of Jefferson. I confess, I never researched or made an effort to verify it. Perhaps it is only legend. But story, or legend, he described the atmosphere, the strain, the debate, and that as men for the first time faced the consequences of such an irretrievable act, the walls resounded with the dread word of treason and its price—the gallows and the headman's axe. As the day wore on the issue hung in the balance, and then, according to the story, a man rose in the small gallery. He was not a young man and was obviously calling on all the energy he could muster. Citing the grievances that had brought them to this moment, he said, "Sign that parchment. They may turn every tree into a gallows, every home into a grave and yet the words of that parchment can never die. For the mechanic in his workshop, they will be words of hope, to the slave in the mines—freedom." And he added, "If my hands were freezing in death, I would sign that parchment with my last ounce of strength. Sign, sign if the next moment the noose is around your neck, sign even if the hall is ringing with the sound of headman's axe, for that parchment will be the textbook of freedom, the bible of the rights of man forever." And then it is said he fell back exhausted. But 56 delegates, swept by his eloquence, signed the Declaration of Independence, a document destined to be as immortal as any work of man can be. And according to the story, when they turned to thank him for his timely oratory, he could not be found nor were there any who knew who he was or how he had come in or gone out through the locked and guarded doors.

Well, as I say, whether story or legend, the signing of the document that day in Independence Hall was miracle enough. Fifty-six men, a little band so unique—we have never seen their like since—pledged their lives, their fortunes and their sacred honor. Sixteen gave their lives, most gave their fortunes and all of them preserved their sacred honor. What manner of men were they? Certainly they were not an unwashed, revolutionary rabble, nor were they adventurers in a heroic mood. Twenty-four were lawyers and jurists, 11 were merchants and tradesmen, nine were farmers. They were men who would achieve security but valued freedom more.

And what price did they pay? John Hart was driven from the side of his desperately ill wife. After more than a year of living almost as an animal in the forest and in caves, he returned to find his wife had died and his children had vanished. He never saw them again, his property was destroyed and he died of a broken heart—but with no regret, only pride in the part he had played that day in Independence Hall. Carter Braxton of Virginia lost all his ships—they were sold to pay his debts. He died in rags. So it was with Ellery, Clymer, Hall, Walton, Gwinnett, Rutledge, Morris, Livingston, and Middleton. Nelson, learning that Cornwallis was using his home for a headquarters, personally begged Washington to fire on him and destroy his home—he died bankrupt. It has never been reported that any of these men ever expressed bitterness or renounced their action as not worth the price. Fifty-six rank-and-file, ordinary citizens had founded a nation that grew from sea to shining sea, five million farms, quiet villages, cities that never sleep—all done without an area re-development plan, urban renewal or a rural legal assistance program.

Now we are a nation of 211 million people with a pedigree that includes blood lines from every corner of the world. We have shed that American-melting-pot blood in every corner of the world, usually in defense of someone's freedom. Those who remained of that remarkable band we call our Founding Fathers tied up some of the loose ends about a dozen years after the Revolution. It had been the first revolution in all man's history that did not just exchange one set of rulers for another. This had been a philosophical revolution. The culmination of men's dreams for 6,000 years were formalized with the Constitution, probably the most unique document ever drawn in the long history of man's relation to man. I know there have been other constitutions, new ones are being drawn today by newly emerging nations. Most of them, even the one of the Soviet Union, contain many of the same guarantees as our own Constitution, and still there is a difference. The difference is so subtle that we often overlook it, but it is so great that it tells the whole story. Those other constitutions say, "Government grants you these rights," and ours says, "You are born with these rights, they are yours by the grace of God, and no government on earth can take them from you."

Lord Acton of England, who once said, "Power corrupts, and absolute power corrupts absolutely," would say of that document, "They had solved with astonishing ease and unduplicated success two problems which had heretofore baffled the capacity of the most enlightened nations. They had contrived a system of federal government which prodigiously increased national power and yet respected local liberties and authorities, and they had founded it on a principle of equality without surrendering the securities of property or freedom." Never in any society has the preeminence of the individual been so firmly established and given such a priority.

In less than twenty years we would go to war because the God-given rights of the American sailors, as defined in the Constitution, were being violated by a foreign power. We served notice then on the world that all of us together would act collectively to safeguard the rights of even the least among us. But still, in an older, cynical world, they were not convinced. The great powers of Europe still had the idea that one day this great continent would be open again to colonizing and they would come over and divide us up.

In the meantime, men who yearned to breathe free were making their way to our shores. Among them was a young refugee from the Austro-Hungarian Empire. He had been a leader in an attempt to free Hungary from Austrian rule. The attempt had failed and he fled to escape execution. In America, this young Hungarian, Koscha by name, became an importer by trade and took out his first citizenship papers. One day, business took him to a Mediterranean port. There was a large Austrian warship under the command of an admiral in the harbor. He had a manservant with him. He had described to this manservant what the flag of his new country looked like. Word was passed to the Austrian warship that this revolutionary was there and in the night he was kidnapped and taken aboard that large ship. This man's servant, desperate, walking up and down the harbor, suddenly spied a flag that resembled the description he had heard. It was a small American war sloop. He went aboard and told Captain Ingraham, of that war sloop, his story. Captain Ingraham went to the American Consul. When the American Consul learned that Koscha had only taken out his first citizenship papers, the consul washed his hands of the incident. Captain Ingraham said, "I am the senior officer in this port and I believe, under my oath of my office, that I owe this man the protection of our flag."

He went aboard the Austrian warship and demanded to see their prisoner, our citizen. The Admiral was amused, but they brought the man on deck. He was in chains and had been badly beaten. Captain Ingraham said, "I can hear him better without those chains," and the chains were removed. He walked over and said to Koscha, "I will ask you one question; consider your answer carefully. Do you ask the protection of the American flag?" Koscha nodded dumbly, "Yes," and the Captain said, "You shall have it." He went back and told the frightened consul what he had done. Later in the day three more Austrian ships sailed into harbor. It looked as though the four were getting ready to leave. Captain Ingraham sent a junior officer over to the Austrian flag ship to tell the Admiral that any attempt to leave that harbor with our citizen aboard would be resisted with appropriate force. He said that he would expect a satisfactory answer by four o'clock that afternoon. As the hour neared they looked at each other through the glasses. As it struck four he had them roll the cannons into the ports and had them light the tapers with which they would set off the cannons—one little sloop. Suddenly the lookout tower called out and said, "They are lowering a boat," and they rowed Koscha over to the little American ship.

Captain Ingraham then went below and wrote his letter of resignation to the United States Navy. In it he said, "I did what I thought my oath of office required, but if I have embarrassed my country in any way, I resign." His resignation was refused in the United States Senate with these words: "This battle that was never fought may turn out to be the most important battle in our Nation's history." Incidentally, there is to this day, and I hope there always will be, a USS Ingraham in the United States Navy.

I did not tell that story out of any desire to be narrowly chauvinistic or to glorify aggressive militarism, but it is an example of government meeting its highest responsibility.

In recent years we have been treated to a rash of noble-sounding phrases. Some of them sound good, but they don't hold up under close analysis. Take for instance the slogan so frequently uttered by the young senator from Massachusetts, "The greatest good for the greatest number." Certainly under that slogan, no modern day Captain Ingraham would risk even the smallest craft and crew for a single citizen. Every dictator who ever lived has justified the enslavement of his people on the theory of what was good for the majority.

We are not a warlike people. Nor is our history filled with tales of aggressive adventures and imperialism, which might come as a shock to some of the placard painters in our modern demonstrations. The lesson of Vietnam, I think, should be that never again will young Americans be asked to fight and possibly die for a cause unless that cause is so meaningful that we, as a nation, pledge our full resources to achieve victory as quickly as possible.

I realize that such a pronouncement, of course, would possibly be laying one open to the charge of warmongering—but that would also be ridiculous. My generation has paid a higher price and has fought harder for freedom than any generation that had ever lived. We have known four wars in a single lifetime. All were horrible, all could have been avoided if at a particular moment in time we had made it plain that we subscribed to the words of John Stuart Mill when he said that "war is an ugly thing, but not the ugliest of things."

The decayed and degraded state of moral and patriotic feeling which thinks nothing is worth a war is worse. The man who has nothing which he cares about more than his personal safety is a miserable creature and has no chance of being free unless made and kept so by the exertions of better men than himself.

The widespread disaffection with things military is only a part of the philosophical division in our land today. I must say to you who have recently, or presently are still receiving an education, I am awed by your powers of resistance. I have some knowledge of the attempts that have been made in many classrooms and lecture halls to persuade you that there is little to admire in America. For the second time in this century, capitalism and the free enterprise are under assault. Privately owned business is blamed for spoiling the environment, exploiting the worker and seducing, if not outright raping, the customer. Those who make the charge have the solution, of course—government regulation and control. We may never get around to explaining how citizens who are so gullible that they can be suckered into buying cereal or soap that they don't need and would not be good for them, can at the same time be astute enough to choose representatives in government to which they would entrust the running of their lives.

Not too long ago, a poll was taken on 2,500 college campuses in this country. Thousands and thousands of responses were obtained. Overwhelmingly, 65, 70, and 75 percent of the students found business responsible, as I have said before, for the things that were wrong in this country. That same number said that government was the solution and should take over the management and the control of private business. Eighty percent of the respondents said they wanted government to keep its paws out of their private lives.

We are told every day that the assembly-line worker is becoming a dull-witted robot and that mass production results in standardization. Well, there isn't a socialist country in the world that would not give its copy of Karl Marx for our standardization.

Standardization means production for the masses and the assembly line means more leisure for the worker—freedom from backbreaking and mind-dulling drudgery that man had known for centuries past. Karl Marx did not abolish child labor or free the women from working in the coal mines in England – the steam engine and modern machinery did that.

Unfortunately, the disciples of the new order have had a hand in determining too much policy in recent decades. Government has grown in size and power and cost through the New Deal, the Fair Deal, the New Frontier and the Great Society. It costs more for government today than a family pays for food, shelter and clothing combined. Not even the Office of Management and Budget knows how many boards, commissions, bureaus and agencies there are in the federal government, but the federal registry, listing their regulations, is just a few pages short of being as big as the Encyclopedia Britannica.

During the Great Society we saw the greatest growth of this government. There were eight cabinet departments and 12 independent agencies to administer the federal health program. There were 35 housing programs and 20 transportation projects. Public utilities had to cope with 27 different agencies on just routine business. There were 192 installations and nine departments with 1,000 projects having to do with the field of pollution.

One Congressman found the federal government was spending 4 billion dollars on research in its own laboratories but did not know where they were, how many people were working in them, or what they were doing. One of the research projects was "The Demography of Happiness," and for 249,000 dollars we found that "people who make more money are happier than people who make less, young people are happier than old people, and people who are healthier are happier than people who are sick." For 15 cents they could have bought an Almanac and read the old bromide, "It's better to be rich, young and healthy, than poor, old and sick."

The course that you have chosen is far more in tune with the hopes and aspirations of our people than are those who would sacrifice freedom for some fancied security.

Standing on the tiny deck of the Arabella in 1630 off the Massachusetts coast, John Winthrop said, "We will be as a city upon a hill. The eyes of all people are upon us, so that if we deal falsely with our God in this work we have undertaken and so cause Him to withdraw His present help from us, we shall be made a story and a byword throughout the world." Well, we have not dealt falsely with our God, even if He is temporarily suspended from the classroom.

When I was born my life expectancy was 10 years less than I have already lived – that's a cause of regret for some people in California, I know. Ninety percent of Americans at that time lived beneath what is considered the poverty line today, three-quarters lived in what is considered substandard housing. Today each of those figures is less than 10 percent. We have increased our life expectancy by wiping out, almost totally, diseases that still ravage mankind in other parts of the world. I doubt if the young people here tonight know the names of some of the diseases that were commonplace when we were growing up. We have more doctors per thousand people than any nation in the world. We have more hospitals than any nation in the world.

When I was your age, believe it or not, none of us knew that we even had a racial problem. When I graduated from college and became a radio sport announcer, broadcasting major league baseball, I didn't have a Hank Aaron or a Willie Mays to talk about. The Spaulding Guide said baseball was a game for Caucasian gentlemen. Some of us then began editorializing and campaigning against this. Gradually we campaigned against all those other areas where the constitutional rights of a large segment of our citizenry were being denied. We have not finished the job. We still have a long way to go, but we have made more progress in a few years than we have made in more than a century.

One-third of all the students in the world who are pursuing higher education are doing so in the United States. The percentage of our young Negro community that is going to college is greater than the percentage of whites in any other country in the world.

One-half of all the economic activity in the entire history of man has taken place in this republic. We have distributed our wealth more widely among our people than any society known to man. Americans work less hours for a higher standard of living than any other people. Ninety-five percent of all our families have an adequate daily intake of nutrients—and a part of the five percent that don't are trying to lose weight! Ninety-nine percent have gas or electric refrigeration, 92 percent have televisions, and an equal number have telephones. There are 120 million cars on our streets and highways—and all of them are on the street at once when you are trying to get home at night. But isn't this just proof of our materialism—the very thing that we are charged with? Well, we also have more churches, more libraries, we support voluntarily more symphony orchestras, and opera companies, non-profit theaters, and publish more books than all the other nations of the world put together.

Somehow America has bred a kindliness into our people unmatched anywhere, as has been pointed out in that best-selling record by a Canadian journalist. We are not a sick society. A sick society could not produce the men that set foot on the moon, or who are now circling the earth above us in the Skylab. A sick society bereft of morality and courage did not produce the men who went through those years of torture and captivity in Vietnam. Where did we find such men? They are typical of this land as the Founding Fathers were typical. We found them in our streets, in the offices, the shops and the working places of our country and on the farms.

We cannot escape our destiny, nor should we try to do so. The leadership of the free world was thrust upon us two centuries ago in that little hall of Philadelphia. In the days following World War II, when the economic strength and power of America was all that stood between the world and the return to the dark ages, Pope Pius XII said, "The American people have a great genius for splendid and unselfish actions. Into the hands of America God has placed the destinies of an afflicted mankind."

We are indeed, and we are today, the last best hope of man on earth.

A World Split Apart

and

Godlessness, the First Step Toward the Gulag

Aleksandr Solzhenitsyn

Aleksandr Solzhenitsyn (1918–2008) was a Russian historian and novelist and an outspoken critic of the Communist totalitarian rule in the Soviet Union. He was sent to prison labor camps and then internal exile for anti-Stalin comments made in a private letter. In 1962 the publication of One Day in the Life of Ivan Denisovich, *a fictionalized account of Solzhenitsyn's time in forced-labor camps, was approved by Soviet Premier Nikita Krushchev. After Krushchev's removal, repression increased and Solzhenitsyn became a non-person. In 1974 he was expelled from the Soviet Union and exiled to the West. He lived first in Europe and then in the U.S., surviving negative Soviet propaganda and several attempts on his life by the KGB. With the fall of the Soviet Union he returned to Russia. During his lifetime Solzhenitsyn published over 30 novels, short stories, and speeches, and is best known in the West for* One Day in the Life of Ivan Denisovich, Cancer Ward, *and* The Gulag Archipelago. *In 1970 he was awarded the Nobel Prize in literature, which at the time he could not accept in person for fear he would not be permitted to return to Russia; he received it in Stockholm in 1974 after his exile. In 1983 he was honored with the Templeton Prize, given to "a living person who has made an exceptional contribution to affirming life's spiritual dimension," and gave as his acceptance speech the second work reproduced here.*

A World Split Apart

Commencement address at Harvard University, delivered June 8, 1978; translated by Irina Alberti.

I am sincerely happy to be here with you on the occasion of the 327th commencement of this old and illustrious university. My congratulations and best wishes to all of today's graduates.

Harvard's motto is "VERITAS." Many of you have already found out and others will find out in the course of their lives that truth eludes us as soon as our concentration begins to flag, all the while leaving the illusion that we are continuing to pursue it. This is the source of much discord. Also, truth seldom is sweet; it is almost invariably bitter. A measure of truth is included in my speech today, but I offer it as a friend, not as an adversary.

Three years ago in the United States I said certain things that were rejected and appeared unacceptable. Today, however, many people agree with what I said.

The split in today's world is perceptible even to a hasty glance. Any of our contemporaries readily identifies two world powers, each of them already capable of destroying each other. However, the understanding of the split too often is limited to this political conception: the illusion according to which danger may be abolished through successful diplomatic negotiations or by achieving a balance of armed forces. The truth is that the split is both more profound and more alienating, that the rifts are more numerous than one can see at first glance. These deep manifold splits bear the danger of equally manifold disaster for all of us, in accordance with the ancient truth that a kingdom—in this case, our Earth—divided against itself cannot stand.

There is the concept of the Third World: thus, we already have three worlds. Undoubtedly, however, the number is even greater; we are just too far away to see. Every ancient and deeply rooted self-contained culture, especially if it is spread over a wide part of the earth's surface, constitutes a self-contained world, full of riddles and surprises to Western thinking. As a minimum, we must include in this China, India, the Muslim world, and Africa, if indeed we accept the approximation of viewing the latter two as uniform.

For one thousand years Russia belonged to such a category, although Western thinking systematically committed the mistake of denying its special character and therefore never understood it, just as today the West does not understand Russia in Communist captivity. And while it may be that in past years Japan has increasingly become, in effect, a Far West, drawing ever closer to Western ways (I am no judge here), Israel, I think, should not be reckoned as part of the West, if only because of the decisive circumstance that its state system is fundamentally linked to its religion.

How short a time ago, relatively, the small world of modern Europe was easily seizing colonies all over the globe, not only without anticipating any real resistance, but usually with contempt for any possible values in the conquered people's approach to life. It all seemed an overwhelming success, with no geographic limits. Western society expanded in a triumph of human independence and power. And all of a sudden the twentieth century brought the clear realization of this society's fragility.

We now see that the conquests proved to be short lived and precarious (and this, in turn, points to defects in the Western view of the world which led to these conquests). Relations with the former colonial world now have switched to the opposite extreme and the Western world often exhibits an excess of obsequiousness, but it is difficult yet to estimate the size of the bill which former colonial countries will present to the West and it is difficult to predict whether the surrender not only of its last colonies, but of everything it owns, will be sufficient for the West to clear this account.

But the persisting blindness of superiority continues to hold the belief that all the vast regions of our planet should develop and mature to the level of contemporary Western systems, the best in theory and the most attractive in practice; that all those other worlds are but temporarily prevented (by wicked leaders or by severe crises or by their own barbarity and incomprehension) from pursuing Western pluralistic democracy and adopting the Western way of life. Countries are judged on the merit of their progress in that direction. But in fact such a conception is a fruit of Western incomprehension of the essence of other worlds, a result of mistakenly measuring them all with a Western yardstick.

The real picture of our planet's development bears little resemblance to all this.

The anguish of a divided world gave birth to the theory of convergence between the leading Western countries and the Soviet Union. It is a soothing theory which overlooks the fact that these worlds are not evolving toward each other and that neither one can be transformed into the other without violence. Besides, convergence inevitably means acceptance of the other side's defects, too. and this can hardly suit anyone.

If I were today addressing an audience in my country, in my examination of the overall pattern of the world's rifts I would have concentrated on the calamities of the East. But since my forced exile in the West has now lasted four years and since my audience is a Western one, I think it may be of greater interest to concentrate on certain aspects of the contemporary West, such as I see them.

A decline in courage may be the most striking feature that an outside observer notices in the West today. The Western world has lost its civic courage, both as a whole and separately, in each country, in each government, in each political party, and, of course, in the United Nations. Such a decline in courage is particularly noticeable among the ruling and intellectual elites, causing an impression of a loss of courage by the entire society. There are many courageous individuals, but they have no determining influence on public life.

Political and intellectual functionaries exhibit this depression, passivity, and perplexity in their actions and in their statements, and even more so in their self-serving rationales as to how realistic, reasonable, and intellectually and even morally justified it is to base state policies on weakness and cowardice. And the decline in courage, at times attaining what could be termed a lack of manhood, is ironically emphasized by occasional outbursts and inflexibility on the part of those same functionaries when dealing with weak governments and with countries that lack support, or with doomed currents which clearly cannot offer resistance. But they get tongue-tied and paralyzed when they deal with powerful governments and threatening forces, with aggressors and international terrorists.

Must one point out that from ancient times a decline in courage has been considered the first symptom of the end?

When the modern Western states were being formed, it was proclaimed as a principle that governments are meant to serve man and that man lives in order to be free and pursue happiness. (See, for example, the American Declaration of Independence.) Now at last during past decades technical and social progress has permitted the realization of such aspirations: the welfare state.

Every citizen has been granted the desired freedom and material goods in such quantity and in such quality as to guarantee in theory the achievement of happiness, in the debased sense of the word which has come into being during those same decades. (In the process, however, one psychological detail has been overlooked: the constant desire to have still more things and a still better life and the struggle to this end imprint many Western faces with worry and even depression, though it is customary to carefully conceal such feelings. This active and tense competition comes to dominate all human thought and does not in the least open a way to free spiritual development.)

The individual's independence from many types of state pressure has been guaranteed; the majority of the people have been granted well-being to an extent their fathers and grandfathers could not even dream about; it has become possible to raise young people according to these ideals, preparing them for and summoning them toward physical bloom, happiness, and leisure, the possession of material goods, money, and leisure, toward an almost unlimited freedom in the choice of pleasures. So who should now renounce all this, why and for the sake of what should one risk one's precious life in defense of the common good and particularly in the nebulous case when the security of one's nation must be defended in an as yet distant land?

Even biology tells us that a high degree of habitual well-being is not advantageous to a living organism. Today, well-being in the life of Western society has begun to take off its pernicious mask.

Western society has chosen for itself the organization best suited to its purposes and one I might call legalistic. The limits of human rights and rightness are determined by a system of laws; such limits are very broad. People in the West have acquired considerable skill in using, interpreting, and manipulating law (though laws tend to be too complicated for an average person to understand without the help of an expert). Every conflict is solved according to the letter of the law and this is considered to be the ultimate solution.

If one is risen from a legal point of view, nothing more is required, nobody may mention that one could still not be right, and urge self-restraint or a renunciation of these rights, call for sacrifice and selfless risk: this would simply sound absurd. Voluntary self-restraint is almost unheard of: everybody strives toward further expansion to the extreme limit of the legal frames. (An oil company is legally blameless when it buys up an invention of a new type of energy in order to prevent its use. A food product manufacturer is legally blameless when he poisons his produce to make it last longer: after all, people are free not to purchase it.)

I have spent all my life under a Communist regime and I will tell you that a society without any objective legal scale is a terrible one indeed. But a society based on the letter of the law and never reaching any higher fails to take full advantage of the full range of human possibilities. The letter of the law is too cold and formal to have a beneficial influence on society. Whenever the tissue of life is woven of legalistic relationships, this creates an atmosphere of spiritual mediocrity that paralyzes man's noblest impulses.

And it will be simply impossible to bear up to the trials of this threatening century with nothing but the supports of a legalistic structure.

Today's Western society has revealed the inequality between the freedom for good deeds and the freedom for evil deeds. A statesman who wants to achieve something highly constructive for his country has to move cautiously and even timidly; thousands of hasty (and irresponsible) critics cling to him at all times; he is constantly rebuffed by parliament and the press. He has to prove that his every step is well founded and absolutely flawless. Indeed, an outstanding, truly great person who has unusual and unexpected initiatives in mind does not get any chance to assert himself; dozens of traps will be set for him from the beginning. Thus mediocrity triumphs under the guise of democratic restraints.

It is feasible and easy everywhere to undermine administrative power and it has in fact been drastically weakened in all Western countries. The defense of individual rights has reached such extremes as to make society as a whole defenseless against certain individuals. It is time, in the West, to defend not so much human rights as human obligations.

On the other hand, destructive and irresponsible freedom has been granted boundless space. Society has turned out to have scarce defense against the abyss of human decadence, for example against the misuse of liberty for moral violence against young people, such as motion pictures full of pornography, crime, and horror. This is all considered to be part of freedom and to be counterbalanced, in theory, by the young people's right not to look and not to accept. Life organized legalistically has thus shown its inability to defend itself against the corrosion of evil.

And what shall we say about the dark realms of overt criminality? Legal limits (especially in the United States) are broad enough to encourage not only individual freedom but also some misuse of such freedom. The culprit can go unpunished or obtain undeserved leniency—all with the support of thousands of defenders in the society. When a government earnestly undertakes to root out terrorism, public opinion immediately accuses it of violating the terrorist's civil rights. There is quite a number of such cases.

This tilt of freedom toward evil has come about gradually, but it evidently stems from a humanistic and benevolent concept according to which man—the master of the world—does not bear any evil within himself, and all the defects of life are caused by misguided social systems, which must therefore be corrected. Yet strangely enough, though the best social conditions have been achieved in the West, there still remains a great deal of crime; there even is considerably more of it than in the destitute and lawless Soviet society. (There is a multitude of prisoners in our camps who are termed criminals, but most of them never committed any crime; they merely tried to defend themselves against a lawless state by resorting to means outside the legal framework.)

The press, too, of course, enjoys the widest freedom. (I shall be using the word "press" to include all the media.) But what use does it make of it?

Here again, the overriding concern is not to infringe the letter of the law. There is no true moral responsibility for distortion or disproportion. What sort of responsibility does a journalist or a newspaper have to the readership or to history? If they have misled public opinion by inaccurate information or wrong conclusions, even if they have contributed to mistakes on a state level, do we know of any case of open regret voiced by the same journalist or the same newspaper? No; this would damage sales. A nation may be the worse for such a mistake, but the journalist always gets away with it. It is most likely that he will start writing the exact opposite to his previous statements with renewed aplomb.

Because instant and credible information is required, it becomes necessary to resort to guesswork, rumors, and suppositions to fill in the voids, and none of them will ever be refuted; they settle into the readers' memory. How many hasty, immature, superficial, and misleading judgments are expressed everyday, confusing readers, and then left hanging?

The press can act the role of public opinion or miseducate it. Thus we may see terrorists heroized, or secret matters pertaining to the nation's defense publicly revealed, or we may witness shameless intrusion into the privacy of well-known people according to the slogan "Everyone is entitled to know everything." (But this is a false slogan of a false era; far greater in value is the forfeited right of people not to know, not to have their divine souls stuffed with gossip, nonsense, vain talk. A person who works and leads a meaningful life has no need for this excessive and burdening flow of information.)

Hastiness and superficiality—these are the psychic diseases of the twentieth century and more than anywhere else this is manifested in the press. In-depth analysis of a problem is anathema to the press; it is contrary to its nature. The press merely picks out sensational formulas.

Such as it is, however, the press has become the greatest power within Western countries, exceeding that of the legislature, the executive, and the judiciary. Yet one would like to ask: According to what law has it been elected and to whom is it responsible? In the Communist East, a journalist is frankly appointed as a state official. But who has voted Western journalists into their positions of power, for how long a time, and with what prerogatives?

There is yet another surprise for someone coming from the totalitarian East with its rigorously unified press: One discovers a common trend of preferences within the Western press as a whole (the spirit of the time), generally accepted patterns of judgment, and maybe common corporate interests, the sum effect being not competition but unification. Unrestrained freedom exists for the press, but not for readership, because newspapers mostly transmit in a forceful and emphatic way those opinions which do not too openly contradict their own and that general trend.

Without any censorship in the West, fashionable trends of thought and ideas are fastidiously separated from those that are not fashionable, and the latter, without ever being forbidden have little chance of finding their way into periodicals or books or being heard in colleges. Your scholars are free in the legal sense, but they are hemmed in by the idols of the prevailing fad. There is no open violence, as in the East; however, a selection dictated by fashion and the need to accommodate mass standards frequently prevents the most independent-minded persons from contributing to public life and gives rise to dangerous herd instincts that block dangerous herd development.

In America, I have received letters from highly intelligent persons—maybe a teacher in a faraway small college who could do much for the renewal and salvation of his country, but the country cannot hear him because the media will not provide him with a forum. This gives birth to strong mass prejudices, to a blindness which is perilous in our dynamic era. An example is the self-deluding interpretation of the state of affairs in the contemporary world that functions as a sort of petrified armor around people's minds, to such a degree that human voices from seventeen countries of Eastern Europe and Eastern Asia cannot pierce it. It will be broken only by the inexorable crowbar of events.

I have mentioned a few traits of Western life which surprise and shock a new arrival to this world. The purpose and scope of this speech will not allow me to continue such a survey, in particular to look into the impact of these characteristics on important aspects of a nation's life, such as elementary education, advanced education in the humanities, and art.

It is almost universally recognized that the West shows all the world the way to successful economic development, even though in past years it has been sharply offset by chaotic inflation. However, many people living in the West are dissatisfied with their own society. They despise it or accuse it of no longer being up to the level of maturity by mankind. And this causes many to sway toward socialism, which is a false and dangerous current.

I hope that no one present will suspect me of expressing my partial criticism of the Western system in order to suggest socialism as an alternative. No; with the experience of a country where socialism has been realized, I shall not speak for such an alternative. The mathematician Igor Shafarevich, a member of the Soviet Academy of Science, has written a brilliantly argued book entitled Socialism; this is a penetrating historical analysis demonstrating that socialism of any type and shade leads to a total destruction of the human spirit and to a leveling of mankind into death. Shafarevich's book was published in France almost two years ago and so far no one has been found to refute it. It will shortly be published in English in the U.S.

But should I be asked, instead, whether I would propose the West, such as it is today, as a model to my country, I would frankly have to answer negatively. No, I could not recommend your society as an ideal for the transformation of ours. Through deep suffering, people in our own country have now achieved a spiritual development of such intensity that the Western system in its present state of spiritual exhaustion does not look attractive. Even those characteristics of your life which I have just enumerated are extremely saddening.

A fact which cannot be disputed is the weakening of human personality in the West while in the East it has become firmer and stronger. Six decades for our people and three decades for the people of Eastern Europe; during that time we have been through a spiritual training far in advance of Western experience. The complex and deadly crush of life has produced stronger, deeper, and more interesting personalities than those generated by standardized Western well-being. Therefore, if our society were to be transformed into yours, it would mean an improvement in certain aspects, but also a change for the worse on some particularly significant points.

Of course, a society cannot remain in an abyss of lawlessness, as is the case in our country. But it is also demeaning for it to stay on such a soulless and smooth plane of legalism, as is the case in yours. After the suffering of decades of violence and oppression, the human soul longs for things higher, warmer, and purer than those offered by today's mass living habits, introduced as by a calling card by the revolting invasion of commercial advertising, by TV stupor, and by intolerable music.

All this is visible to numerous observers from all the worlds of our planet. The Western way of life is less and less likely to become the leading model.

There are telltale symptoms by which history gives warning to a threatened or perishing society. Such are, for instance, a decline of the arts or a lack of great statesmen. Indeed, sometimes the warnings are quite explicit and concrete. The center of your democracy and of your culture is left without electric power for a few hours only, and all of a sudden crowds of American citizens start looting and creating havoc. The smooth surface film must be very thin, then, the social system quite unstable and unhealthy.

But the fight for our planet, physical and spiritual, a fight of cosmic proportions, is not a vague matter of the future; it has already started. The forces of Evil have begun their decisive offensive. You can feel their pressure, yet your screens and publications are full of prescribed smiles and raised glasses. What is the joy about?

How has this unfavorable relation of forces come about? How did the West decline from its triumphal march to its present debility? Have there been fatal turns and losses of direction in its development? It does not seem so. The West kept advancing steadily in accordance with its proclaimed social intentions, hand in hand with a dazzling progress in technology. And all of a sudden it found itself in its present state of weakness.

This means that the mistake must be at the root, at the very foundation of thought in modern times. I refer to the prevailing Western view of the world in modern times. I refer to the prevailing Western view of the world which was born in the Renaissance and has found political expression since the Age of Enlightenment. It became the basis for political and social doctrine and could be called rationalistic humanism or humanistic autonomy: the pro-claimed and practiced autonomy of man from any higher force above him. It could also be called anthropocentricity, with man seen as the center of all.

The turn introduced by the Renaissance was probably inevitable historically: the Middle Ages had come to a natural end by exhaustion, having become an intolerable despotic repression of man's physical nature in favor of the spiritual one. But then we recoiled from the spirit and embraced all that is material, excessively and incommensurately. The humanistic way of thinking, which had proclaimed itself our guide, did not admit the existence of intrinsic evil in man, nor did it see any task higher than the attainment of happiness on earth. It started modern Western civilization on the dangerous trend of worshiping man and his material needs.

Everything beyond physical well-being and the accumulation of material goods, all other human requirements and characteristics of a subtle and higher nature, were left outside the area of attention of state and social systems, as if human life did not have any higher meaning. Thus gaps were left open for evil, and its drafts blow freely today. Mere freedom per se does not in the least solve all the problems of human life and even adds a number of new ones.

And yet in early democracies, as in American democracy at the time of its birth, all individual human rights were granted on the ground that man is God's creature. That is, freedom was given to the individual conditionally, in the assumption of his constant religious responsibility. Such was the heritage of the preceding one thousand years. Two hundred or even fifty years ago, it would have seemed quite impossible, in America, that an individual be granted boundless freedom with no purpose, simply for the satisfaction of his whims.

Subsequently, however, all such limitations were eroded everywhere in the West; a total emancipation occurred from the moral heritage of Christian centuries with their great reserves of mercy and sacrifice. State systems were becoming ever more materialistic. The West has finally achieved the rights of man, and even excess, but man's sense of responsibility to God and society has grown dimmer and dimmer. In the past decades, the legalistic selfishness of the Western approach to the world has reached its peak and the world has found itself in a harsh spiritual crisis and a political impasse. All the celebrated technological achievements of progress, including the conquest of outer space, do not redeem the twentieth century's moral poverty, which no one could have imagined even as late as the nineteenth century.

As humanism in its development was becoming more and more materialistic, it also increasingly allowed concepts to be used first by socialism and then by communism, so that Karl Marx was able to say, in 1844, that "communism is naturalized humanism."

This statement has proved to be not entirely unreasonable. One does not see the same stones in the foundations of an eroded humanism and of any type of socialism: boundless materialism; freedom from religion and religious responsibility (which under Communist regimes attains the stage of antireligious dictatorship); concentration on social structures with an allegedly scientific approach. (This last is typical of both the Age of Enlightenment and of Marxism.) It is no accident that all of communism's rhetorical vows revolve around Man (with a capital M) and his earthly happiness. At first glance it seems an ugly parallel: common traits in the thinking and way of life of today's West and today's East? But such is the logic of materialistic development.

The interrelationship is such, moreover, that the current of materialism which is farthest to the left, and is hence the most consistent, always proves to be stronger, more attractive, and victorious. Humanism which has lost its Christian heritage cannot prevail in this competition. Thus during the past centuries and especially in recent decades, as the process became more acute, the alignment of forces was as follows: Liberalism was inevitably pushed aside by radicalism, radicalism had to surrender to socialism, and socialism could not stand up to communism.

The communist regime in the East could endure and grow due to the enthusiastic support from an enormous number of Western intellectuals who (feeling the kinship!) refused to see communism's crimes, and when they no longer could do so, they tried to justify these crimes. The problem persists: In our Eastern countries, communism has suffered a complete ideological defeat; it is zero and less than zero. And yet Western intellectuals still look at it with considerable interest and empathy, and this is precisely what makes it so immensely difficult for the West to withstand the East.

I am not examining the case of a disaster brought on by a world war and the changes which it would produce in society. But as long as we wake up every morning under a peaceful sun, we must lead an everyday life. Yet there is a disaster which is already very much with us. I am referring to the calamity of an autonomous, irreligious humanistic consciousness.

It has made man the measure of all things on earth— imperfect man, who is never free of pride, self-interest, envy, vanity, and dozens of other defects. We are now paying for the mistakes which were not properly appraised at the beginning of the journey. On the way from the Renaissance to our days we have enriched our experience, but we have lost the concept of a Supreme Complete Entity which used to restrain our passions and our irresponsibility.

We have placed too much hope in politics and social reforms, only to find out that we were being deprived of our most precious possession: our spiritual life. It is trampled by the party mob in the East, by the commercial one in the West. This is the essence of the crisis: the split in the world is less terrifying than the similarity of the disease afflicting its main sections.

If, as claimed by humanism, man were born only to be happy, he would not be born to die. Since his body is doomed to death, his task on earth evidently must be more spiritual: not a total engrossment in everyday life, not the search for the best ways to obtain material goods and then their carefree consumption. It has to be the fulfillment of a permanent, earnest duty so that one's life journey may become above all an experience of moral growth: to leave life a better human being than one started it.

It is imperative to reappraise the scale of the usual human values; its present incorrectness is astounding. It is not possible that assessment of the President's performance should be reduced to the question of how much money one makes or to the availability of gasoline. Only by the voluntary nurturing in ourselves of freely accepted and serene self-restraint can mankind rise above the world stream of materialism.

Today it would be retrogressive to hold on to the ossified formulas of the Enlightenment. Such social dogmatism leaves us helpless before the trials of our times.

Even if we are spared destruction by war, life will have to change in order not to perish on its own. We cannot avoid reassessing the fundamental definitions of human life and society. Is it true that man is above everything? Is there no Superior Spirit above him? Is it right that man's life and society's activities should be ruled by material expansion above all? Is it permissible to promote such expansion to the detriment of our integral spiritual life?

If the world has not approached its end, it has reached a major watershed in history, equal in importance to the turn from the Middle Ages to the Renaissance. It will demand from us a spiritual blaze; we shall have to rise to a new height of vision, to a new level of life, where our physical nature will not be cursed, as in the Middle Ages, but even more importantly, our spiritual being will not be trampled upon, as in the Modern Era.

The ascension is similar to climbing onto the next anthropological stage. No one on earth has any other way left but —upward.

Godlessness, the First Step Toward the Gulag

Address in acceptance of the Templeton Prize, delivered May 10, 1983; translated by Alexis Klimoff

More than half a century ago, while I was still a child, I recall hearing a number of older people offer the following explanation for the great disasters that had befallen Russia: *Men have forgotten God; that's why all this has happened.*

Since then I have spent well-nigh fifty years working on the history of our Revolution; in the process I have read hundreds of books, collected hundreds of personal testimonies, and have already contributed eight volumes of my own toward the effort of clearing away the rubble left by that upheaval. But if I were asked today to formulate as concisely as possible the main cause of the ruinous Revolution that swallowed up some sixty million of our people, I could not put it more accurately than to repeat: *Men have forgotten God; that's why all this has happened.*

What is more, the events of the Russian Revolution can only be understood now, at the end of the century, against the background of what has since occurred in the rest of the world. What emerges here is a process of universal significance. And if I were called upon to identify briefly the principal trait of the *entire* twentieth century, here too, I would be unable to find anything more precise and pithy than to repeat once again: *Men have forgotten God.*

The failings of human consciousness, deprived of its divine dimension, have been a determining factor in all the major crimes of this century. The first of these was World War I, and much of our present predicament can be traced back to it. It was a war (the memory of which seems to be fading) when Europe, bursting with health and abundance, fell into a rage of self-mutilation which could not but sap its strength for a century or more, and perhaps forever. The only possible explanation for this war is a mental eclipse among the leaders of Europe due to their lost awareness of a Supreme Power above them. Only a godless embitterment could have moved ostensibly Christian states to employ poison gas, a weapon so obviously beyond the limits of humanity.

The same kind of defect, the flaw of a consciousness lacking all divine dimension, was manifested after World War II when the West yielded to the satanic temptation of the "nuclear umbrella." It was equivalent to saying: Let's cast off worries, let's free the younger generation from their duties and obligations, let's make no effort to defend ourselves, to say nothing of defending others —let's stop our ears to the groans emanating from the East, and let us live instead in the pursuit of happiness. If danger should threaten us, we shall be protected by the nuclear bomb; if not, then let the world burn in Hell for all we care. The pitifully helpless state to which the contemporary West has sunk is in large measure due to this fatal error: the belief that the defense of peace depends not on stout hearts and steadfast men, but solely on the nuclear bomb. . . .

Today's world has reached a stage which, if it had been described to preceding centuries, would have called forth the cry: "This is the Apocalypse!" Yet we have grown used to this kind of world; we even feel at home in it.

Dostoevsky warned that "great events could come upon us and catch us intellectually unprepared." This is precisely what has happened. And he predicted that "the world will be saved only after it has been possessed by the demon of evil." Whether it really will be saved we shall have to wait and see: this will depend on our conscience, on our spiritual lucidity, on our individual and combined efforts in the face of catastrophic circumstances. But it has already come to pass that the demon of evil, like a whirlwind, triumphantly circles all five continents of the earth. . . .

In its past, Russia did know a time when the social ideal was not fame, or riches, or material success, but a pious way of life. Russia was then steeped in an Orthodox Christianity which remained true to the Church of the first centuries. The Orthodoxy of that time knew how to safeguard its people under the yoke of a foreign occupation that lasted more than two centuries, while at the same time fending off iniquitous blows from the swords of Western crusaders. During those centuries the Orthodox faith in our country became part of the very pattern of thought and the personality of our people, the forms of daily life, the work calendar, the priorities in every undertaking, the organization of the week and of the year. Faith was the shaping and unifying force of the nation.

But in the 17th century Russian Orthodoxy was gravely weakened by an internal schism. In the 18th, the country was shaken by Peter's forcibly imposed transformations, which favored the economy, the state, and the military at the expense of the religious spirit and national life. And along with this lopsided Petrine enlightenment, Russia felt the first whiff of secularism; its subtle poisons permeated the educated classes in the course of the 19th century and opened the path to Marxism. By the time of the Revolution, faith had virtually disappeared in Russian educated circles; and amongst the uneducated, its health was threatened.

It was Dostoevsky, once again, who drew from the French Revolution and its seeming hatred of the Church the lesson that "revolution must necessarily begin with atheism." That is absolutely true. But the world had never before known a godlessness as organized, militarized, and tenaciously malevolent as that practiced by Marxism. Within the philosophical system of Marx and Lenin, and at the heart of their psychology, hatred of God is the principal driving force, more fundamental than all their political and economic pretensions. Militant atheism is not merely incidental or marginal to Communist policy; it is not a side effect, but the central pivot.

The 1920's in the USSR witnessed an uninterrupted procession of victims and martyrs amongst the Orthodox clergy. Two metropolitans were shot, one of whom, Veniamin of Petrograd, had been elected by the popular vote of his diocese. Patriarch Tikhon himself passed through the hands of the Cheka-GPU and then died under suspicious circumstances. Scores of archbishops and bishops perished. Tens of thousands of priests, monks, and nuns, pressured by the Chekists to renounce the Word of God, were tortured, shot in cellars, sent to camps, exiled to the desolate tundra of the far North, or turned out into the streets in their old age without food or shelter. All these Christian martyrs went unswervingly to their deaths for the faith; instances of apostasy were few and far between. For tens of millions of laymen access to the Church was blocked, and they were forbidden to bring up their children in the Faith: religious parents were wrenched from their children and thrown into prison, while the children were turned from the faith by threats and lies. . . .

For a short period of time, when he needed to gather strength for the struggle against Hitler, Stalin cynically adopted a friendly posture toward the Church. This deceptive game, continued in later years by Brezhnev with the help of showcase publications and other window dressing, has unfortunately tended to be taken at its face value in the West. Yet the tenacity with which hatred of religion is rooted in Communism may be judged by the example of their most liberal leader, Khrushchev: for though he undertook a number of significant steps to extend freedom, Khrushchev simultaneously rekindled the frenzied Leninist obsession with destroying religion.

But there is something they did not expect: that in a land where churches have been leveled, where a triumphant atheism has rampaged uncontrolled for two-thirds of a century, where the clergy is utterly humiliated and deprived of all independence, where what remains of the Church as an institution is tolerated only for the sake of propaganda directed at the West, where even today people are sent to the labor camps for their faith, and where, within the camps themselves, those who gather to pray at Easter are clapped in punishment cells—they could not suppose that beneath this Communist steamroller the Christian tradition would survive in Russia. It is true that millions of our countrymen have been corrupted and spiritually devastated by an officially imposed atheism, yet there remain many millions of believers: it is only external pressures that keep them from speaking out, but, as is always the case in times of persecution and suffering, the awareness of God in my country has attained great acuteness and profundity.

It is here that we see the dawn of hope: for no matter how formidably Communism bristles with tanks and rockets, no matter what successes it attains in seizing the planet, it is doomed never to vanquish Christianity.

The West has yet to experience a Communist invasion; religion here remains free. But the West's own historical evolution has been such that today it too is experiencing a drying up of religious consciousness. It too has witnessed racking schisms, bloody religious wars, and rancor, to say nothing of the tide of secularism that, from the late Middle Ages onward, has progressively inundated the West. This gradual sapping of strength from within is a threat to faith that is perhaps even more dangerous than any attempt to assault religion violently from without.

Imperceptibly, through decades of gradual erosion, the meaning of life in the West has ceased to be seen as anything more lofty than the "pursuit of happiness," a goal that has even been solemnly guaranteed by constitutions. The concepts of good and evil have been ridiculed for several centuries; banished from common use, they have been replaced by political or class considerations of short lived value. It has become embarrassing to state that evil makes its home in the individual human heart before it enters a political system. Yet it is not considered shameful to make daily concessions to an integral evil. Judging by the continuing landslide of concessions made before the eyes of our very own generation, the West is ineluctably slipping toward the abyss. Western societies are losing more and more of their religious essence as they thoughtlessly yield up their younger generation to atheism. If a blasphemous film about Jesus is shown throughout the United States, reputedly one of the most religious countries in the world, or a major newspaper publishes a shameless caricature of the Virgin Mary, what further evidence of godlessness does one need? When external rights are completely unrestricted, why should one make an inner effort to restrain oneself from ignoble acts?

Or why should one refrain from burning hatred, whatever its basis—race, class, or ideology? Such hatred is in fact corroding many hearts today. Atheist teachers in the West are bringing up a younger generation in a spirit of hatred of their own society. Amid all the vituperation we forget that the defects of capitalism represent the basic flaws of human nature, allowed unlimited freedom together with the various human rights; we forget that under Communism (and Communism is breathing down the neck of all moderate forms of socialism, which are unstable) the identical flaws run riot in any person with the least degree of authority; while everyone else under that system does indeed attain "equality"—the equality of destitute slaves. This eager fanning of the flames of hatred is becoming the mark of today's free world. Indeed, the broader the personal freedoms are, the higher the level of prosperity or even of abundance—the more vehement, paradoxically, does this blind hatred become. The contemporary developed West thus demonstrates by its own example that human salvation can be found neither in the profusion of material goods nor in merely making money.

This deliberately nurtured hatred then spreads to all that is alive, to life itself, to the world with its colors, sounds, and shapes, to the human body. The embittered art of the twentieth century is perishing as a result of this ugly hate, for art is fruitless without love. In the East art has collapsed because it has been knocked down and trampled upon, but in the West the fall has been voluntary, a decline into a contrived and pretentious quest where the artist, instead of attempting to reveal the divine plan, tries to put himself in the place of God.

Here again we witness the single outcome of a worldwide process, with East and West yielding the same results, and once again for the same reason: Men have forgotten God.

With such global events looming over us like mountains, nay, like entire mountain ranges, it may seem incongruous and inappropriate to recall that the primary key to our being or non-being resides in each individual human heart, in the heart's preference for specific good or evil. Yet this remains true even today, and it is, in fact, the most reliable key we have. The social theories that promised so much have demonstrated their bankruptcy, leaving us at a dead end. The free people of the West could reasonably have been expected to realize that they are beset by numerous freely nurtured falsehoods, and not to allow lies to be foisted upon them so easily. All attempts to find a way out of the plight of today's world are fruitless unless we redirect our consciousness, in repentance, to the Creator of all: without this, no exit will be illumined, and we shall seek it in vain. The resources we have set aside for ourselves are too impoverished for the task. We must first recognize the horror perpetrated not by some outside force, not by class or national enemies, but within each of us individually, and within every society. This is especially true of a free and highly developed society, for here in particular we have surely brought everything upon ourselves, of our own free will. We ourselves, in our daily unthinking selfishness, are pulling tight that noose. . . .

Our life consists not in the pursuit of material success but in the quest for worthy spiritual growth. Our entire earthly existence is but a transitional stage in the movement toward something higher, and we must not stumble and fall, nor must we linger fruitlessly on one rung of the ladder. Material laws alone do not explain our life or give it direction. The laws of physics and physiology will never reveal the indisputable manner in which the Creator constantly, day in and day out, participates in the life of each of us, unfailingly granting us the energy of existence; when this assistance leaves us, we die. And in the life of our entire planet, the Divine Spirit surely moves with no less force: this we must grasp in our dark and terrible hour.

To the ill-considered hopes of the last two centuries, which have reduced us to insignificance and brought us to the brink of nuclear and non-nuclear death, we can propose only a determined quest for the warm hand of God, which we have so rashly and self-confidently spurned. Only in this way can our eyes be opened to the errors of this unfortunate twentieth century and our hands be directed to setting them right. There is nothing else to cling to in the landslide: the combined vision of all the thinkers of the Enlightenment amounts to nothing.

Our five continents are caught in a whirlwind. But it is during trials such as these that the highest gifts of the human spirit are manifested. If we perish and lose this world, the fault will be ours alone.

The Case Against Moral Relativism: "Who's to Judge What's Right or Wrong?"

Louis Pojman

Louis Pojman (1935–2005) was an American philosopher. He earned a Ph.D. in Philosophy from Union Theological Seminary at Columbia University as well as a D.Phil. in Philosophy from Oxford. He authored some 34 books and over 100 articles on topics of philosophy and ethics.

In this article he presents the case, as he sees it, against the validity of moral relativism. His goal is to use evidence to build a logical argument that moral relativism is incorrect. By using a straightforward structure along with examples that are taken from recent history, he is able to provide a cogent, intelligent, and comprehensible analysis of a topic that is often dense, vague, and unclear.

Note: Footnotes are those of the author.

Published 2004

> Like many people, I have always been instinctively a moral relativist. As far back as I can remember... it has always seemed to be obvious that the dictates of morality arise from some sort of convention or understanding among people, that different people arrive at different understandings, and that there are no basic moral demands that apply to everyone. This seemed so obvious to me I assumed it was everyone's instinctive view, or at least everyone who gave the matter any thought in this day and age.
>
> —Gilbert Harman[1]

> Ethical relativism is the doctrine that the moral rightness and wrongness of actions vary from society to society and that there are not absolute universal moral standards on all men at all times. Accordingly , it holds that whether or not it is right for an individual to act in a certain way depends on or is relative to the society to which he belongs. —John Ladd[2]

Gilbert Harman's intuitions about the self-evidence of ethical relativism contrast strikingly with Plato's or Kant's equal certainty about the truth of objectivism, the doctrine that universally valid or true ethical principles exist.[3] "Two things fill the soul with ever new and increasing wonder and reverence the oftener and more fervently reflection ponders on it: the starry heavens above and the moral law within," wrote Kant. On the basis of polls taken in my ethics and introduction to philosophy classes in recent years, Harman's views may signal a shift in contemporary society's moral understanding. The polls show a two-to-one ratio in favor of moral relativism over moral absolutism, with fewer than five percent of the respondents recognizing that a third position

---

[1] Gilbert Harman, "Is There a Single True Morality?" in Morality, Reason and Truth, eds. David Copp and David Zimmerman (Rowman & Allenheld, 1984).

[2] John Ladd, Ethical Relativism (Wadsworth, 1973).

[3] Lest I be misunderstood, in this essay I will generally be speaking about the validity rather than the truth of moral principles. Validity holds that they are proper guides to action, whereas truth presupposes something more. It presupposes Moral Realism, the theory that moral principles have special ontological status. Although this may be true, not all objectivists agree. R. M. Hare, for instance, argues that moral principles, while valid, do not have truth value. They are like imperatives which have practical application but cannot be said to be true. Also, I am mainly concerned with the status of principles, not theories themselves. There may be a plurality of valid moral theories, all containing the same objective principles. I am grateful to Edward Sherline for drawing this distinction to my attention.

between these two polar opposites might exist. Of course, I'm not suggesting that all of these students had a clear understanding of what relativism entails, for many who said they were relativists also contended in the same polls that abortion except to save the mother's life is always wrong, that capital punishment is always wrong, or that suicide is never morally permissible.

Among my university colleagues, a growing number also seem to embrace moral relativism. Recently one of my nonphilosopher colleagues voted to turn down a doctoral dissertation proposal because the student assumed an objectivist position in ethics. (Ironically, I found in this same colleague's work rhetorical treatment of individual liberty that raised it to the level of a non-negotiable absolute). But irony and inconsistency aside, many relativists are aware of the tension between their own subjective positions and their metatheory that entails relativism. I confess that I too am tempted by the allurements of this view and find some forms of it plausible and worth of serious examination. However, I also find it deeply troubling.

In this essay I will examine the central notions of ethical relativism and look at the implications that seem to follow from it. Then I will present the outline of a very modest objectivism, one that takes into account many of the insights of relativism and yet stands as a viable option to it.

1. An Analysis of Relativism

Let us examine the theses contained in John Ladd's succinct statement on ethical (conventional) relativism that appears at the beginning of this essay. If we analyze it, we derive the following argument:

> 1. Moral rightness and wrongness of actions vary from society to society, so there are no universal moral standards held by all societies.
>
> 2. Whether or not it is right for individuals to act in a certain way depends on (or is relative to) the society to which they belong.
>
> 3. Therefore, there are no absolute or objective moral standards that apply to all people everywhere.

1. The first thesis, which may be called the *diversity thesis*, is simply a description that acknowledges the fact that moral rules differ from society to society. The Spartans of ancient Greece and

the Dobu of New Guinea believe that stealing is morally right, but we believe it is wrong. The Roman father had the power of life and death (*just vitae necisque*) over his children, whereas we condemn parents for abusing their children. A tribe in East Africa once threw deformed infants to the hippopotamuses, and in ancient Greece and Rome infants were regularly exposed, while we abhor infanticide. Ruth Benedict describes a tribe in Melanesia that views cooperation and kindness as vices, whereas we see them as virtues. While in ancient Greece, Rome, China and Korea parricide was condemned as "the most execrable of crimes," among Northern Indians aged persons, persons who were no longer capable of walking, were left alone to starve. Among the California Gallinomero, when fathers became feeble, a burden to their sons, "the poor old wretch is not infrequently thrown down on his back and securely held while a stick is placed across his throat and the two of them seat themselves on the ends of it until he ceases to breathe."[4] Sexual practices vary over time and place. Some cultures permit homosexual behavior, while others condemn it. Some cultures practice polygamy, while others view it as immoral. Some cultures condone while others condemn premarital sex. Some cultures accept cannibalism, while the very idea revolts us. Some West African tribes perform clitoridectomies on girls, whereas we deplore such practices. Cultural relativism is well documented, and "custom is the king o'er all." There may or may not be moral principles that are held in common by every society, but if there are any, they seem to be few at best. Certainly it would be very difficult to derive any single "true" morality by observing various societies' moral standards.

2. The second thesis, *the dependency thesis,* asserts that individual acts are right or wrong depending on the nature of the society from which they emanate. Morality does not occur in a vacuum, and what is considered morally right or wrong must be seen in a context that depends on the goals, wants, beliefs, history, and environment of the society in question. As William G. Sumner says,

We learn the morals as unconsciously as we learn to walk and hear

---

[4] Reported by the anthropologist Powers, Tribes of California, p. 178. Quoted in E. Westermarck, Origin and Development of Moral Ideals (London, 1906), p. 386. This work is a mine of examples of cultural diversity.

and breathe, and [we] never know any reason why the [morals] are what they are. The justification of them is that when we wake to consciousness of life we find them facts which already hold us in the bonds of tradition, custom, and habit.[5]

Trying to see things from an independent, noncultural point of view would be like taking out our eyes in order to examine their contours and qualities. There is no "innocent eye." We are simply culturally determined beings.

We could, of course, distinguish between a week and a strong thesis of dependency, for the nonrelativist can accept a certain degree of relativity in the way moral principles are *applied* in various cultures, depending on beliefs, history, and environment. For example, Jewish men express reverence for God by covering their heads when entering places of worship, whereas Christian men uncover their heads when entering places of worship. Westerners shake hands upon greeting each other, whereas Hindus place their hands together and point them toward the person to be greeted. Both sides adhere to principles of reverence and respect but apply them differently. But the ethical relativist must maintain a stronger thesis, one that insists that the moral principles themselves are products of the cultures and may vary from society to society. The ethical relativist contends that even beyond environmental factors and differences in beliefs, a fundamental disagreement exists among societies. One way for the relativist to support this thesis is by appealing to an indeterminancy of translation thesis, which maintains that there is a conceptual relativity among language groups so that we cannot even translate into our language the worldviews of a culture with a radically different language.

In a sense we all live in radically different worlds. But the relativist wants to go further and maintain that there is something conventional about *any* morality, so that every morality really depends on a level of social acceptance. Not only do various societies adhere to different moral systems, but the very same society could (and often does) change its moral views over place and time. For example, the majority of people in the United States now view slavery as immoral, whereas one hundred and

---

[5] W. G. Sumner, Folkways (Ginn & Co., 1906), p.76.

forty years ago they did not. Our society's views on divorce, sexuality, abortion, and assisted suicide have changed somewhat as well—and they are still changing.

3. The conclusion that there are no absolute or objective moral standards binding on all people follows from the first two propositions. Combining cultural relativism (*the diversity thesis*) with *the dependency thesis* yields ethical relativism in its classic form. If there are different moral principles from culture to culture and if all morality is rooted in culture, then it follows that there are no universal moral principles that are valid (or true) for all cultures and peoples at all times.

2. Subjectivism

Some people think that this conclusion is still too tame, and they maintain that morality is not dependent on the society but rather on the individual. As my students sometimes maintain, "Morality is in the eye of the beholder." They treat morality like taste or aesthetic judgments—person relative. This form of moral subjectivism has the sorry consequence that it makes morality a very useless concept, for, on its premises, little or no interpersonal criticism or judgment is logically possible. Suppose that you are repulsed by observing John torturing a child. You cannot condemn him if one of his principles is "torture little children for the fun of it." The only basis for judging him wrong might be that he was a hypocrite who condemned others for torturing. But suppose that another of his principles is that hypocrisy is morally permissible (for him); thus we cannot condemn him for condemning others for doing what he does.

On the basis of subjectivism Adolf Hitler and the serial murderer Ted Bundy could be considered as moral as Gandhi, so long as each lived by his own standards, whatever those might be. Witness the following paraphrase of a tape-recorded conversation between Ted Bundy and one of his victims in which Bundy justifies his murder:

> Then I learned that all moral judgments are "value judgments," that all value judgments are subjective, and that none can be proved either 'right' or 'wrong.' I even read somewhere that the Chief Justice of the United States had written that the American Constitution expressed nothing more than collective value judgments. Believe it or not, I figured out for myself—what

apparently the Chief Justice couldn't figure out for himself—that if the rationality of one value judgment was zero, multiplying it by millions would not make it one whit more rational. Nor is there any 'reason' to obey the law for anyone, like myself, who has the boldness and daring—the strength of character—to throw off its shackles. . . . I discovered that to become truly free, truly unfettered, I had to become truly uninhibited. And I quickly discovered that the greatest obstacle to my freedom, the greatest block and limitation to it, consists in the insupportable 'value judgment' that I was bound to respect the rights of others. I asked myself, who were these 'others'? Other human beings, with human rights? Why is it more wrong to kill a human animal than any other animal, a pig or a sheep or a steer? Is your life more to you than a hog's life to a hog? Why should I be willing to sacrifice my pleasure more for the one than for the other? Surely you would not, in this age of scientific enlightenment, declare that God or nature has marked some pleasures as 'moral' or 'good' and others as 'immoral' or 'bad'? In any case, let me assure you, my dear young lady, that there is absolutely no comparison between the pleasure I might take in eating ham and the pleasure I anticipate in raping and murdering you. That is the honest conclusion to which my education has led me—after the most conscientious examination of my spontaneous and uninhibited self.[6]

Notions of good and bad, or right and wrong, cease to have interpersonal evaluative meaning. We might be revulsed by the views of Ted Bundy, but that is just a matter of taste. A student might not like it when her teacher gives her an F on a test paper, while he gives another student an A for a similar paper, but there is no way to criticize him for injustice, because justice is not one of his chosen principles.

Absurd consequences follow from subjectivism. If it is correct, then morality reduces to aesthetic tastes about which there can be neither argument nor interpersonal judgment. Although many students say they espouse subjectivism, there is evidence that it conflicts with other of their moral views. They typically condemn Hitler as an evil man for his genocidal policies. A contradiction seems to exist between subjectivism and the very concept of morality, which it is supposed to characterize, for morality has to do with *proper* resolution of interpersonal conflict

---

6 This is a paraphrased and rewritten statement of Ted Bundy by Harry V. Jaffa, Homosexuality and the Natural Law (Claremont, CA: The Claremont Institute of the Study of Statesmanship and Political Philosophy, 1990), pp. 3–4.

and the amelioration of the human predicament (both deontological and teleological systems do this, but in different ways . . .). Whatever else it does, morality has a minimal aim of preventing a Hobbesian state of nature . . . , wherein life is "solitary, poor, nasty, brutish, and short." But if so, subjectivism is no help at all, for it rests neither on social agreement of principle (as the conventionalist maintains) nor on an objectively independent set of norms that bind all people for the common good. If there were only one person on earth, there would be no occasion for morality, because there wouldn't be any interpersonal conflicts to resolve or others whose suffering he or she would have a duty to ameliorate. Subjectivism implicitly assumes something of this solipsism, an atomism in which isolated individuals make up separate universes.

Subjectivism treats individuals like billiard balls on a societal pool table where they meet only in radical collisions, each aimed at his or her own goal and striving to do in the others before they themselves are done in. This atomistic view of personality is belied by the facts that we develop in families and mutually dependent communities in which we share a common language, common institutions, and similar rituals and habits, and that we often feel one another's joys and sorrows. As the poet John Donne wrote, "No man is an island, entire of itself; everyman is a piece of the continent."

Radical individualistic ethical relativism is incoherent. If so, it follows that the only plausible view of ethical relativism must be one that grounds morality in the group or culture. This form is called *conventionalism*.

3. Conventionalism

Conventional ethical relativism, the view that there are no objective moral principles but that all valid moral principles are justified (or are made true) by virtue of their cultural acceptance, recognizes the social nature of morality. That is precisely its power and virtue. It does not seem subject to the same absurd consequences which plague subjectivism. Recognizing the importance of our social environment in generating customs and beliefs, many people suppose that ethical relativism is the correct metaethical theory. Furthermore, they are drawn to it for its liberal philosophical stance. It seems to be an enlightened response to the sin of ethnocentricity, and it seems to entail or strongly imply an attitude of tolerance toward other cultures. Anthropologist Ruth Benedict says, that in recognizing ethical relativity, "We shall arrive at a more realistic social faith, accepting as grounds of hope and as new bases for tolerance the coexisting and equally valid patterns of life which mankind has created for itself from the raw materials of existence."[7] The most famous of those holding this position is the anthropologist Melville Herskovits, who argues even more explicitly than Benedict that ethical relativism entails intercultural tolerance.

1. If morality is relative to its culture, then there is no independent basis for criticizing the morality of any culture but one's own.
2. If there is no independent way of criticizing any other culture, then we ought to be *tolerant* of the moralities of other cultures.
3. Morality is relative to its culture. Therefore,
4. We ought to be *tolerant* of the moralities of other cultures.[8]

Tolerance is certainly a virtue, but is this a good argument for it? I think not. If morality simply is relative to each culture, then if the culture in question does not have a principle of tolerance, its members have no obligation to be tolerant. Herskovits seems to be treating the *principle of tolerance* as the one exception to his relativism. He seems to be treating it as an absolute moral principle. But from a relativistic point of view there is no more reason to be tolerant than to be intolerant and neither stance is objectively morally better than the other.

Not only do relativists fail to offer a basis for criticizing those who are intolerant, but they cannot rationally criticize anyone who espouses what they might regard as a heinous principle. If, as seems to be the case, valid criticism supposes an objective or impartial standard, relativists cannot morally criticize anyone outside their own culture. Adolf Hitler's genocidal actions, so long as they are culturally accepted, are as morally legitimate as Mother Theresa's works of mercy. If Conventional Relativism is accepted, racism, genocide of unpopular minorities, oppression of the poor, slavery, and even the advocacy of war for its own sake

---

[7] Ruth Benedict, Patterns of Culture (New American Library, 1934), p. 257.

[8] Melville Herskovits, Cultural Relativism (Random House, 1972).

are as equally moral as their opposites. And if a subculture decided that starting a nuclear war was somehow morally acceptable, we could not morally criticize those people. Any actual morality, whatever its content, is as valid as every other, and more valid than ideal moralities—since the latter aren't adhered to by any culture.

There are other disturbing consequences of ethical relativism. It seems to entail that reformers are always (morally) wrong since they go against the tide of cultural standards. William Wilberforce was wrong in the eighteenth century to oppose slavery; the British were immoral in opposing *suttee* in India (the burning of widows, which is now illegal in India). The early Christians were wrong in refusing to serve in the Roman army or to bow down to Caesar, since the majority in the Roman Empire believed that these two acts were moral duties. In fact, Jesus himself was immoral in breaking the law of His day by healing on the Sabbath day and by advocating the principles of the Sermon on the Mount, since it is clear that few in His time (or in ours) accepted them.

Yet we normally feel just the opposite, that the reformer is a courageous innovator who is right, who has the truth, against the mindless majority. Sometimes the individual must stand alone with the truth, risking social censure and persecution. As Dr. Stockman says in Ibsen's *Enemy of the People,* after he loses the battle to declare his town's profitable but polluted tourist spa unsanitary, "The most dangerous enemy of the truth and freedom among us—is the compact majority. Yes, the damned, compact and liberal majority. The majority has *might*—unfortunately—but *right* it is not. Right—are I and a few others." Yet if relativism is correct, the opposite is necessarily the case. Truth is with the crowd and error with the individual.

Similarly, conventional ethical relativism entails disturbing judgments about the law. Our normal view is that we have a prima facie duty to obey the law, because law in general, promotes the human good. According to most objective systems, this obligation is not absolute but relative to the particular law's relation to a wider moral order. Civil disobedience is warranted in some cases where the law seems to be in serious conflict with morality. However, if moral relativism is true, then neither law nor civil disobedience has a firm foundation. On the one hand, from the side of the society at large, civil disobedience will be morally wrong, so long as the majority culture agrees with the law in question. On the other hand, if you belong to the relevant subculture which doesn't recognize the particular law in question (because it is unjust from your point of view), disobedience will be morally mandated. The Ku Klux Klan, which believes that Jews, Catholics, and Blacks are evil or undeserving of high regard, are, given conventionalism, morally permitted or required to break the laws which protect these endangered groups. Why should I obey a law that my group doesn't recognize as valid?

To sum up, unless we have an independent moral basis for law, it is hard to see why we have any general duty to obey it; and unless we recognize the priority of a universal moral law, we have no firm basis to justify our acts of civil disobedience against "unjust laws." Both the validity of law and morally motivated disobedience of unjust laws are annulled in favor of a power struggle.

There is an even more basic problem with the notion that morality is dependent on cultural acceptance for its validity. The problem is that the notion of a *culture* or *society* is notoriously difficult to define. This is especially so in a pluralistic society like our own where the notion seems to be vague with unclear boundary lines. One person may belong to several societies (subcultures) with different value emphases and arrangements of principles. A person may belong to the nation as a single society with certain values of patriotism, honor, courage, laws (including some which are controversial but have majority acceptance, such as the current law on abortion). But he or she may also belong to a church which opposes some of the laws of the State. He may also be an integral member of a socially mixed community where different principles hold sway, and he may belong to clubs and a family where still other rules are adhered to. Relativism would seem to tell us that where he is a member of societies with conflicting moralities he must be judged both wrong and not-wrong whatever he does. For example if Mary is a U.S. citizen and a member of the Roman Catholic Church, she is wrong (qua Catholic) if she chooses to have an abortion and not-wrong (qua citizen of the U.S.A. if she acts against the teaching of the Church on abortion. As a member of a racist university fraternity, KKK, John has no obligation to treat his fellow Black student as an equal, but as a member of the university community itself (where the principle of equal rights is accepted) he does have the obligation; but as a member of the surrounding community (which may reject the principle of equal rights) he again has no such obligation; but then again as a member of the nation at large (which accepts the principle) he is obligated to treat his fellow with respect. What is the morally right thing for John to do? The question no longer makes much sense in this moral Babel. It has lost its action-guiding function.

Perhaps the relativist would adhere to a principle which says that in such cases the individual may choose which group to belong to as primary. If Mary chooses to have an abortion, she is choosing to belong to the general society relative to that principle. And John must likewise choose among groups. The trouble with this option is that it seems to lead back to counter-intuitive results. If Murder Mike of Murder, Incorporated, feels like killing Bank President Ortcutt and wants to feel good about it, he identifies with the Murder, Incorporated, society rather than the general public morality. Does this justify the killing? In fact, couldn't one justify anything simply by forming a small subculture that approved of it? Ted Bundy would be morally pure in raping and killing innocents simply by virtue of forming a little coterie. How large must the group be in order to be a legitimate subculture or society? Does it need ten or fifteen people? How about just three? Come to think about it, why can't my burglary partner and I found our own society with a morality of its own? Of course, if my partner dies, I could still claim that I was acting from an originally social set of norms. But why can't I dispense with the interpersonal agreements altogether and invent my own morality—since morality, on this view, is only an invention anyway? Conventionalist relativism seems to reduce to subjectivism. And subjectivism leads, as we have seen, to moral solipsism, to the demise of morality altogether.

Should one object that this is an instance of the *Slippery Slope Fallacy*,[9] let that person give an alternative analysis of what constitutes a viable social basis for generating valid (or true) moral principles. Perhaps we might agree (for the sake of

---

[9] The fallacy of objecting to a proposition on the erroneous grounds that, if accepted, it will lead to a chain of states of affairs which are absurd or unacceptable.

argument, at least) that the very nature of morality entails two people making an agreement. This move saves the conventionalist from moral solipsism, but it still permits almost any principle at all to count as moral. And what's more, those principles can be thrown out and their contraries substituted for them as the need arises. If two or three people decide that they will make cheating on exams morally acceptable for themselves, via forming a fraternity "Cheaters Anonymous" at their university, then cheating becomes moral. Why not? Why not rape, as well?

However, I don't think you can stop the move from conventionalism to subjectivism. The essential force of the validity of the chosen moral principle is that it is dependent on choice. The conventionalist holds that it is the choice of the group, but why should I accept the group's silly choice, when my own is better (for me)? Why should anyone give such august authority to a culture of society? If this is all morality comes to, why not reject it altogether—even though one might want to adhere to its directives when other are looking in order to escape sanctions?

4. A Critique of Ethical Relativism

However, while we may fear the demise of morality, as we have known it, this in itself may not be a good reason for rejecting relativism. That is, for judging it false. Alas, truth may not always be edifying. But the consequences of this position are sufficiently alarming to prompt us to look carefully for some weakness in the relativist's argument. So let us examine the premises and conclusion listed at the beginning of this essay as the three theses of relativism.

1. *The Diversity Thesis.* What is considered morally right and wrong varies from society to society, so that there are no moral principles accepted by all societies.

2. *The Dependency Thesis.* All moral principles derive their validity from cultural acceptance.

3. *Ethical Relativism.* Therefore, there are no universally valid moral principles, objective standards which apply to all people everywhere and at all times.

Does any one of these seem problematic? Let us consider the first thesis, the diversity thesis, which we have also called cultural relativism. Perhaps there is not as much diversity as anthropologists like Sumner and Benedict suppose. One can also see great similarities between the moral codes of various cultures. E. O. Wilson has identified over a score of common features,[10] and before him Clyde Kluckhohn has noted much significant common ground between cultures.

> Every culture has a concept of murder, distinguishes this from execution, killing in war, and other "justifiable homicides." The notions of incest and other regulations upon sexual behavior, the prohibitions upon untruth under defined circumstances, of restitution and reciprocity, of mutual obligations between parents and children—these and many other moral concepts are altogether universal.[11]

Colin Turnbull's description of the sadistic, semidisplaced, disintegrating Ik in Northern Uganda supports the view that a people without principles of kindness, loyalty, and cooperation will degenerate into a Hobbesian state of nature.[12] But he has also produced evidence that under the surface of this dying society, there is a deeper moral code from a time when the tribe flourished, which occasionally surfaces and shows its nobler face.

On the other hand, there is enormous cultural diversity and many societies have radically different moral codes. Cultural relativism seems to be a fact, but, even if it is, it does not by itself establish the truth of ethical relativism. Cultural diversity in itself is neutral between theories. For the objectivist could concede complete cultural relativism, but still defend a form of universalism; for he or she could argue that some cultures simply lack correct moral principles.

On the other hand, a denial of complete cultural relativism (i.e., an admission of some universal principles) does not disprove ethical relativism. For even if we did find one or more universal principles, this would not prove that they had any

---

[10] E. O. Wilson, On Human Nature (Bantam Books, 1979), pp. 22–23.

[11] Clyde Kluckhohn, "Ethical Relativity: Sic et Non," Journal of Philosophy, LII (1955).

[12] Colin Turnbull, The Mountain People (New York: Simon & Schuster, 1972).

objective status. We could still *imagine* a culture that was an exception to the rule and be unable to criticize it. So the first premise doesn't by itself imply ethical relativism and its denial doesn't disprove ethical relativism.

We must turn to the crucial second thesis, the dependency thesis. Morality does not occur in a vacuum, but rather what is considered morally right or wrong must be seen in a context, depending on the goals, wants, beliefs, history, and environment of the society in question. We distinguished a *weak* and a *strong* thesis of dependency. The weak thesis says that the application of principles depends on the particular cultural predicament, whereas the strong thesis affirms that the principles themselves depend on that predicament. The nonrelativist can accept a certain relativity in the way moral principles are *applied* in various cultures, depending on beliefs, history, and environment. For example, a raw environment with scarce natural resources may justify the Eskimos' brand of euthanasia to the objectivist, who in another environment would consistently reject that practice. The members of a tribe in the Sudan throw their deformed children into the river because of their belief that such infants *belong* to the hippopotamus, the god of the river. We believe that they have a false belief about this, but the point is that the same principles of respect for property and respect for human life are operative in these contrary practices. They differ with us only in belief, not in substantive moral principle. This is an illustration of how nonmoral beliefs (e.g., deformed children belong to the hippopotamus) when applied to common moral principles (e.g., give to each his due) generate different actions in different cultures. In our own culture the difference in the nonmoral belief about the status of a fetus generates opposite moral prescriptions. The major difference between pro-choicers and pro-lifers is not whether we should kill persons but whether fetuses are really persons. It is a debate about the facts of the matter, not the principle of killing innocent persons.

So the fact that moral principles are weakly dependent doesn't show that ethical relativism is valid. In spite of this weak dependency on nonmoral factors, there could still be a set of general moral norms applicable to all cultures and even recognized in most, which are disregarded at a culture's own expense.

What the relativist needs is a strong thesis of dependency, that somehow all principles are essentially cultural inventions. But why should we choose to view morality this way? Is there anything to recommend the strong thesis over the weak thesis of dependency? The relativist may argue that in fact we don't have an obvious impartial standard from which to judge. "Who's to say which culture is right and which is wrong?" But this seems to be dubious. We can reason and perform thought experiments in order to make a case for one system over another. We may not be able to *know* with certainty that our moral beliefs are closer to the truth than those of another culture or those of others within our own culture, but we may be *justified* in believing that they are. If we can be closer to the truth regarding factual or scientific matters, why can't we be closer to the truth on moral matters? Why can't a culture be simply confused or wrong about its moral perceptions? Why can't we say that the society like the Ik which sees nothing wrong with enjoying watching its own children fall into fires is less moral in that regard than the culture that cherishes children and grants them protection and equal rights? To take such a stand is not to commit the fallacy of ethnocentricism, for we are seeking to derive principles through critical reason, not simply uncritical acceptance of one's own mores.

Many relativists embrace relativism as a default position. Objectivism makes no sense to them. I think this is Ladd and Harman's position, as the latter's quotation at the beginning of this article seems to indicate. Objectivism has insuperable problems, so the answer must be relativism. The only positive argument I know for the strong dependency thesis upon which ethical relativism rests is that of the indeterminacy of translation thesis. This theory, set forth by B. L. Whorf and W. V. Quine,[13] holds that languages are often so fundamentally different from one another that we cannot accurately translate concepts from one to another. But this thesis, while relatively true even within a language (each of us has an idiolect), seems falsified by experience. We do learn foreign languages and learn to translate across linguistic frameworks. For example, people from a myriad

---

[13] See Benjamin Whorf, Language, Thought and Reality (MIT Press, 1956); and W. V. Quine, Word and Object (MIT Press, 1960), and Ontological Relativity (Columbia University Press, 1969).

of language groups come to the United States and learn English
and communicate perfectly well. Rather than a complete hiatus,
the interplay between these other cultures eventually enriches the
English language with new concepts (for example, *forte, foible,
taboo,* and *coup de grâce*), even as English has enriched (or
"corrupted" as the French might argue) other languages. Even if it
turns out that there is some indeterminacy of translation between
language users, we should not infer from this that no translation
or communication is possible. It seems reasonable to believe that
general moral principles are precisely those things that can be
communicated transculturally. The kind of common features that
Kluckhohn and Wilson advance—duties of restitution and
reciprocity, regulations on sexual behavior, obligations of parents
to children, a no-unnecessary-harm principle, and a sense that the
good should flourish and the guilty be punished—these and others
constitute a human experience, a common set of values within a
common human predicament of struggling to survive and flourish
in a world of scarce resources.[14] So it is possible to communicate
cross-culturally and find that we agree on many of the important
things in life. If this is so, then the indeterminacy of translation

---

[14] David Hume gave the classic expression to this idea of a common human nature
when he wrote:
It is universally acknowledged that there is a great uniformity among the actions of
men, in all nations and ages, and that human nature remains still the same, in its
principles and operations. The same events follow from the same causes. Ambition,
avarice, self-love, vanity, friendship, generosity, public spirit; these passions, mixed in
various degrees, and distributed through society, have been, from the beginning of the
world, and still are, the source of all the actions and enterprises which have ever been
observed among mankind. Would you know the sentiments, inclinations, and course
of life of the Greeks and Romans? Study well the temper and actions of the French
and English: you cannot be much mistaken in transferring to the former most of the
observations which you have made with regard to the latter. Mankind are so much the
same, in all times and places, that history informs us of nothing new or strange in that
particular. Its chief use is only to discover the constant and universal principles of
human nature, by showing men in all varieties of circumstances and situations, and
furnishing us with materials, from which we may form our observations, and become
acquainted with the regular springs of human action and behavior. These records of
wars, intrigues, factions, and revolutions, are so many collections of experiments by
which the politician or moral philosopher fixes the principles of his science; in the
same manner as the physician or natural philosopher becomes acquainted with the
nature of plants, minerals, and other external objects, by the experiments which he
forms concerning them. Nor are the earth, water, and other elements examined by
Aristotle and Hippocrates more like to those which at present lie under our
observation than the men described by Polybius and Tacitus are to those who now
govern the world.
Essays, Moral, Political and Literary (Longman, Green, 1875).

thesis, upon which relativism rests, must itself be relativized to the point where it is no objection to objective morality.

5. The Case for Moral Objectivism

If nonrelativists are to make their case, they will have to offer a better explanation of cultural diversity and why we should nevertheless adhere to moral objectivism. One way of doing this is to appeal to a divine law, and human sin, which causes deviation from that law. Although I think that human greed, selfishness, pride, self-deception and other maladies have a great deal to do with moral differences and that religion may lend great support to morality, I don't think that a religious justification is necessary for the validity of moral principles. In any case, in this section I shall outline a modest nonreligious objectivism, first by appealing to our intuitions and secondly by giving a naturalist account of morality that transcends individual cultures.

First, I must make it clear that I am distinguishing moral *absolutism* from moral *objectivism*. The absolutist believes that there are nonoverrideable moral principles which ought never to be violated. Kant's system, or one version of it, is a good example. One ought never to break a promise, no matter what. Act utilitarianism also seems absolutist, for the principle, Do that act that has the most promise of yielding the most utility, is nonoverrideable. An objectivist need not posit any nonoverrideable principles, at least not in unqualified general form, and so need not be an absolutist. As Renford Bambrough put it,

> To suggest that there is a *right* answer to a moral problem is at once to be accused of or credited with a belief in moral absolutes. But it is no more necessary to believe in moral absolutes in order to believe in moral objectivity than it is to believe in the existence of absolute space or absolute time in order to believe in the objectivity of temporal and spatial relations and of judgments about them.[15]

On the objectivist's account moral principles are what William Ross refers to as *prima facie* principles, valid rules of action which should generally be adhered to, but which may be overridden by another moral principle in cases of moral conflict. For example,

---

[15] Renford Bambrough, Moral Skepticism and Moral Knowledge (London: Routledge & Kegan Paul, 1979), p. 33.

while a principle of justice may generally outweigh a principle of benevolence, there are times when enormous good could be done by sacrificing a small amount of justice, so that an objectivist would be inclined to act according to the principle of benevolence. There may be some absolute or nonoverrideable principles, but there need not be many or any for objectivism to be true.[16]

If we can establish or show that it is reasonable to believe that there is at least one objective moral principle which is binding on all people everywhere in some ideal sense, we shall have shown that relativism is probably false and that a limited objectivism is true. Actually, I believe that there are many qualified general ethical principles which are binding on all rational beings, but one will suffice to refute relativism. The principle I've chosen is the following:

A. It is morally wrong to torture people for the fun of it.

I claim that this principle is binding on all rational agents, so that if some agent, S, rejects A, we should not let that affect our intuition that A is a true principle but rather try to explain S's behavior as perverse, ignorant, or irrational instead. For example, suppose Adolf Hitler doesn't accept A. Should that affect our confidence in the truth of A? Is it not more reasonable to infer that Adolf is morally deficient, morally blind, ignorant, or irrational than to suppose that his noncompliance is evidence against the truth of A?

Suppose further that there is a tribe of Hitlerites somewhere who enjoy torturing people. The whole culture accepts torturing others for the fun of it. Suppose that Mother Theresa or Gandhi tries unsuccessfully to convince them that they should stop torturing people altogether, and they respond by torturing the reformers. Should this affect our confidence in A? Would it not be more reasonable to look for some explanation of Hitlerite behavior? For example, we might hypothesize that this tribe lacked a developed sense of sympathetic imagination which is necessary for the moral life. Or we might theorize that this tribe was on a lower evolutionary level than most *Homo sapiens*. Or we might simply conclude that the tribe was closer to a Hobbesian

---

[16] William Ross, The Right and the Good (Oxford University Press, 1930), p. 18f.

state of nature than most societies, and as such probably would not survive. But we need not know the correct answer as to why the tribe was in such bad shape in order to maintain our confidence in A as a moral principle. If A is a basic or core belief for us, we will be more likely to doubt the Hitlerites' sanity or ability to think morally than to doubt the validity of A.

We can perhaps produce other candidates for membership in our minimally basic objective moral set. For example:

1. Do not kill innocent people.
2. Do not cause unnecessary pain and suffering.
3. Do not cheat or steal.
4. Keep your promises and honor your contracts.
5. Do not deprive another person of his or her freedom.
6. Do justice, treating equals equally and unequals unequally.
7. Tell the truth.
8. Help other people, at least when the cost to oneself is minimal.
9. Reciprocate (show gratitude for services rendered).
10. Obey just laws.

These ten principles are examples of the *core morality*, principles necessary for the good life. They are not arbitrary, for we can give reasons why they are necessary for social cohesion and human flourishing. Principles like the Golden Rule, not killing innocent people, treating equals equally, telling truth, promise keeping, and the like are central to the fluid progression of social interaction and the resolution of conflicts of which ethics are about (at least minimal morality is, even though there may be more to morality than simply these kinds of concerns). For example, language itself depends on a general and implicit commitment to the principle of truth telling. Accuracy of expression is a primitive form of truthfulness. Hence, every time we use words correctly we are telling the truth. Without this behavior, language wouldn't be possible. Likewise, without the recognition of a rule of promise keeping, contracts are of no avail an cooperation is less likely to occur. And without the protection of life and liberty, we could not secure other goals.

A moral code or theory would be adequate if it contained a requisite set of these objective principles or the core morality, but there could be more than one adequate moral code or theory which contained different rankings of these principles and other principles consistent with *core morality*. That is, there may be a certain relativity to secondary principles (whether to opt for monogamy rather than polygamy, whether to include a principle of high altruism in the set of moral duties, whether to allocate more resources to medical care than to environmental concerns, whether to institute a law to drive on the left side of the road or the right side of the road, and so forth), but in every morality a certain core will remain, though applied somewhat differently because of differences in environment, belief, tradition, and the like.

The core moral rules are analogous to the set of vitamins necessary for a healthy diet. We need an adequate amount of each vitamin—some humans more of one than another—but in prescribing a nutritional diet we don't have to set forth recipes, specific foods, place settings, or culinary habits. Gourmets will meet the requirements differently than ascetics and vegetarians, but the basic nutrients may be had by all without rigid regimentation or an absolute set of recipes.

Stated more positively, an objectivist who bases his or her moral system on a common human nature with common needs and desires might argue for objectivism somewhat in this manner:

1. Human nature is relatively similar in essential respects, having a common set of needs and interests.

2. Moral principles are functions of human needs and interests, instituted by reason in order to promote the most significant interests and needs of rational beings (and perhaps others).

3. Some moral principles will promote human interests and meet human needs better than others.

4. Those principles which will meet essential needs and promote the most significant interests of humans in optimal ways can be said to be objectively valid moral principles.

5. Therefore, since there is a common human nature, there is an objectively valid set of moral principles, applicable to all humanity.

This argument assumes that there is a common human nature. In a sense, I accept a *strong dependency thesis*—morality *depends* on human nature and the needs and interests of humans in general, but not on any specific cultural choice. There is only one large human framework to which moral principles are relative.[17] I have considered the evidence for this claim toward the end of Section 4, but the relativist may object. I cannot defend it any further in this paper, but suppose we content ourselves with a less controversial first premise, stating that some principles will tend to promote the most significant interests of persons. The revised argument would go like this:

1. Objectively valid moral principles are those adherence to which meets the needs and promotes the most significant interests of persons.

2. Some principles are such that adherence to them meets the needs and promotes the most significant interests of persons.

3. Therefore, there are some objectively valid moral principles.

Either argument would satisfy objectivism, but the former makes it clearer that it is our common human nature that generates the common principles.[18] However, as I mentioned, some philosophers might not like to be tied down to the concept of a common human nature, in which case the second version of the argument may be used. It has the advantage that even if it turned out that we did have somewhat different natures or that other creatures in the universe had somewhat different natures, some of the basic moral principles would still survive.

If this argument succeeds, there are ideal moralities (and not simply adequate ones). Of course, there could still be more than one ideal morality, from which presumably an ideal observer would choose under optimal conditions. The ideal observer may conclude that out of an infinite set of moralities two, three, or more combinations would tie for first place. One would expect that these would be similar, but there is every reason to believe that all of these would contain the set of core principles.

---

[17] In his essay "Moral Relativism" in Moral Relativism and Moral Objectivity (Blackwell, 1996) by Gilbert Harman and Judith Jarvis Thompson, Harman defines moral relativism as the claim that "There is no single true morality. There are many different moral frameworks, none of which is more correct than the others" (p. 5). I hold that morality has a function of serving the needs and interests of human beings, so that some frameworks do this better than others. Essentially, all adequate theories will contain the principles I have identified in this essay.

[18] I owe the reformulation of the argument to Bruce Russell. Edward Sherline has objected (in correspondence) that assuming a common human nature in the first argument begs the question against the relativist. You may be the judge.

Of course, we don't know what an ideal observer would choose, but we can imagine that the conditions under which such an observer would choose would be conditions of maximal knowledge about the consequences of action-types and impartiality, second-order qualities which ensure that agents have the best chance of making the best decisions. If this is so, then the more we learn to judge impartially and the more we know about possible forms of life, the better chance we have to approximate an ideal moral system. And if there is the possibility of approximating ideal moral systems with an objective core and other objective components, then ethical relativism is certainly false. We can confidently dismiss it as an aberration and get on with the job of working out better moral systems.

Let me make the same point by appealing to your intuitions in another way. Imagine that you have been miraculously transported to the dark kingdom of hell, and there you get a glimpse of the sufferings of the damned. What is their punishment? Well, they have eternal back itches which ebb and flow constantly. But they cannot scratch their backs for their arms are paralyzed in a frontal position, so that they writhe with itchiness throughout eternity. But just as you are beginning to feel the itch in your own back, you are suddenly transported to heaven. What do you see in the kingdom of the blessed? Well, you see people with eternal back itches, who cannot scratch their own backs. But they are all smiling instead of writhing. Why? Because everyone has his or her arms stretched out to scratch someone else's back, and, so arranged in one big circle, a hell is turned into a heaven of ecstasy.

If we can imagine some states of affairs or cultures that are better than others in a way that depends on human action, we can ask what are those character traits that make them so. In our story people in heaven, but not in hell, cooperate for the amelioration of suffering and the production of pleasure. These are very primitive goods, not sufficient for a full-blown morality, but they give us a hint as to the objectivity of morality. Moral goodness has something to do with the ameliorating of suffering, the resolution of conflict, and the promotion of human flourishing. If our heaven is really better than the eternal itchiness of hell, then whatever makes it so is constitutively related to moral rightness.

6. An Explanation of the Attraction of Ethical Relativism

Why, then, is there such a strong inclination toward ethical relativism? I think that there are four reasons, which haven't been adequately emphasized. One is the fact that the options are usually presented as though absolutism and relativism were the only alternatives, so conventionalism wins out against an implausible competitor. At the beginning of this paper I referred to a student questionnaire that I have been giving for twenty years. It reads as follows: "Are there any ethical absolutes, moral duties binding on all persons at all times, or are moral duties relative to culture? Is there any alternative to these two positions?" Fewer than five percent suggest a third position and very few of them identify objectivism. Granted, it takes a little philosophical sophistication to make the crucial distinctions, and it is precisely for lack of this sophistication or reflection that relativism has procured its enormous prestige. But, as Ross and others have shown and as I have argued in this paper, one can have an objective morality without being absolutist.

The second reason for an inclination toward ethical relativism is the confusion of moral objectivism with moral realism. A realist is a person who holds that moral values have independent existence, if only as emergent properties. The anti-realist claims that they do not have independent existence. But objectivism is compatible with either of these views. All it calls for is deep intersubjective agreement among humans because of a common nature and common goals and needs.

An example of a philosopher who confuses objectivity with realism is the late J. L. Mackie, who rejects objectivism because there are no good arguments for the independent existence of moral values. He admits, however, that there is a great deal of intersubjectivity in ethics. "There could be agreement in valuing even if valuing is just something people do, even if this activity is not further validated. Subjective agreement would give intersubjective values, but intersubjectivity is not objectivity.[19] But Mackie fails to note that there are two kinds of intersubjectivity, and that one of them gives all that the objectivist wants for a moral theory. Consider the following situations of intersubjective agreement:

---

[19] J. L. Mackie, Ethics: Inventing Right and Wrong (Penguin, 1977), p. 22.

Set A

A1. All the children in first grade at School S would agree that playing in the mud is preferable to learning arithmetic.

A2. All the youth in the district would rather take drugs than go to school.

A3. All the people in Jonestown, British Guyana, agree that the Rev. Jones is a prophet from God, and they love him dearly.

A4. Almost all the people in community C voted for George Bush.

Set B

B1. All the thirsty desire water to quench their thirst.

B2. All humans (and animals) prefer pleasure to pain.

B3. Almost all people agree that living in society is more satisfying than living as hermits alone.

The naturalist contrasts these two sets of intersubjective agreements and says that the first set is accidental, not part of what it means to be a person, whereas the agreements in the second set are basic to being a person, basic to our nature. Agreement on the essence of morality, the core set, is the kind of intersubjective agreement more like the second kind, not the first. It is part of the essence of a human in community, part of what it means to flourish as a person, to agree and adhere to the moral code.

The third reason is that our recent sensitivity to cultural relativism and the evils of ethnocentricism, which have plagued the relations of Europeans and Americans with those of other cultures, has made us conscious of the frailty of many aspects of our moral repertoire, so that there is a tendency to wonder "Who's to judge what's really right or wrong?" However, the move from a reasonable cultural relativism, which rightly causes us to rethink our moral systems, to an ethical relativism, which causes us to give up the heart of morality altogether, is an instance of the fallacy of confusing factual or descriptive statements with normative ones. Cultural relativism doesn't entail ethical relativism. The very reason that we are against ethnocentricism constitutes the same basis for our being for an objective moral system: that impartial reason draws us to it.

We may well agree that cultures differ and that we ought to be cautious in condemning what we don't understand, but this in no way need imply that there are not better and worse ways of living. We can understand and excuse, to some degree at least, those who differ from our best notions of morality, without abdicating the notion that cultures without principles of justice or promise keeping or protection of the innocent are morally poorer for these omissions.

A fourth reason, which has driven some to moral nihilism and others to relativism, is the decline of religion in Western society. As one of Dostoevsky's characters has said, "If God is dead, all things are permitted." The person who has lost religious faith feels a deep vacuum and understandably confuses it with a moral vacuum, or he or she finally resigns to a form of secular conventionalism. Such people reason that if there is no God to guarantee the validity of the moral order, there must not be a universal moral order. There is just radical cultural diversity and death at the end. But even if there turns out to be no God and no immortality, we still want to live happy, meaningful lives during our fourscore years on earth. If this is true, then it matters by which principles we live, and those which win out in the test of time will be objectively valid principles.

In conclusion, I have argued (1) that cultural relativism (the fact that there are cultural differences regarding moral principles) does not entail ethical relativism (the thesis that there are no objectively valid universal moral principles); (2) that the dependency thesis (that morality derives its legitimacy from individual cultural acceptance) is mistaken; and (3) that there are universal moral principles based on a common human nature and a need to solve conflicts of interest and flourish.

So "Who's to judge what's right or wrong?" We are. We are to do so on the basis of the best reasoning we can bring forth, and with sympathy and understanding.[20]

---

[20] Bruce Russell, Morton Winston, Edward Sherline, and an anonymous reviewer made important criticisms on earlier versions of this article, issuing in this revision.

Credits

Unless otherwise noted, all non-original text falls into the category of public domain or of fair use (17 US Code § 107), and all images were reproduced from Wikimedia (commons.wikimedia.org). All websites were accessed between July 1 and 10, 2015. If you are a copyright holder who has not been properly credited, please contact the authors at grappaport@ljcds.org or jonathansammartino@gmail.com.

Dedication: Portraits of Angelo Sammartino, April 1965 and April 2011, from private collection of Jonathan Sammartino.

p. 1: *Grammatica,* Cornelis Cort, 1565, engraving, 23.3 cm x 28 cm, Museum Boijmans van Beuningen, Rotterdam.

p. 59: *Dialectica,* Cornelis Cort, 1565, engraving, 22.7 cm x 28 cm, Museum Boijmans van Beuningen, Rotterdam.

p. 130: *At the Rabbi's,* Carl Schleicher, ca. 1860, oil on panel, 25.5 cm x 31 cm.

p. 139: *Rhetorica,* Cornelis Cort, 1565, engraving, 22.5 cm x 27.9 cm, Museum Boijmans van Beuningen, Rotterdam.

p. 187: image licensed by PresenterMedia (#3352, www.presentermedia .com).

p. 201: image licensed by PresenterMedia (#3399, www.presentermedia.com).

p. 204: *Portrait of a Scholar,* Domenico Fetti, first half of 17th Century, oil on canvas, Old Masters Gallery, Dresden.

p. 207: Holkham Hebrew Bible Genesis title page, Joshua Solomon Soncino, 1491–1492, 32.7 cm x 22.9 cm, Bodeleian Libraries, Oxford, reproduced from http://bodleian.thejewishmuseum.org/?p=47.

pp. 208–251, 343–353: *King James Bible* selections reprinted from Project Gutenberg, http://www.gutenberg.org/ebooks/10.

p. 252: *Achilles tending Patroclus wounded by an arrow,* Sosias, 500BCE, Tondo of an Attic red-figure kylix, Altes Museum, Berlin.

pp. 253–281: Homer, *Iliad,* trans. Samuel Butler, reprinted from Project Gutenberg, http://www.gutenberg.org/ebooks/2199.

p. 282: *Bust of Thucydides,* artist unknown, ca. 430 BCE, marble, 36.8 cm high, Royal Ontario Museum, Toronto.

p. 290: *Death of Socrates,* Jacques-Louis David, 1787, oil on canvas, 129.5 cm × 196.2 cm, Metropolitan Museum of Art, New York.

pp. 291–318: Plato, *Apology,* trans. Benjamin Jowett, reprinted from Project Gutenberg, http://www.gutenberg.org/ebooks/1656.

p. 319: *School of Athens,* Raphael, 1509–1511, fresco, 5.0 m x 7.7 m, detail, Apostolic Palace, Vatican City.

p. 328: Charioteer with two horses, artist unknown, bronze, 25.4 cm x 10.16 cm x 15.24 cm, image reproduced from http://www.emuseum store.com/ Roman-Charioteer-with-Two-Horses-Bonded-Bronze-Small_p_882.html with permission.

pp. 487–490: We Now Demand Our Right to Vote, reprinted from http://womenshistory.about.com/od/stantoneworks/fl/We-Now-Demand-Our-Right-to-Vote-1848.htm.

p. 491: *Abraham Lincoln, Gettysburg Portrait*, Alexander Gardner, November 8, 1863, photograph, Library of Congress digital ID cph.3a53289.

pp. 492–493: Abraham Lincoln, "Second Inaugural Address," reprinted from Our Documents, http://www.ourdocuments.gov/doc.php?flash=true& doc=38&page=transcript.

p. 494: *Portrait of John Stuart Mill*, London Stereoscopic Company, ca. 1870, photograph, Hulton Archive.

pp. 495–497: John Stuart Mill, *On Liberty*, excerpt reprinted from Project Gutenberg, http://www.gutenberg.org/ebooks/34901.

p. 498: *Portrait of Leo Tolstoy*, F.W. Taylor, 1897, photograph, Library of Congress digital ID ppmsca.37767.

pp. 499–556: Leo Tolstoy, *The Death of Ivan Ilych*, trans. Louise and Aylmer Maude, reprinted from University of Adelaide, http://ebooks.adelaide.edu.au/t/tolstoy/leo/t65d/.

p. 557: *Portrait of Emmeline Pankhurst*, ca. 1913, photograph, Matzene, Chicago, Library of Congress digital ID cph.3b38130.

pp. 558–590: "Freedom or Death" is reprinted from http://www.emersonkent.com/speeches/freedom_or_death.htm.

p. 591: Henri Manuel, *Portrait of Marie Curie*, ca. 1920, photogravure, Wellcome Library, London. Reproduced from Wellcome Images http://www.wellcomeimages.org under Creative Commons License 4.0.

p. 594: *Portrait of Ruth Benedict*, World Telegram staff photographer, 1937, photograph, New York World-Telegram & Sun Collection, Library of Congress digital ID cph.3c14649.

pp. 595–603: "Anthropology and the Abnormal" reprinted from *Journal of General Psychology*, 10 (1), 1934, pp. 59–80.

p. 604: *Portrait of Kenneth Burke*, March 14, 1969, Oscar White. Reproduced courtesy of Corbis Images, Inc. Corbis ID: IH023590.

pp. 605–626: "The Rhetoric of Hitler's 'Battle'" reprinted from *The Southern Review, Spring 1939*, pp. 1–21.

p. 627: J. Russell and Sons, *Portrait of Winston Churchill*, 1941, photograph, Library of Congress digital ID cph.3b12010.

pp. 628–637: "Their Finest Hour" is reprinted from The Churchill Centre, http://www.winston churchill.org/resources/speeches/1940-the-finest-hour/their-finest-hour.

pp. 638–649: "The Few" is reprinted from The Churchill Centre, http://www.winston churchill.org/resources/speeches/1940-the-finest-hour/the-few.

p. 650: *Portrait of Simone Weil*, artist unknown, ca 1935, photograph, reproduced with kind permission from the private collection of Sylvie Weil.

p. 676: Portrait of Franklin Delano Roosevelt, Elias Goldensky, 1933, photograph, Library of Congress digital ID cph.3d17121.

Colophon

Introduction to the Fundamental Liberal Arts:
Grammar, Logic, and Rhetoric

Layout and design created in *Pages,* output in Portable Document Format (PDF)

Images prepared and edited in *Adobe Photoshop CS5*

Text set in Arno Pro

Imaged at 300dpi

^Printed by CreateSpace on acid-free 50# paper

^Bound with PUR Adhesive Case Binding